Fodor's 05

BRAZIL
3RD EDITION

Where to Stay and Eat
for All Budgets

Must-See Sights
and Local Secrets

Ratings You Can Trust

Fodor's Travel Publications   New York, Toronto, London, Sydney, Auckland
www.fodors.com

FODOR'S BRAZIL
Editor: Shannon Kelly

Editorial Production: Tom Holton
Editorial Contributors: Carolina Berard, Karla Brunet, Gabriela Dias, Rhan Flatin, José Fonseca, Denise Garcia, Joan Gonzalez, Satu Hummasti, Olivia Mollet, João Pijnappel, Jefferson Santos, Carlos Tornquist, Ana Lúcia do Vale, Brad Weiss
Maps: David Lindroth, *cartographer;* Bob Blake and Rebecca Baer, *map editors*
Design: Fabrizio La Rocca, *creative director;* Guido Caroti, *art director;* Melanie Marin, *senior photo editor*
Production/Manufacturing: Angela L. McLean
Cover Photo (zoo in Manaus, the Amazon): Andrea Pistolesi/The Image Bank/ Getty Images

Third Edition

ISBN 1–4000–1282–1

ISSN 0163–0628

SPECIAL SALES
This book is available for special discounts for bulk purchases for sales promotions or premiums. Special editions, including personalized covers, excerpts of existing books, and corporate imprints, can be created in large quantities for special needs. For more information, write to Special Markets/Premium Sales, 1745 Broadway, MD 6-2, New York, New York 10019 or e-mail specialmarkets@randomhouse.com.

AN IMPORTANT TIP & AN INVITATION
Although all prices, opening times, and other details in this book are based on information supplied to us at press time, changes occur all the time in the travel world, and Fodor's cannot accept responsibility for facts that become outdated or for inadvertent errors or omissions. So **always confirm information when it matters,** especially if you're making a detour to visit a specific place. Your experiences—positive and negative—matter to us. If we have missed or misstated something, **please write to us.** We follow up on all suggestions. Contact the Brazil editor at editors@fodors.com or c/o Fodor's at 1745 Broadway, New York, New York 10019.

PRINTED IN THE UNITED STATES OF AMERICA

10 9 8 7 6 5 4 3 2 1

DESTINATION BRAZIL

Brazil is vast, fascinating, and as full of surprises as it is of samba. It lures you this way with glorious shores and pulls you that way with snowcapped peaks, arid plateaus, and enormous plains. Rio entices with its happy heart and its bossa nova beats. São Paulo invigorates with its ethnic diversity and its energy. Salvador intrigues with its African traditions. And Brasília astonishes with its modern shapes. From the baroque statuary of a colonial church to the statuesque figures of Copacabana, the country's sights captivate your senses and capture your imagination. And just when you think you've seen it all, there's yet another surprise waiting down the road, around the bend, or beyond the next palm tree. Boa viagem!

Tim Jarrell, Publisher

CONTENTS

CloseUps

ON THE ROAD WITH FODOR'S

Our success in showing you many areas of Brazil is a credit to our extraordinary writers. Although there's no substitute for travel advice from a good friend who knows your style, our contributors are the next best thing—the kind of people you would poll for travel advice if you knew them.

Carolina Berard is a journalist, translator, and interpreter based in Curitiba. She is also a tourism guide accredited by Embratur, the tourism office of the Brazilian government. She lived in Brasília for eight years and has also lived in Rio, São Paulo, Ponta Grossa, Curitiba, and in Spain. Carolina's articles have appeared in the online magazines *Brazzil* and *MultARTE Brazilian Culture*. For this book Carolina updated the Brasília and Goiás sections of the Brasília and the West chapter.

São Paulo chapter writer Karla Brunet is a photographer and designer who teaches digital photography in Brazil. Her major passion is travel, and she has done a great deal of it. Her most recent expeditions took her to the Inca sites in South America and to Arabic countries in Africa and Middle East.

Gabriela Dias, a Rio native who lives in São Paulo, is a freelance writer and editor for Brazilian books, magazines, and new media. The enthusiastic music fan and *carioca* lent her expertise to the Side Trips from São Paulo section and the Understanding Brazil chapter.

Amazon updater Rhan Flatin is a naturalist, writer, and photographer. He has spent several years in the Amazon basin directing a college semester abroad program and leading ecotours. Rhan and his wife, Selma, who is from Brazil, live in Vermont.

Denise Garcia, a resident of Rio, is a journalist and a producer of animated cartoons and has traveled and lived around the world. She put her talent to work on the Smart Travel Tips section and the Where to Eat, Nightlife & the Arts, and Sports & the Outdoors sections in the Rio de Janeiro chapter.

Joan Gonzalez, who updated the Salvador and Bahia chapter, has updated Fodor's material for destinations that include Ecuador, Peru, and Bolivia. She also coauthored the first edition of *Fodor's Pocket Los Cabos*. As a freelance writer, she specializes in Latin America and is based in Miami.

Smart Travel Tips updater Olivia Mollet is a freelance writer and regular Fodor's contributor who lives in New York with her husband and two cats.

Jefferson Santos is a Web producer for an online music magazine in Belo Horizonte. He updated the Minas Gerais chapter for this edition.

Carlos Tornquist, who covered The South and the Pantanal and surrounding areas, is an agricultural advisor based in Porto Alegre. He's currently pursuing a PhD in soil science, but still manages some free time for traveling. Carlos has seen much of the New World—from Canada to the tip of Tierra del Fuego.

Compulsive traveler, journalist, and Rio native Ana Lúcia do Vale updated the Exploring, Lodging, Shopping, and Side Trips sections of the Rio de Janeiro chapter. Her career has included producing and directing Brazilian television shows as well as work with a news agency and writing for the *carioca* newspaper *O Dia*.

While living in Brazil, Recife, Natal & Fortaleza updater Brad Weiss guided tours, translated for the financial newspaper *Gazeta Mercantil*, and wrote the Amazon chapter for the first edition of this book. Since then, he has contributed to Fodor's books on Argentina, Costa Rica, and Los Cabos, Mexico. He currently works at the World Tourism Organization in Madrid.

ABOUT THIS BOOK

The best source for travel advice is a like-minded friend who's just been where you're headed. But with or without that friend, you'll be in great shape to find your way around your destination once you learn to find your way around your Fodor's guide.

SELECTION

Our goal is to cover the best properties, sights, and activities in their category, as well as the most interesting communities to visit. We make a point of including local food lovers' hot spots as well as neighborhood options, and we avoid all that's touristy unless it's really worth your time. You can go on the assumption that everything in this book is recommended wholeheartedly by our writers and editors. Flip to On the Road with Fodor's to learn more about who they are. It goes without saying that no property pays to be included.

RATINGS

Orange stars ★ denote sights and properties that our editors and writers consider the very best in the area covered by the entire book. These, the best of the best, are listed in the Fodor's Choice section in the front of the book. Black stars ★ highlight the sights and properties we deem Highly Recommended, the don't-miss sights within any region. In cities, sights pinpointed with numbered map bullets ❶ in the margins tend to be more important than those without bullets.

SPECIAL SPOTS

Pleasures & Pastimes and the text on the chapter title pages focus on experiences that reveal the spirit of the destination. Also watch for Off the Beaten Path sights. Some are out of the way, some are quirky, and all are worthwhile. When the munchies hit, look for Need a Break? suggestions.

TIME IT RIGHT

Check On the Calendar up front and chapters' Timing sections for weather and crowd overviews and best days and times to visit.

SEE IT ALL

Use Fodor's exclusive Great Itineraries as a model for your trip. Follow those that begin each chapter, or mix regional itineraries from several chapters. In cities, Good Walks guides you to important sights in each neighborhood; ▶ indicates the starting points of walks and itineraries in the text and on the map.

BUDGET WELL

Hotel and restaurant price categories from ¢ to $$$$ are defined in the opening pages of each chapter—expect to find a balanced selection for every budget. For attractions we always give standard adult admission fees; reductions are usually available for children, students, and senior citizens. AE, D, DC, MC, V following restaurant and hotel listings indicate whether American Express, Discover, Diners Club, MasterCard, and Visa are accepted.

BASIC INFO

Smart Travel Tips lists travel essentials for the entire area covered by the book; city- and region-specific basics end each chapter. To find the best way to get around, see the transportation section; see individual modes of travel ("Car Travel," "Train Travel") for details.

ON THE MAPS	Maps throughout the book show you what's where and help you find your way around. Black and orange numbered bullets ❶ ❶ in the text correlate to bullets on maps.
BACKGROUND	We give background information within the chapters in the course of explaining sights as well as in CloseUp boxes and in Understanding Brazil at the end of the book. To get in the mood, review Books & Movies. The Portuguese Vocabulary can be invaluable.
FIND IT FAST	Within the book chapters are arranged roughly from north to south starting with the major cities of Rio de Janeiro and São Paulo. Chapters are divided into small regions, within which towns are covered in logical geographical order; attractive routes and interesting places between towns are flagged as En Route. Heads at the top of each page help you find what you need within a chapter.
DON'T FORGET	Restaurants are open for lunch and dinner daily unless we state otherwise; we mention dress only when there's a specific requirement and reservations only when they're essential or not accepted— it's always best to book ahead. Unless we note otherwise, hotels have private baths, phone, TVs, and air-conditioning and operate on the European Plan (a.k.a. EP, meaning without meals). We always list facilities but not whether you'll be charged extra to use them, so when pricing accommodations, find out what's included.
SYMBOLS	

Many Listings

★ Fodor's Choice
★ Highly recommended
⊠ Physical address
✛ Directions
⌖ Mailing address
☎ Telephone
🖷 Fax
⊕ On the Web
✉ E-mail
💳 Admission fee
☉ Open/closed times
► Start of walk/itinerary
Ⓜ Metro stations
🖃 Credit cards

Outdoors

🏌 Golf
⛺ Camping

Hotels & Restaurants

🏨 Hotel
🛏 Number of rooms
⚭ Facilities
🍽 Meal plans
✗ Restaurant
⚑ Reservations
👕 Dress code
◟ Smoking
🍷 BYOB
✗🏨 Hotel with restaurant that warrants a visit

Other

♨ Family-friendly
🛈 Contact information
⇨ See also
⊠ Branch address
☞ Take note

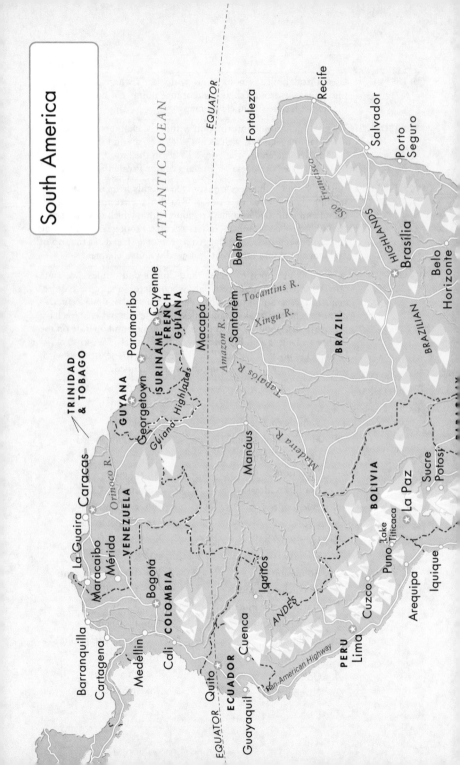

South America

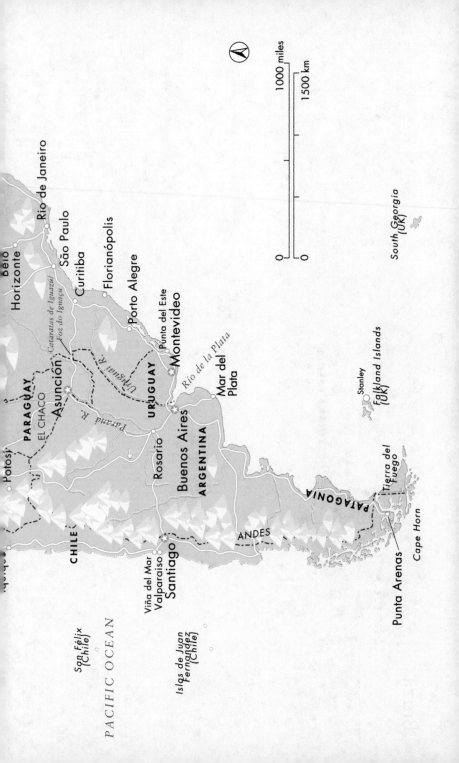

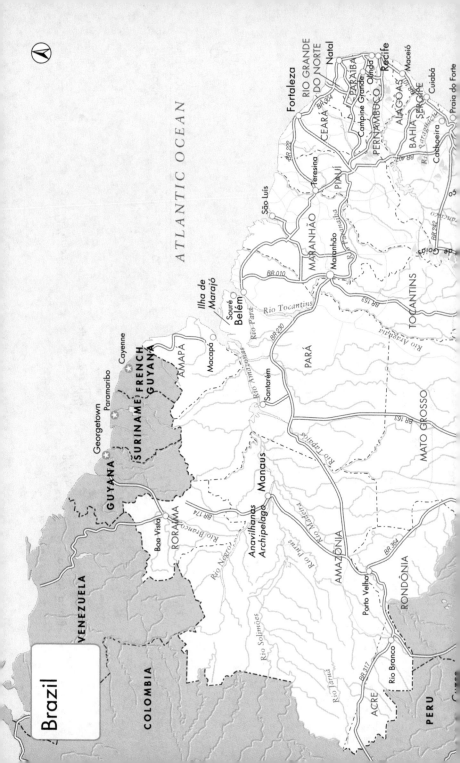

The Amazon

Through the centuries many have tried in vain to conquer Brazil's vast northwest, a mythical land of a thousand rivers dominated by one giant, the Amazon River. Flowing for more than 4,000 mi, this gargantuan waterway is so wide in places you can't see the opposite shore. It is banked by a rainforest that houses the greatest variety of life on earth. Manaus, the capital city of Amazonas State, lies almost exactly at the longitudinal center of the continent. Santarém is less than 500 mi downriver and halfway between Manaus and the Atlantic. Before reaching the ocean, the river splits in two, leading northeast to Macapá and east to Belém. In the 200 mi between the river's opposite banks lies the Ilha do Marajó, the world's largest river island, roughly the size of the U.S. state of Indiana.

Brasília & the West

Built in five years and inaugurated in 1960, Brasília, the nation's capital, lies in the geographical center of the country in a vast, flat region dominated by the *cerrado,* the Brazilian savanna. The cerrado extends west through the sparsely populated "frontier" states of Goiás, Tocantins, Mato Grosso, and Mato Grosso do Sul. The massive Pantanal—an untamable mosaic of swamp and forest teeming with wildlife—is the dominant feature of the far west both in geography and in tourist appeal.

Minas Gerais

Roughly the size of Spain, the inland state of Minas Gerais is northwest of Rio de Janeiro and São Paulo. Near the center of the state is the capital, Belo Horizonte. Just southeast of Belo is the Serra do Espinhaço, where most of the state's gold towns lie a short drive from one another. Diamantina, land of diamonds, is north of Belo Horizonte, and Mariana, founded in 1696, is to the southwest. In the state's southern region spas abound, such as those in Poços de Caldas and Caxambú. Ouro Preto, known for its baroque architecture, is embedded 3,500 feet high in mountains that rise well above 6,200 feet in the Serra do Espinhaço. Tiradentes, with its waterfalls and breathtaking views of the São José Sierra, is 130 mi southwest of Belo Horizonte.

Recife, Natal & Fortaleza

On Brazil's most curvaceous bit of coast nearly 600 mi north of Salvador are two colonial cities: Recife, the capital of Pernambuco, affectionately called the Venice of Brazil, is bathed by the sea and crisscrossed by rivers and bridges dating from the 1640s; Recife can be seen from the hills of Olinda 3½ mi away. About 130 mi to the north is Natal, the capital city of Rio Grande do Norte, where the sun shines an average of 300 days a year. Natal is geographically the closest Brazilian city to Europe and Africa. The state's coastline 50 mi to the south and 180 mi to the north of Natal is dotted with dune-flanked beaches and quiet fishing villages. In the southern part of the state are some of Brazil's most spectacular beaches: Ponta Negra, Alagamar, Cotovelo, Pirangi, and Búzios. In Fortaleza, capital of Ceará, 340 mi north of Natal, you can revel in miles of urban beaches. Thirty miles east of Fortaleza is Iguapé, where dunes are so high and smooth you can ski down their slopes. Seventy miles farther east is Canoa Quebrada, lined with red cliffs and white sands.

Rio de Janeiro

On the map the city of Rio de Janeiro dangles from the south-central edge of the state by the same name. The city cascades down and between dramatic mountains and out to beaches that ribbon the metropolitan area. Rio de Janeiro State bulges from Brazil's southeast coast, just at the point where the country starts to narrow. Rio is best known for its beaches, but inland you'll find several historical towns in relatively cool and lush mountainous settings. The Tijuca Forest, near Barra da Tijuca Beach, has more than 900 species of plants and is home to the open-armed Christ the Redeemer statue atop Corcovado. On the west side is White Rock (Pedra Branca) State Park, four times bigger than Tijuca park, with 30,888 acres of the original Mata Atlântica rainforest. In cities such as Angra dos Reis, Búzios, Cabo Frio, and Parati, white beaches and calm, warm waters abound.

Salvador & Environs

On a huge bay, the city of Salvador, the capital of Bahia State, is divided between valley and hill. The enormous Lacerda Elevator connects the two parts: the Cidade Baixa (Lower City) and the Cidade Alta (Upper City). In the nearby waters of All Saints' Bay, Frades and Itaparica islands date from colonial times. To the west in the state's heartland is Lençóis, a village lying in the splendor of the Chapada Diamantina, a plateau covered with rare flowers and orchids. In the state's southern region lies the once rich cocoa town of Ilheus.

São Paulo

South of Rio de Janeiro State is the industrial coastal state of São Paulo. Beautiful beaches, the large ocean port of Santos, ecological sanctuaries—including some patches of the Mata Atlântica (Atlantic Forest)—all run along its shores. Like the state of Rio, São Paulo's heartland includes mountainous regions covered with charming historical and resort towns. São Paulo's huge, eponymous capital is on a plateau 46 mi from the coast.

The South

The three southernmost states—Paraná, just below São Paulo, followed by Santa Catarina and Rio Grande do Sul—run along the coast and stretch inland to the borders of Uruguay, Argentina, and Paraguay. Together they compose the narrowest section of Brazil's territory, covering 220,000 square mi, an area about the size of France. Curitiba, the capital of Paraná, is on a plateau 50 mi from the sea. Santa Catarina's capital, Florianópolis, literally straddles the Atlantic, its coastal mainland portion connected by a bridge to its offshore island portion. Rio Grande do Sul's capital, Porto Alegre, is halfway between São Paulo and Buenos Aires (about a 1½-hour flight to either destination). Far to the west is the mighty Foz de Iguaçu (Iguaçu Falls).

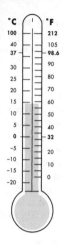

°C		°F
100		212
40		105
37		98.6
30		90
25		80
20		70
15		60
10		50
5		40
0		32
-5		20
-10		10
-15		0
-20		

Prices in beach resorts are invariably higher during the Brazilian summer (November–April). If you're looking for a bargain, stick to the off-season (May–June and August–October; July is school-break month). Rio and beach resorts along the coast, especially in the northeast, suffer from oppressive summer heat November–April, but in Rio the temperature can drop to uncomfortable levels for swimming from June through August.

Climate

Seasons below the equator are the reverse of the north—summer in Brazil runs from December to March and winter from June to September. The rainy season in Brazil occurs during the summer months, but this is rarely a nuisance. Showers can be torrential but usually last no more than an hour or two. The areas of the country with pronounced rainy seasons are the Amazon and the Pantanal. In these regions the rainy season runs roughly from November to May and is marked by heavy, twice-daily downpours.

Rio de Janeiro is on the tropic of Capricorn, and its climate is just that—tropical. Summers are hot and humid. The same holds true for the Brazilian coastline north of Rio, although temperatures are slightly higher year-round in Salvador and the northeastern coastal cities. In the Amazon, where the equator crosses the country, temperatures are in the high 80s to the 90s (30s C) all year. In the south, São Paulo, and parts of Minas Gerais, winter temperatures can fall to the low 40s (5°C–8°C). In the southern states of Santa Catarina and Rio Grande do Sul, snowfalls occur in winter, although they're seldom more than dustings.

⚑ Forecasts **Weather Channel Connection** ☎ 900/932–8437, 95¢ per minute from a Touch-Tone phone ⊕ www.weather.com.

RIO DE JANEIRO

Jan.	84F	29C	May	77F	25C	Sept.	75F	24C
	69	21		66	19		66	19
Feb.	85F	29C	June	76F	24C	Oct.	77F	25C
	73	23		64	18		63	17
Mar.	83F	28C	July	75F	24C	Nov.	79F	26C
	72	22		64	18		68	20
Apr.	80F	27C	Aug.	76F	24C	Dec.	82F	28C
	69	21		64	18		71	22

SALVADOR

Jan.	87F	31C	May	80F	27C	Sept.	78F	26C
	76	24		70	21		69	21
Feb.	88F	31C	June	80F	27C	Oct.	80F	27C
	76	24		67	19		69	21
Mar.	87F	31C	July	78F	26C	Nov.	83F	28C
	77	25		66	19		72	22
Apr.	84F	29C	Aug.	80F	27C	Dec.	86F	30C
	73	23		67	19		77	25

Countrywide events and celebrations related to Brazil's biggest festival, Carnaval, start in January and peak in the days preceding Lent, sometime in February or March. Manaus takes its Carnaval a step further by combining it with the traditions of *boi bumba* (dancing competitions) in a festival known as Carnaboi. Holy Week, in March or April, is marked by many events throughout the country, including Passion plays. Remember: the country's seasons are the reverse of those in the northern hemisphere.

SUMMER

Dec.	Although December 8 is the actual date of the Festa de Nossa Senhora da Conceição, thousands of celebrants start to fill Santarém's streets during the last week of November. The weeklong celebration culminates with a procession through the city.
Jan.	On Ano Novo (New Year's Eve), followers of Candomblé (a spiritualist cult) honor Iemanjá, goddess of the sea, with fireworks, songs, rituals, and offerings along Rio's beaches, particularly Copacabana.
	Salvador's four-day Festival of the Good Lord Jesus of the Seafarers starts on the first Sunday of the month. It features samba and capoeira performances, feasts of Bahian food, and a processional—with hundreds of small vessels—along the coast to Boa Viagem Beach.
Feb.	In Salvador the Festa de Lemanjá is held on the second Sunday of February. Devotees of the Afro-Brazilian Candomblé cult begin singing the sea goddess's praises at the crack of dawn along the beaches.

FALL

Mar.	The Formula I Grand Prix (☎ 011/5044–3000 ⊕ www.gpbrasil.com) is held during March in São Paulo.
	In Salvador, March sees PercPan (⊕ www.percpan.com.br), a percussion festival in which such music notables as Gilberto Gil and Caetano Veloso perform alongside percussion groups.
	In Macapá (Amazon), the most important local holiday is the Festa de São José, a weeklong celebration honoring the city's patron saint. The festivities, which consist mostly of traditional music and dance presentations, end on March 19.
Apr.	April 21 is Tiradentes, a national holiday honoring the father of Brazil's 18th-century independence movement, the Inconfidência. On this date Joaquim José da Silva Xavier, known as Tiradentes (Tooth Puller) because he was a dentist, was executed for treason by the Por-

tuguese crown in Ouro Preto. The city celebrates his life over a four-day period (April 18–21) with many ceremonies.

May	Many communities throughout Brazil celebrate the **Festa do Divino Espírito Santo,** with food donations for the poor, processionals, and folklore festivals. The central-west town of Pirenópolis observes the holiday with the *cavalhadas,* equestrian events that reenact battles between Christians and Moors.

WINTER

June	The **Festas Juninas** celebrations last from mid-June to mid-July and honor St. John (June 24) and St. Peter (June 29). The festivals are noteworthy in Rio de Janeiro State and in several interior regions of the northeast. Typical foods are prepared especially for these occasions. Look for fresh corn and other salty and sweet-corn products (*pamonha, curau, canjica*) as well as sweets made with coconut or peanuts, such as cocada, *cuscuz, pé de moleque* and *paçoca.* Fireworks and barn dances are among the festival traditions.
	In São Paulo the annual **Carlton Dance Festival** starts in June and continues through July.
	During Brasília's **Festa dos Estados,** held the last weekend of June, each of the nation's 26 states gets a chance to showcase its traditions.
	Outside Salvador, the town of Cachoeira celebrates the **Feast of St. John** (June 23–24), which commemorates the harvest season. There are many special music and dance activities, and the children dress up in traditional garb.
	The **Parintins Folk Festival** (June 28–30) takes place 400 km (250 mi) downriver from Manaus and is the Amazon's largest folkloric festival. The chief event is the boi bumba dancing competition between two groups—the Garantidos (who wear red) and the Caprichosos (who wear blue)—that have slightly different styles. Among the more than 40,000 spectators, all wearing the color of their favorite group, there's a mania not unlike that of a soccer match.
July	The **Festival de Inverno** (⊕ www.camposdojordao.com.br) in Campos do Jordão, São Paulo, is one of Brazil's most important classical musical events. Young musicians can learn from more experienced ones, and everyone can watch performances at the Auditório Cláudio Santoro.
	On Ilhabela, July sees the **Semana da Vela** (⊕ www.svilhabela.com.br), which brings sailors from throughout Brazil to the island for competitions.
	During Ouro Preto's weeklong **Festival de Inverno** (⊕ www.unibh.br/eventos) in mid-July, the town is overtaken by musical and theatrical performances.

In the west the Chapada dos Guimarães Festival de Inverno takes place the last week of July. Young hippies flock here for the variety of bands that perform and because this town—as the uncontested geodesic center of South America—has some really good vibes.

During Fortaleza's Regata de Jangadas, held in late July, you can watch fishermen race their *jangada* boats between Praia do Meireles and Praia Mucuripe.

Fortal (⊕ verdesmares.globo.com/fortal), Fortaleza's lively out-of-season Carnaval, is held the last week of July.

The Animamundi International Animation Festival (⊕ www.animamundi.com.br), showcasing national and international animated films, takes place every year in Rio de Janeiro and São Paulo during two weeks in July. Workshops, lectures, and children's programs are also offered.

Aug.

São Paulo's Museu da Imagem e do Som (Museum of Image and Sound) sponsors the Festival Internacional de Curtas-Metragens (International Short Film Festival; ⊕ www.kinoforum.org) in August.

The month also sees São Paulo's annual three-day Free Jazz Festival.

During Ilhabela's August Festival do Camarão, restaurants get together to organize cooking contests and offer lectures.

Salvador's Festin Bahia is a three-day international music festival held every August or September featuring foreign and local performers; past participants have included Maxi Priest, Youssou N'Dour, China Head, Carlinhos Brown, Pepeu Gomes, and Olodum. Many events are free.

In Cachoeira, west of Salvador, the Irmandade da Boa Morte (Sisterhood of the Good Death), once a slave women's secret society, holds a three-day half-Candomblé, half-Catholic festival in mid-August honoring the spirits of the dead.

In Fortaleza each August 15 the Lemanjá Festival honors the water goddess on Praia do Futuro.

Late August sees Fortaleza's Semana do Folclore, the city's folklore week.

SPRING

Sept.

Ouro Preto's giant, weeklong Jubileu do Senhor Bom Jesus do Matosinhos religious festival is held in mid-September.

One of Belém's two out-of-season Carnavals, Paráfolia, takes place at the end of September.

The most interesting and eagerly awaited week on Ilha do Marajó (Amazon) comes in September when Soure hosts the annual ExpoBúfalo. The finest water buffalo in Brazil are brought here to compete in such categories as the prettiest and the best milk producer.

The weeklong Festa do Cairé, held in Alter do Chão (Amazon) the second week of September, features folkloric music and dance presentations.

Oct.

Not only is October 12 the official day (celebrated all over the country and particularly in Aparecida in São Paulo State) of Brazil's patron saint, Nossa Senhora da Aparecida, but it's also Children's Day.

São Paulo's international film festival, Mostra Internacional de Cinema, is held in October. The world-renowned biennial art exhibition (South America's largest), the São Paulo Biennial, is held from mid-October to mid-December in each even-numbered year in Ibirapuera Park.

Porto Alegre's monthlong Feira do Livro (Book Fair; ⊕ www.feiradolivro-poa.com.br) is the largest and most famous event of its kind in Brazil.

Blumenau's Oktoberfest (⊕ www.oktoberfestblumenau.com.br) lasts three weeks and emulates the original in Munich.

The citizens of Recife repeat Carnaval in the weekend-long Recifolia festival; dates vary each year.

On the second Sunday in October thousands of worshipers flock to Belém for the Círio de Nazaré processional honoring the city's patron saint. There's also a procession on the river involving hundreds of boats bedecked in flowers.

Nov.

In November Ouro Preto's Semana do Aleijadinho honors the great 18th-century sculptor whose work adorns many of the city's churches.

The second of Belém's out-of-season Carnavals, Carnabelém, takes place in mid-November.

PLEASURES & PASTIMES

Architecture Although Brazilian architecture has been through many periods, two widely different styles dominate the scene—the baroque and the modern. In the 17th century, to ensure control over gold discovered in Minas Gerais, the Portuguese sent missionaries from traditional Catholic orders to the New World, where new lay brotherhoods, or "third orders," were formed. The lay brothers' attempts to build churches similar to the ones they had known in Europe, with little guidance or experience, led to improvisations and to the unique Brazilian style of baroque. Many churches from this period have simple exteriors that belie interiors of gold-leaf-encrusted carvings so intricate they seem like filigree. As the gold supply diminished, facades became more elaborate—with more sophisticated lines, elegant curves, and large round towers—and their interiors less so as murals were used more than carvings and gold leaf. Besides the many buildings and the 13 churches of Ouro Preto, you can see outstanding examples of baroque architecture in every other Gold Town in Minas.

At the other end of the architectural spectrum is modernism. In the middle of the 20th century, longing to appear a "nation of the future," Brazil discovered the works of architects Lúcio Costa and Oscar Niemeyer (and of landscape designer Roberto Burle Marx). Their linear buildings epitomize functionality and simplicity of design and economy of building materials, at the same time that they embody the vastness of Brazil. Many buildings are set on huge concrete *pilotis* (pillars), leaving large, open areas beneath them. Enormous glass facades and reflecting pools (some are really more the size of small lakes) often add to the sense of space; organic-looking sculptures—either as plump and curvaceous as a cluster of coconuts or as willowy and elongated as palm fronds—add touches of softness. Although the thoroughly planned capital, Brasília, is a mecca of modernism, you can see examples of this style in Rio de Janeiro (Catedral de São Sebastião, Monumento aos Pracinhas, Museu de Arte Moderna), in São Paulo (Edifício Copan, Museu de Arte de São Paulo, Memorial da América Latina), and elsewhere.

Beaches Brazil's Atlantic coast runs more than 7,300 km (4,600 mi), edging the country with sandy, palm-lined shores as well as some dramatic, rugged stretches. Many northeastern *praias* (beaches) offer sweeping, isolated expanses of gloriously high dunes; warm aquamarine waters; and constant breezes. Of course, Rio's famous beaches seem to embody the Brazilians themselves: vibrant, social, joyful, and beautiful. São Paulo's cleanest and best sands are along the north shore, where mountains and bits of Atlantic forest hug small sandy coves. In the south some glorious sands and slightly cooler climes can be found in Paraná State as well as on Ilha de Santa Catarina; still farther south the Mata Atlântica gives way to cliffs that run into the sea. Not all the best beaches are on the ocean. The banks of the Amazon and its tributaries also have splendid sandy stretches.

Carnaval

Carnaval (Carnival) is the biggest festivity of the year. In some areas events begin right after Reveillon (New Year's) and continue beyond the four main days of the celebration (just before the start of Lent) with smaller feasts and parties. At Carnaval's peak, businesses close throughout the country as Brazilians don costumes—from the elaborate to the barely there—and take to the streets singing and dancing. These four explosive days of color include formal parades as well as spontaneous street parties fueled by flatbed trucks that carry bands from neighborhood to neighborhood.

Eating Out

Eating is a national passion. Brazilian restaurants often prepare plates for two people. Ask, when you order, if one plate will suffice. The major cities have restaurants for all tastes, in the streets and shopping malls. Between extremes of sophistication and austere simplicity, each region has its own specialties: exotic fish dishes in the Amazon; African spiced casseroles in Bahia; the well-seasoned bean paste *tutu* in Minas Gerais. Much was inherited from the Portuguese, including the popular fish stews, *caldeiradas,* and beef stews, *cozidos,* boiled with a variety of vegetables. Dried salted meats are common in the interior and northeast of Brazil, but the national dish is *feijoada*. This stew of black beans, pork, sausage, and meat cuts is served with rice, shredded kale or collard greens, orange slices, and *farofa,* manioc flour fried with eggs and onions. *Churrascarias* serve *churrasco,* barbecued chunks of choice meats roasted on spits over an open fire. For a set price you get all the meat and side dishes you can eat, in a *rodízio*-style churrascaria. Rodízio means "going around." The waiters only rest their skewers to slice another piece of meat onto your plate with ritualistic ardor.

Minas cuisine has tutu—and much more. *Feijão tropeiro* (brown beans, bacon, and manioc meal), *lingüiça* (Minas pork sausage), *lombo* (pork tenderloin), *frango ao molho pardo* (chicken in the sauce of its own blood), and *queijo de Minas* (cheese from Minas) are frequently on the menu.

Seafood is the thing in Bahia. A happy mix of African and local flavors, coconut milk, lemon, coriander, tomato, *dendê* (palm oil), onions, dried shrimp, salt, and hot chili peppers can be found in every kitchen. The ubiquitous *moqueca,* cooked in a clay pot over a high flame, has all these ingredients plus the seafood catch of the day. The *vatapá,* a fish purée, is made of bread, ginger, peanuts, cashews, and olive oil. *Caruru* is okra mashed with ginger, dried shrimp, and palm oil. *Ximxim de galinha* demands chicken, peanuts, coconut, and *efo,* a bitter chicorylike vegetable cooked with dried shrimp. (Note that palm oil is high in cholesterol and hard to digest. You can order these dishes without dendê. Restaurants prepare simpler fish or shrimp dishes on demand, even if they're not on the menu.)

Brazilian *doces* (desserts), particularly those of Bahia, are very sweet, descended from the egg-based custards and puddings of Portugal and France. *Cocada* is a shredded coconut caked with sugar; *quindim* is a small tart made from egg yolks and coconut; *doce de banana* (or any other fruit) is the fruit cooked in sugar; *ambrosia* is a lumpy milk and sugar pudding.

Coffee is served black and strong with sugar in demitasse cups and is called *cafezinho*. Requests for *descafeinado* (decaf) will be met with a firm shake of the head "no," a blank stare, or outright amusement—it's just not a Brazilian thing. Coffee is taken with milk—called *café com leite*—only at breakfast. Bottled mineral water is sold in two forms: with and without bubbles (*com gas* and *sem gas,* respectively).

The national drink is *caipirinha,* crushed lime, ice, sugar, and *cachaça,* a liquor distilled from sugarcane. Whipped with fruit juices and condensed milk, cachaça becomes *batida.* Bottled beer is sold in most restaurants, but many Brazilians prefer the tap beer, called *chopp,* sold in most bars and some restaurants. Be sure to try the carbonated soft drink *guaraná,* made with the Amazonian fruit of the same name.

Music

A great variety of rhythms and dances, tunes and lyrics—*axé,* bossa nova, *forró, frevo, lundu, maxixe,* samba, *tropicalismo*—weave a seamless and enchanting blend of European, African, and regional sounds into the popular musical arts. If the famed samba has the Bantu hip-swiveling lundu dance in its vein, it also has maxixe, a polkalike Afro-Portuguese shuffle. The more mournful samba (from the Bantu word *semba,* meaning "gyrating movement") originated in Rio de Janeiro in the early 20th century but wasn't refined until the 1940s, when Rio's Carnaval competitions began. Today its many forms include the pure samba *de morro* (literally, "of the hill"; figuratively, "of the poor neighborhood"), which is performed using only percussion instruments, and the samba *cançao* (the more familiar "samba song").

During the late 1950s the new-wave bossa nova—with Rio composers such as Tom Jobim, Vinícius de Morais, João Gilberto—began to blend mellow Brazilian samba, cool American jazz, and French impressionistic chanson. During the politically turbulent '60s and '70s, musicians inspired by the traditions of the Northeast combined contemporary instruments (including the electric guitar and keyboard) and avant-garde experimentation with samba and other traditional rhythms to produce a new style: tropicalismo. Tunes such as those by Caetano Veloso, Chico Buarque, and Gilberto Gil were upbeat even though the lyrics were highly critical of social injustice and political tyranny. In addition to being linked with tropicalismo, Brazil's Northeast is known for several other musical styles. Many of these have gained popularity throughout the country. Among them are forró (which uses the accordion at its best, and most rhythmic, advantage), axé (a Bahian blend of samba and reggae), and frevo (a fast-paced dance music most associated with Recife's Carnaval).

Soccer   South Americans in general are passionate about *futebol* (soccer), but Brazilians are virtually hysterical about it. Top players are treated like deities. All-time best Pelé retired in the early 1980s and is still revered as a national hero. *O jogo bonito* (the beautiful game) is considered an art form. The best players are supposed to have *jinga*, which lends them a feline, almost swaggering grace. In the professional league, although the games are avidly followed throughout the country, there is chronic corruption and lack of funding. The country's best players leave to display their superlative skills abroad. But the national team has won the World Cup five times, and you can always catch an outstanding game in any large city. If you do attend a match, expect to see Brazilian fans at their passionate best and, alas, sometimes at their worst.

FODOR'S CHOICE

The sights, restaurants, hotels, and other travel experiences on these pages are our editors' top picks—our Fodor's Choices. They're the best of their type in the area covered by the book—not to be missed and always worth your time. In the chapters that follow, you will find all the details.

BEACHES

Barra da Tijuca, Rio. The citizens of Rio adore this urban stretch of sand for its clean, refreshing waters, its cool breezes, and its many nearby amenities.

Búzios, near Rio. Just two hours from Rio, this resort community and its string of gorgeous sands attract the chic and savvy from around the world.

Canoa Quebrada, near Fortaleza. Dunes, red cliffs, and palm groves are among the many charms of this northeastern stretch.

Garopaba, near Florianópolis. This surfer, sand-boarder, and whale-watcher territory is interspersed with modern amenities.

Ilha do Mel, Paranaguá. You must hike to the unspoiled beaches of this island, where cars aren't allowed and the number of visitors is limited each day.

Ilha de Santa Catarina. Any of the 42 beaches on this, the Magic Island, will charm you immediately.

Ilhabela, southeast of São Paulo. This island on the northeast coast of the state has beaches for all tastes, great restaurants and pousadas, and excellent windsurfing, sailing, and scuba diving.

Jericoacoara, northwest of Fortaleza. One of the country's most pristine beaches, Jeri has a 100-foot sand dune and the spectacular Arched Rock.

Praia do Forte, northeast of Salvador. The white sand beaches facing a former fishing village attract more than humans. Loggerhead and Hawksbill turtles return every year to lay their eggs here.

Prainha and Grumari, Rio. These two tiny crescents are so isolated that it's hard to believe they're part of the city.

Stella Maris, Salvador. Sun worshipers and surfers prize this beach's sands and shores; its food kiosks also entice.

RESTAURANTS

$$–$$$$ **Famiglia Mancini, São Paulo.** The atmosphere here is jovial, the decor is unique, and the food is some of the best Italian you'll find in South America's largest city.

$$$	**Olympe, Rio.** Sensitive use of Brazilian ingredients and chefs whose creativity knows no end yield out-of-this-world meals.
$$–$$$	**Le Coq d'Or, Ouro Preto.** The Cordon Bleu–trained executive chef here brings French inspiration to Brazilian cuisine.
$$–$$$	**Trapiche Adelaide, Salvador.** It's almost impossible to have a bad meal in this city, but this restaurant along the harbor still stands out for its unique blend of French and Bahian cuisines and for its fresh fish.
$–$$$	**Al Dente, Porto Alegre.** For many years this has been the pillar of northern Italian cuisine in Porto Alegre.
$–$$$	**Chef Fedoca, Ilha de Santa Catarina.** Locals are fond of this seafood spot for its superb location overlooking the Lagoa da Conceição.
$–$$$	**Durski, Curitiba.** This Polish and Ukrainian enclave feels more like central Europe than Brazil.
$$	**Porcão, Brasília.** This is deservedly one of Brazil's most famous *churrascarias* (Brazilian barbecues).
$$	**Porcão, Rio.** When in Rio, head here for the churrascaria experience: waiters zip among tables, slicing sizzling chunks of grilled beef, pork, and chicken onto your plate.
$–$$	**La Bohème, Fortaleza.** Only one room in this mansion serves as a restaurant. The rest are galleries hung with art.

BUDGET RESTAURANTS

$–$$	**Amigo do Rei, Belo Horizonte.** The service is personalized and the food beyond compare at Brazil's first Persian restaurant.
$–$$	**Casa do Ouvidor, Ouro Preto.** This is the place to sample typical mineira food.
$–$$	**Chalezinho, Belo Horizonte.** This chalet-style, hilltop restaurant attracts couples in search of magical evenings of fondues and music.
$–$$	**Galpão, São Paulo.** The modern setting reflects the good tastes of the architect-owner, and the pizzas are inventive and delicious.
$–$$	**Quatro Sete Meia, Rio.** The seafood in this restaurant, in a fishing village just outside the city, is served both indoors and in a garden outside.
¢–$$	**Fogo Caipira, Campo Grande.** The delicious Pantanal fish and western Brazilian beef dishes here are unforgettable.
$	**Canto da Peixada, Manaus.** This restaurant owes its popularity to masterful preparation of river fish.
$	**Lá em Casa, Belém.** Outstanding interpretations of indigenous Amazon dishes have given this restaurant international renown.

$	**Viradas do Largo, Tiradentes.** This is one of the best restaurants in the country for typical *comida mineira* (Minas cuisine).
¢–$	**Braz, São Paulo.** Old Italy prevails at this pizzeria with delicious pies.
¢–$	**Mangai, Natal.** Sample from over 40 regional specialties at this lively per-kilo restaurant.

HOTELS

$$$$	**Copacabana Palace, Rio.** Old-world elegance joins contemporary amenities and white-glove service.
$$$$	**Fazenda Carmo Camará, Ilha do Marajó.** A stay at this Amazon buffalo farm makes for a memorable experience.
$$$$	**Maison Joly, São Paulo.** Amenities such as a heliport stand out at this Ilhabela establishment.
$$$–$$$$	**Caiman Ecological Refuge, Pantanal.** This deluxe ranch, which promotes ecological awareness, is one of the region's top lodges.
$$$–$$$$	**Gran Meliá São Paulo.** The location is as big a draw as the creature comforts, some of them high-tech.
$$$–$$$$	**Sheraton Porto Alegre.** The city's finest hotel is in the hip Moinhos de Vento neighborhood.
$$–$$$$	**Costão do Santinho Resort, Florianópolis.** This comfortable resort has a beach and a solid roster of amenities.
$$$	**Tropical Cataratas EcoResort, Foz do Iguaçu.** Within a nature preserve and with the thundering roar of the falls in the background, these are the finest accommodations near Iguaçu.
$$–$$$	**Ouro Minas Palace Hotel, Belo Horizonte.** This fine hotel offers elegant surroundings, excellent service, and many amenities.
$$	**Academia de Tênis Resort, Brasília.** This former tennis club is now a resort with chalets, pools, and, of course, tennis courts.
$$	**Bonaparte Hotel Residence, Brasília.** Stylish decor, spacious rooms, and great business services are among the draws.
$$	**Lago Salvador, Manaus.** One of several famed jungle lodges offers seclusion and a sense of unity with the forest as well as simple comforts.
$$	**Manary Praia Hotel, Natal.** This small, smartly designed hotel has impeccable service, and ideal oceanside location, and town's only ecotourism agency.

BUDGET HOTELS

$	**Caesar Towers, Salvador.** Location is key at this apartment–hotel in the trendy Barra district, close to the best beaches in Salvador, and not too far from the historic Pelourinho district.

$ **Pousada Araras EcoLodge, Transpantaneira Highway, south of Cuiabá.** This lodge combines outstanding amenities with ecotours in the northern Pantanal.

$ **Pousada dos Pireneus, Pirenópolis.** Well-heeled families flee stark Brasília for this landscaped resort.

$ **Solar Nossa Senhora do Rosário, Ouro Preto.** Impeccable service and elegant rooms are the hallmarks here.

$ **Solar da Ponte, Tiradentes.** This colonial inn charms you with its immaculate garden and its afternoon teas.

¢ **Ibis, Belo Horizonte.** Just a few yards from Praça da Liberdade, this hotel in the backyard of a historic mansion is a steal.

¢ **Manacá, Belém.** This comfortable, well-situated hotel costs astonishingly little.

¢ **Pousada do Principe, Parati.** As its name implies, this is the inn of a prince—literally.

MONUMENTS

Basilica de Nossa Senhora de Nazaré, Belém. Built of marble, this church holds its own next to Europe's finest.

Catedral Metropolitana Nossa Senhora Aparecida, Brasília. Oscar Niemeyer's masterpiece, a structure resembling a crown of thorns, honors Brazil's patron saint.

Corcovado and Cristo Redentor, Rio. The city's icon gazes out benevolently from Corcovado Mountain.

Edifício Itália, São Paulo. The top of this building offers a 360-degree view and a chance to see how big this city really is.

Hidrelétrica de Itaipú. The world's largest dam tames the mighty Rio Paraná.

Igreja Bom Jesus do Matosinho, Congonhas do Campo. The 12 Old Testament prophets standing before this church are among Brazil's most cherished artworks.

Igreja de São Francisco, Salvador. The ornate carvings and profusion of gold leaf inside this 17th-century church are breathtaking.

Igreja São Francisco de Assis, Ouro Preto. This baroque church's lavish altars and soapstone sculptures are masterpieces.

Memorial JK, Brasília. Immerse yourself in a pyramid containing displays on the city's history. It's also the tomb of Juscelino Kubitschek, the man who made it all happen.

Palácio Catete, Rio. The former presidential palace's details are as incredible as its history.

Teatro Amazonas, Manaus. No other structure better represents the opulence of the rubber boom.

MUSEUMS

Museu Afro–Brasileiro, Salvador. Africa's strong influence on this region of the country is displayed in a fascinating collection of musical instruments, masks, costumes, and artifacts.

Museu de Arte Naif do Brasil, Rio. The canvases that grace the walls bring to art what Brazilians bring to life: verve, color, and joy.

Museu de Arte de São Paulo. MASP is the pride of São Paulo, and its image is linked to the city in the same way that the Eiffel Tower is linked to Paris.

Museu Emílio Goeldi, Belém. In a small chunk of rain forest you'll find interesting flora and fauna as well as a great museum with Indian artifacts.

Museu da Inconfidência, Ouro Preto. This museum commemorates Brazil's first attempt at independence.

Museu da Mineralogia e das Pedras, Ouro Preto. The large collections illustrate Minas's gold and the wealth and variety of its gems.

PARKS & WILDLIFE

Pantanal Wetlands. This vast floodplain is the best place to see wildlife outside sub-Saharan Africa. Its savannas, forests, and swamps are home to more than 600 bird species as well as anacondas, jaguars, monkeys, and other creatures.

Parque Nacional dos Aparados da Serra. The pine-fringed canyons here are often hidden by fog, evoking an otherworldly atmosphere.

Parque Nacional da Chapada Diamantina, west of Salvador. One of Brazil's most spectacular parks, Chapada Diamantina was a former diamond mining center. Today it is a center for hard and soft adventure.

Parque Nacional do Iguaçu. This amazing preserve has one of the world's most fantastic waterfalls.

Parque da Pedreira, Curitiba. Impressive landscaping and unique structures have given an abandoned quarry new life.

Projeto Tamar, Praia do Forte. Each year, September through March, more than 400,000 baby turtles are hatched along this beach northeast of Salvador.

Sítio Roberto Burle Marx, Rio. Inland amid mangrove swamps and jungle, this museum honors Brazil's finest landscape designer.

SMART TRAVEL TIPS

Finding out about your destination before you leave home means you won't squander time organizing everyday minutiae once you've arrived. You'll be more streetwise when you hit the ground as well, better prepared to explore the aspects of Brazil that drew you here in the first place. The organizations in this section can provide information to supplement this guide; contact them for up-to-the-minute details, and consult the A to Z sections that end each chapter for facts on the various topics as they relate to Brazil's many regions. Happy landings!

ADDRESSES

Finding addresses in Brazil can be frustrating, as streets often have more than one name and numbers are sometimes assigned haphazardly. In some places street numbering doesn't enjoy the wide popularity it has achieved elsewhere; hence, you may find the notation "s/n," meaning *sem número* (without number). In rural areas and small towns there may only be directions to a place rather than to a formal address (i.e., street and number). Often such areas do not have official addresses and/or don't need them.

In Portuguese *avenida* (avenue) and *travessa* (lane) are abbreviated (as *Av.* and *Trv.* or *Tr.*), while other common terms such as *estrada* (highway) and *rua* (street) often aren't abbreviated. Street numbers follow street names in Brazilian addresses. Eight-digit postal codes (CEP) are widely used.

In some written addresses you might see other abbreviations. For example, an address might read, "R. Presidente Faria 221-4°, s. 413, 90160-091 Porto Alegre, RS" which translates as 221 Rua Presidente Faria, 4th floor, Room 413 ("s" is short for *sala*), postal code 90160-091, in the city of Porto Alegre, in the state of Rio Grande do Sul. You might also see *andar* (floor) or *edifício* (building).

The abbreviations for Brazilian states are: Acre (AC); Alagoas (AL); Amazonas (AM); Amapá (AP); Bahia (BA); Ceará (CE); Distrito Federal (Federal District, or Brasília; DF); Espírito Santo (ES); Goiás (GO); Maranhão (MA); Minas Gerais

(MG); Mato Grosso do Sul (MS); Mato Grosso (MT); Pará (PA); Paraíba (PB); Pernambuco (PE); Piauí (PI); Paraná (PR); Rio de Janeiro (RJ); Rio Grande do Norte (RN); Rondônia (RO); Roraima (RR); Rio Grande do Sul (RS); Santa Catarina (SC); Sergipe (SE); São Paulo (SP); Tocantins (TO).

AIR TRAVEL

Miami, Newark, New York, and Toronto are the major gateways for flights to Brazil from North America. Several airlines fly directly from London, but there's no direct service from Australia or New Zealand. At this writing, all flights to Brazil from North America and the United Kingdom connect through São Paulo. For airport information *see* São Paulo A to Z *in* Chapter 2.

There's regular jet service within the country between all major cities and most medium-size cities. Remote areas are also accessible—as long as you don't mind small planes. Flights can be long, lasting several hours for trips to the Amazon, with stops en route. The most widely used service is the Varig Ponte Aérea (Air Bridge), the Rio–São Paulo shuttle, which departs every half hour from 6 AM to 10:30 PM (service switches to every 15 minutes during morning and evening rush hours). Plane tickets (one-way) for the Rio–São Paulo shuttle service cost R$50–R$190 ($18–$68); reservations aren't necessary.

AIRPORT TRANSFERS

To ensure your city destination is understood, write it down on a piece of paper and present it to bus or taxi drivers, most of whom don't speak English.

BOOKING

When you book, look for nonstop flights and remember that "direct" flights stop at least once. Try to avoid connecting flights, which require a change of plane. Two airlines may operate a connecting flight jointly, so ask whether your airline operates every segment of the trip; you may find that the carrier you prefer flies you only part of the way.

Within a country as big as Brazil, it's especially important to plan your itinerary with care. Book as far in advance as possible, particularly for weekend travel. Planes tend to fill up on Friday, especially to or from Brasília or Manaus. For more booking tips and to check prices and make online flight reservations, log on to www.fodors.com.

CARRIERS

Varig, Brazil's largest airline, flies nonstop from New York, Los Angeles, Miami, and London to São Paulo. Varig also has nonstop service to Manaus from Miami. TAM, another Brazil-based international carrier, flies nonstop from Miami to São Paulo, with continuing service to Rio and connections to other cities. TAM also offers nonstop service between Miami and Manaus.

American Airlines has an agreement with TAM that allows passengers to accumulate AA miles and awards on TAM flights. United Airlines has a similar agreement with Varig. Continental Airlines flies nonstop from Newark to São Paulo. Delta offers nonstop service from Atlanta to São Paulo. Air Canada, another Varig partner, has nonstop service between Toronto and São Paulo.

British Airways has nonstop service from London to Rio and São Paulo. Continental flies from London to Newark and Houston, with connecting flights to Rio and São Paulo.

From Sydney, Australia, you can fly to Los Angeles, then continue to Brazil on Varig. Another option is to fly Qantas to Buenos Aires, where you connect to Varig and fly on to São Paulo, Rio, Porto Alegre, Florianópolis, Salvador, or Brasília. Air New Zealand offers flights to major Brazilian cities through its partnership with Varig.

Gol is a low-cost airline whose tickets can only be purchased in person and in cash (unless you have a Brazilian credit card). 🛧 Airlines **Air Canada** ☎ 888/247–2262 in North America ⊕ www.aircanada.com. **Air New Zealand** ☎ 800/803-298 in Australia, 0800/737–000 in New Zealand ⊕ www.airnz.co.nz. **American Airlines** ☎ 800/433–7300 in North America, 0845/789–789 in the U.K. ⊕ www.aa.com. **British Airways** ☎ 0845/773–3377 ⊕ www.britishairways.com. **Continental Airlines** ☎ 800/231–0856 in North America, 0800/776-464 in the U.K. ⊕ www.continental. com. **Delta Airlines** ☎ 800/241-4141 in North America ⊕ www.delta.com. **Gol** ☎ 0300/789-2121 in Brazil ⊕ www.voegol.com.br. **Qantas** ☎ 13-13-13 in Australia, 357-8900 in Auckland, 0800/808-767 in rest of New Zealand ⊕ www.qantas.com.au. **TAM** ☎ 888/235-9826 in the U.S., 305/406-2826 in Miami, 0207/707-4586 in the U.K. ⊕ www. tamairlines.com. **United Airlines** ☎ 800/241-6522 ⊕ www.united.com. **Varig** ☎ 800/468-2744 in the U.S., 0208/321-7170 in the U.K. ⊕ www.varig.com.

CHECK-IN & BOARDING
Always **find out your carrier's check-in policy.** Plan to arrive at the airport about two hours before your scheduled departure time for domestic flights and 2½–3 hours before international flights. You may need to arrive earlier if you're flying from one of the busier airports or during peak air-traffic times.

Always **bring a government-issued photo ID** to the airport even when it's not required, a passport is best. **Be prepared to show your passport when leaving Brazil and to pay a hefty departure tax,** which runs about R$78 ($23) for international flights. A departure tax also applies to flights within Brazil. Although the amount varies, figure on R$11–R$22 ($4–$8). Although some airports accept credit cards as payment for departure taxes, it's wise to **have the appropriate amount in reais.**

CUTTING COSTS
The least expensive airfares to Brazil are priced for round-trip travel and must usually be purchased in advance. Airlines generally allow you to change your return date for a fee; most low-fare tickets, however, are nonrefundable. It's smart to call a number of airlines and check the Internet; when you are quoted a good price, book it on the spot—the same fare may not be available the next day, or even the next hour. Always check different routings and look into using alternate airports. Also, price off-peak flights, which may be significantly less expensive than others. Travel agents, especially low-fare specialists (⇨ Discounts and Deals), are helpful.

Many airlines, singly or in collaboration, offer discount air passes that allow foreigners to travel economically in a particular country or region. These visitor passes usually must be reserved and purchased before you leave home. Information about passes often can be found on most airlines' international Web pages, which tend to be aimed at travelers from outside the carrier's home country. Also, try typing the name of the pass into a search engine, or search for "pass" within the carrier's Web site.

Look into discount passes. If you plan to travel a lot within Brazil, buy an air pass from TAM or Varig before you leave home (these can only be purchased outside Brazil). Such passes can save you hundreds of dollars. Varig's Brazil AirPass costs $560 for five coupons, which are valid for 21 days on flights to more than 100 cities within Brazil on Varig or its affiliates, Rio-Sul or Nordeste. You can buy up to four additional coupons (a total of nine) for $100 each. TAM's 21-day Brazilian Air-Pass costs $399 for four coupons, with additional coupons at $100 each.

If you plan to visit more than one of the Mercosur (Southern Common Market) countries—Argentina, Brazil, Paraguay, and Uruguay—the Mercosur Pass presents the greatest savings. It's valid on Aerolineas Argentinas, Varig, and several other carriers. You must visit at least two countries within a minimum of seven days and a maximum of 30 days. Pricing is based on mileage.

Eight versions of the pass are offered, ranging from $225 for flights totaling between 1,450 and 2,300 km (between 1,200 and 1,900 mi) to $870 for flights totaling more than 8,450 km (more than 7,000 mi). Contact participating airlines or tour operators and travel agents who specialize in South American travel for information and purchase.

🗐 **Consolidators** **AirlineConsolidator.com** ☎ 888/468-5385 ⊕ www.airlineconsolidator.com; for international tickets. **Best Fares** ☎ 800/576-8255 or 800/576-1600 ⊕ www.bestfares.com; $59.90 annual membership. **Cheap Tickets** ☎ 800/377-1000 or 888/922-8849 ⊕ www.cheaptickets.com. **Expedia** ☎ 800/397-3342 or 404/728-8787 ⊕ www.expedia.com. **Hotwire** ☎ 866/468-9473 or 920/330-9418

⊕ www.hotwire.com. **Now Voyager Travel** ✉ 45 W.
21st St., 5th floor, New York, NY 10010 ☎ 212/459-1616
🖶 212/243-2711 ⊕ www.nowvoyagertravel.com. **One-
travel.com** ⊕ www.onetravel.com. **Orbitz** ☎ 888/
656-4546 ⊕ www.orbitz.com. **Priceline.com**
⊕ www.priceline.com. **Travelocity** ☎ 888/709-5983,
877/282-2925 in Canada, 0870/111-7060 in the U.K.
⊕ www.travelocity.com.

FLYING TIMES

The flying time from New York is 8½
hours to Rio, 9½ hours to São Paulo.
From Miami it's seven hours to Rio, eight
hours to São Paulo. Most flights from Los
Angeles go through Miami, so add five
hours to the Miami times given; direct
flights to São Paulo from Los Angeles take
about 13 hours. From London it's seven
hours to São Paulo.

Within Brazil it's one hour from Rio to
São Paulo or Belo Horizonte, 1½ hours
from Rio to Brasília, two hours from Rio
to Salvador, and 2½ hours from Rio to
Belém or Curitiba. From São Paulo it's
four hours to Manaus and 1½ hours to
Iguaçu Falls.

HOW TO COMPLAIN

If your baggage goes astray or your flight
goes awry, complain right away. Most carriers require that you **file a claim immediately.** The Aviation Consumer Protection
Division of the Department of Transportation publishes *Fly-Rights,* which discusses
airlines and consumer issues and is available on-line. You can also find articles and
information on mytravelrights.com, the
Web site of the nonprofit Consumer Travel
Rights Center.

🗹 Airline Complaints **Aviation Consumer Protection Division** ✉ U.S. Department of Transportation,
C-75, Room 4107, 400 7th St. SW, Washington, DC
20590 ☎ 202/366-2220 ⊕ airconsumer.ost.dot.gov.
**Federal Aviation Administration Consumer Hot-
line** ✉ for inquiries: FAA, 800 Independence Ave.
SW, Washington, DC 20591 ☎ 800/322-7873
⊕ www.faa.gov.

RECONFIRMING

Check the status of your flight before you
leave for the airport. You can do this on
your carrier's Web site, by linking to a
flight-status checker (many Web booking
services offer these), or by calling your car-

rier or travel agent. Always confirm international flights at least 72 hours ahead of
the scheduled departure time. Reconfirm
flights within Brazil and throughout South
America, even if you have a ticket and a
reservation, as flights here tend to operate
at full capacity.

BIKE TRAVEL

Riding a bike will put you face to face
with the people and landscapes of Brazil.
However, the oft-rugged terrain and varying road conditions pose considerable
challenges. Consider a mountain bike, because basic touring bikes are too fragile
for off-road treks.

In Brazil bike maps are nonexistent, and
there are few rental shops. The establishments that do exist are usually in major
cities and offer only short-term (an hour
or two) rentals. If you're a hard-core cy-
clist, bring your own bike and gear or sign
up for a bike trip through a tour operator.
Many operators within South America
offer trips—sometimes including equipment rental—that range in length from a
half-day to several days.

Always remember to lock your bike when
you make stops. Although some cities,
such as Rio, have bike paths and places
that are perfect for a bike ride, in general,
avoid riding in congested urban areas,
where it's difficult (and dangerous) enough
getting around by car let alone by bike.

BIKES IN FLIGHT

Most airlines accommodate bikes as luggage, provided they are dismantled and
boxed; check with individual airlines
about packing requirements. Some airlines
sell bike boxes, which are often free at
bike shops, for about $15 (bike bags can
be considerably more expensive). International travelers often can substitute a bike
for a piece of checked luggage at no
charge; otherwise, the cost is about $100.
U.S. and Canadian airlines charge
$40–$80 each way.

BUSINESS HOURS

BANKS & OFFICES

Banks are, with a few exceptions, open
weekdays 10–4. Office hours are generally 9–6.

GAS STATIONS

Within cities and along major highways, many gas stations are open 24 hours a day, seven days a week. In smaller towns they may only be open during daylight hours Monday–Saturday.

MUSEUMS & SIGHTS

Many museums are open from 10 or 11 to 5 or 6 (they may stay open later one night a week). Some museums, however, are open only in the afternoon, and many are closed on Monday. Always check before you go.

SHOPS

Generally, small shops are open weekdays from 9 to 7 and on Saturday from 9 to 1 or 2. Centers and malls are often open from 10 to 10. Some centers and malls are open on Sunday.

BUS TRAVEL

The nation's *ônibus* (bus) network is affordable, comprehensive, and efficient—compensating for the lack of trains and the high cost of air travel. Every major city can be reached by bus as can most small to medium-size communities.

Lengthy bus trips anywhere will involve travel over some bad highways, an unfortunate fact of life in Brazil today. Trips to northern, northeastern, and central Brazil tend to be especially trying; the best paved highways are in the southeast, so trips to and within this region may go more smoothly. When traveling by bus, **bring water, toilet paper, and an additional top layer of clothing** (the latter will come in handy if it gets cold, or it can serve as a pillow). Travel light, dress comfortably, and **keep a close watch on your belongings**—especially in bus stations.

CLASSES

Various classes of service are offered, with each increase in price buying plusher seats and more leg room (if you're over 5'10", buy the most expensive ticket available and try for front-row seats).

Buses used for long trips are modern and comfortable (bathrooms and air-conditioning are common amenities), and they stop regularly at reasonably clean roadside cafés. Sleeper buses have fewer seats, allowing the seats to recline more. Note that regular buses used for shorter hauls may be labeled AR CONDICIONADO (AIR-CONDITIONED) but often are not.

CUTTING COSTS

Bus fares are substantially cheaper than in North America or Europe. Between Rio and São Paulo (6½–7 hours), for example, a bus departs every ½ hour and costs about R$33–R$43 ($11–$15); a night sleeper will run about R$61–R$87 ($21–$30). Sometimes competing companies serve the same routes, so it can pay to shop around.

PAYING & RESERVATIONS

Tickets are sold at bus-company offices and at city bus terminals. Note that larger cities may have different terminals for buses to different destinations, and some small towns may not have a terminal at all (you're picked up and dropped off at the line's office, invariably in a central location). **Expect to pay with cash,** as credit cards aren't accepted everywhere. Reservations or advance-ticket purchases generally aren't necessary except for trips to resort areas during high season—particularly on weekends—or during major holidays (Christmas, Carnaval, etc.) and school-break periods. In general, **arrive at bus stations early, particularly for peak-season travel.**

CAMERAS & PHOTOGRAPHY

Brazil, with its majestic landscapes and varied cityscapes, is a photographer's dream. Brazilians are usually amenable to having picture-taking visitors in their midst, but you should always **ask permission before taking pictures in churches or of individuals.**

If you plan to take photos on some of the country's many beaches, bring a skylight (81B or 81C) or polarizing filter to minimize haze and light problems. If you're visiting the Amazon or Pantanal, bring high-speed film to compensate for low light under the tree canopy and invest in a telephoto lens to photograph wildlife; standard zoom lenses in the 35 mm–88 mm range won't capture enough detail.

Casual photographers should consider using inexpensive disposable cameras to reduce the risks inherent in traveling with sophisticated equipment. Single-use cameras with panoramic or underwater functions are also nice supplements to a standard camera and its gear.

The *Kodak Guide to Shooting Great Travel Pictures* (available at bookstores everywhere) is loaded with tips.

▪ Photo Help **Kodak Information Center** ☎ 800/242-2424 ⊕ www.kodak.com.

EQUIPMENT PRECAUTIONS

Don't pack unprocessed film, single-use cameras, or cameras with film inside in checked luggage. High-intensity x-ray machines used to view checked luggage will fog your film. Lower-intensity x-rays for carry-on luggage usually will not harm your film, but play it safe and ask for hand inspection. U.S. airports are required to honor this request, but non-U.S. airports may refuse it. Lead-lined bags can protect film from x-ray scans to some extent. Pack your film in a small bag that is easily removed from your larger luggage in case an inspector requires that your bag go through more than one scan or in case you are forced to check your carry-on luggage. Motion picture film should not pass through even low-intensity x-rays. Process it before traveling or call the airport in advance to arrange for a hand inspection. Digital cameras are not affected by airport x-ray machines.

Keep videotapes and computer disks away from metal detectors. Assume that you will have to remove your laptop from its case. Carry an extra supply of batteries, and be prepared to turn on your camera, camcorder, or laptop to prove to airport security personnel that the device is real.

Always keep film, tape, and computer disks out of the sun, and on jungle trips **keep your equipment in resealable plastic bags** to protect it from dampness. Petty crime is a problem throughout Brazil, particularly in the cities, so **keep a close eye on your gear.**

FILM & DEVELOPING

Bring your own film. It's expensive in Brazil and is frequently stored in hot conditions. Plan on shooting a minimum of one 36-exposure roll per week of travel. If you don't want the hassle of keeping a shot log, make a quick note whenever you start a new roll—it will make identifying your photos much easier when you get home.

VIDEOS

The system used in Brazil is PAL-M. The average price of a blank VHS tape is R$8 ($3) for 60 minutes and R$12 ($4) for 120 minutes. A DV tape (60 minutes) costs about R$30 ($10). Tapes, batteries, cables, and other equipment are readily available in electronics shops, convenience stores, gas stations, newsstands, and even some street-side stalls.

CAR RENTAL

Driving in cities is chaotic at best, mortally dangerous at worst; in the countryside the usually rough roads, lack of clearly marked signs, and language difference are discouraging for driving. Further, the cost of renting can be steep. All that said, certain areas are most enjoyable when explored on your own in a car: the beach areas of Búzios and the Costa Verde (near Rio) and the Belo Horizonte region; the North Shore beaches outside São Paulo; and many of the inland and coastal towns of the south, a region with many good roads.

Always **give the rental car a once-over** to make sure the headlights, jack, and tires (including the spare) are in working condition.

▪ Major Agencies **Alamo** ☎ 800/522-9696 ⊕ www.alamo.com. **Avis** ☎ 800/331-1084, 800/879-2847 in Canada, 0870/606-0100 in the U.K., 02/9353-9000 in Australia, 09/526-2847 in New Zealand ⊕ www.avis.com. **Budget** ☎ 800/527-0700, 0870/156-5656 in the U.K. ⊕ www.budget.com. **Dollar** ☎ 800/800-6000, 0124/622-0111 in the U.K., where it's affiliated with Sixt, 02/9223-1444 in Australia ⊕ www.dollar.com. **Hertz** ☎ 800/654-3001, 800/263-0600 in Canada, 0870/844-8844 in the U.K., 02/9669-2444 in Australia, 09/256-8690 in New Zealand ⊕ www.hertz.com. **National Car Rental** ☎ 800/227-7368, 0870/600-6666 in the U.K. ⊕ www.nationalcar.com.

CUTTING COSTS

Although international car-rental agencies have better service and maintenance track records than local firms (they also provide better breakdown assistance), your best bet at getting a good rate is to **rent on arrival, particularly from local companies.** But reserve ahead if you plan to rent during a holiday period, and check that a confirmed reservation guarantees you a car. (For details on local agencies, see A to Z sections in each chapter.)

Consider hiring a car and driver through your hotel concierge, or make a deal with a taxi driver for extended sightseeing at a long-term rate. Often drivers charge a set hourly rate, regardless of the distance traveled. You'll have to pay cash, but you may actually spend less than you would for a rental car.

INSURANCE

When driving a rented car, you are generally responsible for any damage to or loss of the vehicle. You also may be liable for any property damage or personal injury that you may cause while driving. Before you rent, find out in advance from a car-rental agency what type of proof of insurance you need to carry and check what coverage you already have under the terms of your personal auto-insurance policy and credit cards.

REQUIREMENTS & RESTRICTIONS

In Brazil the minimum driving age is 18.

SURCHARGES

Before you pick up a car in one city and leave it in another, ask about drop-off charges or one-way service fees, which can be substantial. Note, too, that some rental agencies charge extra if you return the car before the time specified in your contract. To avoid a hefty refueling fee, fill the tank just before you turn in the car, but be aware that gas stations near the rental outlet may overcharge. It's almost never a deal to buy the tank of gas that's in the car when you rent it; the understanding is that you'll return it empty, but some fuel usually remains.

CAR TRAVEL

Brazil has more than 1.65 million km (1.02 million mi) of highway, about 10% of it paved. Recent construction has improved the situation, but independent land travel in Brazil definitely has its liabilities. In addition, Brazilian drivers are, to say the least, daredevils. For these reasons, it is recommended that you rely on taxis and buses for short distances and on planes for longer journeys.

Your own driver's license is acceptable— sort of. Police (particularly highway police) have been known to claim that driving with a foreign license is a violation in order to shake down drivers for money. An international driver's license, available from automobile associations, is a *really* good idea. International driving permits (IDPs) are available from the American, Canadian, and New Zealand automobile associations; in the United Kingdom from the Automobile Association and Royal Automobile Club; and in Australia from the Royal Automobile Club or state-run automobile associations. These international permits, valid only in conjunction with your regular driver's license, are universally recognized; having one may save you a problem with local authorities. If you do get a ticket for some sort of violation—real or imagined—don't argue. And plan to spend longer than you want settling it.

Some common-sense rules of the road: before you set out, **establish an itinerary** and **ask about gas stations.** Be sure to **plan your daily driving distance conservatively** and **don't drive after dark.** Always **obey speed limits and traffic regulations.**

EMERGENCY SERVICES

The Automóvel Clube do Brasil (Automobile Club of Brazil) provides emergency assistance to foreign motorists in cities and on highways but only if they're members of an automobile club in their own nation. **Automóvel Clube do Brasil** ⊠ Rua do Passeio, 90, Rio de Janeiro ☎ 021/2240-4191 weekdays 9–7, 021/2262-2141 at other times.

GASOLINE

Gasoline in Brazil costs around R$2.15 (74¢) a liter, which is about $2.75 per

gallon. Unleaded gas, called *especial,* costs about the same. Brazil also has an extensive fleet of ethanol-powered cars.
Ethanol fuel is sold at all gas stations and is priced a little lower than gasoline. However, these cars get lower mileage, so they offer little advantage over gas-powered cars. Stations are plentiful both within cities and on major highways, and many are open 24 hours a day. In smaller towns few stations take credit cards, and their hours are more limited.

PARKING
Finding a space in most cities—particularly Rio, São Paulo, Belo Horizonte, and Salvador—is a major task. It's best to **head for a garage or a lot** and leave your car with the attendant. There are no meters; instead, there's a system involving coupons that you must post in your car's window, which allows you to park for a certain time period (usually two hours). You can buy them from uniformed street-parking attendants or at newsstands. Should you find a space on the street, you'll probably have to pay a fee for parking services. Or you might run into unauthorized street parking offered by the so-called *flanelinhas* (literally, "flannel wearers"), who may charge from R$2 (68¢) to R$5 ($1.71) in advance.

No-parking zones are marked by a crossed-out capital letter *E* (which means *estacionamento,* the Portuguese word for "parking"). These zones, more often than not, are filled with cars that rarely are bothered by the police.

ROAD CONDITIONS
Brazil's federal highways were built between 1964 and 1976, and maintenance was nearly nonexistent in the 1980s. The country's highway department estimates that 40% of the federal highways (those with either the designation *BR* or a state abbreviation such as *RJ* or *SP*), which constitute 70% of Brazil's total road system, are in a dangerous state of disrepair. Evidence of this is everywhere: potholes, lack of signage, inadequate shoulders. Landslides and flooding after heavy rains are frequent and at times shut down entire stretches of key highways. Increasing traffic adds to the system's woes, as does the fact that neither speed limits nor basic rules of safety seem to figure in the national psyche. The worst offenders are bus and truck drivers. If you drive, do so with the utmost caution.

ROAD MAPS
Quatro Rodas is *the* name for maps of Brazil. It has atlases, books, and maps of different sizes for states, regions, and cities. If you're a beach aficionado, look for this company's four-color book of topographical maps of all the nation's beaches.

RULES OF THE ROAD
Brazilians drive on the right, and in general, traffic laws are the same as those in the United States. The use of seat belts is mandatory. The national speed limit is 80 kph (48 mph) but is seldom observed.

CHILDREN IN BRAZIL
Having yours along may prove to be your ticket to meeting locals. Children are welcome in most hotels and restaurants, especially on weekends, when Brazilian families go out for brunch or lunch in droves. Brazil is a country of great cultural diversity, so try to attend one of the many festivals held all over the country throughout the year. These often feature music and dance performances that transcend language barriers and acquaint children with Brazilian folklore. Older kids and teenagers may be captivated by Brazil's plants and animals. Take a guided tour of an urban park or a trek into a national preserve. Such expeditions are a safe, easy way to experience nature.

If you are renting a car, don't forget to arrange for a car seat when you reserve. For general advice about traveling with children, consult *Fodor's FYI: Travel with Your Baby* (available in bookstores everywhere).

FLYING
If your children are two or older, ask about children's airfares. As a general rule, infants under two not occupying a seat fly at greatly reduced fares or even for free. But if you want to guarantee a seat for an infant, you have to pay full fare. Consider

flying during off-peak days and times; most airlines will grant an infant a seat without a ticket if there are available seats. When booking, confirm carry-on allowances if you're traveling with infants. In general, for babies charged 10% to 50% of the adult fare you are allowed one carry-on bag and a collapsible stroller; if the flight is full, the stroller may have to be checked or you may be limited to less.

Experts agree that it's a good idea to use safety seats aloft for children weighing less than 40 pounds. Airlines set their own policies: if you use a safety seat, U.S. carriers usually require that the child be ticketed, even if he or she is young enough to ride free, because the seats must be strapped into regular seats. And even if you pay the full adult fare for the seat, it may be worth it, especially on longer trips. Do **check your airline's policy about using safety seats during takeoff and landing.** Safety seats are not allowed everywhere in the plane, so get your seat assignments as early as possible.

When reserving, request children's meals or a freestanding bassinet (not available at all airlines) if you need them. But note that bulkhead seats, where you must sit to use the bassinet, may lack an overhead bin or storage space on the floor.

WHERE TO STAY

Large hotels often offer a range of supervised activities—picnics, movies, classes, contests—for children of all ages. Many hotels in Brazil allow children under a certain age to stay in their parents' room at no extra charge, but others charge for them as extra adults; be sure to find out the cutoff age for children's discounts.

PRECAUTIONS

Any person under the age of 18 who isn't traveling with both parents or legal guardian(s) must provide a notarized letter of consent signed by the nonaccompanying parent or guardian. The notarized letter must be authenticated by the Brazilian embassy or consulate and translated into Portuguese.

Children must have all their inoculations up to date (those between the ages of three months and six years must have an international polio vaccination certificate) before leaving home. **Make sure that health precautions, such as what to drink and eat, are applied to the whole family.** Not cramming too much into each day will also keep everyone healthier while on the road.

SIGHTS & ATTRACTIONS

Places that are especially appealing to children are indicated by a rubber-duckie icon (🐤) in the margin.

SUPPLIES & EQUIPMENT

Pack things to keep your children busy while traveling. For children of reading age, bring books from home; locally, literature for kids in English is hard to find. Inexpensive art supplies such as crayons (*giz de cera*), paint (*tinta*), and coloring books (*livros de pintar*) are sold in stationery stores, bookstores, newsstands, and some supermarkets and street stalls.

You can find international brands of baby formula (*leite nan*) and diapers (*fraldas*) in drugstores, supermarkets, and convenience shops. The average cost of a 450-gram (16-ounce) container of formula is R$12 ($4). The average price for a package of diapers is R$6 ($2).

COMPUTERS ON THE ROAD

If you're traveling with a laptop, carry a spare battery, a universal adapter plug, and a converter if your computer isn't dual voltage. Ask about electrical surges before plugging in your computer. Keep your disks out of the sun and avoid excessive heat for both your computer and disks. In Brazil carrying a laptop computer signals wealth and could make you a target for thieves; conceal your laptop in a generic bag and keep it close to you at all times.

Internet access is widespread. In addition to business centers in luxury hotels and full-fledged cybercafés, look for computers set up in telephone offices. Rates range from R$9 ($3) to R$15 ($5) an hour. Dial-up speeds are variable, though they tend toward the sluggish.

CONSUMER PROTECTION

Whether you're shopping for gifts or purchasing travel services, **pay with a major**

credit card whenever possible, so you can cancel payment or get reimbursed if there's a problem (and you can provide documentation). If you're doing business with a particular company for the first time, contact your local Better Business Bureau and the attorney general's offices in your state and (for U.S. businesses) the company's home state as well. Have any complaints been filed? Finally, if you're buying a package or tour, always consider travel insurance that includes default coverage (⇨ Insurance).

🚩 **BBBs Council of Better Business Bureaus** ✉ 4200 Wilson Blvd., Suite 800, Arlington, VA 22203 ☎ 703/276-0100 🖶 703/525-8277 ⊕ www.bbb.org.

CRUISE TRAVEL

Cruise itineraries to Brazil change frequently, so contact a travel agent or a cruise company to get the most recent information. Popular Brazilian ports of call include Belém, Fortaleza, Manaus, Recife, Rio, Salvador, and Vitória.

If time (and money) are no object, consider one of the 69-day voyages that have been offered by Fred. Olsen Cruises. Past trips have begun in England, with stops in Portugal and Senegal, crossing to Recife, Brazil, continuing around South America, visiting various ports in Argentina, and then heading to Jamaica, Cuba, the Turks and Caicos Islands, Bermuda, and the Azores en route back to Southampton.

To learn how to plan, choose, and book a cruise-ship voyage, consult *Fodor's FYI: Plan & Enjoy Your Cruise* (available in bookstores everywhere).

🚩 **Cruise Lines Abercrombie & Kent** ☎ 800/323-7308 ⊕ www.abercrombiekent.com. **Amazon Tours and Cruises** ☎ 800/423-2791 or 305/227-2266 ⊕ www.amazontours.net. **Clipper Cruise Line** ☎ 800/325-0010 or 314/655-6700 ⊕ www.clippercruise.com. **Celebrity Cruises** ☎ 800/722-5941 in the U.S. and Canada, 800/018-2525 in the U.K. ⊕ www.celebritycruises.com. **Crystal Cruises** ☎ 800/446-6620 ⊕ www.crystalcruises.com. **Cunard** ☎ 800/528-6273 ⊕ www.cunard.com. **Fred. Olsen Cruises** ☎ 800/661-1119 in the U.S. and Canada, 147/374-2424 in the U.K. ⊕ www.fredolsencruises.co.uk. **Holland America Line** ☎ 877/932-4259 ⊕ www.hollandamerica.com.

Lindblad Expeditions ☎ 800/397-3348 or 212/765-7740 ⊕ www.lindblad.com. **Orient Lines** ☎ 800/333-7300 ⊕ www.orientlines.com. **Radisson Seven Seas Cruises** ☎ 877/505-5370 ⊕ www.rssc.com. **Royal Olympia Cruises** ☎ 800/872-6400 in the U.S. and Canada, 207/440-9090 in the U.K. ⊕ www.royalolympiacruises.com. **Seabourn Cruise Lines** ☎ 800/929-9595 ⊕ www.seabourn.com. **Silversea Cruises** ☎ 800/722-9955 in the U.S. and Canada, 870/333-7030 in the U.K. ⊕ www.silversea.com.

CUSTOMS & DUTIES

Traveling home with items made from animal parts, certain types of wood, or plant fibers can result in big fines and even jail time, so beware. When shopping abroad, keep receipts for all purchases. Upon reentering the country, **be ready to show customs officials what you've bought.** Pack purchases together in an easily accessible place. If you think a duty is incorrect, appeal the assessment. If you object to the way your clearance was handled, note the inspector's badge number. In either case, first ask to see a supervisor. If the problem isn't resolved, write to the appropriate authorities, beginning with the port director at your point of entry.

IN AUSTRALIA

Australian residents who are 18 or older may bring home A$400 worth of souvenirs and gifts (including jewelry), 250 cigarettes or 250 grams of cigars or other tobacco products, and 1,125 ml of alcohol (including wine, beer, and spirits). Residents under 18 may bring back A$200 worth of goods. Members of the same family traveling together may pool their allowances. Prohibited items include meat products. Seeds, plants, and fruits need to be declared upon arrival.

🚩 **Australian Customs Service** 📬 Regional Director, Box 8, Sydney, NSW 2001 ☎ 02/9213-2000 or 1300/363263, 02/9364-7222 or 1800/803-006 quarantine-inquiry line 🖶 02/9213-4043 ⊕ www.customs.gov.au.

IN BRAZIL

In addition to personal items, you're permitted to bring in, duty-free, up to R$1,700 ($500) worth of gifts purchased abroad, including up to 2 liters of liquor. If you plan to bring in plants, you may do so only with documentation authenticated by the consular service.

IN CANADA

Canadian residents who have been out of Canada for at least seven days may bring in C$750 worth of goods duty-free. If you've been away fewer than seven days but more than 48 hours, the duty-free allowance drops to C$200. If your trip lasts 24 to 48 hours, the allowance is C$50. You may not pool allowances with family members. Goods claimed under the C$750 exemption may follow you by mail; those claimed under the lesser exemptions must accompany you. Alcohol and tobacco products may be included in the seven-day and 48-hour exemptions but not in the 24-hour exemption. If you meet the age requirements of the province or territory through which you reenter Canada, you may bring in, duty-free, 1.5 liters of wine or 1.14 liters (40 imperial ounces) of liquor or 24 12-ounce cans or bottles of beer or ale. Also, if you meet the local age requirement for tobacco products, you may bring in, duty-free, 200 cigarettes and 50 cigars. Check ahead of time with the Canada Customs and Revenue Agency or the Department of Agriculture for policies regarding meat products, seeds, plants, and fruits.

You may send an unlimited number of gifts (only one gift per recipient, however) worth up to C$60 each duty-free to Canada. Label the package UNSOLICITED GIFT—VALUE UNDER $60. Alcohol and tobacco are excluded.

🗋 **Canada Customs and Revenue Agency** ✉ 2265 St. Laurent Blvd., Ottawa, Ontario K1G 4K3 ☎ 800/461-9999, 204/983-3500, or 506/636-5064 ⊕ www.ccra.gc.ca.

IN NEW ZEALAND

All homeward-bound residents may bring back NZ$700 worth of souvenirs and gifts; passengers may not pool their allowances, and children can claim only the concession on goods intended for their own use. For those 17 or older, the duty-free allowance also includes 4.5 liters of wine or beer; one 1,125-ml bottle of spirits; and either 200 cigarettes, 250 grams of tobacco, 50 cigars,

or a combination of the three up to 250 grams. Meat products, seeds, plants, and fruits must be declared upon arrival to the Agricultural Services Department.

🗋 **New Zealand Customs** ✉ Head office: The Customhouse, 17–21 Whitmore St., Box 2218, Wellington ☎ 09/300–5399 or 0800/428–786 ⊕ www.customs.govt.nz.

IN THE U.K.

From countries outside the European Union, including Brazil, you may bring home, duty-free, 200 cigarettes or 50 cigars, 1 liter of spirits or 2 liters of fortified or sparkling wine or liqueurs, 2 liters of still table wine, 60 milliliters of perfume, 250 milliliters of toilet water, plus £145 worth of other goods, including gifts and souvenirs. Prohibited items include meat products, seeds, plants, and fruits.

🗋 **HM Customs and Excise** ✉ Portcullis House, 21 Cowbridge Rd. E, Cardiff CF11 9SS ☎ 0845/010–9000 or 0208/929–0152, 0208/929–6731 or 0208/910–3602 complaints ⊕ www.hmce.gov.uk.

IN THE U.S.

U.S. residents who have been out of the country for at least 48 hours may bring home, for personal use, $800 worth of foreign goods duty-free, as long as they haven't used the $800 allowance or any part of it in the past 30 days. This exemption may include 1 liter of alcohol (for travelers 21 and older), 200 cigarettes, and 100 non-Cuban cigars. Family members from the same household who are traveling together may pool their $800 personal exemptions. For fewer than 48 hours, the duty-free allowance drops to $200, which may include 50 cigarettes, 10 non-Cuban cigars, and 150 ml of alcohol (or 150 ml of perfume containing alcohol). The $200 allowance cannot be combined with other individuals' exemptions, and if you exceed it, the full value of all the goods will be taxed. Antiques, which the U.S. Bureau of Customs and Border Protection defines as objects more than 100 years old, enter duty-free, as do original works of art done entirely by hand, including paintings, drawings, and sculptures. This doesn't apply to folk art or handicrafts, which are in general dutiable.

You may also send packages home duty-free, with a limit of one parcel per addressee per day (except alcohol or tobacco products or perfume worth more than $5). You can mail up to $200 worth of goods for personal use; label the package PERSONAL USE and attach a list of its contents and their retail value. If the package contains your used personal belongings, mark it AMERICAN GOODS RETURNED to avoid paying duties. You may send up to $100 worth of goods as a gift; mark the package UNSOLICITED GIFT. Mailed items do not affect your duty-free allowance on your return.

To avoid paying duty on foreign-made high-ticket items you already own and will take on your trip, register them with Customs before you leave the country. Consider filing a Certificate of Registration for laptops, cameras, watches, and other digital devices identified with serial numbers or other permanent markings; you can keep the certificate for other trips. Otherwise, bring a sales receipt or insurance form to show that you owned the item before you left the United States.

🔲 **U.S. Bureau of Customs and Border Protection** ✉ for inquiries and equipment registration, 1300 Pennsylvania Ave. NW, Washington, DC 20229 ⊕ www.customs.gov ☎ 877/287-8667 or 202/354-1000 🖂 for complaints, Customer Satisfaction Unit, 1300 Pennsylvania Ave. NW, Room 5.5D, Washington, DC 20229.

DISABILITIES & ACCESSIBILITY

Although international chain hotels in large cities have some suitable rooms and facilities for people in wheelchairs, and it's easy to hire private cars and drivers for excursions, Brazil isn't very well equipped to handle travelers with disabilities. There are few ramps and curb cuts, and it takes effort and planning to negotiate cobbled city streets, get around museums and other buildings, and explore the countryside.

City centers such as Rio de Janeiro are your best bets; indeed, some areas on the south side of Rio *do* have ramps and wide sidewalks with even surfaces. Legislation concerning people with disabilities has been approved but has yet to be enforced.

There's no central clearinghouse for information on this topic, so the best local resource is the staff at your hotel.

RESERVATIONS

When discussing accessibility with an operator or reservations agent, ask hard questions. Are there any stairs, inside *or* out? Are there grab bars next to the toilet *and* in the shower/tub? How wide is the doorway to the room? To the bathroom? For the most extensive facilities meeting the latest legal specifications, opt for newer accommodations. If you reserve through a toll-free number, consider also calling the hotel's local number to confirm the information from the central reservations office. Get confirmation in writing when you can.

🔲 Complaints **Aviation Consumer Protection Division** (⇨ Air Travel) for airline-related problems. **Departmental Office of Civil Rights** ✉ for general inquiries, U.S. Department of Transportation, S-30, 400 7th St. SW, Room 10215, Washington, DC 20590 ☎ 202/366-4648 🖶 202/366-9371 ⊕ www.dot.gov/ost/docr/index.htm. **Disability Rights Section** ✉ NYAV, U.S. Department of Justice, Civil Rights Division, 950 Pennsylvania Ave. NW, Washington, DC 20530 ☎ ADA information line 202/514-0301, 800/514-0301, 202/514-0383 TTY, 800/514-0383 TTY ⊕ www.ada.gov. **U.S. Department of Transportation Hotline** ☎ for disability-related air-travel problems, 800/778-4838 or 800/455-9880 TTY.

TRAVEL AGENCIES

In the United States, the Americans with Disabilities Act requires that travel firms serve the needs of all travelers. Some agencies specialize in working with people with disabilities.

🔲 Travelers with Mobility Problems **Access Adventures/B. Roberts Travel** ✉ 206 Chestnut Ridge Rd., Scottsville, NY 14624 ☎ 585/889-9096 ⊕ www.brobertstravel.com 🖂 dltravel@prodigy.net, run by a former physical-rehabilitation counselor. **CareVacations** ✉ No. 5, 5110-50 Ave., Leduc, Alberta, Canada, T9E 6V4 ☎ 780/986-6404 or 877/478-7827 🖶 780/986-8332 ⊕ www.carevacations.com, for group tours and cruise vacations. **Flying Wheels Travel** ✉ 143 W. Bridge St., Box 382, Owatonna, MN 55060 ☎ 507/451-5005 🖶 507/451-1685 ⊕ www.flyingwheelstravel.com.

DISCOUNTS & DEALS

Be a smart shopper and compare all your options before making decisions. A plane ticket bought with a promotional coupon from travel clubs, coupon books, and direct-mail offers or purchased on the Internet may not be cheaper than the least expensive fare from a discount ticket agency. And always keep in mind that what you get is just as important as what you save.

DISCOUNT RESERVATIONS

To save money, look into discount reservations services with Web sites and toll-free numbers, which use their buying power to get a better price on hotels, airline tickets (⇨ Air Travel), even car rentals. When booking a room, always **call the hotel's local toll-free number** (if one is available) rather than the central reservations number—you'll often get a better price. Always ask about special packages or corporate rates.

When shopping for the best deal on hotels and car rentals, look for guaranteed exchange rates, which protect you against a falling dollar. With your rate locked in, you won't pay more, even if the price goes up in the local currency.

🛪 Airline Tickets **Air 4 Less** ☎ 800/AIR4LESS; low-fare specialist.

🛪 Hotel Rooms **Accommodations Express** ☎ 800/444-7666 or 800/277-1064 ⊕ www. accommodationsexpress.com. **Steigenberger Reservation Service** ☎ 800/223-5652 ⊕ www.srs-worldhotels.com. **Turbotrip.com** ☎ 800/473-7829 ⊕ www.turbotrip.com.

PACKAGE DEALS

Don't confuse packages and guided tours. When you buy a package, you travel on your own, just as though you had planned the trip yourself. In cities, ask the local visitor's bureau about hotel packages that include tickets to major museum exhibits or other special events.

EATING & DRINKING

Eating is a national passion in Brazil, and portions are huge. In many restaurants plates are prepared for two people; when you order, ask if one plate will suffice. The restaurants we list are the cream of the crop in each price category. Properties indicated by an ✕🏨 are lodging establishments whose restaurant warrants a special trip. Price categories are as follows:

WHAT IT COSTS IN REAIS

CATEGORY	COST*
$$$$	over R$60
$$$	R$45–R$60
$$	R$30–R$45
$	R$15–R$30
¢	under R$15

Prices are for a main course at dinner.

MEALS & SPECIALTIES

Between the extremes of sophistication and austere simplicity, each region has its own cuisine. You find exotic fish dishes in the Amazon, African-spiced dishes in Bahia, and well-seasoned bean mashes in Minas Gerais. In major cities the variety of eateries is staggering: restaurants of all sizes and categories, snack bars, and fast-food outlets line downtown streets and fight for space in shopping malls. Pricing systems vary from open menus to buffets where you weigh your plate. In São Paulo, for example, Italian eateries—whose risottos rival those of Bologna—sit beside pan-Asian restaurants, which, like the chicest spots in North America and Europe, serve everything from Thai *satay* to sushi. In addition, there are excellent Portuguese, Chinese, Japanese, Arab, and Spanish cuisines.

Outside the cities you find primarily typical, low-cost Brazilian meals that consist simply of *feijão preto* (black beans) and *arroz* (rice) served with beef, chicken, or fish. Manioc, a root vegetable that's used in a variety of ways, and beef are adored everywhere. Note that Brazilians eat few vegetables, and these often must be ordered separately.

Many Brazilian dishes are adaptations of Portuguese specialties. Fish stews called *caldeiradas* and beef stews called *cozidos* (a wide variety of vegetables boiled with different cuts of beef and pork) are popular, as is *bacalhau*, salt cod cooked in sauce or grilled. *Salgados* (literally, "salt-eds") are appetizers or snacks served in sit-down restaurants as well as at stand-up *lanchonetes* (luncheonettes). Dried salted meats form the basis of many dishes from the interior and northeast of Brazil, and pork is used heavily in dishes from Minas Gerais. Brazil's national dish is *feijoada* (a stew of black beans, sausage, pork, and beef), which is often served with rice, shredded kale, orange slices, and manioc flour or meal—called *farofa* if it's coarsely ground, *farinha* if finely ground—that has been fried with onions, oil, and egg.

One of the most avid national passions is the *churrascaria*, where meats are roasted on spits over an open fire, usually *rodízio* style. Rodízio means "going around," and waiters circulate nonstop carrying skewers laden with charbroiled hunks of beef, pork, and chicken, which are sliced onto your plate with ritualistic ardor. For a set price you get all the meat and side dishes you can eat.

Brazilian *doces* (desserts), particularly those of Bahia, are very sweet, and many are descendants of the egg-based custards and puddings of Portugal and France. *Cocada* is shredded coconut caked with sugar; *quindim* is a small tart made from egg yolks and coconut; *doce de banana* (or any other fruit) is banana cooked in sugar; *ambrosia* is a lumpy milk-and-sugar pudding.

Coffee is served black and strong with sugar in demitasse cups and is called *cafezinho*. (Requests for *descafeinado* [decaf] are met with a firm shake of the head "no," a blank stare, or outright amusement.) Coffee is taken with milk—called *café com leite*—only at breakfast. Bottled mineral water is sold in two forms: carbonated or plain (*com gas* and *sem gas,* respectively).

⇨ For more information on regional cuisine, *see* Pleasures & Pastimes *at* the beginning of each chapter.

MEALTIMES

It's hard to find breakfast outside a hotel restaurant. At lunch and dinner portions are large. Often a single dish will easily feed two people; no one will be the least bit surprised if you order one entrée and ask for two plates. In addition, some restaurants automatically bring a *couvert* (an appetizer course of such items as bread, cheese or pâté, olives, quail eggs, and the like). You'll be charged extra for this, and you're perfectly within your rights to send it back if you don't want it.

Mealtimes vary according to locale. In Rio and São Paulo, lunch and dinner are served later than in the United States. In restaurants lunch usually starts around 1 and can last until 3. Dinner is always eaten after 8 and in many cases not until 10. In Minas Gerais, the northeast, and smaller towns in general, dinner and lunch are taken at roughly the same time as in the States.

Unless otherwise noted, the restaurants listed in this guide are open daily for lunch and dinner.

PAYING

Credit cards are widely accepted at restaurants in the major cities. In the countryside all but the smallest establishments generally accept credit cards as well. Gratuity is 10% of the total sum, and it is sometimes included in the bill; when it is not, it is optional to give the waiter a tip.

RESERVATIONS & DRESS

Reservations are always a good idea; we mention them only when they're essential or not accepted. Book as far ahead as you can, and reconfirm as soon as you arrive. (Large parties should always call ahead to check the reservations policy.) We mention dress only when men are required to wear a jacket or a jacket and tie.

WINE, BEER & SPIRITS

The national drink is the *caipirinha*, made of crushed lime, sugar, and *pinga* or *cachaça* (sugarcane liquor). When whipped with crushed ice, fruit juices, and condensed milk, the pinga/cachaça becomes a *batida*. A *caipivodka*, or *caipiroska*, is the same cocktail with vodka instead of cachaça. Some bars make both drinks using a fruit other than lime, such as kiwi and *maracujá* (passion fruit). Brazil has many brands of bottled beer. In general, though, Brazilians prefer tap beer, called *chopp*, which is sold in bars and restaurants. Be sure to try the carbonated soft drink *guaraná*, made using the Amazonian fruit of the same name.

ECOTOURISM

Ecotourism is an ever more popular form of travel. Some ecotour operators are more trustworthy than others, however. Those recommended in this guide are good bets (⇨ Tours & Packages). You can also contact the Brazilian Institute of Ecotourism (Instituto Ecoturismo do Brasil, or IEB), a highly respected organization that's dedicated to preserving Brazil's natural resources while promoting tourism. Staffers there should have information about special-interest tours.

🔢 **IEB** ⊠ Rua Minerva 156, Bairro Perdizes, São Paulo ☎ 011/3672-7571 ⊕ www.ecoturismo.org.br.

ELECTRICITY

The current in Brazil isn't regulated: in São Paulo and Rio it's 110 or 120 volts (the same as in the United States and Canada); in Recife and Brasília it's 220 volts (the same as in Europe); and in Manaus and Salvador it's 127 volts. Electricity is AC (alternating current) at 60 Hz, similar to that in Europe. To use electric-powered equipment purchased in the U.S. or Canada, **bring a converter and adapter.** Wall outlets take Continental-type plugs, with two round prongs. Consider buying a universal adapter, which has several types of plugs in one handy unit.

If your appliances are dual-voltage, you'll need only an adapter. Don't use 110-volt outlets marked FOR SHAVERS ONLY for high-wattage appliances such as blow-dryers. Most laptops operate equally well on 110 and 220 volts and so require only an adapter.

EMBASSIES & CONSULATES

🔢 Australia **Australian Embassy** ⊠ SES, Quadra 9 Conjunto 16, Casa 1, 70469-900, Brasília, DF ☎ 061/248-5569 🖷 061/226-1112 ⊕ www.embaixada-australia.org.br. **Australian Consulate** ⊠ Veirano e Advogados Associados, Av. Presidente Wilson 231, 23rd floor, 20030-021 Rio de Janeiro RJ ☎ 021/3824-4624 🖷 021/262-4247 ⊠ Alameda Ministro Rocha Azevedo 456, 2nd floor, Jardim Paulista 01410-000 São Paulo SP ☎ 011/3085-6247 Ext. 204 🖷 011/3082-4140.

🔢 Canada **Canadian Embassy** ⊠ SES, Av. das Nações, Quadra 803, Lote 16, 70410-900, Brasília, DF ☎ 061/321-2171 ⊕ www.dfait-maeci.gc.ca/brazil.

Canadian Consulate ⊠ Atlântica Business Center, Av. Atlântica 1130, 5th floor, Copacabana 22021-000 Rio de Janeiro RJ ☎ 021/2543-3004 🖷 021/2275-2195 ⊠ Brooklin Centro Empresarial Nações Unidas, Av. das Nações Unidas 12901, 16th floor, 04578-000 São Paulo SP ☎ 011/5509-4321 🖷 011/5509-4260.

🔢 New Zealand **New Zealand Embassy** ⊠ SHIS QI-9, Conjunto 16, casa 01 Lago Sul 71625-160 Brasília DF ☎ 061/248-9900 🖷 061/248-9916. **New Zealand Consulate** ⊠ Alameda Campinas 579, 15th floor, Cerqueira Cesar 01404-000, São Paulo, SP ☎ 011/3148-0616 🖷 011/3148-2521 ⊲ consuladonz@nzte.govt.nz.

🔢 United Kingdom **British Embassy** ⊠ SES, Av. das Nações, Quadra 801, Loto 8, Conjunto K, 70408-900, Brasília, DF ☎ 061/225-2710 🖷 061/225-1777. **British Consulate** ⊠ Rua dos Inconfidentes 1075, sala 1302 Savassi 30140-120 Belo Horizonte MG ☎ 031/261-2072 🖷 031/261-0226 ⊠ Rua Presidente Faria 51, 2nd floor, Conjunto 204, 80020-918 Curitiba PR ☎ 041/322-1202 or 041/322-3537 🖷 041/322-1202 or 041/322-3537 ⊠ Edifício Galleria, Av. Conselheiro Aguiar 2941, 3rd floor, Boa Viagem 51020-020 Recife PE ☎ 081/465-0230 🖷 081/465-0247 ⊠ Praia do Flamengo 284, 2nd floor, Flamengo 22210-030 Rio de Janeiro RJ ☎ 021/2555-9640 🖷 021/2555-9671 ⊠ Rua Ferreira de Araújo 741, 2nd floor, Pinheiros 05428-002 São Paulo SP ☎ 011/3816-2303 🖷 011/3811-9981 **Honorary British Consulate** ⊠ Ed. Palladium Center, Av. Governador J. Malcher 815, Conjunto 4101/411 66035-900 Belém PA ☎ 091/222-5074 🖷 091/212-0274 ⊠ Grupo Edson Queiroz, Praça da Imprensa s/n Aldeota 60135-900 Fortaleza CE ☎ 085/244-8888 🖷 085/261-8763 ⊠ Swedish Match da Amazônia S.A., Rua Poraquê 240 Distrito Industrial 69075-180 Manaus AM ☎ 092/613-1819 🖷 092/61-1420 ⊠ Edifício Montreal, Rua Itapeva 110, Conjunto 505 Passo D'Areia 91350-080 Porto Alegre RS ☎ 051/341-0720 🖷 051/341-0720 ⊠ Edifício Estados Unidos, Av. Estados Unidos 18B, 8th floor, Comércio 40010-020 Salvador BA ☎ 071/243-7399 🖷 071/242-7293

🔢 United States **American Embassy** ⊠ Lote 3, Unit 3500, Av. das Nações, 70403-900, Brasília, DF ☎ 061/321-7272 ⊕ www.embaixada-americana.org.br. **American Consular Agency** ⊠ Rua Nogueira Acioly 891, 60110-140 Fortaleza, CE ☎☎ 085/252-1539 **American Consulate** ⊠ Av. Presidente Wilson 147 20030-020 Rio de Janeiro, RJ ☎ 021/2292-7117 ⊠ Rua Padre João Manoel 933,

Cerqueira César 01411-001 São Paulo SP ☎ 011/ 3081-6511 🖷 011/3062-5154

ENGLISH-LANGUAGE MEDIA

Outside the programs on cable TV in large chain hotels, you probably won't find anything in English. In movie theaters British and American films are shown in English with Portuguese subtitles. In major cities large newsstands and bookstores sell most American and a few British publications—albeit at prices much higher than you would pay at home. Some bookstores also carry English-language books.

ETIQUETTE & BEHAVIOR

Although Brazil is a predominately Catholic country, in many places there's an anything-goes outlook. As a rule, coastal areas (particularly Rio and parts of the northeast) are considerably less conservative than inland areas and those throughout the south. People dress nicely to enter churches, and hats are frowned upon during mass.

Whether they tend toward the conservative or the risqué, Brazilians are a very friendly lot. Don't be afraid to smile in the streets, ask for directions, or strike up a conversation with a local (be aware, however, that a Brazilian may give you false directions before admitting that he or she doesn't know where to point you). The slower pace of life in much of the country reflects an unwavering appreciation of family and hospitality (as well as a respect for the heat); knowing this will help you understand why things may take a little longer to get done.

Throughout the country use the thumbs-up gesture to indicate that something is OK. The gesture created by making a circle with your thumb and index finger and holding your other fingers up in the air has a very rude meaning.

GAY & LESBIAN TRAVEL

Brazil is South America's most popular destination for gay and lesbian travelers, and major cities such as Rio de Janeiro, São Paulo, and Salvador have numerous gay bars, organizations, and publications. Realize, however, that the acceptance of same-sex couples in the major cities may be limited to more touristy areas. Outside these destinations use discretion about public displays of affection.

The great Carnaval celebrations include many gay parades. At the end of the year, Mix Brasil International Festival of Sexual Diversity takes place in São Paulo, Rio de Janeiro, and Porto Alegre.

Rio is much like New York City or any other large metropolitan center with regard to acceptance of gays and lesbians. Style Travel, an offshoot of the established Brasil Plus travel agency, is a great source of information on gay and lesbian lodgings, tours, and nightlife options in the area. It can supply knowledgeable, English-speaking gay and lesbian guides and arrange trips to outlying areas. Style Travel is a member of the International Gay and Lesbian Travel Association (IGLTA).

G Magazine is Rio's gay and lesbian glossy magazine. It's available at most newsstands and lists local arts, music, and style events—in Portuguese. Visit the online riogayguide.com for soup-to-nuts information. Rio's gay beach scene is at Bolsa, on Copacabana Beach in front of the Copacabana Palace, and at Ipanema, by Posts 8 and 9, east of Rua Farme de Amoedo, a.k.a. Farme Gay. Locals on these sandy stretches are usually open to questions about what's happening in the gay and lesbian community. Disque Defesa Homossexual is a number set up by the Rio police to aid lesbians and gays who have suffered violence or discrimination.

In Salvador you can get gay and lesbian information and purchase the guide *Guia para Gays* (R$10) from the Grupo Gay da Bahia.

🛈 **Resources Disque Defesa Homossexual** ☎ 021/3399-1111 ⊙ weekdays 10–5. **Grupo Arco-Íris de Conscientização Homossexual** ☎ 021/2552-5995 or 021/9295-7229. **Grupo Gay da Bahia** ✉ Rua do Sodré 45, Centro Salvador BA ☎ 071/322-2552. **Style Travel** ✉ Av. Armando Lombardi 633, loja F, Barra da Tijuca ☎ 021/2494-5858 ⊕ www.styletravel.com.br. **Riogayguide.com** ⊕ www.riogayguide.com.

🛈 **Gay- & Lesbian-Friendly Travel Agencies Different Roads Travel** ✉ 8383 Wilshire Blvd., Suite 520, Beverly Hills, CA 90211 ☎ 323/651-5557 or

800/429-8747 (Ext. 14 for both) 🖨 323/651-3678 ✉ lgernert@tzell.com. **Kennedy Travel** ✉ 130 W. 42nd St., Suite 401, New York, NY 10036 ☎ 212/840-8659 or 800/237-7433 🖨 212/730-2269 ⊕ www. kennedytravel.com. **Now, Voyager** ✉ 4406 18th St., San Francisco, CA 94114 ☎ 415/626-1169 or 800/255-6951 🖨 415/626-8626 ⊕ www.nowvoyager. com. **Skylink Travel and Tour** ✉ 1455 N. Dutton Ave., Suite A, Santa Rosa, CA 95401 ☎ 707/546-9888 or 800/225-5759 🖨 707/636-0951; serving lesbian travelers.

HEALTH

DIVERS' ALERT

Do not fly within 24 hours of scuba diving.

Neophyte divers should have a complete physical exam before undertaking a dive. If you have travel insurance that covers evacuations, **make sure your policy applies to scuba-related injuries,** as not all companies provide this coverage.

FOOD & DRINK

The major health risk in Brazil is traveler's diarrhea, caused by eating contaminated fruit or vegetables or drinking contaminated water. So watch what you eat—on and off the beaten path. Avoid ice, uncooked food, and unpasteurized milk and milk products, and **drink only bottled water** or water that has been boiled for at least 20 minutes, even when brushing your teeth. Don't use ice unless you know it's made from purified water. (Ice in city restaurants is usually safe.) Peel or thoroughly wash fresh fruits and vegetables. Avoid eating food from street vendors.

INFECTIOUS DISEASES

Most travelers to the Amazon return home unscathed apart from a bit of traveler's diarrhea. However, you should visit a doctor at least six weeks prior to traveling to discuss recommended vaccinations, some of which require multiple shots over a period of weeks. If you get sick weeks, months, or in rare cases, years after your trip, make sure your doctor administers blood tests for tropical diseases.

Meningococcal meningitis and typhoid fever are common in certain areas of Brazil—and not only in remote areas like the Amazon. Meningitis has been a problem around São Paulo in recent years. Some of the following ailments are common in Brazil or in certain areas of Brazil and you should take the precautions we advise seriously. Other ailments listed here are extremely rare.

Chagas' Disease: Chagas' is found in rural areas. It is most often transmitted by a reduviid bug, or "kissing bug" that resides in clay and wood walls at night. Infection occurs when an insect carrying Chagas' deposits feces onto food you eat or onto your skin, after which you unintentionally rub it into the bite wound, a cut, your eyes, or your mouth. To reduce risk, don't sleep against walls and always wash or peel fruit and vegetables before eating. Symptoms of Chagas' often appear 10–20 years after infection; they are usually chronic but not deadly, and include heart problems and enlargement of the digestive tract. In rare cases acute symptoms occur soon after infection. Acute symptoms include swelling at the point of infection and fever. The disease can be treated effectively if caught before symptoms become too severe.

Cholera: There's little risk of contracting cholera in the Amazon. The disease can be avoided by being careful of what you eat and drink. The most common culprits are contaminated shellfish, crustaceans, and water. Most people who contract the disease experience only mild diarrhea, but it can cause severe diarrhea, vomiting, and cramping. A telltale sign of cholera is a watery stool with white mucus. Mild cases resolve themselves with fluid replacement; severe cases require antibiotics.

Diarrhea: Diarrhea is a common side effect of travel but is usually not serious. Simple changes in diet or climate can cause diarrhea, but contaminated food and water are also culprits (⇨ Food & Drink, *above*). If you are stricken with diarrhea, be sure to drink lots of water or juice, and avoid caffeine. If you're feeling dehydrated, take a rehydrating solution, available at drugstores, or make your own (⇨ Over-the-Counter Remedies, *below*).

Dengue Fever: Seldom fatal, dengue is nevertheless a serious problem in the

Amazon and in the Pantanal. The virus is caused by bites from infected mosquitoes. You can contract dengue almost anywhere in the Amazon, even in the cities. Infected mosquitoes attack during the day (unlike malarial mosquitoes, which attack at dusk and dawn). Symptoms, which usually have immediate onset, are flulike: fever, chills, and aches. A severe headache, pain behind the eyes, or rash might also occur. There is no treatment for dengue; sufferers are usually hospitalized and closely monitored until the disease runs its course. There is no immunization, but at this writing, the World Health Organization had hinted that a vaccine might become available in the near future. Don't take aspirins to treat dengue—they don't mix well with the virus.

Hepatitis: Vaccines against hepatitis A and B are recommended for travel to Brazil. The hepatitis virus attacks the liver and is transmitted via contaminated food and water, sexual contact, dirty needles (from tattooing, transfusions, or drug taking), and in some rare cases, dirty lavatories. Symptoms include jaundice, fatigue, abdominal pain, dark urine, nausea, diarrhea, and fever.

Intestinal Worms: Intestinal worms are parasites that can enter through your skin or via contaminated food, especially undercooked meat. Fairly common in the Amazon region of Brazil, this ailment is often not serious. Symptoms include diarrhea, loss of appetite, restless sleep, nausea, vomiting, and fever.

Leishmaniasis: Caused by sandfly bites, leishmaniasis is usually contracted in forested areas. Most often, the condition starts as a bump that becomes a sore that is slow to heal. Other, less common forms of the disease can cause swelling of the nose or a serious and sometimes fatal fever. Prevent sandfly bites by sleeping on the second story of buildings (they can't fly very high), wearing pants and long-sleeve shirts in rural, forested areas, and using repellant with DEET.

Malaria: The Amazon is the highest risk area in Brazil for malaria, but most residents of the Amazon have never had the disease. The Centers for Disease Control (CDC) offers some good information but can be overly cautious. It lumps huge areas of the Amazon together and makes no distinction between particularly harmful strains of malaria found in parts of Africa, for example, and the less serious strains found in the Amazon. For destination-specific advice, ask a local doctor or pharmacist. If you find that malaria is a risk where you are going, either change your plans or use lots of bug spray and wear pants and long-sleeve shirts. Especially avoid exposing yourself to mosquitoes around dusk and dawn, when mosquitoes that carry malaria are most active. Symptoms of the disease are flulike: fever, aches, chills, fatigue, and headache, and might include nausea, vomiting, and diarrhea. If malaria is not treated, it can be fatal. Malaria medication does not prevent the disease; it only lessens its effects. The medication itself can have bothersome side effects, such as nausea. Discuss the option with your doctor. If you are experiencing symptoms of malaria but blood tests are negative, make sure your blood tests are being administered *while* you are showing symptoms. The blood test to detect malaria is not effective during dormant phases of the disease.

Rabies: Avoid contact with cats, dogs, and wild mammals to minimize your chance of contracting rabies. If you plan to be in contact with wild or rural animals on your trip, consider getting a rabies vaccination.

Schistosomiasis: Of the many doctors we surveyed in the Amazon, none had ever seen a case of schistosomiasis (also called bilharzia). The disease is caused by a parasite that infects worms in water contaminated by human waste. The parasite can penetrate the skin of a person wading or swimming in contaminated water. Worms then grow inside the blood vessels and lay eggs that can travel to the bladder and intestines. Symptoms might appear within days or up to two months after infection and include a rash or itching around the point of infection, fever, chills, cough, and aches. In extreme cases schistosomiasis causes serious damage to the liver, lungs, bladder, and intestines.

Yellow Fever: A yellow fever vaccination is available and is highly recommended for travel to certain areas of Brazil. The disease is rare, but in 2002 an American died after contracting yellow fever on an Amazon fishing trip; he had not been vaccinated. Mosquitoes transmit yellow fever. Use bug spray and cover up to avoid mosquito bites. Abdominal pain, severe headache, and fever are symptoms of the disease. Yellow fever can be fatal in a matter of days, so seek medical attention right away if you experience these symptoms.

OVER-THE-COUNTER REMEDIES

Mild cases of diarrhea may respond to Imodium (known generically as loperamide) or Pepto-Bismol (not as strong), both of which can be purchased over the counter at a pharmacy (*farmácia*). Rehydrating solutions are available at pharmacies, or you can concoct your own version by mixing one teaspoon of sugar and a quarter teaspoon of salt per liter of water. Drink plenty of purified water or *chá* (tea)—*camomila* (chamomile) is a good folk remedy. In severe cases rehydrate yourself with a salt–sugar solution: ½ teaspoon *sal* (salt) and 4 tablespoons *açúcar* (sugar) per quart of *agua* (water).

Pharmacies also sell antidiarrheal medicines, but an effective home remedy is the same as the rehydrating concoction: a teaspoon of sugar plus a quarter teaspoon of salt in a liter of water.

The word for aspirin is *aspirina*; Tylenol is pronounced *tee-luh-nawl*.

PESTS & OTHER HAZARDS

In forested areas, especially in the Amazon, insects and other pests can cause plenty of annoyance but rarely serious problems. Still, it is advisable to err on the side of caution. In areas with malaria and dengue fever, which are both carried by mosquitoes, take *mosquiteiros* (mosquito nets for beds or hammocks), wear boots and clothing that covers the body, apply repellent containing DEET (non-DEET repellents don't work in the Amazon) to shoes and clothing, and use a spray against flying insects in living and sleeping areas.

Carry an adrenalin kit if you are allergic to bites and stings. Repellant can also ward off ticks and chiggers. Check your clothing and skin when you return from hikes to be sure you haven't brought any stowaways home. Make sure your shoes are empty before putting them on each morning. And if all of these devices fail, anti-itch cream gives you some relief.

Bichos de pé, parasites found in areas where pigs, chickens, and dogs run free, embed themselves in human feet. To avoid these parasites, never walk barefoot in areas where animals are loose.

Sunshine, limes, and skin don't mix well. The oil in lime-skin juice, if left on human skin and exposed to the sun, will burn and scar. If you're using lime and will be exposed to a lot of sun, be sure to wash well with soap and water. Should spots appear on skin areas that have been exposed, pharmacies will know which creams work best to heal the burns. (Note that affected areas shouldn't be exposed to the sun for three months following the burn.)

Heatstroke and heat prostration are common though easily preventable maladies. The symptoms for either can vary but always start with headaches, nausea, and dizziness. If ignored, these symptoms can worsen until you require medical attention. In hot weather be sure to rehydrate regularly, wear loose lightweight clothing, and avoid overexerting yourself.

Aside from the obvious safe-sex precautions, keep in mind that Brazil's blood supply isn't subject to the same intense screening as it is in North America, western Europe, Australia, and New Zealand. If you need a transfusion and circumstances permit it, ask that the blood be screened. Insulin-dependent diabetics or those who require injections should pack enough of the appropriate supplies—syringes, needles, disinfectants—for the entire trip. It's best to resist the temptation to get a new tattoo or body piercing in Brazil, but if you're determined, be sure to carefully inspect the equipment.

SHOTS & MEDICATIONS

For travel anywhere in Brazil, you must have updated vaccines for diphtheria, tetanus, and polio. Children must additionally have current inoculations against measles, mumps, and rubella. For travel to jungle areas and some other regions of the country, vaccinations against hepatitis A and B, meningitis, typhoid, and yellow fever are highly recommended. Consult your doctor about whether to get a rabies vaccination. If you plan to visit remote regions or stay for more than six weeks, **check with the CDC's International Travelers' Hotline.**

Discuss the option of taking antimalarial drugs with your doctor. Note that in parts of northern Brazil, a particularly aggressive strain of malaria has become resistant to one antimalarial drug—chloroquine (Aralen®). Some antimalarial drugs have rather unpleasant side effects—from headaches, nausea, and dizziness to psychosis, convulsions, and hallucinations.

🛈 Health Warnings **National Centers for Disease Control and Prevention (CDC)** ✉ National Center for Infectious Diseases, Division of Quarantine, Travelers' Health, 1600 Clifton Rd. NE, Atlanta, GA 30333 ☎ 877/394-8747 for International Travelers' Hotline, 404/498-1600 for Division of Quarantine, 800/311-3435 for other inquiries 🖷 888/232-3299 ⊕ www.cdc.gov/travel.

HOLIDAYS

Major national holidays include: New Year's Day; Epiphany (Jan. 6); Carnaval (the week preceding Ash Wednesday); Good Friday (the Friday before Easter Sunday); Easter Sunday; Tiradentes Day (Apr. 21); Labor Day (May 1); Corpus Christi (60 days after Easter Sunday); Independence Day (Sept. 7); Our Lady of Aparecida Day (Oct. 12); All Souls' Day (Nov. 1); Declaration of the Republic Day (Nov. 15); and Christmas.

INSURANCE

The most useful travel-insurance plan is a comprehensive policy that includes coverage for trip cancellation and interruption, default, trip delay, and medical expenses (with a waiver for preexisting conditions).

Without insurance you'll lose all or most of your money if you cancel your trip, regardless of the reason. Default insurance covers you if your tour operator, airline, or cruise line goes out of business. Trip-delay covers expenses that arise because of bad weather or mechanical delays. Study the fine print when comparing policies.

If you're traveling internationally, a key component of travel insurance is coverage for medical bills incurred if you get sick on the road. Such expenses aren't generally covered by Medicare or private policies. U.K. residents can buy a travel-insurance policy valid for most vacations taken during the year in which it's purchased (but check preexisting-condition coverage). British and Australian citizens need extra medical coverage when traveling overseas.

Always **buy travel policies directly from the insurance company;** if you buy them from a cruise line, airline, or tour operator that goes out of business you probably won't be covered for the agency or operator's default, a major risk. Before making any purchase, review your existing health and home-owner's policies to find what they cover away from home.

🛈 Travel Insurers In the U.S.: **Access America** ✉ 6600 W. Broad St., Richmond, VA 23230 ☎ 800/284-8300 🖷 804/673-1491 or 800/346-9265 ⊕ www.accessamerica.com. **Travel Guard International** ✉ 1145 Clark St., Stevens Point, WI 54481 ☎ 715/345-0505 or 800/826-1300 🖷 800/955-8785 ⊕ www.travelguard.com.

🛈 Insurance Information In the U.K.: **Association of British Insurers** ✉ 51 Gresham St., London EC2V 7HQ ☎ 020/7600-3333 🖷 020/7696-8999 ⊕ www.abi.org.uk. In Canada: **RBC Insurance** ✉ 6880 Financial Dr., Mississauga, Ontario L5N 7Y5 ☎ 800/565-3129 🖷 905/813-4704 ⊕ www.rbcinsurance.com. In Australia: **Insurance Council of Australia** ✉ Insurance Enquiries and Complaints, Level 3, 56 Pitt St., Sydney, NSW 2000 ☎ 1300/363683 or 02/9251-4456 🖷 02/9251-4453 ⊕ www.iecltd.com.au. In New Zealand: **Insurance Council of New Zealand** ✉ Level 7, 111–115 Customhouse Quay, Box 474, Wellington ☎ 04/472-5230 🖷 04/473-3011 ⊕ www.icnz.org.nz.

LANGUAGE

The language in Brazil is Portuguese, not Spanish, and Brazilians will appreciate it if you know the difference. The two languages are distinct, but common origins mean many words are similar, and fluent speakers of Spanish will be able to make themselves understood. English is spoken among educated Brazilians and, in general, by at least some of the staff at hotels, tour operators, and travel agencies. Store clerks and waiters may speak a smattering of English; taxi and bus drivers won't. As in many places throughout the world, you're more likely to find English-speaking locals in major cities than in small towns or the countryside. In the northeast you may even have difficulty in the cities.

LODGING

When you consider your lodgings in Brazil, add these three terms to your vocabulary: *pousada* (inn), *fazenda* (farm), and "flat" or "block" hotel (apartment-hotel). Flat hotels are popular with Brazilians, particularly in cities and with families and groups. Some have amenities such as pools, but for most folks, the biggest draw is affordability: with kitchen facilities and room for a group, flat hotels offer more for the money.

In the hinterlands it's good to **look at any room before accepting it;** expense is no guarantee of charm or cleanliness, and accommodations can vary dramatically within one hotel. Also, **be sure to check the shower:** some hotels have electric-powered showerheads rather than central water heaters. In theory, you can adjust both the water's heat and its pressure. In practice, if you want hot water you have to turn the water pressure down; if you want pressure, expect a brisk rinse. Careful! Don't adjust the power when you're under the water—you can get a little shock.

If you ask for a double room, you'll get a room for two people, but you're not guaranteed a double mattress. If you'd like to avoid twin beds, ask for a *cama de casal* ("couple's bed"). All rooms have air-conditioning, telephones, and televisions unless we indicate otherwise.

The lodgings we list are the cream of the crop in each price category. We always list the facilities that are available, but we don't specify whether they cost extra; when pricing accommodations, always ask what's included and what costs extra. Properties are assigned price categories based on the range between their least and most expensive standard double rooms at high season (excluding holidays). Properties marked ✕🏨 are lodging establishments whose restaurants warrant a special trip.

Assume that hotels operate on the European Plan (EP, with no meals) unless we specify that they use either the Continental Plan (CP, with a Continental breakfast), Breakfast Plan (BP, with a full breakfast), Modified American Plan (MAP, with breakfast and dinner), Full American Plan (FAP, with all meals), or are all-inclusive (including all meals and most activities). Price categories are as follows:

WHAT IT COSTS IN REAIS

CATEGORY	COST*
$$$$	over R$500
$$$	R$375–R$500
$$	R$250–R$375
$	R$125–R$250
¢	under R$125

*Prices are for a standard double room in high season, excluding taxes.

APARTMENT & VILLA RENTALS

If you want a home base that's roomy enough for a family and comes with cooking facilities, consider a furnished rental. These can save you money, especially if you're traveling with a group. Home-exchange directories sometimes list rentals as well as exchanges.

🏢 International Agents **Hideaways International** ✉ 767 Islington St., Portsmouth, NH 03801 ☎ 603/430–4433 or 800/843–4433 🖷 603/430–4444 ⊕ www.hideaways.com, membership $145. **Villas International** ✉ 4340 Redwood Hwy., Suite D309, San Rafael, CA 94903 ☎ 415/499–9490 or 800/221–2260 🖷 415/499–9491 ⊕ www.villasintl.com.

CAMPING

There are campgrounds all over the country, and some are well situated in areas such as the beach resort of Búzios in Rio de Janeiro State and the beautiful mesa of Chapada dos Gumarães in Mato Grosso State. Those with basic facilities (running water and electricity) cost as little as R$11

($3) a day per person. Some campgrounds also have picnic areas, kitchen and laundry facilities, recycling bins, playgrounds, soccer fields, and courts for volleyball and/or basketball.

Although it isn't illegal to camp outside campgrounds, you should inquire with locals for additional information and permission. Note that most conservation areas have restricted access, and some natural preserves forbid camping altogether.

HOME EXCHANGES

If you would like to exchange your home for someone else's, join a home-exchange organization, which will send you its updated listings of available exchanges for a year and will include your own listing in at least one of them. It's up to you to make specific arrangements.

🏠 Exchange Clubs **HomeLink International** ⌂ Box 47747, Tampa, FL 33647 ☎ 813/975-9825 or 800/638-3841 🖷 813/910-8144 ⊕ www.homelink. org; $110 yearly for a listing, on-line access, and catalog; $70 without catalog. **Intervac U.S.** ✉ 30 Corte San Fernando, Tiburon, CA 94920 ☎ 800/ 756-4663 🖷 415/435-7440 ⊕ www.intervacus.com; $105 yearly for a listing, online access, and a catalog; $50 without catalog.

HOSTELS

No matter what your age, you can save on lodging costs by staying at hostels. There are about 100 hostels scattered across Brazil, all of them affiliated with Hostelling International (HI). Many Brazilian hostels' names are preceded by the letters *AJ* (Albergues de Juventude). The Federação Brasileira dos Albergues de Juventude (FBJA; Brazilian Federation of Youth Hostels) is based in Rio.

Membership in any HI national hostel association, open to travelers of all ages, allows you to stay in HI-affiliated hostels at member rates; one-year membership is about $28 for adults (C$35 for a two-year minimum membership in Canada, £13.50 in the U.K., A$52 in Australia, and NZ$40 in New Zealand); hostels charge about $10–$30 per night. Members have priority if the hostel is full; they're also eligible for discounts around the world, even on rail and bus travel in some countries.

For information about youth hostels in Brazil contact the Associação Paulista de Albergues da Juventude. The association sells a book ($2.50) that lists hostels throughout the country.

🏠 Organizations **Associação Paulista de Albergues da Juventude** ✉ Rua 7 de Abril 386, República, São Paulo 01320-040 ☎ 011/258-0388. **Federação Brasileira dos Albergues de Juventude** ✉ Rua da Assembleia 10, Sala 1211, Centro, Rio De Janeiro, RJ 20011 ☎ 021/2531-2234 or 021/ 2531-1302. **Hostelling International–USA** ✉ 8401 Colesville Rd., Suite 600, Silver Spring, MD 20910 ☎ 301/495-1240 🖷 301/495-6697 ⊕ www.hiayh. org. **Hostelling International–Canada** ✉ 205 Catherine St., Suite 400, Ottawa, Ontario K2P 1C3 ☎ 613/237-7884 or 800/663-5777 🖷 613/237-7868 ⊕ www.hihostels.ca. **YHA England and Wales** ✉ Trevelyan House, Dimple Rd., Matlock, Derbyshire DE4 3YH, U.K. ☎ 0870/870-8808, 0870/770-8868, or 0162/959-2700 🖷 0870/770-6127 ⊕ www.yha.org.uk. **YHA Australia** ✉ 422 Kent St., Sydney, NSW 2001 ☎ 02/9261-1111 🖷 02/ 9261-1969 ⊕ www.yha.com.au. **YHA New Zealand** ✉ Level 4, Torrens House, 195 Hereford St., Box 436, Christchurch ☎ 03/379-9970 or 0800/278-299 🖷 03/365-4476 ⊕ www.yha.org.nz.

HOTELS

All hotels listed have private bath unless otherwise noted.

Hotels listed with EMBRATUR, Brazil's national tourism board, are rated using stars. However, that the number of stars awarded appears to be based strictly on the number of amenities, without taking into account intangibles such as service and atmosphere.

Carnaval (Carnival), the year's principal festival, occurs during the four days preceding Ash Wednesday. For top hotels in Rio, Salvador, and Recife—the three leading Carnaval cities—you must make reservations a year in advance. Hotel rates rise 20% on average for Carnaval. Not as well known outside Brazil but equally impressive is Rio's New Year's Eve celebration. More than a million people gather along Copacabana Beach for a massive fireworks display and to honor the sea goddess Iemanjá. To ensure a room, book at least six months in advance.

Hotels accept credit cards for payment, but first ask if there's a discount for cash. Try to bargain hard for a cash-on-the-barrel discount, then pay in local currency.

RESERVING A ROOM

When you book a room, you pay, in addition to the base fee, tourism fees equaling 10% of the room price plus R$1.50.

Toll-Free Numbers **Best Western** ☎ 800/528-1234 ⊕ www.bestwestern.com. **Choice** ☎ 800/424-6423 ⊕ www.choicehotels.com. **Comfort Inn** ☎ 800/424-6423 ⊕ www.choicehotels.com. **Hilton** ☎ 800/445-8667 ⊕ www.hilton.com. **Holiday Inn** ☎ 800/465-4329 ⊕ www.sixcontinentshotels.com. **Hyatt Hotels & Resorts** ☎ 800/233-1234 ⊕ www.hyatt.com. **Inter-Continental** ☎ 800/327-0200 ⊕ www.intercontinental.com. **Marriott** ☎ 800/228-9290 ⊕ www.marriott.com. **Le Meridien** ☎ 800/543-4300 ⊕ www.lemeridien-hotels.com. **Quality Inn** ☎ 800/424-6423 ⊕ www.choicehotels.com. **Radisson** ☎ 800/333-3333 ⊕ www.radisson.com. **Renaissance Hotels & Resorts** ☎ 800/468-3571 ⊕ www.renaissancehotels.com/. **Sheraton** ☎ 800/325-3535 ⊕ www.starwood.com/sheraton. **Sleep Inn** ☎ 800/424-6423 ⊕ www.choicehotels.com.

MAIL & SHIPPING

Post offices are called *correios,* and branches are marked by name and by a logo that looks something like two interlocked fingers; most are open weekdays 8–5 and Saturday until noon. Mailboxes are small yellow boxes marked CORREIOS that sit atop metal pedestals on street corners. Airmail from Brazil takes at least 10 or more days to reach the United States, possibly longer to Canada and the United Kingdom and definitely longer to Australia and New Zealand.

OVERNIGHT SERVICES

Brazil has both national and international express mail service, the price of which varies according to the weight of the package and the destination. FedEx is available in São Paulo, Rio, and Porto Alegre. In other areas international express mail can be sent with DHL. Keep in mind that "overnight" packages to or from Brazil take several days.

Major Services **DHL** ☎ 0800/701-0833 in Brazil ⊕ www.dhl.com.br. **FedEx** ☎ 011/5641-7788 in São Paulo, 0800/90-3333 elsewhere in Brazil ⊕ www.fedex.com/br_english.

POSTAL RATES

An airmail letter from Brazil to the United States and most parts of Europe, including the United Kingdom, costs about R$2.16 (75¢). Aerograms and postcards cost the same.

RECEIVING MAIL

Mail can be addressed to **poste restante** and sent to any major post office. The address must include the code for that particular branch. American Express will hold mail for its cardholders.

MONEY MATTERS

Top hotels in Rio and São Paulo go for more than R$430 ($125) a night, and meals can—but do not have to—cost as much. Outside Brazil's two largest cities and Brasília, prices for food and lodging tend to drop considerably. Self-service salad bars where you pay by weight (per kilo, about 2.2 pounds) are inexpensive alternatives everywhere, though be sure to choose carefully among them. Taxis can be pricey. City buses, subways, and long-distance buses are all inexpensive; plane fares aren't.

Prices throughout this guide are given for adults. Substantially reduced fees are almost always available for children, students, and senior citizens. For information on taxes, *see* Taxes.

ATMS

Nearly all the nation's major banks have automated teller machines (*caixas automáticos*), for which you must use a card with a credit-card logo. MasterCard/Cirrus holders can withdraw at Banco Itaú, Banco do Brasil, HSBC, and Banco24horas ATMs; Visa holders can use Bradesco ATMs and those at Banco do Brasil. American Express cardholders can make withdrawals at most Bradesco ATMs marked 24 HORAS. To be on the safe side, carry a variety of cards. Note also that if your PIN is more than four digits long and/or uses letters instead of numbers, it might not work. Get a four-digit numerical PIN before your trip. For your card to function in some ATMs, you may need to hit a screen command (perhaps, *estrangeiro*) if you are a foreign client.

CREDIT CARDS

In Brazil's largest cities and leading tourist centers, restaurants, hotels, and shops accept major international credit cards. Off the beaten track, you may have more difficulty using them. Many gas stations in rural Brazil don't take credit cards.

For costly items use your credit card whenever possible—you'll come out ahead, whether the exchange rate at which your purchase is calculated is the one in effect the day the vendor's bank abroad processes the charge or the one prevailing on the day the charge company's service center processes it at home.

Throughout this guide, the following abbreviations are used: **AE**, American Express; **DC**, Diners Club; **MC**, MasterCard; and **V**, Visa.

Reporting Lost Cards **MasterCard/Cirrus** ☎ 0800/891-3294 in Brazil. **Visa/Plus** ☎ 0800/891-3680 in Brazil.

CURRENCY

Brazil's unit of currency is the real (R$; plural: *reais*, though it's sometimes seen as *reals*). One real is 100 centavos (cents). There are notes worth 1, 5, 10, 20, 50, and 100 reais, together with coins worth 1, 5, 10, 25, and 50 centavos and 1 real.

CURRENCY EXCHANGE

At this writing, the real is at 3.63 to the Euro, 5.28 to the pound sterling, 2.88 to the U.S. dollar, 2.18 to the Canadian dollar, 2.24 to the Australia dollar, and 1.95 to the New Zealand dollar.

For the most favorable rates **change money through banks.** Although ATM transaction fees may be higher abroad than at home, ATM rates are excellent because they are based on wholesale rates offered only by major banks. You won't do as well at *casas de câmbio* (exchange houses), in airports or rail or bus stations, in hotels, in restaurants, or in stores.

To avoid lines at airport exchange booths, **get local currency before you leave home.** Don't wait until the last minute to do this

as many banks—even the international ones—don't have reais on hand and must order them for you. This can take a couple of days. Outside larger cities, changing money in Brazil becomes more of a challenge. When leaving a large city for a smaller town, bring enough cash for your trip. For an average week in a Brazilian city, a good strategy is to convert $500 into reais. This provides sufficient cash for most expenses, such as taxis and small purchases and snacks.

Exchange Services **International Currency Express** ✉ 427 N. Camden Dr., Suite F, Beverly Hills, CA 90210 ☎ 888/278-6628 orders ☎ 310/278-6410 ⊕ www.foreignmoney.com.

TRAVELER'S CHECKS

Do you need traveler's checks? It depends on where you're headed. If you're going to rural areas and small towns, go with cash; traveler's checks are best used in cities. Traveler's checks can be exchanged at hotels, banks, casas de câmbio, travel agencies, and shops in malls or stores that cater to tourists. Many small tradesmen are at a total loss when faced with traveler's checks. Note, however, that the rate for traveler's checks is lower than that for cash, and hotels often change them at a rate that's lower than that available at banks or casas de câmbio.

Lost or stolen checks can usually be replaced within 24 hours. To ensure a speedy refund, buy your own traveler's checks—don't let someone else pay for them: irregularities like this can cause delays. The person who bought the checks should make the call to request a refund. Traveler's checks should be in U.S. dollars. Some casas de câmbio accept only American Express traveler's checks, but you should be able to cash checks from other major banks in larger Brazilian cities.

PACKING

If you're doing business in Brazil, you'll need the same attire you would wear in U.S. and European cities: for men, suits and ties; for women, suits for day wear and cocktail dresses or the like for an evening out. For sightseeing, casual clothing and good walking shoes are appropriate; most restaurants don't require formal attire. For beach vacations bring lightweight sportswear, a bathing suit, a beach cover-up, a sun hat, and waterproof sunscreen that is at least SPF 15.

Travel in rain-forest areas requires long-sleeve shirts, long pants, socks, waterproof hiking boots (sneakers are less desirable, but work in a pinch), a hat, a light waterproof jacket, a bathing suit, and plenty of (strong) insect repellent. Other useful items include a screw-top water container that you can fill with bottled water, a money pouch, a travel flashlight and extra batteries, a Swiss Army knife with a bottle opener, a medical kit, binoculars, a pocket calculator, and lots of extra film. A sarong or a light cotton blanket makes a handy beach towel, picnic blanket, and cushion for hard seats, among other things.

In your carry-on luggage, pack an extra pair of eyeglasses or contact lenses and enough of any medication you take to last a few days longer than the entire trip. You may also ask your doctor to write a spare prescription using the drug's generic name, as brand names may vary from country to country. In luggage to be checked, **never pack prescription drugs, valuables, or undeveloped film.** And don't forget to carry with you the addresses of offices that handle refunds of lost traveler's checks. Check *Fodor's How to Pack* (available at on-line retailers and bookstores everywhere) for more tips.

To avoid customs and security delays, carry medications in their original packaging. Don't pack any sharp objects in your carry-on luggage, including knives of any size or material, scissors, and corkscrews, or anything else that might arouse suspicion.

To avoid having your checked luggage chosen for hand inspection, don't cram bags full. The U.S. Transportation Security Administration suggests packing shoes on top and placing personal items you don't want touched in clear plastic bags.

CHECKING LUGGAGE

You're allowed to carry aboard one bag and one personal article, such as a purse or a laptop computer. Make sure what you carry on fits under your seat or in the overhead bin. Get to the gate early, so you can board as soon as possible, before the overhead bins fill up.

Baggage allowances vary by carrier, destination, and ticket class. On international flights you're usually allowed to check two bags weighing up to 70 pounds (32 kilograms) each, although a few airlines allow checked bags of up to 88 pounds (40 kilograms) in first class. Some international carriers don't allow more than 66 pounds (30 kilograms) per bag in business class and 44 pounds (20 kilograms) in economy. On domestic flights the limit is usually 50–70 pounds (23–32 kilograms) per bag. In general, carry-on bags shouldn't exceed 40 pounds (18 kilograms). Most airlines won't accept bags that weigh more than 100 pounds (45 kilograms) on domestic or international flights. Check baggage restrictions with your carrier before you pack.

Airline liability for baggage on international flights is $9.07 per pound or $20 per kilogram for checked baggage (roughly $640 per 70-pound bag) and $400 per passenger for unchecked baggage. You can buy additional coverage at check-in for about $10 per $1,000 of coverage, but it often excludes a rather extensive list of items, shown on your airline ticket.

Before departure, itemize your bags' contents and their worth, and label the bags with your name, address, and phone number. (If you use your home address, cover it so potential thieves can't see it readily.) Include a label inside each bag and **pack a copy of your itinerary.** At check-in, make sure each bag is correctly tagged with the destination airport's three-letter code. Because some checked bags will be opened for hand inspection, the U.S. Transportation Security Administration recommends that you leave luggage unlocked or use the plastic locks offered at check-in. TSA screeners place an inspection notice inside searched bags, which are resealed with a special lock.

If your bag has been searched and contents are missing or damaged, file a claim with the TSA Consumer Response Center as soon as possible. If your bags arrive damaged or fail to arrive at all, file a written report with the airline before leaving the airport.

🔁 Complaints **U.S. Transportation Security Administration Consumer Response Center** ☎ 866/289-9673 ⊕ www.tsa.gov.

PASSPORTS & VISAS

When traveling internationally, carry your passport even if you don't need one (it's always the best form of ID) and **make two photocopies of the data page** (one for someone at home and another for you, carried separately from your passport). If you lose your passport, promptly call the nearest embassy or consulate and the local police.

U.S. passport applications for children under age 14 require consent from both parents or legal guardians; both parents must appear together to sign the application. If only one parent appears, he or she must submit a written statement from the other parent authorizing passport issuance for the child. A parent with sole authority must present evidence of it when applying; acceptable documentation includes the child's certified birth certificate listing only the applying parent, a court order specifically permitting this parent's travel with the child, or a death certificate for the nonapplying parent. Application forms and instructions are available on the Web site of the U.S. State Department's Bureau of Consular Affairs (⊕ www.travel.state.gov).

ENTERING BRAZIL

To enter Brazil, all U.S. citizens, even infants, must have both a passport and a tourist visa (valid for five years). To obtain one, you must submit the following to the Brazilian embassy or to the nearest consulate: a passport that will be valid for six months past the date of first entry to Brazil; a passport-type photo; a photocopy of your round-trip ticket or a signed letter from a travel agency with confirmed round-trip bookings or proof of your ability to pay for your stay in Brazil; and cash, a money order, or a certified check for $100 (there's also a $10 handling fee if anyone other than the applicant submits the visa).

If you're a business traveler, you may need a business visa (valid for 90 days). It has all the same requirements as a tourist visa, but you'll also need a letter on company letterhead—addressed to the embassy or consulate and signed by an authorized representative (other than you)—stating the nature of your business in Brazil, itinerary, business contacts, dates of arrival and departure, and that the company assumes all financial and moral responsibility while you're in Brazil. The fee is $100 (plus the $10 fee if someone other than you submits the visa). In addition to the forms of payment detailed above, a company check is also acceptable.

Canadian nationals, Australians, and New Zealanders also need visas to enter the country. For Canadians the fee is C$72, for New Zealanders NZ$50, and for Australians A$87.50. Citizens of the United Kingdom don't need a visa.

In the United States there are consulates in Boston, Chicago, Houston, Los Angeles, Miami, New York, San Francisco, San Juan, and Washington, D.C. To get the location of the Brazilian consulate to which you must apply, contact the Brazilian embassy. Note that some consulates don't allow you to apply for a visa by mail. If you don't live near a city with a consulate, consider hiring a concierge-type service to do your legwork. Many cities have these companies, which not only help with the paperwork for such things as visas and passports but also send someone to wait in line for you.

PASSPORT OFFICES & EMBASSIES

The best time to apply for a passport or to renew is in fall and winter. Before any trip, check your passport's expiration date, and, if necessary, renew it as soon as possible.

🔁 Australian Citizens **Brazilian Embassy** ⌂ Box 1540, Canberra, ACT 2601 ☎ 616/273-2372. **Passports Australia** ☎ 131-232 ⊕ www.passports.gov.au.

🔁 Canadian Citizens **Brazilian Embassy** ✉ 450 Wilbrod St., Ottawa, Ontario, K1N 6M8 ☎ 613/237-1090. **Passport Office** ✉ to mail in applications: 200 Promenade du Portage, Hull, Québec J8X 4B7 ☎ 819/994-3500 or 800/567-6868 ⊕ www.ppt.gc.ca.

New Zealand Citizens **Brazilian Embassy**
⊠ Box 5432, 10 Brandon St., level 9, Wellington
☎ 04/473-3516 🖷 04/473-3517 ⊕ www.brazil.org.
nz. **New Zealand Passports Office** ☎ 0800/
22-5050 or 04/474-8100 ⊕ www.passports.govt.nz.

U.K. Citizens **Brazilian Embassy** ⊠ 32 Green
St., London, W1K 4AT ☎ 020/7629-6909. **U.K. Passport Service** ☎ 0870/521-0410 ⊕ www.passport.
gov.uk.

U.S. Citizens **Brazilian Embassy** ⊠ 3006
Massachusetts Ave. NW, Washington, DC 20008
☎ 202/238-2700 or 202/238-2800 to cultural section. **National Passport Information Center**
☎ 900/225-5674 or 900/225-7778 TTY (calls are
55¢ per min for automated service or $1.50 per min
for operator service), 888/362-8668 or 888/498-
3648 TTY (calls are $5.50 each) ⊕ www.travel.
state.gov.

REST ROOMS

The word for "bathroom" is *banheiro,*
though the term *sanitários* (toilets) is also
used. *Homens* means "men" and *mul-
heres* means "women." Around major
tourist attractions and along the main
beaches in big cities, you'll find public rest
rooms. In other areas you may have to
rely on the kindness of local restaurant
and shop owners. If a smile and polite request (*"Por favor, posso usar o banheiro?"*) doesn't work, become a
customer—the purchase of a drink or a
knickknack might just buy you a trip to
the bathroom. Rest areas with relatively
clean, well-equipped bathrooms are plentiful along major highways. Still, carry a
pocket-size package of tissues in case
there's no toilet paper. Tip bathroom attendants with a few spare centavos.

SAFETY

For many English-speaking tourists in
Brazil, standing out like a sore thumb is
unavoidable. But there are some precautions you can take. Don't wear a waist
pack or a money belt because thieves can
cut the strap. Instead, distribute your cash
and any valuables (including credit cards
and passport) between a deep front
pocket, an inside jacket or vest pocket,
and a hidden money pouch. Do not reach
for the money pouch in public. Unless
you're out in the wild, if carrying a backpack, put it in front or at least over your
shoulder and hang on tight. Likewise, wallets go in your front pocket.

By day the countryside is safe. Although
there has been a real effort to crack down
on tourist-related crime, particularly in
Rio, petty street thievery is still prevalent
in urban areas, especially in places around
tourist hotels, restaurants, and discos.
Avoid flashing money around. To safeguard your funds, **lock traveler's checks
and cash in a hotel safe,** except for what
you need to carry each day. Ask the manager to sign a list of what you put in a
hotel safe.

Money (and important documents) that
you do carry are best tucked into a money
belt or carried in the inside pockets of
your clothing. Wear the simplest of time-
pieces and **do not wear any jewelry you
aren't willing to lose**—stories of thieves
yanking chains or earrings off travelers
aren't uncommon. When on a crowded
bus or boat, keep your hand on your wal-
let or your eyes on your purse. If you're
taking photos, unless you're with a tour
group, take your photo and then put your
camera away. Don't let it hang around
your neck while you wander around. **Keep
cameras in a secure camera bag,** preferably one with a chain or wire embedded in
the strap. If you're traveling by bus or
boat, or just walking in crowded areas,
carabiners come in handy for clipping
your bag or other items to a luggage rack,
your belt loops, or any other ingenious
place to provide extra security. Always **remain alert for pickpockets,** particularly in
market areas, and **follow local advice
about where it's safe to walk.**

Never leave valuables visible in a car.
Take them inside with you whenever possible, or lock them in the trunk. Talk with
locals or your hotel's staff about crime
whenever you arrive in a new location.
They will be able to tell you if it's safe to
walk around after dark and what areas to
avoid. Most important, **don't bring anything you can't stand to lose.**

Note that Brazilian law requires everyone to have official identification with
them at all times. Carry a copy of your

passport's data page and of the Brazilian visa stamp (leave the actual passport in the hotel safe).

LOCAL SCAMS

Most tourist-related crimes occur in busy public areas: beaches, sidewalks or plazas, bus stations (and on buses, too). In these settings pickpockets, usually young children, work in groups. One or more will try to distract you while another grabs a wallet, bag, or camera. **Beware of children who suddenly thrust themselves in front of you** to ask for money or who offer to shine your shoes. Another member of the gang may strike from behind, grab whatever valuable is available, and disappear in the crowd. It's best not to protest while being mugged. Those on the take are sometimes armed or will tell you that their backup is, and although they're often quite young, they can be dangerous.

WOMEN IN BRAZIL

If you carry a purse, choose one with a zipper and a thick strap that you can drape across your body; adjust the length so that the purse sits in front of you at or above hip level. (Don't wear a money belt or a waist pack.) Store only enough money in the purse to cover casual spending. Distribute the rest of your cash and any valuables between deep front pockets, inside jacket or vest pockets, and a concealed money pouch.

Although women are gradually assuming a more important role in the nation's job force, machismo is still a strong part of Brazilian culture. Stares and catcalls aren't uncommon. Although you should have no fear of traveling unaccompanied, you should still take a few precautions.

Ask your hotel staff to recommend a reliable cab company, and **call for a taxi instead of hailing one on the street,** especially at night. **Dress to avoid unwanted attention.** For example, always wear a cover-up when heading to or from the beach. Avoid eye contact with unsavory individuals. If such a person approaches you, discourage him by politely but firmly saying, "*Por favor, me dê licença*" (pohr fah-**vohr,** meh day lee-**sehn**-see-ah), which means "Excuse me, please," and then walk away with resolve.

SENIOR-CITIZEN TRAVEL

There's no reason why active, well-traveled senior citizens shouldn't visit Brazil, whether on an independent (but pre-booked) vacation, an escorted tour, or an adventure vacation. The country is full of good hotels and competent ground operators to meet your flights and organize your sightseeing. Before you leave home, however, determine what medical services your health insurance will cover outside the United States; note that Medicare doesn't provide for payment of hospital and medical services outside the United States. If you need additional travel insurance, buy it.

To qualify for age-related discounts, mention your senior-citizen status up front when booking hotel reservations (not when checking out) and before you're seated in restaurants (not when paying the bill). Have identification on hand. When renting a car, ask about promotional car-rental discounts, which can be cheaper than senior-citizen rates.

Educational Programs Elderhostel ⊠ 11 Ave. de Lafayette, Boston, MA 02111-1746 ☎ 877/426–8056, 978/323–4141 international callers, 877/426–2167 TTY 📠 877/426-2166 ⊕ www.elderhostel.org.

STUDENTS IN BRAZIL

Although airfares to and within Brazil are high, you can **take buses to most destinations** for mere dollars, and you can usually find safe, comfortable (if sparse) accommodations for a fraction of what it might cost back home. Most Brazilian cities also have vibrant student populations. In stalwart university towns like Ouro Preto in Minas Gerais State, you may find inexpensive lodging at fraternity houses (*repúblicas*). Students are supposed to be given a 50% discount at movie theaters and concert halls, although some places don't observe this practice. Foreign visitors may also qualify for discounts at some sporting events. **Contact a travel agency for full details on discounts and how to qualify for them.**

IDs & Services STA Travel ⊠ 10 Downing St., New York, NY 10014 ☎ 212/627-3111, 800/777-0112 for 24-hr service center 📠 212/627-3387 ⊕ www.

sta.com. **Travel Cuts** ✉ 187 College St., Toronto, Ontario M5T 1P7, Canada ☎ 800/592-2887 in the U.S., 416/979-2406 or 866/246-9762 in Canada 🖷 416/979-8167 ⊕ www.travelcuts.com.

TAXES

Sales tax is included in the prices shown on goods in stores. Hotel, meal, and car rental taxes are usually tacked on in addition to the costs shown on menus and brochures. At this writing, hotel taxes are roughly 5%, meal taxes 10%, and car rental taxes 12%.

Departure taxes on international flights from Brazil aren't always included in your ticket and can run as high as R$86 ($25); domestic flights may incur a R$22 ($7) tax. Although U.S. dollars are accepted in some airports, be prepared to **pay departure taxes in reais.**

TELEPHONES

The number of digits in Brazilian telephone numbers varies widely.

COUNTRY & AREA CODES

The country code for Brazil is 55. When dialing a Brazilian number from abroad, drop the initial zero from the local area code. The country code is 1 for the United States and Canada, 61 for Australia, 64 for New Zealand, and 44 for the United Kingdom. The area code for Rio is 021, for São Paulo 011. Other area codes are listed in the front of local phone directories and in chapter A to Z sections throughout this guide.

DIRECTORY & OPERATOR INFORMATION

For local directory assistance, dial 102. For directory assistance in another Brazilian city, dial the area code of that city plus 121.

INTERNATIONAL CALLS

International calls to and from Brazil are extremely expensive. Hotels also add a surcharge, increasing this cost even more. For international calls, dial 00 + the long-distance company's access code + the country code + the area code and number. For operator-assisted international calls, dial 00–0111. For international information, dial 00–0333.

AT&T, MCI, and Sprint operators are also accessible from Brazil; before you leave home, **get the local access codes** for your destinations. International calls can be made from public phone booths with a prepaid phone card.

LOCAL CALLS

Local calls can be made most easily from pay phones, which take phone cards only. A bar or restaurant may allow you to use its private phone for a local call if you're a customer.

LONG-DISTANCE CALLS

Even with a phone card, you may not be able to make long-distance calls from some pay phones—and the logic behind those that do and those that don't allow such calls varies from region to region, making it as baffling as it is Brazilian. First, do as the locals do: shrug your shoulders and smile. Second, do as the locals say: ask the staff at your hotel for insight. Long-distance calls within Brazil are expensive, and hotels also add a surcharge.

With the privatization of the Brazilian telecommunications network, there's a wide choice of long-distance companies. Hence, to make direct-dial long-distance calls, you must find out which companies serve the area from which you're calling and then get their access codes—the staff at your hotel can help. (Some hotels have already made the choice for you, so you may not need an access code when calling from the hotel itself.) For long-distance calls within Brazil, dial 0 + the access code + the area code and number.

LONG-DISTANCE & INTERNATIONAL SERVICES

AT&T, MCI, and Sprint access codes make calling long-distance relatively convenient, but you may find the local access number blocked in many hotel rooms. First ask the hotel operator to connect you. If the hotel operator balks, ask for an international operator, or dial the international operator yourself. One way to improve your odds of getting connected to your long-distance carrier is to travel with more than one company's calling card (a hotel may block Sprint, for example, but not MCI). If all else fails, call from a pay phone.

Access Codes AT&T Direct ☎ 0800/890-0288 or 0800/888-8288. **MCI WorldPhone** ☎ 000-8012. **Sprint International Access** ☎ 0800/888-7800, 0800/890-8000, or 0800/888-8000.

PHONE CARDS

All pay phones in Brazil take phone cards only. Buy a phone card, a *cartão de telefone*, at a *posto telefônico* (phone office), newsstand, or post office. Cards come with a varying number of units (each unit is usually worth a couple of minutes), which will determine the price. Buy a couple of cards if you don't think you'll have the chance again soon.

PUBLIC PHONES

Public phones are everywhere and are called *orelhões* (big ears) because of their shape. The phones take phone cards only.

TIME

Although Brazil covers several time zones, most Brazilian cities are three hours behind GMT (Greenwich mean time), which means that if it's 5 PM in London, it's 2 PM in Rio and noon in New York. Manaus is an hour behind Rio.

TIPPING

Wages can be paltry in Brazil, so a little generosity in tipping can go a long way. At hotels it can go even farther if you tip in U.S. dollars or pounds sterling (bills, not coins). At restaurants that add a 10% service charge onto the check, it's customary to give the waiter an additional 5% tip. If there's no service charge, leave 15%. In deluxe hotels tip porters R$2 per bag, chambermaids R$2 per day, and bellhops R$4–R$6 for room and valet service. Tips for doormen and concierges vary, depending on the services provided. A good tip would be at least R$22, with an average of R$11. For moderate and inexpensive hotels, tips tend to be minimal (salaries are so low that virtually anything is well received). If a taxi driver helps you with your luggage, a per-bag charge of about R$1 is levied in addition to the fare. In general, tip taxi drivers 10% of the fare.

At a barber shop or beauty salon, a 10%–20% tip is expected. If a service station attendant does anything beyond filling up the gas tank, leave him a small tip of some spare change. Tipping in bars and cafés follows the rules of restaurants, although savvy Brazilians rarely leave a gratuity if they have had only a soft drink or a beer. At airports and at train and bus stations, tip the last porter who puts your bags into the cab (R$1 a bag at airports, 50 centavos a bag at bus and train stations). In large cities you'll often be accosted on the street by children looking for handouts; 50 centavos is an average "tip."

TOURS & PACKAGES

Because everything is prearranged on a prepackaged tour or independent vacation, you spend less time planning—and often get it all at a good price.

BOOKING WITH AN AGENT

Travel agents are excellent resources. But it's a good idea to collect brochures from several agencies, as some agents' suggestions may be influenced by relationships with tour and package firms that reward them for volume sales. If you have a special interest, find an agent with expertise in that area; the American Society of Travel Agents (ASTA; ⇨ Travel Agencies) has a database of specialists worldwide. You can log on to the group's Web site to find an ASTA travel agent in your neighborhood.

Make sure your travel agent knows the accommodations and other services of the place being recommended. Ask about the hotel's location, room size, beds, and whether it has a pool, room service, or programs for children, if you care about these. Has your agent been there in person or sent others whom you can contact?

Do some homework on your own, too: local tourism boards can provide information about lesser-known and small-niche operators, some of which may sell only direct.

BUYER BEWARE

Each year consumers are stranded or lose their money when tour operators—even large ones with excellent reputations—go out of business. So check out the operator. Ask several travel agents about its reputation, and try to **book with a company that has a consumer-protection program.** (Look for information in the company's brochure.) In the United States, members of the National Tour Association and the United States Tour Operators Association are required to set aside funds to cover payments and travel arrangements in the event that the company defaults. It's also a good idea to choose a company that participates in the American Society of Travel Agents' Tour Operator Program; ASTA will act as mediator in any disputes between you and your tour operator.

Remember that the more your package or tour includes, the better you can predict the ultimate cost of your vacation. Make sure you know exactly what is covered, and beware of hidden costs. Are taxes, tips, and transfers included? Entertainment and excursions? These can add up.

🖪 Tour-Operator Recommendations **American Society of Travel Agents** (⇨ Travel Agencies). **National Tour Association** (NTA) ✉ 546 E. Main St., Lexington, KY 40508 ☎ 859/226-4444 or 800/682-8886 🖷 859/226-4404 🌐 www.ntaonline.com. **United States Tour Operators Association** (USTOA) ✉ 275 Madison Ave., Suite 2014, New York, NY 10016 ☎ 212/599-6599 🖷 212/599-6744 🌐 www.ustoa.com.

THEME TRIPS

Among companies that sell theme-trip tours to Brazil, the following are well known, have a proven reputation, and offer plenty of options.

🖪 Amazon Jungle Lodges **Ecotour Expeditions** ☏ Box 128, Jamestown, RI 02835 ☎ 401/423-3377 or 800/688-1822 🖷 401/423-9630 🌐 www.naturetours.com. **Explorers Travel Group** ✉ 1 Main St., Suite 304, Eatontown, NJ 07724 ☎ 800/631-5650 🖷 732/542-9420 🌐 www.explorerstravelgroup.com. **Naturequest** ✉ 30872 S. Coast Hwy., Box 185, Laguna Beach, CA 92651 ☎ 949/499-9561 or 800/369-3033 🖷 949/499-0812 🌐 www.naturequesttours.com. **Swallows and Amazons** ✉ Rua Quintino Bocaiúva 189, sala 13, Centro Manaus 69005-110 🖷🖷 092/622-1246 🌐 www.swallowsandamazonstours.com.

🖪 Amazon River Trips **Abercrombie & Kent** ✉ 1520 Kensington Rd., Suite 212, Oak Brook, IL 60523 🖷 630/954-2944 or 800/323-7308 🖷 630/954-3324 🌐 www.abercrombiekent.com. **Amazon Tours & Cruises** ✉ 275 Fontainebleau Blvd., Suite 173, Miami, FL 33172 🖷 305/227-2266 or 800/423-2791 🖷 305/227-1880 🌐 www.amazontours.net. **Brazil Nuts** ✉ 1854 Trade Center Way, Suite 101A, Naples, FL 34109 🖷 941/593-0266 or 800/553-9959 🖷 941/593-0267 🌐 www.brazilnuts.com. **Clipper Cruise Line** ✉ 11969 Westline Industrial Dr., St. Louis, MO 63146 🖷 314/655-6700 or 800/325-0010 🖷 314/655-6670 🌐 www.clippercruise.com. **Ecotour Expeditions** ☏ Box 128, Jamestown, RI 02835 🖷 401/423-3377 or 800/688-1822 🖷 401/423-9630 🌐 www.naturetours.com. **Explorers Travel Group** ✉ 1 Main St., Suite 304, Eatontown, NJ 07724 🖷 800/631-5650 🖷 401/423-9630 🌐 www.explorerstravelgroup.com. **G.A.P. Adventures** ✉ 19 Duncan St., Suite 401, Toronto, Ontario M5H 3H1, Canada 🖷 416/260-0999 or 800/465-5600 🖷 416/260-1888 🌐 www.GAPadventures.com In U.S. ✉ 760 North Bedford Rd., #246, Bedford Hills, NY 10507 🖷 914/666-4417 or 800/692-5492 🖷 914/666-4839. **Southwind Adventures** ☏ Box 621057, Littleton, CO 80162 🖷 303/972-0701 or 800/377-9463 🖷 303/972-0708 🌐 www.southwindadventures.com. **Tours International** ✉ 12750 Briar Forest Dr., Suite 603, Houston, TX 77077 🖷 281/293-0809 or 800/247-7965 🖷 281/589-0870 🌐 www.toursinternational.com. **Travcoa** ✉ 2350 S.E. Bristol St., Newport Beach, CA 92660 🖷 949/476-2800 or 800/992-2003 🖷 949/476-2538 🌐 www.travcoa.com.

🖪 Bird-Watching **Field Guides** ✉ 9433 Bee Cave Rd., Bldg. 1, Suite 150, Austin, TX 78733 🖷 512/263-7295 or 800/728-4953 🖷 512/263-0117 🌐 www.fieldguides.com. **Focus Tours** ✉ 103 Moya Rd., Santa Fe, NM 87508 🖷 505/466-4688 🖷 505/466-4689 🌐 www.focustours.com. **Swallows and Amazons** ✉ Rua Quintino Bocaiúva 189, sala 13, Centro Manaus 69005-110 🖷🖷 092/622-1246 🌐 www.swallowsandamazonstours.com. **Victor Emanuel Nature Tours** ☏ 2525 Wallingwood Dr., Suite 1003, Austin, TX 78746 🖷 512/328-5221 or 800/328-8368 🖷 512/328-2919 🌐 www.ventbird.com.

🖪 Canoeing **Explorers Travel Group** ✉ 1 Main St., Suite 304, Eatontown, NJ 07724 🖷 800/631-5650 🖷 732/542-9420 🌐 www.explorerstravelgroup.com.

🖪 Culture **Ecotour Expeditions** ☏ Box 128, Jamestown, RI 02835 🖷 401/423-3377 or 800/688-1822 🖷 401/423-9630 🌐 www.naturetours.com.

Fishing **Fishing International** 1825 4th St., Santa Rosa, CA 95404 707/542-4242 or 800/950-4242 707/542-3477 www.fishinginternational. com. **Quest Global Angling Adventures** 3595 Canton Hwy., Suite C11, Marietta, GA 30066 770/971-8586 or 888/891-3474 770/977-3095 www.fishquest.com. **Rod & Reel Adventures** 32617 Skyhawk Way, Eugene, OR 97405 541/349-0777 or 800/356-6982 541/338-0367 www.rodreeladventures.com.

Natural History **Ecotour Expeditions** Box 128, Jamestown, RI 02835 401/423-3377 or 800/688-1822 401/423-9630 www.naturetours. com. **Focus Tours** 103 Moya Rd., Santa Fe, NM 87508 505/466-4688 505/466-4689 www. focustours.com. **Southwind Adventures** Box 621057, Littleton, CO 80162 303/972-0701 or 800/377-9463 303/972-0708 www. southwindadventures.com.

Photography **Focus Tours** 103 Moya Rd., Santa Fe, NM 87508 505/466-4688 505/466-4689 www.focustours.com. **Joseph Van Os Photo Safaris** Box 655, Vashon Island, WA 98070 206/463-5383 206/463-5484 www. photosafaris.com.

Scientific Research Trips **Earthwatch** 3 Clocktower Pl., Suite 100, Box 75, Maynard, MA 01754 978/461-0081 or 800/776-0188 978/461-2332 www.earthwatch.org.

Trekking & Hiking **Brazil Nuts** 1854 Trade Center Way, Suite 101A, Naples, FL 34109 941/593-0266 or 800/553-9959 941/593-0267 www.brazilnuts.com. **Eldertreks** 597 Markham St., Toronto, Ontario M6G 2L7, Canada 416/588-5000 or 800/741-7956 416/588-9839 www.eldertreks.com. **Explorers Travel Group** 1 Main St., Suite 304, Eatontown, NJ 07724 800/631-5650 732/542-9420 www. explorerstravelgroup.com.

Volunteer & Learning **Amizade** 920 William Pitt Union, University of Pittsburgh, Pittsburgh, PA 15260 888/973-4443 www.amizade.org.

TRAIN TRAVEL

Brazil has an outdated and insufficient rail network, the smallest of any of the world's large nations. Although there are commuter rails to destinations around major cities, don't plan on taking passenger trains between major cities. There's one exception: the ride from Curitiba to Paranaguá—in the southern state of Paraná—offers spectacular vistas of ravines, mountains, and waterfalls from bridges and viaducts.

TRAVEL AGENCIES

A good travel agent puts your needs first. Look for an agency that has been in business at least five years, emphasizes customer service, and has someone on staff who specializes in your destination. In addition, **make sure the agency belongs to a professional trade organization.** The American Society of Travel Agents (ASTA)—the largest and most influential in the field with more than 20,000 members in some 140 countries—maintains and enforces a strict code of ethics and will step in to help mediate any agent-client disputes involving ASTA members if necessary. ASTA (whose motto is "Without a travel agent, you're on your own") also maintains a Web site that includes a directory of agents. (If a travel agency is also acting as your tour operator, *see* Buyer Beware *in* Tours and Packages.)

Local Agent Referrals **American Society of Travel Agents (ASTA)** 1101 King St., Suite 200, Alexandria, VA 22314 703/739-2782 or 800/965-2782 24-hr hot line 703/739-3268 www. astanet.com. **Association of British Travel Agents** 68-71 Newman St., London W1T 3AH 020/7637-2444 020/7637-0713 www.abta.com. **Association of Canadian Travel Agencies** 130 Albert St., Suite 1705, Ottawa, Ontario K1P 5G4 613/237-3657 613/237-7052 www.acta.ca. **Australian Federation of Travel Agents** Level 3, 309 Pitt St., Sydney, NSW 2000 02/9264-3299 02/9264-1085 www.afta.com.au. **Travel Agents' Association of New Zealand** Level 5, Tourism and Travel House, 79 Boulcott St., Box 1888, Wellington 6001 04/499-0104 04/499-0786 www. taanz.org.nz.

VISITOR INFORMATION

Learn more about Brazil by checking government-issued travel advisories and country information. For a broader picture consider information from more than one country.

EMBRATUR, Brazil's national tourism organization, doesn't have offices overseas, though its Web site is helpful. For information in your home country, contact the Brazilian embassy or the closest consulate—

some of which have Web sites and staff dedicated to promoting tourism. Cities and towns throughout Brazil have local tourist boards, and some state capitals also have state tourism offices.

🛈 Tourist Information **Brazilian Embassy** 🏛 Box 1540, Canberra, ACT 2601 ☎ 616/273-2372. **Brazilian Embassy** ✉ 450 Wilbrod St., Ottawa, Ontario K1N 6M8 ☎ 613/237-1090. **Brazilian Embassy** ✉ Box 5432, 10 Brandon St., level 9, Wellington ☎ 04/473-3516 📠 04/473-3517 ⊕ www.brazil.org. nz. **Brazilian Embassy in London Tourism Office** ✉ 32 Green St., London W1K 7AT ☎ 020/7629-6909 ⊕ www.brazil.org.uk. **Tourism Office at the Brazilian Embassy** ✉ 3006 Massachusetts Ave. NW, Washington, DC 20008 ☎ 800/727-2945 ⊕ www. braziltourism.org.

🛈 Government Advisories **U.S. Department of State** ✉ Overseas Citizens Services Office, Room 4811, 2201 C St. NW, Washington, DC 20520 ☎ 202/647-5225 interactive hot line or 888/407-4747 ⊕ www.travel.state.gov; enclose a cover letter with your request and a business-size SASE. **Consular Affairs Bureau of Canada** ☎ 800/267-6788 or 613/944-6788 ⊕ www.voyage.gc.ca. **U.K. Foreign and Commonwealth Office** ✉ Travel Advice Unit, Consular Division, Old Admiralty Building, London SW1A 2PA ☎ 020/7008-0232 or 020/7008-0233 ⊕ www. fco.gov.uk/travel. **Australian Department of Foreign Affairs and Trade** ☎ 02/6261-1299 Consular Travel Advice Faxback Service ⊕ www.dfat.gov.au. **New Zealand Ministry of Foreign Affairs and Trade** ☎ 04/439-8000 ⊕ www.mft.govt.nz.

WEB SITES

Do check out the World Wide Web when planning your trip. You'll find everything from weather forecasts to virtual tours of famous cities. Be sure to visit Fodors.com (⊕ www.fodors.com), a complete travel-planning site. You can research prices and book plane tickets, hotel rooms, rental cars, vacation packages, and more. In addition, you can post your pressing questions in the Travel Talk section. Other planning tools include a currency converter and weather reports, and there are loads of links to travel resources.

For good information you may have to search by region, state, or city—and hope that at least one of them has a comprehensive official site of its own. **Don't rule out foreign-language sites**; some have links to sites that present information in more than one language, including English. On Portuguese-language sites, watch for the name of the region, state, or city in which you have an interest. The search terms in Portuguese for "look," "find," and "get" are *olhar* or *achar*, *buscar*, and *pegar*; "next" and "last" (as in "next/last 10") are *próximo* and *último* or *anterior*. Keep an eye out for such words as: *turismo* (tourism), *turístico* (tourist-related), *hoteis* (hotels), *restaurantes* (restaurants), *governo* (government), *estado* (state), and *cidade* (city).

The following sites should get you started: ⊕ www.embratur.gov.br (the official Brazilian tourist board site, with information in English provided by the Brazilian embassy in London), ⊕ www.varig.com (Varig Airlines's site, with English information), ⊕ www.brazilny.org (the official consular Web site in New York, with details about other consulates and the embassy as well as travel information and links to other sites), ⊕ www.brazilinfocenter.org (a Washington, D.C.–based organization that promotes political and business issues rather than tourism, but whose Web site has an incredible number of helpful links), ⊕ www. vivabrazil.com (a site with background and travel info on Brazil's different regions as well as links that will help you arrange your trip). The online magazine *Brazzil*, ⊕ www. brazzil.com, has interesting articles on culture and politics in English.

RIO DE JANEIRO

1

Updated by
Denise Garcia
and Ana Lúcia
do Vale

RIO IS A PULSATING CITY, synonymous with the girl from Ipanema, the dramatic Pão de Açúcar Mountain, and the wild and outrageous Carnaval (Carnival) celebrations. But Rio is also a city of stunning architecture, good museums, and marvelous food; it's a teeming metropolis where the very rich and the very poor live in uneasy proximity and where enthusiasm is boundless—and contagious.

Rio was named—or misnamed—by the crew of a Portuguese ship that arrived here on January 1, 1502. Thinking they had found the mouth of a river, instead of the bay that became known as the Baía de Guanabara (Guanabara Bay), they dubbed the spot Rio de Janeiro (January River). Sixty-five years later, on the feast of St. Sebastian, the city was founded with the official name of São Sebastião do Rio de Janeiro.

In 1736 Brazil's colonial capital was moved to Rio from Salvador, and in 1889, when the country became independent, Rio was declared the capital of the Republic of Brazil. It held this title until 1960, when the federal government was moved to Brasília.

As you leave the airport and head to your hotel, you'll be tossed onto a massive, chaotic, not-so-scenic urban roadway. But by the time you reach breezy, sunny Avenida Atlântica—flanked on one side by white beach and azure sea and on the other by the pleasure-palace hotels that testify to the city's eternal lure—your heart will leap with expectation. Now you're truly in Rio, where the 10 million wicked angels and shimmering devils known as *cariocas* dwell.

The term *carioca* comes from the country's early history, when it meant "white man's house" and was used to describe a Portuguese trading station. Today the word defines more than birthplace, race, or residence: it represents an ethos of pride, a sensuality, and a passion for life. Much of the carioca verve comes from the sheer physical splendor of a city blessed with seemingly endless beaches and sculpted promontories.

Prepare to have your senses engaged and your inhibitions untied. You'll be seduced by a host of images: the joyous bustle of vendors at Sunday's Feira Hippie (Hippie Fair); the tipsy babble at sidewalk cafés as patrons sip their last glass of icy beer under the stars; the blanket of lights beneath Pão de Açúcar; the bikers, joggers, strollers, and power walkers who parade along the beach each morning. Borrow the carioca spirit for your stay; you may find yourself reluctant to give it back.

EXPLORING RIO DE JANEIRO

Numbers in the text correspond to numbers in the margin and on the Rio Centro & Environs map and the Rio de Janeiro City map.

Cariocas divide their city into three sections: Zona Norte (North Zone), Zona Sul (South Zone), and Centro, the downtown area that separates the other two. Except for some museums, churches, and historic sights, most tourist activity is in beach- and hotel-laden Zona Sul. To sense the carioca spirit, spend a day on Copacabana and walk from the Avenida Atlântica to Ipanema. The western extension of Ipanema, Leblon, is an

If you have
3 days

If you only have three days, you must visit Rio's two most famous peaks: try **Pão de Açúcar** ⑳ ☞ your first morning and **Corcovado** ㉑—and the nearby **Museu de Arte Naif do Brasil** ㉓—that afternoon. Weekdays swing by the little **Museu Carmen Miranda** ⑱ to see the Brazilian bombshell's costumes, jewelry, and wild headdresses. In the evening join the fun at a samba show. Set your second day aside for exploring historic Rio and for shopping. On your third day, when the sun and sand have become irresistible, explore **Copacabana** and **Ipanema,** or settle in under a beach umbrella on breezy **Barra da Tijuca.** In the evening try the national dish at Ipanema's Casa da Feijoada.

1

If you have
5 days

On your first day explore Centro, take the cable car to **Pão de Açúcar** ⑳ ☞, and head to a samba show at Plataforma. The next day jump on the cogwheel train to **Corcovado** ㉑ and set aside time for the captivating **Museu de Arte Naif do Brasil** ㉓ near its base before indulging in a Brazilian barbecue at Marius or Porcão. Bike or walk off lunch at Lagoa Rodrigo de Freitas, then slide into a shopping center. On your third day stroll from **Copacabana** to **Ipanema,** stopping en route to order a tropical pizza at Bar Garota de Ipanema or grab an icy drink on **Barra da Tijuca.**

Take an organized favela (shantytown) tour in the afternoon and in the evening dine on feijoada or churrasco. On the fourth day head for **Petrópolis** ㉙ to see the imperial palace, or make the 40-minute drive to **Sítio Roberto Burle Marx** to see the country house and gardens of Brazil's most famous landscaper. Have your concierge check the evening schedule at the Banco do Brasil Cultural Center. On your last day take the Santa Teresa trolley to the **Museu Chácara do Céu** ⑬ before you hop the metrô to the opulent **Palácio do Catete** ⑰ Weekdays wind up the day at the kitschy Museu Carmen Miranda.

If you have
7–10
days

Begin in the Flamengo and Botafogo neighborhoods and at **Pão de Açúcar** ⑳ ☞. Work in visits to the **Museu Carmen Miranda** ⑱ and the **Museu de Arte Moderna** ⑭. On the second day wander through Centro and head for the **Palácio do Catete** ⑰. Then take the trolley to Santa Teresa and the **Museu Chácara do Céu** ⑬. On the third day beach-hop by bus early in the day and then do some shopping. On your fourth day slide out of town to 🚗 **Petrópolis** ㉙ or down the coast to 🚗 **Angra dos Reis** ㉚ or 🚗 **Parati** ㉜ for a day or two. When you return to Rio, visit **Corcovado** and the nearby **Museu de Arte Naif do Brasil** ㉓; spend the afternoon roaming through the **Jardim Botânico** ㉔ or biking around Lagoa Rodrigo de Freitas. Your final days could include an escape to the **Prainha** and **Grumari** beaches and the **Sítio Roberto Burle Marx,** or you could do a favela tour. In the evenings catch a samba revue or a bossa nova or jazz show or head out dancing. If you're in the city on Sunday, wander through Ipanema's Feira Hippie.

affluent, intimate community flush with good, small restaurants and bars (sadly, the water is polluted). The more distant southern beaches, beginning with São Conrado and extending past Barra da Tijuca to Grumari, become richer in natural beauty and increasingly isolated.

Although Rio's settlement dates back nearly 500 years, it's in every respect a modern city. Most historic structures have fallen victim to the wrecking ball, though a few churches and villas are still tucked in and around Centro. As these colonial vestiges are far-flung, consider seeing them on an organized walking or bus tour. You can use the metrô (and comfortable walking shoes) to explore, or the bus is another option. Just be sure you know where you're going, and memorize some key phrases in Portuguese, as bus drivers don't speak English. Police have put a dent in crime, but as in any large city, be cautious and aware.

Timing

Carnaval is the best time to soak in the city's energy. Arrive a few days before the celebrations begin, or stay a few days after they end in order to enjoy the museums and other sights that close for the four days of revelry. Be sure to book your hotel and flight at least one year in advance. To tour the city at a quieter time with gentler temperatures (it usually stays in the 90s during Carnaval) and lower prices, come in the off-season, from May to October (Brazil's winter).

Centro & Environs

What locals generally refer to as Centro is a sprawling collection of several districts that contain the city's oldest neighborhoods, churches, and most enchanting cafés. Rio's beaches, broad boulevards, and modern architecture may be impressive; but its colonial structures, old narrow streets, and alleyways in leafy inland neighborhoods are no less so.

A Good Tour (or Two)

Start at the **Mosteiro de São Bento ❶** ▶ for your first taste of Brazilian baroque architecture. From here move south into the heart of Centro. At the beginning of Avenida Presidente Vargas you'll find the solid **Igreja de Nossa Senhora da Candelária ❷**. From this church there are several options: soccer fans can take a cab or the metrô to **Maracanã** soccer stadium, where the "beautiful game" is played; those who prefer a more bucolic setting can head (by cab or metrô) to **Quinta da Boa Vista;** and history buffs can walk south along Avenida 1° de Março, crossing it and heading west to a network of narrow lanes and alleys highlighted by the **Beco do Comércio ❸**, a pedestrian street. After wandering this area, return to Avenida 1° de Março and walk southeast to the Praça 15 de Novembro, a square that's dominated by the **Paço Imperial ❹**. A few blocks away is the large **Museu Histórico Nacional ❺**.

From the Museu Histórico Nacional, follow Rua Santa Luzia southeast to Avenida Rio Branco, Centro's main thoroughfare. North one block is the Victorian **Biblioteca Nacional ❻**, and one block up from it is the French neoclassical **Museu Nacional de Belas Artes ❼**. In the middle of the next block up and across Rio Branco is the **Teatro Municipal ❽** and its elegant café. Continue north on Rio Branco and turn left on Avenida

Beaches

Rio's beaches define its culture: vibrant, joyful, beautiful. From infants to women in string bikinis—known as *tangas*—and thong-wearing men to senior citizens, the beach culture seduces all. The strands of tawny sand are exercise centers, gathering places, lovers' lanes—in effect, the city's pulse points. And every beach has its own flavor: grande dame Copacabana with its volleyball nets and outdoor cafés; seductive Ipanema; São Conrado with its hang gliders to the hip; expansive Barra da Tijuca. A day at the beach doesn't necessarily mean swimming. Although cariocas wander into the water to surf or cool off, most spend their time crammed on the sand, sunning and socializing.

Carnaval

Of the great carnivals of the world—Venice in Europe, Trinidad and Tobago in the Caribbean, and Mardi Gras in New Orleans—the most amazing may be Brazil's. And although Carnaval celebrations unfold all over this South American country, there's none with more glitter, glitz, or downright decadence than Rio's. During the four official days of the celebration, which ends the day before Lent begins, *escolas de samba* (samba schools, which are actually neighborhood groups, not schools at all) compete in two nights of opulent parades, weaving through the aptly named Sambódromo from sunset to dawn. Costumed revelers writhe at street parties and gala balls to the seductive samba beat. "Costume" is a relative term: some are wildly elaborate; others are barely there.

These competitions draw some of Rio's best percussionists, dozens of lavish floats, and thousands of marchers—including statesmen, beauty queens, veteran samba musicians, soccer personalities, and would-be celebrities (even a few seconds of TV exposure marching with a samba school is enough to launch a modeling or acting career). The joyous free-for-all infects even the most staid.

Side Trips

As tantalizing as the city is, you'll have a far richer taste of Brazil—of both its imperial past and its jet-setting present—if you wander outside town. Just across Guanabara Bay is Niterói, where ancient forts provide a window on history and a great view of Rio. A scenic road leads northeast to Petrópolis and the opulent imperial palace that was the summer home of Brazil's emperor. Swiss-settled Nova Friburgo peeks from a lush valley speckled with waterfalls farther north. Sailboat-jammed Cabo Frio is a popular eastern coastal resort, and although Brigitte Bardot in a bikini may have put nearby Búzios on the map, its 23 beaches, temperate weather, and sophisticated ambience have kept it there.

West of Rio, on Brazil's Costa Verde (Green Coast), Angra dos Reis is the jumping-off point for 365 islands that pepper a picturesque bay. One of the loveliest islands, Ilha Grande, is lapped by emerald waters and retains an unspoiled flavor despite its popularity. The most amazing gem, however, is the southwestern coastal town of Parati, with its 18th-century architecture; the lovely cays sprinkled along its bay have attracted American, European, and Brazilian celebrities.

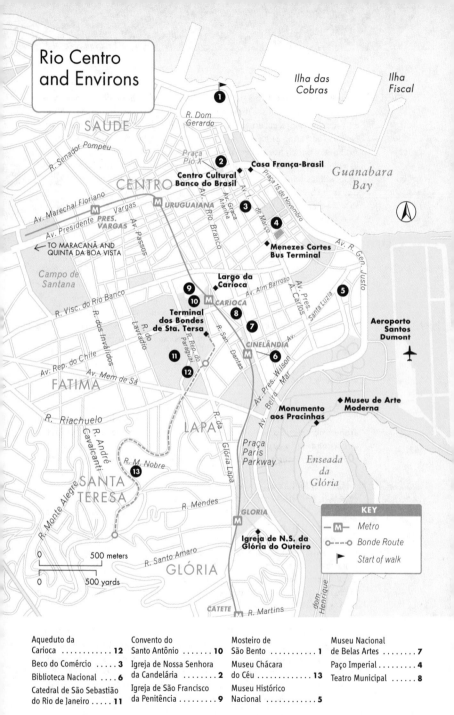

Rio Centro and Environs

Ilha das Cobras

Ilha Fiscal

❶

R. Dom Gerardo

SAUDE

R. Senador Pompeu

Praça Pio X

❷

Casa França-Brasil

Guanabara Bay

Centro Cultural Banco do Brasil

CENTRO

URUGUAIANA

Av. Marechal Floriano

Vargas

Av. Presidente **PRES. VARGAS**

← TO MARACANÃ AND QUINTA DA BOA VISTA

Campo de Santana

R. Visc. do Rio Banco

❸

Av. Graça Aranha

Av. Rio Branco

Praça 15 de Novembro

Av. 1 de Março

❹

Menezes Cortes Bus Terminal

Largo da Carioca

❾

❿

CARIOCA

Terminal dos Bondes de Sta. Tersa

R. do Lavradio

R. dos Inválidos

❽

❼

Av. Alm Barroso

A. Carlos

Av. Pres. Santa Luzia

❺

Av. R. Gen. Justo

Aeroporto Santos Dumont

R. Rep. do Paraguai

R. São Dentas

CINELÂNDIA

❻

Av. Pres. Wilson

FATIMA

Av. Rep. do Chile

Av. Mem de Sá

⓫

⓬

R. Riachuelo

R. André Cavalcanti

LAPA

R. da Glória Lapa

Av. Beira Mar

Monumento aos Pracinhas

♦Museu de Arte Moderna

Praça Paris Parkway

Enseada da Glória

R. M. Nobre

R. Monte Alegre

⓭

SANTA TERESA

R. Mendes

GLORIA

Igreja de N.S. da Glória do Outeiro

dom Henrique

| 0 | 500 meters |
| 0 | 500 yards |

R. Santo Amaro

GLÓRIA

CATETE   R. Martins

KEY

—Ⓜ— Metro

o---•---o Bonde Route

▶ Start of walk

Almirante Barroso. A short walk northwest brings you to the Largo da Carioca, a large square near the Carioca metrô stop. Atop a low hill overlooking it are the **Igreja de São Francisco da Penitência** ❾ and the **Convento do Santo Antônio** ❿. The architecturally striking (or absurd, depending on your viewpoint) **Catedral de São Sebastião do Rio de Janeiro** ⓫ is just south, off Avenida República do Chile, as is the station where you can take a *bonde* (trolley) over the **Aqueduto da Carioca** ⓬ and along charming Rua Joaquim Murtinho into Santa Teresa. This eccentric neighborhood is famed for its cobblestone streets and its popular **Museu Chácara do Céu** ⓭, whose works are displayed in a magnificent former home with beautiful city views.

TIMING & PRECAUTIONS
Although you can follow this tour in a day if you set out early, you might want to break it up into two days or be selective about which museums you fully explore. You can also mix some of the southernmost sights in with those (the Atêrro do Flamengo, Museu de Arte Moderna, or Monumento aos Pracinhas) in the Flamengo, Botafogo, and Pão de Açúcar tours. However you organize your tour, you'll need plenty of energy to get everything in. Leave your camera at your hotel if you're planning to use public transportation. Wear no jewelry, and keep your cash in a money belt or safe pocket.

What to See

▶ ⓬ **Aqueduto da Carioca.** The imposing Carioca Aqueduct, with its 42 massive stone arches, was built between 1744 and 1750 to carry water from the Rio Carioca in the hillside neighborhood of Santa Teresa to Centro. In 1896 the city transportation company converted the then-abandoned aqueduct to a viaduct, laying trolley tracks along it. Since then Rio's distinctive trolley cars (called "bondes" because they were financed by foreign bonds) have carried people between Santa Teresa and Centro. Guard your belongings particularly closely when you ride the open-sided bondes. Every Saturday at 10 the bondes make a longer, 90-minute tour through Santa Teresa. ⊠ *Estação Carioca, Rua Professor Lélio Gama, Centro,* ☎ *021/2240–5709 or 021/2240–5709* ⊠ *Aqueduct R$4, bonde trips R$1* ⊘ *Bondes leave every 15 mins 6 AM–10 PM* Ⓜ *Carioca or Cinelândia.*

❸ **Beco do Comércio.** A network of narrow streets and alleys centers on this pedestrian thoroughfare. The area is flanked by restored 18th-century homes, now converted to offices. The best known is the Edifício Teles de Menezes. A famous arch, the Arco do Teles, links this area with Praça 15 de Novembro. ⊠ *Praça 15 de Novembro 34, Centro* Ⓜ *Uruguaiana.*

❻ **Biblioteca Nacional.** Corinthian columns adorn the neoclassical National Library (built between 1905 and 1908), the first such establishment in Latin America. Its original archives were brought to Brazil by King João VI in 1808. Today it contains roughly 13 million books, including two 15th-century printed Bibles, and manuscript New Testaments from the 11th and 12th centuries; first-edition Mozart scores as well as scores by Carlos Gomes (who adapted the José de Alencar novel about Brazil's Indians, *O Guarani,* into an opera of the same name); books that belonged to Empress Teresa Christina; and many other manuscripts, prints, and drawings. Tours are available in English, but groups with more than 20 people must book the visit in advance. ✉ *Av. Rio Branco 219, Centro* 🕾 *021/2262–8255, 021/2220–9484 for guided tours for groups* ⊕ *www.bn.br* 🖃 *Tours R$2* ☉ *Weekdays 9–8, Sat. 9–3; tours weekdays at 11, 1, and 4* Ⓜ *Cinelândia.*

⓫ Catedral de São Sebastião do Rio de Janeiro. The exterior of this circa-1960 metropolitan cathedral, which looks like a concrete beehive, can be off-putting. The daring modern design stands in sharp contrast to the baroque style of other churches. But don't judge until you've stepped inside. Outstanding stained-glass windows transform the interior—which is 80 meters (263 feet) high and 96 meters (315 feet) in diameter—into a warm yet serious place of worship that accommodates up to 20,000 people. An 8½-ton granite rock lends considerable weight to the concept of an altar. ✉ *Av. República do Chile 245, Centro* 🕾 *021/2240–2869* 🖃 *Free* ☉ *Daily 7–5:30* Ⓜ *Carioca or Cinelândia.*

⓾ Convento do Santo Antônio. The Convent of St. Anthony was completed in 1780, but some parts date from 1615, making it one of Rio's oldest structures. Its baroque interior contains priceless colonial art—including wood carvings and wall paintings. The sacristy is covered with azulejos (Portuguese tiles). Note that the church has no bell tower: its bells hang from a double arch on the monastery ceiling. An exterior mausoleum contains the tombs of the offspring of Dom Pedro I and Dom Pedro II. ✉ *Largo da Carioca 5, Centro* 🕾 *021/2262–0129* 🖃 *Free* ☉ *By appointment only* Ⓜ *Carioca.*

❷ Igreja de Nossa Senhora da Candelária. The classic symmetry of Candelária's white dome and bell towers casts an unexpected air of sanity over the chaos of downtown traffic. The church was built on the site of a chapel founded in 1610 by Antônio de Palma after he survived a shipwreck; paintings in the present dome tell his tale. Construction on the present church began in 1775, and although it was formally dedicated by the emperor in 1811, work on the dome wasn't completed until 1877. The sculpted bronze doors were exhibited at the 1889 world's fair in Paris. ✉ *Praça Pio X, Centro* 🕾 *021/2233–2324* 🖃 *Free* ☉ *Weekdays 8–4, weekends 8–noon* Ⓜ *Uruguaiana.*

❾ Igreja de São Francisco da Penitência. The church was completed in 1737, nearly four decades after it was started. Today it's famed for its wooden sculptures and rich gold-leaf interior. The nave contains a painting of St. Francis, the patron of the church—reportedly the first painting in Brazil done in perspective. ✉ *Largo da Carioca 5, Centro* 🕾 *021/2262–0197* 🖃 *Free* ☉ *Wed–Fri. 8–noon and 2–4* Ⓜ *Carioca.*

off the beaten path

MARACANÃ – From the Igreja de Nossa Senhora da Candelária, walk 3½ blocks to the Uruguaiana station and take the metrô to the world's largest soccer stadium. Officially called Estádio Mário Filho after a famous journalist, it's best known as Maracanã, which is the name of the surrounding neighborhood and a nearby river. The 178,000-seat stadium (with standing room for another 42,000) was built in record time to host the 1950 World Cup. Brazil lost its chance at the cup by losing a match 2–1 to Uruguay—a game that's still analyzed a half-century later. Soccer star Pelé made his 1,000th goal here in 1969. The smaller, 17,000-seat arena in the same complex has hosted Madonna, Paul McCartney, and Pope John Paul II. Guided stadium tours are available. ⊠ *Rua Professor Eurico Rabelo, Gate 16* ☎ *021/2568–9962 or 021/2569–4916* ▭ *Tours R$3* ⊙ *Tours daily 9–5, except on match days* Ⓜ *Maracanã.*

▶ ❶ **Mosteiro de São Bento.** Just a glimpse of this church's main altar can fill you with awe. Layer upon layer of curvaceous wood carvings coated in gold create a sense of movement. Spiral columns whirl upward to capitals topped by cherubs so chubby and angels so purposeful they seem almost animated. Although the Benedictines arrived in 1586, they didn't begin work on this church and monastery until 1617. It was completed in 1641, but such artisans as Mestre Valentim (who designed the silver chandeliers) continued to add details almost through to the 19th century. Every Sunday at 10, mass is accompanied by Gregorian chants. ⊠ *Rua Dom Gerardo 32, Centro* ☎ *021/2291–7122* ▭ *Free* ⊙ *Weekdays 7–11 and 2–5:30.*

★ ❸ **Museu Chácara do Céu.** With its cobblestone streets and bohemian atmosphere, Santa Teresa is a delightfully eccentric neighborhood. Gabled Victorian mansions sit beside alpine-style chalets as well as more prosaic dwellings—many hanging at unbelievable angles from the flower-encrusted hills. Here, too, is the Museum of the Small Farm of the Sky. The outstanding collection of mostly modern works was left—along with the hilltop house that contains it—by one of Rio's greatest arts patrons, Raymundo de Castro Maya. Included are originals by 20th-century masters Picasso, Braque, Dalí, Degas, Matisse, Modigliani, and Monet. The Brazilian holdings include priceless 17th- and 18th-century maps and works by leading modernists. The grounds afford fine views of the aqueduct, Centro, and the bay. ⊠ *Rua Murtinho Nobre 93, Centro* ☎ *021/2507–1932* ▭ *R$2* ⊙ *Wed.–Mon. noon–5.*

need a break? Santa Teresa attracts artists, musicians, and intellectuals to its eclectic slopes. Their hangout is **Bar do Arnaudo** (⊠ Rua Almirante Alexandrino 316-B, Centro ☎ 021/2252–7246), which is always full.

❺ **Museu Histórico Nacional.** The building that houses the National History Museum dates from 1762, though some sections—such as the battlements—were erected as early as 1603. It seems appropriate that this colonial structure should exhibit relics that document Brazil's history. Among its treasures are rare papers, Latin American coins, carriages, cannons, and religious art. ⊠ *Praça Marechal Ancora, Centro* ☎ *021/2550–9224 or 021/2220–2328* ▭ *Tues.–Sat. R$5, free Sun.* ⊙ *Tues.–Fri. 10–5, weekends 2–6* Ⓜ *Carioca or Cinelândia.*

❼ **Museu Nacional de Belas Artes.** Works by Brazil's leading 19th- and 20th-century artists fill the space at the National Museum of Fine Arts. The most notable canvases are those by the country's best-known modernist, Cândido Portinari, but be on the lookout for such gems as Leandro

Joaquim's heartwarming 18th-century painting of Rio (a window to a time when fishermen still cast nets in the waters below the landmark Igreja de Nossa Senhora da Glória do Outeiro). After wandering the picture galleries, tour the extensive collections of folk and African art. ⊠ *Av. Rio Branco 199, Centro* 🕾 *021/2240–0068* ⊕ *www.iphan.gov.br* 💳 *R$4, free Sun.* ⊙ *Tues.–Fri. 10–6, weekends 2–6* Ⓜ *Carioca or Cinelândia.*

❹ **Paço Imperial.** This two-story colonial building with thick stone walls and ornate entrance was built in 1743 and for the next 60 years was the headquarters for Brazil's captains (viceroys), appointed by the Portuguese court in Lisbon. When King João VI arrived, he made it his royal palace. After Brazil's declaration of independence, emperors Dom Pedro I and II called the palace home. When the monarchy was overthrown, the building became Rio's central post office. Restoration work in the 1980s transformed it into a cultural center and concert hall. The building houses a restaurant, a coffee shop, a stationery-and-CD shop, and a movie theater. The square on which the palace sits, Praça 15 de Novembro, known in colonial days as Largo do Paço, has witnessed some of Brazil's most significant historic moments: it is where two emperors were crowned, slavery was abolished, and Emperor Pedro II was deposed. The square's modern name is a reference to the date of the declaration of the Republic of Brazil: November 15, 1889. ⊠ *Praça 15 de Novembro 48, Centro* 🕾 *021/2533–4407* ⊕ *www.pacoimperial.com.br* 💳 *Free* ⊙ *Tues.–Sun. noon–6:30.*

off the beaten path

QUINTA DA BOA VISTA – West of downtown, on the landscaped grounds of a former royal estate, are pools and marble statues, as well as the Museu Nacional and the Jardim Zoológico. Housed in what was once the imperial palace (built in 1803), the museum has exhibits on Brazil's past and on its flora, fauna, and minerals—including the biggest meteorite (5 tons) found in the southern hemisphere. At the zoo you can see animals from Brazil's wilds in re-created natural habitats. Glimpse bats and sloths at the Nocturnal House. ⊠ *Av. Paulo e Silva and Av. Bartolomeu de Gusmão* 🕾 *021/2568–8262 for museum, 021/2569–2024 for zoo* 💳 *Museum R$3; zoo R$5 weekends, R$4 Tues.–Fri.* ⊙ *Museum Tues.–Sun. 10–4; zoo Tues.–Sun. 9–4:30* Ⓜ *São Cristóvão.*

❽ **Teatro Municipal.** Carrara marble, stunning mosaics, glittering chandeliers, bronze and onyx statues, gilded mirrors, German stained-glass windows, brazilwood inlay floors, and murals by Brazilian artists Eliseu Visconti and Rodolfo Amoedo make the Municipal Theater opulent, indeed. Opened in 1909, it's a scaled-down version of the Paris Opera House. The main entrance and first two galleries are particularly ornate. As you climb to the upper floors, the decor becomes more ascetic, a reflection of a time when different classes entered through different doors and sat in separate sections. The theater seats 2,357—with outstanding sight lines—for its dance performances and classical music concerts. ⊠ *Praça Floriano 210, Centro* 🕾 *021/2299–1717, 021/2299–1695 for guided tour* 💳 *Tours R$4* ⊙ *Tours by appointment weekdays 10–5* ⊕ *www.theatromunicipal.rj.gov.br* Ⓜ *Cinelândia or Carioca.*

<table>
<tr><td>

need a break?

</td><td>

Elegance joins good at **Café do Odeon BR** (⊠ Praça Floriano 7, Centro ☏ 021/2240–0746), close to the Teatro Municipal. Appetizers and sandwiches can revitalize after walking downtown. The Odeon BR is one of Rio's most traditional movie theaters and was renovated in 2000. The café's veranda has a view to Praça Cinelândia. To taste a little of the carioca life, try the bar **Carlitos** (⊠ Rua Álvaro Alvim 36, Loja E Centro ☏ 021/2262–6567), on a street parallel to Teatro Municipal. Don't expect a fashionable place but a spot where the *chopp* (draft beer) is good and *batidas* (sweet alcoholic drinks mixed in a blender) come in many flavors—from tropical fruits to gingerbread.

</td></tr>
</table>

Flamengo, Botafogo & Pão de Açúcar

These neighborhoods and their most famous peak—Pão de Açúcar— are like a bridge between the southern beach districts and Centro. Several highways intersect here, making it a hub for drives to Corcovado, Copacabana, Barra, or Centro. The metrô also travels through the area. Although the districts are largely residential, Rio Sul—one of the city's most popular shopping centers—is here, as are some of the city's best museums and public spaces.

The eponymous beach at Flamengo no longer draws swimmers (its gentle waters look appealing but are polluted; the people you see are sunning, not swimming). A marina sits on a bay at one end of the beach, which is connected via a busy boulevard to the smaller beach (also polluted), at Botafogo. This neighborhood is home to the city's yacht club, and when Rio was Brazil's capital, it was also the site of the city's glittering embassy row. The embassies were long ago transferred to Brasília, but the mansions that housed them remain. Among Botafogo's more interesting mansion- and tree-lined streets are Mariana, Sorocaba, Matriz, and Visconde e Silva.

Botafogo faces tiny sheltered Urca, which is separated by Pão de Açúcar from a small patch of yellow sand called Vermelha. This beach is, in turn, blocked by the Urubu and Leme mountains from the 1-km (½-mi) Leme Beach at the start of the Zona Sul.

A Good Tour

Start at the northern end of the lovely, landscaped Atêrro do Flamengo (Flamengo Landfill) at the **Museu de Arte Moderna (MAM)** ⑭ ☞. Nearby is the **Monumento aos Pracinhas** ⑮, which honors the dead of World War II. Wander south along the Atêrro before hopping into a cab and heading inland to the hilltop **Igreja de Nossa Senhora da Glória do Outeiro** ⑯. Get on the metrô at the Glória station and take it one stop to the Catete terminal, or walk south along Rua da Glória da Lapa to Rua da Catete and the **Palácio do Catete** ⑰. From here, either head to the Parque do Flamengo by cab and walk south to the **Museu Carmen Miranda** ⑱, or take the metrô to the Botafogo stop and the nearby **Casa Rui Barbosa** ⑲. Finish the tour by riding the cable car up the **Pão de Açúcar** ⑳ for panoramic views of the bay and the neighborhoods you've just explored.

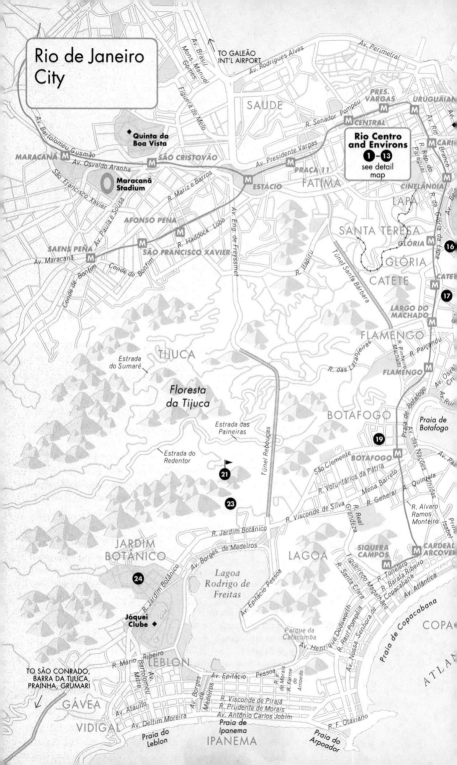

KEY

🚩 Start of walk

Ⓜ Metro

Street Car

Cable Car

This tour takes a full day and involves a lot of walking and time outdoors. You can shorten the itinerary by taking a cab to sights off the Atêrro do Flamengo and/or from one end of the Atêrro to the other. As always, keep your money and other valuables out of sight while strolling.

What to See

⑲ Casa Rui Barbosa. Slightly inland from the Atêrro is a museum in what was once the house of 19th-century Brazilian statesmen and scholar Rui Barbosa (a liberal from Bahia State who drafted one of Brazil's early constitutions). The pink mansion dates from 1849 and contains memorabilia of Barbosa's life, including his 1913 car and an extensive library that's often consulted by scholars from around the world. ⊠ *Rua São Clemente 134, Botafogo* ☎ *021/2537–0036* ☒ *Free* ◷ *Tues.–Fri. 9–4, weekends 2–5* Ⓜ *Botafogo.*

⑯ Igreja de Nossa Senhora da Glória do Outeiro. Set atop a hill, this baroque church is visible from many spots in the city, making it a landmark that's truly cherished by the cariocas. Its location was a strategic point in the city's early days. Estácio da Sá took this hill from the French in the 1560s and then went on to expand the first settlement and found a city for the Portuguese. The church, which wasn't built until 1739, is notable for its octagonal floor plan, large dome, ornamental stonework, and vivid tile work. The church has a small museum inside with baroque art. Tours are given by appointment only. ⊠ *Praça Nossa Senhora da Glória 135, Glória* ☎ *021/2557–4600* ☒ *Church free, museum R$2* ◷ *Tues.–Fri. 9–noon and 1–5, weekends 9–noon* Ⓜ *Glória.*

⑮ Monumento aos Pracinhas. The Monument to the Brazilian Dead of World War II (the nation sided with the Allies during the conflict) is actually a museum and monument combined. It houses military uniforms, medals, stamps, and documents belonging to soldiers. Two soaring columns flank the tomb of an unknown soldier. The first Sunday of each month Brazil's armed forces perform a colorful changing of the guard. ⊠ *Parque Brigadeiro Eduardo Gomes, Flamengo* ☎ *021/2240–1283* ☒ *Free* ◷ *Tues.–Sun. 10–4* Ⓜ *Cinelândia.*

▶ **⑭ Museu de Arte Moderna (MAM).** In a striking concrete-and-glass building, the Modern Art Museum has a collection of some 1,700 works by artists from Brazil and elsewhere. It also hosts significant special exhibitions and has a movie theater that plays art films. ⊠ *Av. Infante Dom Henrique 85, Flamengo* ☎ *021/2240–4944* ⊕ *www.mamrio.org.br* ☒ *Thurs.–Tues. R$8, Wed. R$4* ◷ *Tues.–Fri. noon–6, weekends noon–7* Ⓜ *Cinelândia.*

⑱ Museu Carmen Miranda. This tribute to the Brazilian bombshell is in a circular building that resembles a concrete spaceship (its door even opens up rather than out). On display are some of the elaborate costumes and incredibly high platform shoes worn by the actress, who was viewed as a national icon by some and as a traitor to true Brazilian culture by others. Hollywood photos of Miranda, who was only 46 when she died of a heart attack in 1955, show her in her trademark turban and jewelry. Also here are her records and movie posters and such memorabilia as the silver hand mirror she was clutching when she died. Guided tours are given by appointment, but guides do not speak English. ⊠ *Atêrro do Flamengo park, Av. Rui Barbosa s/n, across from Av. Rui Barbosa 560, Flamengo* ☎ *021/2551–2597* ⊕ *www.sec.rj.gov.br* ⊠ *R$2* ⊙ *Weekdays 11–5, weekends 1–5* Ⓜ *Flamengo.*

need a break? Flamengo has some of Rio's better small restaurants. For authentic Brazilian fare, the bohemian community heads to **Lamas** (⊠ Rua Marquês de Abrantes 18 ☎ 021/2556–0799), which is eight blocks from the Carmen Miranda Museum.

⓱ Palácio do Catete. Once the villa of a German baron, the elegant, 19th-century granite-and-marble palace became the presidential residence after the 1889 coup overthrew the monarchy and established the Republic of Brazil. Eighteen presidents lived here. Gaze at the palace's gleaming parquet floors and intricate bas relief ceilings as you wander through its **Museu da República** (Museum of the Republic). The permanent exhibits include a shroud-draped view of the bedroom where President Getúlio Vargas committed suicide in 1954 after the military threatened to overthrow his government. Presidential memorabilia, furniture, and paintings that date from the proclamation of the republic to the end of Brazil's military regime in 1985 are also displayed. A small contemporary art gallery, a movie theater, a restaurant, and a theater operate within the museum. ⊠*Rua do Catete 153, Catete* ☎*021/2558–6350* ⊠*Tues. and Thurs.–Sun. R$5, free Wed.* ⊙ *Tues.–Fri. noon–5:30, weekends 2–5:30* Ⓜ *Catete.*

FodorśChoice ★

★ ⓴ **Pão de Açúcar.** This soaring 1,300-meter (390-foot) granite block at the mouth of Baía de Guanabara was originally called *pau-nh-acugua* (high, pointed peak) by the indigenous Tupi people. To the Portuguese the phrase seemed similar to *pão de açúcar,* or "sugarloaf"; the rock's shape reminded them of the conical loaves in which refined sugar was sold. Italian-made bubble cars holding 75 passengers each move up the mountain in two stages. The first stop is at Morro da Urca, a smaller, 212-meter (705-foot) mountain; the second is at the summit of Pão de Açúcar itself. The trip to each level takes three minutes. In high season long lines form for the cable car; the rest of the year the wait is seldom more than 30 minutes. ⊠ *Av. Pasteur 520, Praia Vermelha, Urca* ☎ *021/2546–8400* ⊕ *www.bondinho.com.br* ⊠ *R$30* ⊙ *Daily 8 AM–10 PM.*

Parque do Flamengo. Flanking the Baía de Guanabara from the Glória neighborhood to Flamengo is this waterfront park. It gets its name from its location atop an *atêrro* (landfill), and was designed by landscape architect Roberto Burle Marx. Paths used for jogging, walking, and biking wind through it. There are also playgrounds and public tennis and basketball courts. On weekends the freeway beside the park is closed to traffic, and the entire area becomes one enormous public space. ⊠ *Inland of the beach, from Glória to Botafogo* ⊠ *Free* ⊙ *Daily 24 hours* Ⓜ *Glória or Flamengo.*

Zona Sul

Rio is home to 23 *praias* (beaches), an almost continuous 73-km (45-mi) ribbon of sand. All are public and are served by buses and taxis. At intervals along the beaches at Copacabana and Ipanema are small *postos* (bathhouses) with washrooms, showers, and dressing rooms that can be used for about R$2. Kiosks manned by police also pepper the avenues running parallel to the beach, and crime has dropped dramatically as a result.

A Good Beach Strategy

Although the circuit starts to the northeast at the beaches of Flamengo, Botafogo, Urca, and Vermelha, the waters off their shores are often polluted. The best sands are farther south. **Praia do Leme,** which is popular with senior citizens, runs into the city's grande dame, **Praia de Copacabana.** Its 3-km (2-mi) stretch is lined by a sidewalk whose swirling pattern was designed by Roberto Burle Marx. Copacabana has outdoor cafés, high-rise hotels, and juice kiosks. At its end cut around on the small **Praia Arpoador** (favored by surfers), or take Avenida Francisco Otaviano to **Praia de Ipanema.** Note that the final leg of this beach, called Leblon, is polluted, and swimming isn't recommended here.

Beyond Ipanema and Leblon, mountains again form a natural wall separating you from the next beach, little Vidigal. Still more mountains block it from **São Conrado,** a beach where hang gliders land after leaping from a nearby peak. A highway through a mountain tunnel forms the link between São Conrado and the long, spectacular **Praia Barra da Tijuca.** Its waters are clean and cool, and its far end, known as Recreio dos Bandeirantes, was home to a small fishing village until the late 1960s. Beyond are **Prainha,** whose rough seas make it popular with surfers, and the lovely **Praia de Grumari,** whose copper sands are often packed. Just before Prainha, you can take a slight detour to visit the **Museu Casa do Pontal,** Brazil's largest folk-art museum. It's worth continuing down the hill beyond Grumari to the **Sítio Roberto Burle Marx** for an in-depth look at one of Brazil's greatest artists.

City buses and small green minivans pick you up and drop you off wherever you request along the shore. If you're brave enough to drive, the city has established small, affordable parking lots (look for attendants in green-and-yellow vests) along waterfront avenues. There are several organized tours that take in the beaches, and agents at Turismo Clássico can arrange for drivers and guides.

TIMING &
PRECAUTIONS
Although you can tour the shoreline in several hours, consider spending a full day just wandering from Copacabana to Ipanema or sunbathing on Barra da Tijuca. Remember that Rio's beaches aren't just about sunning and swimming; they're also about volleyball games, strolling, biking, and people-watching.

Don't shun the beaches because of reports of crime, but *do* take precautions. Leave jewelry, passports, and large sums of cash at your hotel; avoid wandering alone and at night; and be alert when groups of friendly youths engage you in conversation (sometimes they're trying to distract you while one of their cohorts snatches your belongings). The biggest danger is the sun. From 10 to 3 the rays are merciless, making heavy-duty sunscreen, hats, cover-ups, and plenty of liquids essential; you can also rent a beach umbrella from a vendor or your hotel. Hawkers stroll

RITES ON THE BEACH

THERE IS PERHAPS NO STRANGER SIGHT *than that which takes place on the beaches in many of Brazil's cities each New Year's Eve. Under the warm tropical sky and with the backdrop of the modern city, thousands faithful to the Candomblé religion—vulgarly known as macumba—honor Iemanjá, the goddess of the sea.*

The advent of the new year is a time for renewal and to ask for blessings. The faithful of all ages, colors, and classes pour onto the beaches at around 10 PM, mostly at Copacabana. Some draw mystic signs in the sand. Others lay out white tablecloths with gifts befitting the proud, beautiful goddess: combs, mirrors, lipsticks, hair ribbons, perfumes, wines. Still others bring flowers with notes asking for favors tucked amid the blossoms. Worshipers chant and sing over their offerings and set candles around them.

By 11:30 PM the beaches are a mass of white-clad believers with flickering candles—the shore looks as if it has been invaded by millions of fireflies. At midnight the singing, shrieking, and sobbing is accompanied by fireworks, sirens, and bells. After that the faithful rush to the water for the moment of truth: if the goddess is satisfied with an offering, it's carried out to sea, and the gift giver's wish will come true. If, however, Iemanjá is displeased with an offering, the ocean throws it back; the gift giver must try again another year.

the beaches with beverages—take advantage of their services. Lifeguard stations are found every kilometer. (Note: beach vendors aren't supposed to charge more than R$5.50 for a bottle of beer or other alcoholic beverage, R$3 for a coconut water.)

What to See

Museu Casa do Pontal. If you're heading toward Prainha or beyond to Grumari, consider taking a detour to Brazil's largest folk-art museum. One room houses a wonderful mechanical sculpture that represents all of the *escolas de samba* (samba schools) that march in the Carnaval parades. Another mechanical "scene" depicts a circus in action. This private collection is owned by a French expatriate, Jacques Van de Beuque, who has been collecting Brazilian treasures—including religious pieces—since he arrived in the country in 1946. ⊠ *Estrada do Pontal 3295, Grumari* ☎ *021/2490–3278 or 021/2490–4013* ☎ *R$8* ☉ *Thurs.–Sun. 9:30–5.*

FodorśChoice ★ **Praia Barra da Tijuca.** Cariocas consider the beach at Barra da Tijuca to be Rio's best, and the 18-km-long (11-mi-long) sweep of sand and jostling waves certainly is dramatic. Pollution isn't a problem, and in many places neither are crowds. Barra's water is cooler and its breezes more refreshing than those at other beaches. The waves can be strong in spots; this attracts surfers, windsurfers, and jet skiers, but you should swim with caution. The beach is set slightly below a sidewalk, where cafés and restaurants beckon. Condos have also sprung up here, and the city's largest shopping centers and supermarkets have made inland Barra their home.

At the far end of Barra's beachfront avenue, Sernambetiba, is Recreio dos Bandeirantes, a 1-km (½-mi) stretch of sand anchored by a huge rock, which creates a small protected cove. Its quiet seclusion makes it popular with families. The calm, pollution-free water, with no waves or currents, is good for bathing, but don't try to swim around the rock—it's bigger than it looks.

At this writing, hotels, restaurants, and other tourist attractions are opening in the Barra da Tijuca neighborhood in preparation for the 2007 Pan-American Games, which are to be held here.

Praia de Copacabana. Maddening traffic, noise, packed apartment blocks, and a world-famous beach—this is Copacabana, Manhattan with bikinis. A walk along the neighborhood's classic crescent is a must to see the essence of beach culture, a cradle-to-grave lifestyle that begins with toddlers accompanying their parents to the water and ends with graying seniors walking hand in hand along the sidewalk. It's here that athletic men play volleyball using only their feet and heads, not their hands. Brazilians call it *futevôlei.* As you can tell by all the goal nets, soccer is also popular (Copacabana hosts the world beach soccer championships every January and February). You can swim here, although pollution levels and a strong undertow can sometimes be discouraging.

Copacabana's privileged live on beachfront Avenida Atlântica, famed for its wide mosaic sidewalks, hotels, and cafés. On Sunday two of the avenue's lanes are closed to traffic and are taken over by joggers, rollerbladers, cyclists, and pedestrians. Two blocks inland from and parallel to the beach is Avenida Nossa Senhora de Copacabana, the main commercial street, with shops, restaurants, and sidewalks crowded with the colorful characters that give Copacabana its flavor. ✉ *Av. Princesa Isabel to Rua Francisco Otaviano, Copacabana.*

need a break?   Stop in for a drink at one of Avenida Atlântica's few air-conditioned cafés. The windows of **Manoel & Juaquim** (✉ Av. Atlântica 1936, Copacabana ☎ 021/2236–6768) face the sands, so you can settle in with a cold draft beer or a light meal (the garlic potatoes are unbeatable) while watching carioca life unfold.

Fodor'sChoice ★   **Praia de Grumari.** About five minutes beyond Prainha, off Estrada de Guaratiba, is Grumari, a beach that seems an incarnation of paradise. What it lacks in amenities—it has only a couple of groupings of thatch-roof huts selling drinks and snacks—it makes up for in natural beauty: the glorious red sands of its quiet cove are backed by low, lush hills. Weekends are extremely crowded. Take a lunch break at Restaurante Point de Grumari (⇨ Where to Eat, *below*), which serves excellent fish dishes. ✉ *Grumari.*

Praia de Ipanema. As you stroll along this beach, you catch a cross section of the city's residents, each favoring a particular stretch. One area is dominated by families, another is favored by the gay community. A spot near Copacabana, **Praia do Arpoador** (⊠ Rua Joaquim Nabubo to Rua Francisco Otaviano, Arpoador), tantalizes surfers. Ipanema, nearby Praia do Leblon (whose waters are too polluted for swimming), and the blocks surrounding Lagoa Rodrigo de Freitas are part of Rio's money belt. For an up-close look at the posh apartment buildings, stroll down beachfront Avenida Vieira Souto and its extension, Avenida Delfim Moreira, or drive around the lagoon on Avenida Epitácio Pessoa. The tree-lined streets between Ipanema Beach and the lagoon are as peaceful as they are attractive. The boutiques along Rua Garcia D'Ávila make window-shopping a sophisticated endeavor. Other chic areas near the beach include Praça Nossa Senhora da Paz, which is lined with wonderful restaurants and bars; Rua Vinícius de Moraes; and Rua Farme de Amoedo. ⊠ *Rua Joaquim Nabuco to Av. Epitácio Pessoa, Ipanema.*

need a break?

Have you ever wondered if there really *was* a girl from Ipanema? The song was inspired by schoolgirl Heloísa Pinheiro, who caught the fancy of songwriter Antônio Carlos (a.k.a. Tom) Jobim and his pal lyricist Vinícius de Moraes as she walked past the two bohemians sitting in their favorite bar. They then penned one of last century's classics. That was in 1962, and today the bar has been renamed **Bar Garota de Ipanema** (⊠ Rua Vinícius de Moraes 49-A, Ipanema ☎ 021/2523–3787).

Praia do Leme. A natural extension of Copacabana Beach to the northeast, toward the Pão de Açúcar, is Leme Beach. A rock formation juts into the water here, forming a quiet cove that's less crowded than the rest of the beach. Along a sidewalk, at the side of the mountain overlooking Leme, anglers stand elbow to elbow with their lines dangling into the sea. ⊠ *Av. Princesa Isabel to Morro do Leme, Leme.*

Fodor'sChoice
★

Prainha. The length of two football fields, Prainha is a vest-pocket beach favored by surfers, who take charge of it on weekends. The swimming is good, but watch out for surfboards. On weekdays, especially in the off-season, the beach is almost empty; on weekends, particularly in peak season, the road to and from Prainha and nearby Grumari is so crowded it almost becomes a parking lot. ⊠ *35 km (22 mi) west of Ipanema on the coast road; accessible only by car from Av. Sernambetiba.*

São Conrado. Blocked by the imposing Dois Irmãos Mountain, Avenida Niemeyer snakes along rugged cliffs that offer spectacular sea views on the left. The road returns to sea level again in São Conrado, a natural amphitheater surrounded by forested mountains and the ocean. Development of what is now a mostly residential area began in the late '60s with an eye on Rio's high society. A short stretch along its beach includes the condominiums of a former president, the ex-wife of another former president, an ex-governor of Rio de Janeiro State, and a one-time Central Bank president. The far end of São Conrado is marked by the towering Pedra da Gávea, a huge flattop granite block. Next to it is Pedra

Bonita, the mountain from which gliders depart. (Although this beach was the city's most popular a few years ago, contaminated water has discouraged swimmers.)

Ironically, the neighborhood is surrounded by favelas (shantytowns). Much of the high ground has been taken over by Rio's largest favela, Rocinha, where an estimated 200,000 people live. This precarious city within a city seems poised to slide down the hill. It and others like it are the result of Rio's chronic housing problem coupled with the refusal by many of the city's poor to live in distant working-class neighborhoods. Though the favelas are dangerous for the uninitiated, they have their own internal order, and their tremendous expansion has even upper-class cariocas referring to them not as slums but as neighborhoods. The favelas enjoy prime vistas, and most are constructed of brick. ⊠ *Just west of Leblon.*

Fodor'sChoice
★

Sítio Roberto Burle Marx (Roberto Burle Marx Farm). Beyond Grumari, the road winds through mangrove swamps and tropical forest. It's an apt setting for the plantation-turned-museum where Brazil's famous landscape designer Roberto Burle Marx is memorialized. Marx, the mind behind Rio's mosaic beachfront walkways and the Atêrro do Flamengo, was said to have "painted with plants" and was the first designer to use Brazilian flora in his projects. More than 3,500 species—including some discovered by and named for Marx as well as many on the endangered list—flourish at this 100-acre estate. He grouped his plants not only according to their soil and light needs but also according to their shape and texture. Marx also liked to mix the modern with the traditional—a recurring theme throughout the property. The results are both whimsical and elegant. In 1985 he bequeathed the farm to the Brazilian government, though he remained here until his death in 1994. His house is now a cultural center full of his belongings, including collections of folk art. The grounds also contain his large ultramodern studio (he was a painter, too) and a small, restored colonial chapel dedicated to St. Anthony. ⊠ *Estrada Barra de Guaratiba 2019, Pedra de Guaratiba* ☎ *021/2410–1412* ☒ *R$5* ☽ *By appointment only.*

The Lush Inland

Beyond the sand and sea in the Zona Sul are lush parks and gardens as well as marvelous museums, seductive architecture, and tantalizing restaurants. You can't say you've seen Rio until you've taken in the view from Corcovado and then strolled through its forested areas or beside its inland lagoon—hanging out just like a true carioca.

Numbers in the text correspond to numbers in the margin and on the Rio de Janeiro City map.

A Good Tour

Head first to the imposing **Corcovado** ㉑ ► and its hallmark Cristo Redentor statue. As you slide up the side of the steep mountain in the train, you pass through the lush forested area known as **Floresta da Tijuca.** (To explore the forest more, hire a cab or join a tour that offers both Corcovado and Floresta da Tijuca.) Back down the hill and at the train station again, stroll downhill a short distance to the **Museu de Arte Naif do Brasil** ㉓, which houses a renowned collection of primitive art from around the world. The same street leads uphill to the delightful colonial square called Largo do Boticário—a good place to rest your feet. From here grab a taxi and journey west to the inviting **Jardim Botânico** ㉓, across from which is the Jóckey Clube. The botanical gardens are within walking distance from the Lagoa Rodrigo de Freitas, the giant saltwater lagoon that serves as one of the city's playgrounds—for children and adults alike.

TIMING & PRECAUTIONS   You can see these sights in a day if you start early. Try to visit Corcovado on a clear day; clouds often obscure the Christ statue on its summit. You can join an organized tour or hire a cabbie to take you out for the day (public transportation doesn't conveniently reach these sights). The security is good at Corcovado and Floresta da Tijuca, so you can usually carry your camera without worry. At the Jardim Botânico and the Lagoa Rodrigo de Freitas, however, be alert. Throughout this tour, keep valuables in a money belt or somewhere else out of sight.

What to See

▶ ㉑ **Corcovado.** There's an eternal argument about which view is better, from Pão de Açúcar or from here. Corcovado has two advantages: at 690 meters (2,300 feet), it's nearly twice as high and offers an excellent view of Pão de Açúcar itself. The sheer 300-meter (1,000-foot) granite face of Corcovado (the name means "hunchback" and refers to the mountain's shape) has always been a difficult undertaking for climbers.

Fodor'sChoice ★

It wasn't until 1921, the centennial of Brazil's independence from Portugal, that someone had the idea of placing a statue atop Corcovado. A team of French artisans headed by sculptor Paul Landowski was assigned the task of erecting a statue of Christ with his arms apart as if embracing the city. (Nowadays, mischievous cariocas say Christ is getting ready to clap for his favorite escola de samba.) It took 10 years, but on October 12, 1931, the *Cristo Redentor* (Christ the Redeemer) was inaugurated. The sleek, modern figure rises more than 30 meters (100 feet) from a 6-meter (20-foot) pedestal and weighs 700 tons. In the evening a powerful lighting system transforms it into a dramatic icon.

There are two ways to reach the top: by cogwheel train (R$30, which includes R$5 entrance fee) or by taxi (R$10 per person, plus R$5 entrance fee). The train, built in 1885, provides delightful views of Ipanema and Leblon from an absurd angle of ascent, as well as a close look at thick vegetation and butterflies. (You may wonder what those oblong medicine balls hanging from the trees are, the ones that look like spiked watermelons tied to ropes—they're *jaca*, or jackfruit.) Trains leave the **Cosme Velho station** (✉ Rua Cosme Velho 513, Cosme Velho ☎ 021/2558–1329 ⊕ www.corcovado.com.br) for the steep, 5-km (3-mi), 17-minute ascent. Late-afternoon trains are the most popular; on weekends be prepared for a long wait. To get to the summit, you can climb up 220 steep, zigzagging staircases (which was the only option available prior to 2003), or take an escalator or a panoramic elevator. If you choose the stairs, you pass little cafés and shops selling film and souvenirs along the way. Once at the top, all of Rio stretches out before you. ✉ *Flo-*

resta da Tijuca ☎ *021/2558–1329* 🖃 *R$5* ⊙ *Daily 8:30–6:30; trains depart every 30 mins.*

Floresta da Tijuca (Quagmire Forest). Surrounding Corcovado is the dense, tropical Tijuca Forest. Once part of a Brazilian nobleman's estate, it's studded with exotic trees and thick jungle vines and has a delightful waterfall, the Cascatinha de Taunay. About 180 meters (200 yards) beyond the waterfall is the small pink-and-purple Capela Mayrink (Mayrink Chapel), with painted panels by the 20th-century Brazilian artist Cândido Portinari.

From several points along this national park's 96 km (60 mi) of narrow winding roads the views are breathtaking. Some of the most spectacular are from Dona Marta, on the way up Corcovado; the Emperor's Table, supposedly where Brazil's last emperor, Pedro II, took his court for picnics; and, farther down the road, the Chinese View, the area where Portuguese king João VI allegedly settled the first Chinese immigrants to Brazil, who came in the early 19th century to develop tea plantations. A great way to see the forest is by jeep; you can arrange tours through a number of agencies, such as **Jeep Tour** (🖃 Praça Seve 22, Galpão, São Cristovão ☎ 021/3890–9336, 021/3878–0325, 021/3878–0324, or 021/9977–9610), which is open daily 7 AM–10 PM. Jeep tours are about four hours and cost around R$80. 🖃 *Entrance at Praça Afonso Viseu 561, Tijuca* ☎ *021/2492–2253* 🖃 *Free* ⊙ *Daily 8–6.*

㉔ Jardim Botânico. The 340-acre Botanical Garden contains more than 5,000 species of tropical and subtropical plants and trees, including 900 varieties of palms (some more than a century old) and more than 140 species of birds. The temperature is usually a good 12°C (22°F) cooler in the shady garden that was created in 1808 by Portuguese king João VI during his exile in Brazil. In 1842 the garden gained its most impressive adornment, the Avenue of the Royal Palms, 720-meter (800-yard) double row of 134 soaring royal palms. Elsewhere in the gardens, the Casa dos Pilões, an old gunpowder factory, has been restored and displays objects that pertained to both the nobility and to their slaves. Also on the grounds are a library, a small café, and a gift shop that sells souvenirs with ecological themes. 🖃 *Rua Jardim Botânico 1008* ☎ *021/2294–6012* ⊕ *www.jbrj.gov.br* 🖃 *R$4* ⊙ *Daily 8–5.*

> **need a break?**
>
> Cool off with some homemade ice cream with a tropical twist. The flavors at **Mil Frutas Sorvetes** (🖃 Rua J. J. Seabra, Jardim Botânico ☎ 021/2511–2550) are concocted using such local fruits as *acerola* and jaca.

㉓ Museu de Arte Naif do Brasil. More than 8,000 art naïf works by Brazil's best (as well as works by other self-taught painters from around the world) grace the walls of this lovely colonial mansion that was once the studio of painter Eliseu Visconti. The pieces in what is reputedly the world's largest and most complete collection of primitive paintings date from the 15th century through contemporary times. Don't miss the colorful, colossal 7 × 4–meter (22 × 13–foot) canvas that depicts the city of Rio; it reportedly took five years to complete. This museum sprang from a

FodorśChoice
★

collection started decades ago by a jewelry designer who later created a foundation to oversee the art. ⊠ *Rua Cosme Velho 561, Cosme Velho* ☎ *021/2205-8612 or 021/2205-8547* ☞ *R$8* ☉ *Tues.–Fri. 10–6, weekends noon–6.*

WHERE TO EAT

With more than 900 restaurants, Rio's dining choices are broad, from low-key Middle Eastern cafés to elegant contemporary eateries with award-winning kitchens and first-class service. The succulent offerings in the *churrascarias* (restaurants specializing in grilled meats) can be mesmerizing for meat lovers—especially the places that serve *rodízio* style (grilled meat on skewers is continuously brought to your table—until you can eat no more). Hotel restaurants often serve the national dish, *feijoada* (a hearty stew of black beans and pork), on Saturday—sometimes Friday, too. Wash it down with a *chopp* (the local draft beer; pronounced "shop") or a *caipirinha* (crushed lime, crushed ice, and a potent sugarcane liquor called *cachaça*).

For vegetarians there is an abundance of salad bars, where you pay for your greens by the kilo. And seafood restaurants are everywhere. Note that it's perfectly safe to eat fresh produce in clean, upscale places; avoid shellfish in all but the best restaurants.

Cariocas have scaled back on *almoço* (lunch), which used to be a full meal, and now tend to eat only a *lanche* (sandwich). Dinner is a late affair; if you arrive at 7, you may be the only one in the restaurant. Popular places seat customers until well after midnight on weekends, when the normal closing hour is 2 AM. Cariocas love to linger in *botecos,* plain but pleasant bars that may also serve food, and such establishments abound. Most serve dishes in the $–$$ range, and portions are large enough for two people to share.

Many restaurants have a fixed-price menu as well as à la carte fare. Many also include what is referred to as a *couvert* (cover charge) for the bread and other appetizers placed on the table. Leaving a 10% tip is enough, but check your bill: it may already have been added. Some restaurants don't accept credit cards, and dress is almost always casual.

WHAT IT COSTS In Reais				
$$$$	**$$$**	**$$**	**$**	**¢**
AT DINNER over $60	$45–$60	$30–$45	$15–$30	under $15

Prices are for a main course at dinner.

Brazilian

$$$–$$$$ ✕ **Esplanada Grill.** This churrascaria serves high-quality meat like T-bone steak or *picanha*, a tasty Brazilian cut of beef marbled with some fat. All the grilled dishes come with fried palm hearts, baked potatoes, and rice. An average meal is R$80. ⊠ *Rua Barão da Torre 600, Ipanema*

Where to Eat in
Rio de Janeiro

☏ *021/2512–2970* ▭ *DC, MC, V* Ⓜ *Cardeal Arcoverde, then shuttle bus to Praça General Osório.*

$$$–$$$$ ✕ **Siri Mole.** For typical food from the northeast of Brazil, this is the place. It's a small but absolutely comfortable restaurant that makes exotic dishes such as *acarajé*, a mix of fried smashed white beans and shrimp. Don't miss the *moqueca de siri*, a hot stew made of crabs, orange palm or *dendê* oil (spicy orange palm oil), and coconut milk. ⊠ *Rua Francisco Otaviano 50, Copacabana* ☏ *021/2267–0894* ▭ *AE, DC, MC, V* Ⓜ *Cardeal Arcoverde, then shuttle bus to Praça General Osório.*

$$$ ✕ **Marius.** This well-regarded churrascaria serves more than a dozen types of sizzling meats rodízio style. Marius is famed for taking the usual meat cuts to a higher level of sophistication. There is a great variety of side dishes, including Japanese food and fish. ⊠ *Av. Atlântica 290A, Leme* ☏ *021/2542–2393* ▭ *DC, MC, V.*

★ $$ ✕ **Casa da Feijoada.** Brazil's savory national dish is the specialty here, where huge pots of the stew simmer every day. The restaurant's desserts include a selection of traditional sweets with flavors like banana, guava, or pumpkin. *Quindim*, a coconut, yolk, and sugar cake, and Romeo and Juliet (guava compote with fresh cheese) are two favorite desserts. The caipirinhas are made not only with lime but also with tangerine, passion fruit, pineapple, strawberry, or kiwi. Be careful—they're strong. ⊠ *Rua Prudente de Morais 10, Ipanema* ☏ *021/2523–4994 or 021/2247–2776* ⊕ *www.cozinhatipica.com.br* ▭ *AE, DC, MC, V* Ⓜ *Cardeal Arcoverde, then shuttle bus to Praça General Osório.*

$$ ✕ **Porção.** Waiters at these rodízio-style churrascarias fly up and down
FodorśChoice between rows of linen-draped tables wielding giant skewers laden with
★ sizzling barbecued beef, pork, and chicken. Save room if you can: the papaya cream pudding topped by a bit of cassis shouldn't be missed. ⊠ *Rua Barão da Torre 218, Ipanema* ☏ *021/2522–0999* ⌲ *Reservations not accepted* ▭ *AE, DC, MC, V* Ⓜ *Cardeal Arcoverde, then shuttle bus to Praça General Osório* ⊠ *Av. Armando Lombardi 591, Barra da Tijuca* ☏ *021/2492–2001* ⊠ *Av. Infante Dom Henrique, Parque do Flamengo* ☏ *021/2554–8862* Ⓜ *Flamengo.*

$–$$ ✕ **Bar do Arnaudo.** For more than 30 years residents of beautiful Santa Teresa have flocked to this informal eatery that serves generous portions of Brazilian food. It's a bit far from the city center, but the restaurant has nice views of the city and Guanabara Bay. The goat and broccoli with *pirão* (cassava, or *mandioca*, mush) and rice is one of the traditional dishes served. Portions are large enough to serve two or even three. For dessert, sweetened condensed milk is cooked to a creamy caramel-like paste and served atop slices of *coalho* (a semihard Brazilian cow cheese). ⊠ *Rua Almirante Alexandrino 316-B, Santa Teresa* ☏ *021/2252–7246* ▭ *No credit cards.*

$–$$ ✕ **Barra Grill.** A favorite stop after a long day at Praia Barra, this informal and popular steak house serves some of the best meat in town. Prices for the rodízio-style meals are slightly more expensive on weekends than during the week. Reservations are essential on weekends. ⊠ *Av. Ministro Ivan Lins 314, Barra da Tijuca* ☏ *021/2493–6060* ▭ *AE, DC, MC, V.*

★ $–$$ ✕ **Yorubá.** Exotic and delicious dishes are served at this restaurant, one of the few places that goes beyond traditional African–Brazilian cuisine.

Try the Afro menu, a selection of contemporary West African cuisine. Service can be slow, but you are well rewarded for the wait. The *piripiri* (a spicy rice with ginger, coconut milk, and shrimp) is worth the price of R$65 for two. ⊠ *Rua Arnaldo Quintela 94, Botafogo* ☎ 021/2541–9387 ▤ *No credit cards.*

¢–$ ✕ **Yemanjá.** Typical food from Bahia is served in portions big enough for two here. Try the *bobó de camarão*, made of shrimp and *aipim* (mashed cassava). For dessert opt for the white or black *cocada*, a sugar-and-coconut confection cooked either a short time (white), or a longer time (black). ⊠ *Rua Visconde de Pirajá 128, Ipanema* ☎ 021/2247–7004 ▤ *AE, DC, MC, V* Ⓜ *Cardeal Arcoverde, then shuttle bus to Praça General Osório.*

Cafés

★ ¢–$ ✕ **Garcia & Rodrigues.** Cariocas breakfast at this cozy combination café, delicatessen, liquor shop, and trendy restaurant. At lunchtime choose from a selection of sandwiches, such as marinated salmon, pastrami, or buffalo milk cheese. Dinner, based on French cuisine, is served until 12:30 AM Monday–Thursday and Sunday and until 1 AM Friday and Saturday. ⊠ *Av. Ataulfo de Paiva 1251, Leblon* ☎ 021/2512–8188 ▤ *AE, DC, MC, V.*

★ ¢ ✕ **Colombo.** At the turn of the century this belle epoque structure was Rio's preeminent café, the site of afternoon teas for upper-class *senhoras* and a center of political intrigue and gossip. Jacaranda-framed mirrors from Belgium and stained glass from France add to the art nouveau decor. Portions are generous, but you can also just stop by for a pastry and coffee while you absorb the opulence. ⊠ *Rua Gonçalves Dias 32, Centro* ☎ 021/2232–2300 ▤ *AE, MC, DC, V* ☉ *Closed Sun. No dinner* Ⓜ *Carioca.*

Eclectic

$$–$$$$ ✕ **Alho & Óleo.** Pasta is the hallmark of this place of vivid European inspiration. There are many options, including *picatina alcapone* (spaghetti in cream sauce), beef fillet with lime sauce, and sage-and-ricotta tortellini. Finish with a pear dessert cooked in white wine with vanilla ice cream and chocolate topping. The restaurant is near the Cosme Velho area and the *Cristo Redentor*. ⊠ *Rua Buarque de Macedo 13, Flamengo* ☎ 021/2225–3418 ▤ *AE* Ⓜ *Largo do Machado.*

$–$$ ✕ **Aipo & Aipim.** There are more than 20 salads and hot dishes at this self-serve eatery with live music. After walking through the hot-dish and salad buffet, take your plate up to the grill and pick steaks, chicken, and pork cuts. Waiters take orders for drinks at your table. ⊠ *Nossa Senhora de Copacabana 391, Loja B, Copacabana* ☎ 021/2255–6285 ▤ *AE, DC, MC, V* Ⓜ *Cardeal Arcoverde.*

$ ✕ **Fazendola.** The name means "small farm," and this restaurant is reminiscent of a Brazilian farm with its wooden furniture and dim lighting. Homemade dishes prepared with very fresh ingredients are sold by the kilo. On Saturday you can have the special *paulista* couscous and shrimp, a cornmeal-and-manioc meal cooked to a paste consistency and flavored with olives, tomatoes, palm hearts, green peas, and hard-boiled eggs. For dessert—also sold by the kilo—try the caramel banana with orange syrup or chocolate topping. ⊠ *Rua Visconde da Graça 51, Jardim Botânico* ☎ *021/2512–6062* ⊟ *AE, DC, MC, V* ⊠ *Rua Jangadeiros 14B, Ipanema* ☎ *021/2247–9600* ⊟ *AE, DC, MC, V* Ⓜ *Cardeal Arcoverde, then shuttle bus to Praça General Osório* ⊠ *Rua Maria Angélica 171, Loja 103, Jardim Botânico* ☎ *021/2286–3680* ⊠ *Rua Alexandre Ferreira 220A, Jardim Botânico* ☎ *021/2539–0905.*

¢–$ ✕ **Doce Delícia.** Make your own dish by choosing from 5 to 15 of the 42 combinations of vegetables, side dishes, hot dishes, and fruit. Quiche, salmon, grilled tenderloin, chicken, and cold pasta are some of the choices. Dressings range from the light and yogurt based to innovative creations combining mustard and lemon. There are plenty of vegetarian options. The slick decor and fresh ingredients make this popular a choice for a regular clientele in the trendy area of Ipanema. For a reasonable price you can also pick main dishes from the menu—for example, the chicken breast with honey and rosemary sauce for R$17. ⊠ *Rua Aníbal de Mendonça 55, Ipanema* ☎ *021/2259–0239* ⊟ *V.*

French

★ $$$$ ✕ **Carême.** This charming bistro, decorated in a romantic style, offers several fine prix-fixe menus (R$95 each), including La Cuisine du Bienêtre, which is prepared with organic ingredients. Delicious desserts are created by a staff trained by French confectioners. *Delícia de limão* (lemon delight) is a must. ⊠ *Rua Visconde de Caravelas 113, Botafogo* ☎ *021/2537–5431* ⚲ *Reservations essential* ☉ *No lunch* ⊟ *DC, MC* Ⓜ *Botafogo.*

★ $$$$ ✕ **Le Pré-Catalan.** Considered the best French cuisine in Rio, this is the *carioca* version of the charming Parisian restaurant of the same name in the Bois du Boulogne. This highly reputed establishment has a prix-fixe menu (R$95) with three choices for appetizers, main dish, and dessert that changes every two weeks. ⊠ *Sofitel Rio Palace, Av. Atlântica 4240, Level E, Copacabana* ☎ *021/2525–1160* ⚲ *Reservations essential* ⊟ *AE, DC, MC, V* ☉ *No lunch* Ⓜ *Cardeal Arcoverde.*

★ $$$$ ✕ **Le Saint Honoré.** An extraordinary view of Copacabana Beach from atop Le Meridien hotel accompanies fine French cuisine at Le Saint Honoré. Brazilian fruits and herbs are tucked into dishes such as *les pièces du boucher marquées sauces gamay et béarnaise* (beef fillet with béarnaise and red-wine sauces). ⊠ *Av. Atlântica 1020, 37th floor, Copacabana* ☎ *021/3873–8880* ⚲ *Reservations essential* ⋔ *Jacket and tie* ⊟ *AE, DC, MC, V.*

$$$$ ✕ **Olympe.** The menu's all-Brazilian ingredients are a unique trait of this
FodorśChoice innovative restaurant that blends native flavors with nouvelle techniques.
★ Every dish—from the crab or lobster flan to chicken, fish, and duck prepared with exotic herbs and sauces—is exceptionally light. The passionfruit mousse is a favorite dessert. ⊠ *Rua Custódio Serrão 62, Jardim Botânico* ☎ *021/2537–8582* ⚲ *Reservations essential* ⊟ *AE, DC.*

★ $$ ✕ **Le Champs Elysées.** Try the salmon with spinach cream and onion confit or puff pastry with parfait glacé and apple at this restaurant in the Maison de France cultural institute. Dinner includes an appetizer, main dish, and dessert. ⊠ *Maison de France, Av. Presidente Antônio Carlos 58, 12th floor, Centro* ☎ *021/2220–4713* ⌂ *Reservations essential* ⊟ *AE, DC, MC, V* ⊘ *Closed Sun. No dinner Mon.–Wed.; no lunch Sat.* Ⓜ *Carioca.*

Indian

$–$$ ✕ **Natraj.** One block from Leblon's beachfront, this traditional Indian restaurant has a tasting menu for two, with eight portions of different dishes, a good option for a reasonable price. It can be ordered in vegetarian or nonvegetarian versions. Other suggestions are the many *pulau* (rice) and *dhal* (bean or pea) dishes, which may come with vegetables, coconut, fresh white cheese, or *panir*, and spices, or masala. You can also order à la carte. Good options for starters, the *samosas* are fine pastries with chicken, beef, mixed-vegetable, or potato-and-pea fillings. ⊠ *Av. General San Martin 1219, Leblon* ☎ *021/2239–4745* ⊟ *D, MC, V.*

Italian

★ $$$$ ✕ **Cipriani.** For a superb dining experience, start with a Cipriani, champagne with fresh peach juice (really a Bellini), and move on to an appetizer of snook carpaccio with apple and fennel or a salad of endive marinated in red wine. The pasta dishes are prepared with great care, and the meat and fish entrées are appropriate to their lavish surroundings—with a view to the hotel's beautiful pool. The degustation menu is R$150, or R$220 with wine. ⊠ *Copacabana Palace hotel, Av. Atlântica 1702, Copacabana* ☎ *021/2545–8747* ⌂ *Reservations essential* ⊟ *AE, DC, MC, V* Ⓜ *Cardeal Arcoverde.*

★ $$$–$$$$ ✕ **D'Amici.** This place has the largest wine list in Rio, with 300 labels, ranging from R$26 to R$10,000—for the Romanée Conti—and also serves 30 types of wine by the glass (R$7–R$26). The lamb with arugula risotto is a specialty. ⊠ *Rua Antônio Vieira 18, Leme* ☎ *021/2541–4477* ⊟ *AE, DC, MC, V.*

$–$$$$ ✕ **Margutta.** Just a block from Ipanema Beach, Margutta has a reputation for outstanding Mediterranean-style seafood, such as broiled fish in tomato sauce and fresh herbs or lobster cooked in aluminum foil with butter and saffron risotto. Polenta is made with olive oil and flavored with white truffles. ⊠ *Av. Henrique Dumont 62, Ipanema* ☎ *021/ 2511–0878* ⊟ *AE, MC, DC, V* ⊘ *No lunch weekdays.*

$$–$$$ ✕ **Alfredo.** The pasta here is excellent, especially the fettuccine Alfredo. Start your meal with something from the cold buffet of antipasti, which may include traditional pastas served with a variety of sauces. The restaurant has a view of the hotel pool. ⊠ *Inter-Continental Rio hotel, Av. Prefeito Mendes de Morais 222, São Conrado* ☎ *021/3323–2200* ⊟ *AE, DC, MC, V* ⊘ *No lunch.*

Japanese

$$–$$$$ ✕ **Madame Butterfly.** At this fine Japanese restaurant, start with pumpkin *gyoza* (dumplings) with shrimp, a platter with six servings, or the Beijing duck salad, a mix of greens and shredded duck with tangerine sauce. Main dishes include grilled salmon with honey and miso, and the best sukiyaki in Rio. ⊠ *Rua Barão da Torre 472, Ipanema* ☎ *021/ 2267–4347* ⊟ *AE, D, DC, MC.*

$–$$$$ ✕**Tanaka San.** The cult following of VIPs and demanding palates at Tanaka San is well-deserved. The roasted salmon sashimi with teriyaki sauce, a platter with eight servings, is excellent. For an unusual treat, order the *yosenabe*, a vegetable-and-seafood fondue, which serves three. ⊠ *Rua Bartolomeu Mitre 112, Leblon* ☎ *021/2239–0198* ⊟ *AE, D, MC.*

Mexican

$–$$ ✕**Guapo Loco.** Bustling crowds feast on tamales, enchiladas, and other Mexican favorites until the last customer leaves. Tequila has garnered quite a following in Rio, making Guapo Loco one of the favorite Mexican places due to its good margaritas. ⊠ *Rua Rainha Guilhermina 48, Leblon* ☎ *021/2294–2915* ⊟ *AE, DC, MC, V* ☉ *No lunch weekdays.*

Portuguese

★ $$$–$$$$ ✕**Antiquarius.** This much-loved establishment is famous for its flawless rendering of Portuguese classics. Wander through the antiques shop at the restaurant before settling in at a table. A recommended dish is the *cozido*, a stew with onions, yams, carrots, pumpkin, cabbage, bananas, and more. The *cataplana*, a seafood stew with rice, is also marvelous, and the *perna de cordeiro* (leg of lamb) is the most requested dish on the menu. The wine list impresses even Portuguese gourmands. ⊠ *Rua Aristides Espínola 19, Leblon* ☎ *021/2294–1049* ⌕ *Reservations essential* ⊟ *DC.*

$$–$$$$ ✕**Adega do Valentim.** Generous portions of cod, goat, and stews easily serve two or three people. The appetizers, especially the *bolinho de bacalhau* (fried cod dumplings), are popular. The restaurant is near Rio Sul Shopping Center, on the way from Copacabana Beach to Guanabara Bay. ⊠ *Rua da Passagem 178, Botafogo* ☎ *021/2541–1166* ⊟ *AE, D, DC, MC, V.*

Seafood

★ $$–$$$$ ✕**Satyricon.** Some of the best seafood in town is served at this eclectic Italian seafood restaurant, which also has a branch in Búzios. The *pargo* (fish baked in a thick layer of rock salt) is a specialty, and the sushi and sashimi are well loved. ⊠ *Rua Barão da Torre 192, Ipanema* ☎ *021/ 2521–0627* ⊟ *DC, MC, V* Ⓜ *Cardeal Arcoverde, then shuttle bus to Praça General Osório.*

$$–$$$ ✕**Albamar.** Opened in 1933, Albamar faces Guanabara Bay. The restaurant is owned by the waitstaff, assuring efficient service. The circular green building serves fine seafood and fish. The chef's-style *à moda* dishes are good choices. The menu lists a fish fillet with white-wine sauce, sour cream, shrimp, and mussels, served with mashed potatoes; Spanish-style octopus with potatoes; and six codfish balls. Albamar closes at 6 PM. ⊠ *Praça Marechal Âncora 186, Centro* ☎ *021/2240–8428* ⊟ *AE, DC, MC, V* ☉ *No dinner. Closed Mon.* Ⓜ *Uruguaiana.*

$$–$$$ ✕**Restaurante Point de Grumari.** From Grumari, Estrada de Guaratiba climbs up through dense forest, emerging atop a hill above the vast Guaratiba flatlands. Here you find this eatery famed for grilling fish to perfection.

With its shady setting, glorious vistas, and live music performances (samba, bossa nova, jazz), it's the perfect spot for lunch (open daily 11:30–7) after a morning on the beach and before an afternoon at the Sítio Roberto Burle Marx or the Museu Casa do Pontal. ⊠ *Estrada do Grumari 710, Grumari* ☎ *021/2410–1434* ☼ *No dinner* ▭ *No credit cards.*

$–$$$ ✕ **Quatro Sete Meia.** This restaurant is 30 km (19 mi) west of Copacabana, at the end of a road with stunning coastal views. Simplicity is the soul of the restaurant—whose name is its street number—and the village in which it's set. There are only 11 tables: five indoors and six in a garden at water's edge. The menu lists seven delicious options, including *moquecas* (seafood stews), grilled seafood, and curries. ⊠ *Rua Barros de Alarcão 476, Pedra de Guaratiba* ☎ *021/2417–1716* ⌲ *Reservations essential* ▭ *No credit cards* ☼ *Closed Mon., Tues. No dinner Wed., Thurs.*

FodorsChoice
★

★ **¢–$$** ✕ **Don Camillo.** There's always something new on the menu at this Copacabana beachfront restaurant. Try the baked mix of lobster, shrimp, squid, mussels, tomato, potato, and fresh fish of the day. The Italian atmosphere is completed by a musical group that sings traditional songs. ⊠ *Av. Atlântica 3056, Copacabana* ☎ *021/2549–9958* ⊕ *www.tempero.com. br* ▭ *AE, D, DC, MC, V* Ⓜ *Cardeal Arcoverde.*

¢–$$ ✕ **Shirley.** Homemade Spanish seafood casseroles and soups are the draw at this traditional Copacabana restaurant tucked onto a shady street. Try the *zarzuela*, a seafood soup, or *cazuela*, a fish fillet with white-wine sauce. Don't be turned off by the simple decor (a few paintings hung on wood-paneled walls): the food is terrific. ⊠ *Rua Gustavo Sampaio 610, Leme* ☎ *021/2275–1398* ⌲ *Reservations not accepted* ▭ *No credit cards.*

Vegetarian

$$ ✕ **Celeiro.** One of Rio's few organic restaurants, Celeiro is always full. There are approximately 20 salads on the buffet, as well as a wide selection of pastas. ⊠ *Rua Dias Ferreira 199, Leblon* ☎ *021/2274–7843* ▭ *D, MC, V* ☼ *No dinner.*

$–$$ ✕ **Vegetariano Social Clube.** Vegan restaurants are rare in Rio, and this is by far the most sophisticated. The small eatery has carefully prepared dishes free of any animal products that go much beyond brown rice or burdock. ⊠ *Rua Conde de Bernadotte 26, Loja L, Leblon* ☎ *021/ 2540–6499* ▭ *D, MC, V.*

¢–$ ✕ **Bistrô do Paço.** A good option for a light lunch, the daily buffet of salads (R$12 per person) includes carrot salad with oranges, potatoes, and apples. You also can try an onion, cheese, or spinach quiche. ⊠ *Praça Quinze 48, Centro* ☎ *021/2262–3613* ▭ *AE, D, MC, V* ☼ *No dinner* Ⓜ *Uruguaiana.*

WHERE TO STAY

Most hotels are in Copacabana and Ipanema. Copacabana hotels are close to the action (and the metrô), but the neighborhood is noisier than Ipanema (which is itself noisier than São Conrado and Barra da Tijuca). If you plan to spend time at the beach, your best bet is a hotel along Copacabana, Ipanema, or Barra da Tijuca (Copacabana has the advantage

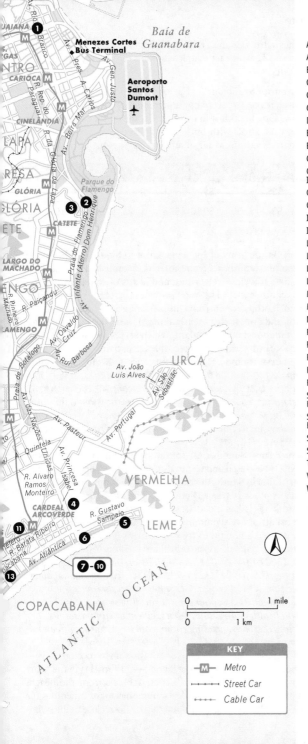

of being on the *metrô*, or subway, line). Note that Rio's "motels" aren't aimed at tourists. They attract couples looking for privacy and usually rent by the hour.

In the days just prior to and during Carnaval, already peak-season rates can double, even triple. Expect to pay a premium for a room with a view. Many hotels include breakfast in the rate, but the quality varies from a full buffet to a hard roll with butter. If you're traveling during peak periods, make reservations as far in advance as possible.

WHAT IT COSTS In Reais					
	$$$$	**$$$**	**$$**	**$**	**¢**
FOR 2 PEOPLE	over $500	$375–$500	$250–$375	$125–$250	under $125

Prices are for a standard double room in high season, excluding taxes.

★ **$$$$**   🏨 **Caesar Park.** In the heart of Ipanema, close to high-class shops and gourmet restaurants, this beachfront hotel has established itself as a favorite of business travelers, celebrities, and heads of state, who appreciate its impeccable service. The hotel provides secretarial services, fax machines, and laptops for in-room use. Among other comforts, the hotel has a bar and pool with a breathtaking view on the top floor, with an excellent Italian restaurant, Galani, which serves a Sunday brunch, feijoada every Saturday, and an impeccable executive lunch, with buffet starters and desserts and à la carte main courses. ⊠ *Av. Vieira Souto 460, Ipanema 22420-000* ☎ *021/2525–2525 or 0800/21–0789, 800/2223–6800 in the U.S.* ⊕ *www.caesarpark-rio.com* ➳ *186 rooms, 32 suites* ⚑ *Restaurant, room service, in-room safes, in-room data ports, cable TV, pool, gym, hair salon, massage, sauna, bar, baby-sitting, dry cleaning, laundry service, business services, meeting room, concierge, free parking* ⊟ *AE, DC, MC, V.*

$$$$ 🏨 **Copacabana Palace.** Built in 1923 for the visiting king of Belgium and
FodorśChoice inspired by Nice's Negresco and Cannes's Carlton, the Copacabana was
★ the first luxury hotel in South America, but it still retains more soul and elegance than any other. Marlene Dietrich, Robert De Niro, and Princess Di have stayed here. It has a neoclassical facade and one of the city's largest and most attractive swimming pools. One of its two restaurants, the Cipriani, is rated among the city's best for its northern Italian cuisine. The Saturday feijoada is extraordinary. ⊠ *Av. Atlântica 1702, Copacabana 22021-001* ☎ *021/2548–7070 or 0800/21–1533, 800/237–1236 in the U.S.* 🖷 *021/2235–7330* ⊕ *www.copacabanapalace. orient-express.com* ➳ *122 rooms, 102 suites* ⚑ *2 restaurants, room service, in-room data ports, in-room safes, cable TV, in-room VCRs, tennis court, pool, health club, sauna, 2 bars, cinema, laundry service, dry cleaning, business services, meeting room, concierge, parking (fee), no-smoking rooms* ⊟ *AE, DC, MC, V* Ⓜ *Cardeal Arcoverde.*

$$$$ 🏨 **Everest Rio.** With standard service but one of Rio's finest rooftop views— a postcard shot of Corcovado and the lagoon—this hotel is in the heart of Ipanema's shopping and dining district, a block from the beach. Back rooms offer sea views. It lacks decor but it has many amenities for business travelers. The restaurant 360°, on the top floor close to the swimming pool, has seafood and some specialties from the south of Brazil. There's a sushi bar on the ground floor. ⊠ *Rua Prudente de Morais 1117, Ipanema 22420-041* ☎ *021/2525-2200 or 0800/24-4485* 🖷 *021/ 2521-3198* ⊕ *www.everest.com.br* ⟿ *156 rooms, 11 suites* ⚐ *Restaurant, room service, in-room data ports, in-room safes, cable TV, pool, sauna, bar, laundry service, dry cleaning, concierge, business services, parking (fee), no-smoking floors* ⊟ *AE, DC, MC, V.*

$$$$ 🏨 **Golden Tulip Ipanema Plaza.** European standards and solid service are the hallmarks of this hotel. The rooms are large, decorated in pastels, and have modern facilities. In the center of Ipanema, very close to the beach, the hotel is on a street known for its wild bars. From the rooftop pool it's possible to see not only the ocean, but also the lagoon and the statue of Christ the Redeemer. ⊠ *Rua Farme de Amoedo 34, Ipanema 22420-020* ☎ *021/3687-2000* 🖷 *021/3687-2001* ⊕ *www. ipanemaplazahotel.com* ⟿ *117 rooms, 18 suites* ⚐ *Restaurant, room service, in-room data ports, in-room safes, cable TV, pool, sauna, health club, dry cleaning, laundry service, business services, meeting room, concierge, parking (fee), no-smoking floors* ⊟ *AE, DC, MC, V* ⦿ *BP.*

$$$$ 🏨 **Inter-Continental Rio.** One of the city's few resorts is in São Conrado, on its own slice of beachfront next to the Gávea Golf and Country Club. Attractions include a cocktail lounge, an Italian restaurant (the Alfredo), and a buffet with feijoada every Saturday. Every room has an original tapestry done by a Brazilian artist and a balcony overlooking the ocean. The nearby mall is much less crowded than those with more central locations. The club floor, on the higher levels, has extra facilities like massage, daily newspapers, and a tearoom. ⊠ *Av. Prefeito Mendes de Morais 222, São Conrado 22610-090* ☎ *021/3323-2200, 800/327-0200 in the U.S.* 🖷 *021/3323-5500* ⊕ *www.interconti.com* ⟿ *391 rooms, 53 suites, 20 cabanas* ⚐ *4 restaurants, room service, in-room data ports, in-room safes, cable TV, golf privileges, 3 tennis courts, 3 pools, health club, hair salon, sauna, 2 bars, piano bar, dance club, shops, dry cleaning, laundry service, concierge, business services, convention center, car rental, travel services, free parking, no-smoking rooms* ⊟ *AE, DC, MC, V.*

$$$$ ✕🏨 **Le Meridien.** Of the leading Copacabana hotels, the 37-story French-owned Meridien is the closest to Centro, making it a favorite of business travelers. Rooms are soundproof and have dark-wood furniture. Some rooms are wheelchair accessible. If you have work to do, the hotel has a complete executive center. Afterward, relax over a meal in Le Saint Honoré restaurant (⇨ above) and then head for the jazz bar, which books some of the best acts in town. ⊠ *Av. Atlântica 1020, Copacabana 22010-000* ☎ *021/3873-8888 or 0800/25-7171* 🖷 *021/3873-8788* ⊕ *www.meridien-br.com/rio* ⟿ *443 rooms, 53 suites* ⚐ *2 restaurants, room service, in-room data ports, in-room safes, cable TV, pool, hair salon, sauna, bar, dry cleaning, laundry service, concierge, business services, free parking, no-smoking floors* ⊟ *AE, DC, MC, V.*

$$$$ 🏨 **Marriott Rio de Janeiro.** The carioca branch of the Marriott chain honors its brand with comfort and modern facilities. Despite its enormous lobby, the rooms here are smaller than at most Marriott hotels. Although aimed for business travelers, its location at Copacabana Beach and high standards of service work for tourists as well. Some rooms look out onto the atrium in this futuristic building; other rooms have sea views. A sushi bar is open for dinner. ⊠ *Av. Atlántica 2600, Copacabana 22041-001* ☎ *021/2545–6500* 🖶 *021/2545–6555* ⊕ *www.marriottbrasil.com* ⤶ *230 rooms, 15 suites* ⚇ *Restaurant, room service, in-room data ports, in-room safes, cable TV, pool, sauna, health club, dry cleaning, laundry service, concierge, meeting rooms, business services, parking (fee), no-smoking rooms* ⊟ *AE, DC, MC, V.*

$$$$ 🏨 **Praia Ipanema.** This hotel isn't deluxe, but it has a great location across from the beach and between Ipanema and Leblon. You can see the sea from all its rooms. Choose the higher floors to enjoy the view and avoid the traffic noise. Take in the dramatic beach view from the pool area on the roof of the 15-story building. You can also catch a breeze from your private balcony (every room has one). ⊠ *Av. Vieira Souto 706, Ipanema 22440-000* ☎ *021/2540–4949* 🖶 *021/2239–6889* ⊕ *www.praiaipanema.com* ⤶ *105 rooms* ⚇ *Pool, room service, in-room data ports, in-room safes, cable TV, sauna, bar, health club, dry cleaning, laundry service, concierge, business services, parking (fee)* ⊟ *AE, DC, MC, V* ⦿ *BP.*

$$$$ 🏨 **Rio Atlântica.** Though it's not luxurious, the Atlântica allows rooftop sunbathing and swimming and has a bar with a view of Copacabana Beach. The service is superb. Excellent restaurants, shopping, and nightlife in Copacabana are all within walking distance. Bathrooms are large and very clean. Standard rooms do not have a view. Oceanfront suites have an oversize balcony. The hotel has been undergoing a slow renovation over the past few years since it changed hands. ⊠ *Av. Atlántica 2964, Copacabana 22070-000* ☎ *021/2548–6332 or 0800/26–6332* 🖶 *021/2255–6410* ⊕ *www.pestanahotels.com.br* ⤶ *103 rooms, 113 suites* ⚇ *Restaurant, room service, in-room data ports, in-room safes, cable TV, pool, health club, 2 bars, dry cleaning, laundry service, concierge, business services, meeting room, free parking, no-smoking rooms* ⊟ *AE, DC, MC, V.*

$$$$ 🏨 **Sheraton Rio Hotel & Towers.** Built so that it dominates Vidigal, between Leblon and São Conrado, this is the only hotel in Rio with a private beach. Guest rooms are decorated in pastels, and all have beach views. All rooms have balconies with sea views and are wheelchair accessible. Floors in the Towers section are reserved for business travelers. Be prepared for numerous taxi rides because of the hotel's isolated location. ⊠ *Av. Niemeyer 121, Vidigal 22450-220* ☎ *021/2274–1122, 0800/21–0750, 800/325–3589 in the U.S.* 🖶 *021/2239–5643* ⊕ *www.sheraton-rio.com* ⤶ *561 rooms, 22 suites* ⚇ *2 restaurants, in-room safes, cable TV, 3 tennis courts, 3 pools, gym, sauna, beach, 2 bars, shops, dry cleaning, laundry service, concierge, business services, meeting room, car rental, travel services, free parking, no-smoking rooms* ⊟ *AE, DC, MC, V* ⦿ *BP.*

$$$$ 🏨 **Sofitel Rio Palace.** Anchoring one end of Copacabana Beach, this hotel was given a top-to-bottom face-lift in 2000 and is once again one of the best on the strip. The building's H shape gives views of the sea, the mountains, or both from the balconies of all rooms. The most reasonably priced rooms face one of the pools opposite the beach. All other units have an ocean view. The first floors are home to Shopping Casino Atlântico, an upscale mall with home accessories, decorative art, and antiques stores. One pool gets the morning sun; the other, afternoon rays.

The rooftop bar areas are always lively. The restaurant Le Pré-Catalan is as good as its Parisian original. Chef Roland Villard, from the French Culinary Academy, is welcoming and creates new dishes every two weeks. ⊠ *Av. Atlântica 4240, Copacabana 22070-002* ☎ *021/2525–1232 or 0800/703–7003, 800/7763–4835 in the U.S.* ⊕ *www.accorhotels.com. br* 🛏 *388 rooms, 32 suites* ⚷ *2 restaurants, in-room data ports, in-room safes, cable TV, 2 pools, health club, sauna, 2 bars, shops, dry cleaning, laundry service, concierge, business services, convention center, free parking, no-smoking rooms* ⊟ *AE, DC, MC, V.*

$$$–$$$$ 🏨 **Excelsior.** This hotel, part of the Windsor chain, may have been built in the 1950s, but its look is sleek and contemporary—from the sparkling marble lobby to the guest-room closets paneled in gleaming jacaranda (Brazilian redwood). Service is top rate. The expansive breakfast buffet is served in the hotel's window-banked restaurant facing the avenue and beach. The equally elaborate lunch and dinner buffets cost roughly R$30. The rooftop bar–pool area offers an escape from the hustle and bustle. Ask for a room with a water view. ⊠ *Av. Atlântica 1800, Copacabana 22021-001* ☎ *021/2545–6000 or 0800/704–2827, 800/444–885 in the U.S.* 🖷 *021/2257–1850* ⊕ *www.windsorhoteis.com.br* 🛏 *233 rooms* ⚷ *Restaurant, room service, in-room data ports, in-room safes, minibars, cable TV, pool, health club, 2 bars, dry cleaning, laundry service, concierge, meeting room, free parking, no-smoking rooms* ⊟ *AE, DC, MC, V* ⦿| *BP* Ⓜ *Cardeal Arcoverde.*

$$$–$$$$ 🏨 **Sol Ipanema.** Another of Rio's crop of tall, slender hotels, this one has a great location (between Rua Vinícius de Moraes and Farme de Amoedo, where there are several bars), anchoring the eastern end of Ipanema Beach. All rooms have motel-style beige carpets and drapes and light-color furniture; deluxe front rooms have panoramic beach views, while back rooms from the eighth floor up, which are the same size, have views of the lagoon and Corcovado. Marble bathrooms are large and clean. ⊠ *Av. Vieira Souto 320, Ipanema 22420-000* ☎ *021/2525–2020* 🖷 *021/2247–8484* ⊕ *www.solipanema.com.br* 🛏 *90 rooms* ⚷ *Restaurant, pool, bar* ⊟ *AE, DC, MC, V* ⦿| *BP.*

$$$ 🏨 **Atlântico Copacabana.** Just three blocks from Copacabana Beach and close to the Siqueira Campos metrô station, this hotel has a great location for the price. Rooms are simple and slightly larger than average. Choose a room on one of the top floors to avoid the street noise of this residential area. ⊠ *Rua Siqueira Campos 90, Copacabana 22031-070* ☎ *021/2548–0011* 🖷 *021/2235–7941* ⊕ *www.atlanticocopacabana.com. br* 🛏 *97 rooms, 18 suites* ⚷ *Restaurant, room service, in-room data ports, in-room safes, cable TV, pool, hair salon, sauna, bar, health club, dry cleaning, laundry service, concierge, business services, parking (fee), no-smoking floors* ⊟ *AE, DC, MC, V* ⦿| *BP* Ⓜ *Siqueira Campos.*

$$$ 🏨 **Sheraton Barra Hotel e Suites.** Opened in 2003, this mammoth gleaming-white hotel has balconies in each room that overlook Barra Beach. The decor is futuristic, with white walls, brushed nickel and mahogany accents, skillful lighting, and clean lines. Rooms have high-speed Internet access. Be prepared to rent a car or spend a good deal on taxis when staying in this neighborhood, as there's no metrô station and unreliable bus service. ⊠ *Av. Lúcio Costa 3150, Barra da Tijuca 22630-010* ☎ *021/*

3139–8000 🖨 *021/3139–8025* ⊕ *www.sheraton.com/barra* 🖅 *263 rooms, 30 suites* ♿ *Restaurant, room service, in-room data ports, cable TV, pool, wading pool, gym, 2 hot tubs, sauna, spa, squash, bar, concierge, business services, meeting rooms, parking (fee)* ⊟ *AE, DC, MC, V.*

$$–$$$ 🏨 **Glória.** A grande dame of Rio's hotels, this classic was built in 1922 and is full of French antiques. What makes it a draw for business travelers—it's a five-minute cab ride from Centro—may discourage sun worshipers since it's a slightly longer cab ride to the beaches. ⊠ *Rua do Russel 632, Glória 22210-010* ☎ *021/2205–7272 or 0800/21–3077* 🖨 *021/2555–7282* ⊕ *www.hotelgloriario.com.br* 🖅 *596 rooms, 20 suites* ♿ *4 restaurants, room service, in-room data ports, some in-room safes, cable TV, 2 pools, gym, sauna, 3 bars, dry cleaning, laundry service, concierge, meeting room, parking (fee), no-smoking rooms* ⊟ *AE, DC, MC, V* ⍾ *BP* Ⓜ *Glória.*

$$–$$$ 🏨 **Luxor Regente Hotel.** The best of the Luxor hotels in Rio, the Regente has drab furnishings but solid service. The restaurant Forno e Fogão has a good feijoada, though it's not as well known as that of the Copacabana Palace. The suites have whirlpool baths. The gym area is small, but the hotel is committed to continually updating its equipment. If you choose a standard room, be sure that it's not one that faces south, without any view at all. Other rooms have beach views onto Avenida Atlântica. ⊠ *Av. Atlântica 3716, Copacabana 22070-001* ☎ *021/2525–2070 or 0800/16–5322* 🖨 *021/2267–7693* ⊕ *www.luxor-hotels.com/regente* 🖅 *233 rooms, 7 suites* ♿ *Restaurant, room service, some in-room data ports, in-room safes, cable TV, pool, sauna, health club, dry cleaning, laundry service, concierge, business services, parking (fee), no-smoking rooms* ⊟ *AE, DC, MC, V* ⍾ *BP.*

$$–$$$ 🏨 **Miramar Palace.** The beachfront Miramar is a strange mix of old and new. Rooms are among the largest in Rio, and public areas are dominated by classic touches, from the Carrara marble floor of the lobby to the spectacular glass chandeliers that light the restaurant. The hotel's 16th-floor bar is notable for its unobstructed view of the entire sweep of Copacabana. ⊠ *Av. Atlântica 3668, Copacabana 22070-001* ☎ *021/2525–0303 or 0800/23–2211* 🖨 *021/2521–3294* ⊕ *www.hotelmiramar.com.br* 🖅 *146 rooms, 10 suites* ♿ *Restaurant, coffee shop, tea shop, room service, in-room data ports, in-room safes, cable TV, bar, dry cleaning, laundry service, concierge, free parking, no-smoking rooms* ⊟ *MC, V* ⍾ *BP.*

$$–$$$ 🏨 **Plaza Copacabana Hotel.** This hotel is at the entrance of Copacabana, close to the beach but also near Rio Sul, one of the most popular malls in the city with restaurants and movie theaters. Its location permits easy transportation to downtown. The hotel still looks new (it opened in 1999) despite its simple decoration. The rooftop gym center and pool have views of Copacabana Beach. ⊠ *Av. Princesa Isabel 263, Copacabana 22011-010* ☎ *021/2586–0000 or 0800/90–2090* 🖨 *021/2543–8071* ⊕ *www.windsorhoteis.com/plaza* 🖅 *234 rooms, 3 suites* ♿ *Restaurant, room service, in-room safes, in-room data ports, cable TV, pool, sauna, free parking, health club, bar, dry cleaning, laundry service, concierge, business services, no-smoking floors* ⊟ *AE, DC, MC, V* ⍾ *BP.*

$$–$$$ 🏨 **Rio Internacional.** The red frame of this beachfront hotel has become a Copacabana landmark. Swiss owned and aimed at business travelers, the hotel offers a rarity for Avenida Atlântica: all rooms have balconies with sea views. All guests are welcomed with a glass of champagne. ⊠ *Av. Atlântica 1500, Copacabana 22021-000* ☎ *021/2543–1555 or 0800/ 21–1559* 🖶 *021/2542–5443* ⊕ *www.riointernacional.com.br* ⤴ *117 rooms, 13 suites* ⚐ *Restaurant, room service, in-room data ports, in-room safes, cable TV, pool, sauna, 2 bars, health club, dry cleaning, laundry service, concierge, business services, parking (fee), no-smoking floors* ⊟ *AE, DC, MC, V* Ⓜ *Cardeal Arco Verde.*

$$–$$$ 🏨 **Windsor Palace Hotel.** Close to the shopping area of Copacabana, the Windsor Palace has a modern but simple style. From the fifth floor up, rooms have balconies, but only those from the 12th floor up have ocean views. Overall, this is a low-budget option with solid services. The rooftop pool has a view of Copacabana beach, and it's just two blocks from the Siqueira Campos metrô station. ⊠ *Rua Domingos Ferreira 6, Copacabana 22050-010* ☎ *021/2545–9000* 🖶 *021/2549–9373* ⊕ *www. windsorhoteis.com/windsor* ⤴ *73 rooms, 1 suite* ⚐ *Restaurant, room service, in-room safes, cable TV, bar, pool, sauna, dry cleaning, laundry service, concierge, meeting room, free parking, no-smoking floors* ⊟ *AE, DC, MC, V* ¶⊙¶ *BP* Ⓜ *Siqueira Campos.*

$$ 🏨 **Leme Othon Palace.** Large rooms and a quiet beachfront location have made this a hotel of choice with repeat visitors. Built in 1964, it has a subdued, conservative air and lacks some modern amenities. Its location near Leme Beach and many transportation choices is the reason to stay here, despite slightly run-down accommodations. The metrô station is eight blocks away. ⊠ *Av. Atlântica 656, Leme 22010-000* ☎ *021/3873–5900* 🖶 *021/3873–5904* ⊕ *www.hoteis-othon.com.br* ⤴ *164 rooms, 26 suites* ⚐ *Restaurant, room service, some in-room data ports, in-room safes, cable TV, bar, dry cleaning, laundry service, concierge, business services* ⊟ *AE, DC, MC, V* Ⓜ *Cardeal Arco Verde.*

$–$$ 🏨 **Arpoador Inn.** This simple pocket-size hotel occupies the stretch of sand known as Arpoador. Surfers ride the waves, and pedestrians rule the roadway—a traffic-free street allows direct beach access. At sunset the view from the rocks that mark the end of the beach is considered one of Rio's most beautiful. The spectacle is visible from the hotel's back rooms (deluxe rooms) that face Arpoador Beach; avoid the front rooms, which are on the noisy side. Built in the '70s, the hotel has since been renovated and has a restaurant on the ground floor overlooking the beach. ⊠ *Rua Francisco Otaviano 177, Ipanema 22080-040* ☎ *021/2523–0060* 🖶 *021/ 2511–5094* ⤴ *50 rooms* ⚐ *Restaurant, room service, in-room safes, cable TV, bar, dry cleaning, laundry service* ⊟ *AE, DC, MC, V* ¶⊙¶ *BP.*

$–$$ 🏨 **Grandville Ouro Verde.** For three decades folks have favored this hotel for its efficient, personalized service. The tasteful Brazilian colonial decor and dark-wood furniture are in step with the emphasis on quality and graciousness. All front rooms face the beach; those in the back on the 6th–12th floors have a view of Corcovado. ⊠ *Av. Atlântica 1456, Copacabana 22021-000* ☎ *021/2543–4123* 🖶 *021/2542–4597* ⊕ *www.grandarrell.com.br/ouroverde/gouro.htm* ⤴ *60 rooms, 1 suite* ⚐ *Restaurant, room service, in-room data ports, in-room safes, cable TV, bar, library, dry cleaning, laundry service, no-smoking rooms* ⊟ *AE, DC, MC, V* Ⓜ *Cardeal Arco Verde.*

$–$$ 🏨 **Guanabara Palace Hotel.** A member of the Windsor chain that was remodeled in 2001, the Guanabara is one of the few solid hotel choices right in Centro. Rooms are reasonably sized and tastefully done in brown and beige. Like the one in its sister hotel, the Excelsior, the restaurant serves elaborate buffet meals. The contemporary rooftop pool area, with its stunning views of Guanabara Bay, absolutely gleams thanks to its pristine white tiles, white trellises, and white patio furnishings. The hotel has 30 meeting rooms. ⊠ *Av. Presidente Vargas 392, Centro 20071-000* ☎ *021/2216–1313* 🖷 *021/2516–1582* ⊕ *www.windsorhoteis. com.br* 🛏 *467 rooms, 3 suites* ⚭ *Restaurant, room service, in-room data ports, in-room safes, cable TV, minibars, pool, health club, sauna, dry cleaning, laundry service, bar, business services, meeting rooms, parking (fee), no-smoking rooms* ☰ *AE, DC, MC, V* ℟ *BP* Ⓜ *Uruguaiana.*

$ 🏨 **Benidorm Place.** Two blocks from Copacabana Beach, this hotel has simple rooms with mahogany furnishings. The rooftop pool is small but faces the Cristo Redentor. ⊠ *Rua Barata Ribeiro 547, Copacabana 22040-000* ☎🖷 *021/2548–8880* ⊕ *www.benidorm.com.br* 🛏 *84 apartments* ⚭ *Dining room, refrigerators, pool, cable TV, bar, parking (fee), no-smoking floor* ☰ *AE, DC, MC, V* ℟ *BP* Ⓜ *Siqueira Campos.*

$ 🏨 **Copacabana Rio Hotel.** Colorful room decor—such as yellow walls paired with blue beds—greets you at this hotel a block for the beach. Rooms have wonderful views of Pedra da Gávea. From the heated rooftop pool you can see Copacabana Beach and Sugarloaf. The Siqueira Campos metrô station is 10 blocks away. ⊠ *Av. Nossa Senhora de Copacabana 1256, Copacabana 22070-010* ☎ *021/2267–9900* 🖷 *021/2267–2271* ⊕ *www.copacabanariohotel.com.br* 🛏 *76 rooms, 8 suites* ⚭ *Restaurant, in-room safes, cable TV, pool, sauna, baby-sitting, concierge, laundry service, meeting room, parking (fee)* ☰ *AE, MC, V* ℟ *BP* Ⓜ *Siqueira Campos.*

$ 🏨 **Debret.** This former apartment building scores points for keeping its prices moderate despite a beachfront location. The decor honors Brazil's past: the lobby has baroque statues and prints depicting colonial scenes, and the rooms are furnished in dark, heavy wood. The hotel has a loyal following among diplomats and businesspeople who are more interested in functionality and low prices than elegance. ⊠ *Av. Atlântica 3564, Copacabana 22060-040* ☎ *021/2522–0132* 🖷 *021/2521–0899* ⊕ *www. debret.com* 🛏 *95 rooms, 11 suites* ⚭ *Restaurant, some in-room data ports, in-room safes, cable TV, bar, dry cleaning, laundry service, no-smoking rooms* ☰ *AE, DC, MC, V* ℟ *BP.*

$ 🏨 **Ipanema Inn.** If you want to stay in Ipanema and avoid the high prices of beachfront accommodations, this no-frills hotel with great service fits the bill. Just a half block from the beach, close to Praça Nossa Senhora da Paz, it's convenient not only for sun worshipers but also for those seeking to explore Ipanema's varied nightlife. ⊠ *Rua Maria Quitéria 27, Ipanema 22410-040* ☎ *021/2523–6092 or 021/2274–6995* 🛏 *54 rooms* ⚭ *Dining room, in-room safes, cable TV, bar, dry cleaning, laundry service* ☰ *AE, DC, MC, V* ℟ *BP.*

$ 🏨 **Leblon Flat Service.** Small, decorated, and furnished apartments have one or two bedrooms and balconies at this hotel-like apartment complex. Leblon beach is nearby. This is a good option for those who want to save money by cooking at home. ⊠ *Rua Professor Antônio Maria Teixeira 33, Leblon 22430-050* ☎ *021/2529–8332 for information, 021/ 2239–4598 for reservations* ☏ *021/2259–2191* ♨ *Coffee shop, kitchens, in-room safes, cable TV, pool, gym, sauna, laundry facilities, bar, meeting room* ☞ *120 apartments* ▤ *AE, DC, MC, V.*

$ 🏨 **Novo Mundo.** A short walk from the Catete metrô station and just five minutes by car from Santos Dumont Airport, this traditional hotel is on Guanabara Bay in Flamengo, near Glória. Convention rooms are popular with the business crowd. Deluxe rooms have a view of the bay and also of the Pão de Açúcar. The traditional restaurant, Flamboyant, has buffet service during the week and feijoada every Saturday. ⊠ *Praia do Flamengo 20, Flamengo 22210-030* ☎ *021/2557–6226 or 0800/ 25–3355* ⊕ *www.hotelnovomundo-rio.com.br* ☞ *208 rooms, 23 suites* ♨ *Restaurant, in-room data ports, in-room safes, refrigerators, cable TV, hair salon, bar, dry cleaning, laundry service, meeting room, parking (fee), no-smoking floor* ▤ *AE, D, MC, V* ⦿| *BP* Ⓜ *Catete.*

$ 🏨 **Royalty Copacabana.** Three blocks from the beach, this hotel is convenient for beachgoers yet removed enough to provide peace and quiet. The back rooms from the third floor up are the quietest and have mountain views; front rooms face the sea. ⊠ *Rua Tonelero 154, Copacabana 22030-000* ☎ *021/2548–5699* ☏ *021/2255–1999* ⊕ *www.royaltyhotel. com.br* ☞ *130 rooms, 13 suites* ♨ *Restaurant, in-room data ports, in-room safes, cable TV, pool, gym, sauna, dry cleaning, laundry service, bar, parking (fee), no-smoking rooms* ▤ *AE, DC, MC, V* ⦿| *BP* Ⓜ *Cardeal Arcoverde.*

$ 🏨 **Toledo.** Although it has few amenities, the Toledo goes the extra mile to make the best of what it does have. The staff is friendly, the service is efficient, and the location—on a quiet backstreet of Copacabana, a block from the beach—isn't bad either. Back rooms from the 9th to the 14th floors have sea views and sliding floor-to-ceiling windows. ⊠ *Rua Domingos Ferreira 71, Copacabana 22050-010* ☎ *021/2257–1990* ☏ *021/ 2257–1931* ⊕ *www.hoteisgandara.com.br* ☞ *92 rooms* ♨ *Coffee shop, in-room safes, cable TV* ▤ *AE, DC, MC, V* ⦿| *BP* Ⓜ *Siqueira Campos.*

$ 🏨 **Vilamar Copacabana.** Opened in 2002, this hotel aims to please budget travelers. The hotel is small (by Rio's standards), as are most of the rooms and the pool. But being only 200 meters (about 660 feet) from the beach, the size of the pool shouldn't be a problem. If you choose rooms on the lower level, be prepared for some noise from the street. ⊠ *Rua Bolívar 75, Copacabana 22061-020* ☎ *021/3461–5601* ☏ *021/ 2547–7528* ⊕ *www.hotelvilamarcopacabana.com.br* ☞ *56 rooms, 14 suites* ♨ *Restaurant, in-room data ports, in-room safes, refrigerators, cable TV, pool, sauna, bar, dry cleaning, laundry service, business services, parking (fee), no-smoking rooms* ▤ *AE, DC, MC, V* ⦿| *BP.*

NIGHTLIFE & THE ARTS

Rio's nightlife is as hard to resist as its beaches. Options range from samba shows, shamelessly aimed at visitors, to sultry dance halls that play *forró*, a music style that originated in Brazil's northeast during World War II. (American GIs stationed at refueling stops opened up their clubs "for all," which, when pronounced with a Brazilian accent, became "forró.") Seek out the sounds of big band, rock, and everything in-between. One of the happiest mediums is *música popular brasileira* (MPB), the generic term for popular Brazilian music, which ranges from pop to jazz. Note that establishments in this carefree city often have carefree hours; call ahead to confirm opening times.

For opera, theater, music, dance, film, and other performing arts listings, pick up the Portuguese-language *Rio Prá Você*, published by Riotur, the city's tourist board. *Este Mês no Rio* (This Month in Rio) and similar publications are available at most hotels, and your hotel concierge is also a good source of information. The Portuguese-language newspapers *Jornal do Brasil* and *O Globo* both publish schedules of events in the entertainment sections of their Friday editions, which may also be found online at www.jb.com.br and www.oglobo.com.br.

Nightlife

Cariocas love to chat while drinking until late hours in bars and restaurants all around town. Brazilian rhythms like samba and forró fill the night with excitement in neighborhoods like Lapa, Copacabana, Ipanema, and Leblon. If you're interested in entertainment of a steamier variety, stroll along Avenida Princesa Isabel at the end of Copacabana—near Le Meridien hotel—to one of the numerous burlesque, striptease, and sex shows. Be warned—some of the female patrons may be prostitutes.

Bars

Bars and lounges often ask for a nominal cover in the form of either a drink minimum or a music charge. *Choperias* (pubs) and *botecos,* bars specializing in draft beer and appetizers, are casual places you can go wearing a swimsuit.

Back in the '60s, regulars Tom Jobim and Vinícius de Moraes, who wrote the song "The Girl from Ipanema," sat at tables at **Bar Garota de Ipanema** (⊠ Rua Vinícius de Moraes 39, Ipanema ☎ 021/2267–5757 Ⓜ Cardeal Arcoverde, then shuttle bus to Praça General Osório), then called Bar Veloso, and longingly watched the song's heroine head for the beach. See if you can guess where they usually sat (hint: it's a table for two near a door). True to its name, **Bar do Hotel** (⊠ Marina Palace hotel, Av. Delfim Moreira 630, Leblon ☎ 021/2540–4990) is a hotel bar that serves lunch and dinner. It gets extremely crowded for drinks on Friday and Saturday nights. The unpretentious beachfront choperia **Barril 1800** (⊠ Av. Vieira Souto 110, Ipanema ☎ 021/2287–0085 Ⓜ Cardeal Arcoverde, then shuttle bus to Praça General Osório) is an Ipanema landmark and is usually jammed with people grabbing an icy beer or cocktail and a snack.

Don't expect anything fancy at **Bracarense** (⊠ Rua José Linhares 85B, Leblon ☎ 021/2294–3549), a small informal place where cariocas linger with their beers on the sidewalk in front of the bar. It's perfect for after a soccer game in Maracanã; many come just to talk about sports. At **Cervantes** (⊠ Av. Prado Júnior 335, Copacabana ☎ 021/2275–6174 ⊙ Closed Mon.), the beer goes well with the house special, French-bread sandwiches filled with beef, pork, and cheese. You may add sauces, onions, or even fruits—a specialty is pork and pineapple. Steaks with rice or french fries are also on the menu. **Chico's Bar** (⊠ Av. Epitácio Pessoa 1560, Lagoa ☎ 021/2523–3514) and the adjoining restaurant, Castelo da Lagoa, are big with affluent carioca singles and couples.

Near the Jóquei Clube, **Hipódromo** (⊠ Praça Santos Dumont, Gávea ☎ 021/2294–0095) has good chopp, honest food, and crowds of young people living it up. **Nova Capela** (⊠ Av. Mem de Sá 96, Lapa ☎ 021/2252–6228 Ⓜ Cinelândia) is a 100-year-old restaurant-bar in Rio's traditional downtown nightlife area. Beer, cachaça, and Brazilian meals and appetizers are served in generous portions. Pizza and draft beer are the mainstays of **Pizzaria Guanabara** (⊠ Av. Ataulfo de Paiva 1228, Leblon ☎ 021/2294–0797 ☴ AE, D, DC, V), which has had a loyal after-midnight crowd for more than 40 years. Artists tend to hang out

★ here. At **Seu Martin** (⊠ Av. General San Martin 1.196, Leblon ☎ 021/2274–0800 ☹ Closed for lunch on Mon.) cocktails, cheesecake, light food, sandwiches, and salad are served to the sound of jazz.

Dance Clubs

Rio's *danceterias* (discos) pulse with loud music and flashing lights. At a number of places, including samba clubs, you can dance to live Brazilian music. *Gafieiras* are old-fashioned ballroom dance halls, usually patronized by an equally old-fashioned clientele. Upon entry to some clubs you're given a card to carry—each successive drink is marked on it. You pay on departure for what you've consumed.

If you prefer to be where the trends are, try **00** (⊠ Av. Padre Leonel Franca 240, Gávea ☎ 021/2540–8041), a restaurant–café–sushi bar with a variety of DJs playing sets of house music, drum and bass, and trance, depending on the DJ. Call to get the program. It's open Tuesday through Sunday; arrive after 10 PM. At the large nightclub **Asa Branca** (⊠ Av. Mem de Sá 17, Lapa ☎ 021/2232–5704 ☴ AE, D, DC, V ☹ Closed Mon., Tues.), modern geometric designs are combined with old-fashioned fixtures. Big bands and popular Brazilian musicians keep the crowd busy from 10 PM until dawn. National and international bands play nearly every night at **Ballroom** (⊠ Rua Humaitá 110, Humaitá ☎ 021/2537–7600 ⊕ www.ballroom.com.br), a concert hall and dance club. Call to check the program. Arrive after midnight.

Bunker (⊠ Rua Raul Pompéia 94, Copacabana ☎ 021/2521–0367) is a dance hall with three lounges. Most of the time two of them are playing different styles of electronic music, with the third blaring rock and roll. Arrive around midnight. There's a small stage for the occasional local bands. Call for schedules. **Estudantina** (⊠ Praça Tiradentes 79, Centro ☎ 021/2232–1149 Ⓜ Presidente Vargas) is an extremely popular nightclub that packs in as many as 1,500 people on weekends to dance to the sound of samba. Brazilian rhythms, drum and bass, rock, and trip-hop are played different nights of the week at **Sítio Lounge** (⊠ Rua Marquês de São Vicente 10, Gávea ☎ 021/2274–2226). The decor is sophisticated and cozy. It used to be an antiques shop, and most of the furniture remains part of the space. It's open from Tuesday to Sunday; arrive after 11 PM.

Gay & Lesbian Bars & Clubs

Rio is a relatively gay-friendly city; the community even has its own gala during Carnaval. Style Travel Agency offers tours targeted to gay and lesbian travelers and has information on local happenings. The hippest cariocas—both gay and straight—hang out in Ipanema and Leblon.

The young energetic crowd at **Bar Bofetada** (⊠ Rua Farme de Amoedo 87–87A, Ipanema ☎ 021/2227–1675) downs chopp and caipirinhas and delicious seafood (the owners are Portuguese) or meat platters large enough to share. Downstairs the tables flow out onto the street; upstairs large windows open to the sky and afford a good view of the action below. The **Galeria Café** (⊠ Rua Teixeira de Mello 31E–F, Ipanema ☎ 021/2523–8250 ⊕ www.galeriacafe.com.br) is a bar with house–techno music for a sophisticated crowd. From Thursday to Saturday it's packed not only inside but has patrons overflowing out onto the sidewalk. The drink minimum is R$10. **Le Boy** (⊠ Rua Paul Pompéia 94, Copacabana ☎ 021/2521–0367 ⊕ www.leboy.com.br) is a gay disco that draws an upscale clientele.

Music Clubs

Although nightclubs often serve food, their main attraction is live music; it's best to eat elsewhere earlier.

Dance to samba rhythms at the compact club **Carioca da Gema** (⊠ Rua Mem de Sá 79, Lapa ☎ 021/2221–0043). At **Mistura Fina** (⊠ Av. Borges de Medeiros 3207, Lagoa Rodrigo de Freitas, Lagoa ☎ 021/2537–2844) fine jazz combines with excellent food. It's open midnight–3 AM. **Plataforma** (⊠ Rua Adalberto Ferreira 32, Leblon ☎ 021/2274–4022), the most spectacular of Rio's samba shows, has elaborate costumes and a variety of musical numbers including samba and rumba. A two-hour show costs about R$100, drinks not included. Downstairs is a hangout for many local luminaries and entertainers. Upstairs you can eat at Plataforma's famed barbecue restaurant. **Rio Scenarium** (⊠ Rua do Lavradio 20, Lapa ☎ 021/2233–3239) occupies three floors of an old townhouse that doubles as an antiques emporium. Dance to some of the best samba and *choro* (instrumental music with improvisational classical guitar) bands around on the spacious dance floor. **Semente** (⊠ Rua Joaquim Silva 138, Lapa ☎ 021/242–5165) is a small but popular samba club. You may rightly associate sultry bossa nova with Brazil, but it's increasingly hard to find venues that offer it. **Vinicius** (⊠ Rua Vinícius de Moraes 39, Ipanema ☎ 021/2287–1497 Ⓜ Cardeal Arcoverde, then shuttle bus to Praça General Osório) is one of the few that do. Along with nightly live samba, jazz, popular music, or bossa nova, it has a good kitchen.

The Arts

Although MPB may have overshadowed *música erudita* (classical music), Rio has a number of orchestras. The Orquestra Sinfônica Brasileira and the Orquestra do Teatro Municipal are the most prominent. Tickets to performing arts events are inexpensive by international standards and may be purchased at the theater or concert hall box offices. Dress is generally smart-casual, although the conservative upper crust still likes to dress elegantly for the Teatro Municipal. Don't wear valuable jewelry or carry lots of cash.

Rio has an avid filmgoing public and a well-regarded film industry (you may catch a flick that later hits the international movie circuit). Films are screened in small *cineclubes,* or state-of-the-art movie theaters (many in shopping malls). Foreign movies are shown in their original language with Portuguese subtitles (only children's films are dubbed). After dark exercise caution in Cinelândia, where there's a large concentration of theaters.

In addition to its many museums, Rio has several privately funded cultural centers. These host changing, often exceptional art and photography exhibits as well as film series, lectures, and children's programs. All the big newspapers have daily cultural sections that tell what's going on in the city—in Portuguese.

Classical Music

Opened in 1922, the **Escola de Música da UFRJ** (⊠ Rua do Passeio 98, Lapa ☎ 021/2240–1391 ⊕ www.musica.ufrj.br Ⓜ Cinelândia), the Music School auditorium, inspired by the Gauveau Hall in Paris, has 1,100 seats where you can listen to chamber music, symphony orchestras, and opera, all free of charge. **Instituto Moreira Salles** (⊠ Rua Marquês de São Vicente 476, Gávea ☎ 021/3284–7400 ⊕ www.ims.com. br), surrounded by beautiful gardens, has just the right atmosphere for listening to classical music. *Projeto Villa-Lobinhos,* whose performances are dedicated to children, is one of their projects. Listen to musicians performing pieces from Bach, Chopin, Debussy, and other classical composers. **Sala Cecília Meireles** (⊠ Largo da Lapa 47, Centro ☎ 021/2224–3913 Ⓜ Cinelândia) is a traditional midsize concert room that hosts classical-music performances.

Concert Halls

The 4,500-seat **ATL Hall** (⊠ Av. Ayrton Senna 3000, Barra da Tijuca ☎021/2430–0790 or 021/2285–0773) hosts music concerts, theater, and dance events. Many pop stars have performed here. Check the daily newspapers for programs. **Canecão** (⊠ Av. Venceslau Brás 215, Botafogo ☎021/2543–1241) is the most traditional venue for the biggest names on the national music scene. It seats up to 5,000 people; reserve a table up front.

Escolas de Samba

Open rehearsals attract crowds of samba enthusiasts to the *escolas de samba* (samba schools) from August to Carnaval (February or March) as fans gather to practice the year's rhythms and lyrics in preparation for the parade. Ticket prices range from R$5 to R$15.

Académicos do Salgueiro (⊠ Rua Silva Teles 104, Andaraí ☎ 021/2288–3065 ⊕ www.salgueiro.com.br) rehearses Saturday at 11 PM. **Beija-Flor** (⊠ Pracinha Wallace Paes Leme 1025, Nilópolis ☎ 021/2791–2866 ⊕ www.beija-flor.com.br) rehearses Thursday at 9 PM. **Estação Primeira de Mangueira** (⊠ Rua Visconde de Niterói 1072 Mangueira ☎ 021/2567–4637 ⊕ www.mangueira.com.br) rehearses Saturday at 11 PM. **Imperatriz Leopoldinense** (⊠ Rua Professor Lacê 235, Ramos

☎ 021/2560–8037 ⊕ www.imperatriz/leopoldinense.com.br) rehearses Sunday at 4 PM.

Império Serrano (✉ Av. Ministro Edgard Romero 114, Madureira ☎ 021/3359–4944 ⊕ www.imperioserrano.art.br) rehearses Saturday at 11 PM. **Mocidade Independente de Padre Miguel** (✉ Rua Coronel Tamarindo 38, Padre Miguel ☎ 021/3332–5823 ⊕ www.mocidade.com.br) rehearses Saturday at 11 PM. **Portela** (✉ Rua Clara Nunes 81, Madureira ☎ 021/2489–6440 ⊕ www.gresportela.com.br) rehearses Wednesday at 9 PM, Saturday at 10 PM, and Sunday at 3 PM. **Caprichosos de Pilares** (✉ Rua Faleiros 1, Pilares ☎ 021/2592–5620 ⊕ www.rioarte.com/caprichosos) rehearses Saturdays at 10 PM. **Unidos de Vila Isabel** (✉ Boulevard 28 de Setembro 382, Vila Isabel ☎ 021/2576–7052) rehearses Saturday at 10 PM.

Film
Part of the *Grupo Estação*, an art-house chain, the **Estação Ipanema** (✉ Av. Visconde de Pirajáa 595, Ipanema ☎ 021/2540–6445) is a charming theater with two auditoriums and a coffee shop in a lively area of small restaurants and bookstores, perfect for hanging out before or after the films. The only movie theater in Rio with a smoking room, **Estaço Paissandu** (✉ Rua Senador Vergueiro 35, Flamengo ☎ 021/2557–4653 Ⓜ Flamengo) allows smokers to enjoy the film through a glass window while sitting on comfortable couches. The auditorium seats up to 435.

★ **Espaço Unibanco de Cinema** (✉ Rua Voluntários da Pátria 35, Botafogo ☎ 021/2266–4491 Ⓜ Botafogo), with three auditoriums, shares space with a coffee shop and a secondhand shop selling books, records, and magazines. Members of the Brazilian film industry hang out here, hosting frequent premieres and events.

In one of the very few remaining houses on the Ipanema beachfront, **Laura Alvim** (✉ Av. Vieira Souto 176, Ipanema ☎ 021/2267–1647 Ⓜ Cardeal Arcoverde, then shuttle bus to Praça General Osório) is a small theater presenting several second-run films. Check the program ★ on your way back from the beach. **Odeon BR** (✉ Praça Mahatma Gandhi 2, Cinelândia ☎ 021/2262–5089 Ⓜ Cinelândia) is one of the most beautiful, charming, and important movie theaters in Brazil. In *Cinelândia* (movieland), a traditional neighborhood in downtown with a concentration of movie theaters, Odeon BR hosts international and Brazilian film exhibits, festivals, and art films. Opened in 1926, the theater has been restored to preserve its original neoclassic architecture. Arrive early to enjoy the coffee shop. **Roxy** (✉ Av. Nossa Senhora de Copacabana 945A, Cinelândia ☎ 021/2529–4848 or 021/2547–4576), in the heart of Copacabana two blocks from the beach, groups three midsize auditoriums that show blockbusters as well as Brazilian films.

Opera
★ **Teatro Municipal** (✉ Praça Floriano, Centro ☎ 021/2262–3501 or 021/2299–1717 ⊕ www.theatromunicipal.rj.gov.br) is the city's main performing arts venue, hosting dance, opera (often with international divas as guest artists), symphony concerts, and theater events year-round—

although the season officially runs from April to December. The theater also has its own ballet company.

Theater

Centro Cultural Banco do Brasil (⊠ Rua 1° de Março 66, Centro ☎ 021/2216–0237 or 021/2216–0626 Ⓜ Uruguaiana), constructed in 1880, was once the headquarters of the Banco do Brasil. In the late 1980s the six-story domed building with marble floors was transformed into a cultural center for plays, art exhibitions, and music recitals. It has a bookstore, three theaters, a video hall, four individual video booths, a movie theater, two auditoriums, a restaurant, a coffee shop, and a tearoom. Guided tours in English may be scheduled. It's open Tuesday–Sunday 10–8.

The traditional **Teatro João Caetano** (⊠ Praça Tiradentes, Centro ☎ 021/2221–0305 Ⓜ Presidente Vargas) holds 1,200 seats and offers a large choice of programs, from drama to dance, inexpensively. **Teatro Villa-Lobos** (⊠ Av. Princesa Isabel 440, Copacabana ☎ 021/2275–6695 or 021/2541–6799), a 463-seat theater, has drama productions and occasional dance performances.

SPORTS & THE OUTDOORS

Auto Racing

Brazilian race-car drivers rank among the world's best and frequently compete in international events. At the **Autódromo Internacional Nelson Piquet** (Nelson Piquet International Racetrack; ⊠ Av. Embaixador Abelardo Bueno, Jacarepaguá ☎ 021/2421–4949), you get a taste of the speed as you watch the checkered flag drop on competitions in the Formula I Grand Prix circuit named after one of the country's most famous racers, Emerson Fittipaldi.

Bicycling & Running

Bikers and runners share the boulevards along the beach and, for cooler and quieter outings, the path around Lagoa Rodrigo de Freitas. On weekends a stretch of Floresta da Tijuca Road is closed to traffic and many cariocas bike or run there. Although hotels can arrange bike rentals, it's just as easy to rent from stands along beachfront avenues or the road ringing the lagoon. Rates are about R$10 per hour. You're usually asked to show identification and give your hotel name and room number, but deposits are seldom required. (Note that helmets aren't usually available.)

Boating & Sailing

Saveiro's Tour (⊠ Rua Conde de Lages 44, Glória ☎ 021/2224–0313 Ⓜ Glória) charters all types of crewed vessels for any length of time. You can arrange an afternoon of waterskiing with a speedboat or a weekend aboard a yacht.

Golf

Golden Green Golf Club (⊠ Av. Canal de Marapendi 2901, Barra da Tijuca ☎ 021/2434–0429 ⊕ www.fgerj.com.br/conheca_golfe/clubes/golden.asp) was the first public golf club in Brazil. You can rent equipment for the six-hole course. The greens fee is R$30 Tuesday–Friday and R$40 weekends and holidays. The club is open 7 AM–10 PM.

Hang Gliding

A 30-minute hang-glider flight at **Just Fly** (☎ 021/2268–0565 or 021/9985–7540), during which you jump from Pedra Bonita in the Parque Nacional da Tijuca and land at Praia do Pepino in São Conrado, costs R$250 including transportation to and from your hotel. For a little more you can have 12 pictures taken. **Superfly** (⊠ Estrada das Canoas 1476, Casa 2, São Conrado ☎ 021/3332–2286) has hang-gliding classes and tandem flights with instructors. A package including pickup at your hotel and 12 photos taken in-flight costs about R$220.

Hiking

Centro Excursionista Brasileiro (⊠ Av. Almirante Barroso 2–8, Centro ☎ 021/2252–9844) provides guides, maps, and gear for hiking expeditions throughout the metropolitan area.

Horse Racing

Races are held year-round in the **Jóquei Clube** (⊠ Praça Santos Dumont 31, Gávea ☎ 021/2512–9988) from Friday to Monday. On Friday and the weekends races start at 2 PM; on Monday the first race is at 7 PM. The big event of the year, the Brazilian Derby, is held the first Sunday of August.

Soccer

You can watch a game at the **Estádio Maracanã** (⊠ Rua Prof. Eurico Rabelo, Maracanã ☎ 021/2568–9962 ⊕ www.suderj.rj.gov.br/maracana/main.asp Ⓜ Maracana), where the fans are part of the spectacle. During the season the top game is played each Sunday at around 5. The four most popular teams are Botafogo, Flamengo, Fluminense, and Vasco da Gama. A game between any of them is soccer at its finest. Tickets are available at the door. Arrive 30 minutes early to get the best seats.

Tennis

There are nine outdoor clay courts at **Fazenda Clube Marapendi** (⊠ Av. das Américas 3979, Barra da Tijuca ☎ 021/3325–2440). All courts are lighted. The club is open weekdays 7 AM–11 PM and weekends 7–5. Prices vary from R$15 to R$50, depending on the day of the week and time of the day. The large, well-equipped health club **Rio Sport Center** (⊠ Av. Ayrton Senna 2541, Barra da Tijuca ☎ 021/3325–6644) has six clay courts (three are covered). Prices ranges from R$20 to R$71 per hour depending on the time of the day. You can also rent equipment and arrange lessons.

SHOPPING

Stroll down streets lined with fashionable boutiques, barter with vendors at street fairs, or wander through one of more than two-dozen air-conditioned malls. Good bets are leather, suede, jewelry, and cool summer clothing in natural fibers. Also look for coffee, art, and samba and bossa nova CDs.

Ipanema is Rio's most fashionable shopping district. Its many exclusive boutiques are in arcades, with the majority along Rua Visconde de Pi-

THE BEAUTIFUL GAME

BRAZILIANS ARE MAD ABOUT **FUTEBOL** (soccer), and players here are fast and skillful. The best possess ginga (literally, "sway"), a quality that translates roughly as a feline, almost swaggering grace. Some of their ball-handling moves are so fluid they seem more akin to ballet—or at least to the samba—than to sport.

Futebol is believed to have been introduced in the late 19th century by employees of British-owned firms. By the early 20th century upper-class Brazilians had formed their own leagues, as had the nation's European immigrants. Because it requires little equipment, the sport also found a following in Brazil's poor communities. You can see young brasileiros everywhere practicing—any of these boys could be a future futebol hero. Brazil has turned out many international stars: the most famous, Pelé, retired more than 20 years ago and is still revered as a national hero. The country's team is consistently included in World Cup competitions and is a repeat titleholder. Nothing inspires more pride in Brazilians than their fifth World Cup win, in Korea and Japan in 2002.

Fans come to games with musical instruments, flags, banners, streamers, talcum powder, and firecrackers. There's no better spot for the brave to witness the spectacle than at the world's largest soccer stadium, Rio's Estádio Maracanã. Here you and 91,999 other people can make merry. Even if you don't have a great view of the field, you'll certainly be a part of the event. The main carioca teams are Flamengo, Vasco da Gama, Fluminense, and Botafogo. A match between any of these teams is a great spectacle.

rajá. Copacabana has souvenir shops, bookstores, and branches of some of Rio's better shops along Avenida Nossa Senhora de Copacabana and connecting streets. For upscale jewelry, head to Avenida Atlântica. Brazil is one of the world's largest producers of gold and the largest supplier of colored gemstones, with deposits of aquamarines, amethysts, diamonds, emeralds, rubellites, topazes, and tourmalines. If you're planning to go to Minas Gerais, do your jewelry shopping there; otherwise, stick with shops that have certificates of authenticity and quality.

Centers & Malls

Although **Barra Shopping** (⊠ Av. das Américas 4666, Barra da Tijuca ☎ 021/3089–1100 ⊕ www.barrashopping.com.br) is about 30 km (19 mi) from the city center, shoppers from all over town head to this mall, one of South America's largest. It has a medical center and a bowling alley as well as shops. The view of the Pão de Açúcar from **Botafogo Praia Shopping** (⊠ Praia de Botafogo 400, Botafogo ☎ 021/2559–9559 ⊕ botafogo-praia-shopping.globo.com Ⓜ Botafogo) is more appealing than the 170 shops and six movie screens at this mall on Botafogo Beach. Some of the restaurants have seats with a panoramic view.

With more than 400 sophisticated shops selling jewelry, fine quality clothing, and more. **Rio Sul** (⊠ Av. Lauro Müller 116, Botafogo ☎ 021/2545–7200 ⊕ www.riosul.com.br) is one of the city's most popular retail complexes. There are also four movie screens and a giant food court. Domestic and international fashions are sold at **São Conrado Fashion Mall** (⊠ Estrada da Gávea 899, São Conrado ☎ 021/3083–0000), which may be Rio's most appealing mall—it's the least crowded and has an abundance of natural light. A newer section, opened in 2002, has giant shops of Emporio Armani, Ermenegildo Zegna, Kenzo, and Petit Lippe. There's a four-screen movie theater.

At **Shopping Center da Gávea** (⊠ Rua Marquês de São Vicente 52, Gávea ☎ 021/2274–9896) several top art galleries—of which the best are Ana Maria Niemeyer, Beco da Arte, Borghese, Bronze, Paulo Klabin, Saramenha, and Toulouse—join a small but select mix of fashionable clothing and leather-goods stores. Four theaters here show the best plays in town. The 230-store **Via Parque** (⊠ Av. Ayrton Senna 3000, Barra da Tijuca ☎ 021/2421–9222) is popular for its outlets and ample parking (nearly 2,000 spaces). In addition to fast-food restaurants and six movie screens, the mall is home to the ATL Hall Theater (⇨ Nightlife and the Arts, *above*).

Markets

In the evenings and on weekends along the median of Avenida Atlântica, **artisans** spread out their wares. You can find paintings, carvings, handicrafts, sequined dresses, and hammocks from the northeast. **Babilônia Feira Hype** (⊠ Jockey Club Brasileiro, Rua Jardim Botânico, Jardim Botânico ☎ 021/2253–9800 or 021/2263–7667 ⊕ www.babiloniahype.com.br) takes place every other weekend from 2 PM to 10 PM. This fair combines fashion, design, art, and gastronomy. It's good not only for shopping but for watching the beautiful people go by. Admission is R$5.

The **Feira Hippie** (⊠ Praça General Osório, Ipanema) is a colorful handicrafts street fair held every Sunday 9–6. Shop for jewelry, hand-painted dresses, T-shirts, paintings, wood carvings, leather bags and sandals, rag dolls, knickknacks, furniture, and samba percussion instruments. The crowded, lively **Feira Nordestina** (Northeastern Fair; ⊠ Campo de São Cristóvão São Cristóvão), which starts every Saturday at 3 and finishes on Sunday at 4, is a social event for northeasterners living in Rio. They gather to hear their own distinctive music, eat regional foods, and buy tools and cheap clothing.

Saturday (9–6) an open-air fair, **Feira de Antiquários da Praça 15 de Novembro,** near the Praça 15 de Novembro has china and silver sets, watches, Asian rugs, and chandeliers. On Sunday (9–5) the same fair goes to Praça Santos Dumont, in Jardim Botânico. Vendors at **Feira do Rio Antigo** (Rio Antique Fair; ⊠ Rua do Lavradio, Centro ☎ 021/2252–2669) sell antiques, rare books, records, and all types of objets d'art on every first Saturday afternoon of the month. They move to the Casa Shopping Center in Barra da Tijuca on Sunday. A street fair, **Feirarte** (⊠ Praça do Lido, Copacabana), similar to the Feira Hippie, takes place weekends 8–6. Cardeal Arcoverde is the closest metrô station to the Feirarte.

Specialty Shops

Art

Contorno (✉ Shopping Center da Gávea, Rua Marquês de São Vicente 52, Loja 261, Gávea ☎ 021/2274–3832) shows eclectic selection of Brazilian art. Several shops and some art galleries at **Rio Design Center** (✉ Av. Ataulfo de Paiva 270, Leblon ☎ 021/3206–9100 ⊕ www.riodesign.com. br), like Anita Schwartz Galeria, have contemporary art.

Beachwear

A bikini shop with many mall locations in addition to the Rio Sul branch, **Blueman** (✉ Rio Sul, Av. Lauro Müller 116, Loja B01, Botafogo ☎ 021/2541–6896 ⊕ www.bluemanbrazil.com.br) carries *tangas* (string bikinis) that virtually define Brazil in much of North America's imagination. Tangas are said to have been invented in Ipanema—and they don't take up much room in your luggage. The market leader in beachwear, **Bum Bum** (✉ Rua Visconde de Pirajá 351, Loja B, Ipanema ☎ 021/ 2521–3859 ⊕ www.bumbum.com.br ✉ Shopping Rio Sul, Rua Lauro Muller 116, Loja 401, Botafogo ☎ 021/2542–9614 ✉ Barra Shopping, Av. das Américas 4666, Loja 134B, Barra da Tijuca ☎ 021/2431–8323) opened in 1979, when the stylist Alcindo Silva Filho, known as Cidinho, decided to create the smallest (and by some accounts, the sexiest) bikinis in town. Two decades later Bum Bum became a solid beachwear brand, still for young people, with cheap items for men and women.

At **Lenny** (✉ Fórum Ipanema, Rua Visconde de Pirajá 351, Loja 114, Ipanema ☎ 021/2523–3796 ⊕ www.lenny.com.br) expect sophistication, comfortable sizes, and lots of fashionable beach accessories. Lenny is quite expensive, but the bikinis are particularly creative. A *très* chic bikini designer, **Salinas** (✉ Rio Sul, Rua Lauro Müller 116, Loja C, Botafogo ☎ 021/ 2275–0793) is the label de rigueur with the fashionable set in Búzios and other resort areas. For bikinis larger than a postage stamp, try **Track & Field** (✉ Rio Sul, Rua Lauro Müller 116, Loja 401 B09, Botafogo ☎ 021/ 2295–5996 ⊕ www.tf.com.br), a sportswear shop.

Beauty

Everything you might need for your hair and skin—from shampoo to sunblock to face creams—can be found at **Época Cosméticos** (✉ Rua Visconde de Pirajá 581, Ipanema ☎ 021/2522–6664). The drugstore **Farma Life** (✉ Av. Ataulfo de Paiva, 644, Loja B, Leblon ☎ 021/511–4937 or 021/239–1178 ⊕ www.farmalife.com.br) has a wide selection of beauty products.

Shampoo Cosméticos (✉ Rua Visconde de Pirajá 581, Ipanema ☎ 021/ 2259–1699) carries popular cosmetics brands from L'Óreal to L'Occitane. If after a day or shopping, your feet are moaning, stop by **Spa do Pé** (✉ Av. Nossa Senhora de Copacabana 1066, Loja C, Copacabana ☎ 021/2523–8430 or 021/2523–2556 ⊕ www.spadope.com.br Ⓜ Siqueira Campos) for a massage, manicure, or a foot treatment.

Cachaça

Academia da Cachaça (✉ Rua Conde Bernadote 26, Loja G, Leblon ☎ 021/ 2239–1542) is not only *the* place in Rio to try caipirinhas—made with dozens kinds of tropical fruits—but is a temple of cachaça. The small bar with extraordinary appetizers from northeast Brazil sells 50 brands of cachaça by the glass or bottle. At **Garapa Doida** (✉ Rua Carlos Góis 234, Loja F, Leblon ☎ 021/2274–8186) learn how to prepare a good caipirinha and to buy everything you need to make it, including glasses, straws, barrels to conserve the alcohol, and cachaça brands from all over the country.

Garrafeira (✉ Rua Dias Ferreira 259, Loja A, Leblon ☎ 021/2512–3336) is a charming liquor store that sells more than 10 kinds of cachaça, including some brands from Piauí and Parati, a state and a city well known for producing good ones. Thirty types of cachaça and imported olives, nuts, apricots, salmon, and more are sold at **Lidador** (✉ Rua da Assembléia 65, Centro ☎ 021/2533–4896 Ⓜ Carioca ✉ Rua Barata Ribeiro 505, Copacabana ☎ 021/2549–0091 Ⓜ Siqueira Campos ✉ Botafogo Praia Shopping, Praia de Botafogo 400, Loja 201, Botafogo ☎ 021/2237–9057 Ⓜ Botafogo).

Clothing

DKNY and other well-known brands of sportswear are sold at **Alice Tapajós** (✉ Fórum de Ipanema, Visconde de Pirajá 35, Loja 116, Ipanema ☎ 021/2247–2594 ✉ São Conrado Fashion Mall, Estrada da Gávea 899, São Conrado ☎ 021/3083–0000 ✉ Barra Shopping, Av. das Américas 4666, Barra da Tijuca ☎ 021/3089–1100 ⊕ www. barrashopping.com.br). **Complexo B** (✉ Rua Francisco Otaviano 67, Loja 42—Galeria River, Copacabana ☎ 021/2521–7126 ⊕ www. complexob.com.br) is a men's sportswear shop created by the stylist Beto Neves. The collection focuses on T-shirts with a touch of humor, with prints of saints and superheroes.

At **Krishna** (✉ Rio Sul, Av. Lauro Müller 116, Loja B30, Botafogo ☎ 021/2542–2443 ✉ São Conrado Fashion Mall, Estrada da Gávea 899, São Conrado ☎ 021/3322–0437) the specialty is classic feminine dresses and separates—many in fine linens, cottons, and silks. Rio's largest chain department store, **Lojas Americanas** (✉ Rua do Passeio 42–56, Centro ☎ 021/2524–00315 ⊕ www.lojasamericanas.com.br Ⓜ Cinelândia ✉ Rua do Visconde de Pirajá 526, Ipanema ☎ 021/2274–0590) has casual fashions for men, women, and children. But it also has a wide selection of toys, records, cosmetics, and sporting goods. **Osklen** (✉ Rua Maria Quitéria 85, Ipanema ☎ 021/2227–2911 ✉ São Conrado Fashion Mall, Estrada da Gávea 899, São Conrado ☎ 021/3083–0000 ✉ Barra Shopping, Av. das Américas 4666, Barra da Tijuca ☎ 021/ 3089–1100 ⊕ www.barrashopping.com.br) is a synonym for sporty casual clothing with a fashionable flair. The clothes—from trousers to coats to tennis shoes—are designed for outdoor use. Two additional branches of the shop are at São Conrado Fashion Mall and Barra Shopping (⇨ Centers & Malls, *above*).

Coffee

Armazém do Café (✉ Rua Visconde de Pirajá 261, Ipanema ☎ 021/ 2287–5742 ✉ Rua Rita Ludolf 87, Loja B, Leblon ☎ 021/2259–0170) is a complete coffee shop with several brands of tasteful and high-quality *ouro negro* (black gold), as coffee was once called in the country because of its economic value. The shop also sells coffee machines. The supermarket **Pão de Açúcar** (✉ Av. Nossa Senhora Copacabana 493, Copacabana ☎ 021/2548–0483 Ⓜ Siqueira Campos) is a good bet for coffee and is cheaper than buying it at a coffee shop. Open 24 hours, **Zona Sul** (✉ Prudente de Morais 49, Ipanema ☎ 021/2523–4746) has a wide selection of coffee and other goods at reasonable prices.

Handicrafts

Inside the Museu do Índio (Museum of the Indian), **Artíndia** (✉ Rua das Palmeiras 55, Botafogo ☎ 021/2286–8899 Ⓜ Botafogo) has handcrafted items made by several Brazilian tribes: toys, necklaces made of seeds and feathers, musical instruments, and traditional Brazilian cooking pans made of iron. The shop is open Tuesday–Friday 10–5:30 and weekends 1–5. Handcrafted items made of everything from porcelain to wood and papier-mâché to clay are available at **Casa do Pequeno Empresário** (✉ Rua Real Grandeza 293, Botafogo ☎ 021/2286–9991 Ⓜ Botafogo), an exhibition center. The metrô station is a 10-block walk away.

Curio L Folclore (✉ Rua Visconde de Pirajá 490, Ipanema ☎ 021/2259–7442), owned by H. Stern jewelry, bursts with primitive paintings, costume jewelry, leather and ceramic crafts, and birds and flowers carved from stone. Quality is high, but take note: some items have been imported from other South American nations. Close to the train station to Corcovado, **Jeito Brasileiro** (✉ Rua Erre 11 A, Cosme Velho ☎ 021/2205–7636) has a great variety of paintings; handcrafted wood, leather, and ceramic items; and also some pieces from the Camurim tribe. The shop is open weekdays 10–7, Saturday 10–1, and Sunday 9–1.

Jewelry

Amsterdam Sauer (✉ Rua Visconde de Pirajá 484, Ipanema ☎ 021/2512–9878, 021/2239–8045 for the museum), one of Rio's top names in jewelry, has top prices. Jules Roger Sauer, the founder of these stores (with branches in Brazil, the United States, and the Caribbean), is particularly known for his fascination with emeralds. The on-site gemstone museum is open weekdays 10–5 and Saturday 9:30–1 (tour reservations are a good idea). For nearly 30 years **Antônio Bernardo** (✉ Fórum Ipanema, Rua Visconde de Pirajá 351, Loja 114, Ipanema ☎ 021/2523–3192 ⊕ www.antoniobernardo.com.br ✉ São Conrado Fashion Mall, Estrada da Gávea 899, São Conrado ☎ 021/3083–0000 ✉ Shopping Center da Gávea, Rua Marquês de São Vicente 52, Gávea ☎ 021/2274–9896) has been making gorgeous jewelry with contemporary designs.

Hans Stern started his empire in 1945 with an initial investment of about $200. Today his interests include mining and production operations as well as 170 stores in Europe, the Americas, and the Middle East. His award-winning designers create truly distinctive contemporary pieces (the inventory runs to about 300,000 items). At the world headquarters of **H. Stern** (✉ Rua Visconde de Pirajá 490, Ipanema ☎ 021/2259–7442), you can see exhibits of rare stones and watch craftspeople transform rough stones into sparkling jewels. There's also a museum you can tour (by appointment only). The shops downstairs sell more affordable pieces and folkloric items.

Leather Goods

Constança Basto (✉ Rua Visconde de Pirajá 371, Loja 206, Ipanema ☎ 021/2247–9932 ✉ Rua 7 de Setembro 48, Centro ☎ 021/2232–9801

Ⓜ Uruguaiana) has women's shoes made of crocodile and snake leather in original styles. Most pairs cost upwards of R$200. **Frankie Amaury** (✉ Fórum de Ipanema, Rua Visconde de Pirajá 351, Loja 106, Ipanema ☎ 021/2522–0633) is *the* name in leather clothing. All kinds of modern yet refined leather jackets, skirts, and trousers are available. Traditional carioca boutique **Mariazinha** (✉ Rio Sul, Av. Lauro Müller 116, Loja C34A, Botafogo ☎ 021/2541–6695 ✉ Rio Visconde de Pirajá 365, Ipanema ☎ 021/2523–2340), almost 40 years old, carries fashionable and modern footwear for women and is one of the city's finest clothing brands that follows international trends. **Mr. Cat** (✉ Botafogo Praia Shopping, Praia de Botafogo 400 ☎ 021/2237–9087 ⊕ www.mrcat.com.br Ⓜ Botafogo) carries some of Rio's best handbags and leather shoes for men and women. **Victor Hugo** (✉ Rio Sul, Av. Lauro Müller 116, Loja B19, Botafogo ☎ 021/2543–9290), a Uruguayan who began making handbags when he came to Brazil in the 1970s, has become famous nationally for his quality leather handbags. The bags are similar in quality to more expensive brands like Louis Vuitton, Gucci, and Prada.

Maps, Newspapers & Magazines

All you could need to entertain and guide yourself in Rio is inside **Livraria Letras & Expressõs** (✉ Rua Visconde de Pirajá 276, Ipanema ☎ 021/2521–6110 ⊕ www.letras.com.br ✉ Av. Ataulfo de Paiva 1292, Loja C, Leblon ☎ 021/2511–5085 or 021/2259–4861). Maps and magazines fill the store; the Ipanema location has a cozy coffee shop on the second floor. The 24-hour **Newstand Lido** (✉ Rua Belfort Roxo 146, Copacabana ☎ 021/2541–6629 Ⓜ Cardeal Arcoverde) sells a wide variety of maps and magazines in English. **Livraria Leonardo da Vinci** (✉ Av. Rio Branco 185, Centro ☎ 021/2533–2237 ⊕ www.leonardodavinci.com.br Ⓜ Carioca), one of Rio's best bookstores for foreign-language titles, this shop has a wide selection of books in English, Spanish, and French.

Music

Samba, jazz, bossa nova, and more are sold at **Gramophone** (✉ Rua 7 de Setembro 92, Loja 105, Centro ☎ 021/2221–2032 Ⓜ Uruguaiana ✉ Shopping Center da Gávea, Rua Marquês de São Vicente 52, Gávea ☎ 021/2274–9896), including difficult-to-find titles. **Modern Sound** (✉ Rua Barata Ribeiro 502 D, Copacabana ☎ 021/2548–5005 ⊕ www.modernsound.com.br Ⓜ Siqueira Campos) was a traditional shop that turned into a self-designated megamusic store. Aside from the 50,000 CD titles—which include lots of rarities—the store carries music equipment and accessories and has a charming bistro, where live music, from jazz to bossa nova, is played by the finest carioca musicians.

Toca do Vinícius (✉ Rua Vinícius de Moraes 129, Loja C, Ipanema ☎ 021/2247–5227) bills itself as a "cultural space and bossa nova salon." The shop, though tiny, does indeed seem like a gathering place for bossa nova aficionados from around the world, and if you're one of them, there's a good chance you'll leave the shop with an e-mail address for at least one new pal. Amid the friendly atmosphere, you can find books (a few in English), sheet music, and T-shirts as well as CDs.

Photo Equipment

All Photo (✉ Rua Barata Ribeiro 344, Copacabana ☎ 021/2235–5461 Ⓜ Siqueira Campos) carries film, batteries, and other camera accessories. At **De Plá** (✉ Av. Nossa Senhora Copacabana 975, Loja 11, Copacabana ☎ 021/2235–6179 Ⓜ Cardeal Arcoverde) you can pick up film and batteries and develop photos for reasonable prices.

RIO DE JANEIRO A TO Z

To research prices, get advice from other travelers, and book travel arrangements, visit www.fodors.com.

AIR TRAVEL

CARRIERS   Nearly three-dozen airlines regularly serve Rio. Several of the international carriers also offer Rio–São Paulo flights. International carriers include Aerolíneas Argentinas, Air Canada, American Airlines, British Airways, Continental, Delta, and United. Varig and VASP are domestic carries that serve international destinations. Varig, TAM, and Gol cover domestic routes. Non-Brazilian citizens must purchase tickets for Gol flights in person and with cash; the advantage is that Gol flights tend to be cheaper.

🛪 Airlines & Contacts **Aerolíneas Argentinas** ☎ 021/3398-3520 or 021/2292-4131 ⊕ www.aeroargentinas.com. **Air Canada** ☎ 021/2220-5354 or 0800/127590 ⊕ www. aircanada.com. **American Airlines** ☎ 021/3398-4053 or 021/2210-3126 ⊕ www.aa.com. **British Airways** ☎ 021/3398-3888 or 021/2221-0922 ⊕ www.ba.com. **Continental Airlines** ☎ 0800/55-4777 ⊕ www.continental.com. **Delta** ☎ 021/2549-1010. **Gol** ☎ 021/3398-5132, 021/3398-5136, or 0300/789-2121 ⊕ www.voegol.com.br. **TAM** ☎ 021/2524-1717 or 021/2524-8102 ⊕ www.tamairlines.com. **United** ☎ 021/3398-2450 or 0800/16-2323 ⊕ www.ual.com. **VASP** ☎ 021/3814-8079 or 0300/789-1010 ⊕ www.vasp.com.br. **Varig** ☎ 021/3398-2122, 021/2510-6650, or 0300/788-7000 ⊕ www.varig.com.

AIRPORTS & TRANSFERS

All international flights and most domestic flights arrive and depart from the Aeroporto Internacional Antônio Carlos Jobim, also known as Galeão. The airport is about 45 minutes northwest of the beach area and most of Rio's hotels. Aeroporto Santos Dumont, 20 minutes from the beaches and within walking distance of Centro, serves the Rio–São Paulo air shuttle and a few air-taxi firms.

🛪 Airport Information **Aeroporto Internacional Antônio Carlos Jobim** (Galeão) ☎ 021/3398-4526. **Aeroporto Santos Dumont** ☎ 021/3814-7070 or 021/3814-7646.

AIRPORT   Special airport taxis have booths in the arrival areas of both airports.
TRANSFERS   Fares to all parts of Rio are posted at the booths, and you pay in advance (about R$41–R$56). Also trustworthy are the white radio taxis parked in the same areas; these charge an average of 20% less. Three reliable special taxi firms are Transcoopass, Cootramo, and Coopertramo.

Buses run by Empresa Real park curbside outside customs at Galeão and outside the main door at Santos Dumont; for R$13.50 they make the hour-long trip from Galeão into the city, following the beachfront drives and stopping at all hotels along the way. If your hotel is inland, the driver will let you off at the nearest corner. Buses leave from the airport every half hour from 5:20 AM to 11 PM. There are also air-conditioned buses—called *frescão* (literally, "fresh")—that leave the Galeão to Barra da Tijuca, passing through Zona Sul (R$5). Two of the taxi firms have vans at the international airport: Cootramo has a van (with 11 seats) to downtown for R$57 and to Copacabana for R$78. Coopertramo does the same for R$70 and R$80, but the van has a capacity to transport 15.

🚐 Taxis & Shuttles **Cootramo** ☎ 021/2560-5442, 021/3976-9944, or 021/3976-9945. **Coopertramo** ☎ 021/2560-2022. **Empresa Real** ☎ 021/2560-7041 or 0800/24-0850. **Transcoopass** ☎ 021/2560-4888.

BUS TRAVEL TO & FROM RIO

Regular service is available to and from Rio. Long-distance and international buses leave from the Rodoviária Novo Rio. Any local bus marked RODOVIÁRIA will take you to the station. You can buy tickets at the depot or, for some destinations, from travel agents. Buses also leave from the more conveniently located Menezes Cortes Terminal, near Praça 15 de Novembro. These buses travel to different neighborhoods of Rio (Barra da Tijuca, Santa Cruz, Campo Grande, and Recreio) and to nearby cities Nieterói, Petrópolis, and Nova Friburgo, among others.

🚌 Bus Information **Rodoviária Novo Rio** ✉ Av. Francisco Bicalho 1, São Cristóvão ☎ 021/2291-5151. **Menezes Cortes Terminal** ✉ Rua São José 35, Centro ☎ 021/2533-8819.

BUS TRAVEL WITHIN RIO

Much has been made of the threat of being robbed on Rio's buses. However, crime has dropped significantly in the last few years; if you're discreet, you shouldn't have any problems. Just don't wear expensive watches or jewelry, carry a camera or a map in hand, or talk boisterously in English. It's also wise to avoid buses during rush hour.

Local buses are inexpensive and can take you anywhere you want to go. (Route maps aren't available, but the tourist office has lists of routes to the most popular sights.) You enter buses at the rear, where you pay the attendant and pass through a turnstile, then exit at the front. Have your fare in hand when you board to avoid flashing bills or wallets. Be aware that bus drivers speak no English, and they drive like maniacs. You should have your money ready (with correct change) when you enter the bus because you enter at the back and pay the *cobrador* (fare collector) immediately.

The upscale, privately run, and air-conditioned Frescão buses run between the beaches, downtown, and Rio's two airports. These vehicles, which look like highway buses, stop at regular bus stops but also may be flagged down wherever you see them. Green minivans run back and forth along beachfront avenues. Fares start at about R$1.40.

CAR RENTAL

Car rentals can be arranged through hotels or agencies and at this writing cost about R$110–R$250 a day for standard models. Major agencies include Avis, Hertz, and Unidas. Localiza is a local agency. Hertz and Unidas have desks at the international and domestic airports.

🚗 Major Agencies **Avis** ✉ Av. Princesa Isabel 350, Copacabana ☎ 021/2543-8579.

Hertz ✉ Av. Princesa Isabel 334, Copacabana ☎ 021/2275-7440 or 0800/701-7300 ✉ Aeroporto Internacional Antônio Carlos Jobim ☎ 021/3398-4338 ✉ Aeroporto Santos Dumont ☎ 021/2262-0612. **Localiza Rent a Car** ✉ Av. Princesa Isabel 214, Copacabana ☎ 021/2275-3340 ✉ Aeroporto Internacional Antônio Carlos Jobim ☎ 021/3398-5445 ✉ Aeroporto Santos Dumont ☎ 021/2533-2677. **Unidas** ☎ 021/4001-2222 for main reservations line ✉ Aeropuerto Santos Dumont, Av. Senador Salgado Filho s/n, Centro ☎ 021/2240-9181 ✉ Av. Princesa Isabel, 166, Copacabana ☎ 021/3685-1212 ✉ Aeropuerto Internacional do Galeão, Estrada do Galeão s/n, Ilha do Governador ☎ 021/3398-2286.

CAR TRAVEL

The carioca style of driving is passionate to the point of abandon: traffic jams are common, the streets aren't well marked, and red lights are often more decorative than functional. Although there are parking areas along the beachfront boulevards, finding a spot can still be a problem. If you do choose to drive, exercise extreme caution, wear seat belts at all times, and keep the doors locked.

Arriving from São Paulo (429 km/266 mi on BR 116) or Brasília (1,150 km/714 mi on BR 040), you enter Rio via Avenida Brasil, which runs into Centro's beachside drive, the Avenida Infante Dom Henrique. This runs along Rio's Baía de Guanabara and passes through the Copacabana Tunnel to Copacabana Beach. The beachside Avenida Atlântica continues into Ipanema and Leblon along Avenidas Antônio Carlos Jobim (Ipanema) and Delfim Moreira (Leblon). From Galeão take the Airport Expressway (known as the Linha Vermelha, or Red Line) to the beach area. This expressway takes you through two tunnels and into Lagoa. Exit on Avenida Epitácio Pessoa, the winding street encircling the lagoon. To reach Copacabana, exit at Avenida Henrique Dodsworth (known as the Corte do Cantagalo). For Ipanema and Leblon there are several exits, beginning with Rua Maria Quitéria.

Turismo Clássico Travel, one of the country's most reliable travel and transport agencies, can arrange for a driver, with or without an English-speaking guide (US$30 per hour). Classico's owners, Liliana and Vera, speak English, and each has 20 years of experience in organizing transportation. They also lead sightseeing tours.

🔢 **Turismo Clássico Travel** ✉ Av. Nossa Senhora de Copacabana 1059, Sala 805, Copacabana ☎ 021/2523-3390.

GASOLINE There's a gas station on every main street in Rio: for example, on Avenida Atlântica in Copacabana, around the Lagoa Rodrigo de Freitas, and at Avenida Vieira Souto in Ipanema. International companies, such as Shell and Esso, are represented. The gas stations run by Brazilian oil company Petrobras are called BR. Ipiranga is another local option. Half the gas stations are open from 6 AM until 10 PM, and half are open 24 hours and have convenience stores. Gas stations don't have emergency service, so ask when you rent whether your car-rental insurance includes it.

🔢 **Gas Stations BR** ✉ Posto de Gasolina Cardeal: Av. Atlântica s/n, Leme ☎ 021/2275-5696 ✉ Posto Santa Clara: Av. Atlântica s/n, Copacabana ☎ 021/2547-1467. **Ipiranga** ✉ Ponei Posto de Gasolina: Av. Borges de Medeiros 3151, Lagoa ☎ 021/2539-1283.

EMERGENCIES

The Tourism Police station is open 24 hours.

Emergency Services **Ambulance and Fire** ☎193. **Police** ☎190 ⊕www.novapolicia. rj.gov.br. **Tourism Police** ✉ Rua Humberto de Campos 315, Leblon ☎ 021/3399-7170. **Medical Clinics** **Cardio Plus** ✉ Rua Visconde de Pirajá 330, Ipanema ☎021/ 2521-4899. **Galdino Campos Cardio Copa Medical Clinic** ✉ Av. Nossa Senhora de Co-pacabana 492, Copacabana ☎ 021/2548-9966. **Medtur** ✉ Av. Nossa Senhora de Co-pacabana 647, Copacabana ☎ 021/2235-3339. **Copa D'Or** ✉ Rua Figueiredo Magalhães 875, Copacabana ☎ 021/2545-3600.

24-Hour Pharmacies **Drogaria Pacheco** ✉ Av. Nossa Senhora de Copacabana 534, Copacabana ☎ 021/2548-1525. **Farmácia do Leme** ✉ Av. Prado Júnior 237, Leme ☎ 021/2275-3847.

ENGLISH-LANGUAGE MEDIA

Bookstores that carry some English-language publications include Le-tras & Expressões, Livraria Argumento, Livraria Kosmos, Saraiva Mega-store, and Sodiler. In Ipanema, newsstands Banca Nossa Senhora da Paz and Banca General Osório sell international newspapers 24 hours a day.

Bookstores **Banca General Osório** ✉ Corner of Praça General Osório and Rua Jan-gadeiros, Ipanema ☎ 021/2287-9248. **Banca Nossa Senhora da Paz** ✉ Rua Visconde de Pirajá 365, Ipanema ☎ 021/2522-0880. **Letras & Expressões** ✉ Rua Visconde de Pirajá 276, Ipanema ☎ 021/2521-6110. **Livraria Argumento** ✉ Rua Dias Ferreira 417, Leblon ☎ 021/2239-5294. **Livraria Kosmos** ✉ Rua do Rosário 155, Centro ☎ 021/ 2224-8616. **Saraiva Megastore** ✉ Rio Sul, Rua Lauro Müller 116, Loja 301 C, Botafogo ☎ 021/2543-7002. **Sodiler** ✉ Aeroporto Internacional Antônio Carlos Jobim ☎ 021/ 3393-9511.

HEALTH

Avoid tap water, though ice in restaurants and bars is safe, as it's usu-ally made from bottled water. Take care not to soak up too much sun. Despite Rio's reputation, crime is no more likely than in any large city. Most crimes involving visitors occur in crowded public areas: beaches, busy sidewalks, intersections, and city buses. Pickpockets, usually chil-dren, work in groups. One will distract you while another grabs a wal-let, bag, or camera. Be particularly wary of children who thrust themselves in front of you and ask for money or offer to shine your shoes. Another member of the gang may strike from behind, grabbing your valuables and disappearing into the crowd.

Another tactic is for criminals to approach your car at intersections. Al-ways keep doors locked and windows partially closed. Leave valuables in your hotel safe, don't wear expensive jewelry or watches, and keep cameras out of sight. Walking alone at night on the beach isn't a good idea; neither is getting involved with drugs—penalties for possession are severe, and dealers are the worst of the worst.

MAIL, INTERNET & SHIPPING

Brazilians are joining the Internet community in increasing numbers, and the staff at many hotels can arrange Internet access for guests. In addi-tion, you can head to several cybercafés around town for coffee while you check your e-mail.

The main post office is in Centro, but there are branches all over the city, including one at Galeão, several on Avenida Nossa Senhora de Copacabana in Copacabana, and one on Rua Visconde de Pirajá in Ipanema. Most are open weekdays 8–5 and Saturday 8–noon. Federal Express and DHL have offices open weekdays, but shipping usually takes longer than just overnight. You can call a day ahead to schedule pickup.

At Café do Ubaldo (Sunday–Thursday 8 AM–midnight and Friday–Saturday 8 AM–2 AM), Web access is R$5 for 30 minutes. At Cyber Coffee (Monday–Saturday 10–10; Sunday 3–9) Web access is R$9.50 for an hour and R$3.50 for each additional 15 minutes.

🛈 Courier Services **DHL** ⊠ Rua Teófilo Otoni 15 A, Centro ☎ 021/2516-0828 or 0800/701-0833. **Federal Express** ⊠ Av. Calógeras 23, Centro ☎ 021/2262-8405 or 0800/903-333.

🛈 Internet Centers **Café do Ubaldo** ⊠ Rua Visconde de Pirajá 276, Ipanema ☎ 021/2521-6110 Ⓜ Cardeal Arcoverde, then shuttle bus to Praça General Osório. **Cyber Coffee** ⊠ Rio Sul Shopping Center, Rua Lauro Muller 16, 3rd floor, Botafogo ☎ 021/2543-6886.

🛈 Post Office **Agência Central** (Main Branch) ⊠ Av. Presidente Vargas 3077 ☎ 021/2503-8467 or 021/2273-5998.

METRÔ TRAVEL

Rio's subway system, the metrô, is clean, relatively safe, and efficient—a delight to use—but it's not comprehensive. Reaching sights distant from metrô stations can be a challenge, especially in summer when the infamous carioca traffic fans what is already 90-degree exasperation. Plan your tours accordingly; tourism offices and some metrô stations have maps.

Trains run daily from 6 AM to 11 PM along two lines: Linha 1 runs north from the Siqueira Campos stop in Copacabana, three blocks from the beach and into downtown, then west to its terminus at the Saens Pena station; Linha 2 starts four stops before Saens Pena at Estácio and heads northwest to Rio's edge at the Pavuna station. A single metrô ticket at this writing costs R$1.47. Combination metrô-bus tickets allow you to take special buses to and from the Botafogo station: the M-21 runs to Leblon via Jardim Botânico and Jóckey; the M-22 goes to Leblon by way of Túnel Velho, Copacabana, and Ipanema.

🛈 Metrô Information **Metrô Rio Information Line** ☎ 021/3982-3600 or 021/3211-6300.

MONEY MATTERS

Generally, exchange rates are better in the city than at the airport, and cash gets better rates than traveler's checks. Most Brazilian banks don't exchange money. One that does is Banco do Brasil. The branch at Galeão offers good exchange rates, but it won't provide credit-card advances.

Casas de câmbio (exchange houses) are found all over the city, especially along the beaches and on Avenida Nossa Senhora de Copacabana and Rua Visconde de Pirajá in Ipanema. Many change money without charging a service fee. Sometimes, depending on the amount of money you wish to exchange, exchange houses have a better rate than the banks. American Express is another option.

Some hotels, such as the Caesar Park and the Copacabana Palace, offer competitive rates but charge a commission if you're not a guest. On weekends hotels may be your best bet because few other places are open. Or try the Banco 24 Horas automatic teller machines (ATMs) throughout town, which dispense reais.

🏦 Banks & Exchange Services **American Express** ✉ Av. Atlântica 1702 B, Copacabana ☎ 021/2548-2148 or 0800/702-0777. **Banco do Brasil** ✉ Rua Bartolomeu Mitre 438 A, Leblon ☎ 021/2512-9992 or 021/2274-4664 ✉ Av. Nossa Senhora de Copacabana 594 ☎ 021/3808-2689 ✉ Aeroporto Internacional Antônio Carlos Jobim, 3rd floor ☎ 021/3398-3652. **Banco 24 Horas ATM** ✉ Av. Nossa Senhora de Copacabana 202 ✉ Av. Nossa Senhora de Copacabana 599 ✉ Av. Nossa Senhora de Copacabana 1366 ✉ Visconde de Pirajá 174, Ipanema. **Casa Universal** ✉ Av. Nossa Senhora de Copacabana 371 E, Copacabana ☎ 021/2548-6696.

TAXIS

Yellow taxis have meters that start at a set price and have two rates. The "1" rate applies to fares before 8 PM, and the "2" rate applies to fares after 8 PM, on Sunday, on holidays, throughout December, in the neighborhoods of São Conrado and Barra da Tijuca, and when climbing steep hills. Drivers are required to post a chart noting the current fares on the inside of the left rear window. Most carioca cabbies are pleasant, but there are exceptions. Remain alert and trust your instincts. Few cab drivers speak English. Pay attention to the meter, as some cab drivers might neglect to turn on the meter and then try to overcharge.

Radio taxis and several companies that routinely serve hotels (and whose drivers often speak English) are also options. They charge 30% more than other taxis but are reliable and usually air-conditioned. Other cabs working with the hotels also charge more, normally a fixed fee that you should agree on before you leave. Reliable radio cab companies include Centro de Taxis, Coopacarioca, and Coopatur.

🚕 Taxi Companies **Centro de Taxis** ☎ 021/2593-2598 or 021/3899-1010. **Coopacarioca** ☎ 021/2518-1818. **Coopatur** ☎ 021/2573-1009.

TELEPHONES

Rio's area code is 021. There are public phones on corners throughout the city. They work with cards that you can buy in a variety of denominations at newsstands, banks, and some shops (some phones also work with credit cards). For long-distance calls there are phone offices at the main bus terminal, Galeão, downtown at Praça Tiradentes 41, and in Copacabana at Avenida Nossa Senhora de Copacabana 540. To make international calls through the operator, dial 000111. For operator-assisted long-distance within Brazil, dial 101; information is 102. You can also make international calls through the long-distance providers Embratel (dial 21 before the number you're calling), Telefonica (dial 15), and Intelig (dial 23). You can make international calls from any public phone that reads D.D.I. (*discagen direta internacional,* or "international calls"). Numbers in Rio have eight digits.

TOURS

You can ride around the Floresta da Tijuca and Corcovado, Angra dos Reis, and Teresópolis in renovated World War II jeeps (1942 Dodge Commanders, Willys F-75s, and others) with the well-organized Atlantic Forest Jeep Tours. Guides speak English, French, German, and Spanish. The company also has a range of ecological tours, including some on horseback. English-speaking guides at Gray Line are superb. In addition to a variety of city tours, the company also offers trips outside town, whether you'd like to go white-water rafting on the Rio Paraíbuna, tour a coffee plantation, or spend time in Petrópolis. Helicopter tours are also an option.

Carlos Roquette is a history teacher who runs Cultural Rio, an agency that hosts trips to 8,000 destinations. Most are historic sites. A guided visit costs around US$110 for four hours, depending on the size of the group. Ecology and Culture Tours offers hiking and jeep tours of Tijuca, Sugar Loaf, Santa Teresa, and various beaches. Guides speak English: morning and afternoon excursions are available. Favela Tour offers a fascinating half-day tour of two favelas. For anyone with an interest in Brazil beyond the beaches, such tours are highly recommended. The company's English-speaking guides can also be contracted for other outings.

Private Tours take you around old Rio, the favelas, Corcovado, Floresta da Tijuca, Prainha, and Grumari in a jeep. Guides are available who speak English, Hungarian, French, and German. Hang glide or paraglide over Pedra da Gávea and Pedra Bonita under the supervision of São Conrado Eco-Aventura.

Helisight gives a number of helicopter tours whose flights may pass over the Cristo Redentor, Copacabana, Ipanema, and/or Maracanã stadium. There are night flights as well; reserve ahead for these daily 9–6.

Rio Hiking tours combine the city sightseeing with nature hikes to the Floresta da Tijuca and other areas. The company also runs nightlife tours in the city and overnight trips to Parati and Ilha Grande.

🪧**Atlantic Forest Jeep Tours** ☏ 021/2495-9827 🖨 021/2494-4761. **Cultural Rio** ☏ 021/9911-3829 or 021/3322-4872 ⊕ www.culturalrio.com.br. **Ecology and Culture Tours** ☏021/2522-1620. **Favela Tour** ☏ 021/3322-2727. **Gray Line** ☏ 021/2512-9919. **Helisight** ✉ Rua Visconde de Pirajá 580, Loja 107 ☏ 021/2511-2141, 021/2542-7895, or 021/2259-6995 ⊕ www.helisight.com.br **Private Tours** ☏🖨 021/2232-9710 ⊕ www.privatetours.com.br. **São Conrado Eco-Aventura** ☏ 021/2522-5586, 021/3902-8558, or 021/9966-7010 ⊕ www.4ventos.com.br. **Rio Hiking** ☏ 021/9721-0594 ⊕ www.riohiking.com.br.

TRAIN TRAVEL

Intercity trains leave from *the* central station that starred in the Oscar-nominated movie of the same name, Estação Dom Pedro II Central do Brasil. Trains, including a daily overnight train to São Paulo, also leave from the Estação Leopoldina Barao de Maria, near Praça 15 de Novembro.

🪧 Train Information **Estação Dom Pedro II Central do Brasil** ✉ Praça Cristiano Otoni on Av. President Vargas, Centro ☏ 021/2588-9494.

VISITOR INFORMATION

The Rio de Janeiro city tourism department, Riotur, has an information booth, which is open 8–5 daily. There are also city tourism desks

at the airports and the Novo Rio bus terminal. The Rio de Janeiro state tourism board, Turisrio, is open weekdays 9–6. You can also try contacting Brazil's national tourism board, Embratur.

🔒 Tourist Information **Embratur** ✉ Rua Uruguaiana 174, Centro ☎ 021/2509-6017 🌐 www.embratur.gov.br. **Riotur** ✉ Rua da Assembléia 10, near Praça 15 de Novembro, Centro ☎ 021/2217-7575 or 0800/707-1808 🌐 www.rio.rj.gov.br/riotur. **Riotur information booth** ✉ Av. Princesa Isabel 183, Copacabana ☎ 021/2542-8080. **Turisrio** ✉ Rua da Ajuda 5, Centro ☎ 021/2215-0011 🌐 www.turisrio.rj.gov.br.

SIDE TRIPS FROM RIO

Rio the state has just as much allure as Rio the city. Across Guanabara Bay, Niterói is a mix of new and old: the ultramodern Museu de Arte Contemporânea is not far from historic forts. A scenic northeast road into the mountains leads to Petrópolis, a city that bears testimony to the country's royal legacy. Beyond, tucked into a lush valley, is charming Nova Friburgo with its Swiss roots. Due east of the city, dangling off the yacht-frequented coast, are the sophisticated resort towns of Cabo Frio and Búzios, where Rio's chic escape for weekends. And to the southwest along the Costa Verde sit the stunning Angra dos Reis—facing the offshore island of Ilha Grande—and the colonial city of Parati, with its 18th-century Portuguese architecture and plethora of offshore islets.

Niterói

㉕ *14 km (9 mi) east of Rio.*

Ranked as having the highest quality of life in Rio de Janeiro State, Niterói, literally, "hidden waters," was founded in 1573. Old and new come together in this city of some 450,000, where both a modern naval industry and traditional fishing help support the economy. Ocean beaches and the Fortaleza de Santa Cruz—an ancient fortress built in 1555 to protect the bay—draw visitors, but so does the ultramodern Museu de Arte Contemporânea. Ferries from Rio's Praça 15 de Novembro cross the bay, arriving at Praça Araribóia in a pleasant 20 minutes.

The must-see **Museu de Arte Contemporânea** was constructed by the well-known architect Oscar Niemeyer (he designed most of Brasília). Opened in the 1990s, the building looks a bit like a spaceship. The modern art museum shelters the collection donated by João Sattamini. Just five minutes from Praça Araribóia (in downtown Niterói where the ferries stop), enjoy a nice walk along the coastline. Upon leaving, try the fresh coconut water sold outside. ⊠ *Estrada de Boa Viagem, Boa Viagem* ☎ *021/2620–2400* ⊕ *www.macniteroi.com* ☎ *R$2* ⊙ *Tues.–Fri. 11–7, Sat. 1–9, Sun. 11–7.*

The **Fortaleza de Santa Cruz** was the first fort built on Guanabara Bay, in 1555. Distributed on two floors are cannons, a sun clock, and the Santa Barbara Chapel—dating from the 17th century. It's best to visit in the cool morning hours. Fifteen minutes from downtown, it's an easy taxi ride (R$25), or there's a bus that goes straight to Jurujuba (No. 33) from the ferry dock. ⊠ *Estrada General Eurico Gaspar Dutra, Jurujuba* ☎ *021/2711–0462* ☎ *R$4* ⊙ *Daily 9–4.*

Built as an lookout point, **Forte Barão do Rio Branco** was armed and turned into a battery in 1567. Inside is the Forte do Imbuí, another fortress, which is a wonderful place to walk, with a great view of Guanabara Bay and Rio. ⊠ *Av. Marechal Pessoa Leal 265, Jurujuba* ☎ *021/ 2711–0366 or 021/2711–0566* ☎ *R$6* ⊙ *Weekends 9–5.*

Cabo Frio

㉖ *168 km (101 mi) east of Rio.*

Set up as a defensive port from which to ship wood to Portugal nearly four centuries ago, Cabo Frio has evolved into a resort town renowned for its fresh seafood. It's also a prime jumping-off point for the endless number of white-sand beaches that crisscross the area around town and the offshore islands. A favorite sailing destination, its turquoise waters are crowded with sailboats and yachts on holidays and weekends. The town itself has attractive baroque architecture.

Praia do Forte is popular thanks to its calm, clear waters and long stretch of sand. On weekends it's jammed with colorful beach umbrellas, swimmers, and sun lovers. Some distance away, Praia Brava and Praia do Foguete lure surfers to their crashing waves. Cabo Frio hotels are not as nice as those in nearby Búzios, so you're better off staying there and making the short trip to Cabo Frio by car or via a 50-minute bus trip (R$2.10).

Restaurants in Cabo Frio tend to be of the by-the-kilo, cheap variety and change frequently. Head to Boulevard Canal for restaurants and nightlife.

Where to Stay

★ $–$$ ☒ **Malibu Palace Hotel.** One of the most traditional hotels in Cabo Frio, the Malibu Palace is simply decorated but has the advantage of being just in front of Praia do Forte, with its blue transparent waters, and in the center of the city some blocks from shops and restaurants. Lunch and breakfast are included. ☒ *Av. do Contorno 900, at Praia do Forte, 28907-250* ☏ *022/2643–1955 or 022/2645–5131* ⊕ *www.malibupalace. com.br* ➪ *110 rooms* ⌂ *Restaurant, room service, in-room data ports, in-room safes, refrigerators, cable TV, 2 pools, sauna, gym, dry cleaning, laundry service, no-smoking rooms* ☰ *AE, DC, MC, V* ⚏ *BP.*

Búzios

27
FodorsChoice
★

25 km (15 mi) northeast of Cabo Frio; 193 km (126 mi) northeast of Rio.

Búzios, a little more than two hours from Rio, is a string of gorgeous beaches that draws resort fans year-round from Europe and South America. This is the perfect place to do absolutely nothing. It was little more than a fishing village until the 1960s, when Brigitte Bardot was photographed here in a bikini. Since then Búzios's rustic charm has given way to *pousadas,* or inns (some of them luxurious, few inexpensive); restaurants; and bars run by people who came on vacation and never left. The balance between the cosmopolitan and the primitive is seductive.

March through June is low season, when temperatures range from about 27°C (80°F) to 32°C (90°F), and prices often drop 30%–40%. The water is still warm, yet the crowds aren't as great; the area seems much more intimate than in the summer months of October through December. Though not a great deal of English is spoken here, a little Spanish or French will get you a long way.

Each of the beaches offers something different: the lovely, intimate Azeda and Azedinha are local favorites (and the spots where you may find topless bathing); Ferradura is known for jet skiing and excellent food kiosks; Lagoinha is referred to as a magic beach and has a natural amphitheater where world-class musicians hold concerts; Brava is the surfers' beach; and Manguinhos is popular with windsurfers.

If you choose not to stay at the Brava Hotel at **Spa Ligia Azevedo,** you can still stop by to indulge in treatments like shiatsu massage, paraffin masks, lymphatic drainage, facials, and manicures. Owner Ligia Azevedo is well known for her Rio beauty center. ☒ *Brava Hotel, Rua 17, lote*

14, quadra O, Praia Brava ☎ *021/2495–9191 or 021/2495–5959* ⊕ *www.ligiazevedo.com.br.*

Where to Stay & Eat

★ **$$$–$$$$** ✕ **Satyricon.** The Italian fish restaurant famous in Rio has opened up shop here as well. The menu's highlight is the expensive but great seafood, including the restaurant's famous rock salt–baked whole fish. ⊠ *Av. José Bento Ribeiro Dantas (Orla Bardot) 500* ☎ *022/2623–1595* ⊟ *AE, DC, MC, V.*

★ **$–$$** ✕ **Cigalon.** The restaurant has a veranda overlooking the beach. You can get lamb steak for R$30, and the cooked lobster with rice and almonds for R$75 is a must. If you're having trouble making up your mind among the tempting options, the tasting menu for R$33 might be your best bet. ⊠ *Rua das Pedras 265* ☎ *022/2623–6284* ⊟ *AE, DC, MC, V.*

¢ ✕ **Chez Michou.** This *crêperie* on the main drag in the center of town is the best place to eat if you want something quick, light, and inexpensive. You can choose from among about 500 crepe fillings and then eat outdoors. At night locals and visitors alike congregate to drink and people-watch. ⊠ *Rua da Pedras 90* ☎ *022/2623–2169* ⊕ *www.chezmichou. com.br* ⊟ *No credit cards.*

★ **$$$** ⌂ **Brava Hotel.** Physical well-being is the focus at this health-conscious hotel and spa. The Spa Ligia Azevedo has group activities like aquatic gymnastics, walks on the beach, and yoga classes, plus personalized fitness programs, physician-prescribed diets, massage, and beauty treatments. Simply decorated and of Mediterranean inspiration, the suites are small, but all have balconies with sea views. Close to Praia Brava, the hotel has a wonderful view of the beach from the pool and the restaurant. The owner recommends a week in the spa to feel the results; it's not hard to take her advice. ⊠ *Rua 17, lote 14, quadra O, Praia Brava, 28950-000* ☎☎ *022/2623–5943 for hotel* ☎ *021/2495–9191 or 021/2495–5959 for spa* ⊕ *www.buziosturismo.com/bravahotel* ⇴ *27 suites* ⌂ *Restaurant, room service, in-room safes, refrigerators, cable TV, pool, spa, dry cleaning, laundry service, no-smoking rooms* ⊟ *AE, DC, MC, V.*

★ **$$$** ⌂ **Galápagos Inn.** Overlooking the Orla Bardot, the most charming place in Búzios—the continuation of Rua das Pedras, where people congregate at night—this hotel also has a view of the sea and, best of all, a view of the sunset. Rooms are comfortable, with decoration inspired by the sea. Verandas have views to João Fernandinho Beach, and there's bar service at the beach. The hotel is included in Brazil's esteemed Roteiros de Charme club, a highly exclusive association of the nation's best places to stay, which also includes the Caesar Park Hotel Ipanema, in Rio. ⊠ *Praia João Fernandinho 3, 28925-000* ☎ *022/2623–6161* ⊕ *www.galapagos. com.br* ⇴ *37 rooms* ⌂ *Restaurant, room service, in-room data ports, in-room safes, refrigerators, cable TV, pool, sauna, bar, dry cleaning, laundry service, no-smoking rooms* ⊟ *AE, DC, MC, V* ⦿ *BP.*

★ **$** ⌂ **Pousada dos Gravatás.** Its location right on Praia de Geribá, a long beach with red sand preferred by surfers, makes this pousada the best budget option in Búzios. Suites have pool and ocean views. Standard apartments are at the back of the pousada, facing an internal patio. Rooms aren't big, but they are comfortable, with decor inspired by the sea. There's bar service on the beach. ⊠ *Rua dos Gravatás 67, Praia de Geribá, 28950-*

000 ☎ *022/2623–1218* ⊕ *www.pousadagravatas.com.br* ↙ *56 rooms* ♨ *Room service, refrigerators, cable TV, 2 pools, sauna, gym, bar* ⊟ *AE, DC, MC, V* ⦿ *BP.*

★ $ ⊡ **Pousada Pedra da Laguna.** Next to Ferradura Beach and in front of Ponta da Lagoinha—a place close to the rocks where the sea forms natural pools—this hotel is included in Brazil's esteemed Roteiros de Charme club, a highly exclusive association of the nation's best places to stay. Although it's a 15-minute walk from Rua das Pedras (or 5 minutes by car), the pousada has spacious apartments with balconies. Only the suites have sea views; rooms overlook the pool. Two rooms are wheelchair accessible. ✉ *Rua 6, lote 6, quadra F, Praia da Ferradura, 28950-000* ☎☎ *022/2623–1965 or 022/2623–2569* ⊕ *www.pedradalaguna. cjb.net* ↙ *25 rooms* ♨ *Restaurant, tennis court, pool, sauna, room service, in-room data ports, in-room safes, refrigerators, cable TV, laundry service* ⊟ *AE, V* ⦿ *BP.*

Nova Friburgo

㉘ *131 km (79 mi) northeast of Petrópolis; 196 km (121 mi) northeast of Rio.*

This summer resort town was settled by Swiss immigrants in the early 1800s when Brazil was actively encouraging European immigration and when the economic situation in Switzerland was bad. Woods, rivers, and waterfalls dot the terrain encircling the city. Homemade liquors, jams, and cheeses pack the shelves of the town's small markets. Cariocas come here to unwind in the cool mountain climate.

A cable car rises more than 600 meters (2,000 feet) to **Morro da Cruz,** which offers a spectacular view of the mountain. ✉ *Praça Teleférica* ☎ *022/2522–4834* 💳 *R$10* ⊙ *Weekends 9–6.*

Where to Stay

$ ⊡ **Hotel Bucsky.** Long walks through the several thousand kilometers of forest that surrounds the hotel are among the draws at this country-house inn. Opened in 1940 by members of a Hungarian family that first established themselves as restaurant owners in Rio, the hotel has a rustic style, with some rooms in pine. Rooms aren't large. The buffet-style restaurant is not luxurious, but it serves good, simple food. The hotel holds gastronomic festivals that center around German and Hungarian cuisines. ✉ *Estrada Rio-Friburgo, Km 76.5, Ponte Saudade 28615-160* ☎ *022/ 2522–5052 or 022/2522–5500* 🖶 *024/2522–9769* ⊕ *www.hotelbucsky. com.br* ↙ *60 rooms, 10 suites* ♨ *Room service, refrigerators, cable TV, miniature golf, tennis court, pool, sauna, laundry service* ⊟ *AE, DC, MC, V* ⦿ *FAP.*

Petrópolis

㉙ *65 km (42 mi) northeast of Rio.*

The hilly highway northeast of the city rumbles past forests and waterfalls en route to a mountain town so refreshing and picturesque that Dom Pedro II, Brazil's second emperor, spent his summers in it. (From 1889 to 1899 it was also the country's year-round seat of government.) Horse-drawn carriages shuttle between the sights, passing flowering gardens, shady parks, and imposing pink mansions.

The **Museu Imperial** is a museum housed in the magnificent 44-room palace that was Dom Pedro's summer home, the colossal structure is filled with polished wooden floors, 19th-century artwork, and grand chandeliers. You can also see the diamond-encrusted gold crown and scepter of Brazil's last emperor, as well as other royal jewels. ✉ *Rua da Imperatriz 220* ☎ *024/2237–8000* 🎫 *R$5* ⏲ *Tues.–Sun. 11–6.*

From the Museu Imperial you can walk three long blocks or take a horse-drawn carriage to **São Pedro de Alcantara,** the Gothic cathedral containing the tombs of Dom Pedro II; his wife, Dona Teresa Cristina; and their daughter, Princesa Isabel. ✉ *Av. Tiradentes* ☎ *No phone* 🎫 *Free* ⏲ *Tues.–Sun. 8–noon and 2–6.*

The **Palácio de Cristal** (Crystal Palace), a stained-glass and iron building made in France and assembled in Brazil, was a wedding present to Princesa Isabel. During the imperial years it was used as a ballroom: it was here the princess held a celebration dance after she abolished slavery in Brazil in 1888. ✉ *Praça da Confluencia, Rua Alfredo Pacha* ☎ *No phone* 🎫 *Free* ⏲ *Tues.–Sun. 9–5.*

Where to Stay & Eat

$ ✕ **Bauernstube.** German food is the backbone of this log cabin–style eatery. The bratwurst and sauerkraut are properly seasoned, and the strudel is an excellent choice for polishing off a meal. ✉ *Av. Dr. Nelson de Sá Earp 297* ☎ *024/2242–1097* 💳 *DC, MC, V* ⏲ *Closed Mon.*

$$$ ✕🏨 **Locanda Della Mimosa.** This cozy pousada has only a few suites, but the service is first class. It's in a romantic and inspiring valley filled with bougainvillea trees and places for long walks. The suites are decorated in a classical style with an imperial touch. Tea is served in the afternoon. The Italian restaurant, open Thursday through Sunday, has a degustation menu ($$$$) of specialties from different regions of Italy. ✉ *Km 71.5, BR 040, Alameda das Mimosas 30, Vale Florido, 25725-490* ☎ *024/2233–5405* 🌐 *www.locanda.com.br* 🛏 *6 suites* 🛎 *Restaurant, room service, cable TV, pool, sauna, bar* 💳 *AE, DC, MC, V* 🍽 *BP* ⏲ *Closed Mon.–Wed.*

$$ ✕🏨 **Pousada de Alcobaça.** Just north of Petrópolis, this is considered by many to be the loveliest inn in the area. The grounds have beautiful gardens and a swimming pool. The kitchen turns out exceptional breakfasts, lunches, and high teas with an emphasis on fresh ingredients. Meals ($–$$$), which include savory pastas, are served in the garden. All rooms in the early-20th-century house are cozy and decorated in a rustic style. ✉ *Agostinho Goulão 298, Corrêas, 25730-050* ☎ *024/2221–1240* 📠 *024/2222–3162* 🛏 *11 rooms* 🌐 *www.pousadadaalcobaca.com.br* 🛎 *Restaurant, room service, cable TV, tennis court, pool, sauna, laundry service* 💳 *AE, DC, MC, V* 🍽 *BP.*

$ ✕🏨 **Pousada Monte Imperial.** A few kilometers from downtown, this Euro-style inn has a lobby with a fireplace and a restaurant–bar. Rooms are cozy and rustic, in an old European style, and have a view of the historic center of the city. Drinks and meals can be taken in the lovely garden. ⊠ *Rua José de Alencar 27, 25610-050* ☎ *024/2237–1664* ⊕ *www.compuland.com.br/poumimpe* ⤴ *14 rooms* ⌂ *Restaurant, fans, cable TV, pool, bar, laundry service; no a/c* ⊟ *AE, DC, MC, V* ⏀ *BP.*

¢ 🏢 **Hotel Margaridas.** This complex, five minutes by foot from the heart of downtown, has well-tended gardens. Simple rooms have views of the town and surrounding hills. If you walk uphill along the hotel's street, you reach the Trono de Fátima, a 3.5-meter (11-foot) sculpture of Nossa Senhora de Fátima Madonna, imported from Italy. ⊠ *Rua Bispo Pereira Alves 235, 25621-970* ☎ *024/2242–4686* ⤴ *12 apartments* ⌂ *Cable TV, pool* ⊟ *No credit cards* ⏀ *BP.*

Angra dos Reis

③⓪ *151 km (91 mi) west of Rio.*

Angra dos Reis, the Bay of Kings, anchors the rugged Costa Verde in an area of beautiful beaches, colonial architecture, and clear emerald waters. Schooners, yachts, sailboats, and fishing skiffs thread among the 365 offshore islands, one for every day of the year. Indeed, Angra dos Reis's popularity lies in its strategic location—ideal for exploring those islands, many of which are deserted patches of sand and green that offer wonderful swimming and snorkeling opportunities. Organized boat tours from shore can take you to favored island haunts.

Where to Stay & Eat

$$$ ✕🏢 **Hotel do Frade & Golf Resort.** Guest-room balconies overlook the sea and a private beach at this modern resort hotel. For those who love sports, the property offers many options, including boat rentals (sailboats, motorboats, catamarans). The hotel can also arrange excursions on the Ilha Grande Bay or to go scuba diving. It's no surprise that seafood is good at the buffet restaurant, Scuna ($$). In the summer other resort restaurants open, serving a variety of international cuisines. ⊠ *Km 513, BR 101, Praia do Frade, 23900-000, 32 km (20 mi) west of Angra do Reis* ☎ *024/3369–9500* ⊕ *www.hoteldofrade.com.br* 🖷 *024/3369–2254* ⤴ *160 rooms* ⌂ *5 restaurants, room service, in-room data ports, in-room safes, refrigerators, cable TV, 18-hole golf course, 7 tennis courts, pool, boating, jet skiing, soccer, bar, cinema, baby-sitting, dry cleaning, laundry service, no-smoking rooms* ⊟ *AE, D, DC, MC, V* ⏀ *FAP.*

$$$ 🏢 **Pestana Angra Hotel.** Electric cars shuttle you from the door of your chalet to the sand of the hotel's private beach. Water activities abound. The 55-square-meter (590-square-foot) chalets have balconies and separate guest rooms. Suites have whirlpool baths, saunas, and beach views. ⊠ *Estrada do Contorno 3700, Retiro, 23900-000* ☎ *024/3367–2654* 🖷 *024/3365–1909* ⊕ *www.pestanahotels.com.br* ⤴ *27 chalets* ⌂ *In-room data ports, in-room safes, refrigerators, cable TV, pool, gym, massage, sauna, beach, boating, jet skiing, bar, concierge, dry cleaning, laundry service, convention center* ⊟ *AE, D, DC, MC, V.*

$$ 🏢 **Hotel do Bosque.** Inside the Parque Perequê and close to the river of the same name, this hotel has boat service to its private beach across the river. Apartments look out onto an internal garden. Only the suites face the river. There's bar service at the beach. ⊠ *Km 533, BR 101, Praia*

de Mambucaba, 23908-000 ☎ *0800/704–3130 or 024/3362–3130 for hotel or 21/2286–9711 for reservations in Rio* ⊕ *www.hoteldobosque. com.br* ➠ *52 rooms, 4 suites* ⚐ *Room service, in-room data ports, refrigerators, cable TV, tennis court, pool, sauna, beach, boating, bar, laundry service* ☰ *AE, DC, MC, V.*

$$ 🏨 **Portogalo Suíte.** Perched on a hill with a wonderful view of the bay, the exposed-brick buildings at this hotel have a rustic appeal. Rooms have balconies with sea view. Although starkly white and cool, with tile floors, the rooms are clean and right by the beach. A cable car takes guests down the hillside to the beach and the marina. ⊠ *Km 71, BR 101, Praia de Itapinhoacanga, 23900-000, 25 km (16 mi) south of town* ☎ *024/3361–4343* 🖷 *024/3361–4361* ⊕ *www.portogalosuite.com. br* ➠ *86 rooms* ⚐ *Room service, in-room data ports, in-room safes, refrigerators, cable TV, 2 tennis courts, pool, sauna, jet skiing, bar, dry cleaning, laundry service* ☰ *AE, D, DC, MC, V.*

Ilha Grande

③① One of the most popular islands in Brazil is the lush, mountainous Ilha Grande. Just 2 km (1 mi), a 90-minute ferry ride from Angra dos Reis or Mangaratiba, it has more than 100 idyllic beaches—sandy ribbons that stretch on and on with a backdrop of tropical foliage. Ferries arrive at Vila do Abraão, and from there you can roam paths that lead from one slip of sand to the next or negotiate with local boatmen for jaunts to the beaches or more remote islets.

A 10-minute walk from Vila do Abraão takes you to the hot waters off Praia da Júlia and Praia Comprida. The transparent sea at Abraãozinho Beach is another 25-minute walk from Vila do Abraão. If you choose to go by boat, don't miss the big waves of Lopes Mendes Beach or the astonishingly blue Mediterranean-like water of Lagoa Azul. Scuba-diving fans should head to Gruta do Acaiá to see turtles and other colorful South American fish.

It's smart to take to the island only what you can carry, as you have to walk to your hotel. But there are men at the pier who make a living helping tourists carry luggage (about R$5 per bag).

Where to Stay & Eat

$$ 🏨 **Recreio da Praia.** A three-minute walk from the pier, this pousada has simply decorated rooms with sofa beds. ⊠ *Rua da Praia, Vila do Abraão, 23960-000* ☎ *024/3361–5266 or 024/3361–5375* ➠ *10 rooms* ⚐ *Restaurant, room service, refrigerators, cable TV, laundry service* ☰ *MC, V* ⦿ *BP.*

$ 🏨 **Farol dos Borbas.** Like all lodging options on the island, Farol dos Borbas has simple rooms, but its advantage is its location 50 meters (155 feet) from the pier where the ferry from Angra dos Reis stops. The hotel has boat service, with tours around the island. ⊠ *Rua da Praia 9, Vila do Abraão, 23960-970* ☎ *024/3361–5260, 024/3361–5261, or 024/ 3361–5866* ⊕ *www.ilhagrandetur.com.br* ➠ *14 rooms* ⚐ *Room service, refrigerators, cable TV* ☰ *D, MC, V* ⦿ *BP.*

Parati

 100 km (60 mi) southwest of Angra dos Reis; 225 km (140 mi) southwest of Rio

This stunning colonial city—also spelled Paraty—is one of South America's gems. Giant iron chains hang from posts at the beginning of the mazelike grid of cobblestone streets, closing them to all but pedestrians, horses, and bicycles. Until the 18th century this was an important transit point for gold plucked from the Minas Gerais—a safe harbor protected from pirates by a fort. (The cobblestones are the rock ballast brought from Lisbon, then unloaded to make room in the ships for their golden cargoes.) In 1720, however, the colonial powers cut a new trail from the gold mines straight to Rio de Janeiro, bypassing the town and leaving it isolated. It remained that way until contemporary times, when artists, writers, and others "discovered" the community and UNESCO placed it on its World Heritage Site list.

Parati isn't a city peppered with lavish mansions and opulent palaces; rather, it has a simple beauty. By the time the sun breaks over the bay each morning—illuminating the whitewashed, colorfully trimmed buildings—the fishermen have begun spreading out their catch at the outdoor market. The best way to explore is simply to begin walking winding streets banked with centuries-old buildings that hide quaint inns, tony restaurants, shops, and art galleries. Parati is jammed with churches, but the most intriguing are the trio whose congregations were segregated by race during the colonial era: the Igreja de Nossa Senhora do Rosário; Igreja de Santa Rita, and Igreja de Nossa Senhora das Dores. Once you've finished your in-town exploration, you can begin investigating what makes this a weekend escape for cariocas: the lush, tropical offshore islands and not-so-distant strands of coastal beach.

The town's slaves built the **Igreja de Nossa Senhora do Rosário** for themselves around 1725 because the other churches in town were reserved for the white population. ☒ *Rua do Comércio* ☎ *024/3371–1467* *R$1, R$2 combination ticket with other Parati churches and Forte Defensor* ☉ *Tues.–Sun. 9–5.*

The neoclassical **Igreja de Nossa Senhora dos Remédios** was built in 1787. It holds the small art gallery Pinacoteca Antônio Marino Gouveia, with paintings of modern artists such as Djanira, Di Cavalcanti, and Anita Malfatti. ☒ *Rua da Matriz* ☎ *024/3371–2946* *R$1, R$2 combination ticket with other Parati churches and Forte Defensor* ☉ *Tues.–Sun. 9–noon and 2–5.*

The oldest church in Parati, the simple and clean-lined **Igreja de Santa Rita** was built in 1722 by and for free mulattoes. Today it houses a small religious art museum (Museu de Arte Sacra). It's a typical jesuitical church with a tower and three front windows. Religious art objects inside the church are constantly being restored. ☒ *Rua Santa Rita* ☎ *024/3371–1620* *R$1, R$2 combination ticket with other Parati churches and Forte Defensor* ☉ *Wed.–Sun. 9–noon and 2–5.*

The **Igreja de Nossa Senhora das Dores,** built in 1800, was the church of the community's small but elite white population. ✉ *Rua Dr. Pereira* ☎ *024/3371–2946* 🎫 *R$1, R$2 combination ticket with other Parati churches and Forte Defensor* 🕐 *Tues.–Sun. 9–5.*

The **Forte Defensor Perpétuo** was built in the early 1700s (and rebuilt in 1822) as a defense against pirates and is now home to a folk-arts center. It sits north of town. ✉ *Morro da Vila Velha* ☎ *No phone* 🎫 *R$1, R$2 combination ticket with Parati churches* 🕐 *Wed.–Sun. 9–5.*

Where to Stay & Eat

$$–$$$ ✕ **Restaurante do Hiltinho.** This is one of the most fashionable restaurants in Parati. Its specialty is *camarão casadinho,* fried colossal shrimp stuffed with hot *farofa* (toasted cassava flour) made with small shrimp. Even if you're familiar with jumbo shrimp, you might be astonished at the size of these. The portions are attractively presented and are big enough for two. The service borders on perfection. ✉ *Rua Marechal Deodoro 233, Centro Histórico de Paraty* ☎ *024/3371–1432* ▭ *AE, DC, MC, V.*

$ 🏨 **Pousada do Ouro.** Inside an 18th-century building with a garden courtyard, this inn is a block from the Igreja da Matriz de Nossa Senhora dos Remédios. Although it's on the beach, only one suite has a sea view. The décor is colonial style; rooms face an internal garden. ✉ *Rua Dr. Pereira 145, Centro Histórico 23970-000* ☎ *024/3371–2033 or 024/3371–1378* 🖶 *024/3371–1311* ⊕ *www.pousadaouro.com.br* 🛏 *18 rooms, 8 suites* ♿ *Restaurant, room service, in-room safes, refrigerators, cable TV, pool, sauna, bar, laundry service* ▭ *AE, DC, MC, V* ⧆*BP.*

★ $ 🏨 **Pousada Pardieiro.** The houses that make up this property are decorated in a 19th-century Brazilian-colonial style. Rooms follow the colonial style, with dark-wood-carved beds and antique bureaus. There's a beautiful patio with birds and orchids. ✉ *Rua do Comércio 74, Centro Histórico, 23970-000* ☎ *024/3371–1370* 🖶 *024/3371–1139* ⊕ *www.pousadapardieiro.com.br* 🛏 *27 rooms* ♿ *Restaurant, room service, in-room safes, refrigerators, cable TV, laundry service, pool, sauna, bar* ▭ *AE, V.*

★ ¢ 🏨 **Pousada Porto Imperial.** In the oldest part of town just behind the Igreja da Matriz de Nossa Senhora dos Remédios, this historic building has rooms that ring a series of courtyards and a swimming pool. The pousada is decorated with a collection of typical Brazilian artwork—ceramics, tapestries, and colonial furniture—and also has a tropical garden filled with bromeliads. ✉ *Rua Tenente Francisco Antônio (Rua do Comércio) s/n, Centro Histórico 23970-000* ☎ *024/3371–2323* 🖶 *024/3371–2111* ⊕ *www.pousadaportoimperial.com.br* 🛏 *48 rooms, 3 suites* ♿ *Restaurant, room service, in-room safes, refrigerators, cable TV, pool, sauna, bar, laundry service* ▭ *AE, MC, V.*

¢ 🏨 **Pousada do Príncipe.** A prince (the great grandson of Emperor Pedro II) owns this aptly named inn at the edge of the colonial city. The hotel FodorśChoice ★ is painted in the yellow and green of the imperial flag, and its quiet, colorful public areas are graced by photos of the royal family. Rooms are small, decorated in a colonial-like style, and face either the internal garden or the swimming pool, which is in the beckoning plant-filled patio. The kitchen is impressive, too; its chef turns out an exceptional feijoada.

✉ *Av. Roberto Silveira 289, 23970-000* ☎ *024/3371–2266* ⊕ *www. pousadadoprincipe.com.br* 🖷 *024/3371–2120* ⌨ *31 rooms, 3 suites* ⌂ *Restaurant, room service, fans, refrigerators, cable TV, some in-room safes, 2 tennis courts, pool, sauna, laundry service; no a/c in some rooms* ▤ *AE, DC, MC, V.*

Side Trips from Rio A to Z

To research prices, get advice from other travelers, and book travel arrangements, visit www.fodors.com.

BOAT & FERRY TRAVEL

To get to Niterói, there are passenger ferries (R$1.80) available at Praça 15 de Novembro in Rio. In 20 minutes you arrive at Praça Araribóia, in downtown Niterói. Barcas S/A boats are bigger and slower than the newer Catamaran Jumbo Cat fleet.

The two ferries to Ilha Grande are run by Barcas S/A. The ferry for Vila do Abraão on Ilha Grande leaves Angra dos Reis, from Cais da Lapa at Avenida dos Reis Magos, daily at 3:15 PM and returns weekdays at 10 AM and weekends at 11 AM the price is R$4.50 one way. Another ferry leaves Mangaratiba, at Avenida Mangaratiba, weekdays at 8 AM and weekends at 9 AM and returns daily at 5:30 PM the price is R$12 one way. Either trip takes an hour and a half.

🚢 **Boat & Ferry Information Barcas S/A** ✉ Praça Araribóia 6–8, Niterói ☎ 021/2719–1892, 021/2620–6766, 021/2533–6661 for Ilha Grande information. **Catamaran Jumbo Cat** ✉ Praça Araribóia s/n, Niterói ☎ 021/2620–8589 or 021/2620–8670.

BUS TRAVEL

Several bus companies, including Auto Viação 1001, depart for Niterói (R$4) from Avenida Princesa Isabel in Copacabana; from Botafogo at the beach; and from the Menezes Cortes Terminal (⇨ Rio de Janeiro A to Z, *above*). Niterói-bound buses continue on to Nova Friburgo. The price from Rio to Nova Friburgo is R$17.30. Única buses leave hourly from Rio's Rodoviária Novo Rio (⇨ Rio de Janeiro A to Z, *above*) and travel to Petrópolis (R$11.38). Costa Verde buses leave Rio daily every hour for Angra dos Reis, and every two hours for Parati. Cabo Frio buses depart from the Novo Rio station. Regional bus service connects Petrópolis with Nova Friburgo (Rodoviária Norte) and Parati with Angra dos Reis. For these buses, just show up at the terminal and buy a ticket for the next departing bus. Reunidas buses have daily trips from São Paulo to Parati ($27.79), departing from the Terminal Tietê in São Paulo (⇨ São Paulo A to Z, *in* Chapter 2).

The prices we list are for air-conditioned buses. Ticket prices for buses without air-conditioning are slightly less (usually just a few reais difference). Make sure you request an air-conditioned bus when you buy your ticket.

Buses, a shuttle service, and airplanes regularly travel between Búzios and Rio. The best option is the shuttle service, which picks you up in Rio in the morning and drops you at your pousada before noon. Contact Turismo Clássico Travel in Rio for reservations. Municipal buses connect Cabo Frio and Búzios. All buses from Búzios depart from the Terminal Auto Viação 1001.

Bus Information Auto Viação 1001 ☎ 021/0300-3131001. **Costa Verde** ☎ 021/2516-2437. **Reunidas** ☎ 011/3619-0910. **Rodoviária Angra dos Reis** ✉ Av. Toscano Brito 110, Balneário ☎ 024/3365-2041. **Rodoviária Niterói** ✉ Av. Feliciano Sodré s/n, Centro ☎ 021/2620-8847. **Rodoviária Nova Friburgo Norte** ✉ Praça Feliciano Costa, 2.5 km (1.5 mi) north of town ☎ 022/2522-06095. **Rodoviária Nova Friburgo Sul** ✉ Ponte da Saudade, 4 km (2.5 mi) south of town ☎ 022/2522-0400. **Rodoviária Parati** ✉ Rua Jango Pádua west of old town ☎ 024/3371-1224. **Rodoviária Petrópolis** ✉ Rua Doutor Porciúcula 75 ☎ 024/2237-6262. **Terminal Auto Viação 1001** ✉ Estrada da Usina Velha 444 ☎ 022/2623-2050. **Turismo Clássico Travel** ☎ 021/2523-3390. **Única** ☎ 021/2263-8792.

CAR TRAVEL

To reach Niterói by car, take the 14-km-long (9-mi-long) Presidente Costa e Silva Bridge, also known as Rio-Niterói. The toll is R$2.70. BR 101 connects the city to the Costa Verde and Parati. Head north and along BR 040 to reach the mountain towns of Petrópolis and Novo Friburgo. Coastal communities Cabo Frio and Búzios are east of Rio along or off RJ 106.

EMERGENCIES

Droga Tudo, in Parati, is open until 10 PM there are no 24-hour pharmacies in town.

Hospitals & Clinics Hospital Municipal Nelson de Sá Earp ✉ Rua Paulino Afonso 45, Centro, Petrópolis ☎ 024/2237-4062. **Hospital Universitário Antônio Pedro** ✉ Rua Marquês do Paraná 303, Centro, Niterói ☎ 021/2620-2828. **Santa Casa de Misericórdia** ✉ Rua Doutor Coutinho 84, Centro, Angra dos Reis ☎ 024/3365-0131. **Santa Casa de Misericórdia** ✉ Av. São Pedro de Alcântara, Pontal, Parati ☎ 024/3371-1623. **Hospital Municipal São José Operário** ✉ Rua Governador Valadares 22, São Cristóvão, Cabo Frio ☎ 022/2643-2732.

Late-Night & 24-Hour Pharmacies Drogaria Pacheco ✉ Av. José Elias Rabha, inside Angra Shopping center, Parque das Palmeiras, Angra dos Reis ☎ 024/3365-4908 **Drogaria Pacheco** ✉ Rua Gavião Peixoto 115, Niterói ☎ 021/2610-7713. **Drogaria Pacheco** ✉ Rua do Imperador 271, Centro, Petrópolis ☎ 024/2237-3133 or 024/2237-5367. **Drogaria do Povo** ✉ Rua Ezio Cardoso da Fonseca 14, Loja 2, Jardim Esperança, Cabo Frio ☎ 022/2629-9282. **Droga Tudo** ✉ Av. Roberto Silveira, Centro, Parati ☎ 024/3371-2965.

MONEY MATTERS

There are banks and ATMs in each community, but it's best to get reais before leaving Rio. Check in advance with your hotel to make sure credit cards are accepted.

Banks Bradesco ✉ Rua do Comércio 196, Centro Angra dos Reis ✉ Av. José Bento R. Dantas 254, Búzios ✉ Av. Assunção 904, Cabo Frio ✉ Rua Gavião Peixoto 108, Niterói ✉ Av. Roberto Silveira s/n, Parati ✉ Rua do Imperador 268, Petrópolis. **Itaú** ✉ Rua Coronel Carvalho 275, Angra dos Reis ✉ Av. José B. R. Dantas s/n, Búzios ✉ Av. Assunção 898, Cabo Frio ✉ Rua Gavião Peixoto 166, Niterói ✉ Av. Roberto Braune 145, Nova Friburgo ✉ Rua Maria J. de Mello 367 Parati ✉ Rua do Imperador 607, Petrópolis.

VISITOR INFORMATION

Tourist offices are generally open weekdays from 8 or 8:30 to 6 and Saturday from 8 or 9 to 4; some have limited Sunday hours, too. The Niterói Tourism Office is open daily 9–6. Information about Ilha Grande can be found at www.ilhagrande.com.br.

🛈 Tourist Information **Angra dos Reis Tourism Office** ⊠ Across from bus station on Rua Largo da Lapa, Angra dos Reis ☎ 024/3365-1175 Ext. 2186 ⊕ www.angra.rj.gov.br. **Búzios Tourism Office** ⊠ Praça Santos Dumont 111, Búzios ☎ 022/2623-2099 ⊕ www. buziosonline.com.br. **Cabo Frio Tourism Office** ⊠ Av. de Contorno, Praia do Forte, Cabo Frio ☎ 024/2647-1689 ⊕ www.cabofrioturismo.rj.gov.br. **Niterói Tourism Office** ⊠ Estrada Leopoldo Fróes 773, São Francisco ☎ 021/2710-2727 ⊕ www.niteroi.rj.gov. br. **Nova Friburgo Tourism Office** ⊠ Praça Dr. Demervel B. Moreira, Nova Friburgo ☎ 022/ 2523-8000 ⊕ www.friweb.com.br. **Parati Tourism Office** ⊠ Av. Roberto da Silveira ☎ 024/ 3371-1897 ⊕ www.paraty.com.br. **Petrópolis Tourism Office** ⊠ Praça da Confluencia 3, Petrópolis ☎ 0800/24-1516 ⊕ www.petropolis.rj.gov.br.

SÃO PAULO

2

TOP CREATURE FEATURE
Parque Zoologico de São Paulo ⇨*p.90*

EASIEST PLACE TO GO WITH THE FLOW
Brotas, for white-water rafting ⇨*p.127*

HOTTEST BEACH AFTER DARK
Nightlife-packed Ubatuba ⇨*p.92*

CRAFTIEST WAY TO SPEND YOUR DAY
Embu handicrafts fair ⇨*p.131*

BEST BREAD FOR THE DOUGH
Esplanada Grill's *pão de queijo* ⇨*p.93*

HARDEST-TO-FIND FIND
Daslu designer boutique ⇨*p.116*

SO HOT THEY'RE COOL
Águas de São Pedro mineral springs ⇨*p.125*

Updated by
Karla Brunet
and Gabriela
Dias

CROWDED BUSES GRIND DOWN streets spouting black smoke, endless stands of skyscrapers block the horizon, and the din of traffic deafens the ear. But native *paulistanos* (inhabitants of São Paulo city; inhabitants of São Paulo State are called *paulistas*) love this megalopolis of 17 million. São Paulo now sprawls across 7,951 square km (3,070 square mi), 1,502 square km (580 square mi) of which make up the city proper. The largest city in South America makes New York City, with its population of 8 million, seem small.

In 1554 Jesuit priests, including José de Anchieta and Manoel da Nóbrega, founded the village of São Paulo de Piratininga and began converting Indians to Catholicism. Wisely set on a plateau, the mission town was protected from attack and was served by many rivers. It remained unimportant to the Portuguese Crown until it became the departure point for the *bandeira* (literally, "flag") expeditions, whose members set out to look for gemstones and gold, to enslave Indians, and, later, to capture escaped African slaves. In the process, these adventurers established roads into vast portions of previously unexplored territory. São Paulo also saw Emperor Dom Pedro I declare independence from Portugal by the Rio Ipiranga (Ipiranga River), near the city.

In the late 19th century São Paulo became a major coffee producer, attracting both workers and investors from many countries. Italians, Portuguese, Spanish, Germans, and Japanese put their talents and energies to work. By 1895, 70,000 of the 130,000 residents were immigrants. Their efforts transformed the place from a sleepy mission post into a dynamic financial and cultural hub. Avenida Paulista was once the site of many a coffee baron's mansion. Money flowed from these private domains into civic and cultural institutions. The arts began to flourish, and by the 1920s São Paulo was attracting such great artists as Mário and Oswald de Andrade, who introduced modern elements into Brazilian art.

In the 1950s the auto industry began to develop and contributed greatly to São Paulo's contemporary cityscape. Over the next 30 years, people from throughout Brazil came seeking jobs, many in the Cubatão Industrial Park—one of the largest in the developing world—just outside the city limits. Today, like many major European or American hubs, São Paulo struggles to meet its citizens' transportation and housing needs, and goods and services are expensive. Yet, even as the smog reddens your eyes, you'll see that there's much to explore. As a city committed to making dreams come true, São Paulo offers top-rate nightlife and dining as well as thriving cultural and arts scenes.

The city faces the Atlantic shore in the southeast region of the state that shares its name. From town it's easy to travel by car or bus to the state's many small, beautiful beaches and beyond to the states of Paraná, Rio de Janeiro, and Minas Gerais. Although most sandy stretches require one- or two-hour drives, good side trips can be as close as the 30-minute trip to Embu.

2

If you have
3 days
On the first day plan a walk along Avenida Paulista, with its many cultural attractions such as the **Museu de Arte de São Paulo (MASP)** ⑱ ⌐ and **Casa das Rosas** ㉓. In the evening you can see a movie at the nearby Espaço Unibanco, or try one of the Italian restaurants. Bixiga, the Italian neighborhood, near the start of Avenida Paulista. Head to Centro on the second day to see such landmarks as the **Edifício Itália** ❷ and **Teatro Municipal** ❹. Don't miss the Latin crafts exhibit at the **Memorial da América Latina**. The best way to visit São Paulo's center is by metrô. On the third day head for the **Parque Ibirapuera** to visit one of its museums or just relax under the trees. After that you can try one of the bars in nearby Itaim Bibi or Vila Olímpia to see how paulistas enjoy their happy hour.

If you have
5 days
In addition to the attractions outlined in the three-day itinerary, take a day to visit the snake museum at Instituto Butantã at the **Universidade de São Paulo** and/or the **Fundação Maria Luisa e Oscar Americano.** These sights are far from one another; it's best to get a cab. You can go by bus, but it's slow going. In the evening get a drink at one of Vila Madalena's bars; here you can see the city's more alternative kind of nightlife. On your last day tour the Museu do Ipiranga and its environs, where Brazil's independence was declared. Afterward, walk by Liberdade neighborhood to see the Japanese shops and have dinner at one of the local restaurants.

If you have
7–10 days
With so many days, you can explore the city as detailed above and take one or more of several side trips. If relaxing is your priority, go for the spas at ⛱ **Águas de São Pedro** ㉚. If shopping is your passion or you want a taste of typical regional food, take a Saturday or Sunday junket by bus or car to the street fair in **Embu** ㉝. If you haven't got time to waste, favor nearby spots such as **Santana de Parnaíba** ㉟, where you can spend one pleasant afternoon visiting historical sites. If the outdoors beckons and you don't mind spending time on the road, head to the island of ⛱ **Ilhabela** ㉞, which offers cozy lodges and diving paradises, or to ⛱ **Brotas** ㉛, with its numerous waterfalls, trails, and river-rafting tours.

EXPLORING SÃO PAULO

Each neighborhood seems a testament to a different period of the city's history. São Paulo's first inhabitants, Jesuit missionaries and treasure-hunting pioneers, lived in the largely pedestrians-only hilltop and valley areas, particularly Vale do Anhangabaú. Later these areas became Centro (downtown district), a financial and cultural center that's still home to the stock exchange and many banks. It's now the focus of revitalization efforts.

The Bela Vista and Bixiga (the city's little Italy) neighborhoods, near Centro, are home to many theaters and bars. In the 19th century many families who made fortunes from coffee built whimsical mansions in the ridge-top Avenida Paulista neighborhood. Beginning with the post–World War II industrial boom, these homes gave way to skyscrapers. Many of the best hotels are also on or near this avenue.

During the economic growth of the 1970s, many businesses moved west, and downhill to a former swamp. You'll find the tall buildings of Avenida Brigadeiro Faria Lima, the stylish homes of the Jardins neighborhood, and the Shopping Center Iguatemi (Brazil's first mall) just off the banks of the Rio Pinheiros. Large-scale construction of corporate headquarters continues south, between the Marginal Pinheiros Beltway and the Avenida Engenheiro Luís Carlos Berrini, not far from the luxurious Shopping Center Morumbi.

Timing

Most cultural events—film and music festivals and art exhibits—happen between July and December. During the South American summer (January–March) the weather is rainy, and floods can disrupt traffic. In summer make reservations for beach resorts as far in advance as possible, particularly for weekend stays. In winter (May–July), follow the same rule for visits to Campos do Jordão.

Centro

Even though the downtown district has its share of petty crime, it's one of the few places with a historical flavor. Explore the areas where the city began and see examples of architecture, some of it beautifully restored, from the 19th century.

Numbers in the text correspond to numbers in the margin and on the São Paulo Centro map.

A Good Tour

Begin your tour at the **Edifício Copan** ❶ ➤, designed by Brazilian architect Oscar Niemeyer. Farther up Avenida Ipiranga is the city's tallest building, the **Edifício Itália** ❷ (you might want to return at the end of the day for a terrific view of the city from the bar or the restaurant on the 41st floor). Continue north along the avenue to the **Praça da República** ❸. Cross Ipiranga and walk down the pedestrians-only Rua Barão de Itapetininga, with its many shops and street vendors. Follow it to the neobaroque **Teatro Municipal** ❹, in the Praça Ramos de Azevedo. Head east across the square to the Viaduto do Chá, a monumental overpass above the Vale do Anhangabaú—the heart of São Paulo. At the end of this viaduct, turn right onto Rua Líbero Badaró and follow it to the baroque **Igreja de São Francisco de Assis** ❺. A short walk along Rua Benjamin Constant will bring you to the **Praça da Sé** ❻, the city's true center and the site of the Catedral Metropolitana da Sé.

You can take the *metrô* (subway) from the station at the cathedral west to the Barra Funda station and the **Memorial da América Latina.** Or you can head north out of Praça da Sé and follow Rua Roberto Simonsen to the **Solar da Marquesa de Santos** ❼, the city's only surviving late-18th-century residence. Nearby is the **Pátio do Colégio** ❽. Walk north along Rua Boa Vista and Rua do Tesouro. Turn right onto Rua Álvares Penteado.

2

Eating Out

More than 12,000 restaurants fill this melting pot of cultures. Japanese and Italian restaurants abound and you can also find Portuguese, German, French, and Spanish cuisines. Paulistanos are proud of their pizza, especially pies topped with mozzarella, arugula, and sun-dried tomatoes. Be sure to try the *beirute*, a Lebanese sandwich served hot on toasted Syrian bread and filled with roast beef, cheese, lettuce, and tomato and sprinkled with oregano. Of course, many restaurants offer traditional Brazilian specialties. Some places specialize in regional food from Bahia (whose spicy dishes are often toned down), Minas Gerais, and elsewhere. *Virado à paulista* (beans, eggs, and collard greens) is a typical São Paulo dish. In the countryside around São Paulo, traditional farm cooking reigns, with rich stews and roasts and freshwater fish dishes. *Pintado na brasa* (charcoal-broiled catfish) is one of these regional classics that you can taste even in city restaurants. When you finish the meal, don't forget to ask for a *cafezinho*: from authentic Italian espressos to regular Brazilian Santos, São Paulo has the best coffees in the country.

Nightlife

Grab a quiet drink on a romantic garden terrace or dance to throbbing techno music till dawn. The chic and wealthy head for establishments, many of which serve food, in the Vila Olímpia and Itaim neighborhoods. The Pinheiros and Vila Madalena neighborhood have a large concentration of Brazilian clubs and bars. The neighborhood of Jardins has many gay and lesbian bars. São Paulo's music clubs often feature jazz and blues artists. On weekends you find samba and *pagode* (similar to samba but with pop-music elements) in clubs throughout the city. At *forró* clubs couples dance close to the fast beat and romantic lyrics of music from the country's northeast.

Parks & Gardens

In Latin America's biggest urban park, Parque Ibirapuera, you can ramble for an entire day without seeing all the grounds, museums, and cultural attractions. On Sunday you may well be accompanied by thousands of paulistanos seeking refuge from all the surrounding concrete. The Fundação Oscar e Maria Luisa Americano has a small forest and a museum. The Parque do Estado (also called the Parque do Ipiranga) surrounds the Museu do Ipiranga and has a beautiful garden.

Side Trips

São Paulo State is full of natural attractions and towns with artistic and historical treasures. Embu is famous for its furniture stores, and artisans from throughout Brazil sell their wares at its enormous weekend street fair. It is less than 30 minutes by car from the city. Santana de Parnaíba, also 30 minutes from São Paulo, is a small town founded in 1580 by explorers known as bandeirantes, and is famous for its narrow streets surrounded by more than 200 preserved colonial houses. A couple of hours away are the healing waters of the spas of Águas de São Pedro. To delve further into the state, go white-water rafting or hike past more than 17 waterfalls around Brotas. In Campos do Jordão imagine yourself at a European mountain retreat. On the island of Ilhabela you can bask on a beautiful beach and swim, snorkel, or dive.

On the next corner is **Centro Cultural Banco do Brasil** ❾. Continue on Rua Álvares Penteado and turn right onto Rua Miguel Couto. Walk a block onto Rua 15 de Novembro. Number 275, on the left, houses **BOVESPA** ❿, the São Paulo Stock Exchange. Near the end of Rua 15 de Novembro, at Rua João Brícola 24, stands the 36-floor **Edifício BANESPA** ⓫. To the northwest is the **Edifício Martinelli** ⓬. Walk two blocks up on Rua São Bento to the **Basílica de São Bento** ⓭, a church constructed at the beginning of the 20th century. Near it is Café Girondino, a good spot for a break. From the basilica, you can take a train north from the São Bento station to the Luz stop and the **Pinacoteca do Estado** ⓮, the state gallery. On Avenida Tiradentes walk north to see the religious art at **Museu de Arte Sacra** ⓯.

TIMING &
PRECAUTIONS

This route requires at least five hours on foot and use of the metrô, which is safe and clean. An early start will allow you to be more leisurely should one sight pique your interest more than another. If you're planning to take taxis or hire a driver, bear in mind that traffic jams are common. Being a tourist in Centro is a bit hazardous. If you keep a low profile and speak at least some Portuguese or Spanish, you'll most likely avoid being the target of thieves. Otherwise, you might feel more comfortable touring with a guide. Whatever you do, leave your Rolex back at the hotel.

What to See

❸ **Basílica de São Bento.** This church, constructed between 1910 and 1922, was designed by German architect Richard Berndl. Its enormous organ has some 6,000 pipes. ✉ *Largo de São Bento* ☎ *011/228–3633* 🎫 *Free* ⊙ *Mon.–Sat. 6–1 and 3–7:30, Sun. 5–1 and 3–6* Ⓜ *São Bento.*

❿ **BOVESPA.** If you leave an ID with the guard at the front desk, you can go up to the mezzanine and watch the hurly-burly of the busy São Paulo Stock Exchange—a hub for the foreign investment Brazil has attracted in its efforts to privatize state-owned companies. Computer terminals in the observation gallery carry the latest stock quotes as well as general information in various languages. BOVESPA offers tours in English, but only to representatives of foreign investment institutions. ✉ *Rua 15 de Novembro 275, Centro* ☎ *011/3233–2000 Ext. 2456, 011/2333–2110 tours* 🎫 *Free* ⊙ *Weekdays 10–1 and 2–4:45* Ⓜ *São Bento.*

> **need a break?**
>
> **Café Girondino** is frequented by BOVESPA traders from happy hour until 11 PM. The bar serves good draft beer and sandwiches. Pictures on the wall depict Centro in its early days. ✉ *Rua Boa Vista 365, Centro* ☎ *011/229–4574* Ⓜ *São Bento.*
>
> **Restaurante do Centro Cultural Banco do Brasil** is a good option for a break before or after appreciating the artwork. Only lunch is served. A café has snacks. ✉ *Rua Álvares Penteado 112, Centro* ☎ *011/3113–3600* Ⓜ *Sé.*

❾ **Centro Cultural Banco do Brasil.** Opened in 2001, this has become a popular space in town for modern and contemporary art. The center has three floors of exhibition rooms, a theater, an auditorium, a movie theater, and a video room. ✉ *Rua Álvares Penteado 112, Centro* ☎ *011/3113–3600* 🎫 *Free* ⊙ *Tues.–Sun. 12–6:30* Ⓜ *Sé.*

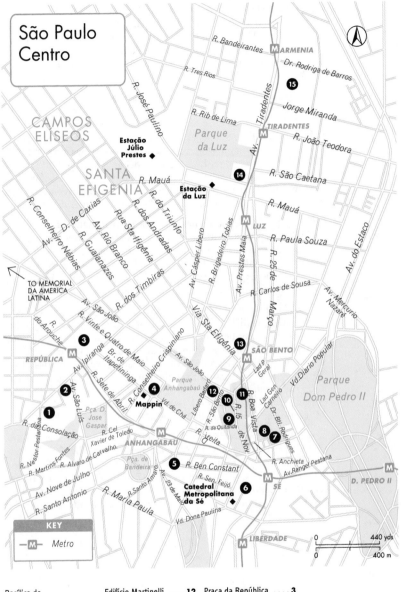

São Paulo
Centro

⓫ Edifício BANESPA. If you can't fit tea or drinks at the top of the Edifício Itália into your Centro tour, get your panoramic view of the city atop the 36-floor BANESPA Building. It was constructed in 1947 and modeled after New York's Empire State Building. A radio traffic reporter squints through the smog every morning from here. ⊠ *Praça Antônio Prado, Centro* ☎ *No phone* 🎟 *Free* ☉ *Weekdays 9–6* Ⓜ *São Bento.*

▶ **❶ Edifício Copan.** The architect of this serpentine apartment and office block, Oscar Niemeyer, went on to design much of Brasília, the nation's capital. The building has the clean, white, undulating curves characteristic of his work. Although many Brazilians prefer colonial architecture, all take pride in Niemeyer's international reputation. The Copan was constructed in 1950, and its 1,850 apartments house about 4,500 people. If you want to shop in the first-floor stores, be sure to do so before dark, after which the area is overrun by prostitutes and transvestites. ⊠ *Av. Ipiranga at Av. Consolação, Centro* ☎ *No phone* Ⓜ *Anhangabaú.*

❷ Edifício Itália. To see the astounding view from atop the Itália Building, you'll have to patronize the bar or dining room of the Terraço Itália restaurant, on the 41st floor. As the restaurant is expensive (and isn't one of the city's best), afternoon tea or a drink is the quickest, least expensive option. Tea is served 3–5:30, and the bar opens at 6. ⊠ *Av. Ipiranga 336, Centro* ☎ *011/3257–6566 for restaurant* Ⓜ *Anhangabaú.*

FodorśChoice
★

⓬ Edifício Martinelli. Amid São Paulo's modern 1950s-era skyscrapers, the Gothic Martinelli Building is a welcome anomaly. The city's first skyscraper, it was built in 1929 by Italian immigrant-turned-count Giuseppe Martinelli. The whimsical penthouse is worth checking out. The rooftop, which has a great view, is open weekdays 10:30–4. To go there, you need permission from the building manager on the ground floor, and you have to leave your ID at the front desk. Then take the elevator to the 34th floor and walk up two more flights. ⊠ *Av. São João 35, Centro* ☎ *No phone* 🎟 *Free* Ⓜ *São Bento.*

❺ Igreja de São Francisco de Assis. The baroque St. Francis of Assisi Church is actually two churches with a common name, one run by Catholic clergy and the other by lay brothers. One of the city's best-preserved Portuguese colonial buildings, it was built from 1647 to 1790. ⊠ *Largo São Francisco 133, Centro* ☎ *011/606–0081* 🎟 *Free* ☉ *Daily 7 AM–8 PM; lay brothers' church weekdays 7–11:30 and 1–8, weekends 7–10* Ⓜ *Sé or Anhangabaú.*

off the beaten path

MEMORIAL DA AMÉRICA LATINA – A group of buildings designed by Oscar Niemeyer, the Latin American Memorial includes the Pavilhão da Criatividade Popular (Popular Creativity Pavilion), which has a permanent exhibition of Latin American handicrafts, and a model showing all the countries in Latin America. The Salão de Atos Building shows the panel *Tiradentes,* about an independence hero from Minas Gerais, painted by Cândido Portinari in 1949 and installed in 1989. ⊠ *Av. Auro Soares de Moura Andrade 664* ☎ *011/3823–4600* ⊕ *www.memorial.org.br* 🎟 *Free* ☉ *Tues.–Sun. 9–6* Ⓜ *Barra Funda.*

⑮ Museu de Arte Sacra. If you can't get to Bahia during your stay in Brazil, the Museum of Sacred Art is a must-see. It houses an extremely interesting collection of wooden and terra-cotta masks, jewelry, and liturgical objects that date from the 17th century to the present. Don't miss the on-site convent, founded in 1774. ⊠ *Av. Tiradentes 676, Centro* ☎ *011/ 3326–1373* 🖃 *R$4* ☉ *Tues.–Fri. 11–6, Sat. and Sun. 10–7* Ⓜ *Luz.*

❽ Pátio do Colégio/Museu Padre Anchieta. São Paulo was founded by the Jesuits José de Anchieta and Manoel da Nóbrega in the College Courtyard in 1554. The church was constructed in 1896 in the same style as the chapel built by the Jesuits. In the small museum you can see some paintings from the colonization period and an exhibition of early sacred art. ⊠ *Pátio do Colégio 84, Centro* ☎ *011/3105–6899* ☉ *Museum Tues.–Sun. 9–5; church Mon.–Sat. 8:15–7, Sun. mass at 10* AM Ⓜ *Sé.*

⑭ Pinacoteca do Estado. The building that houses the State Art Gallery was constructed in 1905. In the permanent collection you can see the work of such famous Brazilian artists as Tarsila do Amaral (whose work consists of colorful, somewhat abstract portraits), Anita Malfatti (a painter influenced by fauvism and German expressionism), Cândido Portinari (whose oil paintings have social and historical themes), Emiliano Di Cavalcanti (a multimedia artist whose illustrations, oil paintings, and engravings are influenced by cubism and contain Afro-Brazilian and urban themes), and Lasar Segall (an expressionist painter). ⊠ *Praça da Luz 2, Centro* ☎ *011/229–9844* ⊕ *www.uol.com.br/pinasp* 🖃 *R$5* ☉ *Tues.–Sun. 10–6* Ⓜ *Luz.*

❸ Praça da República. Republic Square is the site of a huge Sunday street fair, where you'll find arts and crafts, semiprecious stones, food, and often live music. Some artisans display their work all week long, so it's worth a peek anytime. ⊠ *Centro* Ⓜ *República.*

❻ Praça da Sé. Two major metrô lines cross under the large, busy Cathedral Square. Migrants from Brazil's poor northeast often gather to enjoy their music and to sell and buy regional items such as medicinal herbs. It's also the central hangout for street children and the focus of periodic (and controversial) police sweeps to get them off the street. The square and most of the historic area and financial district to its north have been set aside for pedestrians, official vehicles, and public transportation only. ⊠ *Bounded by Rua Quinze de Novembro, Rua Anita Garibaldi, and Av. Rangel Pestana.*

❼ Solar da Marquesa de Santos. This 18th-century manor house was bought by Marquesa de Santos in 1843. It now contains a museum that hosts temporary painting, photo, and sculpture exhibits that usually center on a metropolitan São Paulo theme. ⊠ *Rua Roberto Simonsen 136, Centro* ☎ *011/3106–2218* 🖃 *Free* ☉ *Tues.–Sun. 9–5* Ⓜ *Sé.*

❹ Teatro Municipal. Inspired by the Paris Opéra, the Municipal Theater was built between 1903 and 1911 with art nouveau elements. *Hamlet* was the first play presented, and the house went on to host such luminaries as Isadora Duncan in 1916 and Anna Pavlova in 1919. Plays and operas are still staged here. Buy tickets at the theater; local newspapers have schedules. The fully restored auditorium, resplendent with gold leaf, moss-green velvet, marble, and mirrors, is open only to those attending cultural events, but sometimes you can walk in for a quick look at the vestibule. ⊠ *Praça Ramos de Azevedo, Centro* ☎ *011/223–3022* Ⓜ *Anhangabaú.*

Liberdade

At the beginning of the 20th century, a group of Japanese arrived to work as contract farm laborers in São Paulo State. During the next five decades, roughly a quarter of a million of their countrymen followed, forming what is now the largest Japanese colony outside Japan. Distinguished today by a large number of college graduates and successful businesspeople, professionals, and politicians, the colony has made important contributions to Brazilian agriculture and the seafood industry. Liberdade, which is south of Praça da Sé behind the cathedral, and whose entrance is marked by a series of red porticoes, is home to many first-, second-, and third-generation Nippo-Brazilians. Clustered around Avenida Liberdade are shops with everything from imported bubble gum to miniature robots to Kabuki face paint. The Sunday street fair holds many surprises.

Numbers in the text correspond to numbers in the margin and on the São Paulo City map.

A Good Tour

From the **Praça Liberdade** ⓲, by the Liberdade metrô station, walk south along Rua Galvão Bueno. About six blocks from the square is the intriguing **Museu da Imigração Japonesa** ⓱.

TIMING & PRECAUTIONS The best time to visit Liberdade is on Sunday during the street fair, where Asian food, crafts, and souvenirs are sold. This tour takes about two hours—a little longer if you linger in the museum. Don't follow the tour at night.

What to See

⓱ **Museu da Imigração Japonesa.** The Museum of Japanese Immigration has two floors of exhibits about Nippo-Brazilian culture and farm life and Japanese contributions to Brazilian horticulture. The Japanese are credited with introducing the persimmon, the azalea, the tangerine, and the kiwi to Brazil, among other things. Call ahead to arrange for an English-language tour. ⊠ *Rua São Joaquim 381, Liberdade* ☎ *011/3209–5465* 🎟 *R$3* ⊙ *Tues.–Sun. 1:30–5:30* Ⓜ *São Joaquim.*

⓲ **Praça Liberdade.** On Sunday morning and afternoon Liberdade hosts a sprawling Asian food and crafts fair where the free and easy Brazilian ethnic mix is in plain view; you may see, for example, Afro-Brazilians dressed in colorful kimonos hawking grilled shrimp on a stick. Liberdade also hosts several ethnic celebrations, such as April's Hanamatsuri, commemorating the birth of the Buddha. Apart from the fair and special events, the only other reason to visit this square is to stop by at the nearby Japanese shops and restaurants. ⊠ *Av. da Liberdade and Rua dos Estudantes Liberdade* Ⓜ *Liberdade.*

Avenida Paulista & Bixiga

Money once poured into and out of the coffee barons' mansions that lined Avenida Paulista, making it, in a sense, the financial hub. And so it is today, though instead of mansions there are major banks. Like the barons before them, many of these financial institutions generously support the arts. Numerous places have changing exhibitions—often free— in the Paulista neighborhood. Nearby Bixiga, São Paulo's Little Italy, is full of restaurants.

Numbers in the text correspond to numbers in the margin and on the São Paulo City map.

A Good Tour

Begin your tour at the **Museu de Arte de São Paulo (MASP)** ⑱, which has Brazil's best collection of fine art. Across the street is **Parque Trianon** ⑲, where many businesspeople eat lunch. Leaving the park, veer right onto Avenida Paulista and head for the **Centro Cultural FIESP** ⑳, which frequently has art and theatrical presentations. Farther down Avenida Paulista is the **Espaço Cultural Citibank** ㉑, a gallery with temporary exhibitions. Continue a few more blocks along Avenida Paulista to the **Instituto Cultural Itaú** ㉒, a great place to see contemporary Brazilian art. In the next block is the **Casa das Rosas** ㉓, with yet another noteworthy gallery. From here you can hop a bus or a taxi to the **Museu Memória do Bixiga** ㉔, with its displays on Italian immigration.

TIMING & PRECAUTIONS

This tour takes about five hours, including a visit to MASP and the Museu do Bixiga. Busy, well-lighted Avenida Paulista may well be the safest place in city. Even so, stay alert and hold onto your bags, particularly in Parque Trianon.

What to See

㉓ **Casa das Rosas.** The House of the Roses, a French-style mansion, seems out of place next to the skyscrapers of Paulista. It was built in 1935 by famous paulistano architect Ramos de Azevedo for one of his daughters. The building was home to the same family until 1986, when it was made an official municipal landmark. It was later opened as a cultural center—with changing fine-arts exhibitions and multimedia displays by up-and-coming artists, and it's one of the avenue's few remaining early-20th-century buildings. ⊠ *Av. Paulista 37, Paraíso* ☎ *011/251–5271* ⊕ *www.casadasrosas.sp.gov.br* ⊠ *Free* ⊙ *Tues.–Sun. 1–7* Ⓜ *Brigadeiro.*

⑳ **Centro Cultural FIESP.** The cultural center of São Paulo State's Federation of Industry has a theater, a library of art books, and temporary art exhibits. ⊠ *Av. Paulista 1313, Jardim Paulista* ☎ *011/3253–5877* ⊠ *Free* ⊙ *Tues.–Sun. 9–7* Ⓜ *Trianon.*

㉑ **Espaço Cultural Citibank.** Citibank's cultural space hosts temporary exhibitions of Brazilian art. ⊠ *Av. Paulista 1111, Jardim Paulista* ☎ *011/5576–2744* ⊠ *Free* ⊙ *Weekdays 9–7, weekends 10–5* Ⓜ *Trianon.*

㉒ **Instituto Cultural Itaú.** Maintained by Itaú, one of Brazil's largest private banks, this cultural institute has art shows as well as lectures, workshops, and films. Its library specializes in works on Brazilian art and culture.

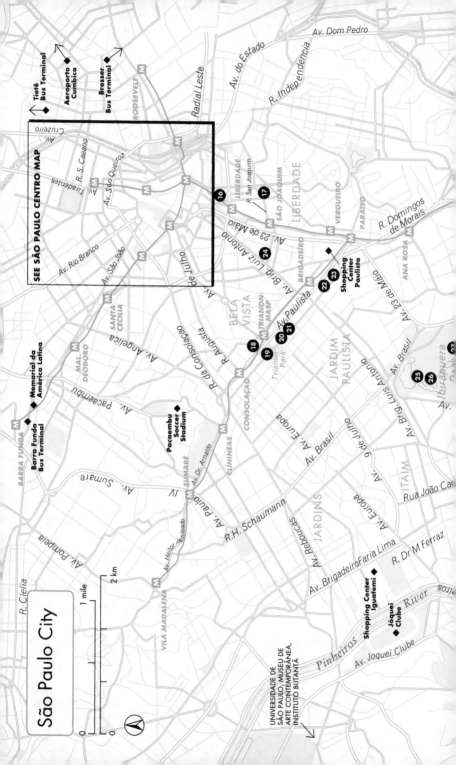

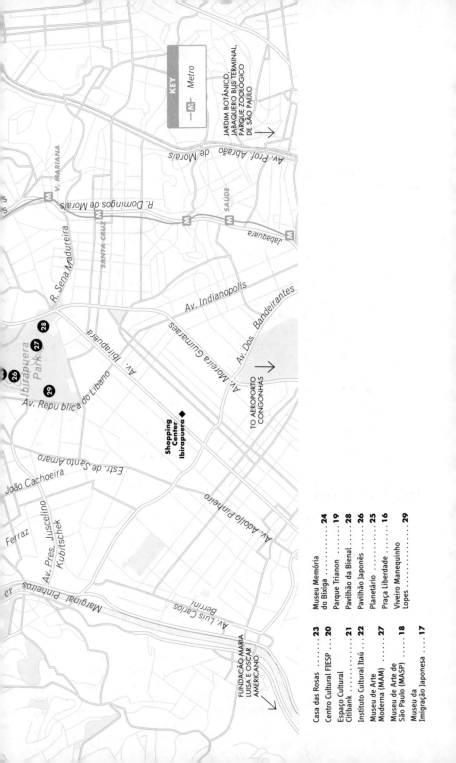

KEY

M — Metro

JARDIM BOTÂNICO,
JABAQUERO BUS TERMINAL,
PARQUE ZOOLÓGICO
DE SÃO PAULO
→

Av. Prof. Abrão de Morais

V. MARIANA

R. Domingos de Morais

SANTA CRUZ

SAÚDE

Jabaquera

R. Sena Madureira

Av. Indianopolis

Av. Dos Bandeirantes

Ibirapuera Park

Av. Ibirapuera

Av. Moreira Guimaraes

TO AEROPORTO
CONGONHAS
→

Av. Republica do Libano

Estr. de Santo Amaro

João Cachoeira

Shopping
Center
Ibirapuera ◆

Av. Adolfo Pinheiro

Ferraz

Av. Pres. Juscelino
Kubitschek

Marginal Pinheiros

Av. Luis Carlos
Berrini

FUNDAÇÃO MARIA
LUISA E OSCAR
AMERICANO

✉ *Av. Paulista 149, Paraíso* ☎ *011/3238–1777* ⊕ *www.itaucultural. org.br* ✉ *Free* ⊙ *Tues.–Sun. 10–7* Ⓜ *Brigadeiro.*

need a break? Before heading to the Museu Memória do Bixiga, try a *baurú* at **Ponto Chic** (✉ Praça Osvaldo Cruz 26, Bixiga ☎ 011/289–1480), a block east of Instituto Cultural Itaú, across Avenida Paulista. The restaurant claims to have invented this sandwich, which is made with roast beef, tomato, cucumber, and steam-heated mozzarella.

⓳ **Museu de Arte de São Paulo (MASP).** A striking low-rise elevated on two

Fodor'sChoice massive concrete pillars 256 feet apart, the São Paulo Museum of Art

★ contains the city's premier collection of fine arts. Highlights include dazzling works by Hieronymus Bosch, Vincent van Gogh, Pierre-Auguste Renoir, and Edgar Degas. Lasar Segall and Cândido Portinari are two of the many Brazilian artists represented in the collection. The huge open area beneath the museum is often used for cultural events and is the site of a Sunday antiques fair. ✉ *Av. Paulista 1578, Bela Vista* ☎ *011/251– 5644* ⊕ *www.masp.art.br* ✉ *R$10* ⊙ *Tues.–Sun. 11–6.*

㉔ **Museu Memória do Bixiga.** This museum, established in 1980, contains objects that belonged to Italian immigrants who lived in the Bixiga neighborhood. On weekends you can extend your tour to include the **Feira do Bixiga,** at Praça Dom Orione, where handicrafts, antiques, and furniture are sold. ✉ *Rua dos Ingleses 118, Bixiga* ☎ *011/3285–5009* ✉ *Free* ⊙ *Wed.–Sun. 2–5.*

⓲ **Parque Trianon.** The park was originally created in 1892 as a showcase for local vegetation. In 1968 Roberto Burle Marx (the Brazilian landscaper famed for Rio's mosaic-tile beachfront sidewalks) renovated it and incorporated new trees. You can escape the noise of the street and admire the flora while seated on one of the benches sculpted to look like chairs. ✉ *Rua Peixoto Gomide 949, Jardim Paulista* ☎ *011/289– 2160* ✉ *Free* ⊙ *Daily 6–6* Ⓜ *Trianon.*

Parque Ibirapuera

Only 15 minutes by taxi from downtown, Ibirapuera is São Paulo's answer to New York's Central Park, though it is slightly less than half the size and gets infinitely more crowded on sunny weekends. In the 1950s the land, which originally contained the municipal nurseries, was chosen as the site of a public park to commemorate the city's 400th anniversary. Oscar Niemeyer was called in to head the team of architects assigned to the project. The park was inaugurated in 1954, and some pavilions used for the opening festivities still sit amid its 160 hectares (395 acres). The park has jogging and biking paths, a lake, and rolling lawns.

A Good Walk

Enter at Gate 9 and walk around the lake to the starry sights at the **Planetário** ㉕. As you exit the planetarium, veer left to the **Pavilhão Japonês** ㉖. Then turn left and follow the path to the Marquise do Ibirapuera, a structure that connects several buildings, including the **Museu de Arte Moderna (MAM)** ㉗ and the **Pavilhão da Bienal** ㉘, which houses the park branch of the Museu de Arte Contemporânea. When you exit the compound, walk toward Gate 7 and the **Viveiro Manequinho Lopes** ㉙, with its many species of Brazilian trees.

TIMING &
PRECAUTIONS The park deserves a whole day, though you can probably do this tour in one afternoon. Avoid the park on Sunday, when it gets really crowded, and after sundown.

What to See

㉗ **Museu de Arte Moderna (MAM).** The permanent collection of the Museum of Modern Art includes more than 2,600 paintings, sculptures (some in a sculpture garden out front), and drawings from the Brazilian modernist movement, which began in the 1920s, when artists were developing a new form of expression influenced by the city's rapid industrial growth. The museum also hosts temporary exhibits that feature works by new local artists and has a library with more than 20,000 books, photographs, videotapes, and CD-ROMs. In a 1982 renovation, Brazilian architect Lina Bo Bardi gave the building a wall of glass, creating a giant window that beckons you to peek at what's inside. ⊠ *Gate 10, Parque Ibirapuera* ☎ *011/5549–9688* ⊕ *www.man.org.br* ⊠ *R$5 (free Tues.)* ☽ *Tues., Wed., Fri. noon–6, Thurs. noon–10, weekends and holidays 10–6.*

> **need a break?** The **Bar do MAM,** inside the Museu de Arte Moderna, has sandwiches, pies, soda, coffee, and tea. The comfortable chairs make it an ideal place to rest in the park, and it's the only place apart from hot dog stands that has food. *(MAM)* ⊠ *Gate 10, Parque Ibirapuera* ☎ *No phone.*

㉘ **Pavilhão da Bienal.** From October through November in every even-numbered year, this pavilion hosts the Bienal (Biennial) art exhibition, which draws more than 250 artists from more than 60 countries. The first such event was held in 1951 in Parque Trianon and drew artists from 21 countries. It was moved to this Oscar Niemeyer–designed building—with its large open spaces and floors connected by circular slopes—after Ibirapuera Park's 1954 inauguration. The pavilion also houses a branch of the **Museu de Arte Contemporânea** (MAC; ☎ 011/5573–9932 ⊕ www. mac.usp.br). There's much more to see at the main branch of the museum, at the University of São Paulo, but this park branch has some temporary exhibits. The museum is open Tuesday–Sunday noon–6; admission is free. ⊠ *Gate 10, Parque Ibirapuera.*

㉖ **Pavilhão Japonês.** An exact replica of the Katsura Imperial Palace in Kyoto, Japan, the Japanese Pavilion is also one of the structures built for the park's inauguration. It was designed by University of Tokyo professor Sutemi Horiguti and built in Japan. It took four months to reassemble beside the man-made lake in the midst of the Japanese-style garden. The main building has displays of samurai clothes, 11th-century sculptures, and pottery and sculpture from several dynasties. Rooms used for traditional tea ceremonies are upstairs. ⊠ *Gate 10, Parque Ibirapuera* ☎ *011/5573–6453* ⊠ *R$3* ☽ *Weekends and holidays 10–5.*

⑤ ㉕ **Planetário.** Paulistanos love the planetarium and frequently fill the 350 seats under its 48-foot-high dome. You can see a projection of the 8,900 stars and five planets (Mercury, Venus, Mars, Jupiter, and Saturn) clearly visible in the southern hemisphere. Shows last 50 minutes and always depict the night sky just as it is on the evening of your visit. Be sure to buy tickets at least 15 minutes before the session begins. ☒ *Gate 10, Av. Pedro Álvares Cabral, Parque Ibirapuera* ☏ *011/5575–5206* ☜ *R$5* ☉ *Weekends and holidays, projections at 3:30 and 5:30.*

㉙ **Viveiro Manequinho Lopes.** The Manequinho Lopes Nursery is where most plants and trees used by the city are grown. The original was built in the 1920s; the current version was designed by Roberto Burle Marx. Specimens are of such Brazilian trees as *ipê, pau-jacaré,* and *pau-brasil,* the tree for which the country was named (the red dye it produced was greatly valued by the Europeans). The Bosque da Leitura (Reading Forest) has a stand that provides books and magazines (all in Portuguese) as well as chairs so people can read among the trees. ☒ *Enter park from Av. República do Líbano, Parque Ibirapuera* ☏ *No phone* ☉ *Daily 5–5.*

Elsewhere in São Paulo

Several far-flung sights are worth a taxi ride to see. West of Centro is the Universidade de São Paulo (USP), which has two very interesting museums: a branch of the Museu de Arte Contemporânea and the Instituto Butantã, with its collection of creatures that slither and crawl. Head southwest of Centro to the Fundação Maria Luisa e Oscar Americano, a museum with a forest and garden in the residential neighborhood of Morumbi. In the Parque do Estado, southeast of Centro, are the Jardim Botânico and the Parque Zoológico de São Paulo.

What to See

Fundação Maria Luisa e Oscar Americano. A private wooded estate is the setting for the Maria Luisa and Oscar Americano Foundation. Paintings, furniture, sacred art, silver, porcelain, engravings, personal possessions of the Brazilian royal family, tapestries, and sculpture are among the objects from the Portuguese colonial and imperial periods. There are some modern pieces as well. ☒ *Av. Morumbi 3700, Morumbi* ☏ *011/ 3742–0077* ⊕ *www.fundacaooscaramericano.org.br* ☜ *R$5* ☉ *Tues.–Fri. 11–5, weekends 10–5.*

Jardim Botânico. The Botanical Gardens contain about 3,000 plants belonging to more than 340 native species. The greenhouse has Atlantic rain-forest species, an orchid house, and a collection of aquatic plants. ☒ *Av. Miguel Stéfano 3031, Parque do Estado* ☏ *011/5073–6300* ☜ *R$2* ☉ *Wed.–Sun. 9–5.*

★ ⑤ **Parque Zoológico de São Paulo.** The 200-acre São Paulo Zoo has more than 3,000 animals, and many of its 410 species—such as the *mico-leão-dourado* (golden lion tamarin monkey)—are endangered. See the monkey houses, built on small islands in the park's lake, and the Casa do Sangue Frio (Cold-Blooded House), with reptilian and amphibious creatures. ☒ *Av. Miguel Stéfano 4241, Parque do Estado* ☏ *011/5073–0811* ⊕ *www.zoologico.com.br* ☜ *R$10* ☉ *Tues.–Sun. 9–5.*

Universidade de São Paulo. Consider taking a stroll around the grounds of the country's largest university (founded in 1934) just to soak in the atmosphere of a Brazilian campus. Art lovers can also visit the main branch of the **Museu de Arte Contemporânea** (MAC; ⊠ Rua da Reitoria 160, Cidade Universitária ☎ 011/3091–3039 ⊕ www.mac.usp.br), where works by world-renowned contemporary European artists Pablo Picasso, Amedeo Modigliani, Wassily Kandinsky, Joan Miró, and Henri Matisse are on display. Look also for the works of well-known Brazilian artists Anita Malfatti, Tarsila do Amaral, Cândido Portinari, and Emiliano Di Cavalcanti. Admission to the MAC is free; it is open Tuesday–Friday 10–5 and weekends 10–4. The smaller branch of the MAC is at the Parque Ibirapuera. In 1888 a Brazilian scientist, with the aid of the state government, turned a farmhouse into a center for the production of snake serum. Today the **Instituto Butantã** (⊠ Av. Vital Brasil 1500, Cidade Universitária ☎ 011/3813–7222) has more than 70,000 snakes, spiders, scorpions, and lizards. It still extracts venom and processes it into serum that's made available to victims of poisonous bites throughout Latin America. Unfortunately, the institute has suffered from underfunding; it's somewhat run-down, and its exhibits aren't as accessible to children as they could be. The institute is open Tuesday–Sunday 9–4:30; admission is R$1.5. ⊠ *Main building: Rua da Reitoria 109, Cidade Universitária ☎ 011/3818–3538 ⊕ www. usp.br ☞ Free ☉ Tues.–Wed. and Fri. 10–7, Thurs. 11–8, weekends 10–4.*

Instituto Tomie Ohtake. Projected by the architect Ruy Ohtake, the institute shows modern and contemporary art. It has exhibition rooms, a video room, a theater, an auditorium, a bookstore, a café, and a restaurant. ⊠ *Rua Coropes 54, Pinheiros ☎ 011/6488–1900 ☞ Free ☉ Tues.–Sun. 11–8.*

Beaches

São Paulo rests on a plateau 72 km (46 mi) inland. If you can avoid traffic, getaways are fairly quick on the parallel Imigrantes (BR 160) or Anchieta (BR 150) highways, each of which becomes one-way on weekends and holidays. Although the port of Santos (near the Cubatão Industrial Park) has *praias* (beaches) in and around it, the cleanest and best beaches are along what is known as the North Shore. Mountains and bits of Atlantic rain forest hug numerous small, sandy coves. Some of the North Shore's most beautiful houses line the Rio-Santos Highway (SP 055) on the approach to Maresias. On weekdays when school is in session, the beaches are gloriously deserted.

Buses run along the coast from São Paulo's Jabaquara terminal, near the Congonhas Airport, and there are once-daily trains from the Estação da Luz to Santos and the sands along the North Shore. Beaches often don't have bathrooms or phones right on the sands, nor do they have beach umbrellas or chairs for rent. They generally do have restaurants nearby, however, or at least vendors selling sandwiches, soft drinks, and beer. All beaches in São Paulo, and most of Brazil, are free and open at all hours.

★ **Praia da Barra do Sahy.** Families with young children favor this small, quiet beach. Its narrow strip of sand (with a bay and a river on one side and rocks on the other) is steep but smooth, and the water is clean and very calm. Kayakers paddle about, and divers are drawn to the nearby Ilha das Couves. Area restaurants serve only basic fish dishes with rice and salad. Note that Barra do Sahy's entrance is atop a slope and appears suddenly—be on the lookout. ⊠ *Rio-Santos Hwy. (SP 055), 165 km (102 mi) southeast of São Paulo.*

Praia do Camburi. The young and the restless flock here to sunbathe, surf, and party. At the center of the beach is a cluster of cafés, ice-cream shops, and bars and the Tiê restaurant. The service may be slow, but Tiê's menu is extensive, and the open-air setup is divine. Another good bet is Bom Dia Vietnã, with its delicious pizzas, sandwiches, sushi, salads, and banana pie. Camburi is just north of Barra do Sahy. If you're coming from the south, use the second entrance; although it's unpaved, it's in better shape than the first entrance. ⊠ *Rio-Santos Hwy. (SP 055), 167 km (104 mi) southeast of São Paulo.*

Praia de Maresias. The beach itself is also nice, with its 4-km (2-mi) stretch of white sand and its clean, green waters that are good for swimming and surfing. Maresias is popular with a young crowd. ⊠ *Rio-Santos Hwy. (SP 055), 180 km (111 mi) southeast of São Paulo.*

Ubatuba. Many of the more than 30 beaches around Ubatuba are truly beautiful enough to merit the long drive. For isolation and peace, try **Prumirim Beach,** which can only be reached by boat; for a little more action try the centrally located **Praia Grande,** with its many kiosks. Ubatuba itself has a very active nightlife. Nearby Itaguá has several gift shops, a branch of the Projeto Tartarugas Marinhas (Marine Turtles Project), and a large aquarium. ⊠ *229 km (148 mi) southeast of São Paulo along Carvalho Pinto and Oswaldo Cruz Hwys.*

WHERE TO EAT

São Paulo's social scene centers on dining out, and there are many establishments from which to choose (new ones seem to open as often as the sun rises), particularly in the Jardins district. You can find German, Japanese, Spanish, Italian, and Portuguese restaurants as well as top-quality French and Indian spots. The innumerable *churrascarias* (places that serve a seemingly endless stream of barbecued meat) are beloved by paulistanos. As in other Brazilian cities, many restaurants serve feijoada on Wednesday and Saturday; top restaurants do it up in fancy buffets.

São Paulo restaurants frequently change their credit-card policies, sometimes adding a surcharge for their use or not accepting them at all. Though most places don't require jacket and tie, people tend to dress up; establishments in the $$ to $$$$ categories expect you to look neat and elegant. A 10% service fee is usually added to restaurant bills.

WHAT IT COSTS In Reais				
$$$$	**$$$**	**$$**	**$**	**¢**
AT DINNER over $60	$45–$60	$30–$45	$15–$30	under $15

Prices are for a main course at dinner.

Brazilian

$$$–$$$$ ✕ **Baby Beef Rubaiyat.** The family that owns and runs this restaurant serves meat from their ranch in Mato Grosso do Sul State. Charcoal-grilled fare—from baby boar (on request at least two hours in advance) and steak to chicken and salmon—is served at the buffet. A salad bar has all sorts of options. Wednesday and Saturday are feijoada nights, and on Friday the emphasis is on seafood. ⊠ *Alameda Santos 86, Paraíso* ☎ *011/289–6366* ⊟ *V* Ⓜ *Paraíso.*

★ **$–$$$** ✕ **Esplanada Grill.** The beautiful people hang out in the bar of this highly regarded churrascaria. The thinly sliced *picanha* steak (similar to rump steak) is excellent; it goes well with a house salad (hearts of palm and shredded, fried potatoes), onion rings, and creamed spinach. The restaurant's version of the traditional *pão de queijo* (cheese bread) is widely viewed as one of the best. ⊠ *Rua Haddock Lobo 1682, Jardins* ☎ *011/3081–3199* ⊟ *AE, DC, MC, V.*

$$ ✕ **Bargaço.** The original Bargaço has long been considered the best Bahian restaurant in Salvador. If you can't make it to the northeast, be sure to have a meal in the São Paulo branch. Seafood is the calling card. ⊠ *Rua Oscar Freire 1189, Cerqueira César* ☎ *011/3085–5058* ⊟ *DC, MC* Ⓜ *Consolação.*

$–$$ ✕ **Consulado Mineiro.** During and after the Saturday crafts and antiques fair in Praça Benedito Calixto, it may take an hour to get a table at this homey restaurant set in a house. Among the traditional mineiro dishes are the *mandioca com carne de sol* (cassava with salted meat) appetizer and the *tutu* (pork loin with beans, pasta, cabbage, and rice) entrée. ⊠ *Rua Praça Benedito Calixto 74, Pinheiros* ☎ *011/3064–3882* ⊟ *AE, DC, MC, V* ☺ *Closed Mon.*

¢–$$ ✕ **Sujinho–Bisteca d'Ouro.** The modest Sujinho serves churrasco without any frills. It's the perfect place for those who simply want to eat an honest, gorgeous piece of meat. The portions are so large here that one dish can usually feed two. A few options on the menu creep into the $$$ price range. ⊠ *Rua da Consolação 2078, Cerqueira César* ☎ *011/3231–5207* ⊟ *No credit cards* Ⓜ *Consolação.*

$ ✕ **Dona Lucinha.** Mineiro dishes—from Minas Gerais State—are the specialties at this modest eatery with plain wooden tables. The classic cuisine is served as a buffet only: more than 50 stone pots hold dishes like *feijão tropeiro* (beans with manioc flour). Save room for a dessert of ambrosia. ⊠ *Av. Chibaras 399, Moema* ☎ *011/5051–2050* ⊟ *AE, DC, MC, V* ⊠ *Rua Bela Cintra 2325, Jardins* ☎ *011/3082–3797* ⊟ *AE, DC, MC, V.*

¢–$ ✕ **Frevo.** Paulistanos of all types and ages flock to this Jardins luncheonette for its *beirute* sandwiches, filled with ham and cheese, tuna, or chicken, and for its draft beer and fruit juices in flavors such as *acerola* (Antilles cherry), passion fruit, and papaya. ⊠ *Rua Oscar Freire 603, Jardins* ☎ *011/3082–3434* ⊟ *AE, DC, MC, V.*

Continental

$–$$$ ✕ **Cantaloup.** That paulistanos take food seriously has not been lost on the folks at Cantaloup. The converted warehouse houses two dining areas:

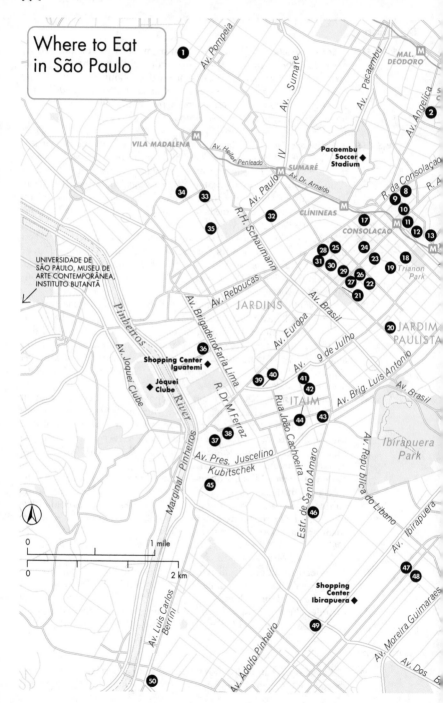

Where to Eat
in São Paulo

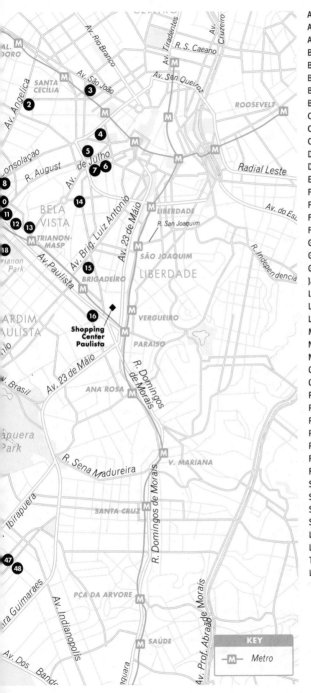

Oversize photos decorate the walls of the slightly formal room, and a fountain and plants make the second area feel more casual. Try the filet mignon with risotto or the St. Peter's beef tenderloin fillet with almonds and spinach. Save room for the papaya ice cream with mango soup or the mango ice cream with papaya soup. ⊠ *Rua Manoel Guedes 474, Itaim Bibi* ☎ *011/3846–6445* ⊟ *AE, DC, MC, V.*

$–$$ ✕ **Paddock.** Both locations of this restaurant are considered ideal for relaxed business lunches; neither is open on weekends. Men and women in suits eat and chat in comfortable armchairs. The Continental cuisine is prepared with finesse; try the lamb with mint sauce or the poached haddock. ⊠ *Av. São Luís 258, Centro* ☎ *011/257–4768* ⊟ *AE, DC, MC, V* ⊗ *Closed weekends.* Ⓜ *Anhangabaú or República* ⊠ *Av. Brigadeiro Faria Lima 1912, Loja 110, Jardim Paulista* ☎*011/3814–3582* ⊟ *AE, DC, MC, V* ⊗ *Closed weekends.*

Eclectic

$$–$$$$ ✕ **La Tambouille.** This Italo-French restaurant with a partially enclosed garden isn't just a place to be seen; it also has some of the best food in town. Among chef André Fernandes's recommended dishes are the linguini with fresh mussels and prawn sauce and the filet mignon *rosini* (served with foie gras and saffron risotto). ⊠ *Av. Nove de Julho 5925, Jardim Europa* ☎ *011/3079–6276* ⊟ *AE, DC, MC, V.*

$–$$ ✕ **Bar des Arts.** A great place for lunch or drinks, and a favorite with businesspeople, the Bar des Arts is in a charming arcade near a flower shop, a wine shop, and a fountain. The Italian dishes are the best options, thanks to the Italian owner. Try the ravioli filled with mozzarella. ⊠ *Rua Pedro Humberto 9, at Rua Horacio Lafer, Itaim Bibi* ☎ *011/ 3849–7828* ⊟ *AE, DC, MC, V* ⊗ *Closed Mon.*

★ **$–$$** ✕ **Mestiço.** Tribal masks peer down from the walls of the large, modern dining room. Consider the Thai *huan-hin* (chicken with shiitake mushrooms in ginger sauce and rice) followed by a dessert of lemon ice cream with *baba de moça* (a syrup made with egg whites and sugar). An eclectic menu also includes Italian, Brazilian, and Bahian dishes. ⊠*Rua Fernando de Albuquerque 277, Consolação* ☎ *011/3256–3165* ⊟ *AE, DC, MC, V* Ⓜ *Consolação.*

$ ✕ **Pitanga.** In a comfortable house in Vila Mariana, Pitanga has a diverse buffet every day (R$22 weekdays, R$25 Saturday, R$18 Sunday). Delicious salads, meat dishes, and feijoada are some of the buffet choices. ⊠ *Rua Original 162, Vila Madalena* ☎ *011/3816–2914* ⊟ *AE, MC, V* ⊗ *Closed Mon.* Ⓜ *Vila Madalena.*

$ ✕ **Ritz.** An animated crowd chatters at this restaurant with Italian, Brazilian, French, and mixed cuisine, as contemporary pop music plays in the background. Although each day sees a different special, a popular dish is *bife à milanesa* (a breaded beef cutlet) with creamed spinach and french fries. ⊠ *Alameda Franca 1088, Jardins* ☎ *011/3088–6808* ⊟ *AE, DC, MC, V* Ⓜ *Consolação.*

¢–$ ✕ **Spot.** The closest thing to a chic diner that you'll find in São Paulo, Spot is just one door up from MASP. The salads and the pasta dishes are good bets; come early, though, as it gets crowded after 10 PM.

⊠ *Alameda Rocha Azevedo 72, Cerqueira César* ☎ *011/283–0946* ▤ *AE, DC, MC, V* Ⓜ *Consolação.*

French

$$–$$$$ ✕ **Freddy.** Leave the grunge and noise of the streets behind in this eatery with the feel of an upscale Parisian bistro. Try the duck with Madeira sauce and apple purée, the pheasant with herb sauce, or the hearty cassoulet with white beans, lamb, duck, and garlic sausage. ⊠ *Praça Dom Gastão Liberal Pinto 111, Itaim Bibi* ☎ *011/3167–0977* ▤ *AE, DC, MC, V* ☻ *No dinner Sun., no lunch Sat.*

$–$$$ ✕ **Bistrô Jaú.** Chef Roberto Eid runs the kitchen and the restaurant here. Businesspeople from Avenida Paulista appreciate the fine decor and the lunch menu, which is superb yet inexpensive (compared with the dinner menu). ⊠ *Alameda Jaú 1606, Jardins* ☎ *011/3085–5573* ▤ *AE, DC, MC, V* Ⓜ *Consolação.*

$–$$$ ✕ **La Casserole.** Facing a little Centro flower market, this charming bistro has been around for generations. Surrounded by wood-paneled walls decorated with eclectic posters, you can dine on such delights as *gigot d'agneau aux soissons* (roast leg of lamb in its own juices, served with white beans) and cherry strudel. ⊠ *Largo do Arouche 346, Centro* ☎ *011/3331–6283* ▤ *AE, DC, MC, V* ☻ *Closed Mon. No lunch Sat.* Ⓜ *República.*

$–$$$ ✕ **Le Coq Hardy.** This upscale restaurant has two chefs: one is a veteran of the top French kitchens in Brazil, and the other spent many years cooking in France. The grilled foie gras and mango, the escargots with mushrooms in an anise-and-wine sauce, and the roast duck are all highly recommended. ⊠ *Rua Jerônimo da Veiga 461, Itaim Bibi* ☎ *011/ 3079–3344* ▤ *AE, DC, MC* ☻ *Closed Sun.*

★ $ ✕ **La Tartine.** An ideal place for a cozy romantic dinner, this small bistro has a good wine selection, movie posters on its walls, and simple but comfortable furniture. The menu changes daily; a favorite is the classic coq au vin, or you can fill up on entrées from beef tenderloin to soups and quiches. It is usually crowded with São Paulo's trendy people, and you might have to wait to get a table on weekends. ⊠ *Rua Fernando de Albuquerque 267, Consolação* ☎ *011/3259–2090* ▤ *V* ☻ *Closed Sun.–Mon.* Ⓜ *Consolação.*

Indian

$–$$$ ✕ **Ganesh.** Many consider this the best Indian restaurant in town. The traditional menu includes curries and *tandoori* dishes from many regions of India. Indian artwork and tapestries fill the interior. ⊠ *Morumbi Shopping Center, Av. Roque Petroni Jr. 1089, Morumbi* ☎ *011/5181–4748* ▤ *AE, DC, MC, V.*

Italian

$$–$$$$ ✕ **Ca' D'Oro.** This is a longtime northern Italian favorite among Brazilian bigwigs, many of whom have their own tables in the old-world-style dining room. Quail, osso buco, and veal-and-raisin ravioli are winners, but the specialty is the Piedmontese *gran bollito misto*, steamed meats and vegetables accompanied by three sauces. ⊠ *Grande Hotel Ca' D'Oro, Rua Augusta 129, Bela Vista* ☎ *011/3236–4300* ⊟ *AE, DC, MC, V* Ⓜ *Anhangabaú.*

$$–$$$$
Fodor'sChoice
★

✕ **Famiglia Mancini.** A huge wheel of provolone cheese is the first thing you see at this warm, cheerful restaurant. An incredible buffet with cheeses, olives, sausages, and much more is the perfect place to find a tasty appetizer. The menu has many terrific pasta options, such as the cannelloni with palm hearts and a four-cheese sauce. ⊠ *Rua Avanhandava 81, Centro* ☎ *011/3256–4320* ⊟ *AE, DC, MC, V* Ⓜ *Anhangabaú.*

$$–$$$$ ✕ **Fasano.** A family-owned northern Italian classic, this restaurant is as famous for its superior cuisine as for its exorbitant prices. The chef, Salvatore Loi, has added to the menu dishes like seafood ravioli with a white wine sauce. The luxe decor—marble, mahogany, and mirrors—has seen better days. ⊠ *Rua Haddock Lobo 1644, Jardins* ☎ *011/3062–4000* ⊟ *AE, DC, MC, V* ☉ *Closed Sun. No lunch.*

$–$$$ ✕ **Gigetto.** The theater posters that adorn the walls are a tribute to the actors who dine here after performing. The modest decor is offset by the elaborate menu's more than 200 delicious options. Try the cappelletti *à romanesca* (with chopped ham, peas, mushrooms, and white cream sauce). ⊠ *Rua Avanhandava 63, Centro* ☎ *011/3256–9804* ⊟ *AE, DC, MC, V* Ⓜ *Anhangabaú.*

$–$$$ ✕ **La Vecchia Cucina.** Chef Sergio Arno changed the face of the city's Italian restaurants with his *nuova cucina*, exemplified by dishes like frogs' legs risotto and duck ravioli with watercress sauce. Well-to-do patrons dine in the glass-walled garden gazebo or the ocher-color dining room decorated with Italian engravings and fresh flowers. ⊠ *Rua Pedroso Alvarenga 1088, Itaim Bibi* ☎ *011/3167–2822* ⊟ *AE, DC, MC, V* ☉ *No dinner Sun., no lunch Sat.*

$–$$$ ✕ **Lellis Trattoria.** Photos of famous patrons (mostly Brazilian actors) hang on the walls, and the doors and bar are made of metal, giving this typical Italian cantina a sophisticated twist. Salmon fillet *marinatta* (in white sauce with potatoes, raisins, and rice) is one of the best choices on the menu. ⊠ *Rua Bela Cintra 1849, Jardim Paulista* ☎ *011/3064–2727* ⊟ *AE, DC, MC, V.*

$–$$ ✕ **Jardim di Napoli.** The white, green, and red of the Italian flag is just about everywhere you look in this restaurant. People come for the unmatchable *polpettone alla parmigiana*, a huge meatball with mozzarella and tomato sauce. There are many other meat dishes, pasta selections, and pizza. ⊠ *Rua Doutor Martinico Prado 463, Higienópolis* ☎ *011/3666–3022* ⊟ *V.*

$–$$ ✕ **Roperto.** Plastic flowers adorn the walls at this typical Bixiga cantina. You won't be alone if you order the traditional and ever-popular fusilli *ao sugo* (with tomato sauce). ⊠ *Rua 13 de Maio 634, Bixiga* ☎ *011/288–2573* ⊟ *DC, MC, V* Ⓜ *Brigadeiro.*

$ ✕ **Don Pepe Di Napoli.** Good and simple Italian food is served here. Choose from a great variety of pastas, salad, and meat dishes. A good option is *Talharina a Don Pepe*, pasta with meat, broccoli, and garlic. ⊠ *Av. Moema 41, Moema* ☎ *011/5051–5100* ⊟ *AE, DC, MC, V.*

Japanese

$$–$$$$ ✕ **Nagayama.** Low-key, trustworthy, and well loved, Nagayama consistently serves excellent sushi and sashimi at both its locations. The chefs like to experiment: the California *uramaki* Philadelphia has rice, cream cheese, grilled salmon, roe, cucumber, and spring onions rolled together. ⊠ *Rua Bandeira Paulista 369, Itaim Bibi* ☎ *011/3079–7553* ▭ *AE, DC, MC* ⊠ *Rua da Consolação 3397, Cerqueira César* ☎ *011/ 3064–0110* ▭ *AE, DC, MC.*

$–$$ ✕ **Nakombi.** Chefs prepare sushi from a *kombi* (Volkswagen van) in the middle of the dining room. In this eclectic environment, tables are surrounded by a small artificial river crowded with fish. The menu includes a good variety of sushi and nonsushi dishes. Try the salmon fillet with *shimeji* mushrooms. ⊠ *Rua Pequetita 170, Vila Olímpia* ☎ *011/ 3845–9911* ▭ *AE, DC, MC, V.*

Lebanese

$–$$ ✕ **Arábia.** For more than 10 years, Arábia has served traditional Lebanese cuisine at this beautiful high-ceilinged restaurant. Simple dishes such as hummus and stuffed grape leaves are executed with aplomb. The lamb melts in your mouth. The reasonably priced "executive" lunch includes one cold dish, one meat dish, a drink, and dessert. Don't miss the pistachio marzipan covered in rose syrup for dessert. ⊠ *Rua Haddock Lobo 1397, Jardins* ☎ *011/3061–2203* ⊕ *www. arabia.com.br* ▭ *AE, DC, MC.*

★ ¢–$ ✕ **Almanara.** Part of a chain of Lebanese semi-fast-food outlets, Almanara is perfect for a quick lunch of hummus, tabbouleh, grilled chicken, and rice. There's also a full-blown restaurant on the premises that serves Lebanese specialties *rodízio* style, where you get a taste of everything until you can ingest no more. ⊠ *Rua Oscar Freire 523, Jardins* ☎ *011/ 3085–6916* ▭ *AE, DC, MC, V.*

Pan-Asian

$–$$ ✕ **Oriental Café.** High ceilings and tile floors convey a sense of space, while flickering candles keep things intimate. Sophisticated dishes like shark's fin soup are the reason this is considered the best pan-Asian restaurant in São Paulo. There are less exotic dishes, such as marinated chicken thighs. ⊠ *Rua José Maria Lisboa 1000, Jardim Paulista* ☎ *011/3060–9495* ▭ *AE, DC, MC, V* ⊗ *Closed Mon. No lunch Tues.–Sat.*

$–$$ ✕ **Sutra.** A coconut tree grows in the middle of this cozy bar–restaurant with sofas and pillows and a huge map of Thailand covering one wall. Vietnamese, Thai, and Japanese cuisines are prepared creatively. *Kaeng kung* (prawns with broccoli and vegetables in a curry–coconut milk sauce) is recommended. Aphrodisiac drinks have names inspired by the Kama Sutra (tabletop cards even have illustrations). The "bamboo splitting," is Absolut, tequila, Cointreau, lemon juice, and Coca-Cola. ⊠ *Rua Salvador Cardoso 20, Itaim Bibi* ☎ *011/3849–4758* ▭ *DC, MC, V* ⊗ *Closed Sun.–Mon. No lunch.*

Pizza

$–$$ ✕ **Pizzaria Camelo.** Though it's neither fancy nor beautiful, Pizzaria Camelo has kept paulistanos enthralled for ages with its wide variety of thin-crust pies. The *chopp* (draft beer) is great, too. Avoid Sunday night, unless you're willing to wait an hour for a table. ⊠ *Rua Pamplona 1873, Jardins* ☎ *011/3887–8764* ▤ *DC, MC, V.*

★ $ ✕ **Galpão.** Lights that shine from behind bottle bottoms embedded in exposed brick walls is one of the interesting design elements in this restaurant owned by an architect. Fast service is also a hallmark. The arugula, sun-dried tomatoes, and mozzarella pizza is one of the best choices. ⊠ *Rua Doutor Augusto de Miranda 1156, Pompéia* ☎ *011/3672–4767* ▤ *DC, MC, V* ⊗ *Closed Mon.*

$ ✕ **Piola.** Part of a chain started in Italy, this restaurant serves good pasta dishes as well as pizza. It's frequented by young people who seem to match the trendy decoration perfectly. ⊠ *Rua Oscar Freire 512, Jardins* ☎ *011/3064–6570* ⊕ *www.piola.com.br* ▤ *AE, DC, MC, V.*

$ ✕ **Speranza.** One of the most traditional pizzerias, this restaurant is famous for its margherita pie. The crunchy *pão de linguiça* (sausage bread) appetizers have a fine reputation as well. ⊠ *Rua 13 de Maio 1004, Bela Vista* ☎ *011/288–8502* ▤ *DC, MC, V.*

¢–$ ✕ **Braz.** Its name comes from one of the most traditional Italian neighFodor'sChoice borhoods in São Paulo. There's a wide selection of crisp-crusted pizzas ★ here; all are delicious, from the traditional margherita to the house specialty, pizza *braz,* with tomato sauce, zucchini, and mozzarella and Parmesan cheeses. The pizzeria is also know for its great *chopp* (draft beer). ⊠ *Rua Grauna 125, Moema* ☎ *011/5561–0905* ▤ *D, MC.*

¢–$ ✕ **Oficina de Pizzas.** Both branches of this restaurant look like something designed by the Spanish artist Gaudí, but the pizzas couldn't be more Italian and straightforward. Try a pie with mozzarella and toasted garlic. ⊠ *Rua Purpurina 517, Vila Madalena* ☎ *011/3816–3749* ▤ *DC, MC, V* ⊠ *Rua Inácio Pereira da Rocha 15, Vila Madalena* ☎ *011/ 3813–8389* ▤ *DC, MC, V.*

¢ ✕ **Pedaço da Pizza.** Pizza is served by the slice here. Choose from the traditional ones such as pepperoni, or an innovation: pizza with oyster mushrooms and cabbage. It is a good late-night stop since it's open until 6 AM on weekends. The place is crowded with paulistas after the movies let out. ⊠ *Rua Augusta 2931, Jardins* ☎ *011/3891–2431* ⊠ *Rua Augusta 1463, Cerqueira César* ▤ *No credit cards* Ⓜ *Consolação.*

Seafood

$–$$$ ✕ **Truta Rosa.** Fresh trout prepared in endless ways makes this small restaurant with a huge fish-shape window a hit. You cross a metal bridge over a small lagoon to reach the dining room, where sashimi and quenelles reel in the customers. ⊠ *Av. Vereador José Diniz 318, Santo Amaro* ☎ *011/5523–7021* ▤ *AE, DC, MC, V* ⊗ *Closed Mon. No dinner Sun.*

$–$$ ✕ **Amadeus.** The quality and preparation of the fish are famous among the business lunch crowd. Appetizers such as fresh oysters and salmon and endive with mustard and entrées like shrimp in a cognac sauce make it a challenge to find better fruits of the sea elsewhere in town. ✉ *Rua Haddock Lobo 807, Jardins* ☎ *011/3061–2859* ⊟ *AE, DC* ☉ *No dinner weekends* Ⓜ *Consolação.*

WHERE TO STAY

São Paulo's hotels are almost exclusively geared to business travelers, both homegrown and foreign. For this reason, most hotels—many of them world-class—are near Avenida Paulista, with a few in the Marginal Pinheiros and charming Jardins neighborhoods. Many hotels offer discounts of 20%–40% for cash payment or weekend stays. Few include breakfast in the room rate. São Paulo hosts many international conventions, so it's wise to make reservations well ahead of your arrival.

WHAT IT COSTS In Reais				
$$$$	$$$	$$	$	¢
FOR 2 PEOPLE over $500	$375–$500	$250–$375	$125–$250	under $125

Prices are for a standard double room in high season, excluding taxes.

$$$$ 🏨 **Hotel Sofitel São Paulo.** Near the Congonhas Airport and Ibirapuera Park, this modern, luxury hotel is noted for its French style. The restaurant serves French cuisine. Dark-wood furniture fills the rooms, many of which have views of park. It's a privilege in São Paulo to be able to see trees from your window. ✉ *Rua Sena Madureira 1355, Bloco 1, Ibirapuera 04021-051* ☎ *011/5574–1100 or 0800/11–1790* 🖷 *011/5575–4544* ⊕ *www. accorhotels.com.br* ⤶ *219 rooms* ⚬ *Restaurant, room service, cable TV, tennis court, pool, gym, sauna, bar, laundry facilities, business services, meeting rooms, helipad, parking (fee)* ⊟ *AE, DC, MC, V.*

★ $$$$ 🏨 **Inter-Continental São Paulo.** This exquisite hotel is by far the most attractive of the city's top-tier establishments. Service is attentive, and both the private and public areas are well appointed. Creams, pastels, and marble come together with seamless sophistication and elegance. ✉ *Av. Santos 1123, Jardins 01419-001* ☎ *011/3179–2600* 🖷 *011/3179–2666* ⊕ *www.interconti.com* ⤶ *160 rooms, 33 suites* ⚬ *Restaurant, room service, cable TV, pool, health club, massage, sauna, bar, business services, helipad, parking (fee)* ⊟ *AE, DC, MC, V* Ⓜ *Trianon.*

$$$$ 🏨 **Renaissance São Paulo.** A stay at this Jardins hotel, a block from Avenida Paulista, puts you close to both shops and businesses. From the street, it has the appeal of a roll of tinfoil, but its interior is graceful and elegant. There are six Renaissance Club floors with 57 suites that include a buffet breakfast, evening hors d'oeuvres, butler service, express check-in and check-out, and fax machines. If you want to arrive in style, the hotel's helipad is key. ✉ *Alameda Santos 2247, Jardins 01419-002* ☎ *011/3069–2233, 800/468–3571 in the U.S.* 🖷 *011/3064–3344* ⊕ *www.renaissancehotels.com* ⤶ *452 rooms, 100 suites* ⚬ *3 restaurants, room service, cable TV, pool, health club, massage, squash, 3 bars, shops, laundry facilities, business services, helipad, travel services, parking (fee)* ⊟ *AE, DC, MC, V* Ⓜ *Consolação.*

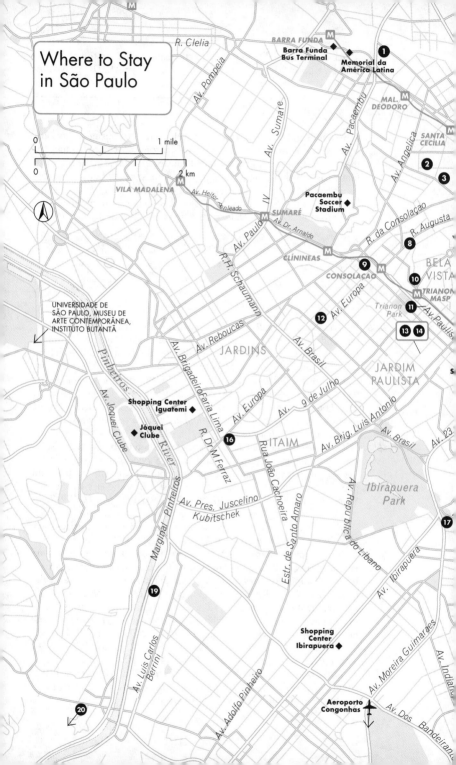

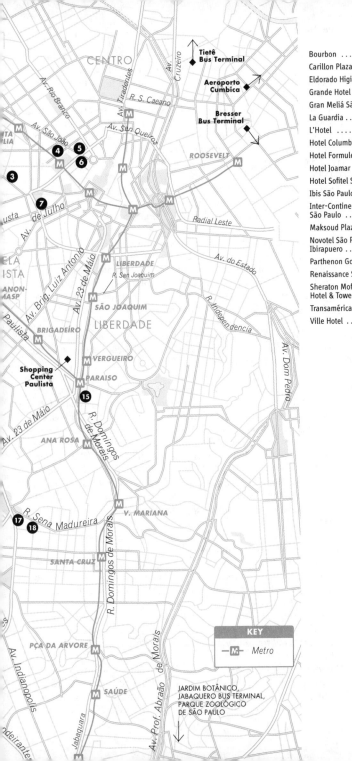

$$$-$$$$ 🏨 **Gran Meliá São Paulo.** This all-suites luxury hotel is in the same build-
Fodor'sChoice ing as São Paulo's world trade center and the D&D Decoração & De-
★ sign Center. Suites have king-size beds, two phone lines, living rooms
with sofas, and small tables that are the perfect places to set up your
laptop. Stay on one of the apartment floors and get special amenities
like pass-key access and bathroom faucets that can be programmed to
maintain your preferred water temperature. Off the large marble lobby
is a bar whose comfortable leather chairs are perfect for unwinding after
a day of meetings or shopping. ⊠ *Av. das Nações Unidas 12559, Brook-
lin 04578-905* ☎ *011/3043–8000 or 0800/15–5555* 🖷 *011/3043–8001*
⊕ *www.solmelia.es* ➯ *300 suites* ⌂ *Restaurant, room service, in-room
data ports, in-room safes, cable TV, tennis court, indoor pool, gym, hair
salon, massage, sauna, paddle tennis, bar, laundry facilities, business ser-
vices, meeting room, parking (fee)* ▤ *AE, DC, MC, V.*

★ **$$$-$$$$** 🏨 **Sheraton Mofarrej Hotel & Towers.** Just behind Avenida Paulista and
next to Parque Trianon, the Mofarrej is part of Sheraton's A-class Lux-
ury Collection hotels. Rooms are a mix of modern and classic styles,
and the four floors that have butler service offer other amenities that
make you feel all the more pampered. Rooms on the west side overlook
the park. ⊠ *Alameda Santos 1437, Jardins 01419-905* ☎ *011/3253–5544
or 0800/11–6000* 🖷 *011/283–0160* ⊕ *www.sheraton-sp.com* ⌂ *2
restaurants, room service, cable TV, indoor pool, gym, massage, sauna,
2 bars, laundry facilities, business services, convention center, parking
(fee)* ▤ *AE, DC, MC, V* Ⓜ *Trianon.*

$$$-$$$$ 🏨 **Transamérica.** Directly across the Rio Pinheiros from the Centro Em-
presarial office complex, the home of many U.S. companies, this hotel
is a comfortable and convenient choice for those working outside Cen-
tro. The skylighted lobby has granite, marble, Persian carpets, palm trees,
leather sofas, and oversize modern paintings; the spacious rooms have
no special charm, but their pastel colors, wood furnishings, and beige
carpeting facilitate relaxation. ⊠ *Av. das Nações Unidas 18591, Santo
Amaro 04795-901* ☎ *011/5693–4511 or 0800/12–6060* 🖷 *011/
5693–4990* ⊕ *www.transamerica.com.br* ➯ *396 rooms, 66 suites*
⌂ *Restaurant, room service, cable TV, 9-hole golf course, 2 tennis
courts, pool, gym, sauna, bar, laundry facilities, business services, park-
ing (fee)* ▤ *AE, DC, MC, V.*

$$-$$$$ 🏨 **L'Hotel.** Close to the major business hubs, this European-style hotel
has rooms and suites decorated in somewhat sterile floral patterns. The
place was modeled after the famous L'Hotel in Paris, and the small number of rooms allows it to focus on providing superior service. Though
at its inception L'Hotel wanted to retain an air of exclusivity, reports
have been mixed as to its success. ⊠ *Alameda Campinas 266, Jardins
01404-000* ☎ *011/283–0500* ⊕ *www.lhotel.com.br* ➯ *82 rooms, 5
suites* ⌂ *2 restaurants, room service, cable TV, pool, health club, sauna,
pub, laundry facilities, business services, meeting room, parking (fee)*
▤ *AE, DC, MC, V* Ⓜ *Trianon.*

$$-$$$$ 🏨 **Maksoud Plaza.** Once *the* place for luxury accommodations in São
Paulo, Maksoud must now share the bill with a bevy of high-end ho-
tels. Still, its decor, comfort, and good location make it one of the top
hotels in the city. The staff provides professional service, the restaurants

are excellent, and the in-house theater and the Maksoud 150 nightclub offer entertainment. ⊠ *Alameda Campinas 1250, Jardins 01404-900* ☎ *011/3145–8000* 🖷 *011/3145–8001* ⊕ *www.maksoud.com.br* 🛏 *416 rooms, 99 suites* ⚲ *6 restaurants, room service, cable TV, indoor pool, health club, 3 bars, nightclub, theater, laundry facilities, business services, parking (fee)* ▤ *AE, DC, MC, V* Ⓜ *Trianon.*

$–$$$$ 🏨 **Grande Hotel Ca' D'Oro.** Owned and run by a northern Italian family for more than 40 years, this old-world-style hotel near Centro has bar-side fireplaces, lots of wood and Persian carpeting, a great variety of classic European design styles, ultrapersonalized service, and the beloved Ca' D'Oro restaurant. All these amenities attract many repeat customers, including quite a few Brazilian bigwigs. ⊠ *Rua Augusta 129, Cerqueira César 01303-001* ☎ *011/3236–4300* 🖷 *011/3236–4311* ⊕ *www.cadoro.com.br* 🛏 *240 rooms, 50 suites* ⚲ *Restaurant, room service, cable TV, indoor pool, gym, sauna, 2 bars, laundry facilities, parking (fee)* ▤ *AE, DC, MC, V* Ⓜ *Consolação.*

$ 🏨 **Bourbon.** Both guests and furnishings are well cared for in this small hotel near the Largo do Arouche, a charming downtown district. A brass-accented basement bar features live piano music. The lobby has upholstered print sofas, an abstract handcrafted black-and-white wall hanging, and granite flooring. Rooms are done in beige and blue and have marvelously large, sunlighted bathrooms. ⊠ *Av. Vieira de Carvalho 99, Centro 01210-010* ☎ *011/3337–2000* 🖷 *011/3331–8187* 🛏 *123 rooms* ⚲ *Restaurant, sauna, bar, parking (fee)* ▤ *AE, DC, MC, V* Ⓜ *República.*

★ $ 🏨 **Eldorado Higienópolis.** In one of the city's oldest and most attractive residential neighborhoods, only a five-minute taxi ride from Centro, this hotel has a large pool and a lobby dressed in travertine marble with a pink-granite floor. The on-site café is lovely, and the rooms are all pleasant; the noise level is lowest in those at the front above the fifth floor or those in back. ⊠ *Rua Marquês de Itu 836, Higienópolis 01223-000* ☎ *011/3361–6888* 🖷 *011/222–7194* ⊕ *www.hoteiseldorado.com.br* 🛏 *152 rooms* ⚲ *Restaurant, room service, cable TV, laundry facilities, pool, bar, parking (fee)* ▤ *AE, DC, MC, V.*

$ 🏨 **Novotel São Paulo Ibirapuera.** Near Ibirapuera Park, with easy access to the city's main streets, Novotel São Paulo Ibirapuera offers solid service. In need of redecoration, it's still a decent choice, just not as great as it once was. ⊠ *Rua Sena Madureira 1355, Ibirapuera 04021-051* ☎ *011/5574–9099* 🖷 *011/5572–3499* ⊕ *www.accorhotels.com.br* 🛏 *80 rooms* ⚲ *Restaurant, room service, cable TV, tennis court, pool, gym, sauna, bar, laundry facilities, business services, meeting rooms, parking (fee)* ▤ *AE, DC, MC, V.*

$ 🏨 **Parthenon Golden Tower.** A full-service establishment with apartment-like amenities, this hotel is popular with business travelers and families alike. The rooms are nicely decorated, and each has a private balcony. ⊠ *Av. Cidade Jardim 411, Pinheiros 01453-000* ☎ *011/3081–6333 or 011/3079–9445* 🖷 *011/3088–3531* ⊕ *www.accorhotels.com.br* 🛏 *73 suites* ⚲ *Restaurant, room service, cable TV, pool, gym, sauna, bar, laundry facilities, meeting room, parking (fee)* ▤ *AE, DC, MC, V.*

¢ 🏨 **Carillon Plaza.** Walk out of the heated hustle and bustle of the Jardins neighborhood and into this hotel's cool lobby, full of mirrors and marble. You can retreat still farther by heading to the rooftop pool for an afternoon of sunbathing or by sinking into a leather chair for a meal in the restaurant. The multilingual staff is very helpful. ⊠ *Rua Bela Cintra 652, Jardins 01415-000* ☎ *011/3257–9233* 🖷 *011/3255–3346* ⊕ *www.redepandehoteis.com.br* ◄⊅ *39 rooms, 10 suites* ♿ *Restaurant, room service, in-room safes, pool, bar, parking (fee)* ⊟ *AE, DC, MC, V* Ⓜ *Consolação*.

¢ ▦ **La Guardia.** If you don't need to be surrounded by luxury, consider this simple, affordable hotel. Rooms are small but comfortable and have thick carpets and marble-top tables. Its a friendly place, and the service is good. ⊠ *Rua Peixoto Gomide 154, Cerqueira César 01409-000* ☎ *011/3255–0600* 🖷 *011/3258–7398* ◄⊅ *28 rooms, 14 suites* ♿ *Restaurant, free parking* ⊟ *AE, DC, MC, V* Ⓜ *Consolação*.

¢ ▦ **Hotel Columbia.** All rooms at this hotel, renovated in late 2002, have a clean functional style. Rooms on the first floor are wheelchair accessible and are designed to accommodate the allergy-prone. ⊠ *Rua dos Timbiras 492, Centro 01208-010* ☎ *011/221–0293* 🖷🖷 *011/3331–3411* ⊕ *www.hotelcolumbia.com.br* ◄⊅ *99 rooms* ♿ *Restaurant, room service, gym, bar, laundry facilities, meeting room, parking (free)* ⊟ *AE, MC, V* Ⓜ *República*.

★ ¢ ▦ **Hotel Formule 1.** One of the first hotels in São Paulo to offer quality and cheap prices, this budget hotel has a simple and practical style. Rooms are small, but each has a queen-size bed with a twin bunk above, a table, and a closet. You pay the same price for 1–3 people in a room. The service and location are good. ⊠ *Rua Vergueiro 1571, Paraiso* ☎ *011/5085–5699* 🖷🖷 *011/5575–8122* ⊕ *www.accorhotels.com.br* ◄⊅ *300* ♿ *Business services, cable TV, parking (fee)* ⊟ *AE* Ⓜ *Paraíso*.

¢ ▦ **Hotel Joamar.** Popular with backpackers, this small hotel in downtown São Paulo was renovated in 2002. It has a clean neat look, with small simple rooms. You can choose from one to three twin beds or a queen-size bed. The hotel is three blocks from the metrô station. ⊠ *Rua Dom José de Barros 187, Centro 01208-010* ☎ *011/221–3611* 🖷🖷 *011/222–1087* ◄⊅ *60 rooms* ♿ *Room service, laundry facilities* ⊟ *AE, MC, V* Ⓜ *República*.

¢ ▦ **Ibis São Paulo Expo.** This large hotel has clean budget rooms. The decoration is contemporary and functional. Rooms have either one queen-size bed or two or three twin beds. The professional staff helps you enjoy your stay here. ⊠ *Rua Eduardo Viana 163, Barra Funda 01133-040* ☎ *011/3824–7373* 🖷 *011/3824–7374* ⊕ *www.accorhotels.com.br* ◄⊅ *280 rooms* ♿ *Restaurant, room service, cable TV, laundry facilities, meeting rooms, free parking* ⊟ *AE, DC, MC, V*.

¢ ▦ **Ville Hotel.** In the lively Higienópolis neighborhood of apartment buildings, bars, and bookstores abutting Mackenzie University, this hotel costs about R$90 a night. The small lobby features a black-and-pink-granite floor, recessed lighting, and leather sofas; rooms are done in pastels and have brown carpeting. ⊠ *Rua Dona Veridiana 643, Higienópolis 01238-010* ☎ *011/3257–5288* 🖷🖷 *011/3241–1871* ⊕ *www.hotelville. com.br* ◄⊅ *54 rooms* ♿ *Restaurant, meeting room, parking (fee)* ⊟ *AE, DC, MC, V*.

NIGHTLIFE & THE ARTS

Nightlife

São Paulo is a city beset by trends, so clubs and bars come and go at a dizzying pace. Though the places listed here were all thriving spots at press time, the nightlife scene is always changing, and it's best to check with hotel concierges and paulistanos you meet to confirm that a place is still open before heading out on the town.

Bars

The most sophisticated (and expensive) places are in the Itaim neighborhood. Vila Madalena is full of trendy places.

Crowded from happy hour to its 2 AM closing, **All Black** (⊠ Rua Oscar Freire 163, Jardins ☎ 011/3088–7990) is an Irish pub with a great variety of international beer brands. Irish soccer paraphernalia decorates the place, and a New Zealand flag betrays one of the owner's roots. This is one of the best places to have a Guinness in São Paulo. The '60s and '70s bohemian decor at **Astor** (⊠ Rua Delfina 163, Vila Madalena ☎ 011/3815–1364) sends you back in time. The owner, after the success of his other two bars, Pirajá and Original, decided to open this place. It has good draft beer, snacks, and meals.

Balcão (⊠ Rua Doutor Melo Alves 150, Jardim Paulista ☎ 011/3088–4630 Ⓜ Consolação) means "balcony," in Portuguese and this place has a sprawling one. If you'd like a little food to accompany your drinks and conversation, try the sun-dried tomato-and-mozzarella sandwich. First opened in 1949, **Bar Brahma** (⊠ Av. São João 677, Centro ☎ 011/3333–0855) used to be the meeting place of artists, intellectuals, and politicians. The decor is a time-warp to the mid-20th-century, with furniture, lamps, and a piano true to the period. This is one of the best places in São Paulo for live music. **Barnaldo Lucrécia** (⊠ Rua Abílio Soares 207, Paraíso ☎ 011/3885–3425 Ⓜ Paraíso) draws crowds with live *música popular brasileira* (MPB; popular Brazilian music). The crowd is intense but jovial.

Elias (⊠ Rua Cayowaá 70, Perdizes ☎ 011/3864–4722) place is a hangout for fans of the Palmeiras soccer team, whose stadium is just a few blocks away. If you want something to eat, the carpaccio is undoubtedly the best choice on the menu. Most patrons stop at **Empanadas** (⊠ Rua Wisard 489, Vila Madalena ☎ 011/3032–2116) for a beer en route to another Vila Madalena bar. It's a good place to "warm up" for an evening out with a quick drink and a bite to eat. Appropriately, the empanadas are particularly appealing. A stop at **Frangó** (⊠ Largo da Matriz de Nossa Senhora do Ó 168, Freguesia do Ó ☎ 011/3932–4818 or 011/3931–4281) makes you feel as if you've been transported to a small town. The bar has 90 varieties of beer, including the Brazilian export beer Xingu. Its rich, molasseslike flavor nicely complements the bar's unforgettable *bolinhos de frango com queijo* (chicken balls with cheese).

★ The fashionable patrons at **Grazie a Dio** (✉ Rua Girassol 67, Vila Madalena ☎ 011/3031–6568 ⊕ www.grazieadio.com.br) may vary in age, but they always appreciate good music. The best time to go is at happy hour for daily live performances. On Saturday it's jazz, and on Friday, bossa nova. The natural decorations, including trees and constellations, complement the Mediterranean food served in the back. **Moça Bonita** (✉ Rua Quatá 633, Vila Olímpia ☎ 011/3846–8136 ⊕ www.mocabonitabar.com.br) is a popular bar with a maritime theme, complete with aquarium and miniature sailboats. The specialties are draft beer and seafood. **Pirajá** (✉ Av. Brigadeiro Faria Lima 64, Pinheiros ☎011/ 3815–6881), known for its draft beer and sandwiches, attracts a crowd of journalists and designers that work nearby. Pictures of Rio line the walls. The action starts at happy hour after 6 PM.

Brazilian Clubs

MPB clubs book quiet, largely acoustic instrumental and vocal music in the style of Milton Nascimento, Chico Buarque, and Gilberto Gil. The emphasis tends to be on samba and bossa nova.

Canto da Ema (✉ Av. Brigadeiro Faria Lima 364, Pinheiros ☎ 011/ 3813–4708 ⊕ www.cantodaema.com.br) is considered the best place to dance forró in town. Here you'll find people of different ages and styles coming together on the dance floor. *Xiboquinha* is the official forró drink, made with *cachaça* (a Brazilian sugarcane-based alcohol), lemon, honey, cinnamon, and ginger. *Carioca* is the term for a person from Rio de Janeiro, and **Carioca Club** (✉ Rua Cardeal Arcoverde 2899, Pinheiros ☎ 011/3812–3782 ⊕ www.cariocaclub.com.br) has the decor of old-style Rio clubs. Its large dance floor attracts an eclectic mix of college students, couples, and professional dancers who move to *samba, gafieira,* and *pagode.*

★ The tiny round tables at **Piratininga** (✉ Rua Wizard 149, Vila Madalena ☎ 011/3032–9775), a small bar-restaurant, are perfect for a quiet rendezvous. The live MPB and jazz music add to the romance. The decor at **Sem Eira Nem Beira** (✉ Rua Fiandeiras 966, Itaim Bibi ☎ 011/ 3845–3444 ⊕ www.semeiranembeira.com.br) was inspired by Brazilian bars circa 1940. The club is famous for its live MPB performances on Friday and Saturday.

Dance Clubs

People tend to go dancing very late, and clubs stay open until 5 or 6 AM. Still, you should arrive early to avoid the lines. Don't worry if the dance floor appears empty at 11 PM; things will start to sizzle an hour or so later.

At **Avenida Club** (✉ Av. Pedroso de Morais 1036, Pinheiros ☎ 011/ 3814–7383) some nights are dedicated to Caribbean rhythms, others to MPB. The large wooden dance floor—one of the finest in town—attracts a crowd of thirtysomethings. **Buena Vista Club** (✉ Rua Atílio Innocenti 780, Vila Olímpia ☎ 011/3045–5245 ⊕ www.buenavistaclub.com.br) is a good place to take dance classes. On Sunday you can learn to dance *Gafieira* and *Zouk.* Live music and DJs heat up the dance floor for hours. The club also has good appetizers and drinks. **Blen Blen Brasil** (✉Rua

Inácio Pereira da Rocha 520, Pinheiros ☎ 011/3812–2890 ⊕ www.
blenblen.com.br) has live music every night except Sunday, from reggae
to salsa to Brazilian rock. The clientele varies depending on the music
(rock generates a younger crowd; salsa an older one). Arrive early and
stay at the bar having a drink and snack before going upstairs to dance.
Brancaleone (✉ Rua Luis Murat 298, Jardim América ☎ 011/3819–8873
⊕ www.brancaleone.com.br) has different music every night, alternating disco, rock, funk, soul, Brazilian pop, and forró. You can take a break
on the patio; refreshments include food as well as drink. At **Dolores Bar**
(✉ Rua Fradique Coutinho 1007, Vila Madalena ☎ 011/3031–3604)
DJs spin funk, soul, and hip-hop tunes for a crowd in its twenties and
thirties. Wednesday and Friday nights are the most popular, and people really do fill up the floor only after the witching hour. Live or
recorded forró is played every night at **KVA** (✉ Rua Cardeal Arcoverde
2958, Pinheiros ☎ 011/3819–2153 ⊕ www.elenkokva.org.br). There
are three stages, two dance floors, and a coffee shop.
Because the venue at **A Lanterna** (✉ Rua Fidalga 531, Vila Madalena
☎ 011/3816–0904 ⊕ www.lanterna.com.br) is a mixture of restaurant, bar, and nightclub, you can go early for dinner and stay late for
dancing. Actors, dancers, and musicians give performances that add to
the entertainment. The walls are decorated with local artists' works. At
★ **Lov.e Club & Lounge** (✉ Rua Pequetita 189, Vila Olímpia ☎ 011/
3044–1613) you might feel that you're on the set of an *Austin Powers*
movie. Before 2 AM the music isn't too loud, and you can sit and talk
on the '50s-style sofas. Then the techno effects keep people on the small
dance floor until sunrise. **Nias** (✉ Rua dos Pinheiros 688, Pinheiros ☎ 011/
3062–3877 ⊕ www.nias.com.br) is one of the few places left where you
can still dance to true rock-and-roll. DJs play tunes from the '80s and
'90s along with current international pop-rock tunes.
Mood Club (✉ Rua Teodoro Sampaio 1109, Pinheiros ☎ 011/3060–9010)
has a bar, a lounge with lots of sofas, and two dancing areas called *The
Home* and *The Hole*. DJs keep things going until 7 AM with electronic
music. Mega club **Piranha** (✉ Rua Turiassu 918, Perdizes ☎ 011/
3873–0744) has three bars and a restaurant, lounge area, garden, and
dance floor. Each weekday has a different crowd depending on the type
of music playing. The DJs play soul, funk, hip-hop, techno, house, and
drum-and-bass from the 80's and 90's. The dance floor has acoustic isolation. **Vila Country** (✉ Av. Francisco Matarazzo 810, Água Branca
☎ 011/3868–5858 Ⓜ Barra Funda) is *the* place to go for American country music and *Sertanejo,* Brazilian country music. The huge club has restaurant, bars, shops, game rooms, and a dance floor. An Old-West theme
permeates the decor.

Gay & Lesbian Bars & Clubs

Alegro (✉ Rua da Consolação 3055, Cerqueira César ☎ 011/3086–0538
Ⓜ Consolação), in the gay nightlife hub of the city, is popular even on
weekdays. It has good food and cocktails, and is popular with the
pre–dance-club crowd. On Saturdays the crowd can reach up to 2,500
people at **Level** (✉ Av. Marques de São Vicente 319, Barra Funda ☎ 011/
3612–4151 Ⓜ Barra Funda). It has a arcade game room, a cyber café,
and lots of house music. **A Lôca** (✉ Rua Frei Caneca 916, Cerqueira César

☎ 011/3120–2055 Ⓜ Consolação) has a large dance floor, a video room, and two bars. A mixed gay and lesbian crowd often dances until dawn and then has breakfast in the club. **Massivo** (✉ Rua Alameda Itu 1548, Jardins ☎ 011/3083–7505 Ⓜ Consolação) is a fabulous underground disco that welcomes gay, lesbian, and straight patrons.

Jazz Clubs

People come to tiny **All of Jazz** (✉ Rua João Cachoeira 1366, Vila Olímpia ☎ 011/3849–1345) to actually *listen* to very good jazz and bossa nova. Local musicians jam here weekly. Call ahead to book a table on weekends. With a name right out of New Orleans, it's no wonder that **Bourbon Street** (✉ Rua Dos Chanés 127, Moema ☎ 011/5561–1643) is where the best jazz and blues bands play. **Café Piu Piu** (✉ Rua 13 de Maio 134, Bixiga ☎ 011/258–8066 ⊕ www.cafepiupiu.com.br) is best-known for jazz, but it also hosts groups that play rock, bossa nova, and even tango. Statues, an antique balcony, and marble tables decorate the place. At **Mr. Blues Jazz Bar** (✉ Av. São Gabriel 558, Jardim Paulista ☎ 011/3884–9356), a traditional jazz, blues, and soul venue, the audience drinks beer and whiskey and eats french fries with Parmesan cheese.

The Arts

The world's top orchestras, opera and dance companies, and other troupes always include São Paulo in their South American tours. Most free concerts—with performances by either Brazilian or international artists—are presented on Sunday in Parque Ibirapuera. City-sponsored events are held in Centro's Vale do Anhangabaú area. State-sponsored concerts take place at the Memorial da América Latina, northwest of Centro.

Listings of events appear in the "Veja São Paulo" insert of the newsweekly *Veja*. The arts sections of the dailies *Folha de São Paulo* and *O Estado de São Paulo* also have listings and reviews. In addition, *Folha* publishes a weekly guide on Friday called "Guia da Folha." Tickets for many events are available at booths throughout the city and at theater box offices. Many of these venues offer ticket delivery to your hotel for a surcharge. **Fun by Phone** (☎ 011/3097–8687 ⊕ www.funbynet.com.br) sells ticket to music concerts, theater, and theme parks. **Ticketmaster.** (☎ 011/6846–6000 ⊕ www.ticketmaster.com.br) also sell tickets by phone and Internet. **Show Ticket at Shopping Center Iguatemi** (✉ Av. Brigadeiro Faria Lima 1191, 3rd floor ☎ 011/3031–2098) sells tickets to the main concerts and performances in town. It's open Monday–Saturday 10 AM–10 PM and Sunday 2–8. **Serviço Social do Comércio** (SESC, Commerce Social Service; ☎ 0800/118–220 ⊕ www.sescsp.org.br) is very active in cultural programming, and many of its events are free.

Classical Music, Dance & Theater Venues

Credicard Hall (✉ Av. das Nações Unidas 17995, Santo Amaro ☎ 011/5643–2500 ⊕ www.credicardhall.com.br) is of the biggest theaters in São Paulo and can accommodate up to 7,000 people. It housed concerts by famous Brazilian and International artists. Tickets can be bought by phone or Internet using the services by Ticketmaster. **Sala São Luiz** (✉ Av. Juscelino Kubitschek 1830, Itaim Bibi ☎ 011/3847–4111) hosts chamber music performances. Opera, ballet, music, and symphony performances are held at **Teatro Alfa** (⊠ Rua Bento Branco de Andrade Filho 722, Santo Amaro ☎ 011/5693–4000 or 0800/55–8191 ⊕ www. teatroalfa.com.br). It's one of the newest theaters in the country, with all the latest sound and lighting technology—and the biggest foreign stars grace the stage. Tickets can be bought by phone and picked up a half hour before the performance.

Fine acoustics make **Teatro Cultura Artística** (⊠ Rua Nestor Pestana 196, Cerqueira César ☎ 011/3258–3616 ⊕ www.culturaartistica.com.br Ⓜ Anhangabaú) perfect for classical music performances. It also hosts dance recitals and plays. Avoid walking from the metro stop at night; take a car instead. **Teatro Faculdade Armando Álvares Penteado (FAAP)** (⊠ Rua Alagoas 903, Pacaembú ☎ 011/3662–1992) presents concerts and Brazilian plays. At **Teatro João Caetano** (⊠ Rua Borges Lagoa 650, Vila Mariana ☎ 011/5573–3774 Ⓜ Santa Cruz) state-sponsored festivals and Brazilian plays take place.

Most serious music, ballet, and opera is performed at **Teatro Municipal** (⊠ Praça Ramos de Azevedo, Centro ☎ 011/222–8698 ⊕ www.prodam. sp.gov.br/theatro Ⓜ Anhangabaú) a classic theater with an intimate gilt and moss-green-velvet interior. There are lyrical performances on Monday at 8:30 and concerts on Wednesday at 12:30. A local cultural organization, the Mozarteum Brasileira Associação Cultural, holds classical music concerts, which include performances by visiting artists, April–October. **Teatro da Universidade Católica (TUCA)** (⊠ Rua Monte Alegre 1024, Sumaré ☎ 011/3670–8453) the Catholic University theater, puts on plays and alternative concerts. **Via Funchal** (⊠ Rua Funchal 65, Vila Olímpia ☎ 011/3846–2300 or 011/3842–6855 ⊕ www.viafunchal. com.br) is capable of seating more than 3,000 people, and is the site of many large international music, theater, and dance shows.

Escola de Samba

From December to February, many *escolas de samba* (literally "sama schools," which are groups that perform during Carnaval) open their rehearsals to the public. Drummers get in sync with the singers, and everyone learns the lyrics to each year's songs. **Rosas de Ouro** (⊠ Av. Cel. Euclides Machado 1066, Freguesia do Ó ☎ 011/3966–0608 or 011/3857–4555 ⊕ www.carnaval-samba.com.br) has one of the most popular escola de samba rehearsals.

Film

Centro Cultural São Paulo (⊠ Rua Vergueiro 1000, Paraíso ☎ 011/3277–3611 Ext. 279 Ⓜ Vergueiro) usually shows a series of films centered on a theme for free or nearly free. It has plays, concerts, and art exhibits. **Cinearte** (⊠ Av. Paulista 2073, Jardim Paulista ☎ 011/3285–3696 Ⓜ Consolação) hosts most of the premieres in town. Brazilian, European, and other non-American films are shown at the **Espaço Unibanco** (⊠ Rua Augusta 1470/1475, Consolação ☎ 011/288–6780 Ⓜ Consolação). The **Unibanco ArtePlex** (⊠ Rua Frei Caneca 569, 3rd floor, Consolação ☎ 011/3472–2365 Ⓜ Consolação) shows Hollywood, European and independent films.

SPORTS & THE OUTDOORS

Brazilians have a reputation for being obsessed with soccer, but in truth, stadiums are normally only full during the finals. Many paulistas prefer to watch soccer on TV at home or in a bar. During the Formula 1 auto race, the city is crowded with foreigners and Brazilians from other states. Paulistas are generally athletic; most work up a sweat in the gym or jogging. Ibirapuera Park is a popular spot for jogging. Check the air quality before you practice outdoor sports. During a dry season, the air can be bad. Don't take your cues from the paulistas—their lungs are made of steel.

Auto Racing

São Paulo hosts a **Formula I** race every March, bringing this city of 4.5 million cars to heights of spontaneous combustion, especially when a Brazilian driver wins. The race is held at **Autódromo de Interlagos** (⊠ Av. Senador Teotônio Vilela 315, Interlagos ☎ 011/5666–8822 ⊕ www.ainterlagos. com), which also hosts other kinds of races on weekends. For ticket information on the Formula I race contact the **Confederação Brasileira de Automobilismo** (⊠ Rua da Glória 290, 8th floor, Rio de Janeiro, RJ 20241-180 ☎ 021/2221–4895 ⊕ www.cba.org.br).

Bicycling

Night Biker's Club (⊠ Rua Pacheco de Miranda 141, Moema ☎ 011/ 3871–2100 ⊕ www.nightbikers.com) offers bike tours of the city at night. In **Parque Ibirapuera,** which has a bike path, you can rent bicycles at a number of places near park entrances for about R$5 an hour. There are also bike lanes on Avenida Sumaré and Avenida Pedroso de Morais. **Sampa Bikers** (⊠ Rua São Sebastião 454, Chácara Santo Antônio ☎ 011/ 5183–9477 ⊕ www.sampabikers.com.br) offers tours in the city and excursions outside town. A day tour starts at a R$50 fee, including transport and lunch.

Climbing

Inspired, perhaps, by the skyscrapers on Avenida Paulista and downtown São Paulo, climbers crowd the gyms and rock-climbing schools that have sprung up around town. Most places offer training and rent equipment. At **Casa de Pedra** (⊠ Rua da Paz 1823, Chácara Santo Antônio ☎ 011/5181–7873 ⊕ www.casadepedra.com.br) the daily fee for using the rock-climbing facilities is R$22, and 90 minutes of instruction is R$45. **Jump** (⊠ Av. Pompéia 568, Pompéia ☎ 011/3675–2300 ⊕ www. jumpacademia.com) gives a three-day climbing course on its open walls. **90 Graus** (⊠ Rua João Pedro Cardoso 107, Aeroporto ☎ 011/5034–8775 ⊕ www.noventagraus.com.br) has climbing courses and individual training.

Golf

The greens fee at the 18-hole **Clube de Campo** (⊠ Praça Rockford 28, Vila Represa ☎ 011/5529–3111) is R$50. It's open Monday, Tuesday,

Thursday, and Friday 7–7. **Golf School** (✉ Av. Guido Caloi 2160, Santo Amaro ☏ 011/5515–3372) is a driving range that has 30-minute classes. For R$18 you get 100 balls.

Horse Racing

Thoroughbreds race at the **São Paulo Jockey Club** (✉ Rua Lineu de Paula Machado 1263, Cidade Jardim ☏ 011/3816–4011), which is open Monday, Wednesday, and Thursday 7:30 PM–11:30 PM and weekends 2–9. Card-carrying Jockey Club members get the best seats and have access to the elegant restaurant.

Scuba Diving

Most dive schools take you to Ilhabela and other places outside town on weekends and offer NAUI and PADI certification courses. **Claumar** (✉ Av. Brigadeiro Faria Lima 4440, Itaim Bibi ☏ 011/3846–3034 ⊕ www.claumar.com.br) has a 15-meter (49-foot) diving tower used during classes in São Paulo. **Deep Sea** (✉ Rua Manoel da Nóbrega 781, Paraíso ☏ 011/3889–7721 ⊕ www.deepsea.com.br) leads small groups on dive trips to Lage de Santos. **Diving College** (✉ Rua Doutor Mello Alves 700, Jardins ☏ 011/3061–1453 ⊕ www.divingcollege. com.br) is one of the oldest diving schools in Brazil and offers all the PADI courses.

Soccer

São Paulo has several well-funded teams with some of the country's best players. The five main teams—São Paulo, Palmeiras, Portuguesa, Corinthians, and Juventus—even attract fans from other states. The two biggest stadiums are Morumbi and the municipally run Pacaembu. Note that covered seats offer the best protection, not only from the elements but also from rowdy spectators. Buy tickets at the stadiums or online at **www.igressofacil.com.br.** Regular games usually don't sell out, but finals do; you can buy tickets up to five days in advance for finals.

Morumbi (✉ Praça Roberto Gomes Pedrosa, Morumbi ☏ 011/ 3749–8000), the home stadium of São Paulo Futebol Clube, has a capacity of 85,000. The first games of the 1950 World Cup were played at the **Pacaembú** (✉ Praça Charles Miller, Pacaembú ☏ 011/3661–9111) stadium, home of the Corinthians team.

Tennis

Tênis Coach (✉ Rua Dr. Francisco Tomás de Carvalho 940, Morumbi ☏ 011/3742–3004) rents courts and has classes for people of all ages.

SHOPPING

People come from all over South America to shop in São Paulo, and shopping is considered an attraction in its own right by many paulistanos. In the Jardins neighborhood, stores that carry well-known brands from around the world alternate with the best Brazilian shops. Stores are open weekdays 9–6:30, Saturday 9–1, and are closed Sunday. Mall hours are generally weekdays 10–10 and Saturday 9 AM–10 PM; malls are open on Sunday during the Christmas season.

Areas

In **Centro,** Rua do Arouche is noted for leather goods. In **Itaim** the area around Rua João Cachoeira has evolved from a neighborhood of small clothing factories into a wholesale- and retail-clothing sales district. Several shops on Rua Tabapuã sell small antiques. Also, Rua Dr. Mário Ferraz is stuffed with elegant clothing, gift, and home-decoration stores. In **Jardins,** centering on Rua Augusta (which crosses Avenida Paulista) and Rua Oscar Freire, double-parked Mercedes-Benzes and BMWs point the way to the city's fanciest stores, which sell leather items, jewelry, gifts, antiques, and art. Jardins also has many restaurants and beauty salons. Shops that specialize in high-price European antiques are on or around Rua da Consolação. A slew of lower-price antiques stores line Rua Cardeal Arcoverde in **Pinheiros.**

Centers & Malls

D&D Decoração & Design Center (⊠ Av. das Nações Unidas 12555, Brooklin Novo ☎ 011/3043–9000 ⊕ www.dedshopping.com.br) shares a building with the World Trade Center and the Gran Meliá hotel. It's loaded with fancy home decorating stores, full-scale restaurants, and fast-food spots. **Shopping Center Ibirapuera** (⊠ Av. Ibirapuera 3103, Moema ☎ 011/5095–2300 ⊕ www.ibirapuera.com.br), once the largest shopping mall in Brazil, has more than 500 stores and three movie theaters.

★ One of the newest shopping malls in São Paulo, **Shopping Pátio Higienópolis** (⊠ Av. Higienópolis 618, Higienópolis ☎ 0800/15–9777) is a mixture of old and new architecture styles. Its design is not as cold as the other malls constructed in the '60s. It has plenty of shops and restaurants. **Shopping Center Iguatemi** (⊠ Av. Brigadeiro Faria Lima 2232, Jardim Paulista ☎ 011/3038–6000 ⊕ www.iguatemisaopaulo.com.br) is the city's oldest and most sophisticated mall and has the latest in fashion and fast food. Four movie theaters often show American films in English with Portuguese subtitles. The Gero Café, built in the middle of the main hall, has a fine menu. **Shopping Center Morumbi** (⊠ Av. Roque Petroni Jr. 1089, Morumbi ☎ 0800/17–7600 ⊕ www.morumbishopping.com.br), in the city's fastest-growing area, is giving Iguatemi a run for its money. That said, it houses about the same boutiques, record stores, bookstores, and restaurants as Iguatemi, though it has more movie theaters (a total of six).

Markets

Almost every neighborhood has a weekly outdoor food market (days are listed in local newspapers), complete with loudmouthed hawkers, exotic scents, and piles of colorful produce.

On Sunday there are **antiques fairs** near the Museu de Arte de São Paulo and (in the afternoon) at the Shopping Center Iguatemi's parking lot. Many stall owners have shops and hand out business cards so you can browse throughout the week at your leisure. An **arts and crafts fair** (⊠ Praça da República, Centro)—selling jewelry, embroidery, leather goods, toys, clothing, paintings, and musical instruments—takes place

Sunday morning. Many booths move over to the nearby Praça da Liberdade in the afternoon, joining vendors there selling Japanese-style ceramics, wooden sandals, cooking utensils, food, and bonsai trees. **Flea markets** with second-hand furniture, clothes, and CDs take place on Saturday at Praça Benedito Calixto in Pinheiros and on Sunday at the Praça Dom Orione in Bela Vista.

Specialty Shops

Antiques

Antiquário Paulo Vasconcelos (⊠ Alameda Gabriel Monteiro da Silva 1881, Jardins ☎ 011/3062–2444) has folk art and 18th- and 19th-century Brazilian furniture, among other treasures. **Edwin Leonard** (⊠ Rua Oscar Freire 146, Jardins ☎ 011/3088–1394) is a collective of three dealers that sell Latin American and European antiques.

Head to **Patrimônio** (⊠ Alameda Ministro Rocha Azevedo 1068, Jardins ☎ 011/3064–1750) for Brazilian antiques at reasonable prices. It also sells some Indian artifacts as well as modern furnishings crafted from iron. **Renato Magalhães Gouvêa Escritório de Arte** (⊠ Rua Pelotas 475, Vila Mariana ☎ 011/5084–7272) sells a potpourri of European and Brazilian antiques, modern furnishings, and art. **Renée Behar Antiques** (⊠ Rua Peixoto Gomide 2088, Jardins ☎ 011/3085–3622 ⊕ www.reneebehar.com.br) has 18th- and 19th-century antiques. It also has temporary exhibitions of antique pieces.

Art

Arte Aplicada (⊠ Rua Haddock Lobo 1406, Jardins ☎ 011/3062–5128) is the place for Brazilian paintings, sculptures, and prints. The staff at **Camargo Vilaça** (⊠ Rua Fradique Coutinho 1500, Vila Madalena ☎ 011/3032–7066) has an eye for the works of up-and-coming Brazilian artists. At **Espaço Cultural Ena Beçak** (⊠ Rua Oscar Freire 440, Jardins ☎ 011/3088–7322 ⊕ www.enabecak.com.br) you can shop for Brazilian prints, sculptures, and paintings and then stop in at the café.

If art *naïf* (literally, "naive" art) is your thing, **Galeria Jacques Ardies** (⊠ Rua do Livramento 221, Vila Mariana ☎ 011/3884–2916 ⊕ www.ardies.com Ⓜ Paraíso) is a must. As the name suggests, art naïf is simple, with a primitive and handcrafted look. At **Galeria Renot** (⊠ Alameda Ministro Rocha Azevedo 1327, Jardins ☎ 011/3083–5933 ⊕ www.renot.com.br) you find oil paintings by such Brazilian artists as Vicente Rego Monteiro, Di Cavalcanti, Cícero Dias, and Anita Malfatti.

Galeria São Paulo (⊠ Rua Estados Unidos 1456, Jardins ☎ 011/3062–8855) is a leader in contemporary, mainstream art. Many a trend has been set at **Mônica Filgueiras Galeria** (⊠ Alameda Ministro Rocha Azevedo 927, Jardins ☎ 011/3082–5292), which has all types of art, but mostly paintings and sculpture.

Beauty

Anna Pegova (⊠ Alameda Lorena 1582 Jardins ☎ 011/3081–2402 or 0800/131345 ⊕ www.annapegova.com.br) is a French beauty-product brand famous in Brazil. The shop has hair, skin, face, and body prod-

★ ucts for men and women. The shops are everywhere in São Paulo; the Jardins store is one of the best. Brazilian brand **O Boticário** (⊠ Rua Pamplona 1345, Jardins ☎ 011/3885–8623 ⊕ www.oboticario.com.br) was created by dermatologists and pharmacists from Curitiba in the '70s. Today it is one of the biggest franchising companies in the country, with products for men, women, and children. The company's *Fundação O Boticário de Proteção a Natureza* (Boticário Foundation for Nature Protection) funds ecological projects throughout Brazil. The shops can be found in most neighborhoods and malls in the city.

Beachwear

Beira Mar Beachwear (⊠ Rua José Paulino 592, Bom Retiro ☎ 011/222–7999 ⊕ www.maiosbeiramar.com.br Ⓜ Tiradentes) was founded in 1948. Since then it has been known for innovative and good-quality products. The Brazilian brand has its own factory and produces a great variety of bikinis and swimming suits. **Track & Field** (⊠ Rua Oscar Freire 959, Jardins ☎ 01/3062–4457 ⊕ www.tf.com.br) is a very good place to buy beachwear and sports clothing. The store sells bikinis and swimsuits from **Cia. Marítima** (⊕ www.ciamaritima.com.br), a famous Brazilian beachwear brand. The shops are in almost every mall in São Paulo.

Books & Maps

A branch of the French media store, **Fnac** (⊠ Av. Pedroso de Moraes 858, Pinheiros ☎ 011/3097–0022 ⊕ www.fnac.com.br) sells CDs, books, and photo and computer equipment. It is a good place to buy maps and travel guides. **Livraria Cultura** (⊠ Av. Paulista 2073, Jardins ☎ 011/3170–4033 ⊕ www.livcultura.com.br Ⓜ Consolação), considered the best place in São Paulo to buy literature on travel, also has a great variety of maps from Brazil and abroad. Branches of **Livraria Saraiva** (⊠ Shopping Ibirapuera, Av. Ibirapuera 3103, Moema ☎ 011/5561–7290 ⊕ www.livrariasaraiva.com.br) can be found in many of the shopping malls in São Paulo. It's a good place to buy maps, books and CDs.

Clothing

Alexandre Herchovitch (⊠ Rua Haddock Lobo 1151, Jardins ☎ 011/3063–2888) is a famous Brazilian designer, and his store has prêt-à-porter and tailor-made clothes. **Anacapri** (⊠ Rua Juquis 276, Moema ☎ 011/5531–8913) sells plus-size women's underwear, swimsuits, and clothes. At **Cori** (⊠ Rua Haddock Lobo 1584, Jardins ☎ 011/3081–5223 ⊕ www.cori.com.br) everyday outfits with classic lines are the specialty.

At designer-label boutique **Daslu** (⊠ Rua Domingos Leme 284, Vila Nova Conceição ☎ 011/3842–3785), mingle with elite ladies who enjoy personalized attention. There's no storefront. **Ellus** (⊠ Rua Oscar Freire 990, Jardins ☎ 011/3061–2900 ⊕ www.ellus.com.br) is a good place to buy men's and women's jeans, sportswear, and street wear. **Fórum** (⊠ Rua Oscar Freire 916, Jardins ☎ 011/3085–6269 ⊕ www.forum.com.br) has a lot of evening attire for young men and women, but it also sells sportswear and shoes.

Le Lis Blanc is Brazil's exclusive purveyor of the French brand Vertigo. Look for party dresses in velvet and sheer fabrics (⊠ Rua Oscar Freire 809, Jardins ☎ 011/3083–2549).

If you have a little money in your pocket, shop at **Maria Bonita** (✉ Rua Oscar Freire 702, Jardins ☎ 011/3082–6649 ⊕ www.mariabonitaextra. com.br), which has elegant women's clothes with terrific lines. At Maria Bonita Extra the prices are a little lower.

At **Petistil** (✉ Rua Teodoro Sampaio 2271, Pinheiros ☎ 011/3816–2865 ⊕ www.petistil.com.br) younger family members aren't forgotten. It sells clothes for infants and children up to 11 years old. The women's clothing at **Reinaldo Lourenço** (✉ Rua Bela Cintra 2167, Jardins ☎ 011/ 3085–8150) is high quality and sophisticated.

Richard's (✉ Rua Oscar Freire 1129, Jardins ☎ 011/3088–8761 Ⓜ Consolação) is one of Brazil's best lines of sportswear. The collection includes outfits suitable for the beach or the mountains. At **Uma** (✉ Rua Girassol 273, Vila Madalena ☎ 011/3813–5559 ⊕ www.uma.com.br) young women are intrigued by the unique designs of the swimsuits, dresses, shorts, shirts, and pants.

The prices at **Vila Romana Factory Store** (✉ Via Anhanguera, Km 17.5, Osasco ☎ 011/3604–5293 ✉ Av. Ibirapuera 3103—Shopping Ibirapuera, Moema ☎ 011/5535–1808 ⊕ www.vilaromana.com.br) for suits, jackets, jeans, and some women's wear (silk blouses, for example) are unbeatable. The store is a 40-minute drive from Centro. The in-town branch is more convenient, but its prices are higher. At **Viva Vida** (✉ Rua Oscar Freire 969, Jardins ☎ 011/3088–0421 ⊕ www.vivavida.com. br) long evening dresses—many done in shiny, sexy, exotic fabrics—steal the show. **Zoomp** (✉ Rua Oscar Freire 995, Jardins ☎ 011/3064–1556 ⊕ www.zoomp.com.br) is famous for its jeans and high-quality street wear. Customers from 13 to 35 mix and match the clothes, creating some unusual combinations.

Handicrafts

Art Índia (✉ Rua Augusta 1371, Loja 117, Cerqueira César ☎ 011/283– 2102 Ⓜ Consolação) is a government-run shop that sells Indian arts and crafts made by tribes throughout Brazil. As its name suggests, **Casa do Amazonas** (✉ Galeria Metropôle, Av. Jurupis 460, Moema ☎ 011/5051–3098 Ⓜ São Luís) has a wide selection of products from the Amazon.

Galeria de Arte Brasileira (✉ Alameda Lorena 2163, Jardins ☎ 011/ 3062–9452) specializes in Brazilian handicrafts. Look for objects made of pau-brasil wood, hammocks, jewelry, T-shirts, *marajoara* pottery (from the Amazon), and lace. **Marcenaria Trancoso** (✉ Rua Harmonia 233, Vila Madalena ☎ 011/3032–3505 ⊕ www. marcenariatrancoso.com.br) sells wooden products that are an elegant mixture of interior design and handicraft. At **Mundareu** (✉ Rua Mourato Coelho 988, Vila Madalena ☎ 011/3032–4649 ⊕ www. mundareu.org.br) browse through quality products made by different types of artisans from all over Brazil.

Jewelry

★ An internationally known Brazilian brand for jewelry, **H. Stern** (✉ Rua Oscar Freire 652, Jardins ☎ 011/3068–8082 ⊕ www.hstern.com.br) has shops in more the 30 countries. This one has designs made especially for the Brazilian stores.

Leather Goods & Luggage

One of the biggest brands for luggage and leather goods in Brazil, **Le Postiche** (⊠ Shopping Villa Lobos, Av. das Nacões Unidas 4777, Pinheiros ☎ 011/3021–0274 ⊕ www.lepostiche.com.br) has 81 shops around the country. You can find one in almost any mall in São Paulo.

Photo Equipment

Consigo (⊠ Rua Conselheiro Crispiniano 105, 1st floor, Centro ☎ 011/3258–4015 Ⓜ República) is one of São Paulo's best shops for photography and lighting equipment.

SÃO PAULO A TO Z

To research prices, get advice from other travelers, and book travel arrangements, visit www.fodors.com.

AIR TRAVEL

CARRIERS Aerolíneas Argentinas has daily flights from Buenos Aires and Madrid and twice-a-week service from Auckland, New Zealand, and Sydney, Australia. Air France has a daily flight from Paris. American Airlines offers three flights a day from Miami and one a day from both New York and Dallas. British Airways flies from London every day but Tuesday and Wednesday. Air Canada flies from Toronto every day but Monday. Continental Airlines flies from New York daily; United Airlines flies daily from Miami, New York, and Chicago.

Rio-Sul and Nordeste connect São Paulo with most major Brazilian cities daily. TAM flies daily to Miami, Paris, and most major Brazilian cities. It serves Mercosur capitals as well. Transbrasil has daily flights to major Brazilian cities. Varig has daily service to many U.S. and Brazilian cities; it also offers regular service to more than 18 countries in Latin America, Europe, Asia, and Australia. GOL, the youngest Brazilian airline, offers budget tickets to major national capitals.

🛂 Airlines & Contacts **Aerolíneas Argentinas** ☎ 011/6445-3806 ⊕ www.aeroargentinas.com. **Air Canada** ☎ 011/3259-9066 ⊕ www.aircanada.com. **Air France** ☎ 011/3049-0909 ⊕ www.airfrance.com. **American Airlines** ☎ 011/3214-4000 ⊕ www.aa.com. **British Airways** ☎ 011/3145-9700 ⊕ www.ba.com. **Continental Airlines** ☎ 0800/55-4777 ⊕ www.continental.com. **GOL** ☎ 0800/701-2131 ⊕ www.voegol.com.br. **Rio-Sul and Nordeste** ☎ 0300/788-7000 or 011/5091-7000 ⊕ www.varig.com. **TAM** ☎ 0300/123-1000 ⊕ www.tamairlines.com. **United Airlines** ☎ 0800/16-2323 or 011/3145-4200 ⊕ www.ual.com. **Varig** ☎ 0300/788-7000 or 011/5091-7000 ⊕ www.varig.com.

AIRPORTS & TRANSFERS

São Paulo's international airport, Aeroporto Cumbica, is in the suburb of Guarulhos, 30 km (19 mi) and a 45-minute drive (longer during rush hour or on rainy days) northeast of Centro. Aeroporto Congonhas, 14 km (9 mi) south of Centro (a 15- to 30-minute drive, depending on traffic), serves regional airlines, including the Rio–São Paulo shuttle. From June to September both airports are sometimes fogged in during the early morning, and flights are rerouted to the Aeroporto Viracopos in Campinas; passengers are transported by bus (an hour's ride) to São Paulo.

🖪 Airport Information **Aeroporto Congonhas** ☎ 011/5090-9000. **Aeroporto Cumbica** ☎ 011/6445-2945. **Aeroporto Viracopos** ☎ 019/725-5000.

AIRPORT TRANSFERS
EMTU *executivo* buses—fancy, green-stripe "executive" vehicles—shuttle between Cumbica and Congonhas (5:30 AM–11 PM, every 30 minutes) as well as between Cumbica and the Tietê bus terminal (5:40 AM–10:10 PM, every 45 minutes); the downtown Praça da República (5:30 AM–11 PM, every 30 minutes); and the Hotel Maksoud Plaza (6:45 AM–11:05 PM every 35 minutes), stopping at most major hotels on Avenida Paulista. The cost is R$16.50. Municipal buses, with CMTC painted on the side, stop at the airport and go downtown by various routes, such as via Avenida Paulista, to the Praça da Sé and the Tietê bus station.

The sleek, blue-and-white, air-conditioned Guarucoop radio taxis take you from Cumbica to downtown for around R$53. *Comum* (regular) taxis charge R$45 from Cumbica and around R$18 from Congonhas. Fleet Car Shuttle (counter at Cumbica Airport's arrivals Terminal 1) is open daily 6 AM–midnight and serves groups of up to 10 people in a van, stopping at one destination of choice. The fee (for the vanload) is about R$90.

🖪 Taxis & Shuttles **EMTU** *executivo* **buses** ☎ 0800/19-0088 or 011/6445-2505. **Fleet Car Shuttle** ☎ 011/945-3030. **Guarucoop radio taxis** ☎ 011/6440-7070.

BUS TRAVEL TO & FROM SÃO PAULO

The four bus stations in São Paulo serve 1,105 destinations combined. The huge main station—serving all major Brazilian cities (with trips to Rio every hour on the half hour) as well as Argentina, Uruguay, Chile, and Paraguay—is the Terminal Tietê in the north, on the Marginal Tietê Beltway. Terminal Bresser, in the eastern district of Brás, serves southern Minas Gerais State and Belo Horizonte. Terminal Jabaquara, near Congonhas Airport, serves coastal towns. Terminal Barra Funda, in the west, near the Memorial da América Latina, has buses to and from western Brazil. All stations have or are close to metrô stops. You can buy tickets at the stations; although those for Rio de Janeiro can be bought a few minutes before departure, it's best to buy tickets in advance for other destinations and during holiday seasons.

🖪 Bus Information **Terminal Barra Funda** ✉ Rua Mário de Andrade 664, Barra Funda ☎ 011/3235-0322. **Terminal Bresser** ✉ Rua do Hipódromo, Brás ☎ 011/3235-0322. **Terminal Jabaquara** ✉ Rua Jequitibas, Jabaquara ☎ 011/3235-0322. **Terminal Tietê** ✉ Av. Cruzeiro do Sul, Santana ☎ 011/3235-0322.

BUS TRAVEL WITHIN SÃO PAULO

There's ample municipal bus service, but regular buses (white with a red horizontal stripe) are overcrowded at rush hour and when it rains. Stops are clearly marked, but routes are spelled out only on the buses themselves. Buses do not stop at every bus stop, so if you are waiting, put out your arm horizontally to flag one down. The fare is R$1.70. You enter at the front of the bus, pay the *cobrador* (fare collector) in the middle, and exit from the rear of the bus. The cobrador gives out *vale transporte* slips, or fare vouchers (with no expiration time), and often has no change.

The green-and-gray SPTrans executivo buses, whose numerical designations all end with the letter *E*, are more spacious and cost around R$2.80 (you pay the driver upon entry). Many *clandestino* buses (unlicensed, privately run) traverse the city. Although not very pleasing to the eye—most are battered white vehicles that have no signs—it's perfectly fine to take them; they charge the same as SPTrans buses.

For bus numbers and names, routes, and schedules for SPTrans buses, purchase the *Guia São Paulo Ruas,* published by Quatro Rodas and sold at newsstands and bookstores for about R$30.

🚍 **Bus Information** **Municipal bus service** ☎ 0800/12-3133. **SPTrans executivo** ☎ 158.

CAR RENTAL
Car-rental rates range from R$60 to R$200 a day. Major international rental companies include Avis and Hertz. Localiza is a major local company.

🚍 **Rental Agencies** **Avis** ✉ Rua da Consolação 335, Centro ☎ 011/288-3733. **Hertz** ✉ Rua da Consolação 439, Centro ☎ 011/3258-8422 or 0800/701-7300. **Localiza** ✉ Rua da Consolação 419, Centro ☎ 0800/99-2000.

CAR TRAVEL
The main São Paulo–Rio de Janeiro highway is the Via Dutra (BR 116 North), which has been repaved and enlarged in places. The speed limit is 120 kph (74 mph) along most of it, and although it has many tolls, there are many call boxes you can use if your car breaks down. The modern Rodovia Ayrton Senna (SP 70) charges reasonable tolls, runs parallel to the Dutra for about a quarter of the way, and is an excellent alternative route. The 429-km (279-mi) trip takes five hours. If you have time, consider the longer, spectacular coastal Rio-Santos Highway (SP 55 and BR 101). It's an easy two-day drive, and you can stop midway at the colonial city of Parati, in Rio de Janeiro State.

Other main highways are the Castelo Branco (SP 280), which links the southwestern part of the state to the city; the Via Anhanguera (SP 330), which originates in the state's rich northern agricultural region, passing through the university town of Campinas; SP 310, which also runs from the farming heartland; BR 116 south, which comes up from Curitiba (a 408-km/265-mi trip); plus the Via Anchieta (SP 150) and the Rodovia Imigrantes (SP 160), parallel roads that run to the coast, each operating one-way on weekends and holidays.

Driving isn't recommended because of the heavy traffic (nothing moves at rush hour, especially when it rains), daredevil drivers, and inadequate parking. If, however, you do opt to drive, there are a few things to keep in mind. Most of São Paulo is between the Rio Tietê and the Rio Pinheiros, which converge in the western part of town. The high-speed routes along these rivers are Marginal Tietê and Marginal Pinheiros. There are also *marginais* (beltways) around the city. Avenida 23 de Maio runs south from Centro and beneath the Parque do Ibirapuera via the Ayrton Senna Tunnel. You can take avenidas Paulista, Brasil, and Faria Lima southwest to the Morumbi, Brooklin, Itaim, and Santo Amaro neighborhoods, respectively. The Elevado Costa e Silva, also called Minhocão, is an elevated road that connects Centro with Avenida Francisco Matarazzo in the west.

In most commercial neighborhoods you must buy hourly tickets (called Cartão Zona Azul) to park on the street during business hours. Buy them at newsstands, not from people on the street. Booklets of 20 tickets cost R$18. Fill out each ticket—you'll need one for every hour you plan to park—with the car's license plate and the time you initially parked. Leave the tickets in the car's window so they're visible to officials from outside. After business hours or at any time near major sights, people may offer to watch your car. Although paying these "caretakers" about R$3 is enough to keep your car's paint job intact, to truly ensure its safety opt for a parking lot. Rates are R$5–R$7 for the first hour and R$1–R$2 each hour thereafter.

EMERGENCIES
The three main pharmacies have more than 20 stores, each open 24 hours— Droga Raia, Drogaria São Paulo, and Drogasil. The police department in charge of tourist affairs, Delegacia de Turismo, is open weekdays 8–8.

🔳 Emergency Services **Ambulance** ☎ 192. **Delegacia de Turismo** ✉ Av. São Luís 91, Centro ☎ 011/3107-8712. **Fire** ☎ 193. **Police (military)** ☎ 190.

🔳 Hospitals **Albert Einstein** ✉ Av. Albert Einstein 627, Morumbi ☎ 011/3745-1233. **Beneficência Portuguesa** ✉ Rua Maestro Cardim 769, Paraíso ☎ 011/3253-5022 Ⓜ Vergueiro. **Sírio Libanês** ✉ Rua. D. Adma Jafet 91, Bela Vista ☎ 011/3155-0200.

🔳 24-Hour Pharmacies **Droga Raia** ✉ Rua José Maria Lisboa 645, Jardim Paulistano ☎ 011/3884-8235. **Drogaria São Paulo** ✉ Av. Angélica 1465, Higienópolis ☎ 011/ 3667-6291. **Drogasil** ✉ Av. Brigadeiro Faria Lima 2726, Cidade Jardim ☎ 011/3812-6276.

ENGLISH-LANGUAGE MEDIA
Most Avenida Paulista newsstands sell major U.S. and European papers as well as magazines and paperbacks in English. Livraria Cultura has a large selection of English books of all types in its store at Conjunto Nacional. Fnac sells many international books and periodicals. Laselva usually receives magazines from abroad earlier than other bookstores. Saraiva's megastore also has English-language titles.

🔳 Bookstores **Fnac** ✉ Av. Pedroso de Morais 858, Pinheiros ☎ 011/3819-2119. **Laselva** ✉ Shopping Ibirapuera, Av. Ibirapuera 3103 ☎ 011/5561-9561. **Livraria Cultura** ✉ Av. Paulista 2073/153, Cerqueira César ☎ 011/3285-4033 Ⓜ Consolação. **Saraiva's** ✉ Shopping Eldorado, Av. Rebouças 3970, Pinheiros ☎ 011/3819-5999.

HEALTH
Don't drink tap water. Ask for juice and ice made with bottled water in restaurants and bars. Don't eat barbecued meats sold by street vendors; even those served in some bars are suspect. The air pollution might irritate your eyes, especially in July and August (dirty air is held in the city by thermal inversions), so pack eye drops.

MAIL, INTERNET & SHIPPING
There's a branch of the *correio* (post office) in Centro. International couriers include DHL and FedEx. At Saraiva Megastore, Internet access is available Monday–Saturday 10–10 and Sunday 2–8; the cost is about

R$8 per hour. The Fnac Internet café is open daily 10–10 and access is about R$7 per hour. Monkey, which specializes in gaming, has 10 shops around the city, with Web access for about R$4 per hour. Play Net charges R$4 per hour for access and has games rooms. Smartbiz charges about R$5 per hour and has electronic music events Fridays and Saturdays.

🖪 Internet Cafés **Coffee & Book at Saraiva Megastore** ⊠ Shopping Eldorado, Av. Rebouças 3970, Pinheiros ☎ 011/3819–1770. **Frans Café at Fnac** ⊠ Av. Pedroso de Morais 858, Pinheiros ☎ 011/3814–2404. **Monkey** ⊠ Rua da Consolação 2961, Jardins ☎ 011/3085–4646 ⊕ www.monkey.com.br. **Play Net** ⊠ Rua Três Rios 90, Bom Retiro ☎ 011/3326–9720 ⊕ www.playnetgame.com.br Ⓜ Tiradentes. **Smartbiz** ⊠ Rua Augusta 2690, Loja 17, Jardins ☎ 011/3082–6937 ⊕ www.smartbiz.com.br

🖪 Post Office **Correio** ⊠ Alameda Santos 2224, Jardins ☎ 011/3085–2394 Ⓜ Consolação.

🖪 Overnight Services **DHL** ⊠ Rua da Consolação 2721, Jardins ☎ 0800/773–0552. **FedEx** ⊠ Av. São Luís 187, Loja 43, Centro ☎ 011/5641–7788 Ⓜ República.

METRÔ TRAVEL

The metrô is safe, quick, comfortable, and clean, but unfortunately it doesn't serve many of the city's southern districts. The blue line runs north–south, the orange line runs east–west, and the green line runs under Avenida Paulista from Vila Mariana to the stations at Sumaré and Vila Madalena, near Avenida Pompéia. The metrô operates daily 5 AM–midnight. Tickets are sold in stations and cost R$1.60 one-way. (You can get discounts on round-trip fares and when you buy 10 tickets at once; note that ticket sellers aren't required to change large bills.) You insert the ticket into the turnstile at the platform entrance, and it's returned to you only if there's unused fare on it. Transfers within the metrô system are free, as are bus-to-metrô (or vice-versa) transfers. You can buy a *bilhete integração* (integration ticket) on buses or at metrô stations for R$2.65. Maps of the metrô system are available from the Departamento de Marketing Institucional, or you can pick up the *Guia São Paulo* at newsstands and bookstores. Call the Metrô for ticket prices, schedules, and locations of metrô stations.

🖪 Metrô Information **Departamento de Marketing Institucional** ⊠ Av. Paulista 1842, 19th floor, Jardins ☎ 011/3371–4933 Ⓜ Consolação. **Metrô** ☎ 011/3286–0111.

MONEY MATTERS

Avenida Paulista is the home of many banks (generally open 10–4), including Citibank. For currency exchange services without any extra fees, try Action. In Centro you can exchange money at Banco do Brasil and at Banespa. Several banks have automatic-teller machines (ATMs) that accept international bank cards and dispense reais.

🖪 Banks & Exchange Services **Action** ⊠ Aeroporto Cumbica, TPS2 arrival floor, Guarulhos ☎ 011/6445–4458 ⊠ Rua Melo Alves 357, Jardins ☎ 011/3064–2910 ⊠ Shopping Paulista, Rua 13 de Maio 1947, Paraíso ☎ 011/288–4222 Ⓜ Brigadeiro. **Banco do Brasil** ⊠ Av. São João 32, Centro ☎ 011/234–1646 Ⓜ República. **Banespa** ⊠ Av. Paulista 1842-Torre Norte, Jardins ☎ 011/3016–9955 Ⓜ Consolação. **Citibank** ⊠ Av. Paulista 1111, Jardins ☎ 011/5576–1190 Ⓜ Trianon-Masp.

SAFETY

Stay alert and guard your belongings at all times, especially at major sights. Avoid wearing shorts, expensive running shoes, or flashy jewelry—all of which attract attention. Also beware of the local scam in which one person throws a dark liquid on you and another offers to help you clean up while the first *really* cleans up!

TAXIS

Taxis in São Paulo are white. Owner-driven taxis are generally well maintained and reliable, as are radio taxis. Fares start at R$3.20 and run R$1.30 for each kilometer (½ mi) or R$.40 for every minute sitting in traffic. After 8 PM and on weekends fares rise by 20%. You'll also pay a tax if the taxi leaves the city, as is the case with trips to Cumbica Airport. Good radio-taxi companies include Chame Taxi, Ligue-Taxi, and Paulista.

🚩 Taxi Companies **Chame Taxi** 🕾 011/3865–3033. **Ligue-Taxi** 🕾 011/3873–2000. **Paulista** 🕾 011/3746–6555.

TELEPHONES

Phone booths are bright green and yellow. Most operate using prepaid cards, but some still use tokens. Both cards and tokens are sold at newsstands. Cards with 30 credits are sold for R$3. Each credit allows you to talk for 3 minutes on local calls and 17 seconds on long-distance calls.

International calls can be made at special phone booths found in Telesp offices around the city. You can choose your own long-distance company. After dialing 0, dial a two-digit company code, followed by the country code and/or area code and number. To call Rio, for example, dial 0, then 21 (for Embratel, a major long-distance and international provider), then 21 (Rio's area code), and then the number. To call the United States, dial 00 (for international calls), 23 (for Intelig, another long-distance company or 21 for Embratel), 1 (country code), and the area code and phone number. For operator-assisted (in English) international calls, dial 000111. To make a collect long-distance call (which will cost 40% more than normal calls), dial 9 + the area code and the number. São Paulo's area code is 11. Phone numbers in the city and state have six, seven, or eight digits. Most cellular phone numbers have eight digits (a few have seven) and start with the numeral 9.

TOURS

You can hire a bilingual guide through a travel agency or hotel concierge (about R$15 an hour with a four-hour minimum), or you can design your own walking tour with the aid of information provided at Anhembi booths around the city. Anhembi also offers Sunday tours of museums, parks, and Centro that are less expensive than those offered in hotels. The tourist board offers three half-day Sunday bus tours, one covering the parks, one centered on the museums, and one focused on the historical downtown area. Officially, none of the board's guides speaks English; however, it may be able to arrange something on request.

Gol Tour Viagens e Turismo and Opcional Tour and Guide Viagens e Turismo offer custom tours as well as car tours for small groups. A half-day city tour costs about R$40 a person (group rate); a night tour—including a samba show, dinner, and drinks—costs around R$100; and day trips to the beach or the colonial city of Embu cost R$80–R$90. The English-speaking staff at Savoy specializes in personalized tours.

Canoar is one of the best rafting tour operators in São Paulo State. Trilha Brazil arranges treks in forests around São Paulo. Reputable operators that offer rain-forest, beach, and island excursions include Biotrip, Pisa Trekking, and Venturas e Aventuras.

🛈 Tour-Operator Recommendations **Biotrip** ✉ Rua Gama Cerqueira 187, Cambuci ☎ 011/3253-7111. **Canoar** ✉ Rua Caetés 410, Sumaré ☎ 011/3871-2282. **Gol Tour Viagens e Turismo** ✉ Av. São Luís 187, Basement, Loja 12, Centro ☎ 011/3256-2388 Ⓜ República. **Opcional Tour and Guide Viagens e Turismo** ✉ Av. Ipiranga 345, 14th floor, Suite 1401, Centro ☎ 011/3259-1007 Ⓜ República. **Pisa Trekking** ✉ Alameda dos Tupiniquins 202, Moema ☎ 011/5571-2525. **Savoy** ✉ Rua James Watt 142, Suite 92, Itaim Bibi ☎ 011/5507-2064 or 011/5507-2065. **Tourist board** ☎ 011/6971-5000. **Trilha Brazil** ✉ Rua Professor Rubião Meira 86, Jardim América ☎ 011/3082-7089. **Venturas e Aventuras** ✉ Rua Minerva 268, Perdizes ☎ 011/3872-0362.

TRAIN TRAVEL

Most travel to the interior of the state is done by bus or automobile. Still, a few places are served by trains. Trains from Estação da Luz, near 25 de Março, run to some metropolitan suburbs and small interior towns. Trains from Estação Barra Funda serve towns in the west of the state. Estação Júlio Prestes, in Campos Elíseos, has trains to the southeast and some suburbs. Estação Roosevelt serves the suburbs only.

🛈 Train Information **Estação Barra Funda** ✉ Rua Mário de Andrade 664, Barra Funda ☎ 011/3612-1527 Ⓜ Barra Funda. **Estação Júlio Prestes** ✉ Praça Júlio Prestes 148, Campos Elíseos ☎ 011/220-8862. **Estação da Luz** ✉ Praça da Luz 1, Luz ☎ 011/3329-9735 Ⓜ Luz. **Estação Roosevelt** ✉ Praça Agente Cícero, Brás ☎ 011/266-4455 Ⓜ Bras.

VISITOR INFORMATION

The most helpful contact is the São Paulo Convention and Visitors Bureau, open 9–6. The sharp, business-minded director, Roberto Gheler, speaks English flawlessly and is extremely knowledgeable. Branches of the city-operated Anhembi Turismo e Eventos da Cidade de São Paulo are open daily 9–6.

The bureaucracy-laden Secretaria de Esportes e Turismo do Estado de São Paulo, open weekdays 9–6, has maps and information about the city and state of São Paulo. SEST also has a booth at the arrivals terminal in Cumbica airport; it's open daily 9 AM–10 PM.

🛈 Tourist Information **Anhembi Turismo e Eventos da Cidade de São Paulo** ✉ Anhembi Convention Center, Av. Olavo Fontoura 1209, Santana ☎ 011/6224-0400 ⊕ www.cidadedesaopaulo.com ✉ Praça da República at Rua 7 de Abril, Centro Ⓜ República ✉ Av. Paulista, across from MASP, Cerqueira César Ⓜ Trianon-Masp ✉ Av. Brigadeiro Faria Lima, in front of Shopping Center Iguatemi, Jardim Paulista ✉ Av. Ribeiro de Lima 99, Luz Ⓜ Luz ✉ bus station, Tietê Ⓜ Tietê ✉ Cumbica Airport Terminals 1 and 2, Aeroporto de Guarulhos. **São Paulo Convention and Visitors Bureau** ✉ Rua Dom José de Barros 17, Centro ☎ 011/289-7588 Ⓜ República. **Secretaria de Esportes e Turismo do Estado de São Paulo** (SEST) ✉ Praça Antônio Prado 9, Centro ☎ 011/3241-5822 Ⓜ São Bento.

SIDE TRIPS FROM SÃO PAULO

Several destinations just outside São Paulo are perfect for short getaways. Embu's weekend crafts fair and many furniture stores are very popular

São Paulo State

MINAS
GERAIS

MATO GROSSO
DO SUL

SÃO PAULO

PARANÁ

ATLANTIC
OCEAN

TO BRASÍLIA

TO BELO
HORIZONTE

TO RIO

TO CURITIBA

0   150 miles
0   240 km

with city inhabitants, and you can see all the sights in an afternoon. Less than one hour away, Santana de Parnaíba mixes historical settings and regional attractions with sophisticated restaurants. For a weekend of relaxation, go northwest to soak up the healing properties of Águas de São Pedro's spas and springs. Farther away, in Brotas, you can go whitewater rafting or hike past waterfalls. If you like mountains, head up in another direction: Campos de Jordão, where cafés and clothing stores are often crowded with oh-so-chic paulistanos. Favor the state's North Shore and Ilhabela (the name means "beautiful island"), if you prefer the beach. The island is part of the Mata Atlântica (Atlantic Rain Forest) and has many waterfalls, trails, and diving spots.

Águas de São Pedro

30 *192 km (120 mi) northwest of São Paulo.*

Although Águas de São Pedro is the smallest city in Brazil, with a mere 3.6 square km (1.4 square mi), its sulfurous waters made it famous countrywide in the 1940s and '50s. The healing hot springs were discovered by chance in the 1920s when technicians were drilling for oil.

Fonte Juventude is the richest in sulfur in the Americas and is often used to treat rheumatism, asthma, bronchitis, and skin ailments. The waters at Fonte Gioconda have minor radioactive elements (and, yes, they are reportedly good for you), whereas Fonte Almeida Salles's have chlorine bicarbonate and sodium (which are said to alleviate the symptoms of diabetes and upset stomachs).

You can access the springs at the *balnéario publico* (public bathhouse) or through its hotel. You can pay to use hotel facilities whether or not you are staying there. Though a number of illnesses respond to the water, most visitors are just healthy tourists soaking in relaxation. Águas de São Pedro is compact, so it's possible to get around on foot.

♨ A walk through the woods in **Bosque Municipal Dr. Octávio Moura Andrade** (⊠ Av. Carlos Mauro) is a chance to relax. Horseback riding costs R$10 for a half hour.

♨ A good option for those with kids is **Thermas Water Park**, with its 11 pools, eight water toboggans, and minifarm. ⊠ *Km 189, SP-304* ☎ *019/ 3482–1011* ⊑ *R$25* ⊙ *Wed.–Sun. 8–6.*

Built in the Swiss style, **Capela Nossa Senhora Aparecida** (⊠ Rua Izaura de Algodoal Mauro, Jardim Porangaba) perches atop the highest part of the city. Twelve pine trees were planted around this chapel to represent the Twelve Apostles.

Balneário Municipal Dr. Octávio Moura Andrade offers immersion baths in sulfurous springwater. You can swim in the pool or sweat in the sauna while you wait for your private soak, massage, or beauty appointment. A snack bar and a gift shop round out the spa services. Guest at the Balnéario's hotel get discounts at the spa. ⊠ *Av. Carlos Mauro* ☎ *019/ 3482–1211* ⊑ *R$6–R$25* ⊙ *Mon.–Sat. 8–noon and 3–7, Sun. 8–2.*

Where to Stay & Eat

$–$$ ✕ **Patagônia.** This restaurant with international cuisine owes its contemporary flavor to the city's gastronomy students who do internships here. Duck, lamb, trout, risotto, and salt cod are the highlights. ⊠ *Av. Presidente Kennedy 876* ☎ *019/3482–1096* ⊟ V ⊙ *No lunch Wed.–Fri. No dinner Sun.*

$$–$$$$ ✕▥ **Grande Hotel São Pedro.** The beautiful art deco building was a casino during the 1940s. Now it's a teaching hotel and restaurant with all the comforts of a full-service spa. Many of the friendly staff members are students—including those who prepare dishes such as salt cod in pistachio sauce. The property is in the middle of a 300,000-square-meter park with more than 1 million trees. ⊠ *Parque Dr. Octávio de Moura Andrade* ☎ *019/3842–1211* 🖷 *019/3842–1665* ⊕ *www.sp.senac.br/ ghp* ⟋ *96 rooms, 16 suites* ♨ *2 restaurants, room service, minibars, cable TV, tennis court, pool, gym, hair salon, sauna, spa, bar, recreation room, video game room, business services, meeting rooms* ⊟ *AE, DC, MC, V.*

¢ ✕▥ **Avenida.** Guests relax on the arcaded veranda of this hotel that resembles a large ranch house. Rooms are plain but spacious. Its restaurant serves home food like *filé cubana* (steak with fried bananas and pineapple) and offers live music on Friday and Saturday. ⊠ *Av. Carlos*

Mauro 246 ☎ *019/3482–1221* 🖷 *019/3482–1223* ⊕ *www.hotelavenida. com.br* ⊃ *53 rooms* ⚷ *Restaurant, room service, fans, pool, Internet, some pets allowed; no air-conditioning* ▤ *No credit cards.*

$ 🏨 **Hotel Jerubiaçaba.** The rooms in this 30-year-old hotel are bathed in light colors and filled with simple furnishings. The 120 rooms are divided into four types, from standard to luxury, but all of them are in a 17,000 square meter green area. ⊠ *Av. Carlos Mauro 168* ☎ *019/ 3482–1411* ⊕ *www.hoteljerubiacaba.com.br* ⊃ *120 rooms, 8 suites* ⚷ *Restaurant, room service, tennis court, pool, hair salon, massage, soccer, bar, recreation room, video game room, playground, business services, meeting rooms, no-smoking floors; no air-conditioning in some rooms* ▤ *AE, DC, MC, V.*

Brotas

50 km (31 mi) from Águas de São Pedro, 242 km (151 mi) northwest of São Paulo.

No one is sure how the city of Brotas got its name. One theory is that its founder, Dona Francisca Ribeiro dos Reis, a Portuguese woman who was a devout Catholic, dedicated the site to her patron saint, Nossa Senhora das Brotas. Other people think the name originated in the abundant water springing from the landscape. (The verb *brotar* means "to sprout.")

The region has approximately 30 *cachoeiras* (waterfalls), many rivers, and endless opportunities for outdoor diversion. Jacaré-Pepira is the main river, which crosses town from east to west. Rafting is the most popular activity, but canyoning (rappelling down a waterfall), cascading (sliding down waterfalls), rappelling, biking, hiking, *bóia* crossing (floating down the river in an inner tube), and canopy walking are also available.

In Brotas most natural attractions are outside town, making a car essential. Most visitors use Brotas as a base and branch out with an arranged agency tour. Admission to some sights is free; if not, the fee is included in the price of a tour. It is essential to make travel arrangements in advance because the town has become an ecotourism mecca and is usually crowded during weekends and holidays. Insect repellent is also essential, especially on afternoon river excursions.

See both artwork and performances at the **Centro Cultural.** This 19th-century house used to be a meeting place for the rich and famous during the golden era of coffee crops in São Paulo. It now hosts a Coffee Museum that displays furniture and objects from those days. ⊠ *Av. Mário Pinotti 584* ☎ *014/653–1122* ▤ *Free* ⊗ *Tues.–Fri. 8–8, Sat. noon–8, Sun. 9–3.*

Seventeen of Brotas's waterfalls are accessible and open to visitors. The **Cachoeira Água Branca** is on D. Calila's Ranch, 22 km (13.6 mi) away from town. Relax and bathe in the fall's collection pool. On-site you can camp (R$5–R$8), or try the homemade liqueur of a small distillery. Like everything else in Brazil, it gets crowded during the summer (January–February). ⊠ *Km 20.5, Estrada Patrimônio* ☎ *014/3653–6267* ⊕ *www.brotasonline.com.br/aguabranca* ▤ *Free* ⊗ *Daily dawn–dusk.*

At **Cachoeira Três Quedas** you can take a short walk to Cachoeira das Andorinhas for a waterfall shower, then follow the trail to Cachoeira da Figueira, a 40-meter (131-foot) waterfall. On the way back stop at the smaller Cachoeirinha das Nascentes to bathe in a collection pool. ⊠*Km 21.5, Estrada Patrimônio* ☎*014/9773–6612* ⊕*www.brotasonline. com.br/cachoeirastresquedas* ⊠ *R$7* ☉ *Daily dawn–dusk.*

Cachoeira Bela Vista is one of three waterfalls formed by small streams. The 20-meter (65-foot) **Bela Vista** and **Cachoeira dos Coqueiros** are easy to get to, but a longer trek is necessary to reach the 40-meter (130-foot) **Cachoeira dos Macacos.** If you are lucky or choose to camp in the area, you may see native *macacos* (monkeys). The per-day camping fee is R$10. For R$26 you get meals and a guided walking tour. ⊠ *Km 16.5, Estrada Patrimônio, 6 km (4 mi) beyond Cachoeira Três Quedas* ☎ *014/ 3653–6183* ⊕ *www.brotasonline.com.br/campingbelavista* ⊠ *R$4* ☉ *Daily dawn–dusk.*

The last stop on the waterfalls road is **Cachoeira do Escorregador,** already on the way to Águas de São Pedro. The waterfall's natural pools are perfect for cooling off after a light hike. Camp sites (R$12 per night) and picnic spots are available, or stop at the snack bar for refreshment. ⊠*Km 36.5, Estrada Patrimônio* ☎*014/9778–4322* ⊕*www.brotasonline. com.br/escorregador* ⊠ *R$5* ☉ *Daily dawn–dusk.*

Where to Stay & Eat

$–$$ ✕ **Restaurante Casinha.** A lake view adds ambience to this family-owned restaurant. Try the delicious *pintado na brasa,* a charcoal-grilled fish made with garlic, onions, and lemon. ⊠ *Av. Lorival Jaubert da Silva Braga 1975* ☎*014/653–1225* ⊕*www.brotas.com.br/restaurantecasinha* ⊟No *credit cards* ☉ *Closed Mon.–Thurs. No lunch Fri., Sat.*

$ ✕ **Malagueta.** Those seeking light fare after a rafting or hiking excursion can find it at Malagueta, which serves grilled meat, salads, and sandwiches. A green-and-red color scheme gives the place an upbeat modern look. *Salada portofino* (lettuce, sun-dried tomatoes, mozzarella, olives, and mustard dressing) is a noteworthy choice. ⊠ *Av. Mário Pinotti 243* ☎ *014/3653–5491* ⊟ *DC, MC, V* ☉ *Closed Mon., Tues. No lunch Wed.–Fri.*

$ ⊞ **Hotel Estalagem Quinta das Cachoeiras.** In front of a park and considered one of the best places in town, this Victorian-style hotel has a staff that prides itself on providing personal attention to their guests. You are treated to a breakfast that includes European pastries and classical music. ⊠*Rua João Rebecca 225, Parque dos Saltos* ☎☎ *014/653– 2497* ⊕ *www.quintadascachoeiras.com.br* ⇌ *14 rooms* ⚬ *Minibars, cable TV, pool, sauna, recreation room; no kids under 14, no smoking* ⊟ *MC, V* ¶⊙¶ *BP.*

¢ ⊞ **Pousada Caminho das Águas.** The owners of this small downtown inn live on-site and provide a friendly place to rest—and a good breakfast. Rooms are decorated in light colors, with cool ceramic-tile floors. ⊠*Av. Mário Pinotti 1110* ☎☎ *014/653–2428* ⊕ *www.cachoeiracassorova. com.br* ⇌ *17 rooms* ⚬ *Fans, minibars, cable TV, pool; no air-conditioning, no room phones* ⊟ *V* ¶⊙¶ *BP.*

Sports & the Outdoors

White-water rafting on the Jacaré-Pepira River is best from November to May. The 9-km (5.6-mi) course ranges in difficulty from Class III to Class IV rapids, with drops of 3–9 feet.

Mata'dentro Ecoturismo e Aventura (⊠ Av. Mário Pinotti 230 ☎ 014/653–1915 ⊕ www.matadentro.com.br) is the oldest rafting operator in town. It also offers canyoning, mountain-biking, and hiking excursions. The basic rafting tour costs R$48, but there are more advanced options such as "raids," which are adventure races and other challenges, and "radical duck," which is an 8- to 10-km run through class II–IV rapids that is done in an inflatable two-person kayak. Tours are given Monday–Sunday 8–8.

Vias Naturais (⊠ Rua João Rebecca 195 ☎ 014/3653–5933 ⊕ www.viasnaturais.com.br) has many river tours, which include night rafting (at R$70 per person for a five-hour program). Horseback riding, hiking, floating, cascading, trekking, canopy walking, bóia crossing, and canyoning are also available.

Campos do Jordão

184 km (114 mi) northeast of São Paulo.

In the Serra da Mantiqueira at an altitude of 5,576 feet, Campos do Jordão and its fresh mountain air are paulistas' favorite winter attractions. In July temperatures drop as low as 32°F (0°C), though it never snows; in warmer months temperatures linger in the 13°C–16°C (55°F–60°F) range.

In the past some people came for their health (the town was once a tuberculosis treatment area), others for inspiration—including such Brazilian artists as writer Monteiro Lobato, dramatist Nelson Rodrigues, and painter Lasar Segall. Nowadays, the arts continue to thrive, especially during July's Festival de Inverno (Winter Festival), which draws classical musicians from around the world.

Exploring Campos do Jordão without a car is very difficult. The attractions are far-flung, except for those at Vila Capivari.

Boulevard Genéve, in the busy Vila Capivari district, is lined with cafés, bars, and restaurants, making it a nightlife hub. You can also find plenty of candy shops full of chocolate (the town's specialty), as well as clothing stores.

Palácio Boa Vista, the official winter residence of the state's governor, has paintings by such famous Brazilian modernists as Di Cavalcanti, Portinari, Volpi, Tarsila do Amaral, and Anita Malfatti. The associated **Capela de São Pedro** (São Pedro Chapel) has sacred art from the 17th and 18th centuries. ⊠ Av. Dr. Adhemar de Barros 300 ☎ 012/262–1122 ☞ R$5 ⊙ Wed., Thurs., weekends 10–noon and 2–5.

Horto Florestal is a natural playground for *macacos-prego* (nail monkeys), squirrels, and parrots, as well as for people. The park has a trout-filled river, waterfalls, and trails—all set among trees from around the world and one of the last *araucária* (Brazilian pine) forests in the state. ⊠ Av. Pedro Paulo ☎ 012/263–3762 ☞ R$3–R$4 ⊙ Daily 8–6.

Outside town, a chair-lift ride to the top of **Morro do Elefante** (Elephant Hill) is a good way to enjoy the view from a 2,295-foot height. ⊠ *Av. José Oliveira Damas s/n* 🕾 *012/263–1530* 🖃 *R$5* ⊘ *Tues.–Fri. 1–5, weekends 9–5:30.*

The athletically inclined can walk 3 km (2 mi) and climb the 300-step stone staircase to **Pedra do Baú** (⊠ Km 25, Estrada São Bento do Sapucaí), a 6,400-foot monolithic trio of rocks inside an ecotourism park north of the city. A trail starts in nearby São Bento do Sapucaí, and it's recommended you hire a guide. In the park you can also practice horseback riding, canopy walking, trekking, or mountain-climbing and spend the night in a dormlike room shared with other visitors.

Where to Stay & Eat

$–$$ ✕ **Baden-Baden.** One of the specialties at this charming German restaurant in the heart of town is sauerkraut *garni* (sour cabbage with German sausages). The typical dish serves two and is almost as popular as Baden-Baden's own brewery, which is open to visitors from 10–5 on weekdays. On weekends, call to set up an appointment. ⊠ *Rua Djalma Forjaz 93, Loja 10* 🕾 *012/263–3610* 🖃 *AE, DC, MC, V.*

$–$$ ✕ **Itália Cantina e Ristorante.** As its name suggests, this place specializes in Italian food. The pasta and the meat dishes are delicious, but you can also try trout, lamb, fondue, and even boar dishes. ⊠ *Av. Macedo Soares 306* 🕾 *012/263–1140* 🖃 *AE, DC, MC, V.*

¢ ✕ **Cyber Café.** At this downtown café it's possible to taste hot cocoa with crepes and pies while you browse the Internet. ⊠ *Rua Djalma Forjaz 100, Loja 15* 🕾 *012/3663–6351* ⊕ *www.cybercafeboulevard.com.br* 🖃 *No credit cards.*

$ 🏨 **Lausanne Hotel.** In an enormous ecopark 7 km (4 mi) outside town, this hotel offers plenty of solitude and the chance to commune with nature. ⊠ *Km 176, Rodovia SP-050* 🕾 *012/262–2985* 🖃 *011/262–2900* ⊕ *www.lausannehotel.com.br* 🛏 *25 rooms* ⚒ *Restaurant, minibars, cable TV, tennis court, pool, soccer, bar, recreation room, Internet, some pets allowed* 🖃 *DC, MC, V.*

$ 🏨 **Pousada Vila Capivary.** A stay at this cozy guest house puts you in the gastronomic and commercial center of Campos. The friendly staff is helpful and efficient. Most apartments have balconies, and the five suites have whirlpool baths. ⊠ *Av. Victor Godinho 131* 🕾 *012/263–1746* 🖃 *012/263–1714* ⊕ *www.villacapivary.com.br* 🛏 *10 rooms, 5 suites* ⚒ *In-room safes, minibars, some in-room hot tubs, cable TV, bar, recreation room* 🖃 *AE, DC, MC, V.*

Shopping

Casa de Chocolates Montanhês (⊠ Praça São Benedito 45, Loja 6 🕾 012/263–1979 ⊕ www.chocolatemontanhes.com.br) is a well-known chocolate shop whose prices start at R$48 per kilo (2 pounds). The best handmade embroidered clothing in town is at **Maison Geneve** (⊠ Rua Djalma Forjaz 100, Lojas 1 a 3 🕾 012/263–2520 ⊕ www.geneve.com. br), open weekdays 10–7 and weekends 10–10. For knit items try **Paloma Malhas** (⊠ Rua Djalma Forjaz 78, Loja 11 🕾 012/262–4504), open weekdays 10–7 and weekends 10–10.

OS BANDEIRANTES

N THE 16TH AND 17TH CENTURIES groups called bandeiras (literally, "flags," but also an archaic term for an assault force) set out on expeditions from São Paulo. Although the bandeirantes (bandeira members) are remembered by some as heroes, their initial goal was to enslave Native Americans. Later, they were hired to capture escaped African slaves and destroy quilombos (communities the slaves created deep in the interior). Still, by heading inland at a time when most colonies were close to the shore, the bandeirantes inadvertently did Brazil a great service.

A fierce breed, they often adopted indigenous customs and voyaged for years at a time. Some went as far as the Amazon River; others discovered gold in present-day Minas Gerais; still others found precious gems. They ignored the 1494 Treaty of Tordesillas, which established a boundary between Spanish and Portuguese lands. (The boundary was a vague north–south line roughly 1,600 km/1,000 mi west of the Cape Verde islands; the Portuguese were to control all lands—discovered or not—east of this line and the Spanish all lands to the west of it.) Other Brazilians followed the bandeirantes, and towns were founded, often in what was technically Spanish territory. These colonists eventually claimed full possession of the lands they settled, and thus Brazil's borders were greatly expanded.

A huge granite monument near Parque Ibirapuera, inaugurated in 1953 to honor the bandeirantes, was sculpted by famous Brazilian artist Victor Brecheret. It is often a site of protests staged by those who don't believe the bandeirantes deserve a monument.

Embu

27 km (17 mi) west of São Paulo.

Founded in 1554, Embu is a tiny Portuguese colonial town of white-washed houses, old churches, wood-carvers' studios, and antiques shops. It hosts a downtown handicrafts fair every Saturday and Sunday. On Sunday the streets sometimes get so crowded you can barely walk. Embu also has many stores that sell handicrafts and wooden furniture; most of these are close to where the street fair takes place.

On weekends it's difficult to find a place to park in Embu, and parking lots can be expensive. Although you can easily walk to all the main sights, the *bondinho* (a "train" whose cars are pulled by a truck) crosses the town and stops at every main square.

Igreja Nossa Senhora do Rosário was built in 1690 and is a nice bet for those who won't have a chance to visit the historic cities of Minas Gerais. The church contains baroque images of saints and is next to a 1730 monastery now turned into a sacred-art museum. ✉ *Largo dos Jesuítas 67* ☎ *011/4704–3490* 🖼 *R$2* ⊙ *Weekdays 1–5, weekends 10–5.*

In the Mata Atlântica you can visit the **Cidade das Abelhas** (City of the Bees), a bee farm with a small museum. You can buy honey while your kids climb the gigantic model of a bee. It's about 10 minutes from downtown; just follow the signs. ⊠ *Km 7, Estrada da Ressaca* ☎ *011/ 4703–6460* ✑ *R$4* ⊘ *Tues.–Sun. 8:30–5.*

Where to Eat

¢–$$ ✕ **O Garimpo.** In a large room with a fireplace or around outdoor tables, choose between Brazilian regional dishes such as the house specialty, *moqueca de badejo* (spicy fish stew), and German classics such as *Eisbein.* ⊠ *Rua da Matriz 136* ☎ *011/4704–6344* ⊟ *AE, DC, MC, V.*

¢–$$ ✕ **Os Girassóis Restaurante e Choperia.** A great variety of dishes is served at this downtown restaurant next to an art gallery. The *picanha brasileira* (barbecued steak with french fries and manioc flour) is recommended. ⊠ *Largo dos Jesuítas 169* ☎ *011/4781–6671* ⊟ *AE, DC, MC, V* ⊘ *No dinner Mon., Tues.*

$ ✕ **Patacão.** In this colonial-style spot you find contemporary versions of country plates, but no salads or juices. Go for the exotic *picadinho jesuítico* (round-steak stew with corn, fried bananas, and raisins sautéed with manioc flour). Unlike most restaurants in the city, Patacão serves one-person portions. ⊠ *Rua Joaquim Santana 95* ☎ *011/4704–2053* ⊟ *No credit cards* ⊘ *Closed Mon.*

Shopping

Atelier Lustres Medieval (⊠ Largo 21 de Abril 183 ☎ 011/4704–2903) specializes in decorator lighting fixtures. The place is 25 years old and has different kinds of table lamps, floor lamps, and ceiling lamps. **Cantão Móveis e Galeria** (⊠ Largo dos Jesuítas 169 ☎ 011/4781–6671) is a good place to buy ceramics, colonial-style furniture, and antique decorations. **Fenix Galeria de Artes** (⊠ Rua Marechal Isidoro Lopes 10 ☎ 011/4704–5634) is a good place to find oil paintings as well as wood and stone sculptures.

Galeria Jozan (⊠ Rua Nossa Senhora do Rosarío 59 ☎ 011/4781–0848) sells unmounted Brazilian gemstones, such as *ametistas* (amethysts) and crystals, which you can have set as you wish. **Guarani Artesanato** (⊠ Largo dos Jesuítas 153 ☎ 011/4704–3200) sells handicrafts made of wood and stone, including sculptures carved from *pau-brasil* (brazilwood). **Real Móveis Rústicos** (⊠ Av. Elias Yazbek 2322 ☎ 011/4781–5857) is one of the largest locations in town at which to buy furniture. The store makes the items it sells.

Ilhabela

FodorśChoice ★ *São Sebastião is 210 km (130 mi) southeast of São Paulo; Ilhabela is 7 km (5 mi)—a 15-min boat ride—from São Sebastião.*

Ilhabela is favored by those who like the beach and water sports; indeed, many championship competitions are held here. This is the biggest sea island in the country, with 22 calm beaches along its western shore, which faces the mainland. The hotels are mostly at the north end, though the best sandy stretches are the 13 to the south, which face the open sea.

There are two small towns on the island: one is where the locals live; the other is where most visitors stay because of its hotels, restaurants, and stores. During the winter months most businesses that cater to tourists, including restaurants, are open only on weekends.

Scuba divers have several 19th- and early-20th-century wrecks to explore—this region has the most wrecks of any area off Brazil's seashore—and hikers can set off on the numerous inland trails, many of which lead to a waterfall (the island has more than 300). Mosquitoes are a problem; bring plenty of insect repellent.

The best way to get around Ilhabela is by car, which you must rent on the mainland. The ferry from São Sebastião transports vehicles as well as passengers to the island. However, public buses do cross the island from north to south daily.

Praia Grande (✉ 6 km/4 mi south of ferry dock) has a long sandy strip with food kiosks, a soccer field, and a small church. At night people gather at **Praia do Curral** (✉ 6 km/4 mi south of Praia Grande), where there are many restaurants and bars—some with live music—as well as places to camp. The wreck of the ship *Aymoré* (1921) can be found off the coast of this beach, near Ponta do Ribeirão.

A small church and many fishing boats add to the charm of **Praia da Armação** (✉ 14 km/9 mi north of ferry dock). The beach was once the site of a factory for processing blubber and other resources from whales caught in the waters around the island. Today windsurfers stick to capturing the wind and the waves.

To reach **Baía dos Castelhanos** (✉ 22 km/14 mi east of the ferry dock), you need a four-wheel-drive vehicle, and if it rains, even this won't be enough. Consider arriving by sailboat, which demands a 1½- to 3-hour trip that can be arranged through local tour operators. With such an isolated location, you can see why slave ships once used the bay to unload their illicit cargo after slavery was banned in Brazil. If you're lucky, you might spot a dolphin.

Where to Stay & Eat

$–$$ ✕ **Ilha Sul.** The best option on the menu is the grilled shrimp with vegetables. Fish and other seafood are also available. ✉ *Av. Riachuelo 287* ☎ *012/3894–9426* ▭ *AE, DC, MC, V* ☉ *Closed Mon.–Thurs. Apr.–June and Aug.–Nov.*

★ $–$$ ✕ **Viana.** This restaurant serves *camarão* (shrimp) prepared in various ways, as well as grilled fish. There are only a few tables, so make a reservation. ✉ *Av. Leonardo Reale 1560* ☎ *012/3896–1089* ▭ *No credits cards* ☉ *Closed Mon.–Thurs. Apr.–June and Aug.–Nov.*

$$$$ ✕🏨 **Maison Joly.** On arrival at this exclusive hotel on top of the Cantagalo Hill, you're given a beach kit complete with mosquito repellent and a hat. Each of the 10 rooms is equipped with something that gives it a theme, such as a piano, a billiard table, or a telescope—and all have balconies facing the sea. The hotel's starred restaurant opens for guests only. ✉ *Rua Antônio Lisboa Alves 278* ☎ *012/3896–1201* 🖨 *012/3896–2364* ⊕ *www.maisonjoly.com.br* 🛏 *10 rooms* ♿ *Restaurant,*

FodorśChoice ★

in-room safes, in-room hot tubs, minibars, cable TV, pool, massage, bar, piano, Internet, meeting rooms; no kids ⊟ *AE, DC, MC, V.*

★ ¢-$ ⊡ **Pousada dos Hibiscos.** North of the ferry dock, this red house has mid-size rooms, all at ground level. The friendly staff serves up a good breakfast and provides poolside bar service. Each room has its own unique decoration, which adds a touch of charm to this cozy lodge. ⊠ *Av. Pedro de Paula Moraes 714* 🕾🕾 *012/3896–1375* ⊕ *www.pousadadoshibiscos. com.br* ⇱ *13 rooms* ⚬ *Fans, in-room safes, minibars, pool, gym, sauna, bar* ⊟ *DC, MC, V.*

Sports & the Outdoors

<table>
<tr><td>BOATING &
SAILING</td><td>Because of its excellent winds and currents, Ilhabela is a sailor's mecca. You can arrange boating and sailing trips through Maremar Turismo (⊠ Av. Princesa Isabel 90 🕾 012/3896–3680 ⊕ www.maremar.tur.br), one of the biggest tour agencies in Ilhabela. Maremar also has sailing courses and other activities, ranging from historical tours to off-road adventures.</td></tr>
</table>

For information on annual boating competitions that Ilhabela hosts, including a popular sailing week, contact **Iate Club de Ilhabela** (⊠ Av. Força Expedicionária Brasileira 299 🕾012/3896–2300). **Ilha Sailing Ocean School** (⊠ Av. Pedro de Paula Moraes 578 🕾 012/3896–1992 ⊕ www. ilhasailing.com.br) has 12-hour sailing courses that cost roughly R$240.

HIKING   The **Cachoeira dos Três Tombos** trail starts at Feiticeira Beach and leads to three waterfalls. **Trilha da Água Branca** is an accessible, well-marked trail. Three of its paths go to waterfalls that have natural pools and picnic areas. You can arrange guided hikes through local agencies such as **Espaço Ecológico** (⊠ Av. Princesa Isabel 605 🕾 012/3896–3557 ⊕ www. espacoecologico.com.br).

SCUBA DIVING   Ilhabela has several good dive sites off its shores. In 1884, the British ship *Darth* sank near **Itaboca** (⊠ 17 km/11 mi south of ferry dock). It still contains bottles of wine and porcelain dishes. **Ilha de Búzios** (⊠ 25 km/15 mi offshore; take boat from São Sebastião), one of the three main Ilhabela islands, is a good place to see a variety of marine life. For beginners the recommended diving spot is the sanctuary off the shore of islet **Ilha das Cabras** (⊠ 2 km/1 mi south of ferry). It has a statue of Neptune at a 22-foot depth.

You can rent equipment, take diving classes, and arrange for a dive-boat trip through **Colonial Diver** (⊠ Av. Brasil 1751 🕾 012/3894–9459 ⊕ www.colonialdiver.com.br). The basic course takes from three to four days and costs around R$750.

SURFING   One of the best places to surf is **Baía de Castelhanos** (⊠ 22 km/14 mi east of ferry dock). **Pacuíba** (⊠ 20 km/12 mi north of ferry dock) has decent wave action. Surfing activities are among the specialties of **Lokal Adventure** (⊠ Av. Princesa Isabel 171 🕾 012/3896–5770 ⊕ www. ilhabela.com.br/lokal), which also promotes tours to isolated communities on the island and rents buggies and motorbikes.

KITE SURFING &   Savvy kite surfers and windsurfers head to **Ponta das Canas,** at the is-
WINDSURFING   land's northern tip. Side-by-side beaches **Praia do Pinto and Armação** (⊠ 12

km/7 mi north of ferry dock) also have favorable wind conditions. You can take windsurfing and sailing lessons at **BL3** (✉ Av. Pedro Paulo de Moraes 1166 ☎ 012/3896–1034 ✉ Armação Beach ☎ 012/3896–1271), the biggest school in Ilhabela. A 12-hour course costs about R$360. For kite surfing try **Tornado Sailing** (✉ Av. Princesa Isabel 423 ☎ 012/3896–2485) instead.

Santana de Parnaíba

42 km (26 mi) northwest of São Paulo.

With more than 200 preserved houses from the 18th and 19th centuries, Santana de Parnaíba is considered the "Ouro Preto from São Paulo"—a town rich with history and colonial architecture. Santana was founded in 1580; by 1625 it was the third village in the state and the most important point of departure for the *bandeirantes*.

In 1901 the first hydroelectric power station in South America was built here. Throughout the 20th century, Santana managed to retain its houses and charm while preserving a local tradition: a rural type of *samba* called "de bumbo," in which the pacing is marked by the *zabumba* (an instrument usually associated with rhythms from the northeastern states of Brazil). The proximity to a couple of São Paulo's finest suburbs grants the region its fine dining. Outdoor lovers feel at home with the canopy-walking and trekking options. On weekends parking is scarce in Santana de Parnaíba, and parking lots can be expensive.

Begin your trip by appreciating the colonial architecture of the **Centro Histórico**, with its more than 200 well-preserved houses. All of them are concentrated around three streets: Suzana Dias, André Fernandes, and Bartolomeu Bueno—two of which are named after famous bandeirantes. The streets still follow the same path as in the 18th century.

Museu Casa do Anhanguera provides an even sharper picture of the bandeirantes era. In a 1600 house (the second oldest in the state) where Bartolomeu Bueno—nicknamed Anhanguera, or "old devil," by the Indians—was born, the museum displays objects and furniture from the past four centuries. ✉ *Largo da Matriz 9* ☉ *Weekdays 8–4:30, weekends 11–5.*

Igreja Matriz de Sant'Anna reminds visitors of the importance of Catholicism in Brazil since colonial times. Built in the same square as Casa do Anhanguera in 1610 and restored in 1880, this baroque church has terracotta sculptures and an altar with gold-plated details. ✉ *Largo da Matriz* ☉ *Daily 8–5.*

Head back to the 21st century by participating in the weekend activities organized by the restaurant **Aldeia Cocar**, which include canopy walking and trekking. A half-hour of canopy walking costs R$30. ✉ *Estrada do Belo Vale 11, Km 32, SP-280* ☎ *011/4192–3073* ☉ *Fri., Sat. 11–11, Sun. 11–5.*

Travessia do Caminho do Sol (☎ 011/4154–2422) is a 240-km (150 mi) trail that passes by 13 villages and crosses small rivers and cane plantations. The trail is considered the local version of the famous Camino de Santiago, in Spain. Call ahead to join a group hike.

Where to Eat

$$$ ✕ **Barone.** The combination of setting (in a 1905 house) and fine contemporary cuisine at this restaurant is not to be missed. Italian and French accents punctuate the menu, which carries lamb-, shrimp-, and boar-based dishes, among several options. ✉ *Praça 14 de Novembro 101* ☎ *011/4154–2679* ▭ *No credit cards* ⊘ *No dinner Mon.–Wed.*

$$–$$$ ✕ **Dom Afonso de Vimioso.** Drink and eat like the Portuguese colonists used to—in the motherland, at least. Options include fine wines and more than 10 dishes made with salt cod. Don't go away without trying typical sweets such as *pastéis de Santa Clara* (yolk and sugar-filled pastries). ✉ *Km 36, Estrada dos Romeiros* ☎ *011/4151–1935* ▭ *AE, DC, MC, V.*

☾ $–$$$ ✕ **Aldeia Cocar.** In a 86,111-square-foot green area, Aldeia offers Brazilian specialties in a native-style atmosphere. *Arrumadinho* (sun-dried meat with mashed pumpkin and collard greens) is an excellent choice. ✉ *Estrada do Belo Vale 11, Km 32, SP-280* ☎ *011/4192–3073* ▭ *V* ⊘ *Closed Mon.–Wed. No lunch Thurs., no dinner Sun.*

$–$$ ✕ **São Paulo Antigo.** In a century-old ranch-style house, taste *caipira* (rural) dishes such as *dobradinha com feijão branco* (intestines and white-bean stew) or *galinha atolada* (rural-style hen stew). The grand finale is a free optional carriage ride around the town's main square. ✉ *Rua Álvaro Luiz do Valle 66* ☎ *011/4154–2726* ▭ *DC, MC, V* ⊘ *No dinner weekdays.*

Side Trips from São Paulo A to Z

To research prices, get advice from other travelers, and book travel arrangements, visit www.fodors.com.

BOAT & FERRY TRAVEL

Make reservations for the ferry from São Sebastião to Ilhabela, particularly December–February. *Balsas* (ferries) run every 30 minutes from 6 AM to midnight and hourly during the night. The fare ranges from R$7.60 (weekdays) to R$11.40 (weekends), including a car.

🖪 **São Sebastião balsa** ✉ Take Av. São Sebastião from town to the coast, São Sebastião ☎ 0800/55-5510.

BUS TRAVEL

Buses to most cities in São Paulo State leave from the Terminal Tietê in the city of São Paulo. These include São Pedro buses, which run daily to Águas de São Pedro; Viação Litorânea buses, which travel five times daily to Ilhabela (via ferry); and Viação Mantiqueira buses, which leave for Campos do Jordão every two hours. Buses to Brotas, operated by Viação Piracicabanam depart three times a day from the Terminal Barra Funda, in the western part of the city. Socicam, a private company, runs all of the city's bus terminals and lists schedules on its Web site. There are no interstate buses to Santana de Parnaíba and Embu. To find out where in São Paulo to catch the correct city bus, dial ☎ 158. For city buses, you can usually buy tickets on the bus.

All bus terminals in the city of São Paulo are connected to metrô stations.
🚩 Bus Information **Socicam** ☎ 011/3235-0322 ⊕ www.socicam.com.br. **São Pedro**
☎ 011/6221-0038. **Terminal Barra Funda** ✉ Rua Mário de Andrade 664, Barra Funda
São Paulo ☎ 011/3235-0322 from 6 AM to 11:30 PM, 011/3612-1782 at other times Ⓜ Barra
Funda. **Terminal Tietê** ✉ Av. Cruzeiro do Sul 1800 Santana, São Paulo ☎ 011/3235-0322
from 6 AM to 11:30 PM Ⓜ Tietê. **Viação Litorânea** ☎ 011/6221-0244. **Viação Mantiqueira** ☎ 011/6221-0244. **Viação Piracicabana** ☎ 011/6221-8711.

CAR TRAVEL

Roads in São Paulo State are in good condition and are well marked;
some of them are toll roads. To make the 30-minute drive from São Paulo
to Embu, drive from Avenida Professor Francisco Morato to Rodovia
Régis Bittencourt and then follow the signs. To reach Santana de Par-
naíba from São Paulo—a 40-minute drive—take the express lane of
Rodovia Castelo Branco and pay attention to the road signs. Águas de
São Pedro is about a 2½-hour drive on SP 330, SP 340, and SP 304. To
reach Campos do Jordão from the city (also a 2½-hour drive), take
Rodovia Carvalho Pinto and SP 123. The drive from São Paulo to São
Sebastião is about 2½ hours; take Rodovia Ayrton Senna, followed by
Rodovia Tamoios to Caraguatatuba, and then follow the signs until you
reach the ferry boat to Ilhabela. Brotas is three hours from São Paulo
on SP 330 and SP 340, SP 310, and SP 225.

EMERGENCIES

🚩 Hospitals & Clinics **Centro de Saúde** ✉ Rua Padre Bronislau Chereck 15, Ilhabela
☎ 012/3896-1222. **Fundação de Saúde** ✉ Rua Antônio Feijó 52, Águas de São Pedro
☎ 019/3482-1721. **Pronto Socorro Municipal** ✉ Av. Elias Yazbek 1415, Embu ☎ 011/
4704-5744. **Santa Casa** ✉ Rua Fernão Dias Falcão 100, Santana de Parnaíba ☎ 011/
4154-2234. **Santa Teresinha** ✉ Av. Rua Barbosa 703, Brotas ☎ 014/653-1200. **São Paulo**
✉ Rua Agripino Lopes de Morais 1100, Campos do Jordão ☎ 012/262-1722.
🚩 Hot Lines **Ambulance** ☎ 912. **Fire** ☎ 193. **Police** ☎ 190.
🚩 24-Hour Pharmacies **Drogaria Estância** ✉ Av. Carlos Mauro 368, Águas de São
Pedro ☎ 019/3482-1478. **Drogaria Nossa Senhora das Dores** ✉ Av. Rui Barbosa 517,
Centro, Brotas ☎ 014/653-1619. **Drogaria Nova Esperança** ✉ Rua da Padroeira 73, Il-
habela ☎ 012/472-1183.

ENGLISH-LANGUAGE MEDIA

Ponto das Letras, in Ilhabela, has a small café-bookstore with international magazines.
🚩 Bookstore **Ponto das Letras** ✉ Rua Dr. Carvalho 146, Ilhabela ☎ 012/3896-2104.

MONEY MATTERS

Embu has a branch of Bradesco, as does Águas de São Pedro. Brotas is
served by Banco do Brasil, just like Santana de Parnaíba, which also has
Unibanco, Banespa, and Bradesco. In Campos do Jordão there's an ATM
at the Parque Centro Shop; banks include Bradesco and Itaú. Ilhabela
has both Banespa and Bradesco branches. It is best to change money in
São Paulo.
🚩 Banks **Banco do Brasil** ✉ Av. Rodolfo Guimarães 673, Brotas. **Banespa** ✉ Rua
Dr. Carvalho 98, Ilhabela. **Bradesco** ✉ Praça Cel. Julião M. Negrão 29, Ilhabela ✉ Rua

Boulevard Francisco P. Carneiro 28, Campos ✉ Rua Maranhão 44, Embu ✉ Rua João B. Azevedo 269, Águas de São Pedro. **Itaú** ✉ Av. Pelinca 19 Campos.

TOURS

Lokal Adventure leads tours of Ilhabela by boat, bike, horse, or jeep. Another Ilhabela operator is Maremar, which has scuba-diving, jeep, horse-back-riding, and hiking tours. HS Turismo offers five tours in or around Campos do Jordão. Also in Campos do Jordão, trains depart from Estação Ferroviária Emílio Ribas on tours of the city and its environs, including the 47-km (29-mi) trip to Reino das Águas Claras, where there's a park with waterfalls.

🚩 Tour-Operator Recommendations **Estação Ferroviária Emílio Ribas** ✉ Av. Dr. Januário Miráglia, Vila Capivari, Campos do Jordão ☎ 012/262-1531. **HS Turismo** ✉ Rua Carlina Antonia Sirin 65, Campos do Jordão ☎ 012/262-2759. **Lokal Adventure** ✉ Av. Princesa Isabel 171, Ilhabela ☎ 012/3896-5770. **Maremar** ✉ Av. Princesa Isabel 90, Ilhabela ☎ 012/3896-3680.

VISITOR INFORMATION

🚩 Tourist Information **Águas de São Pedro Informações Turísticas** ✉ Av. Carlos Mauro in front of Balneário, Águas de São Pedro ☎ 019/3482-1811 ⊕ www.aguasdesaopedro. sp.gov.br. **Brotas Informações Turísticas-Centro Cultural** ✉ Av. Mário Pinotti 584, Brotas ☎ 014/653-1107 ⊕ www.brotas.tur.br. **Campos do Jordão Tourist Office** ✉ At entrance to town, Campos do Jordão ☎ 012/3664-2755 ⊕ www.portaldecampos.com. br. **Embu Secretaria do Turismo** ✉ Largo 21 de Abril 139, Embu ☎ 011/4704-6077 ⊕ www. embu.sp.gov.br. **Ilhabela Secretaria do Turismo** ✉ Rua Bartolomeu de Gusmão 140, Ilhabela ☎ 012/3896-1091 ⊕ www.ilhabela.sp.gov.br.

THE SOUTH

3

Updated by
Carlos G.
Tornquist

EXPECT THE UNEXPECTED IN THE SOUTHERN STATES of Paraná, Santa Catarina, and Rio Grande do Sul. The climate is remarkably cooler (the highest elevations even get a couple of inches of snow every year) and the topography more varied than in the rest of Brazil. Further, you're as likely to find people of German and Italian ancestry as Portuguese. And as Brazil's breadbasket, the Região Sul (southern region) has a standard of living comparable to many developed nations.

The southern section of the Serra do Mar, a mountain range along the coast, stretches well into Rio Grande do Sul. It looks like one green wall—broken only by the occasional canyon or waterfall—separating the interior from the shore. Most mountainsides are still covered with the luxuriant Mata Atlântica (Atlantic Rain Forest), which is as diverse and impressive as the forest of the Amazon. The Serra do Mar gives way to hills that roll gently westward to the valleys of the *rios* (rivers) Paraná and Uruguay. Most of these lands were originally covered with dense subtropical forests interspersed with natural rangelands such as the Campos Gerais, in the north, and the Brazilian pampas, in the south.

Although Portugal controlled the continent's Atlantic coast from the Amazon to the Rio de la Plata delta for more than a century after discovering Brazil, the Spanish influence was greatly felt throughout the interior. In the late 1500s Jesuit missionaries ventured into the valleys of the rios Paraná, Paraguay, and Uruguay, converting (and dominating) the region's native Guarani peoples. The Jesuits and their converts lived in self-sustaining *missões* (mission communities) built around magnificent churches. In the late 1600s these settlements were increasingly attacked by *bandeirantes* (slave hunters and adventurers), who sought labor for the gold mines of Minas Gerais.

By 1750, when the Treaty of Madrid, which recognized Portuguese rule in what is roughly today's Brazil, was signed, the Jesuits were gone, the native peoples were either enslaved or dispersed in the wilderness, and most of the missões were in ruins. Border issues were more or less resolved, and Portuguese settlement increased. In these early days cattle raising was the activity of choice. A large number of *charqueadas* (ranches where cattle was slaughtered and the meat salted and sun-dried by slaves before export) evolved in the late 1800s. This business was so profitable that "cattle barons" turned small cities into bustling commercial hubs. Although not as significant today, cattle culture still dominates these southern areas.

Perhaps the greatest transformation in the region followed the arrival of German and Italian colonizers. These immigrants brought along centuries of old-world farming and wine-making traditions. Many also contributed greatly to urbanization and industrialization, which in turn brought about socioeconomic improvements still evident today.

About the Restaurants

Café colonial is the elaborate 5 PM tea that's very popular among the Germans and a dieter's nightmare (the term is also used to refer to the establishment where it is served). Coffee and tea are served—for a set price—with a variety of breads, pies, German kuchen, honey, butter, and

If you have 5 days

Base yourself in ⊡ **Florianópolis**, taking time to visit the colonial forts and the bustling northern beaches on a schooner tour on your first day. Save the second day for the southern beaches and a trek to **Lagoinha do Leste.** On the third day take time to visit **Porto Belo** or **Garopaba** for diving, surfing, or whale-watching. On Day 4 fly to the remarkable ⊡ **Foz do Iguaçu** and explore both the Brazilian side of the falls and the **Itaipú Dam** in one day. Spend your last day exploring the Argentine side of the falls.

If you have 7 days

Start off in ⊡ **Curitiba** ①–⑦ ⌐, using Day 1 to visit Niemeyer's **Novo Museu** ⑦ and the **Jardim Botânico** and the other city parks; take the next day to travel by train to **Paranaguá** through the scenic Serra da Graciosa. Then head out for a three-day visit to ⊡ **Foz do Iguaçu**. If you opt to drive, make a stop at **Vila Velha State Park.** From Foz fly to ⊡ **Florianópolis** ⑭ for two days on the beaches of the island and the historical forts. Make sure to hike to the tiny secluded beach of Lagoinha do Leste.

If you have 10 days

For your explorations of southern Brazil in ⊡ **Foz do Iguaçu**, reserve two days to visit both the Brazilian and Argentine side of the falls and the **Itaipú Dam.** Then move on to ⊡ **Curitiba** ①–⑦ to experience the European atmosphere and temperate climate; be sure to go to the **Novo Museu** ⑦. On Day 4 take the train tour to **Paranaguá** returning to Curitiba in the evening. Next fly to ⊡ **Florianópolis** to enjoy its many beaches by land on Day 5 and on a schooner tour the following day. Take Day 7 to go either to **Porto Belo** or **Garopaba** ⑯ for whale-watching and snorkeling, or go to **Blumenau** to experience German culture in southern Brazil. The following day fly to ⊡ **Porto Alegre** ⑧–⑮. Then head north for a visit to the Serra Gaúcha for one day. On your last day see the fantastic canyons at **Parque Nacional dos Aparados da Serra** or get acquainted with the South's early history at the missions.

---

several kinds of jelly. For dessert there are fruit creams (puréed fruit mixed with cream) and ice cream.

About the Hotels

The south has a great variety of hotels and inns, though upscale facilities are limited. Except for in the smallest towns and most remote areas, however, you shouldn't have a problem finding comfortable accommodations. *Pousadas,* simple inns usually in vintage houses, are common, particularly in beach towns. A recent trend associated with ecotourism is the *hotel-fazenda,* a farm with guest facilities that often include meals, horseback riding, and visits to local attractions in its rates. Southern beaches attract many Argentine tourists, so seaside cities might become crowded from December through March, depending on the exchange rate between the currencies. There's usually enough lodging for this influx of visitors (though you'd be wise to reserve in advance), but traffic on highways and crowding on beaches can be nightmares.

WHAT IT COSTS In Reais				
	$$$$	**$$$**	**$$**	**$**	**¢**
RESTAURANTS	over $60	$45–$60	$30–$45	$15–$30	under $15
HOTELS	over $500	$375–$500	$250–$375	$125–$250	under $125

Restaurant prices are for a dinner entrée. Hotel prices are for two people in a standard double room in high season, excluding taxes.

Exploring the South

Touring this region—roughly the size of France—in a short time is a challenge, even though the transportation network is relatively efficient. The major hubs include Curitiba, capital of the region's northernmost state of Paraná, and the Foz do Iguaçu, way to the west; Florianópolis, the capital of the central Santa Catarina State; and Porto Alegre, capital of the southernmost state of Rio Grande do Sul.

The region can be divided into two large but more or less homogeneous areas—the coast and the interior—both of which should be visited. The coast has great beaches, forested slopes, canyons, the peaks and valleys of the Serra do Mar, and Santa Catarina's German colonies. Trips to the interior can include Iguaçu, Vila Velha and Curitiba in Paraná, the missões and the mountains of Rio Grande do Sul.

Timing

December through March is invariably hot and humid. Rainfall is high and evenly distributed throughout the year, although some years have had extremely rainy El Niño–related summers. January and February are top vacation months, so expect crowded beaches, busy highways, and higher prices. Winter (April–November) brings much cooler temperatures, sometimes as low as the upper 20s in the higher elevations at night. Cold fronts blowing in from Patagonia can bring gray, blustery days.

PARANÁ

The state of Paraná is best known for the Foz do Iguaçu, a natural wonder, and the Itaipú Dam, an engineering marvel. At one time the rolling hills of the state's plateau were covered with forests dominated by the highly prized Paraná pine, an umbrella-shape conifer. Most of these pine forests were logged by immigrants half a century ago, and the cleared land of the immense interior is now where soybeans, wheat, and coffee are grown. (Still, be on the lookout for the occasional Paraná pine.) The state has a very short coastline, but the beaches and the Serra do Mar are spectacular. Curitiba, the upbeat capital, ranks as a top Brazilian city in efficiency, innovative urban planning, and quality of life.

3

Gaúcho Cuisine

Southern Brazilians may be essentially carnivorous people, but their cuisine is eclectic: rice and beans sit on southern tables right beside Italian or German dishes. In the state capitals and larger cities you can find a variety of international cuisines, though not as readily as you can in São Paulo or Rio. Seafood is very popular along the coast, but don't expect elaborate recipes or seasonings. Still, the *churrasco* (barbecue), by far the most renowned southern dish and now popular throughout the country, originated in Rio Grande do Sul. This tradition is carried on in *churrascarias* (restaurants that specialize in grilled meats), where waiters bring skewers full of different meats to your table until you can eat no more—a system known as *espeto-corrido* (called *rodízio* in the north-central states). In the old days a gaúcho's daily rations consisted of beef or mutton—charbroiled on skewers over pit fires—and *mate* (a tea made from the leaves of the *ilex paraguayensis* tree), also called *chimarrão* in Rio Grande do Sul. Mate remains as popular as coffee in the south today. The *barreado* is a lesser-known dish from coastal Paraná. The original recipe called for stewing beef, bacon, potatoes, and spices for several hours in a clay pot made airtight with moistened manioc flour.

Natural Wonders

You can see the power of nature at work at one of Brazil's best-known wonders: the Foz do Iguaçu (Iguaçu Falls), at the southwestern tip of Paraná. Vila Velha, a series of strange sandstone formations in the center of Paraná, might remind you of the eerily moving landscapes of the western United States. The Serra do Mar and Superagüi regions have Mata Atlântica and almost pristine marine ecosystems. In the Aparados da Serra region of Rio Grande do Sul, gargantuan canyons are the result of millions of years of erosion.

The coastline from Paraná to the city of Torres in Rio Grande do Sul has spectacular scenery dotted with great beaches. The landscape is dominated by bays, coves, and hills that end abruptly in the sea. There are a few offshore islands, of which the largest and most visited is Ilha de Santa Catarina. South of Torres, and extending well into Uruguay, Brazil's southern neighbor, the coastline is basically a 644-km-long (400-mi-long) sandy stretch interrupted only by a few river deltas and lagoons.

Southern Wines

The slopes of the Serra Gaúcha (a mountain district in Rio Grande do Sul) were settled by Italians whose wine-making traditions flourished in the region's fertile soil. Recent agricultural and industrial developments have dramatically improved the quality of the wines from Rio Grande do Sul. The best varieties come from Caxias do Sul and Bento Gonçalves and can rightfully compete with their more renowned Chilean and Argentine counterparts.

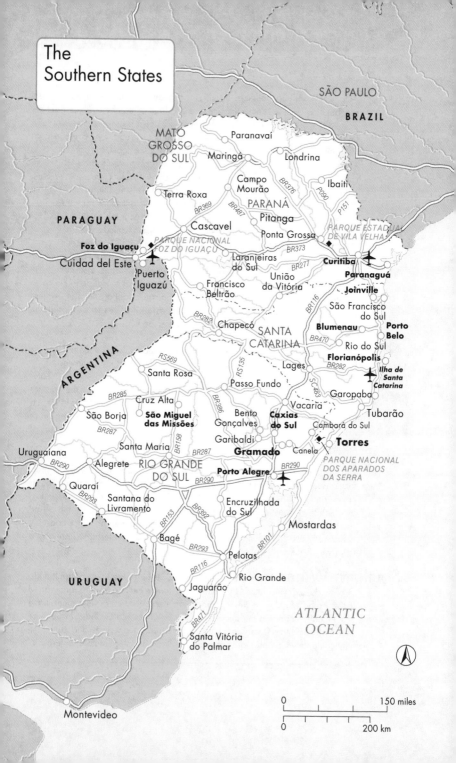

The Southern States

SÃO PAULO

BRAZIL

MATO GROSSO DO SUL

Paranavaí

Maringá

Londrina

Ibaiti

Campo Mourão

Terra Roxa

PARANÁ

Pitanga

Ponta Grossa

Parque Estadual de Vila Velha

PARAGUAY

Cascavel

Foz do Iguaçu

PARQUE NACIONAL FOZ DO IGUAÇU

Laranjeiras do Sul

Curitiba

Paranaguá

Cuidad del Este

Puerto Iguazú

Francisco Beltrão

União da Vitória

Joinville

São Francisco do Sul

Chapecó

SANTA CATARINA

Blumenau

Porto Belo

Rio do Sul

Florianópolis

ARGENTINA

Santa Rosa

Passo Fundo

Lages

Ilha de Santa Catarina

Cruz Alta

Garopaba

São Borja

São Miguel das Missões

Bento Gonçalves

Vacaria

Caxias do Sul

Tubarão

Santa Maria

Garibaldi

Cambora do Sul

Uruguaiana

Alegrete

RIO GRANDE DO SUL

Gramado

Canela

Torres

PARQUE NACIONAL DOS APARADOS DA SERRA

Porto Alegre

Quaraí

Santana do Livramento

Encruzilhada do Sul

Mostardas

Bagé

Pelotas

URUGUAY

Rio Grande

Jaguarão

ATLANTIC OCEAN

Santa Vitória do Palmar

Montevideo

BR369
BR487
BR376
P090
P151
BR373
BR277
BR116
BR282
RS569
RS135
SC483
BR470
BR282
BR285
BR396
BR287
BR158
BR287
BR290
BR290
BR293
BR153
BR302
BR290
BR101
BR293
BR116
BR471

| 0 | | | 150 miles |
| 0 | | | 200 km |

Curitiba

408 km (254 mi) south of São Paulo, 710 km (441 mi) north of Porto Alegre.

A 300-year-old city, Curitiba is on the Paraná plateau, at an elevation of 2,800 feet. It owes its name to the Paraná pinecones, which were called *kur-ity-ba* by the native Guaranis. In a region that already differs considerably from the rest of the country, the city of 1.5 million is unique for its temperate climate (with a mean temperature of 16°C/61°F) and the 50% of its population that is of non-Iberian European ancestry.

With one of the highest densities of urban green space in the world, Curitiba is known as the environmental capital of Brazil. This is not only because of its array of parks but also because since the 1980s it has had progressive city governments that have been innovative in their urban planning—a process spearheaded by former mayor and architect Jayme Lerner. The emphasis on protecting the environment has produced an efficient public transportation system and a comprehensive recycling program that are being used as models for cities around the globe.

Numbers in the text correspond to numbers in the margin and on the Curitiba Setor Histórico map.

Setor Histórico

A GOOD TOUR Start your tour in the downtown Setor Histórico (Historic District) at the **Museu Paranaense** ❶ ▶. Then circle the block and take Rua Monsenhor Celso north to the Praça Tiradentes. The **Catedral Metropolitana** ❷ is on the opposite side of the square. Continue a couple of blocks north on Rua do Rosário to the Largo da Ordem, where you will find the **Memorial de Curitiba** ❸. A few steps uphill is the site of the **Igreja de São Francisco** ❹ and its Museu de Arte Sacra. Walk one block southwest to find **Società Giuseppe Garibaldi** ❺, on the northern side of Praça Garibaldi. Right behind the society building are the ruins of São Francisco de Paula Church. You can then retrace your steps to the Largo da Ordem, walk three blocks east on Rua São Francisco, and then go north on Rua Presidente Faria to the **Passeio Público** ❻. Alternatively, you can leave the Setor Histórico and head west to explore the **Santa Felicidade** neighborhood—with its many restaurants and shops—or go to the futuristic **Novo Museu (Museu de Arte do Paraná)** ❼, one of the latest creations of Brasilia's architect Oscar Niemeyer.

TIMING You can follow the tour in two hours, but allow half a day to fully see the sights. Shopping or people-watching in a park can fill up the rest of the day.

WHAT TO SEE ❷ **Catedral Metropolitana.** The cathedral, also called Basílica Nossa Senhora da Luz dos Pinhais, is on the site where the city was founded in 1693. The present neo-Gothic structure was finished in 1893 and was built according to the plan of an unknown cathedral in Barcelona, Spain. ⊠ *Praça Tiradentes s/n* ☎ *041/222–1131* ☜ *Free* ⊙ *Daily 7 AM–9 PM.*

❹ **Igreja de São Francisco.** St. Francis, Curitiba's oldest church, was built in 1737 and was fully restored in 1981. Check out its gold-plated altar

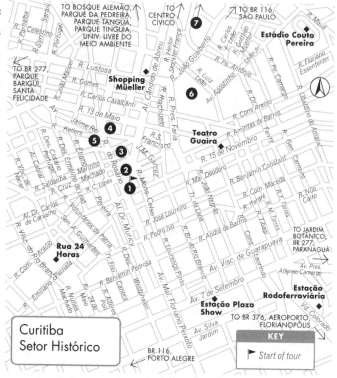

Curitiba
Setor Histórico

KEY

► *Start of tour*

before ducking into the attached **Museu de Arte Sacra** (Sacred Art Museum), with its baroque religious sculptures made of wood and terra-cotta. ⊠ *Largo da Ordem s/n* ☎ *041/223–7545 for church, 041/321–3265 for museum* ◻ *Free* ☉ *Tues.–Fri. 9–6, weekends 9–2.*

❸ **Memorial de Curitiba.** The triangular-shape building with glass walls has three stories with space for art exhibits and workshops. The ground level has a theater and several sculptures by local artists representing the city's history. ⊠ *Rua Claudino dos Santos s/n* ☎ *041/323–8594* ⊕ *www.fundacaoculturaldecuritiba.com.br* ◻ *Free* ☉ *Weekdays 9–6, Sat 9–1.*

need a break?

Rua 24 Horas. To satisfy your hunger, head for Rua 24 Horas, a short downtown alley that's sheltered by a glass roof (with interior lighting) supported by a steel structure. The entrance is marked by stylish clocks that hint at the appealing ambience inside. You'll find souvenir shops and newsstands as well as coffeehouses and bars whose tables spill out onto the walkway. All are open 24 hours a day, seven days a week. ⊠ *Rua Coronel Mena Barreto between Rua Visconde de Rio Branco and Rua Visconde de Nacar, Centro* ☎ *041/225–1732.*

► ❶ **Museu Paranaense.** Founded in 1876, the State Museum of Paraná moved several times before installing its collections in this imposing art nouveau building, which served as city hall from 1916 to 1969. The permanent displays contain official documents, ethnographic materials of the native Guarani and Kaigang peoples, coins and photographs, and archaeological pieces related to the state's history. ✉ *Praça Generoso Marques s/n* ☎ *041/321–4727* ✆ *Free* ⊘ *Weekdays 9–5, weekends 10–4.*

❼ **Novo Museu.** This museum is a creation of Oscar Niemeyer, the architect of Brasília. It incorporates a collection of the works of Paraná's artists from the former Museu de Arte do Paraná with temporary modern art exhibits. Niemeyer's futuristic building design includes a long rectangular building, formerly a school. The main building, a suspended eye-shape structure overlooking the adjacent John Paul II woods has the major modern art exhibit. ✉ *Rua Marechal Hermes 999, Centro Cívico* ☎ *041/254–6633* ⊕ *www.novomuseu.org.*

❻ **Passeio Público.** Opened in 1886, the Public Thoroughfare was designed as a botanical and zoological garden. It soon became a favorite place for the affluent to spend their weekend afternoons. The main gate is a replica of that at the Cimetière des Chiens in Paris. Although it's no longer the official city zoo, you can observe several Brazilian primates and birds still kept in the park, as well as majestic sycamores, oaks, and the famed Brazilian *ipê amarelo.* ✉ *Main Gate: Rua Pres. Faria at Pres. Carlos Cavalcanti* ☎ *041/222–2742* ✆ *Free* ⊘ *Tues.–Sun. 6 AM–8 PM.*

off the beaten path

SANTA FELICIDADE – What was once an Italian settlement (it dates from 1878) is now one of the city's most popular neighborhoods. It has been officially designated as Curitiba's "gastronomic district," and, indeed, you'll find some fantastic restaurants—as well as wine, antiques, and handicrafts shops—along Via Veneto and Avenida Manuel Elias. The area also has some colonial buildings, such as the Igreja Matriz de São José (St. Joseph's Church).

❺ **Società Giuseppe Garibaldi.** The stately neoclassical mansion housing the Garibaldi Society—a philanthropic organization that once helped a great many Italian immigrants—was built with the help of donations from the Italian government and finished in 1890. Today the society sponsors a folkloric dance group and a choir. ✉ *Praça Garibaldi s/n* ☎ *041/ 323–3530* ✆ *Free* ⊘ *By appointment only.*

Parks, Gardens & Forests

It would be a shame to visit Brazil's environmental capital without seeing one of its many parks. In addition to the Passeio Público, you can visit the Jardim Botânico (east from downtown). Also recommended are the Bosque Alemão, Parque da Pedreira, Parque Tangüá, Parque Tingüí, and Universidade Livre do Meio Ambiente (they're clustered northwest of Centro and the Setor Histórico). Tour on your own or as part of the 2½-hour Linha Turismo bus tour.

PARKS TO SEE **Bosque Alemão.** The 8-acre German Woods—which, as its name suggests, is a park honoring German immigration—is on a hill in the Jardim Schaffer neighborhood. On its upper side is the Bach Oratorium, a small concert hall that looks like a chapel; it's the site of classical music performances. The park also has a viewpoint with a balcony overlooking downtown, a library with children's books, and a path through the woods called Hans and Gretel Trail. Named after the Grimm Brothers' tale, the trail has the story depicted in 12 paintings along the way, ending at the Mural de Fausto, where there's a stage for music shows. ⊠ *Rua Nicolo Paganini at Rua Francisco Schaffer, Jardim Schaffer* ☎ *041/338–6835* ⊡ *Free* ⊙ *Park daily sunrise–sunset. Library Mon.–Sat. 8–6.*

Jardim Botânico. Although not as old and renowned as its counterpart in Rio, the Botanical Garden has become a trademark of Curitiba. Its most outstanding feature is the tropical flora in the two-story steel greenhouse that resembles a castle. The Municipal Botanical Museum, with its library and remarkable collection of rare Brazilian plants, is also worth visiting. There are several paths for jogging or just wandering. ⊠ *Rua Eng. Ostoja Roguski s/n, Jardim Botânico* ☎ *041/328–1800* ⊡ *Free* ⊙ *Gardens daily 6 AM–8 PM. Museum weekdays 8–5.*

FodorśChoice
★ **Parque da Pedreira.** This cultural complex was built in the abandoned João Gava quarry and adjacent wooded lot. The quarry itself was converted to an amphitheater that can accommodate 60,000 people. The 2,400-seat **Opera de Arame** (Wire Opera House), also on the grounds here, is built of tubular steel and wire mesh and is surrounded by a moat. National and international musical events have given this facility world renown. ⊠ *Rua João Gava s/n, Pilarzinho* ☎ *041/354–2662* ⊡ *Free* ⊙ *Tues.–Sun. 8 AM–9 PM.*

Parque Tangüá. Tangüá Park, opened in 1996, is the latest addition to Curitiba's recreational scene and the most visited. Its interesting landscaping includes a pond in an abandoned quarry that creates the backdrop for a tunnel (dug 45 meters/160 feet into the rock wall), an artificial waterfall, and a walkway over the water. ⊠ *Rua Eugenio Flor s/n, Pilarzinho* ☎ *041/350–9163* ⊡ *Free* ⊙ *Daily sunrise–sunset.*

Parque Tingüí. One of the city's most pleasant parks was designed to protect the upper basin of the Rio Barigüí from urban encroachment. It's best known as the site of the Ukrainian Memoria—a reproduction of a wooden church with onion domes built by Ukrainian Catholic immigrants in 1900 in the town of Prudentópolis, 250 km (155 mi) away. There is also a shop with traditional Ukrainian handicrafts. ⊠ *Rua Dr. Bemben s/n, Pilarzinho* ☎ *041/335–2112* ⊡ *Free* ⊙ *Daily 6–8.*

Universidade Livre do Meio Ambiente. The Free University of the Environment, in the Bosque Zaninelli (Zaninelli Woods), opened in 1992 during the UN Conference on the Environment and Development being held in Rio. Its main objective is to promote environmental awareness through courses, conferences, and seminars. The impressive main structure is built of eucalyptus wood and has a scenic overlook on its top level. Several paths through the woods make the Bosque Zaninelli a popular place to wander. ⊠ *Rua Victor Benato 210, Pilarzinho* ☎ *041/254–5548* ⊡ *Free* ⊙ *Daily 7–6.*

Where to Stay & Eat

$$–$$$$ ✕ **Boulevard.** The sophisticated atmosphere and excellent wine selection of this highly regarded small French restaurant won't fail to impress. Try the wild boar ribs with herbs, truffles, and mustard sauce. ⊠ *Rua Voluntários da Pátria 539, Setor Histórico* ☎ *041/224–8244* ☰ *AE, DC, MC, V* ⌖ *Reservations essential* ☉ *Closed Sun. No lunch Sat.*

$–$$$ ✕ **Durski.** This family-run restaurant has brought traditional Polish and
Fodor'sChoice Ukrainian food center stage. The impeccable service by staff in tradi-
★ tional attire, as well as the borscht, pierogi, and *bigos* (a round loaf of bread stuffed with sausages and sauerkraut), transport you to central Europe. Another highlight is the home-brewed low-alcohol beer, made of sugar, egg whites, and hops. ⊠ *Rua Jaime Reis 254, Setor Histórico* ☎ *041/225–7893* ⌖ *Reservations essential* ☰ *AE, DC, MC, V* ☉ *Closed Mon. No dinner Sun.*

$–$$ ✕ **Marinheiro.** This is by far the best seafood in town. The shrimp dishes or the *garoupa* flambé—served with a spicy cream sauce—deserves your attention. ⊠ *Av. Bispo D. José 2315, Batel* ☎ *041/243–3828* ☰ *AE, V* ☉ *Closed Mon. No dinner Sun.*

$ ✕ **Devon's.** The service is excellent at this rodízio-style churrascaria. It's very popular with businesspeople and visitors to the Centro Cívico area. ⊠ *Rua Lysimaco Ferreira da Costa 436, Centro Cívico* ☎ *048/ 254–7073* ☰ *DC, MC, V* ☉ *No dinner Sun.*

$ ✕ **Estrela da Terra.** In a colonial house, this restaurant is *the* place to try the local *barreado* (beef, bacon, potatoes, and spices stewed for several hours in a clay pot that is made airtight with moistened manioc flour) on weekends. The weekly menu also contains choices from other regions. ⊠ *Rua Jaime Reis 176, Setor Histórico* ☎ *041/225–5007* ☰ *AE, DC, MC, V* ☉ *No dinner.*

$ ✕ **Madalosso.** An enormous, hangerlike building that seats 4,800 houses the best-known restaurant in Santa Felicidade. The prix-fixe Italian menu includes a large selection of pastas and sauces, meat dishes, and salads. ⊠ *Rua Manoel Ribas 5875, Santa Felicidade* ☎ *041/372–2121* ☰ *AE, DC, MC, V* ☉ *No dinner Sun.*

¢–$ ✕ **Schwarzwald.** One of the city's most popular German restaurants, Schwarzwald has carved a name for itself with great draft beer, including bocks, which are hard to find. Highly recommended entrées are the house version of *eisbein* (pig's leg served with mashed potatoes), *kassler* (beef fillet with a cream sauce), and duck with red cabbage. ⊠ *Rua Claudino dos Santos 63, Setor Histórico* ☎ *041/223–2585* ☰ *AE, DC, MC, V.*

¢–$ ✕ **Baviera.** In the basement of an imposing house on a hillside, this is a popular choice for those visiting the Setor Histórico. Baviera is essentially a pizzeria, but the menu also includes Brazilian-style steak, grilled chicken, and hamburgers. ⊠ *Rua Augusto Stellfeld 18, Setor Histórico* ☎ *041/232–1995* ☰ *AE, DC, MC, V.*

★ **$$** ▥ **Grand Hotel Rayon.** A spacious lobby welcomes you to Curitiba's most sophisticated hotel. Superbly furnished standard rooms have soundproof windows and two phone lines, which are a blessing for the business traveler. Service is impeccable, and the location—in the heart of the financial district and right next to Rua 24 Horas—is convenient. ⊠ *Rua Visconde de Nacar 1424, Centro 80411-201* ☎ *041/322–6006 or 0800/*

41–8899 ⌂*041/322–4004* ⊕*www.rayon.com.br* ⤳*136 rooms, 11 suites* ⚴ *2 restaurants, coffee shop, room service, cable TV, outdoor pool, gym, sauna, bar, business services, meeting room, travel services* ▤ *AE, DC, MC, V* |○| *CP.*

$–$$ ⊡ **Bourbon & Tower.** Much like its counterpart in Foz do Iguaçu, this hotel is recommended for the sophisticated business or leisure traveler. The decor is sober, with custom antique-style furniture and textured wallpaper. The restaurant Le Bourbon serves French-Swiss dishes, but the Brazilian *feijoada* is the Saturday special. ⊠ *Rua Candido Lopes 102, Centro 80010-050* ☎*041/322–4001 or 0800/11–8181* ⌂*041/322–2282* ⊕ *www.bourbon.com.br* ⤳ *157 rooms, 10 suites* ⚴ *Restaurant, coffee shop, gym, cable TV, indoor pool, sauna, bar, business services, convention center* ▤ *AE, DC, MC, V* |○| *CP.*

$ ⊡ **Duomo Park Hotel.** Everything is shiny and comfortable at this small hotel. The rooms and suites are unusually spacious. Bathrooms are heated—hard to find in Brazil, but welcome in the cold Curitiba winters. Another draw is the location: one step from Rua 24 Horas. ⊠ *Rua Visconde de Rio Branco 1710, Centro 80420-200* ☎ *041/322–6655 or 0800/41–1816* ⌂*041/224–1816* ⊕*www.bristol-hotelaria.com.br* ⤳*40 rooms, 8 suites* ⚴ *Restaurant, bar, cable TV, business services, meeting room, airport shuttle* ▤ *AE, DC, MC, V* |○| *CP.*

$ ⊡ **Slaviero Braz Hotel.** The hotel is in a landmark building overlooking the walkway of Rua das Flores. Rooms are large, with wood paneling and matching furniture. Beds are king size, with colorful spreads and cushions that invite you to relax. Note that rooms in the east wing are smaller and oddly shaped, and elevators there are cramped because of the original building plan. The second-floor Getúlio bar-café is a popular gathering spot for businesspeople. ⊠ *Av. Luiz Xavier 67, Centro 80020-020* ☎ *041/322–2829 or 0800/41–3311* ⌂ *041/322–2829* ⊕ *www. hotelslaviero.com.br* ⤳ *89 rooms, 2 suites* ⚴ *Restaurant, bar, cable TV, business services, gym, meeting rooms* ▤ *AE, DC, MC, V* |○| *CP.*

¢ ⊡ **Íbis Curitiba.** The Íbis leads the city's roster of budget lodging. The hotel combines comfort and efficiency in cream-color rooms with a nofrills approach to the extras. Be prepared to carry your own luggage. The reception desk and the restaurant are in restored historic houses that are detached from the main building. Íbis is one of the few hotels in Curitiba to offer rooms for guests with disabilities. ⊠ *Rua Mateus Leme 358, Centro Cívico 80020-050* ☎*041/324–0469 or 0800/11–1790* ⌂*041/324–3404* ⊕*www.accor.com.br* ⤳*80 rooms* ⚴ *Restaurant, bar, cable TV* ▤ *AE, DC, MC, V.*

¢ ⊡ **InterPalace.** What once was a school in downtown Curitiba, near Taetro Guaíra and Setor Histórico, is now a great budget choice. Rooms are basic, but extremely spacious and comfortable. ⊠ *Av XV de Novembro 950, Centro 80060-000* ☎*041/223–5282* ⌂*041/225–2224* ⊕*www. interpalace.com.br* ⤳ *70 rooms* ⚴ *Restaurant, convention center; no a/c in some rooms* ▤ *AE, DC, MC, V* |○| *CP.*

Nightlife & the Arts

Curitiba has a bustling cultural scene, a reflection of the European background of many of its citizens. Complete listings of events are published in the *Gazeta do Povo*, the major daily newspaper.

In what was once a railway terminal, the **Estação Plaza Show** (✉ Av. 7 de Setembro 2775, Centro ☎ 041/322–5356) is a 210,000-square-meter (700,000-square-foot) covered area with a colorful and noisy collection of bars and restaurants, amusement parks, and more than 100 shops. The small Museu Ferroviário (Railway Museum), a cineplex, and daily live musical shows add to the center's charm. The complex is open daily 10 AM–2 AM. The **Teatro Guaíra** (✉ Rua 15 de Novembro s/n, Centro ☎ 041/322–2628), formerly the Teatro São Teodoro (circa 1884), was totally rebuilt in its present location and reopened in 1974. It has a modern, well-equipped 2,000-seat auditorium, as well as two smaller rooms. Shows include plays, popular music concerts, and the occasional full-fledged opera.

Sports & the Outdoors

Curitiba has three professional soccer clubs: Coritiba, Atlético Paranaense, and Paraná Clube. Check local newspaper listings for upcoming game times and locations. Many of the area's parks have paths for jogging and bicycling.

Arena da Baixada (✉ Rua Eng. Rebouças 3113, Água Verde ☎ 041/333–4747) is home for Atlético Paranaense Club. It's the most modern sports facility in the country, with a 32,000-seat capacity, to be expanded to 50,000 in the future. **Estádio Couto Pereira** (✉ Rua Ubaldino do Amaral 37, Alto da Glória ☎ 041/362–3234) is the 60-year-old home of Coritiba FC and holds 40,000 fans. **Parque Barigüi** (✉ Av. Candido Hartmann at Av. Gen. Tourinho, off Km 1, BR 277 ☎ 041/339–8975) contains soccer fields, volleyball courts, and paths spread throughout 310 acres.

Shopping

Curitiba Outlet Center (✉ Rua Brigadeiro Franco 1916, Batel ☎ 041/224–1900) has a large array of clothing shops with rock-bottom prices. This government-sponsored shop offers a variety of wicker, clay, wood, and leather crafts as well as more traditional items such as Ukrainian *pessankes* (painted eggshells) and indigenous ornaments. Handmade toys are also available. **Feito Aqui-Artesanato do Paraná** (✉ Alameda Dr. Muricy 950, Centro ☎ 041/222–6361). Interact directly with the artisans every Sunday at the **Feira de Artesanato** (✉ Praça Garibaldi, Setor Histórico) from 9 to 3. **Shopping Center Müller** (✉ Rua Candido de Abreu 127, São Francisco ☎ 041/224–0510) is the city's prime shopping location, with branches of national chains, upscale fashion and jewelry stores, as well as small handicraft shops, restaurants and cafés, bookstores, and movie theaters.

Paranaguá

90 km (56 mi) southeast of Curitiba.

Most of Brazil's coffee and soybeans are shipped out of Paranaguá, the nation's second-largest port, which also serves as chief port for landlocked Paraguay. Downtown holds many examples of colonial architecture and has been designated an official historic area. The city, founded in 1565 by Portuguese explorers, is 30 km (18 mi) from the

Atlantic on the Baía de Paranaguá. The bay area is surrounded by Mata Atlântica, of which a great swatch on the northern side is protected; several islands in the bay also have rain forests as well as great beaches. You'll find other less scenic but popular sandy stretches farther south, toward the Santa Catarina border.

Although you can reach Paranaguá on BR 277, consider taking the more scenic Estrada da Graciosa, which follows the route taken by 17th-century traders up the Serra do Mar. This narrow, winding route—paved with rocks slabs in some stretches—is some 30 km (18 mi) longer than BR 277, but the breathtaking peaks and slopes covered with rain forest make the extra travel time worthwhile.

Igreja Nossa Senhora do Rosário, the city's first church, was destroyed, sacked, and rebuilt several times, but its facade (circa 1578) is original. ⊠ *Largo Monsenhor Celso s/n* ☎ *No phone* ⌑ *Free* ⊙ *Daily 7 AM–9 PM.*

The **Museu de Arqueologia e Etnologia** (Archaeology and Ethnology Museum) occupies a building that was part of a Jesuit school founded in 1752. The Jesuits left around 1768 when the Marques de Pombal from Portugal, trying to eliminate the power of the Catholic church, had them expelled from the Portuguese kingdom (which included Brazil at that time). The collection includes pieces found in excavations in the area, most belonging to the Sambaqui, a coastal-dwelling native people, and temporary art exhibits. ⊠ *Rua General Carneiro 66* ☎ *041/422–8844* ⌑ *R$2* ⊙ *Tues.–Sun. 1–5.*

FodorśChoice   The 10-km-long (6-mi-long) **Ilha do Mel** (Honey Island), a state park in
★   the Baía de Paranaguá, is the most popular destination on Paraná's coast. It's crisscrossed by hiking trails—cars aren't allowed, and the number of visitors is limited to 5,000 at any one time—and has two villages, Encantadas and Nova Brasília, and several pristine beaches. Local lore has it that the east shore's Gruta das Encantadas (Enchanted Grotto) is frequented by mermaids. On the south shore check out the sights around Farol das Conchas (Lighthouse of the Shells) and its beach. From Forte de Nossa Senhora dos Prazeres (Fort of Our Lady of Pleasures), built in 1767 on the east shore, take advantage of the great views of the forest-clad northern bay islands. The most scenic ferry rides leave from Paranaguá at 8 AM and 5 PM; they take one hour and cost R$20. Additional ferries depart from Pontal do Sul, 49 km (30 mi) east of Paranaguá, by appointment. Prices range from R$50 to R$100. To ensure admission in the high season (December–March), it's best to book an island tour before you leave Curitiba. ⊠ *Ferries depart from Rua General Carneiro s/n* ☎ *041/424–4548.*

The northern shore of Baía de Paranaguá is also home to the 92,000-acre **Parque Nacional de Superagüí** and its complex system of coves, salt-water marshes, and forested islands—including Ilha Superagüí and Ilha das Peças. Most of these pristine settings contain animal and bird species unique to the Mata Atlântica are closed to visitation. You can, however, see a lot of bird and animal species by basing yourself in the fishing village of Guaraqueçaba—reached by a three-hour ferry ride from Paranaguá's harbor—and then touring the bay and trails around the park.

Your best bet for viewing wildlife is to explore the islands on a guided boat tour. ⊠ *Park administration: 2 km (1 mi) north of Guaraqueçaba. Ferry dock: Rua Paula Miranda s/n* ☎ *041/482–1282 park, 041/482–1285 ferry* ⊠ *Park free, ferry R$150–R$250* ☉ *Park daily 9–6; ferries by appointment.*

Where to Stay & Eat

¢–$ ✕ **Casa do Barreado.** As its name suggests, this small, homey family-run restaurant specializes in the traditional barreado, including an unusual chicken variety called *galinha na púcura.* Although the restaurant is officially open only on weekends, you can call ahead to arrange a dinner during the week. ⊠ *Rua José Antônio Cruz 78* ☎ *041/423–1830* ⚒ *Reservations essential* ⊟ *No credit cards* ☉ *Closed weekdays.*

$ ✕🏨 **Camboa.** In the historic district, Camboa has comfortable facilities and a dedicated staff. Modern architecture and cheerful colors blend with the colonial surroundings. Ask to be on the north side for a bay view. Continental cuisine, with an emphasis on French, is served in the restaurant ($–$$). ⊠ *Rua João Estevão s/n, 83203-020* ☎ *041/423–2121 or 0800/703–1163* 🖷 *041/423–2121* ⊕ *www.hotelcamboa.com. br* ⏎ *114 rooms, 6 suites* ⚒ *Restaurant, coffee shop, cable TV, boating, 2 tennis courts, volleyball, soccer, indoor pool, pool, gym, sauna, 2 bars, recreation room, shops, business services, playground, meeting room* ⊟ *AE, DC, MC, V* ⦿❙ *CP.*

¢ ✕🏨 **Tia Bela Pousada and Restaurant.** Right on the waterfront of the historic district, this small pousada allows easy access to the boats and ferries. The apartments are basic, yet cozy and neatly decorated. The friendly staff serves a king's breakfast in the morning before you depart to your explorations to visit the area attractions. The restaurant ($) has barreado and seafood dishes. ⊠ *Rua General Carneiro, 83203-000* ☎🖷 *041/424–3783* ⏎ *5 rooms* ⚒ *Restaurant, fans, room TVs; no a/c in some rooms* ⊟ *No credit cards* ⦿❙ *CP.*

Parque Estadual de Vila Velha

97 km (60 mi) northwest of Curitiba.

The 22 towering rock formations of the 7,670-acre Vila Velha State Park stand in sharp contrast to the green rolling hills of the Campos Gerais, Paraná's high plains. Three hundred million years of rain and wind have carved these sandstone formations, whose names—the Lion, the Cup, the Mushroom, the Sphinx—reflect their shapes. You can visit these natural monuments on foot or in a tractor-pulled wagon along a well-marked 2½-km (1½-mi) trail that starts a mile from the visitor center. Traversing the path and viewing the formations on foot takes about two hours. ⊠ *Km 514, BR 376* ☎ *042/228–1138* ⊠ *R$3* ☉ *Daily 8–6.*

Where to Stay & Eat

$ ✕ **La Taverne.** This is a great choice for pasta, pizzas, and beef in downtown Ponta Grossa, north of the Parque Vila Velha. The *picanha,* grilled steak served with a mushroom-and-herb sauce, is the highlight. ⊠ *Rua Sete de Setembro 1136, Ponta Grossa, 23 km (13 mi) northwest of park* ☎ *042/224–3534* ⚒ *Reservations essential* ⊟ *AE, MC, V.*

¢ ✕ **Pampeana.** This busy, *espeto-corrido*-style (called *rodízio* in the north-central states) churrascaria is the perfect place to satisfy a hearty appetite acquired after touring Parque Estadual de Vila Velha. It has a great salad bar for those not crazy about the meat excesses of churrasco. ⊠ *Km 373, BR 376, Ponta Grossa* ☎ *042/229–2881* ⊟ *DC, MC, V* ⊘ *No dinner Sun.*

¢–$ ✕⊞ **Vila Velha Palace.** The best luxury option in the city, Vila Velha Palace is also the largest hotel in the central region of Paraná State. Among the amenities is free access to the city's golf course. Rooms are ample and elegant, with queen-size beds. The house restaurant ($) serves Brazilian fare. ⊠ *Rua Balduino Taques 123, Ponta Grossa 84040-000* ▦▦ *042/225–2200* ⊕ *www.hospedare.com.br/vilavelha* ⤴ *92 rooms, 2 suites* ⚐ *Restaurant, bar, golf privileges, sauna, gym, business services, meeting rooms* ⊟ *AE, DC, MC, V* ⦶ *CP.*

¢–$ ⊞ **Hotel Fazenda Capão Grande.** The 150-year-old Fazenda Capão Grande is a fully functional ranch that breeds *criollo* horses. You can fully experience gaucho traditions, from churrasco to cattle driving—a great way to round out your visit to Vila Velha. There are trails and waterfalls to explore within the farm. Riding classes are available. ⊠ *19 km (12 mi) along an unpaved road off Km 511, BR 376, Ponta Grossa* ▦▦ *042/228–1198* ⤴ *8 rooms* ⚐ *Dining room, lounge, horseback riding* ⊟ *No credit cards* ⦶ *FAP.*

¢ ⊞ **Planalto Palace.** This budget hotel in downtown Ponta Grossa is a preferred choice for business travelers. It has comfortable rooms and a reliable staff eager to inform you about the attractions of the Campos Gerais region. ⊠ *Rua 7 de Setembro 652, Ponta Grossa 84010-350* ☎ *042/225–2122* 🖷 *042/225–2122* ⤴ *66 rooms* ⚐ *Cable TV, bar, gym, business services, meeting rooms* ⊟ *AE, DC, MC, V* ⦶ *CP.*

Foz do Iguaçu

637 km (396 mi) west of Curitiba, 544 (338 mi) west of Vila Velha.

The Foz do Iguaçu cascades in a deafening roar at a bend in the Rio Iguaçu where southwestern Paraná State meets the borders of both Argentina and Paraguay. This Brazilian town and the Argentine town of Puerto Iguazú are the hubs for exploring the falls (the Paraguayan town of Ciudad del Este is also nearby).

The avalanche of water actually consists of some 275 separate falls (in the rainy season they can number as many as 350) that plunge 80 meters (250 feet) onto the rocks below. The backdrop is one of dense, lush jungle, pitch-black basalt, and rainbows, ferns, and butterflies. The falls and the lands around them are protected by Brazil's Parque Nacional do Iguaçu and Argentina's Parque Nacional Iguazú (where the falls are referred to by their Spanish name, the Cataratas de Iguazú).

The Brazilians are blessed with the best panoramic view of the falls (allow half a day to traverse the catwalks and stop at the lookouts); the Argentine side—where most of the falls are actually situated—offers better up-close experiences. Allow another half day for this tour. Local tour operators run trips that take you to both. To set your own pace, take one of the regularly scheduled buses to the Brazilian park and then take a taxi across the international bridge, Ponte Presidente Tancredo Neves, to Argentina. Note that immigration authorities keep the region under close watch, and you will have to go through immigrations and customs. To avoid delays, make sure you have a valid visa before attempting to cross the Argentina–Brazil border either way.

The summer months (November–March) are hot and humid, so if you're bothered by the heat, plan to visit between April and October. Be aware, however, that high waters from heavy rainfall on the upper Iguaçu River basin occasionally restrict access to some walkways. Whatever time of year you visit, bring raingear: some paths take you extremely close to the falling water, where the spray can leave you drenched.

Fodor'sChoice
★

The **Parque Nacional do Iguaçu** extends 25 km (16 mi) along a paved highway southwest of downtown Foz do Iguaçu. Park administration is handled by a private operator, which runs the visitor center and all tourist service and facilities. ATMs, a snack bar, a souvenir shop, and information and currency exchange are available at the center. You cannot drive into the park—park at the entrance by the visitor center and take a 11-km (7-mi) double-decker shuttle trip from there. Parties larger than 15 must hire a designated tour guide. The shuttle departs every 10 minutes and drops you by the trailhead, where the luxurious Tropical Cataratas EcoResort stands. The path to the falls is about 2 km (1 mi) long, and its walkways and staircases lead through the rain forest to concrete and wooden catwalks. (Much of the park's 457,000 acres are protected rain forest that is off-limits to visitors and home to the last viable populations of jaguars as well as of rare bromeliads and orchids). There is a smaller visitor center with a snack bar, restaurant, and souvenir kiosk at the end of the trail, where you take the shuttle buses back to the main visitor center.

At the Salto Macuco (Macuco Falls) in the park, the crystal-clear waters of the Rio Macuco, a small tributary of the Iguaçu River, fall 18 meters (60 feet) into a natural pool. The only way to visit the falls is on a tour that takes about two hours and costs roughly R$120 per person. The trip requires a 7-km (5-mi) ride in a four-wheel-drive vehicle, followed by a short hike through the forest and a breathtaking 30-minute Zodiac ride on the Iguaçu to the falls.

Highlights of the Brazilian side of the falls include the Salto Santa Maria, from which catwalks branch off to Salto Deodoro and Salto Floriano, where you'll be doused by the spray. The end of the catwalk puts you right at the tallest and most popular falls, Garganta do Diabo (Devil's Throat), which extend for 3 km (1½ mi) in a 270-degree arch; the water thunders down 54 meters (180 feet). ⊠ *Km 17, Rodovia das Cataratas* ☎ *045/572-2261* ✉ *Park R$18, parking R$6.50* ◎ *Mon. 1–6, Tues.–Sun. 8–6.*

In Argentina's **Parque Nacional Iguazú** (☎ 03757/42–2722), there are a couple of major *circuitos* (routes). The Circuito Inferior (Lower Circuit) is a loop trail that leads to the brink of several falls. It starts off the main path leading from the visitor center, which is open daily from

7 AM to 8 PM. Wear your bathing suit on this route so you can take a dip in the calm pools at the trail's edge. The Circuito Superior (Upper Circuit) is a 900-meter-long (3,000-foot-long) path that borders the ridge on the river's south side, along the top of the falls.

The Argentine side offers the chance to view Devil's Throat from a different perspective. From Puerto Canoas, 4 km (2½ mi) upriver from the visitor center, a small fleet of Zodiacs will take you to the remnants of the ½-km-long (¼-mi-long) catwalk that once spanned the river to the falls. Much of this structure was washed away by floods. An overlook lets you watch the mighty waters of the Iguaçu disappear right in front of you.

There are other notable sights near the national park, including the privately run **Parque das Aves** (Bird Park). Here, on 36 acres of mostly untouched tropical forest right outside the national park, are 8-meter-high (25-foot-high) aviaries with 160 species of birds, as well as reptiles and a butterfly collection. A gift shop and a restaurant round out the facilities. ⊠ *Km 17, Rodovia das Cataratas* ☎ *045/529–8282* ⌨ *R$18* ☉ *Daily 9–6.*

Fodor's Choice ★

About 21 km (13 mi) up the Rio Paraná (which flows into the Rio Iguaçu just below the falls) is a great achievement of Brazilian civil engineering: the mighty **Hidrelétrica de Itaipú** (Itaipú Hydroelectric Power Plant) and the Itaipú Dam. It is the world's largest hydroelectric power plant, at 8 km (5 mi) long; its powerhouse alone is 2 km (1 mi) long. Twenty-five percent of Brazil's electricity is produced here. Watch a 15-minute video about the construction of the dam at the visitor center and join the hour-long guided bus tour of the complex—visits to the power plant have to be booked in advance. ⊠ *Km 11, Av. Tancredo Neves* ☎ *045/520–5252* ⌨ *Free* ☉ *Mon.–Sat. 8–6.*

At the **Ecomuseu de Itaipú,** funded by the dam's operator Itaipú Binacional, you can learn about the geology, archeology, and efforts to preserve the flora and fauna of the area since the dam was built. ⊠ *Km 10, Av. Tancredo Neves* ☎ *045/520–5817* ⌨ *Free* ☉ *Daily 8–6.*

Where to Stay & Eat

Near the borders of two other countries, the town of Foz do Iguaçu has a cosmopolitan atmosphere that's reflected in the cuisine. For a city of its size, the options are great. There's also one noteworthy hotel on the Argentine side—the Internacional Cataratas de Iguazú. For convenience, most visitors stay in the establishments that line BR 469 (Rodovia das Cataratas), the highway that runs from the city of Foz do Iguaçu to the national park and the falls. All major hotels can make arrangements for tours.

★ **$–$$$** ✕ **Zaragoza.** In a quiet neighborhood on a tree-lined street, this cozy restaurant, owned by a Spanish immigrant, is very popular with the international crowd as well as the locals. The fare includes the seafood paella, the house specialty, as well as several delicious fish options. The *surubi,* a regional fish, definitely merits a try. ⊠ *Rua Quintino Bocaiúva 882* ☎ *045/574–3084* ▤ *AE, V.*

$–$$ ✕ **Cantina 4 Sorelle.** The warm and cheerful atmosphere at this Italian restaurant makes it very popular among the locals. The efficient staff serves pasta dishes and pizzas. Try the *tortellone anatra ubriaco* (duck-filled pasta with spinach, tomato, and mozzarella in a wine–cognac reduction). ⊠ *Rua Alm Barroso 1336* ☎ *045/523–1707* ☴ *AE, DC, MC, V.*

$ ✕**Cataratas Iate Clube.** One of the draws here is that this is the only restaurant where you can dine with the Paraná River as the backdrop. The fish rodízio includes the best *moqueca de surubi* (stew made with surubi, a local fish) and *piapara ao vinagrete* (fried *piapara* fish marinated in vinegar sauce) in Foz do Iguaçu. ⊠ *Km 0.5, Av. Gen. Meira* ☎ *045/523–2335* ☴ *No credit cards.*

¢ ✕ **Bufalo Branco.** This is the city's finest and largest churrascaria. The picanha stands out from the 20-plus grilled meat choices. The salad bar is well stocked, a boon for vegetarians. ⊠ *Av. Rebouças 530* ☎ *045/523–9744* ☴ *AE, DC, MC, V.*

$$$ ✕🖬 **Tropical Cataratas EcoResort.** Not only is this stately hotel *in* the national park, with wonderful views of the falls from the front-side apartments, but it also provides the traditional comforts of a colonial-style establishment: large rooms, terraces, vintage furniture, and hammocks. The main building, declared a National Heritage Site, is surrounded by verandas and gardens. The Itaipú restaurant ($$–$$$$) serves a traditional Brazilian dinner, with feijoada and a variety of side dishes. Any entrées featuring fish from the Paraná basin are also recommended. ⊠ *Km 25, Rodovia das Cataratas, 85850-970* ☎ *045/521–7000 or 0800/701– 2670* 🖷 *045/522–1717* ⊕ *www.tropicalhotel.com.br* ⤸ *200 rooms* ♨ *2 restaurants, cable TV, coffee shop, 2 tennis courts, gym, bar, pool, playground, volleyball, shops, airport shuttle* ☴ *AE, DC, MC, V* ⍾ *CP.*

FodorsChoice ★

★ **$$–$$$** ✕🖬 **Sheraton Internacional Iguazú.** Half the rooms in this top-notch hotel over the Argentine border have direct views of the falls, so be sure to ask for a view when you make a reservation. Floor-to-ceiling windows let the inspiring scene into the lobby, restaurants, and bars; even the pool has a vista. The handsomely decorated Garganta del Diablo restaurant ($$–$$$$) serves a memorable trout wrapped in pastry and the Argentine version of the *surubí* follows suit. ⊠ *Parque Nacional Iguazú, Km 4, Ruta 12, Puerto Iguazú, Argentina* ☎ *0757/21100* 🖷 *0757/21090* ⤸ *180 rooms, 4 suites* ♨ *2 restaurants, cable TV, 3 tennis courts, biking, pool, 2 bars, meeting room, airport shuttle* ☴ *AE, DC, MC, V* ⍾ *CP.*

$$ ✕🖬 **Bourbon Foz do Iguaçu Resort & Convention Center.** The decor of this hotel is elegant, in light yellow tones, and the upper floors have views of the national park's lush rain forest in the distance. Most of the spacious rooms and guest facilities are in the main building; suites occupy the top floors of an adjacent tower. On the ground floor is a small shopping center. Hotel grounds have a jogging path that runs through a patch of rain forest. The highly regarded restaurant, Tarobá ($–$$$), serves international fare. ⊠ *Km 2½, Rodovia das Cataratas, 85863-000* ☎ *045/529–0123 or 0800/45–1010* 🖷 *045/529–0000* ⊕ *www.bourbon. com.br* ⤸ *298 rooms, 13 suites* ♨ *3 restaurants, cable TV, coffee shop, 2 tennis courts, indoor pool, 2 outdoor pools, health club, gym, sauna, soccer, bar, shops, meeting rooms, convention center, car rental, travel services, no-smoking rooms* ☴ *AE, DC, MC, V* ⍾ *CP.*

★ **$$** 🏨 **Iguaçu Golf Club and Resort.** Even the most demanding visitors find the Iguaçu Golf Club unforgettable. The resort hosts a national pro golf tournament annually. Accommodations are in small eight-room buildings surrounded by spacious and plush gardens with tropical vegetation—a preview of what lies beyond in the national park. If you're traveling with family or a group of friends, ask for one of the separate guest houses. ⊠ *Km 7, Rodovia das Cataratas, 85863-000* ☎ *045/529–9999* 🖶 *045/529–8888* ⊕ *www.iguassugolf.com.br* ⤳ *67 rooms, 4 guest houses* ♨ *Restaurant, cable TV, driving range, 18-hole golf course, putting green, pool, health club, hot tub, bar, lounge, shops, airport shuttle* 🖃 *AE, DC, MC, V* |◯| *CP.*

¢ 🏨 **Florença Iguaçu.** In a sprawling wooded lot on the road to the national park, Florença combines budget rates with excellent service. Rooms are large and have walk-in closets and views of the gardens. ⊠ *Km 13, Rodovia das Cataratas, 85863-000* ☎ *045/529–7755* 🖶 *045/529–8877* ⊕ *www.hotelflorenca.com* ⤳ *63* ♨ *Restaurant, cable TV, pool, volleyball, tennis court, bar, meeting room, playground* 🖃 *AE, DC, MC, V* |◯| *CP.*

¢ 🏨 **Foz Plaza.** This reliable budget choice has standard but comfortable rooms, and although the decor isn't tasteful, the staff is attentive. ⊠ *Rua Mal. Deodoro 1819, 85851-030* ☎ *045/523–1448* 🖶 *045/523–1448* ⤳ *64 rooms* ♨ *Restaurant, cable TV, recreation room, pool, sauna, bar* 🖃 *AE, V* |◯| *CP.*

¢ 🏨 **Foz Presidente.** The main draw of this budget hotel is the downtown location, with easy access to all attractions and the business district. Rooms are nondescript but comfortable, with queen-size beds, and look out onto downtown Foz. ⊠ *Av. Marechal Floriano 1851, 85851-030* ☎ *045/523–2318* 🖶 *045/523–2318* ⊕ *www.fozpresidentehoteis.com* ⤳ *115 rooms* ♨ *Cable TV, bar, lounge, pool* 🖃 *AE, DC, MC, V* |◯| *CP.*

SANTA CATARINA

The state of Santa Catarina, the South's smallest state, has almost 485 km (300 mi) of coastline (with many gorgeous beaches). The capital, Florianópolis, is on Ilha de Santa Catarina, an island with 42 beaches and many world-class hotels and resorts that has become a major travel destination in Brazil. North and south of Florianópolis along the coast are other great destinations where thousands of Brazilian and foreign tourists flock every summer. Santa Catarina is also home to the German settlements of Blumenau and Joinville, in the northern valleys. These highly industrialized cities still retain some of their German flavor, including a popular Oktoberfest.

Joinville

105 km (65 mi) northeast of Blumenau, 195 km (121 mi) north of Florianópolis.

Founded by German immigrants 150 years ago, Joinville is Santa Catarina's largest city. It's a bustling convention, industrial, and international trade center that relies on the nearby seaport of São Francisco do Sul.

Where to Stay & Eat

★ ¢–$ ✗▣ **Tannenhof.** This hotel is one of the region's best and largest, with emphasis on serving the business traveler. Some executive rooms are outfitted with desktop computers and two phone lines. The architecture imitates traditional German-enxaimel style. Rooms are decorated accordingly, with classic Alpine furnishings and lush velvet curtains. You can dine on German fare at the 11th-floor Weishof restaurant (¢–$$), which also serves up a panoramic view of the city and the nearby hills. Or try a late-afternoon café colonial. ⊠ *Rua Visconde de Taunay 340, Centro 89201-420* ☎ *047/433–8011 or 0800/99–8011* 📠 *047/433–8011* ⊕ *www.tannenhof.com.br* ⟿ *100 rooms, 3 suites* ⟍ *Restaurant, cable TV, pool, gym, bar, lounge, meeting room, business services* ⊟ *AE, DC, MC, V* ⟲ *CP.*

Blumenau

250 km (156 mi) northwest of Florianópolis.

Blumenau—the cradle of the prosperous Vale do Itajaí region—is a pleasant place, with clean streets and friendly people who take great pride in their community. The name of this city of more than 260,000 is indicative of its German origins. Downtown has been restored to preserve its early German architectural style—*enxaimel* (half-timber, half-brick construction)—and the annual Oktoberfest has attracted crowds from all over the south since its inception in 1984. Events spill from the festival site into downtown (around Rua 15 de Novembro) for three weeks, when almost 100,000 gallons of beer and matching amounts of wurst and sauerkraut are consumed.

For insight into the history of German immigration, check out the **Museu da Família Colonial** (Colonial Family Museum). The house, which was built in 1864 for the Gaertner family, some of the first settlers to the area, contains a collection of everyday objects that belonged to the city's first residents; its garden has many examples of regional flora. ⊠ *Rua Duque de Caxias 78* ☎ *047/322–1676* 📠 *R$3* ⊙ *Tues.–Fri. 8–6, Sat. 9–4, Sun. 9–noon.*

The Blumenau area is home to an important glassware industry, whose high-quality products are aimed at the discriminating customer. At **Glaspark** you can see artisans at work, learn about the industry at a museum, and buy designer glassware at reasonable prices. ⊠ *Rua Rudolf Roedel 147, Salto Weisbach* ☎ *047/327–1261* 📠 *Free* ⊙ *Mon.–Sat. 9–6.*

Where to Stay & Eat

$ ✗ **Frohsinn.** On the outskirts of town is one of the best German restaurants in the region. The stuffed duck served with mashed potatoes, cassava, and red cabbage is a regional specialty. ⊠ *Rua Gertrud Sierich s/ n, Morro do Aipim* ☎ *047/322–2137* ⊟ *AE, DC, MC, V* ⊙ *Closed Sun.*

$ ✗▣ **Plaza Blumenau.** Check in if you're looking for upscale accommodations, spacious rooms, and great facilities. The Terrace restaurant ($–$$) serves international cuisine with an emphasis on things German. ⊠ *Rua 7 de Setembro 818, Centro 89010-200* ☎ *047/231–7000 or 0800/ 47–1213* 📠 *047/231–7001* ⊕ *www.plazahoteis.com.br* ⟿ *123 rooms,*

CloseUp

THE SOUTH'S GERMAN SETTLERS

A USTRIAN-BORN EMPRESS DONA LEOPOLDINA, *wife of Dom Pedro I (Brazil's first emperor), in the early 1820s envisioned the vast, sparsely populated Brazilian countryside settled with the kind of farmers she knew from Europe. Although European farmers had a poor track record in the tropics, it was felt that southern Brazil's cooler, subtropical climate wouldn't be so inhospitable. Agents hired by the Brazilian crown were dispatched to central Europe, where they touted the wonders of Brazil and the abundance of its "farmland" (actually covered by dense forest, home to native peoples—such as the Guarani and Kaigang—and wild animals like the South American puma). Beginning in 1824 and continuing for more than 50 years, thousands of Europeans—many of them German—were lured to central and eastern Rio Grande do Sul and to eastern Santa Catarina.*

High-end estimates place the number of German settlers in the 200,000–300,000 range (exact figures are hard to come by because of poor record keeping by the Brazilian authorities and the tendency for colonists to indicate the region—Hunsrück, Pommern, Pfalz—from which they came rather than simply "Germany," which was not unified as a single country until 1871). Most who came were poor or landless farmers who faced famine in their homelands. Some were craftsmen who provided the goods and services needed to truly create settlements. The first New World community was established in São Leopoldo (named after Dona Leopoldina), 31 km (19 mi) north of Porto Alegre on the Rio dos Sinos (Bells River). This and the valley of the Rio Itajaí in Santa Catarina became cradles of Brazil's German immigrants.

The Germans brought their unswerving work ethic, their knowledge of intensive cash-crop agriculture, and their rich culture—much of which still thrives. Recent studies indicate that at least 500,000 Brazilians speak some German (usually dialects that speakers of the standard language would find hard to understand). Further, the Lutheran religion is still practiced by many people with German ancestry. Researchers of Rio Grande do Sul's rich folklore are keen to acknowledge that the rhythms of some regional music can be traced back to German polkas. German cuisine is so much a part of the region that hardly anyone here can conceive of a churrasco without pork sausages and Kartoffeln Salat (potato salad). And pastries are an essential part of the German-bred café colonial. Although most small local breweries have been incorporated into large national companies, prior to the 1970s the southern states had a long list of them. In addition, German immigrants and their descendants were behind such internationally renowned Brazilian companies as Varig Airlines, the steel company Gerdau, and the jeweler H. Stern.

If you visit such communities as Blumenau, Joinville, São Leopoldo, Novo Hamburgo, Gramado, Lageado, and Santa Cruz do Sul, you'll certainly experience a bit of Europe in Brazil. Indeed, Blumenau and Santa Cruz host large Oktoberfests. Crowds of German-Brazilians flock to these festivals to dance to their traditional rhythms (polkas and waltzes) and indulge in sausages, sauerkraut, and beer.

8 suites ☝ *Restaurant, cable TV, pool, gym, bar, business services, meeting rooms, no-smoking rooms* ☰ *AE, DC, MC, V* ⦿ *CP.*

¢ ✕⊞ **Hotel Glória.** This best buy has rooms that are basic but comfortable and an attentive staff. The elegant British-style lobby—with wood paneling, wrought-iron lamps, and large leather chairs—is unique in Brazil. What really makes the place popular is the on-site KaffeHaus Glória (¢–$$), which serves the traditional, lavish café colonial, with 50 kinds of pies and cakes. ⊠ *Rua 7 de Setembro 954, Centro 89010-280* ☎ *047/326–1988* 🖷 *047/326–5370* ⊕ *www.hotelgloria.com.br* ⮐ *105 rooms* ☝ *Restaurant, coffee shop, cable TV, bar, meeting rooms* ☰ *AE, DC, MC, V* ⦿ *CP.*

Shopping

H Shopping Center (⊠ Rua 15 de Novembro 759, Centro ☎ 047/326–2166) sells its own glassware and china, all at below-market prices.

Porto Belo

69 km (43 mi) north of Florianópolis.

The seafront town of Porto Belo lies at the base of a peninsula dotted with beaches, bays, and coves, and it has a great reputation among Argentine and Paraguayan tourists for its natural beauty, great beaches, and many water sports. It is a port of call for some of the Buenos Aires–Rio cruise lines. The calm waters of the Porto Belo bay are a haven of nautical sports—scuba diving, snorkeling, sailing. Fishing is very popular here, too. Porto Belo is the ideal place to make your base for exploring the paradisiacal landscapes of the region.

Where to Stay & Eat

¢ ✕⊞ **Baleia Branca.** There are plenty of amenities to recommend this hotel, but the short distance to the beach is certainly the highlight. Expect impeccable service from one of the first hotels to open in the area. The chalets are a comfortable options for larger parties. The highly regarded restaurant ($) won't fail to impress either. ⊠ *Alameda Nena Trevisan 98, 88210-000* ☎ *047/369–4011* 🖷 *047/369–4114* ⊕ *www.hotelbaleiabranca. com.br* ⮐ *43 apartments, 11 chalets* ☝ *Restaurant, beach, pool, sauna, soccer, bar, playground, meeting room* ☰ *V.*

Ilha de Santa Catarina

It's no wonder that every summer thousands of Argentines and Paraguayans travel almost 1,000 km (600 mi) to enjoy the breathtaking beaches and warm waters off the shore of the Ilha de Santa Catarina. They add to a constant influx of Brazilians, making this one of the country's top tourist destinations. Called Magic Island by locals and enthusiastic visitors alike, Ilha de Santa Catarina is joined to the mainland by two bridges: the modern, multilane Ponte Colombo Sales and the 60-year-old Ponte Hercilio Luz—the latter now condemned. The island has more than 42 easy-to-reach beaches. There are not only plenty of opportunities for scuba diving, surfing, sailing, and parasailing but also chances to view nature along trails with the ocean as backdrop, from beaches (the whale-watching is good), or even from a higher perspective—strapped into a parasail. Note that Brazilians tend to refer to all of Santa Catarina island as "Florianópolis," and all the beaches and forts on the island are under the city's jurisdiction.

Beaches

Fodor'sChoice
★ The island's northern *praias* (beaches) are considered the best—and are therefore the busiest—because of their warm waters. Impressive seascapes dominate the Atlantic beaches, and southern beaches have fewer sun worshipers and a more laid-back atmosphere.

You're strongly advised to explore the sophisticated **Praia do Canasvieiras**, which has calm, warm waters and great services and facilities. **Praia Jurerê**, home to an upscale resort and condominiums, normally has bigger waves than its neighbors. The increased development of beachfront hotels, restaurants, and shops has attracted many out-of-state visitors. **Praia dos Ingleses** (English Beach) acquired its name because a British sailboat sank here in 1700. Although it is a narrow beach, the unparalleled lineup of hotels and restaurants for all budgets makes makes Praia dos Ingleses one of the most popular beaches on the island. In summer Spanish with an Argentine accent is the local language. **Praia do Santinho** is a mile-long stretch of sand backed by green hills at the far-northeastern corner of the island. It was a secluded, laid-back neighborhood until a major resort opened in the 1990s.

Surfers have staked claims to **Praia da Joaquina**, the beach where several surfing events take place, including one round of the world professional circuit. Nudism is tolerated at **Praia Mole**, with white sands that mostly attract surfers and foreign tourists. You can paraglide here, and there are a number of beachfront bars. **Praia do Matadeiro**, quite popular among surfers, is a small beach surrounded by breathtaking hills. It can only be reached by a footpath from the Armação village.

The SC 404 highway takes you to **Lagoa da Conceição** (Our Lady of Conception Lagoon), 12 km (8 mi) east of downtown Florianópolis, which has a busy nightlife and dining district, most of whose streets are packed with people on weekend evenings. The region provides a combination fresh- and saltwater environment for water sports.

If you're seeking peace (and you don't mind colder waters and less development), head south through the Beira-Mar Sul (the southbound highway that connects downtown to the airport and beyond) to **Riberão da Ilha, Pântano do Sul**, and **Praia da Lagoinha do Leste.**

Follow SC 401 southwest and make your first stop **Riberão da Ilha**, one of the oldest Portuguese settlements on the island. Its little fishing village with colonial houses overlooking the balmy ocean and the forest-clad mountains on the continent beyond is a rare find in this otherwise bustling island.

Alternatively, head southeast to **Pântano do Sul**, a small beach community surrounded by hills with good restaurants and fishing-boat rides to other beaches and smaller islands nearby. Secluded **Praia da Lagoinha do Leste** is a breathtaking beach that you can only reach by boat or by a steep, 5-km (3-mi) path that starts at Pântano do Sul.

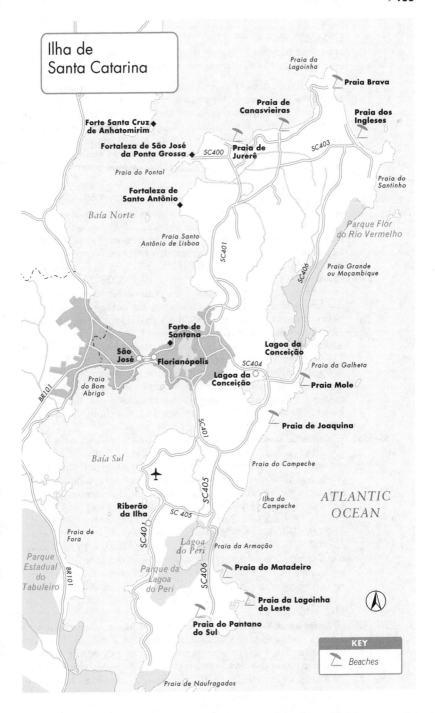

Ilha de Santa Catarina

Praia da Lagoinha

Praia Brava

Praia de Canasvieiras

Praia dos Ingleses

Forte Santa Cruz de Anhatomirim ◆

Fortaleza de São José da Ponta Grossa ◆

SC400

Praia de Jurerê

SC403

Praia do Pontal

Praia do Santinho

Fortaleza de Santo Antônio ◆

Baía Norte

Praia Santo Antônio de Lisboa

SC401

Parque Flor do Rio Vermelho

SC406

Praia Grande ou Moçambique

Forte de Santana ◆

Lagoa da Conceição

São José

Florianópolis

SC404

Praia da Galheta

Lagoa da Conceição ○

Praia Mole

Praia do Bom Abrigo

BR101

Praia de Joaquina

Baía Sul

SC401

Praia do Campeche

SC405

Ilha do Campeche

ATLANTIC OCEAN

Riberão da Ilha

SC 405

Praia de Fora

SC401

Lagoa do Peri

Praia da Armação

Parque Estadual do Tabuleiro

BR101

Parque da Lagoa do Peri

SC406

Praia do Matadeiro

Praia da Lagoinha do Leste

Praia do Pantano do Sul

Praia de Naufragados

KEY

Beaches

Forts

In the early days of the colony, the Portuguese built forts on the Baía Norte and Baía Sul to protect their investment. Today these forts can only be reached by taking a schooner tour.

One of the best-preserved forts open to the public is **Fortaleza de São José**. **Forte Santa Cruz de Anhatomirim** was built in 1744, opposite Fortaleza de São José at the entrance to the Baía Norte. It has a historical photo exhibit as well as a small aquarium. **Fortaleza de Santo Antônio** has marked trails to follow up to the fort. Check out the tropical vegetation along the way. The **Forte de Santana,** under Hercílio Luz Bridge, houses a firearms museum run by the state military police.

Where to Stay & Eat

$–$$$ ✕ **Chef Fedoca.** This restaurant, part of a marina complex, has a grand
Fodor'sChoice view of the Lagoa da Conceição, with surrounding green hills as the back-
★ drop. The fare, organized by Chef Fedoca, a diver himself, includes a wide variety of seafood, with shrimp *moquecas* (stews) as a highlight. ⊠ *Marina Ponta da Areia, Rua Sen. Ivo D'Aquino Neto 133, Lagoa da Conceição, Florianópolis* ☎ *048/232–0759* 🖃 *V* ☺ *Closed Mon.*

$–$$ ✕ **Arante.** At this rustic beachfront restaurant it's the tradition that before leaving, customers pin notes to the walls of their impressions of this restaurant—and the walls are covered with them. The Brazilian seafood buffet served at lunch is flawless; don't pass up the *pirão de caldo de peixe* (black beans cooked with a fish sauce), one of the dinner options. ⊠ *Rua Abelardo Gomes 254, Pântano do Sul, Florianópolis* ☎ *048/237–7022* 🖃 *No credit cards* ⌔ *Reservations essential* ☺ *Closed Mon.*

$ ✕ **Gugu.** This off-the-beaten path restaurant combines no-frills service and decor with an outstanding seafood menu. You can have the steamed oysters as an appetizer and move on to the seafood stew, the talk of the island. ⊠ *Rua Antonio Dias Carneiro 147, Sambaqui, Florianópolis* ☎ *048/335–0288* 🖃 *D, MC, V* ☺ *No lunch Mon.*

$$–$$$$ 🏨 **Costão do Santinho Resort.** The island's most sophisticated resort of-
Fodor'sChoice fers many facilities and a terrific location on Santinho Beach, 35 km (22
★ mi) north of Florianópolis. The ocean view from rooms that face north is one reason to stay here; the surrounding 100-acre Atlantic forest is another (a trail leads to petroglyphs on the hill). The older buildings have full apartments with kitchens, available for longer stays. ⊠ *Rua Ver. Onildo Lemos 2505, Praia do Santinho, Florianópolis 88001-970* ☎ *048/261–1000 or 0800/701–9000* 🖷 *048/261–1236* ⊕ *www.costao. com* 🛏 *451 rooms* ⌕ *3 restaurants, kitchens, cable TV, 8 tennis courts, paddle tennis, 2 indoor pools, 4 outdoor pools, spa, gym, hot tub, massage, sauna, beach, snorkeling, hiking, soccer, volleyball, 2 bars, lounge, recreation room, shops, children's programs, playground, business services, airport shuttle, travel services, convention center* 🖃 *AE, DC, MC, V* ⵏⵓⵎ *MAP.*

$$$ 🏨 **Jurerê Beach Village.** On the sophisticated Jurerê Beach, this hotel is a prime destination for South American visitors, especially those from Argentina. The four- to eight-person guest houses usually require a minimum stay of one week in high season (December–March). The world-class facilities and efficient staff make each guest feel like a homeowner

at Jurerê. And all this is just steps from the sand. ⊠ *Alameda Carlos Nascimento 646, Praia de Jurerê, Florianópolis 88053-000* ☏ *048/ 261–5111 or 0800/48–0110* 🖷 *048/262–5200* ⊕ *www.jurere.com.br* ⌁ *202 apartments, 40 guest houses* ⚘ *Restaurant, kitchen, cable TV, beach, tennis court, 2 pools, health club, sauna, snorkeling, jet skiing, soccer, volleyball, bar, playground, business services* ▭ *AE, DC, MC, V* ⧖ *CP.*

$$–$$$ 🖾 **Praia Mole.** With the Lagoa da Conceição on one side and Praia da Joaquina on the other, the location is unique. Neatly decorated rooms in light colors enhance the green exterior. Colonial-style furnishings, and paintings by local artists contrast with the casual atmosphere. An almost unending lineup of amenities in a 16-acre wooded lot makes this a prime choice for relaxation. In high season (December–February) a four-day minimum stay is required. ⊠ *Estrada Geral da Barra da Lagoa 2001, Praia Mole, Florianópolis 88062-970* ☏ *048/232–5231* 🖷 *048/ 232–5482* ⊕ *www.praiamole.com.br* ⌁ *74 rooms, 18 chalets* ⚘ *Restaurant, cable TV, 2 pools (1 indoor), aerobics, massage, sauna, marina, boating, tennis court, paddle tennis, bar, convention center, no-smoking rooms* ▭ *AE, DC, MC, V* ⧖ *BP.*

$$ 🖾 **Lexus Internacional Ingleses.** Although it has much to offer, this midsize hotel's main attraction is its location on the popular (therefore crowded in high season) Praia dos Ingleses, 34 km (21 mi) northeast of downtown Florianópolis. The pool is one step from the beach, making the Lexus a great place to enjoy the warm northern waters. Choose the bay-facing apartments with balconies where you can hang your hammock and feel the sea breeze. Some apartments have a barbecue grill. ⊠ *Rua Dom João Becker 859, Praia dos Ingleses, Florianópolis 88058-601* ☏ *048/269–2622* 🖷 *048/269–2622* ⌁ *63 rooms* ⚘ *Restaurant, kitchenette, cable TV, indoor pool, outdoor pool, sauna, beach, volleyball, bar* ▭ *AE, DC, MC, V* ⧖ *CP.*

Sports & the Outdoors

The island has a great lineup of sports options. Jet skiing is popular on Lagoa da Conceição, but you must obtain a license by taking a weeklong course from the Brazilian coast guard—something most visitors won't have the time for.

Marina Ponta da Areia (⊠ Rua Sen. Ivo D'Aquino Neto 133, Lagoa da Conceição ☏ 048/232–2290) is the place for boat and jet-ski rentals. Snorkeling and scuba diving are very popular on the northern beaches; check out **Parcel Dive Center** (⊠ Av. Luiz B. Piazza 2243, Ponta das Canas, Florianópolis ☏ 048/284–5564 ⊕ www.parcel.com.br) for diving lessons and for equipment sale, maintenance, and rentals. The cost to rent basic gear is about R$250 a day. **OpenWinds** (⊠ Av. das Rendeiras 1672, Lagoa da Conceição, Florianópolis ☏ 048/232–5004 ⊕ www.openwinds.com.br) offers surf and windsurfing classes; it also has a gear sales and maintenance shop. **Parapente Sul** (⊠ Rua João Antônio da Silveira 201, Lagoa da Conceição, Florianópolis ☏ 048/232–0791 ⊕ www.parapentesul.com.br), a center for parasailing—a popular sport on this mountainous, windy island—leads tandem flights with an instructor for about R$150. For the enthusiasts, a full course is available.

Nightlife

Outside the city proper, the lively Lagoa da Conceição neighborhood has popular bars and live-music venues. During the summer expect heavy car and pedestrian traffic. **John Bull Pub** (⊠ Av. das Rendeiras 1046, Lagoa da Conceição, Florianópolis ☎ 048/232–8535 ⊕ www. johnbullpub.com.br) is *the* place for live music on the island. A roster of local and nationally known bands performs, from blues, rock and roll, and reggae to Brazilian popular music. It's also a great place for drinks and snacks.

Florianópolis

300 km (187 mi) southeast of Curitiba, 476 km (296 mi) northeast of Porto Alegre.

The city of Florianópolis played an important part in the history of the island of Santa Catarina. Settled by colonists from the Azores Islands, it was the southernmost post of Portuguese empire for some time, and it was the site of several skirmishes with the Spanish before the border disputes were settled. You might be lured by the beaches–which rank among the most beautiful in Brazil—but downtown Florianópolis also offers worthwhile attractions.

The **Alfândega** (Old Customs House), which dates from 1875, is the city's best example of neoclassical architecture. It now houses an artists' association and a handicrafts shop that sells *rendas de bilro* (handwoven tapestries) and pottery. ⊠ *Rua Cons. Mafra 141, Centro* ☎ *048/224–6082* ⛛ *Free* ⊙ *Weekdays 9–7, Sat. 9–noon.*

Beyond the Alfândega is the picturesque, 100-year-old **Mercado Público** (Public Market), a Portuguese colonial structure with a large central patio. The renovated market—which is filled with stalls selling fish, fruit, and vegetables—still preserves its Arabian-bazaar atmosphere. ⊠ *Rua Cons. Mafra 255, Centro* ☎ *048/225–3200* ⛛ *Free* ⊙ *Mon.–Sat. 7 AM–9 PM.*

need a break? Despite being small and cramped, **Box 32** (⊠ Mercado Público, Rua Cons. Mafra 255, Centro ☎ 048/224–5588) is *the* meeting place for everyone from businesspeople to students. You'll find more than 800 kinds of liquor, including the Brazilian mainstay, *cachaça* (a sugarcane-based alcohol). Be sure to try the house specialty, *bolinho de bacalhau* (a cod appetizer).

The **Museu Histórico de Santa Catarina** is housed in the 18th-century Palácio Cruz e Souza, a mixture of baroque and neoclassical styles. The palace, whose stairways are lined with Carrara marble, was once the governor's home and office. The sidewalks around the building are still paved with the original stones brought from Portugal. The museum's collection delineates the state's history with documents, personal items, and artwork that belonged to former governors. ⊠ *Praça 15 de Novembro 227, Centro* ☎ *048/221–3504* ⛛ *Free* ⊙ *Tues.–Fri. 10–6, weekends 10–4.*

A great sight to visit by schooner is the **Baía dos Golfinhos** (Dolphin Bay). A few nautical miles up the coast from the island, this bay is home to hundreds of *botos-cinza* (gray dolphins). They tolerate boats moving in very close to them. *See* Tours *in* The South A to Z for information about schooner tours.

Where to Stay & Eat

★ **$-$$** ✕ **La Pergoletta.** A variety of fresh pasta dishes is the highlight here. Try the pasta with shrimp, *kani kama* (ground crabmeat), and white-wine sauce. ⊠ *Trv. Careirão 62, Centro* ☎ *048/224–6353* ⚑ *Reservations essential* ➡ *V* ⊗ *Closed Mon.*

¢ ✕ **Ataliba.** With 20-odd years in the business, you can expect nothing less than excellent service at this rodízio-style churrascaria. The meat selections—more than 20 kinds, from beef to mouton and rabbit—and the salad bar are both outstanding. ⊠ *Rua Irineu Bornhausen 5050, Agronomica* ☎ *048/333–0990* ➡ *AE, DC, MC, V* ⊗ *No dinner Sun.*

$ ⌂ **Íbis Florianópolis.** Íbis is a welcome retreat if you're looking for service and basic facilities like those you can find back home. "Functionality with comfort" is the motto here. It is one of the few hotels to offer rooms for people with disabilities. ⊠ *Av. Rio Branco 37, Centro 88015-200* ☎ *048/216–0000* ⊟ *048/216–0001* ⊕ *www.accorhotels.com.br* ⇙ *198 rooms* ⚬ *Restaurant, cable TV, gym, bar, lounge, business center, Internet* ➡ *AE, DC, MC, V.*

¢ ⌂ **Baía Norte Palace.** Lush suites with hot tubs and await for discerning guests. Rooms are meticulously furnished, and those facing west have a grand view of the bay and Hercílio Luz bridge. From here, quick access to the business district or the beaches is guaranteed. ⊠ *Av. Beira-Mar Norte 220, Centro, 88000-000* ☎ *048/229–3144 or 0800/48–0202* ⊟ *048/225–3227* ⊕ *www.baianorte.com.br* ⇙ *99 rooms, 9 suites* ⚬ *Restaurant, coffee shop, cable TV, outdoor pool, gym, bicycles, bar, meeting room, travel services, airport shuttle* ➡ *AE, DC, MC, V* ⓧ *CP.*

Shopping

For modern shops in a world-class mall, try **Beira-Mar Shopping Center** (⊠ Rua Bocaiúva 2468, Centro ☎ 048/224–1563). If you're looking for beach apparel, a good spot is **Via Lagoa Shopping** (⊠ Rua Henrique Veras do Nascimento s/n, Lagoa da Conceição).

Garopaba

Fodor's Choice *91 km (57 mi) south of Florianópolis, 380 (238 mi) northwest of Porto*
★ *Alegre.*

Around Garopaba you can find great beaches and sand dunes, green hills and rocky cliffs that end right in the ocean. Praia do Rosa and Praia da Ferrugem have acquired national recognition for their awesome beauty and laid-back atmosphere. This is also prime sand-boarding and surfing territory, but watching the *baleia-franca* (right whales) breeding grounds off the coast—scheduled to become a protected area—is quickly becoming popular. The warm waters here attract whales from Patagonia (especially from Peninsula Valdéz) July through October.

Where to Stay & Eat

$ ✕⌂ **EcoResort Vida, Sol e Mar.** This pousada combines easy access to the beach and several amenities, including OnoKaii ($-$$), one of the best seafood restaurants south of Florianópolis. An in-house operator works in conjunction with Instituto Baleia Franca—a nongovernmental environmental organization—to offer whale-watching boat trips (R$100/person). Surfing classes are also available. ⊠ *Km 6, Estrada Geral da Praia do Rosa, Praia do Rosa* ☎ *048/355–6111* ⊕ *www.vidasolemar.com.br* ⇨ *14 rooms* ⌂ *Restaurant, horseback riding, beach, bar* ⊟ *MC, V.*

---

off the beaten path

LAGUNA – Sixty-two kilometers (38 mi) south of Garopaba on BR 101, the city of Laguna is the second-oldest Portuguese settlements in the state of Santa Catarina. Most downtown buildings reflect the early colonial days. Known for its many beaches, Laguna has one of the liveliest Carnaval festivities of southern Brazil. The city is right on the shores of Lagoa Imaruí (Imaruí Lake), which connects to the Atlantic 5 km (3 mi) farther east. You can drive or hire a boat on the beaches to get to the Imaruí Lake delta, where exploring the imposing Santa Marta Lighthouse and nearby beaches is well worth a day's outing.

RIO GRANDE DO SUL

The state of Rio Grande do Sul is almost synonymous with the *gaúcho,* the South American cowboy who is glamorized as much as his North American counterpart. There's more to this state, however, than the idyllic cattle-country lifestyle of the early days. As it is one of Brazil's leading industrial areas, its infrastructure rivals that of any country in the northern hemisphere. Its mix of Portuguese, German, and Italian cultures is evident in the food and architecture. Indeed, to be gaúcho (which is a term for all people and things from this state) may mean to be a vintner of Italian heritage from Caxias do Sul or an entrepreneur of German descent from Gramado as much as a cattle rancher with Portuguese lineage out on the plains.

The state capital, Porto Alegre, is a sophisticated metropolis of 1.3 million that rivals Curitiba in quality of life. This important industrial and business center has universities, museums, and convention centers. It is also one of the greenest cities in Brazil, with many parks and nature preserves. The slopes of the Serra Gaúcha were settled by Italian immigrants; thanks to their wine-making skills, the state now produces quality wines, particularly in the Caxias do Sul and Bento Gonçalves areas. Along the coast, basaltic cliffs drop into a raging Atlantic and provide an impressive backdrop for the sophisticated seaside resort of Torres. Farther inland, straddling the state's highest elevations, is the Aparados da Serra National Park, which has canyons with breathtaking views.

Porto Alegre

476 km (296 mi) southwest of Florianópolis, 760 km (472 mi) southwest of Curitiba, 1,109 km (690 mi) southwest of São Paulo.

Porto Alegre's hallmark is the hospitality of its people, a trait that has been acknowledged over and over by visitors, earning it the nickname Smile City. The capital of one of Brazil's wealthiest states, it has many streets lined with jacaranda trees that create violet tunnels when in full spring bloom.

The city was founded on the banks of the Rio Guaíba in 1772 by immigrants from the Azores. The Guaíba is actually a 50-km-long (31-mi-long) lagoon formed by four rivers that merge a few miles upstream of the city. The city has an important port, connected to the Atlantic by the Lagoa dos Patos.

Exploring Porto Alegre

From Morro de Santa Teresa (Santa Teresa Hill), you get a grand view of the skyline as it confronts the expanse of the Rio Guaíba. From this spot and the numerous riverfront parks, the great spectacle of Porto Alegre's sunset is inspirational. As local poet Mário Quintana put it: "Skies of Porto Alegre, how could I ever take you to heaven?" For another great perspective of Centro, consider taking a riverboat tour of the Rio Guaíba and its islands, which are part of a state park.

The heart of Porto Alegre lies within a triangle formed by Praça da Alfândega, the Mercado Público, and the Praça da Matriz. Not only is this the main business district, it's also the site of many cultural and historical attractions. Outside this area, Casa de Cultura Mário Quintana and Usina do Gasômetro are very active cultural centers, with movies, live performances, art exhibits, and cafés.

Numbers in the text correspond to numbers in the margin and on the Porto Alegre Centro map.

A GOOD WALK On the side of Praça da Alfândega facing the river are two neoclassical structures: the **Museu de Arte do Rio Grande do Sul** ❽ ▶ and the **Memorial do Rio Grande do Sul** ❾. The adjacent brownish building with imposing Roman columns is **Centro Cultural Santander** ❿. From the square head north on Avenida 7 de Setembro to the open space in front of the Prefeitura (the Fonte Talavera de la Reina was donated by the Spanish community of Rio Grande do Sul in 1935). On the opposite side of Avenida Borges de Medeiros is the **Mercado Público** ⓫. Follow Avenida Borges de Medeiros south to the Viaduto Otávio Rocha, the city's first overpass, and climb the stairway to Avenida Duque de Caxias. One block to your right is the **Museu Júlio de Castilhos** ⓬, where you can catch a glimpse of gaúcho culture. A couple of blocks west, on Praça da Matriz, are the **Catedral Metropolitana Nossa Senhora Madre de Deus** ⓭ and the adjacent **Palácio Piratini** ⓮. Finish your tour at **Theatro São Pedro** ⓯.

TIMING You can follow this tour—and visit the museums—in about five hours.

WHAT TO SEE **Catedral Metropolitana Nossa Senhora Madre de Deus.** Although its construction began in 1921, this cathedral wasn't completed until 1986. Its predominant style is Italian Renaissance, but note the twin bell towers, which were inspired by 17th-century Jesuit missions. The facade's mosaic panels were made in the Vatican ateliers. ⊠ *Rua Duque de Caixas 1047, Centro* ☏ *051/3228–6001* ⊡ *Free* ☉ *Daily 7–noon and 2–7.*

⓾ **Centro Cultural Santander.** This stately building has headquartered some local banks in its 100-year existence. Now owned by Banco Santander

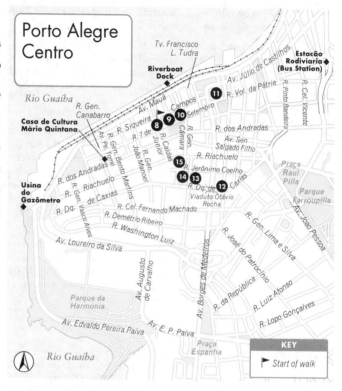

Porto Alegre Centro

Tv. Francisco L. Tudra

Riverboat Dock

Estacão Rodiviaria ◆ (Bus Station)

Av. Júlio de Castilhos

Av. Vol. da Pátria

R. Cel. Vicente

R. Pinto Bandeira

Rio Guaíba

R. Gen. Canabarro

Av. Mauá

Campos Setembro

Casa de Cultura Mário Quintana

R. Siqueira

R. 7 de Junior

R. Caldas

R. Gen. Câmara

R. Gen.

R. dos Andradas

Av. Sen Salgado Filho

Av. Pe. Tomé

R. Gen. Bento Martins

R. João Manoel

R. Riachuelo

R. Jerônimo Coelho

Praça Raul Pilla

R. dos Andradas

R. Riachuelo

R. Dq. de Caxias

Viaduto Otávio Rocha

R. Dq. de Caxias

Parque Farroupilha

Av. João Pessoa

Usina do Gazômetro

R. Cel. Fernando Machado

R. Demétrio Ribeiro

R. Washington Luiz

R. Gen. Lima e Silva

R. José do Patrocínio

Av. Loureiro da Silva

Av. Augusto de Carvalho

Av. Borges de Medeiros

R. da República

R. Luiz Afonso

R. Lopo Gonçalves

Parque da Harmonia

Av. Edvaldo Pereira Paiva

Av. E. P. Paiva

Praça Espanha

Rio Guaíba

KEY
▶ Start of walk

of Spain, it has been transformed into a cultural center and gallery for temporary exhibits. Guided tours (Portuguese only) show the intricate ironwork of the entrance door and second-floor balcony as well as the ceiling's neoclassical paintings. One curiosity: the massive bank vault now contains a small movie theater. ⊠ *Praça da Alfândega s/n, Centro* ☎ *051/3287–5500* ◱ *Free* ☉ *Daily 9–5.*

❾ Memorial do Rio Grande do Sul. Built at the turn of the 20th century, the building was declared a national architectural landmark in 1981. It now houses a state museum. Although overall the style is neoclassical, German-baroque influences are strong; the asymmetrical corner towers with their bronze rotundas are said to resemble Prussian army helmets. A permanent exhibit focuses on the state's history and the lives of important gaúchos, and on the second floor there's one of Brazil's largest collections of documents and manuscripts about Brazilian society. ⊠ *Praça da Alfândega s/n, Centro* ☎ *051/3225–8490* ◱ *Free* ☉ *Daily 9–5.*

⓫ Mercado Público. The neoclassical Public Market was constructed in 1869. It has undergone repeated renovations, the last of which added the glass roof that now covers the central inner plaza. With these changes, some of the produce stalls have been replaced by souvenir shops, cafés, and restaurants—taking away a bit of the boisterous bazaar ambience—but increasing the options for the visitor. ⊠ *Largo Glenio Peres s/n, Centro* ⊙ *Mon.–Sat.* 7 AM–11 PM.

▶ ⑧ **Museu de Arte do Rio Grande do Sul.** In the 1990s the old, neoclassical customs building was restored to house this art museum. German immigrant Theo Wiederspahn designed this and several other of the city's early buildings. A collection of his sketches and blueprints is on display. You can also see paintings, sculptures, and drawings by Brazilian artists from several periods. Two works of Di Cavalcanti—one of the country's most renowned painters—are exhibited as well as several pieces by local sculptor Xico Stockinger. ⊠ *Praça da Alfândega s/n, Centro* ☏ *051/3227-2311* ⊠ *Free* ⊙ *Tues.–Sun. 10–7.*

⑫ **Museu Júlio de Castilhos.** The small Júlio de Castilhos Museum displays an impressive collection of gaúcho documents, firearms, clothing, and household utensils. The home belonged to Governor Julio de Castilhos, who lived here at the turn of the 20th century, before the Palácio Piratini was built. ⊠ *Rua Duque de Caxias 1231, Centro* ☏ *051/3221-3959* ⊠ *Free* ⊙ *Tues.–Fri. 10–5, weekends 1–5.*

⑭ **Palácio Piratini.** The Piratini Palace is the stately governor's mansion, which also houses executive offices. The structure's Roman columns convey a solidity and permanence uncommon in official Brazilian buildings. Duck into the main room to see the murals (depicting gaúcho folktales) by Italian artist Aldo Locatelli. ⊠ *Praça da Matriz s/n, Centro* ☏ *051/3210-4100* ⊠ *Free* ⊙ *Weekdays 9–5.*

⑮ **Theatro São Pedro.** In a 130-year-old building that was thoroughly renovated in the 1980s, São Pedro hosts theatrical and musical performances—including those of the theater's own chamber orchestra (March–December). The popular Café Orquestra das Panelas, on the balcony above the lobby, has an ample view of the Praça da Matriz, the cathedral, and Palácio Piratini. ⊠ *Praça da Matriz s/n, Centro* ☏ *051/3227-5100* ⊠ *Free; ticket prices vary* ⊙ *Closed Mon.*

| off the beaten path | **PARQUE ESTADUAL DE ITAPOÃ** – Fifty-seven kilometers (35 mi) south of Porto Alegre, where the Rio Guaíba flows into Lagoa dos Patos, Itapoã State Park protects 12,000 acres of granitic hills and sandy beaches. At Ponta de Itapoã (Itapoã Point) there's a century-old lighthouse. Although the infrastructure is minimal, being able to bathe in the river, walk along marked trails, and watch magnificent sunsets attracts many visitors. Rare cacti and bands of *bugio* (howler monkeys) add to the list of local natural highlights. Boat tours to the park beaches and lighthouse depart from the marina in the small village of Itapoã, 45 km (28 mi) south of Porto Alegre. ⊠ *Park entrance: Km 1, Estrada das Pombas, Viamão* ☏ *051/494–8083* ⊠ *R$5.50* ⊙ *Wed.–Sun. 8–6.* |

Where to Stay & Eat

$–$$$

FodorśChoice

★

✕ **Al Dente.** This small restaurant serves northern Italian cuisine. Try the *garganelli* (a variety of pasta from from Naples) with salmon in wine sauce or the fettuccine *nere* (black fettuccine) with caviar sauce. ⊠ *Rua*

Mata Bacelar 210, Auxiliadora ☎ *051/3343–1841* ▤ *AE, D, MC, V* ⊘ *Closed Sun. No lunch weekdays.*

★ **$–$$$** ✕ **Il G.** For several years Il Gattopardo (with an abbreviated trade name) has been a trendy dinner spot. It caters to the business crowd, with an essentially international fare that's heavy on Italian. Pasta dishes reign supreme. ⊠ *Rua Felicíssimo de Azevedo 950, Higienópolis* ☎ *051/ 3325–5244* ▤ *AE, DC, MC, V* ⊘ *Closed Sun. No lunch Sat.*

$–$$ ✕ **Galpão Crioulo.** At one of Porto Alegre's largest churrascarias, everything is done the traditional way. The restaurant serves rodízio fare with a salad buffet whose premium beef is more tender than that of most of its competitors. If rodízio is too much for you, ask for the *miniespeto* (one small skewer with a sampler of all meats). Gaúcho musical performances in the evening and a *chimarrão* (type of indigenous tea)–tasting stand round out the highlights. ⊠ *Rua Loureiro da Silva s/n, Parque da Harmonia, Centro* ☎ *051/3226–8194* ▤ *AE, DC, MC, V.*

¢–$ ✕ **Café do Porto.** At one of Porto Alegre's trendiest restaurants, several types of coffee are served, along with drinks, sandwiches, and pastries. Highly recommended is the antipasto *sott'olio* (Italian rolls with dried tomatoes and red and yellow peppers). Combine this with a glass of chardonnay from the regional vineyard, Casa Valduga, or with the house cappuccino. ⊠ *Rua Padre Chagas 293, Moinhos de Vento* ☎ *051/ 3346–8385* ▤ *AE, DC, MC, V.*

¢ ✕ **Ilha Natural.** This is the place to compensate for the likely excesses of rodízio-style churrasco. This vegetarian buffet has carved a name for itself in the downtown business district for its variety of salads and vegetable stews, as well as for the ubiquitous rice and beans. ⊠ *Rua General Camara 60, Centro* ☎ *051/3224–4738* ▤ *No credit cards* ⊘ *Closed weekends. No dinner.*

$–$$ ✕▥ **Holiday Inn Porto Alegre.** The first member of the Holiday Inn family in southern Brazil is in the booming business district of Bela Vista, which not too long ago was a purely residential neighborhood. The decor is modern; rooms have king-size beds. Chef's Grill ($–$$$), the house restaurant with Italian leanings, is increasingly popular on this side of the city. ⊠ *Av. Carlos Gomes 565, Bela Vista 90450-000* ☎ *051/ 3378–2727 or 0800/99–3366* 🖷 *051/3378–2700* 🗗 *172 rooms* ⌂ *Restaurant, coffee shop, cable TV, gym, bar, business services, meeting rooms, no-smoking rooms, Internet* ▤ *AE, DC, MC, V.*

$–$$ ✕▥ **Plaza San Rafael.** The Plaza has long been one of the city's most sophisticated hotels. All suites have whirlpool baths whose hot water is supplied by a thermal spring in the basement. All rooms have wireless Internet service. The restaurant Le Bon Gourmet ($$$–$$$$) has the best French cuisine in town and is very popular with international visitors. One highlight is the juicy fillet Camembert with a mushroom sauce. The Plaza Grill ($$–$$$) serves international fare. ⊠ *Rua Alberto Bins 514, Centro 90030-040* ☎ *051/3220–7000 or 0800/51–2244* 🖷 *051/3220–7001* ⊕ *www.plazahoteis.com.br* 🗗 *261 rooms, 23 suites* ⌂ *2 restaurants, cable TV, indoor pool, gym, sauna, in-room hot tubs, in-room data ports, bar, business services, travel services, convention center, meeting rooms, Internet, no-smoking rooms* ▤ *AE, DC, MC, V* ⑩ *MAP.*

$$$–$$$$ Sheraton Porto Alegre. In the fashionable neighborhood of Moinhos
FodorśChoice de Vento, the Sheraton sets the city's standard of luxury. The level of
★ comfort is outstanding, from the lobby to the top-floor rooms. In the
Brazil Suite you'll find 18th-century-style wooden furniture and copies
of paintings by the French artist Debret, whose works depict rural
scenes of colonial Brazil. The restaurant, Clos du Moulin, offers Mediter-
ranean fare, which is accompanied by live piano performances each
evening. Shoppers take note: the hotel is in the same complex as the Moin-
hos de Vento Mall. ⊠ *Rua Olavo Barreto Viana 18, Moinhos de Vento*
90570-010 ☎ *051/3323–6000 or 0800/11–1345* 🖷 *051/3323–6010*
⊕ *www.sheraton-poa.com.br* 🛏 *156 rooms, 22 suites* ᐸ *Restaurant,*
in-room data ports, in-room safes, minibars, cable TV, health club, bar,
concierge, business services, convention center, meeting rooms, Inter-
net, no-smoking rooms ⊟ *AE, DC, MC, V* ⑩ *CP.*

★ **$–$$** Blue Tree Towers. A haven for well-traveled guests, in the quiet residential Mont Serrat neighborhood, Blue Tree has spacious rooms with
modern decor. Those at the back have superb views of downtown and
the Guaíba. You can ask that a basic office be set up in your room. The
Gaia restaurant serves Japanese fare. ⊠ *Rua Lucas de Oliveira 995, Mont*
Serrat 90940-011 ☎ *051/3333–0333 or 0800/15–0500* 🖷 *051/*
3330–5233 ⊕ *www.bluetree.com.br* 🛏 *130 rooms, 2 suites* ᐸ *Restau-*
rant, cable TV, pool, health club, sauna, bar, business services, meeting
rooms, Internet, no-smoking rooms ⊟ *AE, DC, MC, V* ⑩ *CP.*

$ Everest Palace Hotel. This unassuming central hotel is close to the mu-
seums and cathedral. The staff is well trained and can help you find tours
and activities. The top-floor restaurant, popular with businesspeople,
has relaxing glimpses of the Guaíba riverfront. ⊠ *Av. Duque de Cax-*
ias 1357, Centro 90010-283 ☎ *051/3215–9500 or 0800/99–0095*
🖷 *051/3228–4792* ⊕ *www.everest.com.br* 🛏 *153 rooms* ᐸ *Restaurant,*
cable TV, bar, business services, meeting rooms, Internet, no-smoking
rooms ⊟ *AE, DC, MC, V.*

¢ Continental Business. Tourists are lured to this downtown budget option despite its many business amenities, such as two phone lines for
every room. The hotel is close to attractions and the bus terminal, and
access to the airport is quick and easy. ⊠ *Praça Otávio Rocha 49, Cen-*
tro 90010-000 ☎ *051/3212–1618* 🖷 *051/3228–2463* ⊕ *www.*
hoteiscontinental.com.br 🛏 *126 rooms* ᐸ *Restaurant, cable TV, bar,*
Internet, no-smoking rooms ⊟ *AE, DC, MC, V.*

Nightlife & the Arts

Porto Alegre has a very active cultural life. Complete listings of entertainment and cultural events are published in the daily papers *Zero Hora*
and *Correio do Povo.*

The **Casa de Cultura Mário Quintana** (⊠ Rua dos Andradas 736, Centro
☎ 051/3221–7147) occupies what was Porto Alegre's finest hotel at the
turn of the 20th century, the Majestic. The building has two art-film cinemas, one theater, and several exhibit rooms. The popular Café Con-
certo Majestic, on the seventh floor, has regular jazz and classical music
performances and is a popular happy-hour place. **Dado Bier** (⊠ Bourbon Country Center, Av. Túlio de Rose 100, Três Figueiras ☎ 051/

3378–3000) started off as the city's first microbrewery. Local fashionistas and international tourists hang out at what is now an entertainment complex with a restaurant serving international fare and Dado Tambor, a live-music venue and dance club; the cover charge is R$20. The **Usina do Gasômetro** (⊠ Av. João Goulart 551, Centro ☏ 051/3227–1383) with its conspicuous 110-meter (350-foot) brick smokestack, was the city's first coal-fired powerhouse—built in the early 1920s, when the city experienced rapid growth. Today it's a cultural center with theaters, meeting rooms, and exhibit spaces on the bank of the Rio Guaíba. A terrace café overlooking the river is the perfect place to take in a sunset. The center is open daily 8 AM–midnight.

Sports & the Outdoors

Clube Veleiros do Sul (⊠ Av. Guaíba 2941, Asunção ☏ 051/3346–4382) takes advantage of the great expanse of the Guaíba waters to offer sailing classes and boat rentals. **Estádio Beir-Rio** (⊠ Av. Padre Cacique 891, Praia de Belas ☏ 051/3231–4411), with a capacity of 70,000, is home of Internacional—one of the city's major *futebol* (soccer) clubs. **Estádio Olímpico** (⊠ Largo dos Campeões s/n, Azenha ☏ 051/3217–4466) is the stadium of Grêmio Football Portoalegrense, the city's other major futebol team. It seats 60,000.

Shopping

At the **Brique da Redenção,** on Rua José Bonifácio (southeast side of Parque Farroupilha), you can find antiques and crafts. The entire street is closed to vehicles and taken over by dealers and artisans every Sunday from 10 to 3. **Moinhos Shopping** (⊠ Rua Olavo Barreto Vianna 36, Moinhos de Vento ☏ 051/3346–6013) is the smallest of the city's malls and caters to the sophisticated consumer. There is a six-theater cineplex on-site, and a Sheraton hotel is attached. **Shopping Center Iguatemi** (⊠ Rua João Wallig 1831, Três Figueiras ☏ 051/3334–4500), the oldest of the world-class malls in the city, was extensively expanded in the late 1990s. It includes branches of large chain stores as well as high-end specialty shops. Look for traditional leather crafts, gaúcho apparel, and souvenirs at **Rincão Gaúcho** (⊠ Rua dos Andradas 1159, Centro ☏ 051/3224–1004). If you don't have the time to venture into Brazilian wine country, look for a sample to buy at **Vinhos do Mundo** (⊠ Rua João Alfredo 557, Cidade Baixa ☏ 051/3226–1911).

Caxias do Sul

150 km (93 mi) north of Porto Alegre.

Caxias do Sul is the heart of the state's Italian region, where the first immigrants set foot in 1875. The mild climate and fertile soil helped spur development through agriculture. Now industry (especially the motor and furniture industries) is the leading economic activity in the area, although the production of grapes and other temperate fruits is still important.

The **Museu da Casa de Pedra** (Stone House Museum) was the residence (circa 1878) of the Lucchesi family, one of the first Italian families to arrive in the region. The basalt walls and hewn-wood window frames and doors are testaments to the hardiness of the early days. ⊠ *Rua Matteo Gianella at Av. Ruben Alves* ☎ *054/228–3344 Ext. 1925* 🎫 *Free* ☉ *Tues.–Sun. 9–5.*

Igreja São Pelegrino, finished in 1953, has 14 religious murals, including 12 depicting the *via crucis* (stations of the cross) painted by Italian classical painter Aldo Locatelli, who came to Rio Grande do Sul on a Vatican assignment and eventually became one of the state's most renowned artists. Another highlight is the replica of Michelangelo's *Pietá,* donated in 1975 by the Italian government to celebrate the centennial of immigration (1975). ⊠ *Rua Itália 50* ☎ *No phone* 🎫 *Free* ☉ *Daily 7 AM–9 PM.*

Where to Stay & Eat

$ ✕ **La Vindima.** The city's most traditional eatery, this restaurant is nationally recognized for the *galeto al primo canto* (young fried chicken served with an herb cream sauce). The pasta is homemade, with locally produced wheat flour and eggs, "like in the olden days." If you're not driving, try the house wine; if you are driving, the house grape juice is also good. ⊠ *Rua Borges de Medeiros 446, Caxias do Sul* ☎ *051/ 3221–1696* ▭ *V* ☉ *Closed Sun.*

$ 🏨 **Reynolds International.** Impeccable service has become a hallmark at this small establishment, and a downtown location adds to the convenience. Because of this, it is attracting more and more international businesspeople. Rooms are spacious, with an emphasis on functionality. ⊠ *Rua Dr. Montaury 1441, Caxias do Sul 95100-970* ☎ *054/223–5844* 📠 *054/ 223–5843* ⊕ *www.reynolds.com.br* ⤴ *47 rooms* ⌂ *Restaurant, cable TV, gym, bar, business services, meeting rooms, Internet, parking* ▭ *AE, DC, MC, V* ⏏◯❘ *CP.*

Vale dos Vinhedos

124 km (77 mi) north of Porto Alegre

The Serra Gaúcha produces 90% of Brazilian wine. Grapevines grow throughout the hilly terrain, but the heart of the winemaking country is within the municipality of Bento Gonçalves. Because the best-known Brazilian wineries are within a few miles in this region, the name Vale dos Vinhedos (Vineyard Valley) has become synonymous with quality wines.

Wineries

Casa Valduga is run by Luiz Valduga and his sons. Together they produce Seculum and Premium wines (the cabernets are highly regarded). During the summer you can take a tour of the family-owned vineyards and shop other house products such as grape juice and fruit jellies. ⊠ *Km 6, RS 444, Vale dos Vinhedos, Bento Gonçalves* ☎ *054/453–1154* 🎫 *Free* ☉ *Tours Dec.–Feb. by appointment; wine tastings weekdays 8–11 and 2–6, weekends 9–5.*

Vinícola Cordelier offers guided tours through the facilities, which end in a wine-tasting session. It's smaller than the other wineries in the area and gives more personal attention. ⊠ *Km 210, RS 470, Bento Gonçalves* ☎ *054/453–2333* 🎫 *Free* ☉ *Weekdays 9–4, weekends 9–5.*

The Miolo family has carved a name for itself in the Brazilian wine industry with the **Vinícola Miolo**. The on-site restaurant—which adds to the fare Italian folk songs sung by a small choir—and inn are among the best in the region. Tours of the premises include the vineyards and tasting the award-winning Miolo Reserva wines, which include outstanding chardonnays and cabernet sauvignons. ☒ *Km 9, RS 444, Bento Gonçalves* ☎ *054/459–1233* 🎫 *Free* ☉ *Tours daily 9–5.*

Where to Stay & Eat

$ ✕ **Osteria Mamma Miolo.** This restaurant is connected to the Miolo Winery. In addition to local versions of Italian fare, you'll also find such game as wild boar on the menu. Try the Miolo Reserva Chardonnay as an accompaniment for your dinner. ☒ *Km 9, RS 444, Bento Gonçalves* ☎ *054/459–1233* 🖃 *MC, V.*

$ ✕🖫 **Pousada Valduga.** The Valduga winery maintains three redbrick houses with large, comfortable rooms overlooking the vineyards. The breakfast is almost a full café colonial. The restaurant, which is closed weekdays, serves the best of Brazilian–Italian fare, such as cappelletti soup and pork polenta. ☒ *Km 6, RS 444, Bento Gonçalves 95700-000* ☎ *054/453–1154* 🖶 *054/453–1444* ⊕ *www.casavalduga.com.br* ⇗ *15 rooms* ⚭ *Restaurant, wine shop* 🖃 *D, MC, V.*

Gramado

115 km (72 mi) northeast of Porto Alegre.

It was no doubt Gramado's mild mountain climate that attracted German settlers to the area in the late 1800s. They left a legacy of German-style architecture and traditions that attract today's travelers. Ample lodging options and a seemingly endless choice of restaurants and café colonials have given this city a reputation with conventioneers and honeymooners. Every August the city hosts the Festival de Cinema da Gramado, one of Latin America's most prestigious film festivals. At Christmastime the city is aglow with seasonal decorations and musical performances—the Natal Luz (Christmas Lights) festivities. During peak periods it can be difficult to find lodgings if you haven't made arrangements in advance.

Where to Stay & Eat

$$–$$$ ✕ **Gasthof Edelweiss.** The rustic atmosphere at this superb German restaurant is the ideal setting for duck *à la viennese* (with an orange-flavor cream sauce)—the house specialty. Some tables are in the wine cellar, which has more than 1,000 wine bottles. ☒ *Rua da Carriere 1119, Lago Negro* ☎ *051/3286–1861* 🖃 *AE, DC, MC, V.*

¢–$ ✕🖫 **Bavária.** If you're looking for a peaceful, natural setting, this is a good choice: the hotel is within a private park just off the busy shopping district. A small restaurant ($–$$$) of the same name serves German fare and is highly recommended. ☒ *Rua da Bavária 543, 95670-000* ☎ *051/3286–1362* 🖶 *051/3286–1362* ⇗ *56 rooms* ⚭ *Restaurant, cable TV, indoor pool, sauna, paddle tennis, soccer, bar, Internet* 🖃 *DC, MC, V.*

BRAZILIAN WINE

THE FIRST GRAPEVINES WERE BROUGHT TO BRAZIL IN 1532 by early Portuguese colonists, but it was the Jesuits who settled in the south decades later who were the first to establish true vineyards and wineries (to produce the wine needed for the Catholic mass). It wasn't until Italian immigrants arrived that Brazil's viticulture gained any importance. With the blessing of Italian-born empress Teresa Cristina, wife of Dom Pedro II, the first group of immigrants from northern Italy arrived in 1875. In the next decades, at least 150,000 Italians came to settle the mountainous region of Rio Grande do Sul—the Serra Gaúcha. These newcomers were the first to produce significant quantities of wine, thereby establishing a truly Brazilian wine industry.

Although the region is suitable for growing grapes, the rainfall is often excessive from January to March—when the grapes reach maturity. This has traditionally made local winegrowers true heroes for being able to produce decent wines despite difficult conditions. Traditional grapes such as merlot and cabernet were grown to some extent, but most of the wine produced originated from less impressive American stock—Concord and Niagara grapes. These average wines are still produced for local markets.

New agricultural techniques and hybridization of grapes have brought modern viticulture to the area and allowed a dramatic expansion of higher quality grapes. This has significantly improved wine quality and attracted such international industry heavyweights as Almadén, Moët et Chandon, and Heublein. Almadén broke new ground and established vineyards in the hills near the city of Santana do Livramento (about 480 km/300 mi southwest of Porto Alegre, on the Uruguay border), where, according to current agricultural knowledge, climate and soils are more apt to produce quality grapes. Other wineries are following its steps. There are more than 100 cantinas (winemakers) in Rio Grande do Sul, primarily in the Vale dos Vinhedos (Vineyard Valley) near Bento Gonçalves. The wine producers' association of the Vale dos Vinhedos has created a system similar to that used in European countries for controlled-origin wines to promote and warrant the quality of their products. The following wines have received mentions in the 2002 contest supervised by the Office International de la Vigne et du Vin (International Bureau of Wine): Casa Valduga Spumanti Brut (from Casa Valduga); Salton Espumante moscatel (from Salton), Aurora Espumante Gran Millesime Champenoise (from Cooperativa Vin'cola Aurora); Miolo Terranova shiraz and Reserva cabernet sauvignon (from Miolo); Marco Luigi merlot (from Marco Luigi); Boscato Reserva cabernet sauvignon (from Boscato); Miolo Reserva chardonnay (from Miolo); Cordelier Reserva chardonnay (from Cordelier).

★ $–$$ 🏨 **Serra Azul.** This prestigious hotel's name is almost synonymous with Gramado. It's the preferred choice of Brazilian TV and movie stars during the winter film festival. The location is prime for browsing the myriad clothing shops and enjoying café colonials and restaurants. The owners have a ranch outside the city, where you can experience the gaúcho lifestyle as part of your hotel package. ⊠ *Rua Garibaldi 152, 95670-000* ☎ *054/*

286–1082 🖷 *054/286–3374* 🗪 *151 rooms, 18 suites* ☖ *Restaurant, cable TV, indoor pool, massage, sauna, bar, Internet* ▤ *AE, DC, MC, V.*

¢ 🖷 **Pousada Zermatt.** This charming old inn has a cozy atmosphere with affordable rates and is well away from the noisy downtown district. ⊠ *Rua da Fé 187, Bavaria 95670-000* ☎ *051/3286–2426* 🖷 *051/3286–2426* 🗪 *9 rooms* ☖ *Cable TV, bar* ▤ *MC, V.*

Canela

8 km (5 mi) east of Gramado, 137 km (85 mi) north of Porto Alegre.

Gramado's "smaller sister" is much quieter and more low-profile. Brazilians most immediately associate this city of 35,000 with the Caracol Waterfall, but it has many more attractions, including one of the largest Paraná pine trees on record and great shopping opportunities for cotton and wool-knit apparel, handmade embroidered items, and handicrafts. The impressive views of the forest-clad valleys with meandering rivers also bring many tourists.

The **Parque Estadual do Caracol** (Caracol State Park) has an impressive 120-meter (400-foot) waterfall that cascades straight down into a horseshoe-shape valley carved out of the basaltic plateau. For the best views try the lookout atop the 100-foot tower (R$3). The park also includes 50 acres of native forests with several well-marked paths, dominated by Paraná pine and an environmental education center for children. The entrance area is somewhat overcrowded with souvenir shops and snack tents. ⊠ *Km 9, Estrada do Caracol* ☎ *054/282–3035* 🎫 *R$5* ⊗ *Daily 9–7.*

Parque da Ferradura is a private nature preserve that has three lookouts to the Vale da Ferradura (Horseshoe Valley), formed by Rio Santa Cruz. You can walk trails in more than 500 acres of pine forests through hilly countryside. Spotting deer, anteaters, and badgers is quite common. ⊠ *Km 15, Estrada do Caracol* ☎ *0800/51–2153 or 054/9969–6785* 🎫 *R$10* ⊗ *Daily 9–6.*

Parque do Pinheiro Grosso is a small park that attracts hundreds of tourists, who come to see the 150-foot towering Paraná pine tree. ⊠ *Km 5, Estrada do Caracol* ☎ *No phone* 🎫 *Free* ⊗ *Daily 9–5.*

Where to Stay & Eat

$ ✕ **Al Pesto.** This Italian eatery serves the traditional Brazilian–Italian *galeto* (fried chicken) as well as many homemade pasta options. ⊠ *Rua Helmut Schmidt 109* ☎ *054/1211* ▤ *No credit cards* ⊗ *Closed Mon–Tues. No dinner Sun.*

$ ✕ **Castelinho Caracol.** The lofty two-story building surrounded by flower gardens is the oldest enxaimel house in the region, built in 1913 by the Franzen family, which ran a woodshop on the property for many years. Now this is the place for a hearty café colonial when returning from the Caracol Falls. Behind the house there's a small museum with woodworking tools and farming equipment from the early days of German immigration. ⊠ *Km 6, Estrada do Caracol* ☎ *No phone* ▤ *No credit cards* ⊗ *No dinner.*

$–$$ ⊞ **Laje de Pedra.** Built near a cliff, this hotel has impressive views of the Vale do Quilombo from its west wing. On weekends it regularly hosts a variety of musical performances. Rooms in the main building are rather small and somewhat outdated. ⊠ *Km 3, Av. Pres. Kennedy, 95680-000* ☎ *054/282–4300 or 0800/51–2153* 🖷 *054/282–4400* ⊕ *www.lajedepedra.com.br* 🗘 *250 rooms, 8 suites* △ *Restaurant, cable TV, tennis court, indoor pool, outdoor pool, health club, gym, massage, sauna, spa, bar, theater, children's programs, Internet, meeting rooms* 🖃 *AE, DC, MC, V.*

en route

If you are heading east of Canela on RS 235 to visit the canyons at Aparados da Serra National Park, consider staying in **São Francisco de Paula.** This mountain town, once a stopover for the cattle drives from the south to São Paulo, has many pousadas and hotels—more than you will find near the national park. The town's pride is Lago São Bernardo (St. Bernard Lake), just one step from downtown, with a paved walking path around it.

Parque Nacional dos Aparados da Serra

Fodor'sChoice
★

47 km (29 mi) north of Gramado, 145 km (91 mi) north of Porto Alegre.

This national park was created to protect Itaimbezinho (the Tupi-Guarani language word for "cut rock"), one of the most impressive canyons that dissect the plateau in the north of Rio Grande do Sul State. Another park (Parque Nacional da Serra Geral) was established to protect the other great canyons, such as Malacara and Fortaleza. Winter (June–August) is the best time to take in the spectacular canyon views as there's less chance of fog. The main entrance of the park, the Portaria Gralha Azul, is 20 km (13 mi) southeast of Cambará do Sul, the small town that serves as the park's hub. A visitor center provides information on regional flora and fauna, as well as the region's geology and history. Beyond the entrance, you come to grassy meadows that belie the gargantuan depression ahead. A short path (a 45-minute walk, no guide necessary) takes you to the awesome Itaimbezinho Canyon, cut deep into the basalt bedrock to create the valley 725 meters (2,379 feet) below. The longest path takes you into the canyon's interior. Hire a guide, as it's impossible to navigate the longest trails without one. They can also make arrangements for other trips in the region. The park allows only 1,500 visitors each day, so it's best to arrive early, especially in the summer months. ⊠ *20 km (12 mi) southeast of Cambará do Sul on unpaved road* ☎ *051/3251–1262 or 051/3251–1277, 051/3251–1320 for tour guides (Cambará Visitor Center)* 🖭 *R$6 per person, R$5 parking ticket* ⊗ *Wed.–Sun. 9–5.*

Where to Stay & Eat

¢ ✕ **Fogão Campeiro.** This churrascaria in a picturesque pine bungalow offers the ubiquitous southern Brazilian espeto-corrido, in addition to a fixed-price buffet with less advertised gaúcho dishes such as *arroz de carreteiro* (rice with dried beef), *farofa* (cassava flour), and cooked cassava. Traditional-music performances take place on Friday and Saturday. ⊠ *Rua José Trindade 351* ☎ *051/3251–1012* 🖃 *No credit cards* ⊗ *Closed Mon.*

$ 🏠 **Refúgio Preda Afiada.** The most comfortable lodging on the down side of the canyons, this pousada has established its niche among adventure tourists, who depart from here to explore the Malacara Canyon and beyond. All northwest-facing rooms have balconies with views of the canyon walls. ⊠ *Estrada da Vila Rosa s/n* ☎☎ *048/532–1059 or 051/ 3338–3323* ⤴ *9 rooms* ⚴ *Dining room, snack bar, hiking, horseback riding, lounge; no a/c, no room phones, no room TVs* 🖃 *No credit cards* ⎟⊙⎟ *MAP.*

¢ 🏠 **Pousada das Corucacas.** Step into the region's rugged world by staying at this inn on a working gaúcho ranch—the 1,200-acre Fazenda Baio Ruano. This pousada has no frills but offers cozy guest rooms with central heating (rare in the countryside), an ample lounge with a fireplace, and a great view of the surrounding hills, which are covered with native pastures and dotted with Paraná pine trees. There are waterfalls and woods in the area: consider exploring them on horseback and perhaps venturing in to the canyons beyond. ⊠ *Km 1, Estrada Ouro Verde, 95481-970* ☎ *054/251–1128 or 054/9956–7042* ⤴ *14 rooms* ⚴ *Dining room, horseback riding; no a/c, no room phones, no room TVs* 🖃 *No credit cards* ⎟⊙⎟ *MAP.*

Torres

205 km (128 mi) northeast of Porto Alegre.

The beaches around the city of Torres are Rio Grande do Sul's most exciting. The sophistication of the seaside areas attracts international travelers, particularly those from Argentina and Uruguay. Some of the best beaches are Praia da Cal, Praia da Guarita, and Praia Grande. The Parque Estadual da Guarita (Watchtower State Park), 3 km (2 mi) south of downtown, was set aside to protect the area's unique vegetation as well as the basalt hills that end abruptly in the Atlantic. Locals like to fish from these cliffs. A mile offshore, Ilha dos Lobos (Seawolf Island) is a way station for sea lions in their annual migrations along the south Atlantic coast.

Where to Stay & Eat

¢–$$ ✕ **Restaurante Parque da Guarita.** The thatched roof and tropical garden of this restaurant blend in perfectly with its beach setting. Seafood is the specialty here, and you can partake of your meal while enjoying the magnificent view of the surf with the cliffs as a backdrop. ⊠ *Km 2, Estrada do Parque da Guarita* ☎ *051/3664–1056* 🖃 *DC, MC, V* ⊗ *No dinner Mar.–Nov.*

$ 🏠 **Solar da Barra Hotel.** In one of the best hotels in the city the decor is not distinguished, but rooms are large and comfortably furnished. Services are akin to those normally found only in larger resorts. Sightseeing boat trips to Ilha dos Lobos can be arranged by the hotel. ⊠ *Rua Plínio Kroeff 465, Mampituba 95560–000* ☎ *051/3664–1811 or 0800/ 54–16100* 🖶 *051/3664–1090* ⊕ *www.solardabarra.com.br* ⤴ *178 rooms* ⚴ *Restaurant, cable TV, 2 pools (1 indoor), sauna, bar, night-*

club, meeting room, Internet, soccer, volleyball, paddle tennis, playground ▣ *AE, DC, MC, V.*

São Miguel das Missões

482 km (300 mi) northwest of Porto Alegre.

Jesuit missionaries moved from Paraná Valley to the upper Uruguayan River basin around 1700. In the following decades the local Guarani peoples were converted to Christianity, leading them to abandon their seminomadic lifestyle and to congregate around the new missions. Seven of these existed in what is now Brazil, and several more were in Argentina and Paraguay—all linked by a closely knit trade and communication route. Historians have claimed that at the peak of their influence, the Jesuits actually had created the first de facto country in the Americas, complete with a court system and elections. This important historical period was depicted in *The Mission,* starring Robert De Niro. Later in the century the missions were raided by slave hunters and Portuguese militia. The Jesuits fled, and the Guaranis were either taken as slaves or disappeared into unexplored country.

São Miguel das Missões is the best-preserved and best-organized Jesuit mission in Brazil. Circa 1745 an impressive church was built of reddish basalt slabs brought by the Guaranis from quarries miles away. The ruins are now a UNESCO World Heritage Site. There is a small museum on the grounds designed by Lucío Costa (who was instrumental in the development of Brasília). It holds religious statues carved by the Guaranis, as well as other pieces recovered from archaeological digs. Admission to the site includes a sound-and-light show that tells the mission's story, at 8 PM in summer and 6 PM in winter.

Tours of the missions can be booked through any tour operator in Porto Alegre. Other mission sites with ruins are São Lourenço and São Nicolau; however, there is much less to be seen at these sites, and access is difficult. ⊠ *Parque Histórico de São Miguel. From Porto Alegre follow BR 386 to Carazinho, then BR 285 to the São Miguel exit. From there drive 11 km (7 mi) to mission site via BR 466* ☎ *055/3381–3259* ▣ *R$3* ☉ *Museum daily 8–6; grounds daily 8 AM–dusk.*

Where to Stay & Eat

¢ ✕ **Churrascaria Barichello.** This typical gaúcho restaurant is the best option in town. Savor the espeto-corrido, with more than a dozen kinds of meat. ⊠ *Av. Borges do Canto 1519* ☎ *055/381–1327* ▣ *No credit cards.*

★ ¢ ▦ **Wilson Park Hotel Missões.** A world-class hotel catering to the discriminating tourist, the Wilson Park has large rooms painted in pastel colors, with colonial-style furnishings. Arched doorways echo the design of the mission a few blocks away. The well-trained staff is knowledgeable about the missions and other attractions in the region. ⊠ *Rua São Miguel 664, 98865-000* ☎ *055/3381–2000* ⌨ *78 rooms* ☆ *Restaurant, cable TV, pool, horseback riding, bar, Internet, no smoking rooms* ▣ *AE, MC, V* ◉| *CP.*

THE SOUTH A TO Z

To research prices, get advice from other travelers, and book travel arrangements, visit www.fodors.com.

AIR TRAVEL

CARRIERS No international airlines serve Curitiba or Foz do Iguaçu directly from Canada, the United Kingdom, or the United States. The domestic airlines that fly to Curitiba are TAM, Varig, Gol, and VASP. Foz do Iguaçu is served by TAM, Varig, and VASP. TAM also serves Ciudad del Este, in Paraguay, across the border from the falls. Domestic air carriers that serve the Santa Catarina region include TAM, Gol, Varig, and VASP. Airlines that serve Rio Grande do Sul include Aerolíneas Argentinas, TAM, Gol, Varig, and VASP.

Several airlines have code-share agreements. So technically you can fly United or American Airlines to Porto Alegre, although the planes are owned by Varig or TAM. The closest airport to São Miguel das Missões is 60 km (38 mi) away, in Santo Angelo. It's served daily by OceanAir flights from Porto Alegre and São Paulo.

🛂 Airlines & Contacts **Aerolíneas Argentinas** 🕾 051/3221-3300 in Rio Grande do Sul. **Gol** 🕾 041/322-5655 in Curitiba, 045/523-5205, 045/523-3836 in Foz do Iguaçu, 041/381-1579 elsewhere in Paraná, 0300/789-2121 in Santa Catarina, 051/3358-2028 in Rio Grande do Sul. **TAM** 🕾 041/381-1620, 041/219-1270 in Curitiba, 045/523-8500 or 045/523-3533 in Foz do Iguaçu, 048/223-3391 or 041/236-0086 in Santa Catarina, 051/3286-5834 or 051/3358-2052 in Rio Grande do Sul. **OceanAir** 🕾 051/3358-2393 or 0300/789-8160 in Rio Grande do Sul. **Varig** 🕾 041/322-1343 in Curitiba, 045/523-2155 or 045/529-6601 in Foz do Iguaçu, 041/381-1600 elsewhere in Paraná, 048/236-1121 or 048/236-1779 in Santa Catarina, 051/3358-7200 or 051/3358-7999 in Rio Grande do Sul. **VASP** 🕾 041/221-7422 in Curitiba, 045/523-7161 in Foz do Iguaçu, 041/382-0345 elsewhere in Paraná, 048/236-3033 in Santa Catarina, 051/3371-4496 or 051/3225-6111 in Rio Grande do Sul.

AIRPORTS & TRANSFERS

Curitiba's Aeroporto Internacional Afonso Pena (CWB) is 21 km (13 mi) east of the city. A cab ride to downtown is around R$30. In addition, there's (minibus) service for R$5 that leaves from Rua 24 Horas and Estação Rodoferroviária.

The Aeroporto Internacional Foz do Iguaçu (IGU) is 13 km (8 mi) southeast of downtown. The 20-minute taxi ride should cost R$35, the 45-minute regular bus ride about R$1.75. Note that several major hotels are on the highway to downtown, so a cab ride from the airport may be less than R$25. A cab ride directly to the Parque Nacional in Brazil costs R$60, and a full tour including both the Brazilian and Argentine sides of the falls costs R$160 (tickets not included).

The Aeroporto Internacional Hercílio Luz (FLN) is 12 km (8 mi) south of downtown Florianópolis. Taking a cab into town will run about R$22. In addition, there's *amarelinho* (minibus) service for R$5.

Porto Alegre's Aeroporto Internacional Salgado Filho (POA) is one of the most modern air terminals of Brazil. It is only 8 km (5 mi) northeast of downtown. At a booth near the arrivals gate, you can prepay (R$35) for a ride to town in special airport cars, full-size white sedans with a blue stripe. Regular city cabs (red-orange in color) have meters; a ride to downtown should cost around R$20. There's also a minibus shuttle into town for R$1.30.

🛈 Airport Information Aeroporto Internacional Afonso Pena ✉ Av. Rocha Pombo, São José dos Pinhais, Curitiba ☎ 041/381-1515. **Aeroporto Internacional Foz do Iguaçu** ✉ Km 13, Rodovia das Cataratas ☎ 045/521-4200. **Aeroporto Internacional Hercílio Luz** ✉ Km 12, Av. Deomício Freitas, Florianópolis ☎ 048/236-0879. **Aeroporto Internacional Salgado Filho** ✉ Av. Severo Dulius 90010, Porto Alegre ☎ 051/3358-2000.

BUS TRAVEL

For the most part, each city is served by a different bus company. For long-distance trips it's best to opt for special services, often called *executivo* or *leito* (pullman) buses, which have air-conditioning, wide reclining seats, and rest rooms. Regular buses are 20%–30% less but aren't nearly as comfortable.

PARANÁ Curitiba's main bus station is the Estação Rodoferroviária. Catarinense buses travel to Blumenau (4 hours) and Joinville (1½ hours). Penha buses run to and from São Paulo (5 hours). For trips to Porto Alegre (12 hours), try Pluma. Sulamericana buses make the 10-hour trip to Foz do Iguaçu. The Terminal Rodoviário in Foz do Iguaçu is 5 km (3 mi) northeast of downtown. For trips to Florianópolis (14 hours), contact Catarinense. Pluma buses make the 16-hour journey to São Paulo. For trips to Curitiba (10 hours), try Sulamericana.

🛈 Bus Information Catarinense ☎ 041/224-9368 in Curitiba, 045/223-2996 in Foz do Iguaçu. **Estação Rodoferroviária** ✉ Av. Afonso Camargo 330, Curitiba ☎ 041/320-3000. **Penha** ☎ 041/322-8811. **Pluma** ☎ 041/223-3641 in Curitiba, 045/522-2515 in Foz do Iguaçu. **Sulamericana** ☎ 041/373-1000 in Curitiba, 045/522-2050 in Foz do Iguaçu. **Terminal Rodoviário** ✉ Av. Costa e Silva s/n, Foz do Iguaçu ☎ 045/522-3633.

SANTA CATARINA Several bus companies have regular service to and from Florianópolis's Terminal Rodoviário Rita Maria. For the 12-hour journey to São Paulo, the 3½-hour trip to Joinville, or the two-hour trip to Blumenau, try Catarinense. Pluma buses travel to Curitiba (5 hours). For trips to Porto Alegre (6 hours), try União Cascavel/Eucatur.

🛈 Bus Information Catarinense ☎ 048/222-2260. **Pluma** ☎ 048/223-1709. **Terminal Rodoviário Rita Maria** ✉ Av. Paulo Fontes 1101, Florianópolis ☎ 048/224-2777. **União Cascavel/Eucatur** ☎ 048/224-2080.

RIO GRANDE DO SUL All bus lines to the interior—and to other states and countries—use the ugly, overcrowded Estação Rodoviária. Penha has service to São Paulo (19 hours). Pluma buses travel to Curitiba (12 hours). Florianópolis (6 hours) is served by Santo Anjo/Eucatur. To reach Foz do Iguaçu (14 hours), try Unesul. Regular bus service to São Miguel das Missões is not designed for tourists—the buses are not comfortable and are painfully slow; instead, book a tour from Porto Alegre and fly or take a charter bus.

🛈 Bus Information Estação Rodoviária ✉ Largo Vespasiano Veppo s/n ☎ 051/3210-0101. **Penha** ☎ 051/3225-0933. **Pluma** ☎ 051/3224-9291. **Santo Anjo/Eucatur** ☎ 051/3228-8900. **Unesul** ☎ 051/3228-0029.

BUS TRAVEL WITHIN THE SOUTHERN CITIES

Within the region's cities, the bus is the preferred form of public transportation. You can reach virtually any neighborhood, and the fares are modest. Still, you must use caution, as crime can be a problem on little-traveled routes or during off-peak hours.

In Curitiba, the Linha Turismo is a special bus line maintained by the city that follows a 2½-hour circular route, which allows three stops along the way for the same fare. Buses depart every 30 minutes from 9 to 5:30 from the Praça Tiradentes, stopping at 22 attractions. Plan to spend an entire day on this route. There are taped descriptions of the sights (available in three languages—including English), and the fare is R$10. You can contact the Prefeitura-Turismo for more information.

In Foz do Iguaçu, Linha Cataratas and Parque Nacional buses depart hourly (8–6) from the Terminal Urbano for the visitor center at the park entrance. The fare is about R$1.75. Buses for Puerto Iguazú, Argentina, and Ciudad del Este, Paraguay, depart from the same terminal.

In Florianópolis a quick, convenient way to visit the beaches is by amarelinho (also known as executivo), or express minibuses, which cost about R$3.50. They leave regularly from designated terminals places around Praça XV.

Porto Alegre has an extensive bus system (although not a central station) as well as *lotação* (express minibus) service. The lotaçãoes leave from several spots in Centro and cost about R$2 for most routes. For more information call Informações Municipais.

🚍 Bus Information **Informações Municipais** ⊠ Porto Alegre ☎ 051/158. **Prefeitura-Turismo** ⊠ Curitiba ☎ 041/156. **Terminal Urbano** ⊠ Av. Juscelino Kubitschek s/n, across from army barracks, Foz do Iguaçu ☎ 0800/45–1516. **Terminal Urbano** ⊠ Praça 15 de Novembro s/n, Centro, Florianópolis ☎ 048/1517.

CAR RENTAL

Don't expect to find vehicles in the luxury range of the car spectrum. Automatic transmission is not normally available, and there's a surcharge for air-conditioning.

🚗 Major Agencies **Avis** ⊠ In Paraná: Aeroporto Internacional Afonso Pena, Av. Rocha Pombo, São José dos Pinhais, Curitiba ☎ 041/381–1381 ⊠ Av. Salgado Filho 1491, Curitiba ☎ 041/296–1889 ⊠ Km 16.5, Rodovia das Cataratas, Foz do Iguaçu ☎ 045/523–1510. ⊠ In Santa Catarina: Aeroporto Internacional Hercílio Luz, Av. Deomício Freitas, Km 12, Florianópolis ☎ 048/236–1426 ⊠ Av. Silva Jardim 495, Florianópolis ☎ 048/225–7777. ⊠ In Rio Grande do Sul: Aeroporto Internacional Salgado Filho, Av Severo Dulius 90010, Porto Alegre ☎ 051/3371–4514 ⊠ Av. Ceará 444, Porto Alegre ☎ 051/3342–0400. **Hertz** ⊠ In Paraná: Aeroporto Internacional Afonso Pena, Av. Rocha Pombo, São José dos Pinhais, Curitiba ☎ 041/381–1382 ⊠ Av. Nossa Senhora Aparecida 3731, Curitiba ☎ 041/369–8000. ⊠ In Santa Catarina: Aeroporto Internacional Hercílio Luz, Av. Deomício Freitas, Km 12, Florianópolis ☎ 048/236–9955 ⊠ Rua Bocaiuva 2125, Florianópolis ☎ 048/224–9955. ⊠ In Rio Grande do Sul: Aeroporto Internacional Salgado Filho, Av Severo Dulius 90010, Porto Alegre ☎ 051/3337–7755.

🚗 Local Agency **Localiza** ⊠ In Paraná: Km 16.5, Rodovia das Cataratas, Foz do Iguaçu ☎ 045/529–6300 ⊠ Av. Juscelino Kubitschek 2878, Foz do Iguaçu ☎ 045/522–1608. ⊠ In Santa Catarina: Aeroporto Internacional Hercílio Luz, Av. Deomício Freitas, Km

12, Florianópolis ☎ 048/236-1244 ✉ Av. Paulo Fonte 730, Florianópolis ☎ 048/225-5558. ✉ In Rio Grande do Sul: Aeroporto Internacional Salgado Filho, Av. Severo Dulius 90010, Porto Alegre ☎ 051/3358-2346 ✉ Av. Carlos Gomes 190, Porto Alegre ☎ 051/3328-3150 ✉ Km 13, Estrada Catuipe, Santo Angelo, 60 km (38 mi) from São Miguel das Missões ☎ 055/3312-1000.

CAR TRAVEL

The southern states have extensive highway systems connecting major cities and tourist destinations. Be prepared for stretches that aren't in top condition; some are being renovated, and there may be delays. When planning a road trip, ask at the nearest Polícia Rodoviária (Highway Patrol) station for guidance. These are by the main roads, usually a few miles from major cities. Privatized toll roads in Rio Grande do Sul and Paraná are generally in good shape, but you'll have to pay R$3–R$7.

You can drive from Curitiba to Foz do Iguaçu on BR 277, which traverses Paraná State. It's a long drive, but this toll highway is kept in good shape. To visit Vila Velha State Park, a detour must be made on BR 376 toward Ponta Grossa. The BR 101 is the most direct route from Curitiba to other southern communities, but it's one of the country's busiest roads (there's lots of truck traffic night and day). The single-lane stretch south of Florianópolis is extremely dangerous, especially during the vacation months of January and February.

BR 116, the Mountain Route, runs from Curitiba to Porto Alegre. Built 40 years ago, it was the first highway connecting the region with the rest of the country. Although it's scenic for much of the way—and a little shorter than other routes—it's also narrow, with many curves and many trucks.

The 482-km (300-mi) route from Porto Alegre to São Miguel das Missões is along single-lane roads, but they are generally in good condition. Expect heavy truck traffic.

Traffic in Curitiba, Florianópolis, and Porto Alegre isn't as hectic as in São Paulo or Rio, so driving won't be overly daunting. Finding a place to park is relatively easy, except, of course, in the downtown districts during business hours. Parking lots are abundant in the cities, and one-hour tickets cost about R$4.

EMERGENCIES

🚹 Emergency Contacts **Ambulance** ☎ 192. **Emergency** ☎ 100 in Curitiba. **Fire** ☎ 193. **Police** ☎ 190.

🚹 Hospitals **Hospital Cajuru** ✉ Av. São José 300, Curitiba, Paraná ☎ 041/360-3000. **Hospital Internacional** ✉ Av. Brasil 1637, Foz do Iguaçu, Paraná ☎ 045/523-1404. **Hospital Pronto Socorro** ✉ Av. Osvaldo Aranha s/n, Porto Alegre, Rio Grande do Sul ☎ 051/3316-9600. **Hospital Universitário** ✉ Av. Beira-Mar Norte, Trindade, Florianópolis, Santa Catarina ☎ 048/331-9100.

🚹 24-Hour Pharmacies **Farmácia PanVel** ✉ Av. 24 de Outubro 722, Moinhos de Vento, Porto Alegre, Rio Grande do Sul ☎ 051/3222-0188. **Farmácia Rita Maria** ✉ Av. Paulo Fontes 1101, Terminal Rita Maria, Florianópolis, Santa Catarina ☎ 048/222-5016.

FarmaRede ✉ Av. Brasil 46, Foz do Iguaçu, Paraná ☎ 045/523-1929. **HiperFarma** ✉ Rua P. Antonio Polito 1028, Curitiba, Paraná ☎ 041/286-5511

ENGLISH-LANGUAGE MEDIA

Few bookstores stock English-language books. When they're available, expect only a limited selection of paperbacks. Foreign newspapers are rarely available; you might have more success with popular international magazines.

In Curitiba try Livraria O Livro Técnico. Florianópolis has the Livraria Alemã and Catarinense. In Porto Alegre good bets are Prosa i Verso, which has a limited selection of classics and run-of-the-mill paperbacks, and Saraiva Mega Store, which carries paperbacks, travel guides, and several popular magazines.

🕮 Bookstores **Livraria Alemã** ✉ Rua Felipe Schmidt 14, Florianópolis ☎ 041/224-0178. **Livraria Catarinense** ✉ Beiramar Shopping, Rua Bocaiuva 2468, Florianópolis ☎ 048/324-2519. **Livraria Siciliano** ✉ Rua Candido de Abreu 127, Curitiba ☎ 041/324-3343. **Prosa i Verso** ✉ Quinta Avenida Shopping Center, Av. Mostardeiro 120, Porto Alegre ☎ 051/3222-2409. **Saraiva Mega Store** ✉ Shopping Center Praia de Belas, Av. Praia de Belas 1181, Porto Alegre ☎ 051/3231-6868.

HEALTH

Here, in Brazil's most developed region, tap water is safe to drink in most areas. It's usually highly chlorinated, so you may prefer the taste of bottled water. As in the rest of Brazil, avoid eating unpeeled fruit.

MAIL, INTERNET & SHIPPING

🕮 Courier Services **FedEx** ✉ Rua Nossa Senhora da Penha 435, Curitiba ☎ 041/362-5155 ✉ Rua Coronel Américo 912, Florianópolis ☎ 048/240-6232 ✉ Av. Ceará 255, Porto Alegre ☎ 051/3325-1333. **UPS** ✉ Rua Visconde do Rio Branco 279, Porto Alegre ☎ 051/3346-6655.

🕮 Internet Centers **Digital Land** ✉ Av. das Cataratas 1118, Foz do Iguaçu ☎ 045/523-4245. **Saraiva Mega Store** ✉ Shopping Center Praia de Belas, Av. Praia de Belas 1181, Menino Deus, Porto Alegre ☎ 051/3231-6868.

🕮 Post Offices **Correios** ✉ Av. Marechal Deodoro 298, Curitiba ☎ 041/310-2159. **Correios** ✉ Praça Getúlio Vargas 72, Foz do Iguaçu ☎ 045/523-0327. **Correios** ✉ Praça 15 de Novembro 242, Florianópolis ☎ 048/159. **Correios** ✉ Rua Siqueira Campos 1100, Porto Alegre ☎ 051/3220-8800.

MONEY MATTERS

In general, banks are open weekdays 10–4 in major cities, 10–3 in the countryside, though major airport branches have extended hours for currency exchange (daily 8 AM–9 PM); some also have weekend hours. ATMs dispense only reais; for security reasons most ATMs shut down after 8 PM and restart after 6 AM; usually ATMs at airports and main branches will accept international bank or credit cards. Banco 24 Horas ATMs are linked with Cirrus/Maestro network; Banco do Brasil and HSBC ATMs are connected with Plus/Pulse.

🕮 Banks in Paraná **Banco ABN-AMRO Real** ✉ Av. Candido de Abreu 304, Centro Cívico, Curitiba ☎ 041/252-2233. **Banco do Brasil** ✉ Aeroporto Internacional Afonso Pena, Av. Rocha Pombo, São José dos Pinhais, Curitiba ☎ 041/381-1515 ✉ Av. Brasil 1377,

Foz do Iguaçu ☎ 045/521-2500. **BankBoston** ✉ Av. Mal. Deodoro 869, Centro, Curitiba ☎ 041/322-5052. **STTC** ✉ Av. das Cataratas 1419, Foz do Iguaçu ☎ 045/574-2527.

🏛 Banks in Santa Catarina Amplestur ✉ Rua Jerônimo Coelho 293, Loja 01, Centro, Florianópolis ☎ 041/224-9422. **Banco do Brasil** ✉ Praça 15 de Novembro 20, Florianópolis ☎ 048/222-7000 ✉ Aeroporto Internacional Hercílio Luz, Av. Dep. Diomício Freitas s/n, Florianópolis ☎ 048/236-1717.

🏛 Banks in Rio Grande do Sul Banco do Brasil ✉ Rua Uruguai 185, Centro, Porto Alegre ☎ 051/3214-7500 ✉ Aeroporto Internacional Salgado Filho, Av. Severo Dulius 90010, Porto Alegre ☎ 051/3371-1822. **Citibank** ✉ Praça Maurício Cardoso 176, Porto Alegre ☎ 051/3222-4488. **Exprinter** ✉ Rua Hiláario Ribeiro 292, Porto Alegre ☎ 051/3346-4111.

Casa Brasil ✉ Aeroporto Internacional Salgado Filho, Av Severo Dulius 90010, Porto Alegre ☎ 051/3358-2346.

SAFETY

Crime is low compared with the northern parts of the country. However, you should guard your belongings on city buses and in crowded public spaces—especially bus terminals, which are havens for pickpockets. Be extra cautious at night, especially when leaving a nightclub or bar.

TAXIS

Taxis in Brazil are normally independently owned, and most are locally organized into cooperatives that maintain phone numbers and dispatchers (hence, the moniker *radio taxis*). These outfits have booths in all airports, with posted rates (regulated by city authorities) for specific destinations; you pay up front for the ride to town. Although it's best to call for a cab in town to avoid delays, you can hail passing taxis. Cabs have meters, but to avoid surprises, before departing ask for an estimate of the fare to your destination. In Foz do Iguaçu independent tour operators (certified by the city government) offer their services outside hotel lobbies. These special cabs are usually large sedans with air-conditioning. The driver doubles as a tour guide, and you can tailor the route and pace according to your interests. A half-day trip to the Argentinean Foz side of the falls from downtown costs about R$160.

🏛 Taxi Companies Curitiba radio-taxi service ☎ 0800/707-7676 or 041/376-7676. **Foz do Iguaçu radio-taxi service** ☎ 045/523-4800. **Florianópolis radio-taxi service** ☎ 197. **Porto Alegre radio-taxi service** ☎ 051/3334-7444 or 051/3266-3636.

TELEPHONES

Area codes in the region are 41 for Curitiba, 45 for Foz do Iguaçu, 48 for Florianópolis, and 51 for Porto Alegre. Fax and Internet services are available at hotels and major post offices.

TOURS

PARANÁ In Curitiba try Best Ways (which runs Serra Verde Express) for train tickets to the Paranaguá Bay and tours of the attractions including the national park; check OneTur for other Paraná state sights.

STTC Turismo in Foz do Iguaçu is reliable. Macuco Safari arranges Zodiac trips to Salto Macuco and on to the main falls. Helisul Táxi Aéreo offers helicopter tours of the falls between 9 and 6 and, if you like, of

Itaipú Dam. The shortest flight (10 minutes) costs US$60 per person (with a minimum of three passengers).

Best Ways ⊠ Estação Rodoferroviária, Gate 8, Curitiba ☎ 041/323-4007. **OneTur** ⊠ Rua Mal. Floriano 228, Suite 1107, Centro, Curitiba ☎ 041/224-8509 ⊕ www.onetur. com.br. **Helisul Táxi Aéreo** ⊠ Km 16.5, Rodovia das Cataratas, Foz do Iguaçu ☎ 045/ 529-7474 ⊕ www.helisul.com. **Macuco Safari** ⊠ Km 21, Rodovia das Cataratas, Foz do Iguaçu ☎ 045/574-4244. **STTC Turismo** ⊠ Av. Morenitas 2250, Padre Monti, Foz do Iguaçu ☎ 045/523-1115 ᐸ 045/523-3137 ⊕ www.sttcturismo.com.br.

SANTA CATARINA In Florianópolis try Amplestur for van tours of the city, the beaches, and destinations around the continent. Scuna Sul operates a schooner, on which you can take tours, especially of the northern part of the island. A highly recommended tour includes a stop for snorkeling off Ilha do Arvoredo, a nature preserve. For the more adventurous traveler there is a larger schooner outfitted for a 12-hour trip around the island, which costs R$120.

Amplestur ⊠ Rua Jerônimo Coelho 293, Loja 01, Centro, Florianópolis ☎ 041/224-9422 ⊕ www.amplestur.com.br. **Scuna Sul** ⊠ Rua Antonio Heil s/n, Canasvieiras, Florianópolis ☎ 048/266-1810.

RIO GRANDE DO SUL In Porto Alegre tours of the city, to the Serra Gaúcha, of the coast, and to the missions can all be arranged by Hamburguesa and Unesul Turismo. Cisne Branco and Noiva do Mar run day and night boat trips on the Guaíba. Caá-Etê Expeditions is a good choice for adventure trips—rafting, horseback riding, or hiking excursions—to the national and state parks.

Caá-Etê Expeditions ⊠ Av. Protásio Alves 2715, Suite 905, Porto Alegre ☎ 051/ 3338-3323 ⊕ www.caa-ete.com.br. **Cisne Branco** ⊠ Port of Porto Alegre, Main Gate, Av. Mauá 1050, Porto Alegre ☎ 051/3224-5222. **Noiva do Mar** ⊠ Usina do Gasômetro, Av. Pres João Goulart 551, Porto Alegre ☎ 051/3212-5979. **Hamburguesa** ⊠ Rua Alberto Bins 514, Suite 10 [Hotel Plaza San Rafael lobby], Porto Alegre ☎ 051/3211-5088. **Unesul Turismo** ⊠ Rua Vigário José Inácio 621, Porto Alegre ☎ 051/3228-8111.

TRAIN TRAVEL

One of Brazil's few passenger rail lines runs from Curitiba to Paranaguá—a fabulous 110-km (69-mi) trip. Trains traverse the Serra do Mar slope from 1,000 meters (3,300 feet) down to 5 meters (17 feet) through bridges and tunnels. There are great views of the peaks, waterfalls, and Atlantic rain forest, which covers most of the slopes on the way. Two stops, at the historic towns of Marumbi and Morretes, complete this great route. Two kinds of trains operate: the faster motorcar *litorina* makes the trip in 3½ hours, departs from Curitiba at 9 AM (Friday–Sunday and holidays), returns from Paranaguá at 3:30 PM, and costs R$75; the trip by regular train takes four hours, departs at 8 AM (except Monday), returns at 4 PM, and costs R$25. Note that in the low season (April–November), both trains run only on weekends and holidays. To make arrangements, contact Serra Verde Express.

Train Information Serra Verde Express ⊠ Estação Rodoferroviária, Gate 8, Curitiba ☎ 041/323-4008 ⊕ www.serraverdeexpress.com.br.

VISITOR INFORMATION

Paraná Turismo in Curitiba is open Monday and Tuesday 1 PM–7 PM at the Centro Cívico location and daily 8 AM–10 PM at its Afonso Pena airport location. A reliable independent source about what's going on in Florianópolis is *Guia Floripa*, which is free and can be obtained at newsstands or online at www.guiafloripa.com.br.

🚩 Tourist Information in Paraná **FozTur** ✉ Rua Alm. Barroso 1300, 2nd floor, Foz do Iguaçu ☎ 0800/45-1516 ✉ Aeroporto Internacional Foz do Iguaçu, Km 13, ☎ 045/521-4276. **Paraná Turismo** (State Tourism Board) ✉ Rua Dep. Mário de Barros 1290, Centro Cívico, Curitiba ☎ 041/254-7273, 041/1516 Teletur [24-hr hot line] ⊕ www.pr.gov.br/turismo ✉ Aeroporto Internacional Afonso Pena, Av. Rocha Pombo s/n, São José dos Pinhais ☎ 045/381-1153.

🚩 Tourist Information in Santa Catarina **Portal Turístico** ✉ Rua Eng. Max de Souza 236, Coqueiros, mainland side of Ponte Colombo Sales (Colombo Sales Bridge), São José ☎ 048/271-7000 or 048/3025-1900 ⊕ www.pmf.sc.gov.br/turismo ✉ Terminal Rodoviária Rita Maria, Av. Paulo Fontes 1101, Centro, Florianópolis ☎ 048/244-5822. **SanTur** (State Tourism Authority) ✉ Rua Felipe Schmidt 249, 9th floor, Florianópolis ☎ 048/244-5822 or 048/244-1516 ⊕ www.sc.gov.br/santacatarina/turismo/contrastes/index.html.

🚩 Tourist Information in Rio Grande do Sul **Serviço de Atenção ao Turista** (SAT) ✉ Mercado Público, Largo Glênio Peres s/n, Centro, Porto Alegre ☎ 0800/51-7686 or 051/3333-1873 ✉ Mercado do Bom Fim, Av. Oswaldo Aranha s/n, Bom Fim, Porto Alegre ☎ 051/3333-1873. **Secretaria de Turismo** (State Tourism Authority) ✉ Centro Administrativo, Av. Borges de Medeiros 1501, 10th floor, Porto Alegre ☎ 051/3288-5400 ⊕ www.turismo.rs.gov.br ✉ Aeroporto Internacional Salgado Filho, Av. Severo Dulius 90010, Porto Alegre ☎ 051/3358-2000 ✉ Estação Rodoviária, Largo Vespasiano Veppo s/n, Porto Alegre ☎ 051/3225-0677.

MINAS GERAIS

4

Updated by
Jefferson
Santos

THE CENTRAL MOUNTAINOUS REGION OF BRAZIL IS DOMINATED BY THIS STATE, whose name ("general mines") was inspired by the area's great mineral wealth. In the 18th century the vast precious-metal reserves of Minas Gerais made the state, and particularly the city of Ouro Preto (also seen as Ouro Prêto, an archaic spelling), the de facto capital of the Portuguese colony. That period of gold, diamond, and semiprecious-stone trading is memorialized in the historic towns scattered across the mountains and remains a tremendous source of pride for the *mineiros* (inhabitants of the state). Minas Gerais is one of the most calm and conservative states of Brazil. Many say that it's because of the mountains that surround the state, which are also said to make the mineiro an introspective and friendly person. Yet Minas Gerais has also been a hotbed for movements that have triggered political, economic, and cultural development.

Exploration of Minas Gerais began in the 17th century, when *bandeirantes* (bands of adventurers) from the coastal areas came in search of slaves and gold. Near the town of Vila Rica, they found a black stone that was later verified to be gold (the coloring came from the iron oxide in the soil). Thus Vila Rica came to be called Ouro Preto (Black Gold), and at the beginning of the 18th century Brazil's first gold rush began. Along with the fortune seekers came Jesuit priests, who were later exiled by the Portuguese (for fear they would try to manipulate the mineral trade) and replaced by *ordens terceiros* ("third," or lay, orders). By the middle of the century the Gold Towns of Minas were gleaming with new churches built first in the baroque-rococo style of Europe and later in a baroque style unique to the region.

Minas, as it is known, was also blessed with a local artistic genius, Antônio Francisco Lisboa. The son of a Portuguese architect and a former slave, Lisboa was born in 1738 in what is today Ouro Preto. As an adult he acquired the nickname Aleijadinho (Little Cripple) because of an illness that left him deformed. Working in cedarwood and soapstone, Aleijadinho carved the passion of his beliefs in sculptures that grace churches throughout the state.

By the end of the 18th century the gold had begun to run out, and Ouro Preto's population and importance decreased. The baroque period ended at the start of the 19th century, when the Portuguese royal family, in flight from the conquering army of Napoléon Bonaparte, arrived in Brazil, bringing with them architects and sculptors with different ideas and artistic styles. Ornate twisted columns and walls adorned with lavish carvings gave way to simple straight columns and walls painted with murals or simply washed in white.

Though the Gold Towns are awe inspiring, Minas Gerais has other attractions. Roughly six hours south of the state capital of Belo Horizonte, several mineral-spa towns form the Circuito das Águas (Water Circuit). Thought to have healing powers, the natural springs of places like São Lourenço and Caxambu have attracted the Brazilian elite for more than a century. Close by is the unusual town of São Tomé das Letras—a place where UFOs are said to visit and where mystics and bohemians wait for the dawn of a new world.

Although justifiably proud of their state's artistic accomplishments, mineiros are also passionate about their politics. Minas Gerais has produced many of Brazil's most famous leaders, including Tiradentes, who led Brazil's first attempt at independence; Juscelino Kubitschek, the president who made Brasília happen; and Tancredo Neves, who helped restore Brazilian democracy in the mid-1980s.

Today Minas is Brazil's second most industrialized state, after São Paulo. The iron that darkened the gold of Ouro Preto remains an important source of state income, along with steel, coffee, and auto manufacturing. Although some of its once heavily wooded areas have been stripped bare, Minas still has diverse and amazingly pristine ecosystems, including Atlantic forests, rain forests, wetlands, and grasslands. The traffic that the mines brought here in the 17th century thrust Brazil into civilization, and now, well into the wake of the gold rush, a steady sense of progress and a compassion for the land remain.

Exploring Minas Gerais

The peaks of the Serra do Mantiqueira separate Minas from Rio de Janeiro and give way to the Paraíba Valley. Although Minas is large, its major attractions, including Belo Horizonte, Ouro Preto, and the mineral-spa towns, are in the state's southeast, within driving distance of one another. The key historic cities—called the Gold Towns—are in the Serra do Espinhaço range, with Ouro Preto at 1,220 meters (4,000 feet) above sea level.

Timing

The busiest and often most exciting times to travel are during the Christmas, Easter, and Carnaval periods—although Carnaval is much more subdued here than in Bahia or Rio. July, when the weather is cool and dry, is winter break month and another peak season. To avoid crowds, travel from April to June or August to November. Discounts may be available during these months, although fewer services will be offered.

About the Restaurants

Mineiros tend to eat dinner after 8 (often closer to 10). Restaurants are busiest on weekends and may require reservations; many close on Monday.

About the Hotels

In the interior of Minas Gerais, especially in the historical cities and state parks, there are two types of traditional habitations for tourists: the *pousadas* (inns), with simpler and familiar rooms, and the *fazendas* (farms), which can be a fun option. In many cases hotel services aren't as good as they could be, but in recent years mineiros have been paying more attention to the importance of the tourism and improving the quality of lodgings. That said, most hotels remain small, lack English-speaking staffs, and have few of the amenities common in American and European chains. When you book, you'll likely be given a choice between a standard and a luxury room; the *apartamento de luxo* (luxury room) may be slightly larger, with air-conditioning and a better-equipped bathroom. Significant weekend discounts are common in Belo Horizonte.

If you have **5 days**	Start your trip in ⊡ **Belo Horizonte** ①–⑧, capital and main city of Minas Gerais. On your first day, do our Good Walk and get to know the city. At night, look for a pub or another cultural option. On Day 2, spend your day at the Feira de Artesanato on Avenida Afonso Pena. The following day, rent a car and head to the historical cities. Take the day to know **Sabará** and **Mariana**, the oldest city of the state. Spend your last two days in ⊡ **Ouro Preto** ⑨–⑲ exploring its rich architecture, shopping, and absorbing the local folklore.
If you have **7 days**	Follow the five-day itinerary above. For your remaining days you can either head north to ⊡ **Diamantina** (about 380 km/240 mi) or south through **Congonhas** and 130 km (80 mi) south to the charming town of ⊡ **Tiradentes**.
If you have **10 days**	Spend a day in ⊡ **Belo Horizonte** ①–⑧. On the second day head to ⊡ **Diamantina** and explore the city on your third day. On the fouth day, take a leisurely trip along the Estrada Real nearly 400 km (250 mi) to ⊡ **Ouro Preto** ⑨–⑲, exploring the villages, such as **Sabará**, on the way. Stay in Ouro Preto for two more days. Take a trip to **Mariana**, only a few kilometers away. On the seventh day head to ⊡ **Tiradentes** through **Congonhas** ㉓. Shop for arts and crafts in Bichinho. On Day 9 head to the spa towns for the remainder of your trip. Be aware that innkeepers in places like **São Lourenço** and **Caxambu** will do their best to convince you that a few days in their towns aren't nearly enough—the waters' curative properties are said to only take effect after 20 or so days.

WHAT IT COSTS In Reais				
	$$$$	**$$$**	**$$**	**$**	**¢**
RESTAURANTS	over $60	$45–$60	$30–$45	$15–$30	under $15
HOTELS	over $500	$375–$500	$250–$375	$125–$250	under $125

Restaurant prices are for a dinner entrée. Hotel prices are for two people in a standard double room in high season, excluding taxes.

BELO HORIZONTE

444 km (276 mi) northwest of Rio and 741 km (460 mi) southeast of Brasília.

With more than 2 million inhabitants, Belo Horizonte, the capital of the state of Minas Gerais, still lives up to its nickname, the Garden City, which it earned in the 1940s and '50s, when the main avenue, Afonso Pena, was lined with huge trees. Also affectionately called Beagá (or BH) by residents, the city can look both like a metropolis—with traffic jams, tall buildings, and urban noise—and, in its tranquil downtown neighborhoods, like a simple country town.

Minas Gerais is better known for its historical towns, but Belo Horizonte is not an old city. Inspired by cities like Paris and Washington, Belo Horizonte was inaugurated in 1897 and was the first planned modern city in the country. That year the state capital moved to the city from Ouro Preto, whose location—wedged between mountains—did not allow for an expansion of the capital in line with the prosperity of the state. The construction of a new capital was a sign that modernity had arrived in the state and a celebration of the triumph of the new Brazilian republic over the old Portuguese monarchy.

Growth was slow at first but picked up speed in the 1920s, after World War I. At that time, with industries finally prospering, the city gained monuments like the Praça Sete's obelisk, knows as *Pirulito* (restored in 2003) and the Santa Tereza viaduct. Belo Horizonte also emerged on the Brazilian cultural scene with poets such as Carlos Drummond de Andrade and Pedro Nava, among others. In the 1940s, under the administration of mayor Juscelino Kubitschek, one of the most famous and respected Brazilian politicians, Belo Horizonte gained status as a metropolis. Kubitschek hired the young architect Oscar Niemeyer, who created some of landmarks of the city, including the Pampulha's Architectural Complex.

Today Belo Horizonte, the third-biggest city in Brazil, is distinguished by its politics and its contributions to the arts. In the early 20th century the Brazilian political system was referred to as Café com Leite ("Coffee with Milk"), because the presidency was alternately held by natives of São Paulo (where much of Brazil's coffee is produced) and natives of Minas Gerais (the milk-producing state). The current system is more diverse, but mineiros are still very influential in the country's politics. Minas Gerais is also home to some of the most respected Brazilian theater companies, such as Grupo Galpão, and dance companies (Grupo Corpo, for one), and also to some of the most famous pop bands—such as Skank, Pato Fu, and Jota Quest. The artistic tradition is emphasized by the many festivals dedicated to all forms of art, from comic books to puppet theater and short movies to electronic music. The arts and nightlife scene, along with the stunning modern architecture, are reasons to visit Belo Horizonte before or after traversing Minas Gerais's peaceful countryside.

Exploring Belo Horizonte

Minas Gerais is a mountainous state, and you should be prepared for lots of hills when walking around Belo Horizonte. The central and original section of the city, which was planned in the 19th century, is surrounded by Avenida Contorno. The city's main attractions are downtown and in the southern zone. During the day these areas are not too crowded. To get to other neighborhoods, like Pampulha, you should take a taxi.

A Good Walk

On Avenida Afonso Pena in the center of Belo Horizonte the **Palácio das Artes** ❶ ▶ incorporates the main theaters and art galleries of the city. In front of the Conservatório (Music Conservatory), the neighboring **Parque Muncipal** ❷, with its many trees, is an excellent place for a walk.

4

Architecture

In the 17th century the Portuguese, to ensure their control of the mining industry when gold was discovered in Minas Gerais, exiled the traditional religious orders, which led to the formation of third orders. Attempts by these lay brothers to build churches on European models resulted in improvisations (they had little experience with or guidance on such matters) and, hence, a uniquely Brazilian style of baroque. Many churches from this period have simple exteriors that belie interiors whose gold-leaf-encrusted carvings are so intricate they seem like filigree.

As the gold supply diminished, facades became more elaborate—with more sophisticated lines, elegant curves, and large round towers—and their interiors less so, as murals were used more than carvings and gold leaf. Today you can see several outstanding examples of baroque architecture, many of them attributed to the legendary Aleijadinho, in Ouro Preto (where there are 13 such churches) and the other Gold Towns of Minas.

Mineiro Cuisine

The mainstay of *comida mineira* (the cuisine of Minas) is *tutu*, a tasty mash of beans with roast pork loin, pork sausage, chopped collard greens, manioc meal, and boiled egg served with meat dishes. Another favorite is *feijão tropeiro*, a combination of beans, manioc meal, roast pork loin, fried egg, chopped collard greens, and thick pork sausage. Among meat dishes, pork is the most common, in particular the famed *lingüiça* (Minas pork sausage) and *lombo* (pork tenderloin), which is often served with white rice and/or corn porridge. The most typical chicken dish is *frango ao molho pardo,* broiled chicken served in a sauce made with its own blood. Another specialty is *frango com quiabo,* chicken cooked in broth with chopped okra. The region's very mild white cheese is known throughout Brazil simply as *queijo de Minas* (Minas cheese). Of course, *caipirinhas* (drinks of crushed ice, crushed lime, sugar, and *cachaça,* a sugarcane-based liquor) go well with all the regional dishes.

Gemstones

Minas Gerais produces most of the world's colored gemstones, including the grande dame of them all—the imperial topaz, which is found nowhere else. It comes in shades of pink and tangerine, and the clearer the stone the better the quality. The state's mines also produce amethysts, aquamarines, tourmalines, and emeralds.

The stones are cut, polished, and incorporated into jewelry in cities like Ouro Preto and Belo Horizonte, where you can buy authenticated pieces—often at heavily discounted prices—from top jewelers. Note that gems vary widely in quality and value; don't buy them on the streets, and be wary about buying them from smaller shops (get recommendations first).

Shopping

Hand-carved wood and soapstone figures and other objects are sold by street vendors in all the historic cities. Other typical handicrafts include pottery and tapestries, in particular the handwoven *arraiola* tapestries for which the area around Diamantina is famous. Of course, you should always be on the lookout for interesting jewelry.

On Sunday morning you'll find this part of the avenue crowded with tents for the Feira Artesanato. Take the Avenida Augusto de Lima, in front of the park's entrance, until you cross the Rua da Bahia, with its many historic buildings, which binds together two of the most bohemian neighborhoods of Belo Horizonte: Santo Antônio and Santa Tereza. The neo-Gothic building at the corner is **Centro de Cultura de Belo Horizonte ❸**.

Head southwest five blocks on Rua da Bahia. Along the way you can see the Minas Gerais Writers Academy, the Vivaldi Moreira Auditorium, and the **Basílica de Lourdes ❹**. Turn left to find the **Praça da Liberdade ❺**, a good place to rest and appreciate the diverse architectural styles of the complex, including the **Palácio da Liberdade ❻**, the **Museu de Mineralogia ❼**, the Biblioteca Pública Luiz de Bessa (the Public Library), and the Niemeyer Building, one of the most beautiful examples of the modernist architecture in the city.

Take Praça José Mendes Júnior, the small street to the right of the Palácio da Liberdade, and walk a short ways to the Minas Tênis Clube. This art deco building was the venue of many high-society parties during the 1950s and '60s. Turn left onto Rua Espírito Santo until you arrive at the pleasant Rua Felipe dos Santos, in the Lourdes district. Keep walking to Rua Marília de Dirceu and turn left. Cross Avenida Contorno, where Rua Marília de Dirceu becomes Avenida Prudente de Morais. On your right, two blocks south, is the **Museu Histórico Abílio Barreto** ❽. Visit the museum and grab a snack at its coffee shop.

TIMING Reserve two hours for this walk. If you want to explore the Parque Municipal, add one more hour. Add another hour for the Sunday-morning Feira do Artesanato.

What to See

❹ **Basílica de Lourdes.** Conceived when the capital was founded but only inaugurated in 1923, Our Lady of Lourdes Church was elevated to the category of basilica by Pope Pius XII in 1958. Its Gothic architecture has received some adaptations, but it is still a magnificent building. ✉ *Rua da Bahia 1596, Lourdes* ☎ *031/3218–7676* ✆ *Free* ⊙ *Mon.–Thurs. 7 AM–9 PM, Fri. 2 PM–9 PM, weekends 7 AM–9 PM.*

❸ **Centro de Cultura de Belo Horizonte.** The city's only example of the neo-Gothic style of Portuguese inspiration, this building was built in 1914 in order to house the first legislative assembly of the capital as well as the public library. In 1997 it was transformed into a cultural space, where local visual artist exhibitions take place. ✉ *Rua da Bahia 1149, Centro* ☎ *031/3277–4014* ✆ *Free* ⊙ *Weekdays 9–9, Sat. 9–6, Sun. 2–4.*

Conjunto Arquitetônico da Pampulha. This modern complex was designed by Oscar Niemeyer and built in the 1940s on the banks of Lagoa da Pampulha. Inaugurated in 1943, the **Casa do Baile** (Ballroom House; ✉ Av. Otacílio Negrão de Lima 751, Pampulha ☎ 031/3277–7443) was a popular dance hall. It closed its doors shortly after the casino. Today the Casa do Baileis is an art gallery. At **Igreja de São Francisco de Assis** (Church of St. Francis of Assisi; ✉ Km 12, Av. Otacílio Negrão de Lima, Pampulha ☎ 031/3441–9325) has 14 panels, comprising the most important works painted by Portinari. The church is open daily 8–6. One of Niemeyer's first projects was the **Museu de Arte da Pampulha** (Pampulha Art Museum; ✉ Av. Otacílio Negrão de Lima 16585, Pampulha ☎ 031/3443–4533 ⊕ www.map.art.br), which has landscaped gardens by Burle Marx. The building was a casino until 1946, when gambling was prohibited in Brazil. Transformed into a museum in 1957, the building also has multimedia rooms, a small theater, a library, and a coffee shop. It's open Tuesday through Sunday 9–7; admission is free.

Mercado Central (Central Market). There are more than 400 stores in this market, inaugurated in 1929. You can find almost everything—from groceries to typical products from Minas Gerais, such as cheese, guava and milk sweets, arts and crafts, medicinal herbs and roots, and even pets. Many people (including local celebrities) stop by the popular bars inside the market to drink a beer and sample the famous appetizers, such as liver with onions. ✉ *Av. Augusto de Lima 744, Centro* ☎ *031/3274–9434* ⊕ *www.mercadocentral.com.br* ✆ *Free* ⊙ *Mon.–Sat. 7–6, Sun. 7–noon.*

Museu de Artes e Ofícios. In the main building of the Praça da Estação, in the center of the city, this museum houses almost 2,000 rudimentary

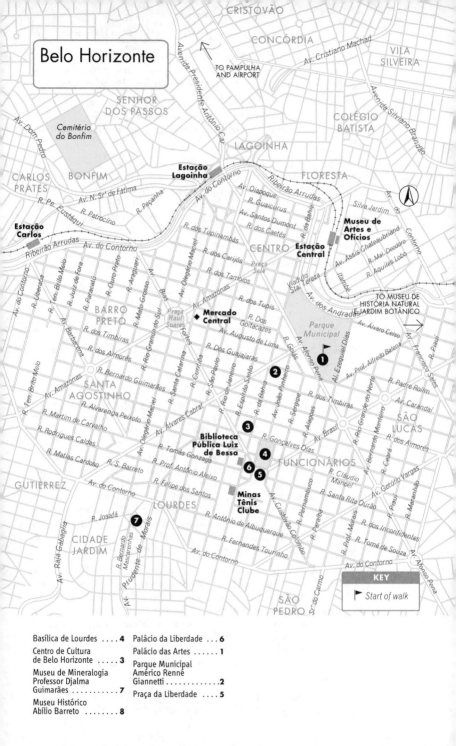

Belo Horizonte

TO PAMPULHA
AND AIRPORT

KEY

► Start of walk

tools and other items from the 17th to the 20th centuries used by Brazilian laborers. ⊠ *Rua Rui Barbosa s/n, Centro* ☎ *031/3213–0003* ⊕ *www.museudearteseoficios.com.br* 🖃 *Free* ☉ *Tues.–Fri. 1–6, Sat. 1–5.*

Museu de História Natural e Jardim Botânico. Although it has an area of more than 600,000 square meters (6,400 square feet), with Brazilian fauna, flora, archaeology, and mineralogy, the museum's main attraction is the Presépio do Pipiripau (Pipiripau Crèche). This ingenious work of art narrates Christ's life in 45 scenes, with 580 moving figures. It was built by Raimundo Machado de Azevedo, who began assembling it in 1906 and finished in 1984. The Instituto do Patrimônio Histórico e Artístico Nacional (National Institute of the History and Arts) deemed it artistic patrimony in 1984. ⊠ *Rua Gustavo da Silveira 1035, Santa Efigênia* ☎ *031/3482–9723* 🖃 *R$2* ☉ *Tues.–Fri. 8–11:30 and 1–4, weekends 9–4.*

❼ Museu de Mineralogia Professor Djalma Guimarães. More than 3,000 pieces extracted from sites all over the world are on display in the mineralogy museum, which is housed in a postmodern steel-and-glass building. ⊠ *Av. Bias Fortes 50, Funcionários* ☎ *031/3271–3415* 🖃 *Free* ☉ *Tues.–Sun. 9–5.*

❽ Museu Histórico Abílio Barreto. Attached to an old colonial mansion, the Abílio Barreto Historical Museum (MHAB) has permanent and temporary expositions about the city of Belo Horizonte. Its comfortable coffee shop is open until midnight. ⊠ *Av. Prudente de Morais 202, Cidade Jardim* ☎ *031/3227–8573* 🖃 *Free* ☉ *Tues.–Sun. 10–5.*

❻ Palácio da Liberdade. Built in 1898, the French-style Liberdade Palace is the headquarter of the Minas Gerais's government and is the official residence of the governor. Of note are the gardens by Paul Villon, the Louis XV–style banquet room, the paintings in Noble Hall, and a panel by Antônio Pereira. The palace is open for public visitation the last Sunday of every month. ⊠ *Praça da Liberdade s/n, Funcionários* ☎ *031/ 3250–6011* 🖃 *Free* ☉ *Last Sun. of month, 8:30–2.*

❶ Palácio das Artes. Designed by Oscar Niemeyer and built in 1970, the Palace of the Arts is the most important cultural center in Belo Horizonte. Comprising three theaters, three art galleries, a movie theater, a bookstore, a coffee shop, and the Centro de Artesanato Mineiro (Mineiro Artisan Center), which has such contemporary Minas handicrafts as wood and soapstone carvings, pottery, and tapestries—all for sale. The main theater, Grande Teatro, stages music concerts, plays, operas, ballets, and other productions by Brazilian and foreign artists. ⊠ *Av. Afonso Pena 1537, Centro* ☎ *031/3237–7399* 🖃 *Free* ☉ *Daily 10–8.*

❷ Parque Municipal Américo Renné Giannetti. With 45 acres of green area, the Parque Municipal (municipal park) Américo Renné Giannetti, inspired by the design of French parks, was inaugurated in 1897. It shelters an orchid house, a school, a playground, and the Francisco Nunes Theater, a beautiful modern building designed by the architect Luiz Signorelli in the 1940s that still presents theatrical play and musical performances. With more than 50 tree species, the Municipal Park is highly recommended for walks. ⊠ *Av. Afonso Pena s/n, Centro* ☎ *031/3277–4749 for park, 031/3224–4546 for Francisco Nunes theater* ☷ *Free* ⊙ *Tues.–Sun. 6–6.*

❺ **Praça da Liberdade** (Liberdade Square). When the city was founded, this square was created to house public administration offices. Today, in addition to centenarian palm trees, fountains, and a bandstand, the square also has neoclassical, art deco, modern, and postmodern buildings. ⊠ *Between Avs. João Pinheiro and Cristóvão Colombro, Funcionários.*

Where to Eat

$$ ✕ **Splêndido Ristorante.** The food and the service at this cosmopolitan restaurant are exceptional. The kitchen blends French and northern Italian cuisines, and it's assured that anyone who's anyone will show up here at some point during a visit to Belo Horizonte. ⊠ *Rua Levindo Lopes 251, Savassi* ☎ *031/3227–6446* ☷ *AE, DC, MC* ⊙ *No lunch Sat. No dinner Sun.*

★ **$$** ✕ **Vecchio Sogno.** What is widely considered Belo Horizonte's best Italian restaurant attracts a well-heeled clientele. Tuxedo-clad waiters serve selections from the extensive wine list as well as steak, seafood, and pasta dishes. Consider the grilled fillet of lamb with saffron risotto in a mushroom-and-garlic sauce; the gnocchi *di mare*, with spinach and potatoes, topped with a white clam and scallop sauce; or the *badejo*, a local white fish baked and dressed in a seafood sauce. ⊠ *Rua Martim de Carvalho 75, Santo Agostinho* ☎ *031/3292–5251 or 031/3290–7585* ☷ *AE, DC, MC, V* ⊰ *Reservations essential* ⊙ *No lunch Sat. No dinner Sun.*

★ **$–$$** ✕ **Amici Miei.** This casual Italian eatery is popular with Brazilians celebrating the end of the workday. The restaurant is often packed both inside and on the large outdoor patio; you may need to wait for the staff to find you a table. Start with the *champignon Recheado* (a large mushroom stuffed with shrimp and prosciutto), followed by *tournedo Amici Miei* (filet mignon wrapped in bacon and marinated in garlic and olive oil). ⊠ *Rua Tome de Souza 1331, Funcionários* ☎ *031/3282–4992* ☷ *DC, MC, V.* ⊙ *Closed Sun. No lunch weekdays.*

$–$$ ✕ **Amigo do Rei.** The first Persian restaurant of Brazil appeared in Parati, Rio de Janeiro, but it moved to the capital of Minas Gerais in 2002. The homey place has only 21 seats. The owner, Cláudio, is the host, and his wife, Nasrin, is the chef. Before your order is ready, the waiter will be happy to inform you about Iranian culture. A recommended dish is the *fessenjhuhn,* small meat spheres with nuts and pomegranate, rice with saffron, and the typical borani gravy, made of zucchini. ⊠ *Rua Quintiliano Silva 118, Santo Antônio* ☎ *031/3296–3881* ☷ *V* ⊙ *Closed Mon.–Tues. No lunch.*

Fodor'sChoice ★

$–$$ ✕ **Chalezinho.** There's only one reason to come here: romance. The dimly lighted chalet, with its elegant piano music (accompanied by the occasional saxophone), is a magical retreat in the hills above town. The specialty is fondue; the filet mignon cooked in a bowl of sizzling oil and paired with any of eight delicious sauces is a treat. Afterward, order a chocolate fondue, which comes with a mouthwatering selection of fruits waiting to be dipped. When you finish, step outside to the Praça dos Amores (Lovers' Plaza) for a kiss under the moonlit sky. ⊠ *Alameda da Serra 18, Vale do Soreno–Novo Lima* ☎ *031/3286–3155* ☷ *AE, DC, MC, V* ⊙ *No lunch.*

Fodor'sChoice ★

$ ✕ **Dona Lucinha.** Roughly 35 traditional Minas dishes are offered in this cafeteria-style eatery. Though there's not much charm, the self-service concept helps to keep the price down to a prix-fixe R$19. Children get significant discounts. ⊠ *Rua Padre Odorico 38, São Pedro* ☎ *031/ 3227-0562* ▤ *AE, DC, MC, V* ☼ *No dinner Sun.* ⊠ *Rua Sergipe 811, Savassi* ☎ *031/3261-5930* ▤ *AE, DC, MC, V* ☼ *No dinner Sun.*

$ ✕ **Restaurante Varandão.** On the 25th floor of the Othon Palace hotel, this romantic restaurant has spectacular urban vistas. Start off with a cocktail at one of the outdoor candlelighted tables before coming inside for dinner, where a generous buffet serves as the dining room's centerpiece. On weekends the chef serves an innovative "soapstone barbecue," where you choose thinly sliced meats to grill on a hot soapstone; your meal also comes with potatoes, sauces, and toast. Live Brazilian music accompanies dinner nightly. ⊠ *Av. Afonso Pena 1050, Centro* ☎ *031/ 3247-0000* ▤ *AE, DC, MC, V.*

¢–$ ✕ **Casa dos Contos.** The menu at this gathering place for local journalists, artists, and intellectuals is unpretentious and varied, ranging from fish and pasta to typical mineira dishes. In keeping with its bohemian clientele, Casa dos Contos serves well past midnight. ⊠ *Rua Rio Grande do Norte 1065, Funcionários* ☎ *031/3261-5853* ▤ *AE, DC, MC, V.*

¢–$ ✕ **Chico Mineiro.** Dining Minas Gerais–style means ample portions of such hearty dishes as *tutu à mineira* (mashed beans with roast pork loin, pork sausage, chopped collard greens, and boiled egg). Nowhere is it better prepared than at this traditional restaurant in the Savassi neighborhood, home to Belo's liveliest nightspots. Lunch sees a self-service mineira buffet for a fixed price of R$13, including dessert. ⊠ *Rua Alagoas 626, Savassi* ☎ *031/3261-3237* ▤ *AE, DC, MC, V.*

¢–$ ✕ **Restaurante Top Beer.** This trendy restaurant–bar makes an ideal launchpad for your evening. Students and executives alike plan their night out while sipping caipirinhas on the large outdoor patio. The inside dining room is an inviting tropical enclave, with fountains and trees surrounding the tables. The pasta dishes and grilled steaks are commendable. ⊠ *Rua Tomé de Souza 1121, Savassi* ☎ *031/3282-7755* ▤ *AE, DC, MC, V.*

Where to Stay

$$–$$$
FodorsChoice
★
▦ **Ouro Minas Palace Hotel.** Though not centrally located, this hotel has comfortable and appealing rooms, with large beds and well-appointed bathrooms. The hotel offers numerous amenities uncommon in Belo Horizonte, including a pool with waterfalls and a multilingual staff. ⊠ *Av. Cristiano Machado 4001, Ipiranga* ☎ *031/3429-4001* 🖷 *031/3429-4002* ⊕ *www.ourominas.com.br* 📞 *343 rooms, 44 suites* ⑂ *Restaurant, cafeteria, room service, in-room data ports, in-room safes, minibars, refrigerator, cable TV, pool, health club, massage, Turkish baths, piano bar, nightclub, recreation room, shop, baby-sitting, laundry service, Internet, business services, convention center, car rental, no-smoking floors* ▤ *AE, DC, MC, V* ❍| *BP.*

$–$$ ▦ **Othon Palace.** The Othon has the best location of any hotel in Belo Horizonte. Although aging (it opened in 1978), renovations are ongoing, and the level of service remains high. Rooms have very little character but are comfortable and enjoy spectacular city views, including the tree-lined Parque Municipal. The rooftop pool and bar are the best in town, and the on-site Restaurante Verandão is excellent. ⊠ *Av. Afonso Pena 1050, Centro* ☎ *031/3247–0000 or 0300/789–8809* 🖷 *031/3247–0001* ⊕ *www.hoteis-othon.com.br* 📑 *266 rooms, 19 suites* ⚴ *Restaurant, room service, in-room safes, minibars, refrigerators, cable TV, pool, gym, massage, sauna, bar, laundry service, concierge floor, Internet, business services, convention center, meeting room, no-smoking floor* ▤ *AE, DC, MC, V* ⎰⎱ *BP.*

$ 🛏 **Mercure Lourdes.** On a main city avenue, close to the Savassi area and not very far from Belo Horizonte's central region, the Mercure hotel is very popular among executives and artists. Its seven convention rooms occasionally stage music concerts. The restaurant's menus include French, Italian, and international food. If possible, choose a room on one of the higher floors for a privileged view of the city. ⊠ *Av. do Contorno 7315, Lourdes* ☎ *031/3298–4100* 🖷 *031/3298–4105* ⊕ *www.accorhotels.com.br* 📑 *374 rooms* ⚴ *2 restaurants, cafeteria, room service, in-room data ports, in-room safes, microwaves, refrigerator, cable TV, pool, gym, sauna, steam room, bar, piano bar, laundry service, Internet, business services, convention center, meeting rooms, no-smoking floors* ▤ *AE, D, MC, V* ⎰⎱ *BP.*

★ $ 🛏 **Merit Plaza.** This downtown hotel is an excellent value, particularly for business travelers in need of modern amenities and a convenient location. Granite covers the contemporary atrium lobby, and guest rooms have soundproof walls, large beds, and well-appointed bathrooms. ⊠ *Rua dos Tamoios 341, Centro* ☎ *031/3201–9000* 🖷 *031/3271–5700* ⊕ *www.meritplaza.com.br* 📑 *115 rooms, 2 suites* ⚴ *Restaurant, café, in-room data ports, bar, business services* ▤ *AE, DC, MC, V* ⎰⎱ *BP.*

¢–$ 🛏 **Grandarrell Minas Hotel.** The lobby of this centrally located hotel, one of the city's oldest, is often crowded with conventioneers. Rooms are comfortable, if a bit dark; many, however, have the same view of the city and surrounding mountains that you'll find from the small rooftop pool and bar. ⊠ *Rua Espírito Santo 901, Centro* ☎ *0800/31–1188 or 031/3248–1000* 🖷 *031/3248–1100* ⊕ *www.grandarrell.com.br* 📑 *241 rooms, 4 suites* ⚴ *Restaurant, cafeteria, dining room, room service, in-room ports, in-room safes, minibars, refrigerators, cable TV, pool, gym, sauna, steam room, bar, piano bar, shop, laundry service, Internet business services, convention center, meeting room* ▤ *AE, DC, MC, V* ⎰⎱ *BP.*

★ ¢–$ 🛏 **Hotel Wimbledon.** An elegant yet warm atmosphere and a central location are two of this hotel's draws. Guest rooms have polished hardwood floors, local artwork, and modern bathrooms; luxury rooms have whirlpool baths. Attentive service makes this hotel feel more like a bed-and-breakfast. There's a rooftop pool and bar—the perfect spot for an afternoon drink. ⊠ *Av. Afonso Pena 772, Centro* ☎ *031/3222–6160 or 0800/31–8383* 🖷 *031/3222–6510* ⊕ *www.wimbledon.com.br* 📑 *69 rooms, 1 suite* ⚴ *Restaurant, room service, in-room data ports, in-room safes, minibars, refrigerator, cable TV, pool, bar, laundry services, Internet, business services, no-smoking floor* ▤ *AE, DC, MC, V* ⎰⎱ *BP.*

¢–$ 🛏 **Wembley Palace.** This aging high-rise offers clean (albeit small) rooms, reliable service, and a central location. ⊠ *Rua Espírito Santo 201, Cen-*

tro ☎ *031/3273–6866* 📠 *031/3273–1601* ⊕ *www.hotelwembley.com.
br* ⤳ *105 rooms, 2 suites* ♿ *Restaurant, room service, in-room data
ports, minibars, refrigerator, cable TV, bar, laundry services, Internet,
convention center, no-smoking floor* ⊟ *AE, DC, MC, V* ⦿ *BP.*

¢ ⊡ **Hotel Amazonas Palace.** Clean, simply furnished, reasonably priced
rooms are the bill at this downtown hotel. On the 11th floor is a good
restaurant that has a nice view of the city. ⊠ *Av. Amazonas 120, Centro* ☎ *031/3201–4644* 📠 *031/3212–4236* ⤳ *76 rooms* ♿ *Cafeteria,
dining room, room service, refrigerator, cable TV, 2 bars, baby-sitting,
laundry services, Internet, business center, convention center, no-smoking rooms* ⊟ *AE, DC, MC, V* ⦿ *BP.*

¢ ⊡ **Ibis.** Constructed in the backyard of an old mansion, this economic hotel
Fodor'sChoice opened in 2003. The mansion, just yards from the Praça da Liberdade,
★ has been well maintained and now has a charming lobby. Prices are lower
than at comparable hotels, and the rooms are simple but well equipped.
For an additional R$6 breakfast is provided daily in the hotel lobby. ⊠ *Rua
João Pinheiro 602, Savassi* ☎ *0800/703–7001* ⊕ *www.accorhotels.com.
br* ⤳ *130 rooms* ♿ *In-room data ports, in-room safes, refrigerators,
cable TV, bar, Internet, convention center* ⊟ *AE, D, MC, V.*

Nightlife & the Arts

Belo Horizonte is a city of bars. No other city in Brazil has as many bars
and coffee shops—there are 14,000, or one for every 150 inhabitants.
And this isn't a recent trend: the first bar appeared in 1893, four years
before the city was inaugurated. The bar culture is the core of the city's
nightlife. There is even a contest every year in April, called Comida di
Buteco (the Bar Food Contest), to reward the best appetizers and the
coldest beer.

THE ARTS **Espaço Belas Artes** (⊠ Rua Gonçalves Dias 1581, Lourdes ☎ 031/
3213–5594) screens foreign and art films. Inaugurated in 2003, the **Marista
Hall** (⊠ Av. Nossa Senhora do Carmo 200, Savassi ☎ 031/3228–7500
⊕ www.maristahall.com.br) presents concerts by famous Brazilian and
foreign musical artists. With the capacity to hold 3,700 people, the place
is also used for volleyball and basketball games. The center of cultural
life in Belo Horizonte is the downtown **Palácio das Artes** (⊠ Rua Afonso
Pena 1537, Centro ☎ 031/3237–7399 ⊕ www.palaciodasartes.com.br),
where ballet companies and symphony orchestras perform. The box office is open only when performances are coming up. Art movies and European films are the main attractions of **Usina de Cinema** (⊠ Rua Aimorés
2424, Santo Agostinho ☎ 031/3337–5566).

NIGHTLIFE For some of Brazil's best cachaças and one of the city's best views, try
Alambique Cachaçaria (⊠ Av. Raja Gabaglia 3200, Chalé 1D, Estoril
☎ 031/3296–7188). **Arrumação** (⊠ Av. Assis Chateaubriand 524, Floresta ☎ 031/3088–3952) is a traditional bar that's owned by Brazilian
comedian and actor Saulo Laranjeira. With some luck you can run into
in one of the artists of the Clube da Esquina at **Bar Brasil** (⊠ Rua
Aimorés 108, Funcionários ☎ 031/3287–3256). It's open until the last
customer leaves. **Bolão** (⊠ Rua Mármore 695, Santa Tereza ☎ 031/
3461–6211) is a bar and restaurant in a quiet district next to Centro.
Its clientele is bohemians, poets, and such musicians as the rock band

Sepultura. A good house draft beer and an excellent feijoada are served Saturday at **Botequim Maria de Lourdes** (✉ Rua Bárbara Heliodora 141, Lourdes ☎ 031/3292–6905). The oh-so-chic **Cafezinho** (✉ Rua Cláudio Manoel 583, Funcionários ☎ 031/3261–6032) is open until midnight every day. Casual **Café com Letras** (✉ Rua Antônio de Albuquerque 781, Savassi ☎ 031/3225–9973) is a good place to listen to live jazz bands (every Sunday) and quiet music.

Established in 1962, **Cantina do Lucas** (✉ Av. Augusto de Lima 233, Loja 18, Centro ☎ 031/3226–7153) is a cultural landmark of Belo Horizonte. A popular nightclub for "GLS," which stands for "gays, *lésbicas, e simpatizantes* (gays, lesbians, and sympathizers)" is **Josefiné** (✉ Rua Antônio de Albuquerque 729, Savassi ☎ 031/3225–2307 or 031/3225–2353). **Lapa Multshow** (✉ Rua Álvares Maciel 312, Santa Efigênia ☎ 031/3241–2074 or 031/3241–5953) is a place you can find typical Brazilian rhythms such as samba and forró. One of the best bars in town is **Mercearia do Lili** (✉ Rua João Evangelista 696, Santo Antônio ☎ 031/3296–1951), which operates in a small grocery store in a bohemian area. During the day the shop sells eggs, cereals, and soap. When the night comes, tables are placed on the sidewalk, and the owner serves iced beer and incomparable appetizers. Weekly party **Movimento Balanço** (✉ Rua Diabase 205, Prado ☎ 031/3225–5888) is one of the hottest spots in town to dance to Brazilian music. Have fun, but be prepared for long lines every Saturday.

Inside the Ponteio Mall **Na Sala** (✉ Rodovia BR 356, 2500, Loja 120D, Santa Lúcia ☎ 031/3286–4705) is the most modern and well-equipped nightclub in the city. It is the premier club for house music in Belo Horizonte. A hip and young crowd ranging in age from 18 to mid-thirties gathers at **A Obra** (✉ Rua Rio Grande do Norte 1168, Savassi ☎ 031/3261–9431), a basement-level pub with a dance floor. Music styles vary from indie rock to classic rock and more, but it's always the best place to go for something other than mainstream music. **Utópica Marcenaria** (✉ Av. Raja Gabaglia 4700, Santa Lúcia ☎ 031/3296–2868) is a furniture store and an architecture office during the day, but from Tuesday to Saturday nights it is a venue for jazz, blues, and Brazilian and Cuban rhythms. It also has a very cool decor, with chairs hung from the ceiling.

Sports & the Outdoors

FUTEBOL The **Estádio Mineirão** (✉ Av. Antônio Abrão Carão 1001, Pampulha ☎ 031/3499–1100) is Brazil's third-largest stadium and the home field for Belo's two professional *futebol* (soccer) teams: Atlético Mineiro and Cruzeiro. Admission to the stadium for a look around (there are no guided tours) is R$1; it's open daily 9–5, except when there's a match. Prices for match tickets vary depending on the type of seat and how important the match is. Expect to pay R$10–R$30 or more for a big game.

HORSEBACK **Nossa Tropa** (☎ 031/3295–5884 or 031/9972–8505) arranges day treks
RIDING on horseback into the mountains surrounding Belo. The daily trips include breakfast and a snack and cost R$50. Reserve at least one week in advance.

RUNNING Most of the city's parks offer good, if short, jogging paths, and running is common during the day. One exception is **Parque das Mangabeiras** (⊠Av. Bandeirantes, s/n Mangabeiras ☎031/3277–8272), on the slopes of Serra do Curral. At 568 acres, it's one of the largest urban parks in the country. The park is open Tuesday through Sunday 8–6. Shaded lawns and a sparkling lake make the **Parque Municipal** (⊠ Av. Afonso Pena s/n, Centro ☎ 031/3277–4749) a good place to jog. It's open Tuesday through Sunday 6–6.

SPELUNKING For amateur spelunkers the mountains of Minas are replete with caves to be explored, though they must be seen with a guided tour. The largest and most popular cavern, with six large chambers, is the **Gruta de Maquiné** (☎ 031/3715–1078), 113 km (70 mi) northwest of Belo Horizonte near the town of Cordisburgo. Admission is R$6, and the cavern is open daily 8–5. The **Gruta da Lapinha** (☎ 031/3689–8422) is only 36 km (22 mi) north of Belo, near the city of Lagoa Santa, on the road leading from Confins Airport. You can tour the cave any day 9:30–5; the entry fee is R$5.

Shopping

In the fashionable Savassi and Lourdes neighborhoods you'll find the city's best antiques, handicrafts, and jewelry stores. For clothing head to one of the major shopping centers. On Saturday morning Avenida Bernardo Monteiro (between Rua Brasil and Rua Otoni) is the site of an antiques fair and food market, offering a taste of mineiro cuisine. On Sunday morning head for the large (nearly 3,000 vendors) arts-and-crafts fair in front of the Othon Palace hotel, on Avenida Afonso Pena.

ANTIQUES **Arte Sacra Antiguidades** (⊠Rua Alagoas 785, Savassi ☎031/3261–7256) has a fine selection of Minas antiques.

CLOTHING For a range of fashions hit the malls and shopping centers (⇨ *below*). If you are looking for clothes influenced by Minas Gerais culture, pay a visit to the store of designer **Ronaldo Fraga** (⊠ Rua Raul Pompéia 264, São Pedro ☎ 031/3282–5379). **Santíssima** (⊠ Rua Tomé de Souza 815, Savassi ☎ 031/3261–9487) sells secondhand clothing and accessories. At **Aramez** (⊠ Rua Paraíba 1395, Savassi ☎ 031/3225–2661) you can find outfits created by young Brazilian designers.

HANDICRAFTS **Brasarts** (⊠ Rua Curitiba 2325, Lourdes ☎ 031/3291–5220) has a good selection of handicrafts. **Serjô** (⊠ Rua Antônio de Albuquerque 749, Savassi ☎ 031/3227–5251) sells handicrafts from different regions of Minas Gerais. The **Centro de Artesanato Mineiro** (⊠ Av. Afonso Pena 1537, Centro ☎ 031/3272–8572), in the Palácio das Artes, offers a wide range of regional crafts. In the main hall of the theater **Cine Belas Artes** (⊠ Rua Gonçalves Dias 1581, Lourdes ☎ 031/9696–1095) there is a small store of aboriginal arts and crafts, plus a coffee shop and a bookstore. Modern colored objects made by up-and-coming Brazilian artists are found in the **Divina Obra** (⊠Rua Paraíba 1358, Loja 11, Savassi ☎ 031/3281–5757).

JEWELRY & Gems are the obvious focus in an area famous for its mines; just be sure
GEMSTONES to buy only from reputable dealers. If you're going to Ouro Preto, wait

to buy until you get there—prices and selection are better. **H. Stern** (⊠ Diamond Mall, Av. Olegário Maciel 1600, Loja OM82–83, Lourdes ☎ 031/3292–9158) is one of Brazil's leading names for gems. **Gemas Palace** (⊠ Galeria Othon Palace, Rua Tupis 25, Loja 05, Centro ☎ 031/3224–7730) is a good jewelry bet. **Raymundo Vianna** (⊠ Av. Presidente Carlos Luz 3001, Loja 3040, Caiçara ☎ 031/3415–6981) has a fine reputation for jewelry.

MALLS & CENTERS **Bahia Shopping** (⊠ Rua de Bahia 1022, Centro ☎ 031/3247–6940) is a good place to shop for men's and women's clothing. In the downtown area, **Shopping Cidade** (⊠ Rua Rio de Janeiro 910, Centro ☎ 031/3274–8300) is one of the most frequented malls. You can buy almost anything, from clothes to electronics. Many shops sell designer togs for men and women in Belo Horizonte's most exclusive mall, **BH Shopping** (⊠ BR 356, Loja 3049, Belvedere ☎ 0800/31–9001).

SIDE TRIPS FROM BELO HORIZONTE

Two hours southeast of Belo is Ouro Preto, a UNESCO World Heritage Site. The country's de facto capital during the gold-boom years, it was also the birthplace of Brazil's first independence movement: the Inconfidência Mineira. Today a vibrant student population ensures plenty of year-round activity, and there are plenty of lodging, dining, and shopping options.

All the Gold Towns—Ouro Preto, Mariana, Tiradentes, and Congonhas—are characterized by winding cobblestone streets, brilliant baroque churches, impressive mansions and museums, and colorful markets. Smaller than Ouro Preto but no less charming is Tiradentes, which truly seems to have stopped in time about midway through the 18th century. Between Ouro Preto and Tiradentes lies Congonhas, whose basilica is guarded by Aleijadinho's extraordinary sculptures of the 12 Old Testament prophets. In each of the towns you visit, from Sabará to Mariana to Diamantina, you'll discover a rich cultural history that sheds considerable light on colonial Brazil.

Parque Nacional do Caraça

123 km (77 mi) southeast of Belo Horizonte.

The symbol of the Parque Nacional do Caraça (whose name means "big face," in homage to the park's mountain, which resembles a giant) is the *lobo guará,* a wolf threatened by extinction that makes the rounds in the park at night searching for food. Beyond the natural attractions—waterfalls, caves (like Gruta do Centenário, one of the world's largest quartzite caves), and natural pools—the Caraça National Park also offers historical attractions. The park, which shelters a convent constructed in the 18th century, also sheltered a seminary that caught fire in 1968. After the accident the building was transformed into an inn and small museum. A Igreja de Nossa Senhora Mãe dos Homens (Church of Our Lady, Mother of Men), built at the end of the 19th century, has French stained-glass windows, rare organ, baroque altars, and a painting of the Last Supper made by artist Athaiçde. In the park administration office it's possible to book a guided walking tour. ⊠ *From Belo Horizonte take BR 262 to Santa Bárbara* ☎ *031/3837–2698* 🖅 *R$10 per vehicle* ⊙ *Daily 7–5.*

Where to Stay

¢ 🏨 **Hospedaria do Caraça.** The park's hotel and restaurant are in the old school, which was destroyed by a fire in 1968 and rebuilt soon after. The rooms are simple—some can accommodate five people—and are divided between two floors. Choose one on the second floor, with a view of the park and the mountain, or one of the three standard apartments. Groups of 15–40 people can rent one of the three houses in the park. Meals, which are served in the convent by priests, have very tight schedules: breakfast is 7–8:30, lunch noon–1:30, and dinner 6:30–7:30. Reservations are essential. ⊠ *Parque Natural do Caraça, Km 25,* ☎ *031/ 3837–2698* 🖅 *51 rooms* ♿ *Restaurant, pool, shop, laundry service; no room phones* ☰ *MC, V* ⦿ *FAP.*

Parque Nacional Serra do Cipó

96 km (60 mi) northeast of Belo Horizonte.

Highlights of the Serra do Cipó National Park include the roaring Cachoeira da Farofa, a waterfall, and the sprawling Canyon das Bandeirantes. Numerous bird species as well as wolves, jaguars, anteaters, monkeys, and the poisonous *sapo de pijama* (colored pajama frog) make up the area's wildlife. Although it is difficult to reach and is lacking in infrastructure, the park has a beautiful landscape and ecological wealth that make it worth the trip. Facilities are poor, so consider visiting the area as part of an organized tour. If you're an intrepid traveler, you can rent a car; call the park's visitor center for some information, and head out on your own. ⊠ *Take MG 10 north from Belo Horizonte toward Lagoa Santa* ☎ *031/3718–7228 or 031/3718–7237 for visitor center* 🖅 *R$3* ⊙ *Daily 8–2.*

Where to Stay

Expect basic and rustic (no air-conditioning), though clean, accommodations near the park. The area's best hotel is **Cipó Veraneio** (⊠ Km 95, Rodovia MG 10, Jaboticatubas, 2 km (1 mi) south of park entrance ☎ 031/3718–7000 ⊕ www.cipoveraneiohotel.com.br), inside the park. Basic rates are between R$110 and R$150 per night and include breakfast and dinner. You can bed and board at the working farm **Fazenda Monjolos Pousada** (⊠ Km 100, Rodovia MG 10, Santana do Riacho, 4 km (2½ mi) south of park entrance ☎ 031/3718–7011 ⊕ www. fazendamonjolos.com.br), which gives horseback riding tours. Rooms are R$150 per night and all meals are included. Camping facilities are available at **Véu da Noiva** (⊠ Parque Nacional Serra do Cipó, Km 101, Rodovia MG 10, Santana do Riacho ☎ 031/3799–1177 or 031/ 3274–2749 for reservations in Belo Horizonte) for R$13 per night. Reservations are recommended, especially around holidays and weekends. During Carnaval the Véu da Noiva can accommodate 2,000 people per day. If you're searching for peace and quiet, stay on weekdays.

Diamantina

290 km (180 mi) northeast of Belo Horizonte.

Diamantina took its name from the diamonds that were extracted in great quantities here in the 18th century. Perhaps because of its remote setting in the barren mountains close to the *sertão* (a remote arid region), Diamantina is extremely well preserved, although its churches lack the grandeur of those in other historic towns. Its white-wall structures stand in pristine contrast to the iron red of the surrounding mountains. The principal attraction in Diamantina is the simple pleasure of walking along the clean-swept cobblestone streets surrounded by colonial houses—note the overhanging roofs with their elaborate brackets.

The city was the home of two legendary figures of the colonial period: diamond merchant João Fernandes and his slave mistress, Xica da Silva, today a popular figure in Brazilian folklore. According to legend, Xica had never seen the ocean; so her lover built her an artificial lake and then added a boat. Two area attractions are linked with her; to see them, you should contact the Casa da Cultura to arrange a guided tour.

The **Casa de Xica da Silva** was the official residence of João Fernandes and Xica da Silva from 1763 to 1771 and contains colonial furniture and Xica's private chapel. ⊠ *Praça Lobo Mesquita 266* ☎ *038/3531–2491* 🖃 *Free* ☺ *Tues.–Sat. noon–5:30, Sun. 9–noon.*

The **Igreja Nossa Senhora do Carmo** is a church built in 1751 as a gift from Fernandes to his mistress. Supposedly, Xica ordered that the bell tower be built at the back of the building so the ringing wouldn't disturb her. The altar has gold-leaf paneling, and the organ has 514 pipes. ⊠ *Rua do Carmo s/n* ☎ *No phone* 🖃 *R$1* ☺ *Tues.–Sat. 9–noon and 2–6, Sun. 9–2.*

The **Museu do Diamante,** the city's diamond museum, in a building that dates from 1789, displays equipment used in colonial-period mines. Other items on exhibit include instruments made to torture slaves as well as sacred art from the 16th to the 19th centuries. There are guided tours of the rooms where diamonds were classified and separated. ⊠ *Rua Direita 14* ☎ *038/3531–1382* 🖃 *R$1* ☺ *Tues.–Sat. noon–5:30, Sun. 9–noon.*

The **Casa de Juscelino Kubitschek** was the childhood home of one of Brazil's most important 20th-century presidents and the man who built Brasília. ⊠ *Rua São Francisco 241* ☎ *038/3531–3607* 🖃 *Free* ☺ *Tues.–Sat. 9–5, Sun. 9–2.*

On Rua da Glória notice the covered wooden **footbridge** connecting the second stories of two buildings that once served as the headquarters of the colonial governors.

Where to Stay & Eat

¢–$ ✕ **Cantina do Marinho.** This well-respected restaurant specializes in comida mineira. Favorites are pork steak with tutu and pork tenderloin with *feijão tropeiro* (brown beans, bacon, and manioc meal). There's an à la carte menu as well as a self-service buffet for a fixed price of R$7.50, including dessert. ⊠ *Rua Direita 113* ☎ *038/3531–1686* ▤ *No credit cards.*

¢ 🏨 **Tijuco.** This historic-district inn is paradoxically housed in an Oscar Niemeyer–designed structure. It's considered the best hotel in town; views of the city from this hotel certainly are outstanding. ⊠ *Rua Macau do Meio 211* ☎ *038/3531–1022* 📞 *27 rooms* 🍴 *Café, room service, fans, refrigerator, laundry services, convention center* ▤ *AE, DC, MC, V* ❘O❘*BP.*

Nightlife

Diamantina enjoys a special distinction as Brazil's center of serenading. At night, particularly on the weekends, romantics gather in a downtown alley known as Beco da Mota, the former red-light district and now home to several popular bars frequented by students and young professionals. Strolling guitar players also gather on Rua Direita and Rua Quitanda.

Sabará

19 km (12 mi) east of Belo Horizonte.

Sabará's churches drive home the enormous wealth of Minas Gerais during the gold-rush days. In this former colonial town, today a sprawling suburb of 90,000, historic buildings are scattered about, requiring you either to join a tour or to drive. The interiors of the baroque churches are rich in gold-leaf paneling.

In the main square sits the unfinished **Igreja de Nossa Senhora do Rosário dos Pretos** (Church of Our Lady of the Rosary of the Blacks; circa 1767), which was built, like its counterpart in Ouro Preto, by slaves. Here, however, they ran out of gold before the project could be completed. When slavery was abolished in 1888, the church was left as a memorial. ⊠ *Praça Melo Viana s/n* ☎ *031/3671–1523* 💲 *R$1* ⊙ *Tues.–Sun. 8–11 and 1–5.*

The ornate **Igreja de Nossa Senhora da Conceição** (Church of Our Lady of the Immaculate Conception), though small, is Sabará's main church and an outstanding example of Portuguese baroque architecture combined with elements of Asian art. Its simple exterior gives no indication of the wealth inside, typified by its luxurious gold altar and lavishly decorated ceiling. At this writing, the church is undergoing renovations but is still open for public visits. ⊠ *Praça Getúlio Vargas s/n* ☎ *031/ 3671–1724* 💲 *R$1* ⊙ *Weekdays 9–5, weekends 9–noon and 2–5.*

Igreja de Nossa Senhora do Ó (Our Lady of Ó Church), one of Brazil's oldest and smallest churches, contains paintings said to have been completed by 23 Chinese artists brought from the former Portuguese colony of Macau. Other signs of Asian influence include the Chinese tower and the gilded arches. ⊠ *Largo do Ó s/n* ☎ *031/3671–1724* 💲 *R$1* ⊙ *Weekdays 9–5, weekends 9–noon and 2–5.*

In the **Igreja de Nossa Senhora do Carmo** (Church of Our Lady of Carmel) are pulpits, a choir loft, and a doorway all designed by the famed Aleijadinho. This is one of several Minas churches that were the result of a collaboration between Aleijadinho and painter Manuel da Costa Ataíde,

CloseUp

THE PASSION OF ALEIJADINHO

IT'S A TESTAMENT TO THE CREATIVE SPIRIT that Brazil's most famous artist couldn't use his hands or feet. Born in 1738 in Vila Rica (today's Ouro Preto) to a Portuguese architect and a black slave, Antônio Francisco Lisboa developed a passion for art through exposure to his father's projects. In his mid-thirties he developed an illness (some say leprosy, others syphilis; most assume it was arthritis) that led to a life of torment. Nicknamed Aleijadinho (Little Cripple), he shunned human contact, going out only at night or before dawn. With the help of some assistants, he traveled between towns, sculpting and overseeing church construction. He died on November 18, 1814, and was buried in the church he attended as a child.

There's no hint of Aleijadinho's pain in the delicate, expressive features of his soapstone and cedarwood figures. Indeed, his art is distinguished by a striking liveliness and deep religious faith. His most cherished works, such as the larger-than-life Old Testament prophets at the church in Congonhas, were created with a hammer and chisel strapped to his wrists, a feat often compared to the suffering of Christ. After those in Congonhas, his best works are in Ouro Preto, where he designed the brilliant Igreja São Francisco de Assis, among other things.

a brilliant artist in his own right. ☒ *Rua do Carmo s/n* ☏ *031/3671–2417* 🖾 *R$1* ⊙ *Tues.–Sat. 9–11:30 and 1–5:30, Sun. 1–6.*

Ouro Preto

97 km (60 mi) southeast of Belo Horizonte.

The former gold-rush capital is the best place to see the legendary Aleijadinho's artistry. Now a lively university town, it has been preserved as a national monument and a World Heritage Site. The surrounding mountains, geometric rows of whitewashed buildings, cobblestone streets and red-tile roofs that climb the hillsides, and morning mist and evening fog all give Ouro Preto an evocative air, as if at any moment it could be transported back three centuries.

In its heyday Ouro Preto was one of Brazil's most progressive cities and the birthplace of the colony's first stirrings of independence. A movement called the Inconfidência Mineira was organized to overthrow the Portuguese rulers and establish an independent Brazilian republic. It was to have been led by a resident of Ouro Preto, Joaquim José da Silva Xavier, a dentist known as Tiradentes (Tooth Puller). But the Minas rebellion never got off the ground. In 1789 word of Tiradentes's intentions reached the capital, Rio de Janeiro; he was hanged and drawn and quartered, and his followers were either imprisoned or exiled.

Exploring Ouro Preto

Ouro Preto has several museums as well as 13 colonial *igrejas* (churches) that are highly representative of mineiro baroque architecture. The Minas style is marked by elaborately carved doorways and curving lines. Most distinctive, though, are the interiors, richly painted and decorated lavishly with cedarwood and soapstone sculptures. Many interiors are unabashedly rococo, with an ostentatious use of gold leaf, a by-product of the region's mineral wealth.

All the town's sights are within easy walking distance of the central square, Praça Tiradentes, which teems with gossiping students, eager merchants, and curious visitors. From here the longest walk you'll make takes about 15 minutes. Note that many museums and churches are closed Monday.

Pay attention to the addresses, because the main streets of Ouro Preto have two names: one from the 18th century, still used by the city's inhabitants, and the other an official name, used on maps but not very popular. Therefore, Rua Conde de Bobadela is better known as Rua Direita, Rua Senador Rocha Lagoa as Rua das Flores, and Rua Cláudio Manoel as Rua do Ouvidor. Street signs sometimes use the official name and sometimes have two signs, each with a different name. We used the official names in this guide.

Numbers in the text correspond to numbers in the margin and on the Ouro Preto map.

A GOOD WALK Start at **Praça Tiradentes** ⌐, in the center of Ouro Preto. South of the square is the **Museu da Inconfidência** ⑨. Two blocks west, on Rua Brigadeiro Mosqueira, is the **Teatro Municipal** ⑩. Across from theater is the **Igreja de Nossa Senhora do Carmo** ⑪, with major works by Aleijadinho and Ataíde, and its neighboring **Museu do Oratório** ⑫.

Head back to Praça Tiradentes. Two blocks east is the distinctive twin-tower **Igreja de São Francisco de Assis** ⑬. Two blocks farther east is the **Igreja de Nossa Senhora da Conceição** ⑭ and its small Aleijadinho museum. From here head east on Rua da Conceição, which becomes Rua Santa Efigênia, to the **Igreja de Santa Efigênia** ⑮. Retrace your steps to Praça Tiradentes one more time. Walk north across the plaza to **Museu da Mineralogia e das Pedras** ⑯, inside the Escola de Minas. There are several restaurants and coffee shops in Rua Direita, a few meters from Praça Tiradentes. Choose one for lunch or a snack.

Head west on Rua Senador Rocha Lagoa (better known as Rua das Flores). One block ahead, on the corner of Rua José, is **Casa dos Contos** ⑰, the city's original mint. Continuing south on the same street, which becomes Rua Randolfo Bretas, you come to the **Igreja de Nossa Senhora do Pilar** ⑱, with its baroque interior. Head northwest on Rua Randolfo Bretas followed by Rua Getúlio Vargas to the less ornate but equally intriguing **Igreja de Nossa Senhora do Rosário dos Pretos** ⑲.

TIMING This is an all-day tour. Start out early, as some churches are only open in the morning. Unless you're an ecclesiastic, plan to spend about 20 minutes in each church and 30–45 minutes in each museum.

WHAT TO SEE **Casa dos Contos.** The colonial coinage house contains the foundry used ⑰ to mint the coins of the gold-rush period as well as examples of coins and period furniture. The museum building is considered one of the best examples of Brazilian colonial architecture. ⊠ *Rua São José 12* ☎ *031/ 3551–1444* ✉ *R$1* ⊙ *Tues.–Sat. 12:30–5:30, Sun. 9–3.*

⑪ **Igreja de Nossa Senhora do Carmo.** Completed in 1772, the impressive Our Lady of Carmel Church contains major works by Aleijadinho and Ataíde. It was originally designed by Aleijadinho's father, himself an architect, but was later modified by Aleijadinho, who added additional baroque elements, including the characteristic soapstone sculptures of angels that are above the entrance. ⊠ *Praça Tiradentes s/n* ☎ *031/ 3551–4735* ✉ *R$1* ⊙ *Tues.–Sun. 9–10:45 and noon–4:45.*

⑭ **Igreja de Nossa Senhora da Conceição.** The lavishly gilded Our Lady of the Conception Church, completed in 1760, contains the tomb of Aleijadinho as well as a small museum dedicated to the artist. ⊠ *Praça Antônio Dias s/n* ☎ *031/3551–3282* ✉ *R$4* ⊙ *Tues.–Sun. 8:30–noon and 1:30–5, Sun. noon–5.*

⑱ **Igreja de Nossa Senhora do Pilar.** Built around 1711 on the site of an earlier chapel, this is the most richly decorated of Ouro Preto's churches and one of Brazil's best examples of baroque religious architecture. It's said that 400 pounds of gold leaf were used to cover the interior. ⊠ *Praça Monsenhor Castilho Barbosa s/n* ☎ *031/3551–4735* ✉ *R$3* ⊙ *Tues.–Sun. 9–10:45 and noon–4:45.*

⑲ **Igreja de Nossa Senhora do Rosário dos Pretos.** The small, intriguing Church of Our Lady of the Rosary of the Blacks was built by slaves, some of whom bought freedom with the gold they found in Ouro Preto. According to legend, the church's interior is bare because the slaves ran out of gold after erecting the baroque building. ⊠ *Largo do Rosário s/n* ☎ *031/ 3551–1209* ✉ *Free* ⊙ *Tues.–Sun. 9–10:45 and noon–4:45.*

⑮ **Igreja de Santa Efigênia.** On a hill east of Praça Tiradentes, this interesting slave church was built over the course of 60 years (1730–90) and was funded by Chico-Rei. This African ruler was captured during Brazil's gold rush and sold to a mine owner in Minas Gerais. Chico eventually earned enough money to buy his freedom—in the days before the Portuguese prohibited such acts—and became a hero among slaves throughout the land. The clocks on the facade are the city's oldest, and the interior contains cedar sculptures by Francisco Xavier de Brito, Aleijadinho's teacher. ⊠ *Rua de Santa Efigênia s/n* ☎ *031/3551–5047* ✉ *R$2* ⊙ *Tues.–Sun. 8:30–4:30.*

⑬ **Igreja de São Francisco de Assis.** Considered Aleijadinho's masterpiece, this
Fodor'sChoice church was begun in 1766 by the Franciscan Third Order and not com-
★ pleted until 1810. In addition to designing the structure, Aleijadinho was responsible for the wood and soapstone sculptures on the portal, high altar, side altars, pulpits, and crossing arch. The panel on the nave ceiling rep-

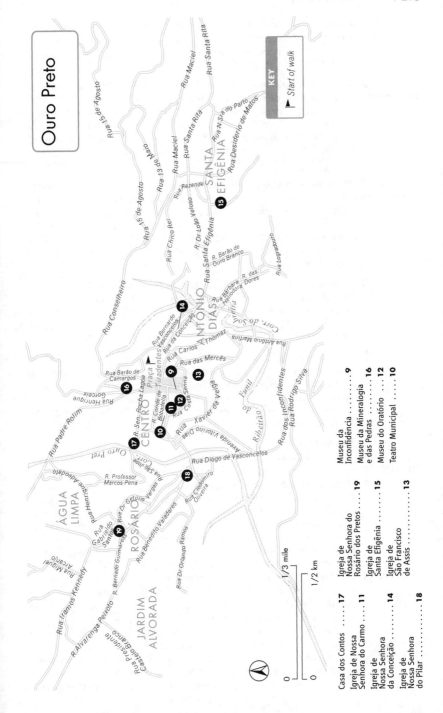

Ouro Preto

KEY

▲ *Start of walk*

Casa dos Contos **17**
Igreja de Nossa
Senhora do Carmo **11**
Igreja de
Nossa Senhora
da Conceição **14**
Igreja de
Nossa Senhora
do Pilar **18**

Igreja de
Nossa Senhora do
Rosário dos Pretos **19**
Igreja de
Santa Efigênia **15**
Igreja de
São Francisco
de Assis **13**

Museu da
Inconfidência **9**
Museu da Mineralogia
e das Pedras **16**
Museu do Oratório ... **12**
Teatro Municipal **10**

resenting the Virgin's glorification was painted by Ataíde. Cherubic faces, garlands of tropical fruits, and allegorical characters carved into the main altar are still covered with their original paint. ⊠ *Largo de Coimbra s/n* ☎ *031/3551–5683* ⌨ *R$4* ☉ *Tues.–Sun. 8:30–noon and 1:30–5.*

❾ Museu da Inconfidência. A former 18th-century prison as well as the onetime city hall, this museum commemorates the failed Inconfidência Mineira rebellion with many artifacts. Among the displays are furniture, clothing, slaves' manacles, firearms, books, and gravestones, as well as works by Aleijadinho and Ataíde. The museum also holds the remains of the unlucky revolutionaries. ⊠ *Praça Tiradentes 139* ☎ *031/3551–1121* ⌨ *R$5* ☉ *Tues.–Sun. noon–5:30.*

FodorsChoice ★

⓰ Museu da Mineralogia e das Pedras. Housed opposite the Museu da Inconfidência in the former governor's palace and inside the current Escola de Minas (School of Mines), the Mineral and Rock Museum contains an excellent collection of precious gems (including diamonds), gold, and crystals. The minerals have been organized according to their rarity, color, and crystallization. ⊠ *Praça Tiradentes 20* ☎ *031/3559–1531* ⌨ *R$4* ☉ *Tues.–Fri. noon–5, weekends 9–1.*

FodorsChoice ★

⓬ Museu do Oratório. Established in the old house of the St. Carmel Novitiate, this museum celebrates sacred art from the 18th and 19th centuries. Some of the oratories, which reflect ideas of religious beauty from the period, have been displayed at the Louvre. ⊠ *Rua Costa Senna 28* ☎ *031/3551–5369* ⌨ *R$2* ☉ *Daily 9:30–11:50 and 1:30–5:30.*

❿ Teatro Municipal. The former opera house, built between 1746 and 1769, still presents shows and plays, making it Latin America's oldest municipal theater still in operation. There's no regular schedule for performances, however; check with the Associação de Guias for information on events. ⊠ *Rua Brigadeiro Musqueira s/n* ☎ *031/3591–3224* ⌨ *R$1* ☉ *Tues.–Sun. noon–6.*

Where to Eat

$–$$ ✕ **Le Coq d'Or.** The finest restaurant in Minas Gerais and one of the best in Brazil is in Ouro Preto's Solar Nossa Senhora do Rosário hotel. An elegant atmosphere with formal place settings, attentive service, and soft Brazilian music makes it ideal for a quiet, romantic dinner. The executive chef trained in Paris at the renowned Cordon Bleu culinary institute before introducing creative French-inspired cuisine to Brazilian gourmands. The ever-changing menu always includes an innovative selection of meat and fish dishes, and the wine list is excellent. ⊠ *Rua Getúlio Vargas 270, Rosário* ☎ *031/3551–5200* ⊟ *AE, DC, MC, V.*

FodorsChoice ★

¢–$$ ✕ **O Profeta.** The friendly staffers at this cozy restaurant serve up mineira and international dishes. On weekends there's also live MPB (*música popular brasileira,* or Brazilian popular music). ⊠ *Rua Conde de Bobadela 65, Centro* ☎ *031/3551–4556* ⊟ *AE, DC, MC, V.*

$ ✕ **Casa do Ouvidor.** Atop a jewelry store in the heart of the historical district, this popular restaurant has garnered several awards for such regional dishes as tutu à mineira, feijão tropeiro, and *frango com quiabo* (chicken cooked in broth with chopped okra). Portions are huge, so come with an empty stomach and be prepared for a noisy, ever-crowded din-

FodorsChoice ★

ing room. ⊠ *Rua Conde de Bobadela 42, Centro* ☎ *031/3551–2141* ☰ *AE, DC, MC, V.*

$ ✕ **Piacere.** If you want to escape from the typical *comida mineira*, the Piacere is an excellent option. This Italian restaurant has modern decor, which contrasts with the architecture of the basement in which it is housed. ⊠ *Rua Getúlio Vargas 241, Rosário* ☎ *031/3551–4297* ☉ *Closed Mon. No lunch Tues.–Sat.; no dinner Sun.*

★ **¢-$** ✕ **Café Geraes.** This cozy bilevel café is at the center of Ouro Preto's artistic and intellectual life. Students sip wine and feast on delicious sandwiches, soups, and other snacks. The pastries and the coffees are equally appealing. ⊠ *Rua Conde de Bobadela 122, Centro* ☎ *031/3551–1405* ☰ *DC, MC.*

★ **¢** ✕ **Chafariz.** Regional cuisine is served buffet style in this informal eatery near the Casa dos Contos. The small, colorful dining room has hardwood floors, wood-beam ceilings, and wooden tables draped with blue, green, or white tablecloths. ⊠ *Rua São José 167, Centro* ☎ *031/ 3551–2828* ☉ *No dinner* ☰ *AE, DC, MC, V.*

Where to Stay

Some families in Ouro Preto rent rooms in their homes, although usually only during Carnaval and Easter, when the city's hotels fill up. For a list of rooms to rent, contact the **Associação de Guias** (⊠ Rua Padre Rolim s/n, São Cristóvão, Ouro Preto ☎ 031/3551–2655). The association also provides information on places to camp.

★ **$-$$** ▥ **Pousada do Mondego.** This small, intimate inn is next to the Igreja de São Francisco de Assis in a house that dates from 1747. You'll find period furnishings, a colonial ambience, and highly personalized service. The hotel also gives two-hour city tours in a 1930s minibus, and it has its own antiques store and art gallery. ⊠ *Largo de Coimbra 38, Centro* ☎ *031/3551–2040, 021/2287–1592 Ext. 601 for reservations in Rio* 🖨 *031/3551–3094* ⊕ *www.roteirosdecharme.com.br* ⬠ *24 rooms* △ *Restaurant, room service, fan, in-room safes, refrigerator, bar, shop, Internet, business services, convention center, travel services, some pets allowed; no a/c* ☰ *AE, DC, MC, V* ⧈ *BP.*

$ ▥ **Estalagem das Minas Gerais.** As it's near a nature preserve, this place is perfect for those who like to hike or walk in the woods. Rooms are modern, and those in front have wonderful views of the valley. The luxury chalets have two floors and granite details. Each can accommodate as many as five people with a double bed upstairs, single beds downstairs, and two bathrooms. The restaurant serves regional fare. ⊠ *Km 90, Rodovia dos Inconfidentes,* ☎ *031/3551–2122* 🖨 *031/3551–2709* ⬠ *114 rooms, 32 chalets* △ *Restaurant, dining room, room service, refrigerator, cable TV, 2 pools, gym, sauna, steam room, squash, bar, piano bar, library, playground, laundry services, Internet, business services, convention center; no a/c* ☰ *AE, DC, MC, V* ⧈ *BP.*

$ ▥ **Luxor Ouro Preto Pousada.** With stone walls that date back 200 years, beautiful wood floors, and gracious antique furnishings, this hotel has the feeling of a 19th-century lodge. The lobby leads to a small, romantic restaurant: typical mineira cooking is served to the lucky few at tables. Guest rooms enjoy views of the city, and some have original paintings by famous Minas artist Chanina. ⊠ *Rua Dr. Alfredo Baeta 16, Antônio Dias* ☎☎ *031/3551–2244* ⊕ *www.luxorhoteis.com.br* ⇱ *19 rooms* ⚐ *Restaurant, room service, fan, in-room data ports, refrigerator, recreation room, baby-sitting, laundry services, Internet, some pets allowed* ⊟ *AE, DC, MC, V* ⦿| *BP.*

$ ▦ **Pousada Clássica.** Opened in 2000, this pousada is in an elegant house a few yards from the main churches and museums. The rooms are comfortable, and one of the suites, in the front of the building, has a hydromassage bathtub. The city view from the balconies is spectacular, but the noise coming from the Rua Direita's bars, frequented by college students, can be a bother. For more tranquillity, choose the apartments in the back, but note that views are not as good. ⊠ *Rua Conde de Bobadela 96, Centro* ☎ *031/3551–3663* 🖷 *031/3551–6593* ⊕ *www.pousadaclassica. com.br* ⇱ *25 rooms, 2 suites* ⚐ *Restaurant, room service, refrigerator, cable TV, laundry service, Internet, some pets allowed* ⊟ *D, MC, V* ⦿|*BP.*

$ ▦ **Solar Nossa Senhora do Rosário.** Superior service and the world-class
Fodor'sChoice Le Coq d'Or restaurant are among this hotel's draws. The beautiful 19th-
★ century building feels like a bed-and-breakfast, with elegant yet comfortable decor, quiet floors, and charming guest rooms. When you're not exploring the town, have a swim in the luxurious hilltop pool or stop by the atrium for afternoon tea. The hotel even has a section of the mine that originally was on this site, discovered during renovations. ⊠*Rua Getúlio Vargas 270, Rosário* ☎ *031/3551–5200* 🖷 *031/3551–4288* ⊕ *www.hotelsolardorosario.com.br* ⇱ *28 rooms, 9 suites* ⚐ *Restaurant, room service, in-room data ports, in-room safes, refrigerator, cable TV, pool, gym, steam room, bar, laundry services, Internet, business services, convention center, some pets allowed* ⊟ *AE, DC, MC, V* ⦿| *BP.*

¢ ▦ **Colonial.** Close to the main square, this is a good example of the small no-frills inns found in most historic cities. What you'll get is a very basic, clean room for a low price. Room 1 has a loft and can sleep up to five people. ⊠ *Trv. Camilo Veloso 26, Centro* ☎ *031/3551–3133* 🖷 *031/ 3551–3361* ⇱ *18 rooms* ⚐ *Restaurant, room service, fans, refrigerator, laundry service; no a/c* ⊟ *AE, DC, MC, V* ⦿| *BP.*

¢ ▦ **Grande Hotel de Ouro Preto.** As its name suggests, the Grande is Ouro Preto's largest hotel—it's immense by local standards, though room sizes are comparable to those at other hotels. The hotel is also the town's premier modernist structure—a curving two-story building on concrete pillars designed by world-acclaimed architect Oscar Niemeyer. Cultural purists and aesthetes consider it an eyesore, however. ⊠ *Rua Senador Rocha Lagoa 164, Centro* ☎ *031/3551–1488* 🖷 *031/3551–5028* ⊕ *www.hotelouropreto.com.br* ⇱ *35 rooms* ⚐ *Restaurant, room service, fan, refrigerator, pool, bar, shop, laundry services, Internet, convention center; no a/c* ⊟ *AE, DC, MC, V* ⦿| *BP.*

★ ¢ ▦ **Pousada Ouro Preto.** Popular with backpackers, this pousada has small rooms individually decorated with local art. Its open-air halls have flowers and paintings of Ouro Preto; the terrace in front of the lobby offers a peaceful view of the city center. The English-speaking staff does laundry for free. ⊠ *Rua das Mercês 72, Antônio Dias* ☎☎ *031/ 3551–3081* ⇱ *17 rooms* ⚐ *Room service, refrigerators, laundry service, some pets allowed; no a/c* ⊟ *DC, MC, V* ⦿| *BP.*

¢ ▣ **Pousada Recanto das Minas.** Its hilltop location at the edge of town is both a blessing and a curse. A stay at this comfortable pousada affords lovely views, but the walk to and from it is somewhat strenuous. It's a popular place with families and other groups. For more privacy and peace, opt for a simple but cozy chalet instead of a room in the main building. ⊠ *Rua Manganês 287, São Cristóvão* ☎☎ *031/3551–3003* ⤳ *11 rooms, 25 chalets* ⚭ *Room service, refrigerator, 2 pools, sauna, steam room, billiards, bar, recreation room, laundry service, Internet, business services; no a/c* ⊟ *AE, DC, MC, V* ⦿I *BP.*

¢ ▣ **Pousada Toledo.** This simple inn with 18th-century architecture has colonial-style furnishings and solid service. If the surroundings put you in the mood for authentic antiques, head for the shop next door. ⊠ *Rua Conselheiro Quintiliano 395, Centro* ☎ *031/3551–3366* ᗺ *031/ 3551–5915* ⤳ *13 rooms* ⚭ *Room service, fans, refrigerators, laundry service; no a/c* ⊟ *AE, V* ⦿I *BP.*

Nightlife & the Arts

Even if the food and the service at **Acaso 85** (⊠ Largo do Rosário 85, Rosário ☎ 031/3551–2397) don't impress you, the incredibly high ceilings, stone walls, and medieval ambience will. It's popular with the late-night crowd. **Bardobeco** (⊠ Trv. do Arieira 15, Centro ☎ No phone) is the city's best *cachaçaria,* with more than 40 brands of cachaça, including the owner's own Milagre de Minas.

The best place for information about theater, arts, and musical performances is the **Associação de Guias** (⊠ Rua Padre Rolim s/n, São Cristóvão ☎ 031/3551–2655). **Fundação das Artes de Ouro Preto** (FAOP; ⊠ Rua Getúlio Vargas 185, Rosário ☎ 031/3551–2014), the local arts foundation, hosts various art and photographic exhibitions throughout the year.

Shopping

HANDICRAFTS   There are numerous handicrafts stores on Praça Tiradentes and its surrounding streets. At the daily **handicrafts fair,** in front of the Igreja de São Francisco de Assis, vendors sell soapstone and wood carvings, paintings, and other goods.

For sculpture head to **Bié** (⊠ Praça Professor Amadeu Barbosa 129 ☎ 031/3551–2309). **Beco da Mãe Chica** (⊠ Beco da Mãe Chica 29 ☎ 031/3551–2511) has a good selection of unique sculptures. For authentic Minas antiques and handicrafts, visit **Bureau d'Art** (⊠ Largo do Rosário 41, Rosário ☎ 031/3551–7438). If you're looking for religious souvenirs, don't miss **Ciríaco** (⊠ Largo do Rosário 41, Rosário ☎ 031/3551–7438). **Z Nelson** (⊠ Rua Antônio de Albuquerque 51, Pilar ☎ 031/3551–6434) sells crafts and religious objects.

JEWELRY &   One of the best places in Brazil to purchase gems, especially the rare
GEMSTONES   imperial topaz, is **Ita Gemas** (⊠ Rua Conde de Bobadela 139, Centro ☎ 031/3551–4895). An excellent store for authenticated gems—including imperial topazes, emeralds, and tourmalines—is **Luiza Figueiredo Jóias** (⊠ Rua Conde de Bobadela 48, Centro ☎ 031/3551–2487). At **Brasil Gemas** (⊠ Praça Tiradentes 74 ☎ 031/3551–2976) you can visit the stonecutting and jewel assembly workshop.

en route

Between Ouro Preto and Mariana lies **Mina de Ouro de Passagem,** Brazil's oldest gold mine. During the gold rush thousands of slaves perished here because of its dangerous, backbreaking conditions. Although the mine is no longer in operation, you can ride an old mining car through 11 km (7 mi) of tunnels and see exposed quartz, graphite, and black tourmaline. Buses travel here from Ouro Preto (catch them beside the Escola de Minas) and cost about R$2.25; taxis are less than R$23. ⊠ *Road to Mariana, 4 km (3 mi) east of Ouro Preto* ☎ *031/3557–5000* 🕮 *R$15* ⊘ *Mon.–Tues. 9–5, Wed.–Sun. 9–5:30.*

Mariana

11 km (7 mi) east of Ouro Preto, 110 km (68 mi) southeast of Belo Horizonte.

The oldest city in Minas Gerais (founded in 1696) is also the birthplace of Aleijadinho's favorite painter, Manuel da Costa Ataíde. Mariana, like Ouro Preto, has preserved much of the appearance of an 18th-century gold-mining town. Its three principal churches showcase examples of the art of Ataíde, who intertwined sensual romanticism with religious themes. The faces of his saints and other figures often have mulatto features, reflecting the composition of the area's population at the time. Today Mariana is most visited for the weekly organ concerts at its cathedral.

The **Catedral Basílica da Sé,** completed in 1760, contains paintings by Ataíde, although it's best known for its 1701 German organ, transported by mule from Rio de Janeiro in 1720. The instrument was a gift from Dom João V and there are only two of its kind in the world. Concerts take place Friday at 11 AM and Sunday at 12:15 PM. ⊠ *Praça Cláudio Manoel s/n* ☎ *031/3557–1216* 🕮 *R$1 donation* ⊘ *Tues.–Sun. 8–noon and 2–6:30.*

Behind the cathedral is the **Museu Arquidiocesano de Arte Sacra de Mariana,** which claims to have the largest collection of baroque painting and sculpture in the state, including wood and soapstone carvings by Aleijadinho and paintings by Ataíde. ⊠ *Rua Frei Durão 49* ☎ *031/3557–2516* 🕮 *R$3* ⊘ *Tues.–Sun. 8:30–noon and 1:30–5.*

Although the 1793 **Igreja de São Francisco de Assis** (Church of St. Francis of Assisi) has soapstone pulpits and altars by Aleijadinho, its most impressive works are the sacristy's ceiling panels, which were painted by Ataíde. They depict, in somber tones, the life and death of St. Francis of Assisi and are considered by many to be the artist's masterpiece. Sadly, however, they've been damaged by termites and water. ⊠ *Praça Minas Gerais* ☎ *031/3557–1023* 🕮 *R$2* ⊘ *Tues.–Sun. 9–noon and 1–5.*

The **Igreja da Nossa Senhora do Carmo** (Our Lady of Carmel Church), with works by Ataíde and Aleijadinho, is noteworthy for its impressive facade and sculpted soapstone designs. Ataíde is buried at the rear of the church. At this writing, it is closed for renovations following a huge fire. ⊠ *Praça Minas Gerais* ☎ *031/3557–1635* ⊘ *Daily 8–5.*

Congonhas do Campo

50 km (31 mi) west of Mariana, 94 km (58 mi) south of Belo Horizonte.

★ To see Aleijadinho's crowning effort, head to the small Gold Town of Congonhas do Campo. Dominating Congonhas is the hilltop pilgrimage church **Igreja Bom Jesus do Matosinho,** built in 1757 and the focus of great processions during Holy Week. At the churchyard entrance are Aleijadinho's 12 life-size Old Testament prophets carved in soapstone, a towering achievement and one of the greatest works of art from the baroque period. The prophets appear caught in movement, and every facial expression is unforgettable. Leading up to the church on the sloping hillside are six chapels, each containing a scene of the stations of the cross. The 66 figures in this remarkable procession were carved in cedar by Aleijadinho and painted by Ataíde. ⊠ *Praça da Basílica s/n* ☎ *031/3731–1590* ⊠ *Free* ⊙ *Tues.–Sun. 6–6.*

Tiradentes

129 km (80 mi) south of Congonhas do Campo, 210 km (130 mi) southwest of Belo Horizonte.

Probably the best historic city to visit after Ouro Preto, Tiradentes was the birthplace of a martyr who gave the city its name (it was formerly called São José del Rei) and retains much of its 18th-century charm. Life in this tiny village—nine streets with eight churches set against the backdrop of the Serra de São José—moves slowly. This quality attracts wealthy residents of Belo Horizonte, Rio, and São Paulo, who have sparked a local real estate boom by buying up 18th-century properties for use as weekend getaways or to transform them into *pousadas* or restaurants.

In addition to the excellent selection of handicrafts—some 20 shops line Rua Direita in the town center—the principal attraction is the **Igreja de Santo Antônio.** Built in 1710, it contains extremely well-preserved gilded carvings of saints, cherubs, and biblical scenes. The church's soapstone frontispiece—a celebration of baroque architecture—was sculpted by Aleijadinho. ⊠ *Rua Padre Toledo s/n* ☎ *032/3355–2149* ⊠ *Donations accepted* ⊙ *Daily 9–noon and 2–5.*

Where to Stay & Eat

$$–$$$ ✕ **Theatro da Villa.** On the site of an old Greek-style amphitheater, this restaurant offers dinner theater Tiradentes style. The menu is filled with international fare, including meat and fish dishes. Most performances involve local folk music and dance. ⊠ *Rua Padre Toledo 157* ☎ *032/ 3355–1275* 🚫 *No credit cards* ⊙ *Closed Mon. No lunch.*

★ **$**   ✕ **Estalagem.** The Estalagem draws rave reviews for its feijão tropeiro and *frango ao molho pardo* (broiled chicken served in a sauce made with its own blood), just two of the dishes that are part of the self-service, fixed-price buffet. Although it's small, it has an elegant atmosphere. Light music and a quiet, attentive staff make for a relaxing meal. ⊠ *Rua Ministro Gabriel Passos 280* ☎ *032/3355–1144* 🚫 *No credit cards* ⊙ *Closed Mon.*

$ ✗ **Tragaluz.** This mix of store, coffee shop, and restaurant serves unusual dishes, like chopped meat with cheese and potatoes. The desserts are delicious—try the fried banana with ice cream and chestnuts. ⊠ *Rua Direita 52* ☎ *032/3355–1424* ▤ *AE, V* ⊘ *Closed Tues.*

$ ✗ **Viradas do Largo.** One of the best restaurants in the country for typical comida mineira, the Viradas do Largo (or Restaurante da Beth) serves dishes such as chicken with *ora pro nobis* (a Brazilian cabbage) and feijão tropeiro with pork chops. Some of the ingredients, such as the *borecole* (kale), are cultivated in the restaurant's backyard. The portions are generous, enough for three or four people, but you can ask for a half order of any dish. The restaurant is also a market, with typical arts and crafts from Minas Gerais. Reservations are recommended on weekends. ⊠ *Rua do Moinho 11* ☎ *032/3355–1111 or 032/3355–1110* ▤ *D, MC, V.*

Fodor'sChoice ★

★ **$** ▦ **Pouso Alforria.** Alforria enjoys a quiet, peaceful location with a fabulous view of the São José Mountains. The light-filled lobby—with its stone floors, high ceilings, and beautiful Brazilian artwork (some of it from Bahia)—leads to a charming breakfast space and courtyard. Rooms have considerable natural light and are individually decorated; mattresses are firm and bathrooms modern. ⊠ *Rua Custódio Gomes 286* ☎☎ *032/3355–1536* ⊕ *www.pousoalforria.com.br* ⇔ *9 rooms* ⚫ *Room service, in-room data ports, refrigerators, cable TV, pool, bar, laundry service, Internet; no a/c, no kids under 16* ▤ *DC, MC* ⊚ *BP.*

¢–**$** ▦ **Solar da Ponte.** In every respect—from the stunning antiques to the comfortable beds to the elegant place settings—this inn is a faithful example of regional style. Breakfast and afternoon tea (included in the rate) are served in the dining room, overlooking well-tended gardens. With advance notice, the English owner and his Brazilian wife can arrange historical, botanical, and ecological tours on foot or horseback. ⊠ *Praça das Mercês s/n* ☎ *032/3355–1255, 021/2287–1592 for reservations in Rio* ▦ *032/3355–1201* ⇔ *12 rooms* ⚫ *Room service, fans, in-room safes, refrigerators, cable TV, pool, massage, steam room, bar, library, recreation room, laundry service, Internet, business services; no a/c, no kids under 12* ▤ *AE, DC, MC, V* ⊚ *BP.*

Fodor'sChoice ★

¢ ▦ **Pousada Três Portas.** This pousada is in an adapted colonial house—with hardwood floors and locally made furniture and artwork—in the historic center of Tiradentes. The owner runs a small puppet theater adjacent to the breakfast room. Rooms are clean and modern. Note that prices jump dramatically on weekends. ⊠ *Rua Direita 280A* ☎ *032/3355–1444* ▦ *032/3355–1184* ⊕ *www.pousadatresportas.com.br* ⇔ *8 rooms, 1 suite* ⚫ *Room service, fan, in-room data ports, refrigerators, cable TV, pool, steam room, 2 bars, children's programs, laundry service, business services; no a/c* ▤ *No credit cards* ⊚ *BP.*

The Arts

Cultural life in Tiradentes revolves around the **Centro Cultural Yves Alves** (⊠ Rua Direita 168 ☎ 032/3355–1503), which has theatrical performances, films, concerts, and art exhibitions. On weekends the **Theatro da Villa** (⊠ Rua Padre Toledo 157 ☎ 032/3355–1275) has musical shows that accompany dinner.

Shopping

Local artwork is the biggest draw here, with painters and sculptors famous throughout Brazil working in their gallerylike studios. The main street for galleries and antiques shops is Rua Direita.

ART **Atelier José Damas** (✉ Rua do Chafariz 130 ☎ 032/3355–1578) belongs to Tiradentes's most famous artist. He paints local scenes—such as a train winding through the mountains or a dusty afternoon street—on canvas and on stones. The small and quiet city **Bichinho** (✉ 6 km/4 mi northeast of Tiradentes) is recognized in the region for the quality of its arts and crafts. Ask at your hotel for directions.

JEWELRY & Although not as upscale as the stores in Ouro Preto, **Artstones** (✉ Rua
GEMSTONES Ministro Gabriel Passos 22 ☎ 032/3355–1730) carries imperial topazes, emeralds, quartz, and tourmalines and also has some finished jewelry.

THE MINERAL-SPA TOWNS

Known for the curative properties of their natural springs, a collection of mineral-spa towns in southern Minas Gerais forms the Circuito das Águas (Water Circuit). For more than a century people in need of physical, mental, and spiritual rejuvenation have flocked to these mystical towns, bathing in the pristine water parks and drinking from the bubbling fountains. Today they're especially popular among older, wealthier Brazilians, who come to experience the fresh air and beautiful landscapes and to get relief for their hypertension, arthritis, allergies, diabetes, and various stomach problems.

You'll be told that a minimum of three weeks of drinking the waters is required for their healing powers to take hold (don't try drinking three weeks' worth of water in a day, unless you want to leave with more ailments than when you arrived). Usually, a one- or two-day visit is enough to experience a helpful placebo effect.

Parque Nacional da Serra do Canastra

320 km (200 mi) southwest of Belo Horizonte.

Serra do Canastra National Park was created to preserve the springs of Rio São Francisco, one of the most important rivers in South America, which cuts through five Brazilian states. Its main attractions are its waterfalls, including the 186-meter (610-foot) Casca D'Anta. The park is in the city of São Roque de Minas, almost on the border with São Paulo State. The Brazilian Institute of the Environment (IBAMA) manages the park from its headquarters in São Roque de Minas. The ecological group Os Canastras has a good Web site (in Portuguese) about the Serra da Canastra and region: www.canastra.com.br. ✉ *From Belo Horizonte take MG 050 southwest to Pium-i, then take the road to São Roque de Minas; entrance to park is 33 km (21 mi) west of São Roque de Minas* ☎ *037/3433–1195 for IBAMA* ✍ *R$3* ☾ *Daily 8–6.*

Where to Stay

The park has a camping area. Cheap and more comfortable options are the simple inns in neighboring cities.

$ ⊡ **Paraíso da Serra.** Just 500 meters (¼ mi) from the main attraction at Parque Nacional da Serra do Canastra—the waterfall Casca D'Anta—this pousada has beautiful views from its rooms. ⊠ *Serra da Canastra, Portaria 4* ☎ *037/9988–8004* ⊕ *www.pousadaparaisodaserra.com.br* ⤳ *8 rooms* ♨ *Restaurant, cafeteria, dining room, room service, fans, minibars, refrigerators, 2 pools, steam room, bicycles, horseback riding, bar, shop, baby-sitting, children's programs, playground, laundry service, business services, some pets allowed, no-smoking rooms; no a/c, no phone in some rooms, no TV in some rooms* ▤ *No credit cards* ⦿ *FAP.*

¢ ⊡ **Pousada da Limeira.** On the bank of the São Francisco River, 15 km (9 mi) from the waterfall Casca D'Anta, this is a simple but comfortable pousada. ⊠ *Km 07, Estrada Cachoeira Casca D'Anta, Vargem Bonita* ☎🖥 *037/3435–1118* ⊕ *www.pousadadalimeira.com.br* ⤳ *13 rooms* ♨ *Fans, pool, lake, exercise equipment, billiards, laundry service, Internet; no a/c, no room phones, no room TVs* ▤ *No credit cards* ⦿ *BP.*

São Lourenço

387 km (240 mi) south of Belo Horizonte.

The most modern of the mineral-spa towns is a good base from which to visit the other Circuito das Águas communities. From here taxis and tour operators happily negotiate a day rate for the circuit, usually around $50.

São Lourenço's **Parque das Águas** (Water Park) includes a picturesque lake with art deco pavilions, fountains, and gorgeous landscaping. The center of activity is its *balneário,* a hydrotherapy spa where you can immerse yourself in bubbling mineral baths and marble surroundings. There are separate bath and sauna facilities for men and women, and you can also get a massage. ⊠ *Praça Brasil s/n* ☎ *035/3332–3066* 🎫 *R$2.50* ☉ *Park daily 8–6. Balneário daily 8–noon and 2–5.*

If your experience at the park fails to rid you of all physical and mental illness, head to the **Templo da Eubiose,** the temple of a spiritual organization dedicated to wisdom and perfection through yoga. The Eubiose believe this will be the only place to survive the end of the world. ⊠ *Praça da Vitória s/n* ☎ *035/3331–1333* 🎫 *Donations accepted* ☉ *Weekends 2–4.*

Where to Stay & Eat

$–$$ ✗🖥 **Hotel Brasil.** This luxury hotel is just across from the Parque das Águas at the Praça Duque de Caxias. It has its own pools, fountains, and mineral waters. Ask for a room with a park view. The restaurant's fixed-price buffet serves regional fare. ⊠ *Alameda João Lage 87* ☎ *035/3332–2000* 🖥 *035/3331–1536* ⊕ *www.hotelbrasil.com.br* ⤳ *142 rooms* ♨ *Restaurant, cafeteria, room service, minibar, refrigerators, cable TV, tennis court, 5 pools, health club, billiards, Ping-Pong, soccer, volleyball, bar, piano bar, nightclub, recreation room, shop, baby-sitting, children's programs, playground, laundry services, Internet, convention center, meeting room, some pets allowed, kennel; no a/c in some rooms* ▤ *DC, MC, V* ⦿ *FAP.*

★ $ ✕⊡ **Emboabas Hotel.** About a half hour's walk from the Parque das Águas, this gracious fazenda is more like a private estate than a rural farm. Its carefully decorated rooms have bucolic views; at night the only sounds you hear are those of various animals roaming the countryside. Occasional performances take place in the fazenda's theater, and there are numerous other activities to keep you amused. The restaurant has fixed-price buffets of at least three regional dishes as well as salads and dessert. ✉ *Alameda Jorge Amado 350* ☎ *035/3332–4600* 🖷 *035/ 3332–4392* ⊕ *www.emboabashotel.com.br* 🛏 *57 rooms, 3 suites* ⚒ *Restaurant, cafeteria, room service, fans, in-room data ports, refrigerators, cable TV, tennis court, 3 pools, gym, hair salon, massage, sauna, steam room, billiards, horseback riding, soccer, squash, volleyball, 2 bars, piano bar, cinema, dance club, library, recreation room, theater, baby-sitting, children's programs, playground, laundry services, Internet, business services, convention center, some pets allowed; no a/c* ⊟ *MC, V* ⦿I *FAP.*

¢ ✕⊡ **Pousada Le Sapê.** The pousada's six tiny rooms are reasonable, low-budget options for a night or two. All rooms are very simple but have verandas and hammocks. The hotel restaurant, open to the public only in summer, specializes in comida mineira. ✉ *Via Ramon s/n* ☎ *035/ 3331–1142* 🛏 *6 rooms* ⚒ *Restaurant, fans, minibars, 2 pools, soccer, volleyball, playground; no a/c, no room phones* ⊟ *No credit cards* ⦿I *BP.*

¢ ⊡ **Hotel Fazenda Vista Alegre.** The many facilities and the low price of accommodations at this farm compensate for the lack of proximity to the water park (around 4 km/3 mi away). You can go boating on the lake in front of the cottages. If you're interested, the employees can teach you how to milk a cow. The chalets, in front of the lake, can house up to five people. The hotel also has rooms for two or four people. ✉ *Km 1, Estrada Aeroporto Conquista* ☎ *035/3332–4730* 🖷🖷 *035/3332–4730* ⊕ *www.hfvistaalegre.com.br* 🛏 *9 chalets, 35 suites* ⚒ *Restaurant, dining room, room service, fans, refrigerators, cable TV, 2 pools, lake, massage, sauna, steam room, boating, fishing, bicycles, billiard, horseback riding, Ping-Pong, soccer, bar, recreation room, shop, children's program, playground, laundry service, Internet, business services, some pets allowed; no a/c, no room phones* ⊟ *V* ⦿I *FAP.*

Caxambu

30 km (19 mi) northeast of São Lourenço.

A 19th-century town once frequented by Brazilian royalty, Caxambu remains a favorite getaway for wealthy and retired *cariocas* (residents of Rio). Although most people spend their time here relaxing in bathhouses and drinking curative waters, you can also browse in the markets where local sweets are sold or take a horse-and-buggy ride to a fazenda.

Towering trees, shimmering ponds, and fountains containing various minerals—each believed to cure a different ailment—fill the **Parque das Águas.** Lavish pavilions protect the springs, and the balneário, a beautiful Turkish-style bathhouse, offers saunas and massages. In addition, hundreds of thousands of liters of mineral water are bottled here daily and distributed throughout Brazil. ⊠ *Town center* ☎ *035/3341–3999* 🖃 *R\$2* ⊙ *Park daily 7–6. Balneário Tues.–Sat. 8–noon and 3–5, Sun. 8–noon.*

Overlooking the springs is the **Igreja Isabel da Hungria.** The small Gothic church was built by Princess Isabel, daughter of Dom Pedro II, after the springs were believed to have restored her fertility. ⊠ *Rua Princesa Isabel s/n* ☎ *035/3341–1582* 🖃 *Donations accepted* ⊙ *Daily 8–noon.*

You could take a **chairlift** (Wednesday–Monday 9–5; R\$5) from near the bus station to the peak of Cristo Redentor, where there's a small restaurant and an impressive city view.

Where to Stay & Eat

★ \$–\$\$ ✕ **La Forelle.** Inside the Fazenda Vale Formoso hotel, La Forelle is the best restaurant in town. Besides typical food from Minas Gerais, it also serves Danish cuisine. The specialty of the house is baked trout with potatoes. The filet mignon, the salmon, and the shrimp are among the extensive menu's stellar entrées. You can also find delicious fondues and freshly made breads. ⊠ *Km 8, Estrada do Vale Formoso* ☎ *035/3343–1900* 🖃 *DC, MC, V* ⊙ *Closed Mon.–Thurs. No lunch Fri., no dinner Sun.*

\$–\$\$ 🏨 **Hotel Glória.** Although it's just across from Caxambu's Parque das Águas, this luxury resort has its own rehabilitation pool and sauna as well as a variety of sports amenities. Rooms are well equipped and have marble baths. Meals are served in an antiques-filled dining room. ⊠ *Av. Camilo Soares 590* ☎☎ *035/3341–3000* ⊕ *www.hotelgloriacaxambu.com.br* 🖫 *120 rooms* ⌂ *Restaurant, cafeteria, room service, fans, in-room safes, refrigerators, cable TV, tennis court, 2 pools, gym, massage, health club, hair salon, sauna, steam room, billiards, Ping-Pong, soccer, squash, 3 bars, piano bar, cinema, recreation room, video game room, shop, babysitting, children's programs, playground, laundry services, Internet, convention center; no a/c in some rooms* 🖃 *DC, MC, V* ⦿❘ *FAP.*

¢–\$ 🏨 **Fazenda Vale Formoso.** A 19th-century coffee plantation transformed into a hotel, this fazenda hotel is in a huge—more than 740 acres—surrounded by mountains, lakes, and virgin forest. The original machinery of the plantation is on display, and some of it is still working, such as the 19th-century water-operated sawmill. The farm also has a cachaça distillery. ⊠ *Km 8, Estrada do Vale Formoso* ☎☎ *035/3343–1900* ⊕ *www.hotelvaleformoso.com.br* 🖫 *17 rooms* ⌂ *Restaurant, room service, fans, minibars, refrigerators, cable TV, 2 pool, lake, steam room, boating, fishing, bicycles, mountain bikes, billiards, horseback riding, soccer, volleyball, 2 bars, video game room, laundry services, Internet, business services, convention center, some pets allowed; no a/c, no kids under 12* 🖃 *D, MC, V* ⦿❘ *FAP.*

São Tomé das Letras

54 km (33 mi) northwest of Caxambu.

With its tales of flying saucers, its eerie stone houses that resemble architecture from outer space, and its 7,500 inhabitants who swear to years of friendship with extraterrestrials, São Tomé das Letras may be one of the oddest towns on earth. Set in a stunning mountain region, it attracts mystics, psychics, and flower children who believe they've been spiritually drawn here to await the founding of a new world. Most visitors make São Tomé a day trip from Caxambu, smartly escaping nightfall's visiting UFOs.

A center of religious activity and one of the few nonstone buildings in São Tomé, **Igreja Matriz** is in São Tomé's main square and contains frescoes by Brazilian artist Joaquim José de Natividade. Next to the Igreja Matriz is the **Gruta de São Tomé,** a small cave that, in addition to its shrine to São Tomé, features some of the mysterious inscriptions for which the town is famous. Just 3 km (2 mi) from São Tomé, two **caverns,** Carimbado and Chico Taquara, both display hieroglyphs. A short walk from the caves put you in view of Véu da Noiva and Véu da Eubiose, two powerful waterfalls.

MINAS GERAIS A TO Z

To research prices, get advice from other travelers, and book travel arrangements, visit www.fodors.com.

AIR TRAVEL
Belo Horizonte, with its two airports, is the gateway to Minas Gerais. A flight from Rio de Janeiro or São Paulo to Belo Horizonte is less than an hour. By bus or car the trip takes approximately eight hours. Many parts of the Brazilian highways aren't very well maintained, and the truck traffic between Belo Horizonte and the two main Brazilian cities is constant. Flying is by far the easier option.

CARRIERS American Airlines flies from Miami and New York to São Paulo and on to Confins. TAM and Gol has domestic flights to and from Pampulha. In addition to connecting Belo Horizonte with other Brazilian cities, Varig has service to Confins from New York and other American cities. VASP also offers domestic flights into both airports.

🛂 Airlines **American Airlines** ☎ 0300/789-7778 ⊕ www.aa.com.br. **Gol** ☎ 0300/789-2121 ⊕ www.voegol.com.br. **TAM** ☎ 0300/123-1000 ⊕ www.tamairlines.com. **Varig** ☎ 0300/788-7000 ⊕ www.varig.com.br. **VASP** ☎ 0300/789-1010 ⊕ www.vasp.com.br.

AIRPORTS
Aeroporto Internacional Tancredo Neves—also known as Aeroporto de Confins—is 39 km (24 mi) north of Belo Horizonte and serves domestic and international flights. Taxis from Confins to downtown cost about R$50 and take roughly a half hour. There are also *executivo* (air-conditioned) buses that leave every 45 minutes and cost R$10. Aeroporto Pampulha is 9 km (5 mi) northwest of downtown and serves domestic flights. A taxi ride from here to downtown costs about R$10.

🛂 Airport Information **Aeroporto Internacional Tancredo Neves** ⊠ MG 10, Confins ☎ 031/3689-2700. **Aeroporto Pampulha** ⊠ Praça Bagatelle 204, Pampulha, Belo Horizonte ☎ 031/3490-2001.

BUS TRAVEL
Belo Horizonte's municipal bus system is safe and efficient, although buses are crowded during rush hour (7–9 and 5–7). They're clearly num-

bered, and you can get route information at Bhtrans. Fares depend on the distance traveled but are always less than R$2.

Frequent buses (either air-conditioned executivos or warmer, less comfortable, but cheaper coaches) connect Belo Horizonte with Rio (R$60–R$90; seven hours), São Paulo (R$50–R$80; eight hours), and Brasília (R$60–R$110; 12 hours). Get advance tickets at holiday times. All buses arrive at and depart from (punctually) the Rodoviária. Bus companies include Cometa, for Rio and São Paulo; Gontijo, for São Paulo; Itapemirim, for Brasília; and Útil, for Rio.

Coaches connect Belo Horizonte with Ouro Preto (R$12; 2–3 hours), Diamantina (R$30; five hours), and São João del Rei (R$20; three hours). Mariana can be reached from Ouro Preto (R$2.25; 30 minutes), Tiradentes from São João del Rei (R$4.50; 30 minutes). From Belo Horizonte a bus to São Lourenço or Caxambu takes roughly seven hours and costs about R$36. To reach São Tomé das Letras, you must change buses in Três Coracões; the entire journey takes 5½ hours.

Companies with regular service from Belo Horizonte include Gardênia, for São Lourenço; Pássaro Verde, for Ouro Preto, Diamantina, and Mariana; and Sandra, for Congonhas and São João del Rei. All buses leave Belo Horizonte from the Terminal Rodoviário Israel Pinheiro da Silva (better know as the *rodoviaria,* or bus station).

🚌 Bus Information **Bhtrans** ☎ 031/3277-6500 ⊕ www.bhtrans.pbh.gov.br. **Cometa** ☎ 031/3201-5611 ⊕ www.viacaocometa.com.br. **Gardênia** ☎ 031/3475-1010. **Gontijo** ☎ 031/3201-6130 ⊕ www.gontijo.com.br. **Itapemirim** ☎ 031/3271-1019. **Ouro Preto bus station** ✉ Rua Padre Rolim 661 ☎ 031/3559-3252. **Pássaro Verde** ☎ 0300/789-4400 ⊕ www.passaroverde.com.br. **Terminal Rodoviário Israel Pinheiro da Silva** ✉ Av. Afonso Pena at Praça Rio Branco, Centro, Belo Horizonte ☎ 031/3271-3000 or 031/3271-8933. **Sandra** ☎ 031/3201-2927. **Útil** ☎ 0800/702-0008.

CAR RENTAL

Rental cars cost between R$89 and R$262 per day, depending on whether mileage is included. Agencies include Localiza and Lokamig.

🚗 Rental Agencies **Localiza** ✉ Aeroporto de Confins, Belo Horizonte ☎ 031/3689-2070 ⊕ www.localiza.com.br ✉ Av. Bernardo Monteiro 1567, Funcionários, Belo Horizonte ☎ 0800/99-2000 or 031/3247-7957. **Lokamig** ✉ Aeroporto de Confins, Belo Horizonte ☎ 031/3689-2020 ⊕ www.lokamig.com.br ✉ Av. Contorno 8639, Belo Horizonte ☎ 031/3335-8977.

CAR TRAVEL

BR 040 connects Belo Horizonte with Rio (444 km/276 mi), to the southeast, and Brasília (741 km/460 mi), to the northwest; BR 381 links the city with São Paulo (586 km/364 mi). The roads are in good condition, although exits aren't always clearly marked.

Belo Horizonte's rush-hour traffic can be heavy, and parking can be difficult (for on-street parking you must buy a sticker at a newsstand or bookshop). Narrow cobblestone streets inside the historical cities, however, weren't designed for cars, and some alleys can make for a tight squeeze. Parking isn't a problem in the smaller communities, except during holidays.

The historic cities and spa towns for the most part are connected by fairly decent minor routes to one of the region's main highways. There's no ideal direct route from Belo Horizonte to Diamantina; your best bet is north on BR 040 and then east on BR 259. Sabará is slightly east of Belo, just off BR 262. From Belo you can take BR 040 south and BR 356 (it becomes MG 262) east to Ouro Preto and beyond to Mariana. To reach Tiradentes from Belo, take BR 040 south (Congonhas do Campo is on this route) and then BR 265 west. São Lourenço, Caxambu, and São Tomé das Letras are south of Belo off BR 381, parts of which are under construction. As an alternative, you can take BR 040 south to BR 267 west.

EMERGENCIES

🔳 General Emergencies **Ambulance or Police** ☎ 190. **Fire** ☎ 193.

🔳 Hospital **Hospital João XXIII** ✉ Av. Alfredo Balena 400, Sta. Efigênia, Belo Horizonte ☎ 031/3239-9200.

🔳 24-Hour Pharmacy **Drogaria Araújo** ☎ 031/3270-5000 in Belo Horizonte.

HEALTH

There are no major health concerns in Minas Gerais, although you should drink bottled rather than tap water. (Despite the curative properties of the mineral waters in the spa towns, don't drink too much when you first arrive unless you want to cleanse your system thoroughly.)

MAIL & INTERNET

Belo Horizonte's main post office is open weekdays 9–7, Saturday 9–1. Internet service is slowly making its way to the region and may be available at your hotel's business center. In Belo Horizonte the Internet Club Café lets you hook up for about R$20 an hour.

🔳 Internet Center **Internet Club Café** ✉ Rua Fernandes Tourinho 385, Savassi, Belo Horizonte ☎ 031/3282-3132.

🔳 Post Office **Belo Horizonte** ✉ Av. Afonso Pena 1270, Centro Belo Horizonte ☎ 0800/570-0100.

MONEY MATTERS

Outside Belo Horizonte, exchanging currency can be challenging and expensive, so change money before you arrive or plan to do it at your hotel. You can change money at Confins Airport weekdays 10–6 and Saturday 10–4 (you're out of luck if you arrive on Sunday). Banco Sudameris has good exchange rates. Banco do Brasil also offers exchange services, though the rates aren't the best.

🔳 Banks **Banco do Brasil** ✉ Rua Rio de Janeiro 750, Centro, Belo Horizonte ☎ 031/3217-3000 ⊕ www.bb.com.br. **Banco Sudameris** ✉ Av. João Pinheiro 214, Centro, Belo Horizonte ☎ 031/3277-3134 ⊕ www.sudameris.com.br.

SAFETY

Petty crime is an issue in Belo Horizonte, though not as much as it is in Rio or São Paulo. Use common sense: avoid waving your money around or wearing expensive jewelry. The historic cities and mineral-spa towns are among Brazil's safest places.

TAXIS

Taxis in Belo Horizonte are white and can be hailed or called. The meter starts at about R$3 and costs about R$1 for every kilometer traveled (slightly higher at night and on weekends). Two reputable companies are BH Taxi and Coopertaxi.

In the historic towns it's hard to drive on the narrow cobblestone streets, so taxis aren't abundant. Besides, these towns are small enough to explore on foot. You'll find plenty of eager taxis in both Caxambu and São Lourenço waiting to take you around the Circuito das Águas. A taxi between São Lourenço and Caxambu runs about R$100; it's about R$200 to São Tomé das Letras.

🚩 Taxi Companies **BH Taxi** ☎ 031/3215-8081. **Coopertaxi** ☎ 0800/99-2424 or 031/ 3421-2424.

TELEPHONES

The area code for the region around Belo Horizonte is 031. If you don't want to place long-distance calls from your hotel, you can make them from the *posto telefônico* (phone office), found in airports and bus stations throughout Minas. Office hours are generally 7 AM–10 PM. In Belo Horizonte the main Telemar office is open 24 hours.

🚩 Long-Distance Services **Telemar** ⊠ Av. Afonso Pena 4001, Serra ☎ 031/3229-2922 or 104 ⊕ www.telemar.com.br.

TOURS

CLN Tourism and Transportation Services offers exceptional tours of Ouro Preto and the historic cities. CLN's Cláudio Neves speaks fluent English, knows a great deal about the region's history, and can arrange airport pickup and other transportation.

AMETUR, the Association of Rural Tourism, is a group of respected, trustworthy ranch owners who have converted their fazendas into accommodations with luxurious yet down-home surroundings. You can visit one or more of these ranches, where relaxation, swimming, horseback riding, walks in the woods, and home-cooked meals are the orders of the day. Suzana Sousa Lima runs AMETUR as well as her own fazenda, Boa Esperança, which has been rated among the top accommodations in the country.

AMO-TE, Minas's Association of Ecological Tourism, offers many fascinating tours. A great way to get acquainted with the history and topography of Minas is on a one- to five-day horseback trip with AMO-TE's Tulio. His English is perfect, his knowledge impressive, and his horses— native Mineiros themselves—have a unique step (not unlike the lambada) that makes extensive trips more comfortable than you might imagine.

The Associação de Guias, formed by Ouro Preto's professional tour guides, can provide general information on the city weekdays 8–6. Its well-informed, courteous guides also conduct six- to seven-hour walking tours (in English) of the historic area. Be prepared for some hiking up and down numerous hills.

🚩 **AMETUR** ⊠ Rua Alvarenga Peixoto 295/102, Lourdes, Belo Horizonte 🏠🏠 031/ 3275-2139. **AMO-TE** ⊠ Rua Professor Morais 624, Apartamento 302, Centro, Belo Horizonte ☎ 031/3344-8986. **Associação de Guias** ✉ Rua Padre Rolim s/n, São Cristóvão, Ouro Preto ☎ 031/3551-2655. **Associação de Guias de Turismo** ✉ Praça Tancredo Neves s/n, Mariana ☎ 031/3557-1158.

CLN Tourism and Transportation Services ✉ Rua Dr. Antônio Ibrahim 103A, Ouro Preto ☎☎ 031/3551-6311 or 031/9961-1220.

TRAVEL AGENTS

Sangetur is an all-purpose agency that can help you rent a car, make travel arrangements or hotel reservations, and book city tours. YTUR Turismo can arrange hotel bookings, transportation plans, and tours of Belo Horizonte and beyond.

🚩 Travel Agencies **Sangetur** ✉ Rua Inconfidentes 732, Loja 1, Funcionários, Belo Horizonte ☎ 031/3261-1055 ⊕ www.sangetur.com.br. **YTUR Turismo** ✉ Av. do Contorno 8000, Loja 2, Lourdes, Belo Horizonte ☎ 031/3275-3233 ⊕ www.ytur.com.br.

VISITOR INFORMATION

In Belo Horizonte, Belotur, the municipal tourist board, is open daily 8 AM–10 PM at the airports and weekdays 8–7 elsewhere. Turminas, the state tourism authority, supplies information on the historic cities and other attractions weekdays 12:30–6:30.

Diamantina's Casa da Cultura has information on the town, including all cultural events. It's open weekdays 8–6, Saturday 9–5, and Sunday 9–noon. In Ouro Preto contact the Associação de Guias (open daily 8 AM–10 PM), which has an office on the edge of town, or the tourist information desk (open daily 8–6) in the center of town. In Mariana contact the Associação de Guias de Turismo for general information on the city. Its hours are Tuesday–Saturday noon–5:30. In Tiradentes the Secretária de Turismo is the best place to go for information (weekdays 8–6).

São Lourenço has a small tourist kiosk in front of the water park. It's open weekdays 8–11 and 1–6. In Caxambu there's an equally small tourist desk that's open weekdays 8–6.

🚩 Belo Horizonte Visitor Information **Belotur** ✉ Rua Pernambuco 284, Funcionários ☎ 031/3277-9797 ⊕ www.belotur.com.br ✉ Mercado das Flores at Av. Afonso Pena and Rua da Bahia, Centro ☎ 031/3277-7666 ✉ Rodoviária, Av. Afonso Pena at Praça Rio Branco, Centro ☎ 031/3277-6907 ✉ Confins Airport ☎ 031/3689-2557. **Turminas** ✉ Praça Rio Branco 56, Centro, Belo Horizonte ☎ 031/3272-8581 ⊕ www.turminas. mg.gov.br.

🚩 Historic Towns Visitor Information **Associação de Guias de Turismo** ✉ Praça Tancredo Neves s/n, Mariana ☎ 031/3557-1158. **Associação de Guias** ✉ Praça Tiradentes 41, Ouro Preto ☎ 031/3559-3269. **Caxambu Tourist Desk** ✉ Rua João Carlos 100, Caxambu ☎ 035/3341-1298 ⊕ www.caxambu.mg.gov.br. **Diamantina Casa da Cultura** ✉ Praça Antônio Eulálio 53, Diamantina ☎ 038/3531-1636. **Posto de Informação Turística** ✉ Praça Tiradentes 41, Centro, Ouro Preto ☎ 031/3559-3269. **São Lourenço Tourist Kiosk** ✉ Praça João Lage s/n, São Lourenço ☎ 035/3349-8459. **Tiradentes Secretária de Turismo** ✉ Rua Resende Costa 71, Tiradentes ☎ 032/3355-1212.

BRASÍLIA &
THE WEST

5

Updated by
Carolina
Berard, João
Carlos
Pijnappel,
Carlos G.
Tornquist

VISITING BRASÍLIA IS LIKE LEAPING INTO THE FUTURE. Rising from the red earth of the 3,000-foot Planalto Central (Central Plateau) and surrounded by the *cerrado* (Brazilian savanna) is one of the world's most singular cities. Its structures crawl and coil along the flat landscape and then shoot up in shafts of concrete and glass that capture the sun's rays.

The idea of moving the capital to the interior dates from the early days of Brazil's independence, but it wasn't until 1955 that the scheme became more than just a possibility. Many said Brasília couldn't be built; others simply went ahead and did it. The resolute Juscelino Kubitschek made it part of his presidential campaign platform. On taking office, he organized an international contest for the city's master plan. A design submitted by urban planner Lúcio Costa was selected, and he and his contemporaries—including architect Oscar Niemeyer and landscape artist Roberto Burle Marx—went to work. With a thrust of energy, the new capital was built less than five years later quite literally in the middle of nowhere.

Costa once mused, "The sky is the sea of Brasília." He made sure that the city had an unhindered view of the horizon, with buildings whose heights are restricted, wide streets and avenues, and immense green spaces. The sky here is an incredible blue that's cut only by occasional clusters of fleecy clouds. The earth is such an amazing shade of red that it seems to have been put here just for contrast. At night it's hard to tell where the city lights end and the stars begin. On a visit to Brazil, the renowned contemporary architect Frank O. Gehry said, "It's a different city. I call it holy land, an untouchable icon of architecture."

Brasília is a great place for those interested in architecture and in a different city. Everything is divided into sectors (hotels, residences, swimming places, etc.), and the streets were designed without traditional sidewalks. Because of this, Brasília has long been known as "the city without corners."

All around this wonderland of modernity nestles the old Brazil—the land of soybean plantations, beef cattle, and sluggish rivers. Nevertheless, those who flock to the rugged yet beautiful west have their eyes on the future. The surreal collection of migrants includes opportunists with get-rich-quick schemes; frontier folk with hopes of a solid, stable tomorrow; mystics and prophets who swear by the region's spiritual energy; and dreamers who are convinced that extraterrestrials visit here regularly. For most earthly visitors, however, the high point of the west is the Pantanal, a flood plain the size of Great Britain that's home to an amazing array of wildlife and the ever-present possibilities for adventure.

Exploring Brasília & the West

Brasília is 1,600 km (1,000 mi) from the Atlantic, on the flat plateau known as the Planalto Central. This is the domain of the vast cerrado, whose climate and vegetation are akin to those of the African savanna. The capital is actually in the Distrito Federal (Federal District), a 55,000-square-km (21,000-square-mi) administrative region. Also in this district are the *cidades-satélite* (satellite cities), which originated as residential areas for Brasília workers but which now qualify as cities in their own right. Cidades-satélite are essentially the suburbs of Brasília.

The Distrito Federal is flanked by Goiás State, part of the country's agricultural heart and the starting point for two massive Amazon tributaries, the rios Araguaia and Tocantins. Still farther west, the states of Mato Grosso and Mato Grosso do Sul have a large share of Brazil's agribusiness. They also contain the Pantanal, an area of watery terrain and rich, unique wildlife that has been the target of a major preservation effort. It has become one of Brazil's top tourist destinations.

About the Restaurants

Brazilians rarely eat breakfast out, but hotels have good continental breakfasts, with fresh fruit, bread, juice, cereal, meat, and cheese. Restaurants close around 1 or 2 AM. Waitstaff in Brasília bring water and bread to the table only on request. Buffet restaurants and by-the-kilo buffets are excellent options because you can eat good food at reasonable prices and you can try many dishes. Gratuity is 10% of the total sum and it is sometimes included in the bill; when it is not, a tip is not expected (but still appreciated).

As the capital, Brasília attracts citizens from throughout the country as well as dignitaries from around the world. Hence, you can find a variety of regional cuisines as well as international fare. In the west the dishes aren't as interesting or as flavorful as those found elsewhere in the country. That said, however, the food is hearty, and the meals are large; affordable all-you-can-eat buffets are ubiquitous.

About the Hotels

Brasília's master plan called for its hotels to be built in commercial areas. Many hotels cater primarily to businesspeople and government officials, and few fall into budget categories. But since 2000 new hotels of all categories have proliferated. Budget options such as *pousadas* (inns) are mainly in Asa Sul (South Wing) and in the hotel sectors. Upscale hotels can be found in the Hotel Sectors and along the shores of Lago Paranoá. Stay in one of the Hotel Sectors to be close to a number of good, inexpensive restaurants.

The frontier towns west of Brasília have few deluxe accommodations. Inside the Pantanal, the *fazendas* (farms) where most people stay are quite spartan; pack a pillow and bug spray (not all fazendas have netting for their beds). If roughing it doesn't thrill you, there are a few jungle lodges that are full-blown resorts with all the expected amenities.

In Brasília hotels are emptier during school vacations (July, December, and especially January). Since many people living here are from other cities, everybody travels during holidays. It is hard to get a room in Brasília hotels when there is a big political event in the city, such as a presidential inauguration (every four years in January) or a world congress. On the other hand, popular holidays such as Carnaval are much less hectic than in other cities.

When you book a room, in addition to its normal fee, you also pay 10% of the value plus R$1.50 for tourism fees.

5

If you have
5 days

Brasília & Chapada dos Veadeiros Start in ⬚ **Brasília ❶–㉓**. Take a day to see the city either on your first or last day. Go to Alto Paraíso de Goiás by car or by plane, and explore the **Parque Nacional da Chapada dos Veadeiros** with a local guide. Spend at least three days trekking around the waterfalls, the Moon Valley, the Morada do Sol (Dwelling of the Sun), the Zen Backwoods, and the Crystal River. On your last day in Goiás, walk through the Vila de São Jorge—a small village 2 km (1 mi) outside the park's entrance that is known for ecotourism—before returning to Brasília.

If you have
5 days

Brasília & the Pantanal Spend two days exploring ⬚ **Brasília ❶–㉓**: the Plano Piloto, including the **Eixo Monumental**, the **Praça dos Três Poderes**, the shores of the **Lago Paranoá**, and the **Parque da Cidade ❺**. On the third morning fly to ⬚ **Cuiabá**. Make sure you get a direct flight, otherwise this 1½-hour trip will take more than six hours. Sign up for an overnight trip into the **Pantanal** to spot wildlife and maybe to fish for piranha.

If you have
7 days

For ⬚ **Brasília ❶–㉓** set aside two days to explore the Plano Piloto and to tour the **Parque Nacional da Brasília**, the **Jardim Botânico**, and the **Catetinho**. On the third day make an early departure to ⬚ **Pirenópolis**, a colonial town just outside the capital. On the following day fly from Brasília to either ⬚ **Cuiabá** or ⬚ **Campo Grande** and spend the remaining time exploring the **Pantanal**.

If you have
10
days

Spend four leisurely days in ⬚ **Brasília ❶–㉓** exploring the Plano Piloto and visiting the **Parque Nacional da Brasília,** the cult communities, and **Pirenópolis**. On the fifth day fly to either ⬚ **Cuiabá** or ⬚ **Campo Grande** and schedule a four-day (three-night) trip into **Bonito** and the **Pantanal**. Such treks include riverboat rides, freshwater snorkeling, horseback rides, fishing, bird-watching, photography safaris, and cooking your very own piranha stew.

WHAT IT COSTS In Reais				
	$$$$	$$$	$$	$	¢
RESTAURANTS	over $60	$45–$60	$30–$45	$15–$30	under $15
HOTELS	over $500	$375–$500	$250–$375	$125–$250	under $125

Restaurant prices are for a dinner entrée. Hotel prices are for two people in a standard double room in high season, excluding taxes.

Timing

In Brasília and much of the west you can count on clear days and comfortable temperatures from March to July (the mean temperature is 22°C/75°F). The rainy season runs from December to February; in August and September the mercury often rises to 38°C (100°F). When congress adjourns (July and January–February), the city's pulse slows noticeably.

In the Pantanal peak season is synonymous with the dry season (July–October, which coincides with southern Brazil's winter, though temperatures rarely drop below 27°C/80°F). At this time the rivers have receded, the roads are easier to traverse, the mosquito population has dwindled, and the birds are nesting. You won't see as much wildlife during the wet season, but you will experience the swamp in all its impenetrable glory.

BRASÍLIA

Brazil's capital was moved from Salvador to Rio in 1763 so that the Portuguese court could be near the center of all the mining and exporting activity. In 1960 it was moved from coastal Rio to Brasília in an attempt to awaken the center of this sleeping giant.

As far back as 1808, Brazilian newspapers ran articles discussing Rio's inadequacies and proposing a new interior capital: "Our present capital is in a corner of Brazil and contact between it and Pará or other far removed states is extremely difficult. Besides, Rio subjects the government to enemy invasion by any maritime power." In 1892 congress authorized the overland Cruls Expedition to find a central locale where "a city could be constructed next to the headwaters of big rivers" and where "roads could be opened to all seaports." Within three months the expedition leaders had chosen one of the plateaus in the southeastern Goiás region. Despite this and several other attempts to establish a location and to move the capital, nothing was done for more than 60 years.

In the mid-1950s a sharp politician named Juscelino Kubitschek made the new capital part of his presidential campaign agenda, which was summarized in the motto "Fifty Years in Five." When he was elected president in 1956, he set the wheels in motion. After a site was selected (in Goiás, as proposed by the 1892 expedition), President Kubitschek flew to the inhospitable Planalto Central, had mass said on the building site, stayed the night, set up work committees, and put Niemeyer in charge of architectural and urban development. Lúcio Costa's master plan was chosen through an international contest, but when work on his project officially began in February 1957—with Kubitschek's deadline only 38 months away—3,000 workers were already at the site building the airport and Niemeyer's design for the Palácio do Planalto, the president's palace.

Building a new seat of power for Latin America's largest nation, complete with a modern infrastructure, was a monumental undertaking. In the first days of the construction, few of the necessary materials could be obtained on the Planalto Central. Before paved roads were built, supplies were flown in from the eastern cities. Thousands of workers came to the region; most came from the poor northeast, which was perennially stricken by droughts, making plenty of cheap labor available. Immigrants were unskilled; all were willing to face any hardship for a paycheck. They learned fast and worked hard. Wooden shacks and army tents sprang up around the construction site. The largest settlement, known as Freetown (now the cidade-satélite called Nucleo Bandeirante), was home to close to 15,000 workers and their families. It

5

Architecture Urban planning, engineering, architecture, and landscape design were applied so harmoniously in Brasília that the city seems like one gigantic sculpture. Lúcio Costa had a simple, original concept: "Brasília was conceived by the gesture of those who mark a place on a map: two axes intersecting at a right angle, that is, the sign of a cross mark." From above, his original Plano Piloto (Pilot, or Master, Plan) portion of the city looks like an airplane (it has also been described as a bow and arrow).

Costa had several objectives, among them: do away with a central downtown, where all the commercial and government facilities were separate from residential areas; design highways that were as accident-free as possible; and ensure that the vast horizon would always be visible. The latter goal complemented Oscar Niemeyer's idea of architecture as "a manifestation of the spirit, imagination, and poetry." Though his buildings are often massive, they're generally low and linear and set in grand spaces—conveying a sense of both light and lightness. Such structures epitomize functionality and simplicity (of design) and economy (of building materials); they also embody the vastness of Brazil. Many are set on huge concrete *pilotis* (pillars), leaving large open areas beneath them where people gather socially. Enormous glass facades and reflecting pools often add to the sense of space; organic-looking sculptures—either as plump and curvaceous as a cluster of coconuts or as willowy and elongated as palm fronds—add touches of softness. To complete the package, the Plano Piloto's most important gardens (some are more like waterscapes) were planned by landscape designer Roberto Burle Marx, who emphasized the use of Brazilian vegetation in natural arrangements. The works of Costa, Niemeyer, and Burle Marx fully articulate the longing expressed by Brazilian leaders in the mid-20th century to portray Brazil as a "nation of the future."

Natural Wonders Brazil's vast cerrado has small trees, shrubs, and grasses that are adapted to the harshness of the dry season, when temperatures in some parts rise well above 38°C (100°F) and humidity drops to a desert low of 15%. Palm species usually stand out among the shrubby vegetation—thick bunches of *buriti* usually grow around springs and creeks. Cacti and bromeliads are also abundant. Look also for the *pequi*, a shrub that produces berries used in local cuisine. Since development it has become harder to spot such species of cerrado wildlife as deer, jaguars, and anteaters. Emus, however, can be seen wandering through pastures and soybean plantations. In the lush Pantanal wetlands it's easy to see birds (more than 600 species flock here), monkeys, *jacarés* (caiman alligators), and fish—including the famous piranha. You may also catch a glimpse of *capivaras* (capybaras, the world's largest rodents; adults are about 60 cm/2 feet tall), wild boar, anteaters, and many types of snakes (including the *sucuri*, or anaconda). The elusive jaguars, however, require touring further into the Pantanal. With a bit of luck and patience, you might spot one of these magnificent felines, which are still surrounded by legend and folk lore.

was a rough place where anything went as long as there was money to pay for it.

Back in Rio opposition to the new capital was loud and heated. Debates in the senate turned into fistfights, and committees were continuously conducting investigations into all the spending. Government employees were unhappy about the impending move. Some feared that Rio's business would drastically decline and its real-estate values would drop dramatically once the city ceased to be the capital. Others simply didn't want to leave the glorious beaches and the many and familiar services. Kubitschek's government countered all this with inducements: 100% salary increases, tax breaks, earlier-than-usual retirement ages, free transportation and moves to the capital, ridiculously low rents on Brasília's new residences, and even discounts on new home furnishings.

Despite all the odds, Kubitschek's deadline was met, and on April 21, 1960, the city was inaugurated. The day began with mass in the uncompleted cathedral and ended with a fireworks display, during which the president's name burned in 15-foot-high letters.

Despite the expenses of building the city and the initial criticism, Brasília has become a comfortable, functional capital. Highways run directly from it to several regions, including the farther-flung states that once were so isolated from the capital. Kubitschek's vision of a nation looking westward from the coast became a reality. His project set off a new era of pioneering and colonization.

Exploring Brasília

Numbers in the text correspond to numbers in the margin and on the Brasília map.

Shaped like an airplane, the *Plano Piloto* (pilot plan) is both the name of the urban design conceived by Lúcio Costa for Brasília and the area of the city that resulted from that plan. The Plano Piloto was to have four basic features: well-ventilated housing near green spaces; work spaces that were separate from housing; spaces for cultural activities, near residential space; and the separation of vehicle and pedestrian pathways.

Addresses in the Plano Piloto might make even surveyors scratch their heads. There are the usual streets, avenues, and plazas with numbers or letters. There are sometimes compass points: *norte* (north), *sul* (south), *leste* (east), *oeste* (west). And there are also such things as *setores* (S.; sectors), *trechos* (sections), *quadras* (Q.; squares), *blocos* (Bl.; blocks, but really more akin to buildings), *lotes* (Lt.; lots), *lojas* (Lj.; literally, "shops" or "stores," but here a type of subdivision within a larger building), and *conjuntos* (Cj.; yet another type of building subdivision). Although the original layout is very logical, it can be hard to get chapter-and-verse addresses, making them seem illogical.

The Eixo (pronounced *ay*-shoo) Monumental, the city's "fuselage," is lined with government buildings, museums, and monuments as well as banks, hotels, and shops. It runs roughly from the Praça do Cruzeiro to the Esplanada dos Ministérios, at the tip of which is the Praça dos

Três Poderes. Intersecting the Eixo Monumental, near the Esplanada dos Ministérios, is the Eixo Rodoviário. It and the areas just off it form the city's "wings." The Asa Sul, or South Wing, is almost totally built up; the Asa Norte, or North Wing, still has spaces for development.

The Eixo Rodoviário has a line of *superquadras* (supersquares) made up of two (usually) quadras numbered from 100 to 116, 200 to 216, or 300 to 316 and consisting of six-story blocos. New quadras numbered 400 and above have been added outside the initial plan. In and around the two main axes are streets and avenues that connect still more residential and commercial areas, parks and gardens, and the Lago Paranoá (formed by a dam built about 16 km/10 mi southeast of the Plano Piloto and divided into the Lago Sul and Lago Norte districts). Along the outer shores of this lake are several residential areas. These include the Setores de Habitações Individuais (Individual Habitation Sectors) and the Setores de Mansões (Mansion Sectors).

It's best to tackle the Eixo Monumental and the Esplanada dos Ministérios first and then to visit the Praça dos Três Poderes. The sights in these areas are easy to reach by bus, cab, or organized tour. Staying at a hotel in the nearby Setor Hoteleiro Norte or Setor Hoteleiro Sul (SHN or SHS; Hotel Sector North or Hotel Sector South) keeps traveling time to a minimum. If you have time, get a taxi to the Entorno (literally, "surroundings"), the city's suburbs and cidades-satélites. Before heading out, get as detailed an address as possible, check that your cabbie knows where to go, and agree on a fare up front. Renting a car is also a good idea, since cabs can be expensive and the bus system is only good in certain areas.

Eixo Monumental

Most of the Plano Piloto's major sights are along or just off the grand 8-km-long (5-mi-long) Eixo Monumental and its multilane boulevards. The distances are too far to see everything on foot, so if you want to explore on your own rather than as part of a tour, you'll have to combine walking with bus and/or cab rides.

A GOOD TOUR   Start at the **Praça do Cruzeiro** ❶ ➤ at the Eixo Monumental's northwestern end. It's an easy 600-foot walk to Niemeyer's **Memorial JK** ❷, where you can learn about the man who made Brasília happen. From here it's another short walk to the **Memorial dos Povos Indígenas** ❸, a round structure containing indigenous artifacts. If you're interested in history and geography, hop a cab for the **Instituto Histórico e Geográfico** ❹ and then take a break in the nearby **Parque da Cidade** ❺. Alternatively, you can continue (by taxi or bus) to the other Eixo Monumental sights, starting with the **Torre de TV** ❻, one of the best places to buy souvenirs and enjoy a great view of the city.

Head southeast and cross the Eixo Rodoviário to the pyramid that houses the **Teatro Nacional Cláudio Santoro** ❼. At the other side of the Eixo Monumental and a little farther southeast is the unique **Catedral Metropolitana de Nossa Senhora da Aparecida** ❽, a Niemeyer masterpiece. You're just a few steps from the Esplanada dos Ministérios, a gigantic corridor formed by 17 identical government buildings lined up along either side of the Eixo Monumental. The buildings that face each other at the far end of the Esplanada (just before the Praça dos Três Poderes) are two more world-renowned Niemeyer works: the **Palácio do Itamaraty** ⑨ and **Palácio da Justiça** ⑩. Take a cab to **Pontão do Lago Sul** ⑪, an outdoor area where you can rest in front of a panoramic view, and to the modern-design **Ponte JK** ⑫, the city's most aesthetically striking bridge, alternately known as Terceria Ponte do Lago Sul (Third Bridge in Lago Sul).

TIMING & PRECAUTIONS You need at least a day (6–8 hours) to visit and fully appreciate all the sights. Although you'll probably ride as well as walk, wear comfortable shoes and drink plenty of water, particularly if you're exploring in the hotter months. Note that all government buildings frown on shorts, tank tops, and the like, so dress comfortably but conservatively.

WHAT TO SEE

❽

Fodor'sChoice

★

Catedral Metropolitana de Nossa Senhora da Aparecida. The city's only cathedral is a Niemeyer masterpiece that was finished in 1967. The circular structure consists of 16 reinforced concrete "fingers" that arch skyward. They support huge panes of glass that shelter a subterranean church awash in natural light. Inside, *Os Anjos* (*The Angels*)—an aluminum sculpture by Brazilian modern artist Alfredo Ceschiatti—hovers above the altar. The *cruz* (cross) used at the city's first mass is also here. Above ground, the cathedral resembles a crown of thorns and is surrounded by a reflecting pool. Its entrance is guarded by four majestic bronze statues, also by Ceschiatti, *Os Evangelistas* (*The Evangelists*). The outdoor carillon is a gift of the Spanish government. ⊠ *Esplanada dos Ministérios* ☎ *61/224–4073* ⊡ *Free* ⊙ *Daily 8–6.*

❹ **Instituto Histórico e Geográfico.** The small collection of photographs and memorabilia in the saucer-shape History and Geography Institute documents the city's story with emphasis on the period from the demarcation of the area to the inauguration. The exhibition includes a vintage Jeep used by Kubitschek to visit the construction site in the late 1950s. ⊠ *Av. W-5, SEPS 703/903* ☎ *61/226–7753* ⊡ *Free* ⊙ *Tues.–Sun. 8–noon and 2–6.*

❷

Fodor'sChoice

★

Memorial JK. This Niemeyer structure is a truncated pyramid and has a function similar to its Egyptian counterpart: it's the final resting place of former president Juscelino Kubitschek (JK), the city's founding father, who died in 1981. The mortuary chamber has a lovely stained-glass roof by local artist Marianne Peretti. JK's office and library from his apartment in Rio have been moved to the memorial's north wing. The bronze statue of JK—his hand raised as if in blessing—surrounded by a half-shell (a trademark of Brasília) looks down upon the Eixo Monumental and makes this one of the capital's most moving monuments. Permanent and changing exhibits here document the city's construction. ⊠ *Praça do Cruzeiro at Eixo Monumental Oeste* ☎ *61/225–9451* ⊡ *R$2* ⊙ *Tues.–Sun. 9–6* ⊕ *www.memorialjk.com.br.*

❸ **Memorial dos Povos Indígenas.** Another Niemeyer project, slated to contain a memorial to native peoples, was transformed into an art museum at completion by the city government. A popular uproar ensued, and the building was overtaken by indigenous peoples' organizations. The cylindrical structure has a spiraling ramp around a center plaza and houses a small museum with crafts made by the Kayapó and the Xavante, and other indigenous peoples who once lived on the cerrado and now dwell in the Xingu area of the Amazon. ⊠ *Eixo Monumental Oeste* ☎ *61/ 223-3760* ✉ *Free* ⊙ *Weekdays Tues.–Sun. 9–6, weekends 11–5.*

★ ➒ **Palácio do Itamaraty.** For the home of the Foreign Ministry, Niemeyer designed a glass-enclosed rectangular structure with a detached concrete shelter whose facade is a series of elegant arches. The whole complex rests amid a Burle Marx–designed reflecting pool that augments the sense of spaciousness and isolation. The building and the water create a perfect backdrop for the *Meteoro (Meteor)*, a round, abstract Carrara-marble sculpture by Brazilian-Italian artist Bruno Giorgi. On the guided tour of the interior, you see an astounding collection of modern art—including paintings by Brazilian artists like Candido Portinari—and a Burle Marx tropical garden. Make reservations for tours. ⊠ *Esplanada dos Ministérios* ☎ *61/411-6159* ✉ *Free* ⊙ *Tours (in English) weekdays 2–4:30, weekends 10–3:30.*

➓ **Palácio da Justiça.** The front and back facades of Niemeyer's Justice Ministry have waterfalls that cascade between its arched columns. Inside there's an important library (not open to the public) that contains one of the few complete original sets of Shakespeare's works—a gift from Queen Elizabeth to Kubitschek. ⊠ *Esplanada dos Ministérios* ☎ *61/429-3877* ✉ *Free* ⊙ *Tours (in English) weekdays 10–noon and 3–5.*

➎ **Parque da Cidade.** A few blocks from the Instituto Histórico and Geográfico, you can relax in the shade of City Park, a collaborative effort by Costa, Niemeyer, and Burle Marx. Recent improvements include a state-of-the-art lighting system and more security guards, making an evening walk, run, or bike ride along a path more agreeable than ever. There's also a go-cart racetrack. ⊠ *Entrances at Q. 901 S and Q. 912 S* ☎ *61/225-2451* ⊙ *Daily 24 hrs.*

⌐ ➊ **Praça do Cruzeiro.** Set at a commanding height above the Eixo Monumental, this small solemn plaza is where the city's first mass was held, on May 3, 1957. The site's original cross is now at the Cathedral Metropolitana.

➐ **Teatro Nacional Cláudio Santoro.** Another of Niemeyer's "pyramid projects," this theater is adorned with an array of concrete cubes and rectangles designed by Brazilian architect Athos Bulcão. Its three stages host a variety of performances, and its several small art galleries offer changing exhibits. ⊠ *SCN, via N2* ☎ *61/325-6240* ✉ *Free* ⊙ *Daily 3–8.*

➏ **Torre de TV.** The *salão panorâmico* (observation room) of this 670-foot TV tower has spectacular views, particularly at night. On a lower level, the small **Museu Nacional das Gemas** has an impressive collection of Brazilian gems, a shop that sells stones and crafts, and a café with a view of the Eixo. This is a great place to buy souvenirs. Guided tours are available in English. ⊠ *Eixo Monumental* ☎ *61/323-1881 museum* ✉ *Salão panorâmico free, museum R$3* ⊙ *Deck Mon. 2–9, Tues.–Sun. 9–9; museum weekdays 1–6.*

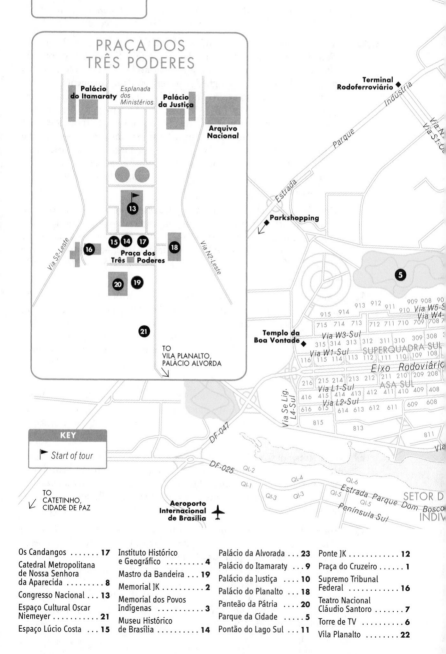

Brasilia

PRAÇA DOS
TRÊS PODERES

Palácio
do Itamaraty
Esplanada
dos
Ministérios
Palácio
da Justiça

Arquivo
Nacional

Terminal
Rodoferroviário

Parkshopping

Praça dos
Três Poderes

TO
VILA PLANALTO,
PALÁCIO ALVORDA

KEY

▶ Start of tour

TO
CATETINHO,
CIDADE DE PAZ

Templo da
Boa Vontade

Via W5-S
Via W4-
Via W3-Sul
Via W1-Sul
SUPERQUADRA SUL

Eixo Rodoviário

Via L1-Sul
ASA SUL
Via L2-Sul

Via Se Lig.
L4-Sul

DF-047

DF-025

Estrada Parque Dom Bosco
Península Sul

SETOR D
INDIV

Aeroporto
Internacional
de Brasília

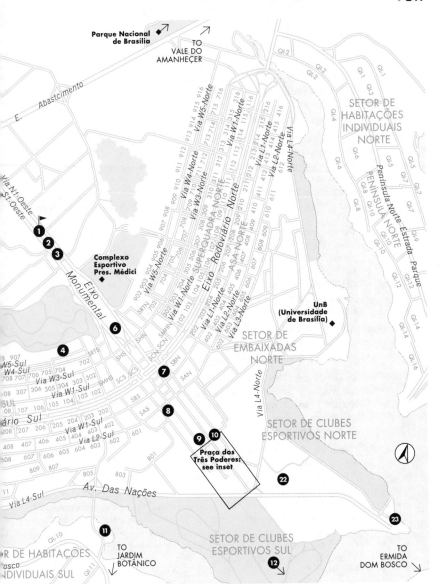

Parque Nacional de Brasília

TO VALE DO AMANHEÇER

SETOR DE HABITAÇÕES INDIVIDUAIS NORTE

PENÍNSULA NORTE

E. Abastcimento

Via N1-Oeste
Via S1-Oeste

Via W5-Norte
Via W4-Norte
Via W3-Norte
Via W1-Norte
Via L1-Norte
Via L2-Norte
Via L4-Norte

SUPERQUADRA NORTE
Eixo Rodoviário Norte
ASA NORTE

Complexo Esportivo Pres. Médici

Eixo Monumental

Peninsula Norte Estrada Parque

UnB (Universidade de Brasília)

SETOR DE EMBAIXADAS NORTE

W5-Sul
W4-Sul
Via W3-Sul
Via W1-Sul

Via L1-Norte
Via L2-Norte
Via L3-Norte

ário Sul

Via W1-Sul
Via L2-Sul

Via L4-Norte

SETOR DE CLUBES ESPORTIVOS NORTE

Via L4-Sul

Av. Das Nações

Praça dos Três Poderes: see inset

R DE HABITAÇÕES osco NDIVIDUAIS SUL

TO JARDIM BOTÂNICO

SETOR DE CLUBES ESPORTIVOS SUL

TO ERMIDA DOM BOSCO

Praça dos Três Poderes

Buildings housing the government's three branches symbolically face each other in the Plaza of the Three Powers, the heart of the Brazilian republic. Here both power and architecture have been given balance as well as a view of Brasília and beyond. Indeed, the cityscape combined with the planalto's endless sky have made the plaza so unusual that Russian cosmonaut Yuri Gagarin once remarked, "I have the impression of landing on a different planet, not on Earth!"

A GOOD TOUR   Start at the plaza's western end, where twin high-rises and two bowl-shape structures make up the **Congresso Nacional** ⓭ ▶. Directly in front of it is the **Museu Histórico de Brasília** ⓮, whose facade is adorned with a sculpture of Kubitschek. To one side of the museum and beneath the plaza is the **Espaço Lúcio Costa** ⓯, with exhibits depicting the planner's ideas for the city, beyond which you'll find the **Supremo Tribunal Federal** ⓰. To the other side of the museum is Giorgi's famous sculpture *Os Candangos* ⓱, which sits in front of the **Palácio do Planalto** ⓲, the executive office. Heading eastward across the plaza, you'll come to the **Mastro da Bandeira** ⓳ and the **Panteão da Pátria** ⓴. Head eastward along the path in the lawn to the **Espaço Cultural Oscar Niemeyer** ㉑, where several of the renowned architect's projects are displayed and explained. From here you can head beyond the plaza by cab to the **Vila Planalto** ㉒ neighborhood and on to the **Palácio da Alvorada** ㉓.

TIMING   All the plaza's sights are close to one another, so you can easily complete this tour on foot in about four hours. Trips by taxi or bus to the Vila Planalto and the Palácio da Alvorada make this a full-day tour.

WHAT TO SEE   *Os Candangos.* This 25-foot-tall bronze sculpture by Giorgi has become
⓱   the symbol of Brasília. The laborers, many from the northeast, who built the city from scratch were called *candangos*. The statue, which consists of graceful elongated figures holding poles, is right across from the Palácio do Planalto.

▶ ⓭   **Congresso Nacional.** One of Niemeyer's most daring projects consists of two 28-story office towers for the 500 representatives of the Câmara dos Deputados (House of Representatives) and the 80 members of the Senado (Senate); a convex structure, where the Câmara meets; and a concave structure, where the Senado convenes. The complex is connected by tunnels to several *anexos* (office annexes) and contains works by such Brazilian artists as Di Cavalcanti, Bulcão, and Ceschiatti as well as French designer Le Corbusier. The indoor gardens were done by Burle Marx. An hourly guided tour takes you through major sites within the building. Guided tours in English are available. ✉ *Praça dos Três Poderes* 🕿 *61/318–5107* ✉ *Free* 🕑 *Weekdays 9:30–11:30 and 2:30–4:30, weekends 9–3:45.*

㉑   **Espaço Cultural Oscar Niemeyer.** This branch of the Oscar Niemeyer Foundation—which is based in Rio and was created to preserve and present the architect's work—houses a collection of sketches and drafts as well as a database with texts and images from Niemeyer's archives. The small auditorium hosts a variety of presentations, which have included talks by the architect himself—after all, this is also the site of his

Brasília office. ⊠ *Praça dos Três Poderes, Lt. J* ☎ *61/226–6797* ✉ *Free* ⊙ *Closed for renovations at this writing; call ahead.*

⑮ Espaço Lúcio Costa. As a tribute to the urban planner who masterminded Brasília, this underground complex was added to the plaza in the late '80s. It has a 1,500-square-foot display of the city's blueprint, and you can read Costa's original ideas for the project (the text is in Portuguese and English). ⊠ *Praça dos Três Poderes* ☎ *61/321–9843* ✉ *Free* ⊙ *Tues.–Sun. 9–6.*

⑲ Mastro da Bandeira. This 300-foot steel flagpole supporting a 242-square-foot Brazilian flag is the only element of Praça dos Três Poderes that was not designed by Niemeyer. In the morning, on the first Sunday of the month, members of the armed forces take part in a *troca da bandeira* (flag change) ceremony. This is a good spot to contemplate the Brazilian flag's elements. The green background symbolizes the forests that once spanned much of the country. The yellow diamond represents the gold-mining period that so influenced the nation's history. The blue circle in the center is a homage to the great blue skies that dominate the territory; inside it are 27 stars—one for each state and the Federal District—from the southern skies and a white band with the national motto, *"Ordem e Progresso"* ("Order and Progress").

⑭ Museu Histórico de Brasília. Brasília's first museum has a small collection of pictures of the city and writings about it by such luminaries as Pope Pius XII, Kubitschek, and Niemeyer. The statue of Kubitschek on its facade is a 1960 work of Brazilian sculptor José Pedrosa. ⊠ *Praça dos Três Poderes* ☎ *61/325–6244* ✉ *Free* ⊙ *Tues.–Sun. 9–6.*

㉓ Palácio da Alvorada. At the tip of a peninsula projecting into Lago Paranoá, the president's official residence—with its trademark slanting supporting columns of white marble—was Niemeyer's first project and was finished in June 1958. Incredible as it may seem, many presidents chose not to live here, preferring other government buildings in the city. You can't go inside, but you can appreciate the grand view of the palace and gardens from the reflecting pool next to the gate. The interior is not open to the public. ⊠ *SHTN, Via Presidencial s/n.*

⑱ Palácio do Planalto. Niemeyer gave this highly acclaimed structure an unusual combination of straight and slanting lines, a variation of the design of Palácio da Alvorada. The access ramp to the main entrance is part of the national political folklore because of the many slips and falls it has provoked. ⊠ *Praça dos Três Poderes* ☎ *61/411–2317* ✉ *Free* ⊙ *Sun. 9:30–1.*

★ **⑳ Panteão da Pátria.** Designed by Niemeyer in 1985, this building honors the nation's heroes, including the beloved Tancredo Neves (it's also known as the Panteão Tancredo Neves), whose untimely death prevented him from being sworn in as Brazil's first democratically elected president after the military dictatorship ended. Inside the curved structure, which resembles a dove, are works by Bulcão and João Camara. One set of panels, *Os Inconfidentes,* depicts the martyrs of the 18th-century Inconfidência Mineira movement, which was organized in Minas Gerais State to overthrow the Portuguese and establish an independent Brazilian republic. ⊠ *Praça dos Três Poderes* ☎ *61/325–6244* 🖼 *Free* ☉ *Tues.–Sun. 9–6.*

16 **Supremo Tribunal Federal.** The Brazilian Supreme Court has the structural lightness that is the backbone of Niemeyer's work. The *Tribunal Pleno*, the highest court in Brazil, convenes on the ground floor. The top floor houses an 80,000-volume library, which you can visit on a guided tour. The 10-foot granite statue set to the left of the main entrance is *The Justice*, by Ceschiatti. ⊠ *Praça dos Três Poderes* ☎ *61/217–3000* 🖼 *Free* ☉ *Weekends 10–3:30.*

22 **Vila Planalto.** Not far from the Palácio da Alvorada, this neighborhood was where the architects, engineers, topographers, accountants, and other professionals stayed while Brasília was under construction. They all lived in prefabricated wooden houses that are representative of an architectural trend within modernism called *racionalismo carioca* (Rio's rationalism), based on Le Corbusier's work. Some of the houses still can be seen along Avenida dos Engenheiros (Avenue of the Engineers). Vila Planalto is a down-to-earth middle- to low-income residential area that maintains a boomtown spirit. It's the perfect place to find a *buteco* (bar) for a late-evening *seresta* (impromptu musical soirée).

Beyond the Plano Piloto

If you have the time, head beyond the Plano Piloto and explore Lago Paranoá's outer perimeter, which has parks, gardens, and several interesting neighborhoods. Here you encounter the cult communities that reflect Brasília's mystical side. In 1883 an Italian priest named Dom Bosco (St. John Bosco) had a vision of a new civilization rising around a lake between the 15th and 20th parallels. "This will be the promised land," he proclaimed. The futuristic architecture; the location between the 15th and 16th parallels in the vast, eerie cerrado; and the fantastic sky views reinforced by the flatness of the region have led many to believe that Brasília is the realization of Bosco's vision. (Bosco never actually set foot in Brazil, making his vision seem even more mysterious.) Since its inception the city has attracted a variety of religious groups.

★ **Catetinho.** When Rio was the capital, the president resided in the Palácio Catete (Catete Palace). Although the new capital was being built, Kubitschek's temporary lodging was called the *Catetinho* (Little Catete). The barrackslike wooden edifice was built in 10 days during the summer of 1956. A nearby landing strip allowed the president to fly in from Rio for his frequent inspections. The building is a must-see museum for those interested in the city's history. It's surrounded by woods in which there's a small springwater pool where the president and his entourage once bathed. ⊠ *Km 0, BR 040, 16 km (10 mi) southeast of Estação Rodoviária* ☎ *61/338–8694* 🖼 *Free* ☉ *Daily 9–5.*

Cidade da Paz. Partly subsidized by the Federal District government, the City of Peace is home to a branch of the Universidade Holística Internacional (International Holistic University), whose goal is to "contribute to the awakening of a new conscience and a new world view." The community occupies the 500-acre Granja do Ipé, 26 km (16 mi) southeast of the Plano Piloto and once the country manor of General

Golbery do Couto e Silva, whom many consider the éminence grise behind the military regime (1964–85). The buildings on the grounds now accommodate university offices, meditation rooms, art galleries, and artisans shops. There are also three thermal pools and waterfalls. ⊠ *Km 30, BR 040* ☎ *61/380–1202* ⌨ *Free* ⊗ *Weekdays 9–4.*

Ermida Dom Bosco. This lakefront sanctuary is dedicated to the saint who inspired so many of those who settled in the new capital. The project is attributed to Niemeyer, though he denies it vehemently. It's adjacent to the impressive postmodern architecture of the Mosteiro São Bento (São Bento Monastery). A scenic overlook with a view of the Plano Piloto and a tranquil Burle Marx–designed garden make it an ideal place to watch the sun set. There's an environmental preserve on the monastery grounds; the entrance is before the ermida's gate. ⊠ *Lago Sul, S. de Mansões Dom Bosco, Cj. 12, 24 km (15 mi) east of the Plano Piloto* ☎ *61/367–4505* ⌨ *Free* ⊗ *Daily dawn–dusk.*

Jardim Botânico. The Botanical Gardens are in a 9,000-acre ecological reserve 27 km (17 mi) south of the Plano Piloto that's only partially open to the public. Three marked trails educate you about Brazilian vegetation, and there's an herb garden with almost 100 types of native medicinal plants. ⊠ *Lago Sul, Km 12, Estrada de Unaí* ☎ *61/366–2141* ⌨ *R$1.50* ⊗ *Tues.–Sun. 9–5.*

Parque Nacional de Brasília. The 60,000-acre Brasília National Park, also called Parque da Água Mineral (Mineral Water Park), is in the northeastern area of the Federal District. The typical cerrado vegetation includes grasslands, woodland savannas, and taller gallery woods on the bottomlands. A 5-km (3-mi) trail through mostly flat terrain starts at the visitor center, where you can pick up maps and brochures. The park also has two pools (fed by natural springs), dressing rooms, and picnic and barbecue areas. ⊠ *EPIA, 9 km (6 mi) from bus terminal* ☎ *61/465–2016* ⌨ *R$3* ⊗ *Daily 8–4.*

Templo da Boa Vontade. This temple is adjacent to the national headquarters of the Legião da Boa Vontade (Goodwill Legion), a religious and philanthropic organization. The pyramid-shape building is open to all denominations for worship or meditation. At the top sits a 21-kilogram (46-pound) quartz crystal, the largest ever found in Brazil. ⊠ *SGAS 915, Lt. 75/6, 8 km (5 mi) south of Eixo Monumental* ☎ *61/245–1070* ⌨ *Temple free, Egyptian room R$2* ⊗ *Temple daily 24 hrs; Egyptian room, gallery, memorial place, and noble room daily 10–6.*

Vale do Amanhecer. The most famous of the cult communities, the Valley of the Dawn, is near Planaltina, a cidade-satélite 40 km (25 mi) north of the Plano Piloto. The community was established in 1969 by Neiva Zelay, known as Tia Neiva, a onetime truck driver who died in 1985 and who reportedly had extrasensory powers. Each day the community's grounds are the site of rituals conducted by followers of a variety of faiths and philosophies. About 1,000 people live here. ⊠ *Km 10, DF 15* ☎ *61/389–7220* ⌨ *Free* ⊗ *Grounds daily 10 AM–midnight; services daily 12:30–2:30.*

★ ⑫ **Ponte JK.** Inaugurated in late 2002, the third bridge in Lago Sul is a combination of utility—it links the Clubs Sector to Lago Sul—and beauty, as its architecture is consistent with the city's modernist aesthetic. Its lakeshore location and promenade attract many people to walk and enjoy the sunset. ⊠ *S. de Clubes Sul, between QL 24 and 26.* 🖅 *Free* ☉ *Daily 24 hrs.*

Pontão do Lago Sul. Brasília may not have beaches, but it does have a shore. This large parklike area is in front of Lago Paranoá and has space to jog, to walk, and to rest, but the interesting bars and restaurants, shops, and beautiful view are the main attractions. Thousands of people head here each weekend. The entrance to the lakefront area is styled after the Arc de Triomphe in Paris, a controversial move, since Brasília has modern architecture. You need a car to get here. ⊠ *SHIS QL 10, Lago Sul.* 🕾 *61/364–0580* 🖅 *Free* ☉ *Daily 8–midnight.*

Where to Eat

BRAZILIAN
$$
Fodor'sChoice
★

✕ **Porcão.** One of the most famous *churrascarias* (barbecue restaurants) in Brazil, Brasília's Porcão is a large place that seats more than 1,000 people. Close to the lake, it has many rooms for special and/or private events. It is *rodízio* style, meaning that waiters bring various types of meat off the spit to your table every few minutes. You can also have salad, sushi, seafood, and regional specialties. ⊠ *SCES trecho 02, Cj. 35, S. de Clubes Sul* 🕾 *61/223–2002* 🖅 *AE, DC, MC, V.*

★ **$–$$**

✕ **Antigamente.** This colonial house was brought stone by stone from the town of Diamantina in Minas Gerais. The restaurant's location—not far from the shore of Lago Paranoá—and the *comida mineira* (food typical of Minas Gerais) are reasons enough to come. Try the *galinha à D. Carlota Joaquina* (chicken with red sauce) or the *ouro velho de Goiás* (butter-fried chicken nuggets). There's a fixed-price buffet option at lunch. At dinner live Brazilian music accompanies your meal. ⊠ *Lago Sul, SCS, Trecho 4, Cj. 5, Lt. 1-B* 🕾 *61/323–3245* 🖅 *AE, DC, MC, V* ☉ *Closed Mon. No dinner Sun.*

$–$$

✕ **Feitiço Mineiro.** Do you enjoy Brazilian music? Then go to this restaurant that, besides offering high-quality *mineira food* (food from the state of Minas Gerais), has live music, often bossa nova, every night. Try the *costelinha ao Véio Chico* (fried ribs with manioc) while you wait for the shows. ⊠ *CLN 306 Bl. B, Lj. 45 and 51* 🕾 *61/272–3032* 🖅 *DC, MC, V* ☉ *No dinner Sun.*

$

✕ **Churrascaria do Lago.** At this rodízio-style churrascaria, waiters bring meat to your table until you tell them to stop. As the name indicates, it's on the lakefront; it has been here, near the Palácio da Alvorada, since the city's early days. This is a favorite with politicians. Reservations are essential for dinner. Beach clothes are not allowed. ⊠ *Lago Norte, SHTN, Cj. 1-A* 🕾 *61/306–2266* 🖅 *AE, DC, MC, V* ☉ *No dinner Sun.*

ECLECTIC
$–$$$$

✕ **O Convento.** From the outside O Convento doesn't look like a restaurant, mainly because the residential area it's in forbids outdoor signs—hence the small plaque near its doorbell. Its name comes from its location—in a house built with material from a convent. The furnishings are 18th century, and the waiters are dressed as monks. The fare is international, with a Brazilian accent—the *camarão rosa grelhado* (grilled shrimp with butter sauce and tropical fruits) is highly recommended. ⊠ *SHIS, QI. 9, Cj. 9, Casa 4, Lago Sul* ☎ *61/248–1211* ⌕ *Reservations essential.* ▤ *MC, V* ☺ *Closed Mon. No dinner Sun.*

★ **$–$$$$** ✕ **La Via Vecchia.** The powers-that-be favor this restaurant in the Bonaparte Hotel for its quiet atmosphere and superb decor. Specialties include *piccole cotolette di agnello* (mutton in a cream sauce made with cassis and port) and the grilled seafood combination served with a fruit risotto. Reservations are essential for dinner. ⊠ *SHS Q. 02, Bl. I* ☎ *61/321–7635 or 61/225–2010* ▤ *AE, DC, MC, V* ☺ *Closed Sun. No lunch Sat.*

$–$$$ ✕ **The Falls.** As its name suggests, this restaurant, in the basement of the Naoum Plaza Hotel, has a decor that includes artificial waterfalls that cascade amid vegetation. The ambience is as much of a draw as the food, which includes such exquisite dishes as the *sinfonia de peixes*, a "fish symphony" of Brazilian seafood, rice, and *pirão* (beans and cassava flour). ⊠ *SHS, Q. 05, Bl. H/I* ☎ *61/322–4545* ▤ *AE, DC, MC, V.*

$ ✕ **Carpe Diem.** If you are a bibliophile or a fan of the arts, you might enjoy the constant book launchings and exhibits at this restaurant frequented by politicians and academics. The menu includes *feijoada* (meat stew with black beans) and a special buffet on Sunday. It is close to the Southern and Northern Hotel sectors. ⊠ *SCLS 104, Bl. D, Lj. 1* ☎ *61/ 225–8883* ▤ *AE, DC, MC, V.*

FRENCH ✕ **La Chaumière.** For more than 30 years, this small but cozy restaurant
★ **$$–$$$** has been highly regarded for its classical French fare—especially for the beef fillet with green pepper sauce and the grilled fillet with Roquefort sauce. ⊠ *SCLS, Q. 408, Bl. A, Lt. 13* ☎ *61/242–7599* ▤ *AE, D, MC* ☺ *Closed Mon. No lunch Sat.; no dinner Sun.*

GERMAN ✕ **Fritz.** In business for decades, this restaurant is synonymous with Ger-
$–$$$ man cuisine. Try the *Eisbein* (pig's leg with mashed potatoes) or *Ente mit Blaukraut und Apfelpurée* (duck cooked in wine served with red cabbage and applesauce). ⊠ *SCLS, Q. 404, Bl. D, Lj. 35* ☎ *61/223–4622* ▤ *AE, DC, MC, V* ☺ *No dinner Sun.*

ITALIAN ✕ **Villa Borghese.** The cantina ambience and fantastic cuisine (including
¢–$$$ many freshly made pastas) make you feel as if you're in Italy. The *tagliatelli negro* (pasta with squid ink), served with a garlic, herb, and shrimp sauce, is divine. ⊠ *SCLS, Q. 201, Bl. A, Lj. 33* ☎ *61/226–5650* ▤ *DC, MC, V* ☺ *Closed Mon.*

SPANISH ✕ **La Torreta.** If you enjoy Spanish food it is worth checking out this fa-
$$ mous restaurant. Its success can be attributed to the personalized service and the variety of dishes—including the traditional *paella*—and wines from Spain, Argentina, Chile, and Brazil. ⊠ *CLS 402, Bl. A, Lj. 9, Asa Sul* ☎ *61/321–2516* ▤ *AE, MC, V* ☺ *No dinner Sun.*

Where to Stay

★ **$$–$$$** 🏨 **Naoum Plaza Hotel.** Brasília's most sophisticated hotel attracts heads of state (Prince Charles, Nelson Mandela, and Fidel Castro have stayed in the Royal Suite) and their diplomats. Rooms have tropical-wood furniture and beige color schemes. The service is impeccable. Two upscale restaurants, the Falls and Mitsubá (with Japanese fare), add to the hotel's appeal. ⊠ *SHS, Q. 05, Bl. H/I, 70322-914* ☎ *61/322–4545 or*

0800/61–4844 🖷 *61/322–4949* ⊕ *www.naoumplaza.com.br* ⊋ *171 rooms, 16 suites* ⚘ *2 restaurants, coffee shop, room service, cable TV, pool, gym, sauna, bar, business services, meeting rooms, travel services, Internet, free parking* ▤ *AE, DC, MC, V* ⦿ *BP.*

$$ ▦ **Academia de Tênis Resort.** What was once merely a tennis club on the
Fodor'sChoice shore of Lago Paranoá has, over the course of 30 years, become a
★ sprawling resort. Suites are in chalets on landscaped grounds with gardens and wooded areas. Chalets are surrounded by palm trees and arranged around the pools, some free-form with waterfalls. Some suites have whirlpool baths. ⊠ *SCES, Trecho 4, Cj. 5, Lt. 1-B, 70200-000* 🕾 *61/ 316–6161* 🖷 *61/316–6268* ⊕ *www.atr-df.com.br* ⊋ *222 suites* ⚘ *6 restaurants, coffee shop, room service, cable TV, 21 tennis courts, indoor pool, 6 outdoor pools, gym, sauna, 3 bars, business services, meeting room, theater, Internet, free parking* ▤ *AE, DC, MC, V* ⦿ *BP.*

$$ ▦ **Bonaparte Hotel Residence.** A sober granite lobby with sophisticated
Fodor'sChoice accent lighting make the Bonaparte an appealing choice. All rooms
★ could be considered small apartments, with plush carpeting, king-size beds, and large bathtubs in every bathroom. The business services here are outstanding, and the on-site restaurant, La Via Vechia, is one of the best in town. ⊠ *SHS, Q. 02, Bl. J, 70322-900* 🕾 *61/218–6600 or 0800/61–9991* 🖷 *61/321–1831* ⊕ *www.bonapartehotel.com.br* ⊋ *267 rooms* ⚘ *2 restaurants, coffee shop, room service, cable TV, pool, gym, sauna, bar, business services, convention center, Internet, free parking* ▤ *AE, DC, MC, V* ⦿ *BP.*

$$ ▦ **Hotel Nacional.** Echoing Brasília's modernist architecture, the Hotel Nacional, though slightly outdated, is still one of the city's best options. It has accommodated any number of distinguished guests, including Queen Elizabeth. The Taboo Grill is a great place for grilled meat or seafood, and the Tropical Coffee shop offers a different buffet table for each day of the week. ⊠ *SHS, Q. 01, Bl. A 70322-900* 🕾 *61/321–7575* 🖷 *61/ 223–9213 or 0800/644–7070* ⊕ *www.hotelnacional.com.br* ⊋ *346 rooms* ⚘ *Restaurant, coffee shop, room service, cable TV, indoor pool, gym, sauna, bar, nightclub, business services, meeting rooms, travel services, Internet, free parking* ▤ *AE, DC, MC, V* ⦿ *BP.*

$$ ▦ **Metropolitan.** This low-key hotel has a lower price tag than its sister property, the Bonaparte. The rooms are fully furnished apartments. It's convenient to the Brasília Shopping mall and gives special rates for extended stays. The Francisco Norte restaurant is highly recommended. ⊠ *SHN Q. 02, Bl. H, 70710-030* 🕾 *61/424–3500 or 0800/61–3939* 🖷 *61/327–3938* ⊕ *www.atlantica-hotels.com* ⊋ *115 apartments* ⚘ *Restaurant, cable TV, pool, gym, sauna, bar, meeting rooms, Internet, free parking* ▤ *AE, DC, MC, V* ⦿ *BP.*

★ **$–$$** ▦ **Kubitschek Plaza.** High-caliber service and upscale amenities are the hallmarks here. The lobby is decorated with antiques, Persian rugs, and original paintings by renowned Nippo-Brazilian artist Tomie Otake. Rooms are comfortable and have a sedate modern decor. After a hard day conducting affairs of state and/or business, many people head for the on-site Plaza Club, a restaurant–bar with a dance floor. ⊠ *SHN, Q. 02, Bl. E, 70710-908* 🕾 *61/329–3333 or 0800/61–3995* 🖷 *61/ 328–9366* ⊕ *www.kubitschek.com.br* ⊋ *246 rooms* ⚘ *2 restaurants,* *coffee shop, room service, cable TV, indoor pool, gym, sauna, 3 bars, business services, meeting rooms, travel services, Internet, free parking* ▭ *AE, DC, MC, V* ⏐⊙⏐ *BP.*

$ ⊞ **Aracoara Hotel.** One of Brasília's oldest and most traditional hotels played a role in the country's history: João Figueiredo made this the de facto presidential residence for a while in the late '70s. Although it's starting to show its age, it's still a worthy choice. The restaurant combines international fare with live Brazilian music. ⊠ *SHN, Q. 05, Bl. C, 70710-300* ☎ *61/424–9222 or 0800/61–4881* ⛱ *61/424–9200* ⟿ *114 rooms, 16 suites* ⟁ *Restaurant, coffee shop, cable TV, sauna, bar, meeting rooms, Internet, free parking* ▭ *AE, DC, MC, V* ⏐⊙⏐ *BP.*

★ $ ⊞ **Blue Tree Park.** Staying so far from the city can be worthwhile to experience this spacious luxury hotel. On the Paranoá Lake shore, near the Palácio da Alvorada, the modern-design hotel is surrounded by greenery. Many events are held here, since the convention center can accommodate up to 750 people and the ballroom up to 1,000 people. ⊠ *SHTN Trecho 01, Cj. 1B, Bl. C, 70800-200* ☎ *61/424–7000* ⛱ *61/424–7001* ⊕ *www.bluetree.com.br* ⟿ *380 rooms* ⟁ *Restaurant, coffee shop, room service, cable TV, pool, gym, sauna, sports courts, bar, business services, convention center, Internet, free parking* ▭ *AE, DC, MC, V* ⏐⊙⏐ *BP.*

$ ⊞ **Eron Brasília Hotel.** Rooms at this hotel have such high-tech amenities as full stereo systems. Request a room on the 10th floor or higher to avoid traffic noise. The Restaurante Panorâmico and its piano bar have a grand view of the Eixo Monumental and are popular with political types. ⊠ *SHN, Q. 05, Bl. A, 70710-300* ☎ *61/329–4000 or 0800/61–0999* ⛱ *61/326–2698* ⊕ *www.eronhotel.com.br* ⟿ *170 rooms, 10 suites* ⟁ *Restaurant, in-room data ports, cable TV, gym, bar, nightclub, meeting rooms, travel services, Internet, free parking* ▭ *AE, DC, MC, V* ⏐⊙⏐ *BP.*

$ ⊞ **Hotel das Nações.** You can spend some of the money you save by staying at this budget hotel, which has been around since the city's early days, at the nearby Pátio Brasil mall. Who needs abundant facilities and imaginative decor when you can go shopping? ⊠ *SHS, Q. 4, Bl. I, 70300-300* ☎ *61/322–8050* ⛱ *61/225–7722* ⟿ *126 rooms* ⟁ *Refrigerators, bar, free parking* ▭ *AE, DC, MC, V* ⏐⊙⏐ *BP.*

$ ⊞ **Monumental Bittar.** Although it has few frills, this hotel is a good budget choice. Rooms have a tasteful decor that makes them feel cozy, bathrooms are large, and the staff is dedicated. ⊠ *SHN, Q. 3, Bl. B, 71710-911* ☎ *61/328–4144* ⛱ *61/328–4144* ⟿ *99 rooms* ⟁ *Restaurant, bar, cable TV, free parking* ▭ *AE, DC, MC, V* ⏐⊙⏐ *BP.*

$ ⊞ **San Marco.** If you're looking for functionality and reliability, stay at the San Marco. You can bask in the central Brazilian sun, taking in the Eixo Monumental, at the rooftop pool. The adjacent restaurant, La Gondola, serves international fare. ⊠ *SHS, Q. 05, Bl. C, 70710-300* ☎ *61/321–8484 or 0800/61–8484* ⛱ *61/226–3055* ⊕ *www.sanmarco.com.br* ⟿ *191 rooms, 4 suites* ⟁ *Restaurant, cable TV, pool, gym, sauna, bar, meeting room, travel services, Internet, free parking* ▭ *AE, DC, MC, V* ⏐⊙⏐ *BP.*

¢   ⊞ **SAN Park.** This hotel is a convenient budget option for those en route to other destinations who do not need to stay downtown. Bathrooms are small, and facilities are basic but up-to-date. ⊠ *SAAN, Q. 3, Bl. D, 70300-300* ☎ *61/361–0077* 🖷 *61/361–0088* 🖘 *56 rooms* ♨ *Restaurant, fans, sauna, free parking; no a/c* 🖃 *AE, DC, MC, V* ⦿❘ *BP.*

Nightlife & the Arts

NIGHTLIFE **Beirute** (⊠ SCLS 109, Bl. A, Lj. 02/04 ☎ 61/244–1717), an eclectic bar-restaurant with an Arabian flair, has been in business since 1966. During its first decade it drew politicians for postsession discussions; today it attracts intellectuals and is gay- and lesbian-friendly. Embassy personnel gather at the stylish **Café Cassis** (⊠ SCLS 214, Bl. B, Lj. 22 ☎ 61/346–7103), which has a newsstand with foreign magazines and newspapers. **Gates Pub** (⊠ SCLS 403, Bl. B, Lj. 34 ☎ 61/322–9301) is popular with those who appreciate jazz and blues. For drinks and light food, go to **Marietta Café** (⊠ SCLS 210 Bl. C, Lj. 6 ☎ 61/244–8344), famous for its natural sandwiches and fruit juices.

In Brasília's clubs some nights are devoted to such northeastern Brazilian rhythms as *forró*—the result of the large number of *nordestinos* (northeasterners) who settled here. **Café Cancun** (⊠ Liberty Mall, SCN Q. 02, Bl. D, Lj. 52 ☎ 61/327–1566) is known for its variety of music. Each day of the week is dedicated to a certain type, and you can dance to forró, *axé* (music from Bahia), and techno.

THE ARTS The **Clube do Choro** (⊠ Eixo Monumental ☎ 61/327–0494) theater presents good Brazilian music. The main building of the **Fundação Brasileira de Teatro** (Brazilian Theatrical Foundation; ⊠ SDS, Bl. C, Lj. 30 ☎ 61/226–0182) has two theaters for plays and concerts: the Teatro Dulcina de Moraes and the Teatro Conchita de Moraes. The **Teatro Nacional Cláudio Santoro** (⊠ SBN, Via N2 ☎ 61/325–6109, 61/325–6105 symphony tickets) has three stages and several practice rooms used by the Orquestra Sinfônica do Teatro Nacional, which performs here from March through November.

Sports & the Outdoors

Most spectator sporting events are held in the Centro Desportivo Presidente Medici complex, on the north side of the Eixo Monumental.

AUTO RACING The **Autódromo Internacional Nelson Piquet** (☎ 61/273–6586), named after three-time Formula I champion and Brasília native Nelson Piquet, has a 5-km (3-mi) racetrack that hosts such events as Formula III and stock car races.

BASKETBALL & **Ginásio Nilson Nelson** (☎ 61/225–4775) is a large arena with 17,000 seats
VOLLEYBALL right on Eixo Monumental. It's used for volleyball and basketball games as well as for musical events.

GOLF At the tip of Eixo Monumental, not far from the Palácio da Alvorada, you can golf on the 18-hole course at the **Clube de Golfe de Brasília** (⊠ SCES, Trecho 2, Lt. 2 ☎ 61/224–2718). Guests at some hotels have free access to the course; all others pay R$60 on weekdays and R$90 on weekends.

HIKING If you just want to wander along a trail, head to the **Parque Nacional de Brasília** (⊠ EPIA, 9 km/6 mi from bus terminal ☎ 61/233–4055). To learn about local vegetation while you walk, try one of the three trails at the **Jardim Botânico** (✉ Lago Sul, S. de Mansões Dom Bosco, Cj. 12 ☏ 61/366–2141 ⊕ www.jardimbotanico.df.gov.br). It is open weekdays 1:30–5:30 and weekends 9–4:30. Besides learning about the nature and the cerrado, you can buy plant seeds, tea, T-shirts, and other items.

SOCCER   The modern, 66,000-seat **Estádio Mané Garrincha** (☏ 61/225–9860) is where Gama FC plays, a second-tier *futebol* (soccer) team that has occasionally risen to the major league. **Ginásio Cláudio Coutinho** (☏ 61/225–5977) is a small, 6,000-seat facility used mostly for practice by national teams.

SWIMMING   Some 35 km (22 mi) south of the Eixo Monumental is the **Cachoeira da Saia Velha** (✉ BR 040, Saida Sul ☏ 61/627–0000), a natural preserve with cerrado vegetation and several waterfalls. Admission is free. The **Parque Nacional de Brasília** (✉ EPIA, 9 km/6 mi northwest of the Estação Rodoviária ☏ 61/465–2016) has pools filled with mineral water. Take your dip in the morning to beat the crowds.

TENNIS   You can get in a match or take classes at the **Academia de Tênis Resort** (✉ SCES, Trecho 4, Lt. 1-B ☏ 61/316–6161), daily 8–4. Court fees are about R$30 per hour (equipment included); lessons are R$55 per hour.

Shopping

There are two major shopping districts along the Eixo Monumental: the Setor Comercial Norte (SCN; Northern Commercial Sector) and the Setor Comercial Sul (SCS; Southern Commercial Sector). In addition, almost every *superquadra* has its own commercial district.

CENTERS & MALLS   Housed in an odd arch-shape building, **Brasília Shopping** (✉ SCN, Q. 05 ☏ 61/328–2122), the most sophisticated mall in the city, has several international chain stores, as well as movie theaters, restaurants, and snack bars. The mall is close to both hotel sectors and is open Monday–Saturday 10–10 and Sunday 2–10. The **Conjunto Nacional Brasília** (✉ SDN, Cj. A ☏ 61/316–9700) is one of the nation's first malls. Its central location (across from the Teatro Nacional and bus terminal) and glitzy neon facade make it one of the most visited, though you won't find many international brand names here. It's open Monday–Saturday 10–10.

Pátio Brasil Shopping (✉ SRTV, Q. 701 ☏ 61/314–7400) often has free concerts and is very close to most hotels. It has a full range of shops and movie theaters and is open Monday–Saturday 10–10:30. Close to the lake, **Pier 21** (✉ SCES, Trecho 2, Cj. 32 ☏ 61/223–0234) has a large food court, a movie theater with 13 screens, and a playground for children. If you want to shop, though, other malls have more options. It's open Monday–Saturday 10–10. **Parkshopping** (✉ SAI/Sudoeste, Q. A-1 ☏ 0800/61–4444), Brasília's largest shopping center, has 183 shops as well as a Burle Marx–designed central garden, the site of many cultural events. It's open Monday–Saturday 10–10.

MARKETS   The **Feira de Antiguidades** (Antiques Fair; ✉ Centro Comercial Gilberto Salomão, SHIS, QI. 5) is held on the last weekend of each month from 8 to 6 and offers a great variety of decorative objects. At the **Feira de Artesanato** (Artisans' Fair; ✉ Foot of Torre de TV, Eixo Monumental) you can find semiprecious-stone jewelry, bronze items, wood carvings, wicker crafts, pottery, and dried flowers. It's held weekends 9–6. A few stalls might open during the week. It is worth going for a short visit to the **Feira Mista** (Miscellaneous Fair; ⊠ HIGS 703/704), where you can find clothes and food. It's only open on Saturday from 8 to 6.

GEMSTONES   For quality stones head to the **Museu Nacional das Gemas** (⊠ Torre de TV, Eixo Monumental ☎ 61/322–3227 Ext. 201). Its shop is open Tuesday–Friday 10–6.

GOIÁS

In the geographical heart of Brazil, far from the sea, but with mysterious sources of sulfurous and saltwater, the state of Goiás was founded in the early 18th century by *bandeirantes* (pioneers), who went there in search of precious metals and stones. In its major towns the state retains traces of the gold rush, an era when the region prospered thanks to the riches extracted from its mines.

When the gold boom ended, livestock farming became important and Goiás was a major producer, with cattle rearing its main source of income, followed by industrial production and general trade. The capital, Goiânia, was slated as the political and economic center of the state. The construction of the federal capital, Brasília, on Goiás territory has made communications with the center of the country easier and has improved access to all parts of the state. In 1988 the state of Goiás was divided, and 40% of its northern territory became the new state of Tocantins.

Exploring Goiás means getting to know some of its historic cities, which started as settlements around gold mines, such as Goiás Velho and Pirenópolis, examples of colonial Brazil in their architecture and local culture. To the south is the hinterland of Caldas Novas, the world's largest hydrothermal resort. North of Brasília is the region of the Chapada dos Veadeiros, with its strange rock formations, fantastic waterfalls, and moonlike sceneries that surround the town of Alto Paraíso (High Paradise), considered by spiritualists to be the city of the third millennium.

Goiânia

209 km (130 mi) southwest of Brasília.

Much like Brasília, Goiânia is a planned metropolis, though it was built in the 1930s. The capital of the important farming state of Goiás, today it is one of Brazil's 10 largest cities, with more than 1 million people. Green areas have been incorporated into the city plan, though accelerated population growth has infringed on some of these spaces. Goiânia might never make it to UNESCO's list of World Heritage Sites, but it's a good stepping-off point for the hot springs of Caldas Novas and the nearby Pousada do Rio Quente resort. It has also acquired a reputation for its nightlife due to its many options: bars, cafes, dance clubs, parties, and music festivals.

The **Museu Antropológico da UFG** (University Anthropology Museum) has a large collection of indigenous artifacts. ✉ *Praça Universitária 1166, S. Universitário* ☎ *62/209–6004* 🏷 *Free* ◷ *Tues.–Fri. 9–5.*

Near the middle of town is the **Bosque dos Buritis,** a large wooded park. Stroll beside its man-made lakes, sit by its fountains (wear bug spray, as the mosquitoes can be fierce), or visit the small **Museu de Arte** (Art Museum), in its northwestern corner. The park isn't safe at night. ✉ *S. Oeste* ☎ *62/541–1190 museum* 🏷 *Free* ◷ *Park daily 9–6, museum Tues.–Sun. 9–6.*

off the beaten path

POUSADA DO RIO QUENTE RESORTS – This resort complex 175 km (109 mi) south of Goiânia in the municipality of Rio Quente (Hot River) consists of two hotels and a water park. The park itself makes a nice day trip from Goiânia. There are also on-site restaurants and bars. Consult the well-informed staff about transportation options. ✉ *Off GO 507* ☎ *64/452–8000* ⊕ *www.viverpousada.com.br* 🏷 *R$25* ◷ *Park Tues.–Sun. 9–5.*

Where to Stay & Eat

$–$$ ✕ **Piquiras.** This popular, upscale, eclectic restaurant is best known for its *peixe na telha* (fried *surubi* fish fillet, served with *pirão*—beans in a thick sauce—and rice). It has two locations: the original is in the quiet Piquiras neighborhood down the street from the Castro's Park hotel; the other branch is in the Marista section of town. Be prepared for the automatic spritzer, designed to help keep you cool during the day; at night your biggest concern will be making reservations. ✉ *Av. República do Líbano 1758, S. Oeste* ☎ *62/251–8168* ▭ *AE, DC, MC, V* ✉ *Rua 146 464, S. Marista* ☎ *62/281–4344* ▭ *AE, DC, MC, V.*

¢–$$ ✕ **Aroeiras.** The main draw of Aroeiras is *tartaruga a moda Araguaia* (Araguaian-style turtle served in its shell, with a spicy sauce and rice), a delicacy from the Araguaia River basin. The brick house is built in the style of Goiás's country houses, with a tile roof and high ceilings, and the brick walls are hung with paintings by local artists. You can also dine on the patio, where water winds around a miniaqueduct. ✉ *Rua 146 No. 570, S. Marista* ☎ *62/241–5975* ▭ *AE, DC, MC, V.*

★ $–$$ ✕⌂ **Castro's Park.** Goiânia's top-of-the-line hotel caters to wealthy businesspeople during the week; on weekends families lounge by the pool. Rooms are modern, though small and nondescript. The Ipê, one of the on-site restaurants, serves a great *feijoada* (traditional Brazilian stew of pork, black beans, rice, and spices) on Saturday. ✉ *Av. República do Líbano 1520, S. Oeste, 74115-30* ☎ *62/223–7766* 🖷 *62/225–7070* ⊕ *www.castrospark.com.br* ⌁ *161 rooms, 16 suites* ⌂ *2 restaurants, minibars, cable TV, pool, sauna, bar, business services, convention center, travel services* ▭ *AE, DC, MC, V.*

$$$$ ⌂ **Pousada do Rio Quente Resorts.** This complex of four hotels plus a water park has a bevy of activities, such as tennis, horseback riding, and fishing. There are also on-site restaurants and bars. All the hotels are reasonably close to each other (the farthest are 4 km/2.5 mi apart). Throughout the year there are cultural festivals such as the *festas juninas* (June parties), which celebrate rural Brazilian culture, or the parties dedicated to Japanese, Italian, and German cultures, to name a few. ⊠ *Off GO 507, 175 km (109 mi) south of Goiânia, Rio Quente* ☎ *62/ 452–8000* 🖷 *62/452–8575* ⊕ *www.viverpousada.com.br* ⟳ *122 rooms in Hotel Turismo, 259 in Hotel Pousada, 398 in Suite & Flat, 47 in Hotel Chalet* ⚷ *Cable TV, tennis court, pool, bars, children's programs* 🚭 *AE, DC, MC, V.*

¢ 🔟 **Bandeirantes.** The rooms in this hotel are pleasant enough and have decent bathrooms. The lack of a pool is what keeps the price below its competitors. The hotel's location is both a draw and a disadvantage: it's near the center of town, but it's in a neighborhood that can be noisy and unsafe at night. ⊠ *Av. Anhangüera 5106, S. Central* ☎☎ *62/212– 0066* ⟳ *70 rooms, 3 suites* ⚷ *Restaurant, bar, meeting room* 🚭 *AE, DC, MC, V.*

Nightlife

Goiânia has a vibrant nightlife: the Setor Marista and Setor Oeste harbor several bars, restaurants, and dance clubs where crowds of all ages take advantage of the cool evenings. **Cervejaria Goyaz** (⊠ Rua T 5 at Av. 85, S. Marista ☎ 62/281–0770) has a good beer selection and live music on weekends. **Draft Casual Bar** (⊠ Rua 22 at Rua 23, S. Oeste ☎ 62/ 214–4455) is a great choice for drinks and dancing.

Shopping

Across from the Estação Rodoviária (bus station) is the massive **Centro de Tradições e Artesanato** (⊠ Av. Goiás at Praça do Trabalhador, S. Norte Ferroviário ☎ 62/229–3676), which has a wide selection of locally made ceramics, baskets, and wood carvings as well as stall upon stall of semiprecious stones. It's open daily 8–8. On Saturday the **Feria da Lua** crafts market is held in the Praça Tamanadré. On Sunday you can shop at the **market** in the Praça Cívica.

Caldas Novas

165 km (102 mi) south of Goiânia, 380 km (236 mi) west of Brasília.

In the crater of a 600-million-year-old volcano, Caldas Novas is the world's greatest hydrothermal resort. The hot waters were discovered only in the early 1700s by adventurers seeking gold and precious stones. Together with Rio Quente, it has the largest number of hotels, resorts and water park resorts of Brazil's midwestern region. Among the therapeutic properties of the water are stress release, muscle relaxation, relief of digestive and rheumatic diseases, and stimulation of the endocrinal glands.

Where to Stay & Eat

$ ✕ **Restaurante Bella Nápoles.** This Italian restaurant and pizzeria offers 28 types of food, including salad and barbecue, plus tropical fruit for dessert. ⊠ *Av. Orcalino Santos 136* ☎ *64/453–1620* 🚭 *No credit cards.*

¢ ✕ **Restaurante e Churrascaria Picanha na Brasâ.** More than 20 à la carte dishes are available at this restaurant with a self-service buffet. Brazilian barbecue and *peixe na telha* (fish with tomatoes, potatoes, and cheese) are served. ⊠ *Rua Luís José Pereira 95* ☎ *64/453–7318* 🚭 *V.*

$–$$ 🏠 **Hotel Parque das Primaveras.** Playgrounds, waterfalls, and a minizoo make this hotel in the middle of a park and ideal place to entertain children. You can choose from four types of units, including a comfortable chalet, where artificial rain and fans take the place of air-conditioning. The "luxury" and "super luxury" rooms are carpeted, and more nicely decorated than the basic rooms. All rooms have whirlpool baths. ⊠ *Rua do Balneário 1* 🕾 *64/453–1355* 🖷 *62/453–1294* ⊕ *www.hpprimaveras. com.br* ⤶ *23 rooms, 1 chalet* ♿ *In-room safes, minibars, refrigerators, cable TV, outdoor hot tub, sauna* ▭ *V* ⫷◎⫸ *MAP.*

$–$$ 🏠 **Thermas di Roma Hotel Clube.** This huge complex has eight thermal swimming pools, a water park, and rooms and apartments of all sizes. There's an astonishing panoramic view of the cerrado and the *Serra de Caldas Novas* (Caldas Novas Mountains). Rooms are bright white, with stone flooring; some have patios. ⊠ *Rua São Cristóvão s/n* 🕾 *64/453–1718* ⊕ *www.diroma.com.br* ⤶ *234 rooms, 4 suites* ♿ *Restaurant, refrigerators, cable TV, 8 pools, hot tub, sauna, hair salon* ▭ *V.*

Pirenópolis

131 km (81 mi) north of Goiânia, 159 km (99 mi) west of Brasília.

Settled in the 18th century at the height of the Goiás gold rush, Pirenópolis was abandoned by the early 19th century after most of its gold was mined. Some locals say the years of isolation were a blessing, as they've helped to preserve the town's character: most streets in the historic downtown district retain the original pavement, which has slivers of quartzite, an abundant mineral that's still quarried north of town. In 1989 the federal government gave national monument status to what was once virtually a ghost town, drawing attention from the tourism industry. On weekends people flee from the modern concrete and glass of nearby Goiânia and Brasília to immerse themselves in Pirenópolis's colonial flavor. The town has several blocks of historic houses, churches, charming restaurants, and quaint resorts, along with several well-respected jewelers.

The **Praça da Matriz** is part of the old neighborhood of the city. It is worth a visit to check out historic structures such as the cathedral (Igreja Matriz), the oldest in town, and the Teatro de Pirenópolis (Pirenópolis Theater). ⊠ *Rua do Rosário at Rua Direita.*

The once-handsome, colonial **Igreja Nossa Senhora do Rosário–Matriz** is the oldest church in Goiás (c. 1728–32), but a fire almost destroyed it on September 5, 2002, and the church is now at the beginning of a long restoration process. ⊠ *Praça da Matriz, Rua do Rosário, at Rua do Bonfim* 🕾 *No phone.*

Across Praça da Matriz from the church is the restored **Teatro de Pirenópolis,** built in 1899. Local plays and some from Brasília are mounted here. ⊠ *Rua Com. Joaquim Alves, Praça da Matriz* 🕾 *62/331–1299, 62/331–2729 for tourist information.*

Down the street from the Praça da Matriz is the **Museu das Cavalhadas** with displays of the outlandish medieval costumes worn by participants in the Festa do Divino Espírito Santo. First celebrated in 1891, this three-day event, which has the atmosphere of a Renaissance fair, takes over the town six weeks after Easter Sunday. Among the roster of activities is a staged battle between Moors and Christians (the Christians win every year). The museum is in a private home—Dona Maria Eunice, the owner, will guide you. ⊠ *Rua Direita 39* ☎ *62/331–1166* ☒ *R$2* ☉ *Fri.–Sun. 9–5.*

The most striking of all the town's churches is the **Igreja Nosso Senhor do Bonfim** (c. 1750–54). Its stunning interior (the altars and Christ statue are particularly beautiful) was brought from Salvador by slaves in 1755. ⊠ *Rua do Bonfim, near intersection of Rua Aurora* ☎ *No phone* ☒ *Free.*

Cachoeiras Bonsucesso is the most popular of the several waterfalls and swimming holes in the Rio das Almas because it's closest to town. A campsite, soccer fields, beach volleyball courts, and trails surround the falls. ⊠ *Rua do Carmo, 7 km (4 mi) north of town* ☎ *62/321–1217* ☒ *R$3* ☉ *Daily 8–6.*

The historic sugar mill and farmhouse, **Fazenda Babilônia** has been a National Heritage Site since 1965. Peek into Brazil's agricultural past—dominated by the sugar and molasses trade for more than a century—and try the *café colonial goiâno* (Goiás brunchlike version of southern Brazil's café colonial, an elaborate 5 PM tea). You can also go horseback riding on the grounds. ⊠ *GO 431, 24 km (15 mi) west of town* ☎ *62/9974–0026* ☒ *R$2* ☉ *Weekends and holidays 8–5.*

Fazenda Vagafogo is a 57-acre ecological preserve with a medium-size waterfall that crashes into a natural pool, a small forest, hiking trails, and a little café near the visitor center at the entrance. The owner, Eduardo Ayer, serves a highly recommended brunch of fruits and farm produce Friday through Sunday. ⊠ *Rua do Carmo, 6 km (4 mi) north of town center* ☎ *62/9969–3090* ☒ *R$3* ☉ *Tues.–Sun. 8–5.*

The **Reserva Ecológica Vargem Grande** is slightly out of the way, but this private nature preserve is worth the trip, with two incredible waterfalls as well as swimming holes in Ribeirão do Inferno (Hell's Creek, a tributary of Rio das Almas). ⊠ *11 km (7 mi) along road to Parque Estadual da Serra dos Pireneus* ☎ *62/331–1171* ☒ *R$4* ☉ *Daily 8:30–5.*

Where to Stay & Eat

$–$$ ✗ **Restaurante e Pizzaria Pireneus.** Lunch options at this outstanding eatery include Goiás-style barbecue (beef roasted over coals or on a grill, instead of using riodízio-style skewers). At dinner the restaurant takes advantage of its traditional brick stove and becomes a pizzeria. ⊠ *Praça da Matriz 31, in front of the church* ☎ *62/331–1577* ☐ *MC, V* ☉ *Closed Mon.–Tues.*

$ ✗ **Le Bistrô.** Light, eclectic food is served at this charming place with a good variety of wine and drinks. The owner is a friendly woman from Bahia, and if you find her there, she will be glad to give you all the information you need about the region. ⊠ *Rua do Rosário* ☎ *62/331–2150* ☐ *No credit cards* ☉ *Closed Mon.–Thurs.*

¢–$ ✕ **Aravinda.** This eatery is also a "spiritual" center—the raspy-voice aging-hippie owner is the town's mother figure. The food is colorful and tasty with an emphasis on vegetarian fare; the highlight is delicious fish dishes, particularly the *peixe na telha,* served with tomatoes, potatoes, rice, and more. There's live music—anything from blues to salsa—on weekends. ⊠ *Rua do Rosário 25* ☎ *62/331–2409* ▣ *No credit cards* ⊗ *Closed Mon.–Tues.*

¢–$ ✕ **Caffe & Tarsia.** Probably the best restaurant in town, Caffe & Tarsia is run by a young Italian man and his Brazilian wife. A wide variety of quality Mediterranean dishes is served; there's a self-service buffet on Saturday. Sit at the far end and enjoy the vines on the roof, which daily are covered with ice so they can endure the hot climate of the cerrado. Live music on weekends. ⊠ *Rua do Rosário 34* ☎ *62/331–1274* ▣ *V* ⊗ *Closed Mon.–Thurs.*

¢ ✕ **As Flor.** Popular with locals because of the affordable buffet-style service, As Flor serves traditional Brazilian fare—both the lunch and the dinner menu consist mainly of cured meats with rice and beans. ⊠ *Sizenando Jaime 16* ☎ *62/331–1276* ▣ *No credit cards* ⊗ *Closed weekends.*

¢ ✕▦ **Hotel Quinta de Santa Bárbara.** Across from the Igreja Nosso Senhor do Bonfim is this family-oriented resort with colonial-style bungalows. Each has two rooms with comfortable beds and flagstone floors; a veranda has views of the town that are particularly beautiful at sunset. The open-air all-you-can-eat restaurant serves excellent Goiás specialties cooked in a massive kilnlike stove. ⊠ *Rua do Bonfim 1* ▦▦ *62/331–1304* ⤴ *20 rooms* ⌂ *Restaurant, minibars, cable TV, 2 pools, sauna, fishing, bar* ▣ *V.*

$ ▦ **Pousada dos Pireneus.** Some people come here on weeklong quests to
lose weight; others bring their families for weekend retreats. The main lodge—which is reminiscent of an adobe structure from the southwestern United States—contains the restaurant and bar, which looks out at the pools, tennis courts, and beyond the landscaped grounds to town. Rooms are in what can only be described as a 17th-century condo complex; ground-floor quarters have decks and hammocks. ⊠ *Chácara Mata do Sobrato* ☎ *62/331–1345* ▦ *62/331–1462* ⤴ *103 rooms* ⌂ *Restaurant, cable TV, tennis court, 2 pools, aerobics, massage, sauna, spa, bicycles, horseback riding, bar, recreation room, shops, convention center* ▣ *AE, DC, MC, V* ⼁◯⼁ *MAP.*

$ ▦ **Pousada Walkeriana.** This pousada is named after *Cattleya walkeriana*—one of several rare Brazilian orchids on display in the garden. The main building housed different city government offices over the years before it was declared an Architectural Heritage Site in 1990. There is an antiques shop specializing in furniture in the west wing, and the pousada's small, comfortable rooms are furnished with pieces from the shop. ⊠ *Praça do Rosário 2, Centro* ▦▦ *62/331–1260* ⤴ *16 rooms* ⌂ *Cable TV, pool, bar, shop* ⊕ *www.pireneus.com.br* ▣ *V* ⼁◯⼁ *CP.*

Nightlife

Most nightlife is along or just off the **Rua do Rosário,** which is closed to vehicular traffic on weekends, when bar and restaurant tables take over the narrow sidewalks and the street proper. The liveliest bars are Lanchonete da Chiquinha, Varanda, and Choperia Santo Graal. **Leve Encanto** (⊠ Rua do Rosário 23 ☎ No phone) has French-style crepes and pancakes—perfect pick-me-ups after a long night. For a late-night snack head to **Pizza Trotramundos** (⊠ Rua do Rosário 32 ☎ 62/331–1559) for the house special (pizza with olives, mushrooms, and ham).

Shopping

The number of art and antiques shops in Pirenópolis keeps growing, but the jewelry shops around the commercial district remain the highlight of the town. **Ateliê Cláudia Azeredo** (⊠ Rua Direita 58 ☎ 62/331–1328) sells designer furniture and tapestries. **Galleria** (⊠ Rua do Bom Fim 18 ☎ 62/331–1483) has jewelry made from gold, silver, and semiprecious stones. **Pica Pedra** (⊠ Beira Rio at Rua do Rosário ☎ No phone) specializes in silver and stones, especially emeralds, amethysts, and quartz. At **Shanti** (⊠ Rua do Bom Fim 20 ☎ 62/9969–3161) you can shop for local handicrafts and indulge in an ice cream or an espresso.

Parque Nacional da Chapada dos Veadeiros

250 km (155 mi) north of Brasília.

In Araí plate, whose formation 1.8 billion years ago makes it the oldest geological part of the continent, the plateaus of the Chapada dos Veadeiros form, according to NASA, the most luminous point seen from the Earth's orbit. This is due to the quantity of quartz crystals present in the soil, in addition to several other metals and minerals. The area is famous for its waterfalls, hiking trails, and unforgettable landscape. Placenames in the Chapada dos Veadeiros are suggestive of its beauty: Crystal River, the Zen Backwoods, the Abyss Waterfall, and Moon Valley. You must be accompanied by a guide to explore the park; you can make arrangements at the park's entrance.

Alto Paraíso (High Paradise), Chapada dos Veadeiros's main town, is at the intersection of Routes GO 118 and GO 327. The majority of the residents of Alto Paraíso are Brazilians from outside the region and foreigners, mostly Europeans. It is considered a center of mysticism, spiritualism, and ecotourism. Crossed by Parallel 14, as is Machu Picchu, in Peru, Alto Paraíso has fantastic stories about flying saucers and extraterrestrial beings.

Where to Stay & Eat

¢–$ ✕ **Jambalaya.** The most refined restaurant in town, Jambalaya has a superb view of the county from its hilltop location. It has a self-service buffet at lunchtime and à la carte dishes for dinner, a good variety of wine (mostly Italian), and international food. There are music and events on weekends. ⊠ *S. Mirante Estância Paraíso* ☎ 62/446–1456 ▭ *V.*

¢–$ ✕ **Oca Lila.** In the evening during high season, this restaurant is packed with youngsters. It's worth the wait for the varied health-food menu, which includes many sandwiches and pizzas. Live music plays on weekends. ⊠ *Av. João Bernardes Rabelo 449* ☎ 62/446–1773 ▭ *V.*

¢ ✕ **Creperia Alfa & Ômega.** Sweet and savory pancakes with healthy ingredients are the draw here. Salads, pasta, and fondues are also on the menu. The atmosphere is friendly, with international music. The service is slow but thoughtful. ⊠ *Av. Ary Valadão Filho S/N* ☎ *62/446–1163* ▤ *V*.

¢ ✕ **Jatô**. Local artists and intellectuals meet over vegetarian and traditional Goiás dishes. Lunch is a self-service buffet, with six types of meat, as well as *arroz integral* (whole-grain rice) and salad. ⊠ *Rua Coleto Paulino 522* ☎ *61/446–1339* ▤ *V* ⊗ *No dinner*.

$ ▦ **Casa das Flores**. Exotic attractions like Arabian dance and live Brazilian music add to the romance of this attractive inn. Stay in rooms or two-story cabanas. ⊠ *Vila de São Jorge,* ☎ *61/234–7493* ⊕ *www.pousadacasadasflores.com.br* ⊷ *8 apartments, 13 cabanas* ⚒ *Restaurant, pool, sauna, bar; no a/c in some rooms* ▤ *No credit cards* ◉❙ *MAP*.

¢–$ ▦ **Camelot Inn**. It seems as if King Arthur's castle, complete with ramparts and parapets, has been transported to the cerrado with this thematic inn. Each room's decor is based on a different character from the Knights of the Round Table legend. You can enjoy the rivers and the waterfalls of the area or take a walk around the hills. ⊠ *Km 168, Rodovia GO 118, 73770-000* ☎ *62/446–1449* ⊕ *www.pousadacamelot.com.br* ⊷ *20 rooms* ⚒ *Cable TV, 3 pools, hot tub, massage, sauna, shop, bar, heliport* ▤ *MC, V* ◉❙ *BP*.

¢ ▦ **Alfa & Ômega**. The owner, one of the first settlers in this town, is a father figure in the region. This interesting place has a meditation area, Indian decoration, and ayurvedic massage. Its chaletlike modules are each divided into four rooms, and the most sophisticated apartments have an inner garden. ⊠ *Rua Joaquim de Almeida 15, 73770-000* ☎ *62/446–1225* 🖷 *62/446–1935* ⊕ *www.veadeiros.com.br* ⊷ *12 rooms* ⚒ *Pool, massage, sauna; no room phones* ▤ *V*.

Cidade de Goiás

150 km (93 mi) northwest of Goiânia, 320 km (200 mi) west of Brasília.

The city of Goiás, better known as Goiás Velho, was founded in 1727 by the *bandeirantes* (explorers whose initial goals were to enslave Indians and, later, to capture African slaves who had escaped into the interior), who settled here when they found gold and diamonds. By order of the king of Portugal, a mint was built here in 1774 to process the large amounts of gold found in the Serra Dourada (Golden Sierras)—a mountain range surrounding the city. The town kept growing well into the 1800s but became stagnant as the gold, silver, and gemstones disappeared.

It was the state's capital until 1937, when the government moved to a more central location in the new planned city of Goiânia; Goiás seemingly lost its importance overnight. Thanks to this sudden downfall, most of the baroque-colonial architecture in the downtown area was preserved. The town has also completed a restoration project in which all the power lines in the area were buried and the stone pavement and several buildings were refurbished; UNESCO World Heritage Site status is forthcoming.

Cidade de Goiás is the site of the Procissão do Fogaréu (Fire Procession), a popular Holy Week celebration. Hooded participants toting burning stakes reenact Christ's descent from the cross and burial. In addition, much like Pirenópolis, Goiás is an important handicrafts center.

The **Chafariz de Cauda,** a baroque fountain, was built around 1778 to provide water for the population and the horses and mules that hauled supplies and gold. Water was drawn from the Chapéu de Padre mine and carried by ingenious pipes carved in stone blocks—some are on display at the Palácio Conde dos Arcos. ⊠ *Praça Brasil Caiado s/n.*

The handsome baroque **Igreja São Francisco de Paula,** built in 1761, is the oldest church in Goiás. The murals, depicting the life of St. Francis, were painted by local artist André da Conceição in 1870. ⊠ *Praça Zacheu Alves de Castro s/n* ☎ *Free* ☉ *Wed.–Fri. 1–5, weekends 9–1.*

The imposing two-story **Museu das Bandeiras** (c. 1766) housed the regional government, court, and jail for almost 200 years. A 20-minute guided tour shows a cell, as well as a collection of vintage furniture, church relics, and indigenous artifacts. ⊠ *Praça Brasil Caiado s/n* ☎ *62/371–1087* ☎ *R$3* ☉ *Tues.–Sat. 1–5, Sun. 8–noon.*

The **Palácio Conde dos Arcos** housed the Goiás executive government from 1755 until the capital moved to Goiânia in 1937. Now the government returns here for three days every July in recognition of the city's historical importance. A guided tour highlights the history of the city and state. ⊠ *Praça Tasso Camargo 1* ☎ *62/371–1200* ☎ *R$2* ☉ *Tues.–Sat. 8–5, Sun. 8–noon.*

Goiás's most important poet, Cora Coralina (1889–1985), started writing at 19 but published her first book when she was 75. The **Casa de Cora Coralina,** a collection of her belongings, writings, and letters from fellow poets, is in the house owned by her family since 1784. ⊠ *Rua D. Cândido 20* ☎ *62/371–1990* ☎ *R$2* ☉ *Tues.–Sat. 9–5, Sun. 8–noon.*

Where to Stay & Eat

¢–$ ✕ **Flor do Ipê.** This simple homey restaurant may be nondescript when it comes to decor, but it is the best place to experience *comida goiânia,* such as *arroz com pequi* (rice with berries) and *galinhada* (chicken and rice with spices and berries). ⊠ *Rua Boa Vista 32-A* ☎ *62/372–1133* ⊟ *No credit cards* ☉ *Closed Mon. No dinner Sun.*

¢ ⌷ **Pousada do Ipê.** This cozy place next to the Chafariz da Carioca (Carioca Fountain) allows you to blend easily into the local way of life because it is in the center of town, close to the old church and the museums. ⊠ *Rua do Fórum 22,* ☎ *62/371–2065* ⋥ *23 rooms* ♢ *Restaurant, bar, pool, hot tub; no a/c in some rooms* ⊟ *No credit cards.*

★ ¢ ⌷ **Vila Boa.** On a hill outside town, this pousada has great views. Although accommodations are standard, this is the best option in town, and the staff makes every possible effort to make your stay comfortable. ⊠ *Av. Dr. Deusdete Ferreira de Moura, Morro do Chapéu de Padre* ☎ *62/371–1000* 🖶 *62/371–1000* ⋥ *33 rooms* ♢ *Restaurant, pool, bicycles, bar* ⊟ *No credit cards.*

Sports & the Outdoors

The hills of Serra Dourada are covered with dense forest and are a great place to hike. There are also waterfalls and swimming holes in the creeks and the Rio Vermelho (Red River). **Balneário Santo Antônio** (✉ Km 125, GO 070) is a popular bathing spot near town. The Rio Vermelho also has rapids and a first-come, first-served camping site that is free. **Pé no Chão Excursionismo** (☎ 62/372–1782) organizes guided tours and rafting trips.

Shopping

Associação dos Artesãos de Goiás (✉ Largo do Rosário s/n ☎ 62/371–1116) sells pottery, wicker, and terra-cotta pieces, all by local artists.

THE WEST

The virtually untamed west consists of the frontier states of Goiás, Mato Grosso, and Mato Grosso do Sul. Although the settlers were mostly after gold and precious stones, agriculture and ranching are the mainstays now. The cerrado is Brazil's breadbasket, and the landscape is one large chessboard of crops and pastures. The main hubs—such as Goiânia, Cuiabá, and Campo Grande—are, for the most part, sophisticated trading outposts for farmers and ranchers. Tourism has begun to flourish as more and more people discover the charms of the colonial towns of Pirenópolis, Goiás, and Miranda in Mato Grosso do Sul, the quasi-mystical mesa of Chapada dos Guimarães; the haven of Bonito, with its great water sports; and, of course, the wildlife paradise of the Pantanal.

The Pantanal Wetlands

Right in the middle of South America, the gigantic flood plain of the Rio Paraguai and its tributaries cover about 225,000 square km (140,000 square mi), two-thirds of which are in Brazil. Much of the land is still owned by ranching families that have been here for generations. The Portuguese had begun colonizing the area by the late 18th century; today it's home to more than 21 million head of cattle and some 4 million people (most of them living in the capital cities). Yet there's still abundant wildlife in this mosaic of swamp, forest, and savanna. From your base at a *fazenda* (ranch) or lodge—with air-conditioning, swimming pools, and well-cooked meals—you can experience the *pantaneiro* lifestyle, yet another manifestation of the cowboy culture. Folklore has it that pantaneiros can communicate with the Pantanal animals.

It's widely held that the Pantanal is the best place in all of South America to view wildlife, and it is slated to become a UNESCO Biosphere Reserve. More than 600 species of birds live in the Pantanal during different migratory seasons, including *araras* (hyacinth macaws), fabulous blue-and-yellow birds that can be as long as 3 feet from head to tail; larger-than-life rheas, which look and walk like aging modern ballerinas; the *tuiuiú,* known as the "lords of the Pantanal" and one of the largest birds known (their wingspan is 5–6 feet), which build an intricate assemblage of nests (*ninhais*) on trees; as well as cormorants, ibis, herons, kingfishers, hawks, falcons, and egrets, to name a few. You're also sure to spot *capivaras* (capybaras; large South American rodents),

tapirs, anteaters, marsh and jungle deer, maned wolves, otters, and one of the area's six species of monkey.

The amphibian family is well represented by *jacarés* (caiman alligators), whose population of 200 per square mile is a large increase from the 1970s, when poaching had left them nearly extinct. (The skin of four animals made just one pair of shoes.) Jacarés are much more tranquil than their North American and African relatives—they don't attack unless threatened. Almost blind and deaf, and lacking a sense of smell, caimans catch the fish they eat by following vibrations in the water. It's hard to spot jaguars and pumas during the day; a night photographic safari is the best way to try your luck. Native guides (some are actually converted hunters) take you safely to the animals' roaming areas. Sightings are not uncommon in the fazendas that go the extra mile to protect their fauna. Though all commercial hunting and the pelt trade in wild species has been illegal since 1967, some ranchers still kill jaguars that prey on livestock. Don't let scary tales about *sucuri* (anacondas), which can grow to 30 feet in length, worry you. Sightings of the snakes are extremely rare and instances of them preying on humans are even rarer.

October is the beginning of the Pantanal's rainy season, which peaks in March but lasts through May (later in El Niño years). The land is much greener and more ravishing in the rainy season than at other times of the year, but the wildlife is harder to spot. In the dry season (July–October), when some trees shed their leaves and grasses die, land animal sightings are more frequent. As the waters continue to disappear, fish get caught in the remaining pools and attract a great variety of animals, especially birds. The best fishing season is May through October, and considering the more than 240 varieties of fish in the area, anglers won't be disappointed. *Piraputanga* and *dourado* are the most prized catches, but the abundant *pacú*, *pintado*, and *traíra* are also popular. Piranhas are endemic to the area, but much like caimans, seldom cause trouble—they only attack animals or humans with open wounds. Nevertheless, always check with locals before venturing into unknown waters.

Bonito

277 km (172 mi) southwest of Campo Grande.

The hills around this small town of 15,000, whose name rightly means "beautiful," are the on the southern edge of the Pantanal, not too far from the Bodoquena Mountain range. The route to the Pantanal from Campo Grande is longer via Bonito (a total of about 200 mi) than if you headed directly west to Miranda and Corumbá, but you are well compensated with top-notch hotels that starkly contrast with the rustic Pantanal lodgings. In Bonito you can swim and snorkel among schools of colorful fish in the headwaters of several crystal-clear rivers. Fishing, rafting, rappelling, hiking, and spelunking are popular activities in this area. Tourism has boomed since the 1990s. There are great handicraft shops with art done by native peoples of Mato Grosso and by local artists.

At **Parque Ecológico Baía Bonita** you can go snorkeling along a 1-km (½-mi) section of the Baía Bonita River, where you can see an incredible diversity of Pantanal fish. There is a small museum describing the region's ecosystems. Equipment rental and lunch are included in the admission price. ⌧ *Km 7, Estrada para Jardim* ☎ *No phone* ✉ *R$150 per day* ⊗ *Daily 9–5.*

The 160-foot-deep **Gruta do Lago Azul** (Blue Lagoon Grotto) has a crystal-clear freshwater lake at the bottom and smaller side caves in the calcareous rock. The best time to visit is from mid-December to mid-January, when sunlight beams down the entrance, reflecting off the water to create an eerie turquoise glow. See stalagmites and stalactites in various stages of development. ⌧ *Fazenda Jaraguá, 20 km (12 mi) west of Bonito on road to Campo dos Índios* ☎ *No phone* ✉ *R$10* ⊗ *Daily 9–5.*

To experience what lies ahead in the Pantanal, check the rafting tour of **Rio Formoso.** The approximately 1½-hour (actual length depends on river water flow) trip takes you through clear waters and some rapids while you observe the fish and the birds of the Pantanal. You might also see and hear bands of *macaco-prego* (nail monkeys), the region's largest primates. The tour ends at Ilha do Padre (Priest's Island), where there's a complex of waterfalls emerging through thick riverine vegetation. To best appreciate this attraction, make sure there hasn't been any rain in the previous days—the river gets quite muddy. ⌧ *Hotel Fazenda Cachoeira, 11 km (7 mi) east of Bonito on road to Ilha do Padre.* ☎ *067/255–1213* ✉ *R$35* ⊗ *Tours by appointment.*

Where to Stay & Eat

$–$$ ✕ **Cantinho do Peixe.** Despite its modest appearance, this establishment is your best choice for Pantanal fish. The highlight is *pintado*, which is prepared in 24 ways. The cheese sauce is a good accompaniment to any of the available fish. ⌧ *Rua 31 de Março 1918* ☎ *067/255–3318* ▭ *No credit cards* ⊗ *Closed Sun.*

★ **$$$$** ✕▦ **Zagaia Eco-Resort Hotel.** This resort has international-class facilities that serve you well for short and longer stays. The main building was inspired by the architecture of the Kadiweu Indians. The rooms—in single-story bungalows—are large and cozy, with colorful furnishings and native ornaments. Most rooms have great views of the gardens and forest-covered hills that lie beyond the complex. The restaurant serves international fare, but Pantanal fish are always available. ⌧ *Km 0, Rodovia Bonito–Três Morros* ☎ *067/255–1280, 0800/99–4400 for reservations* 🖷 *067/255–1710* ⊕ *www.zagaia.com.br* ⇝ *70 rooms, 30 suites* ⌂ *Restaurant, refrigerators, cable TV, tennis court, 3 pools, gym, hair salon, massage, sauna, bicycles, hiking, horseback riding, soccer, volleyball, bar, shops, playground, business services, convention center, meeting rooms, airstrip, travel services* ▭ *AE, DC, MC, V* ⎟⊙⎟ *MAP.*

$ ▦ **Pousada Rancho Jarinu.** A family business, Rancho Jarinu has friendly owners who go to great lengths to help you feel at home and choose the best tour. The redbrick and tile-roof building helps keep the air cool, a boon in the heat of the tropics. You're just steps from the main business district in Bonito. ⌧ *Rua 24 de Fevereiro 1965, 79290-000*

☎ 067/255–2094 ⊕ *www.pousadaranchojarinu.com.br* ⊷ *9 rooms* ⚐ *Pool, cable TV, travel services; no room phones* ⊟ *V.*

Shopping

Além da Arte (⊠ Rua Pilad Rebuá 1966 ☎ 067/255–1485) has beautiful bamboo and feather handicrafts and colorful ceramics made by Kadiweu and Terena peoples.

Miranda

205 km (128 mi) west of Campo Grande.

This tiny settlement on the Miranda River grew into a city after the construction of the railway linking São Paulo to Corumbá and on to Bolivia. In its heyday the railway was called *Ferrovia da Morte* (Death Railway) because of the many cattle thieves, train robbers, and smugglers that rode the rails. Since the 1980s the railway has been closed to passengers. At this writing, there is a project, pending government funding, to open a portion of the railway for a tourist *trem do Pantanal* (Pantanal Train) between Campo Grande and Corumbá. Ecotourism is Miranda's main source of revenue. Comfortable pousadas and farms allow you to get acquainted with the *pantaneiro* lifestyle. The Rio Miranda area has abundant fauna, including a sizable population of jaguars. Here is a great opportunity to practice *focagem,* a local version of a photographic safari: as night falls, guides take you into the Pantanal in 4x4 pickup trucks with powerful searchlights that mesmerize the animals for some time, so you can get a really close look.

Where to Stay & Eat

¢–$ ✕ **Cantina Dell'Amore.** Make this small restaurant your choice for pasta—with the owner's original tomato sauce recipe—and fish. You can also try caiman meat here. Owner Angelo Dell'Amore, an Italian expatriate who came to the Pantanal as a professional hunter and later became a caiman breeder, entertains you with his tales. ⊠ *Rua Barão do Rio Branco 515* ☎ *067/242–2826* ⊟ *No credit cards.*

$$$–$$$$ 🏨 **Caiman Ecological Refuge.** This 100,000-plus-acre ranch pioneered
Fodor'sChoice the idea of ecotourism in the Pantanal. The service is excellent—from
★ the professional manner of the kitchen and bar staffs to the knowledgeable guides, all of whom hold a degree in biology or a related science and most of whom speak English. Lodges are spread out over the ranch. The main lodge has the nicest common areas. The Baiazinha (Small Bay) lodge, which is surrounded almost entirely by water, is another great choice. Activities include horseback rides through the wetlands, boat trips to islands on the refuge's vast holdings, and *focagem* of the fauna. Rates include transfers from Campo Grande's airport. ⊠ *37 km (23 mi) north of Miranda, 235 km (146 mi) west of Campo Grande* ☎ *067/687–2102, 011/3079–6622 for reservations in São Paulo* 🖶 *067/ 687–2103* ⊕ *Rua Campos Bicudo, 98-112 São Paulo 04536-010* ☎ *011/3079–6622* 🖶 *011/3079–6037* ⊕ *www.caiman.com.br* ⊷ *29 rooms* ⚐ *Restaurant, pool, bicycles, boating, hiking, horseback riding, volleyball, bar, airstrip; no room TVs, no room phones* ⊟ *AE, DC, MC, V* ¶◎¶ *FAP.*

$–$$$ ⛺ **Fazenda Rio Negro.** This 25,000-acre farm gained notoriety and helped further the cause of wildlife conservation when a popular Brazilian soap opera (incidentally called *Pantanal*) was shot here. The farm now belongs to the Brazilian chapter of Conservation International, which preserves its wildlife and habitat. The good regional food is one lure of this rustic but charming farm built in 1920. Although facilities aren't up to international hotel standards, rooms are comfortable and kept spotless by the attentive staff. The only way to reach this property is by plane (roughly R$650) from either Campo Grande or Aquidauana. ⊠ *About 200 km (125 mi) northwest of Campo Grande* 🕾 *067/751–5191; 067/751–5248 for reservations in Campo Grande* ⊕ *www.fazendarionegro.com.br* 📞 *10 rooms* ⚒ *Dining room, boating, hiking, horseback riding, airstrip; no room TVs, no room phones* ▭ *No credit cards* ⏐⊙⏐ *FAP.*

¢ ⛺ **Pousada Águas do Pantanal.** In a old house with period furniture, this inn is a recommended budget choice in the city. You receive a warm welcome by the friendly staff and the owner, Fátima, who also runs a travel agency next to the inn. The hearty breakfast, with several kinds of bread, jelly, and pastries, is a rarity in a region where buttered bread and coffee are the norm. ⊠ *Av. Afonso Pena 367, Centro 79380-000* 🕾 *067/242–1314* 🖷 *067/242–1242* ⊕ *www.aguasdopantanal.com.br* 📞 *17 rooms* ⚒ *Pool, travel services; no a/c in some rooms, no room phones, no room TVs* ▭ *No credit cards* ⏐⊙⏐ *CP.*

Sports & the Outdoors

As more and more tourists are coming to the Pantanal, the last reluctant ranchers are beginning to see tourism as a viable economic alternative, which means you can visit a working ranch or farm for a day without having to stay as guest. **Fazenda San Francisco** (⊠ BR 262, 36 km/22 mi west of Miranda on BR 262 🕾 067/242–1088 ⊕ www.fazendasanfrancisco.tur.br/turism/turism.html) is a 15,000-hectare (37,065-acre) working ranch where you can go on a photo safari in the morning and a boat tour on Rio Miranda in the afternoon for R$80. The fee includes a *pantaneiro* lunch—rice and beans with beef and vegetables. **Reserva das Figueiras** (⊠ BR 262, 20 km/12 mi west of Miranda 🕾 067/9988–4082 Miranda, 067/326–9070 Campo Grande ⊕ www.reservadasfigueiras.com.br) offers guided wildlife sighting trips via canoe on Rio Salobra for R$60.

Corumbá

435 km (272 mi) west of Campo Grande.

This port city on the Rio Paraguai's banks is a couple of miles from the Bolivian border. Often called the "capital of the Pantanal," the 100,000-inhabitant city itself is not particularly pretty, with the exception of the riverfront area where you can see some 19th-century buildings (which are National Historic Landmarks) and the wetlands well into Bolivia. Corumbá means "faraway place" in the Tupi language, and the main lures of this far-flung region are the chartered fishing trips in fully outfitted riverboats and the yachts that travel up the Paraguay river into the heart of the Pantanal. Waters are clearest and fish are most concentrated during the dry season (May–September).

Corumbá's most significant historical building, and a Brazilian military outpost to this day, is **Forte Coimbra**. The fort was built in late 1700 overlooking the Paraguay river, which was then the de facto borderline. This was the westernmost outpost of the Portuguese empire in those days. Check out the massive British- and American-made cannons and the great views of the river and adjacent lowlands from one of the four turrets. To visit the fort, it is best to book a tour with local travel agents, as reservation are required. ✉ *3-hr boat trip from Porto Morrinhos, which is 72 km (39 mi) southeast of Corumbá on BR 262* ☎ *067/231–9866* ✆ *Free* ⊘ *By appointment only.*

off the beaten path

ESTRADA-PARQUE – Eight kilometers (5 mi) south of Corumbá on BR 262 is the intersection with an unpaved road known as Park Road. This is the remaining section of the first road into the region, blazed in the late 1800s to bring telegraph lines to the wild frontier. This 120-km (75-mi) dirt road, which merges with BR 262 near the Rio Miranda, is a great chance to see Pantanal wildlife outside scheduled tours. As you traverse the Estrada Parque—be sure to attempt this only with a four-wheel-drive vehicle during the day—you can spot caimans, tuiuiús (also known as jabiru), and other birds and occasionally deer and anteaters. Along the way there are several great places for fishing. Near the Paraguay River ferry and the Miranda River bridge are rustic pousadas, campgrounds, and a few hotels.

Where to Stay & Eat

$ ✕ **Peixaria do Lulu.** This family-run business adds personal flavor to the regional cuisine. The fare is essentially Pantanal fish, which can be fried, grilled, or stewed and is served with several side dishes such as *pirão* (black beans with cassava flour). ✉ *Rua Don Aquino Correia 700* ☎ *067/232–2142* ✍ *Reservations essential* ▭ *No credit cards* ⊘ *Closed weekends.*

¢ ⊡ **Nacional Palace.** This hotel is the best in the region, with comfortable rooms and reliable air-conditioning—an absolute requirement in the tropical heat. Amenities are few, but service is good, and the staff is helpful in recommending local attractions and tours. ✉ *Rua América 936, 79301-060* ☎ *67/231–6868* 🖷 *067/231–6202* ☄ *100 rooms* ⚘ *Cable TV, pool, bar, playground, business center, Internet, meeting rooms* ▭ *AE, DC, MC, V.*

Sports & the Outdoors

Corumbá is known across the country as port of call for comfortable riverboats and yachts with weeklong fishing trips—called locally *barcos-hotel* (hotel boats). Daily sightseeing trips are also available. A great travel agency and tour operator is **Pérola do Pantanal** (☎ *067/231–1470* ⊕ www.peroladopantanal.com.br), which has several boats and yachts of different sizes, including the largest on the Paraguay river, the *Kalypso*. This luxury riverboat has 28 cabins with air-conditioning, plus a pool, a restaurant, a satellite phone link, and freezers for the fish you catch.

Transpantaneira Highway

From Poconé, 103 km (64 mi) south of Cuiabá, the highway runs 149 km (93 mi) southward to Poconé to Porto Jofre.

The Rodovia Transpantaneira (MT 080) was originally planned to cut a north–south line through the Pantanal. Lack of funds and opposition from environmentalists resulted in a stalemate. Today the road dead-ends at the banks of the Cuiabá River, in a village called Porto Jofre, about 150 km (93 mi) south of the town of Cuiabá. Still, the Transpantaneira makes it possible to observe the abundant fauna and plush vegetation of the northern part of the wetlands. A large number of fazendas and pousadas organize popular activities such as fishing and photo safaris.

This "highway" is actually a dirt road with some 125 log bridges that allow the annual floods to flow in the natural system without major interference. Even during dry season traversing the Transpantaneira is time consuming and relatively dangerous. The bridges on the last section, from the Pixaim village to Porto Jofre, are the most precarious. Sections of some bridges have caved in while cars were passing over them. It's best to join an organized tour; leave the driving to experienced guides in four-wheel-drive vehicles and concentrate on the region's fascinating landscapes.

Where to Stay

$ ⨉▦ **Pousada Araras EcoLodge.** Rooms are cozy and impeccably clean at
Fodor'sChoice this ecolodge, and the restaurant serves great Pantanal fish. Environ-
★ mental education and awareness is the motto here: this pousada goes the extra mile to keep the environmental impact of tourism to a minimum and explains why and how they do it. One highlight is the 3,000-foot wooden walkway over the wetlands that ends on a 75-foot-high lookout, well above the treetops. From there you have a bird's-eye view of the surroundings. There's a two-day minimum stay, which leaves you time to join the trekking, canoe, horseback, or other tours of the area. ⊠ *Km 33, Rodovia Transpantaneira, Pixaim* ☎ *065/682–2800* 🖷 *065/682–1260* ⊕ *www.araraslodge.com.br* 🖙 *15 rooms* ⚐ *Restaurant, pool, boating, marina, fishing, hiking, horseback riding, bar, airport shuttle; no room TVs, no room phones* ▤ *V* ⊙ *FAP.*

$ ▦ **Pantanal Mato Grosso Hotel.** This member of the Best Western chain is one of the northern Pantanal's more upscale choices. Its rooms may be sparsely decorated but are comfortable enough to make your stay pleasant. The hotel arranges fishing expeditions, guided treks on horseback or on foot, and visits to the Campo Largo ranch, an adjoining working ranch owned by the hotel. Two- to four-night packages are available, but you can take advantage of some activities on a day-use basis. Book several weeks ahead, particularly in high season (June–October). ⊠ *Km 65, Rodovia Transpantaneira, Pixaim* ☎☎ *065/391–1324 or 065/628–1500* ⊕ *www.hotelmatogrosso.com.br* 🖙 *35 rooms* ⚐ *Restaurant, pool, boating, marina, fishing, hiking, horseback riding, bicycles, airport shuttle, airstrip; no room TVs* ▤ *AE, DC, MC, V* ⊙ *FAP.*

Cuiabá

1,130 km (700 mi) west of Brasília, 1,615 km (1,000 mi) northwest of São Paulo.

The capital of Mato Grosso is well known for being the hottest city in Brazil: mean annual temperature is a sizzling 27°C (81°F). Daily highs surpass 45°C (113°F) several times during the year. The city name comes from the Bororo native people, who lived in the area—it means "place where we fish with spears." Originally settled in the 18th century, when gold was found in the nearby rivers, Cuiabá is at a crossroad: it is the southernmost gateway to the Cerrado and the Amazon beyond and the northern gateway to the Pantanal. You can visit one of several museums while you're waiting for a tour into the wetlands or to Chapada dos Guimarães, a mountain range with impressive gorges, waterfalls, and vistas.

The **Museu História Natural e Antropologia,** close to the center of town, is really a complex of museums with everything from ancient Indian artifacts to contemporary art. ☒ *Palácio da Instrução, Praça da República* ☎ *065/321–3391* ▣ *R$5* ◔ *Weekdays 12:30–5:30.*

Northeast of the town's main square is the **Museu de Pedras Ramis Bucair,** with a stunning collection of area fossils and stones, including what's purportedly a meteorite. ☒ *Rua Galdino Pimentel 195* ▣ *R$5* ◔ *Weekdays 7–11 and 1–4.*

Slightly outside town is the **Museu Rondon,** known informally as the Museu do Índio (Indian Museum). Displays include photos of and objects from the indigenous peoples—the Bororo, Pareci, Xavante, and Txukarramãe—of Mato Grosso. The museum is on the UFMT (Universidade Federal do Mato Grosso) campus, whose grounds also contain a zoo populated by Pantanal wildlife. ☒ *Av. Fernando Correia da Costa, 4 km (2 mi) east of town* ☎ *065/615–8489* ▣ *R$2* ◔ *Weekdays 8–11 and 2–5.*

Where to Eat

$–$$ ✕ **Getúlio Grill.** For those who have had their share of fish from the Pantanal, this is a good choice. The menu is full of churrasco fare, but other options such as fillet *a Parmegianna* are highly recommended. There is a dance club on the second floor. ☒ *Av. Getulio Vargas 1147, Goiabeiras* ☎ *065/624–9992* ◔ *Closed Mon.* ▤ *AE, DC, MC, V.*

¢–$ ✕ **Morro de St. Antônio.** This surf-and-turf place has a Polynesian vibe and caters to a yuppie crowd. Many entrées are enough for two people. Dinner is served nightly until 1 AM; on weekends this is a good place to drink and be merry into the wee hours. ☒ *Av. Isaac Póvoas 1167, Centro* ☎ *065/622–0502* ▤ *AE, DC, MC, V.*

★ ¢–$ ✕ **Peixaria Popular.** This is the place in town for Pantanal fish; don't miss the delicious *piraputanga*, either prepared in a stew or fried. Other options are the *pintado* (a large freshwater fish) and *pacu* (a smaller fish that resembles a piranha). All orders include a side serving of pirão and *banana frita* (fried bananas). ☒ *Av. São Sebastião 2324, Goiabeiras* ☎ *065/322–5471* ▤ *MC, V* ◔ *No dinner Sun.*

¢–$ ✕ **Regionalíssimo.** In the same building as the Casa do Artesão, a shop filled with indigenous artifacts, this self-service eatery has regional cuisine as well as Brazilian staples such as rice and beans. After a hearty meal you can browse for ceramics, baskets, and wood handicrafts. ✉ *13 de Junho 314, Porto* ☎ *065/623–6881* ▭ *DC, MC, V* ⊘ *Closed Mon. No dinner.*

Where to Stay

$ ✕▢ **Paiaguás Palace.** Rooms are simple and rather small but charming. The top-floor restaurant, which has a buffet of international fare, is highly regarded by local businesspeople and has good views—on clear nights you can see the plains. Location is one of the main draws of this hotel; it's right in the business district with easy access to the airport. ✉ *Av. Rubens de Mendonça 1718, Bosque da Saúde* ☎ *065/642–5353* 🖷 *065/ 642–2910* ⊕ *www.hotelpaiaguas.com.br* ⮣ *121 rooms* ♤ *Restaurant, gym, bar, business services, travel services, Internet* ▭ *AE, DC, MC, V* ¶ *CP.*

$–$$ ▢ **Eldorado Cuiabá.** A vision of glass and brass (no gold, as the name would suggest), this hotel has some of the best rooms in town. The pleasant decor, air-conditioning, and cable TV are a welcome break from the surrounding sparse Pantanal fazendas. ✉ *Av. Isaac Póvoas 1000, Centro 78045-640* ☎ *065/624–4000 or 0800/17–1888* 🖷 *065/624–1480* ⊕ *www.hoteiseldorado.com.br/hcuiaba.htm* ⮣ *141 rooms, 6 suites* ♤ *Restaurant, cable TV, pool, bar, shops, business services, convention center, Internet, meeting rooms* ▭ *AE, DC, MC, V* ¶ *CP.*

¢ ▢ **Áurea Palace.** The amenities are few, but this hotel is clean, and the staff is reliable. Each room has two single beds. Make this your choice if you have a tight budget. ✉ *Rua Gen Mello 63, Bandeirantes* ☎ *065/ 623–5008* 🖷 *065/3027–5728* ⮣ *75 rooms* ♤ *Restaurant, refrigerators, pool, bar, Internet; no room TVs* ▭ *AE, V* ¶ *CP.*

Nightlife

Toward the newer part of the city, along Avenida C.P.A. and side streets, there are many sports bars and nightclubs. If you're looking for a wholesome evening, try one of the many ice cream parlors, such as **Alaska** (✉ Rua Pedro Celestino 215). **Entrentanto** (✉ Rua Mal. Floriano 401 ☎ 065/623–3786) has tables in a tree-lined garden and has daily performances of Brazilian and international pop music. Snack on Brazilian appetizers.

Shopping

For Indian handicrafts try the shop run by the Brazilian Indian agency FUNAI: **Artíndia** (✉ Rua Pedro Celestino 301 ☎ 065/623–1675). For wicker, cotton, and ceramic crafts from local artists, go to **Casa do Artesão** (✉ Rua 13 de Junho 315 ☎ 065/321–0603). The shop inside the **Museu de Pedras Ramis Bucair** (✉ Rua Galdino Pimentel 195) sells semiprecious stones, such as emeralds, tourmalines, and agates. **Goiabeiras Shopping** (✉ Av. Lava Pés 500, Duque de Caxias ☎ 065/624–4760) has more than 50 shops of all kinds.

Chapada dos Guimarães

74 km (40 mi) north of Cuiabá.

This quasi-mystical mesa is the area's most popular attraction after the Pantanal, and much of it is protected by a national park. Traveling northeast of Cuiabá, you see the massive sandstone formations from miles away, rising 3,000 feet above the flat cerrado landscape. After navigating the steep and winding MT 251 through breathtaking canyons to reach the top of the mesa, you discover the pretty town of Chapada dos Guimarães, which still retains some of its colonial charm.

If you have time, arrange a guided visit to **Caverna Aroe Jari.** The cave's name means "home of souls" in the Bororo language. This mile-long sandstone cave (one of Brazil's largest) can only be reached after a 4.8-km (3-mi) hike through the cerrado. Contact **Ecoturismo Cultural** (⊠ Praça Dom Wunibaldo 464 ☎ 065/301–1393 ⊕ www.chapadadosguimaraes. com.br/ecoturis.htm) to arrange for a tour guide. ⊠ *45 km (30 mi) east of town on gravel road to Campo Verde.*

The **Igreja de Nossa Senhora de Santana do Sacramento** is a handsome colonial church (circa 1779) with some exceptional gold-plated interior flourishes. ⊠ *Praça Central* ☎ *No phone* ☉ *Daily 7 AM–9 PM.*

In 1972 satellite images proved that the continent's true center was not in Cuiabá, where a monument had been built, but right here at **Mirante do Centro Geodésico,** on the mesa's edge. If the geodesic center doesn't hold spiritual meaning for you, come for the fantastic vista; on a clear day you can see as far as the Pantanal. ⊠ *8 km (5 mi) southwest of town.*

Along the road to Chapada dos Guimarães from Cuiabá, you pass the **Portão do Inferno** (Hell's Gate), a scenic viewpoint over the chasm that was created by the Rio Cuiabá's waters eroded the mesa. ⊠ *48 km (30 mi) northeast of Cuiabá.*

Parque Nacional da Chapada dos Guimarães. Beyond the Portão do Inferno you come to the park's **visitor center** (⊠ Km 51, MT 251 ☎ 065/301–1133), which is open daily 8–5. One step from the visitor center, the **Cachoeira Véu de Noiva** (Bridal Veil Falls), with a 250-foot freefall, is the most impressive of the five falls in the park. You can enjoy lunch at the nearby open-air restaurant. Beyond this point there are hills, caves, more falls, and archeological sites. ⊠ *13 km (8 mi) west of town* ☎ *065/301–1113* 🎟 *R$3* ☉ *Daily 8–5.*

Where to Stay & Eat

$–$$ ✕ **Nivo's Fogão Regional.** The restaurant is true to its motto, QUALIDADE: INGREDIENTE FUNDAMENTAL DE BOA COZINHA, which translates as "quality: the basic ingredient of good cooking." The fish entrées such as pacu and *dourado* are delicious and are always served with pirão and *farofa de banana* (cassava flour with bananas). ⊠ *Praça Dom Wunibaldo 63* ☎ *065/791–1284* 🖃 *V* ☉ *Closed Mon. No dinner.*

$ ✕ **Morro dos Ventos.** This restaurant is right on the edge of the cliff. Enjoy the scenery as you enjoy one of the regional dishes such as *vaca atolada* (cow stuck-in-the-mud), beef ribs served in cooked cassava chunks. The restaurant is in a condominium complex, and you have to pay a R$5 entrance fee. ⊠ *Road to Campo Verde, 1 km (½ mi) east of town* ☎ *065/301–1030* ⚐ *Reservations essential* ☐ *V* ☉ *No dinner.*

$ ⚷ **Pousada Penhasco.** Clinging to the mesa's edge, this small resort may be far from the Chapada dos Guimarães's town center, but it has tremendous views of the cerrado. The sunny rooms are in cabins scattered about the property. All rooms have access to verandas with great vistas. The staff frequently arranges soccer matches at the on-site field and en masse outings to area sights. If you want to explore on your own, you can borrow a bike. ⊠ *Av. Penhasco s/n, Bom Clima* ☎ *065/624–1000 in Cuiabá* ☎☎ *065/301–1555* ⊕ *www.penhasco.com.br* ⇌ *36 rooms* ⚐ *Restaurant, cable TV, 2 pools, sauna, bicycles, hiking, soccer, bar, playground, meeting rooms; no room phones* ☐ *V* ☉ *CP.*

Campo Grande

1025 km (638 mi) west of São Paulo, 694 km (430 mi) south of Cuiabá.

Nicknamed the Cidade Morena (Brunette City) because of the reddish-brown earth on which it sits, this relatively young city (founded in 1899) was made the capital of Mato Grosso do Sul in 1978, when the state separated from Mato Grosso. Campo Grande's economy traditionally relied on ranching, but in the 1970s farmers from the south settled in the region, plowed the flat lands, and permanently changed the landscape. Now ecotourism is booming in the region. The number of foreign and Brazilian visitors to Campo Grande, the gateway to the southern Pantanal and the town of Bonito, is increasing each year.

To get acquainted with Mato Grosso's indigenous population, which includes more than 50,000 Terenas, Kaiowas, Guaranis, and Kadiweu, visit the **Memorial da Cultura Indígena,** a 25-foot-high bamboo *maloca* (Indian hut) built in the middle of an urban Indian reservation (Aldeia Marçal de Souza), the first urban reservation in Brazil. You can shop for pottery and tapestries. The reservation is in the Tiradentes neighborhood. ⊠ *BR 262, exit to Tres Lagoas* ☎ *067/725–4822.*

Founded by Salesian missionaries, the **Museo Dom Bosco,** known as the Museu do Índio, has more than 5,000 indigenous artifacts of the Bororo, Kadiweu, and Carajás native peoples. Noteworthy are the taxidermy exhibits of the Pantanal fauna and the formidable seashell collection. Don't miss the bug room, whose walls are covered from floor to ceiling with insects of every type. ⊠ *Rua Barão do Rio Branco 1843* ☎ *067/312–6491* ⊞ *R$3* ☉ *Tues.–Sat. 8–6, Sun. 8–noon and 2–6.*

Where to Eat

$–$$ ✕ **Casa Colonial.** In a colonial-style house is one of Campo Grande's best restaurants, which serves eclectic fare with a strong leaning toward Italian cuisine. ⊠ *Rua Afonso Pena 3997* ☎ *067/383–3207* ☐ *AE, DC, MC, V* ☉ *No lunch Mon.*

¢–$$ ✕ **Fogo Caipira.** This is the place for regional cuisine. Call ahead for stuffed

Fodor'sChoice pintado or piraputanga. The standout here is the *picanha grelhada na* ★ *pedra* (grilled picanha steak). The *carreteiro* (rice with sun-dried meat)

is also recommended. ⊠ *Rua José Antôonio Pereira 145, Centro* ☏ *067/ 324–1641* ▭ *AE, DC, MC, V.*

¢–$$ ✕ **Radio Clube.** One of the fanciest places in town, this restaurant–night-club adds some energy to the somewhat lifeless Praça da República. You can stop by for a drink or a meal of Continental fare. ⊠ *Rua Padre João Cripa 1280* ☏ *067/321–0131* ▭ *AE, DC, MC, V* ⊘ *Closed Mon.*

Where to Stay

$ ⊞ **Jandaia.** The Jandaia is so thoroughly modern that it almost seems out of place in this wild-west town. Though it has little character—it's geared toward businesspeople, so convenience wins over aesthetics—it does have all the facilities and amenities you'd expect at a deluxe hotel. The upscale Imperium restaurant, on the second floor, serves international fare with Brazilian options. ⊠ *Rua Barão do Rio Branco 1271, 79002-174* ☏ *067/721–7000* 🖷 *067/721–1401* ⊕ *www.jandaia.com. br* 📲 *130 rooms, 10 suites* ♨ *2 restaurants, pool, gym, bar, meeting room* ▭ *AE, DC, MC, V.*

¢ ⊞ **Hotel Internacional.** Though modest, this budget option is clean and well maintained; what's more, management doesn't feel compelled to jack up the rates just because there's a pool. The dormitorylike rooms have firm single beds and private bathrooms. The only problem here is the location near the bus station—a part of town that can be dangerous at night. ⊠ *Rua Allan Kardac 223, 79008-330* ☏ *067/784–4677* 🖷 *067/721–2729* 📲 *100 rooms* ♨ *Restaurant, pool, bar* ▭ *AE, DC, MC, V.*

¢ ⊞ **Metropolitan.** Well located near Avenida Afonso Pena, this hotel is popular with business travelers. Rooms are nicely decorated. The tile floors make the rooms feel extra cool—you might even forget to turn on the air-conditioning. ⊠ *Av Pres. Ernesto Geisel 5100, 79006-000* ☏ *067/ 389–4600* 🖷 *067/389–4601* ⊕ *www.hotelintermetro.com.br* 📲 *80 rooms* ♨ *Cable TV, pool, bar, meeting room* ▭ *AE, DC, MC, V.*

Nightlife

Campo Grande is wilder than Cuiabá; parts of town (particularly the area near the bus station) are downright dangerous and best avoided at night. On the better side of the tracks is **Choperia 4 Mil** (⊠ Av. Afonso Pena 4000 ☏ 067/325–9999), a microbrewery that caters to an eclectic crowd of all styles and ages. It's open for drinks and snacks Wednesday–Sunday from happy hour until after midnight. **Iris** (⊠ Av. Afonso Pena 1975 ☏ 067/784–6002) is one of the few cybercafés in the west. You can surf the Web (for about R$14 per hour) every night until 10, or leaf through one of the week-old English-language magazines. The dance club **D-Edge** (⊠ Rua Arthur Jorge 326 ☏ 067/324–2861) plays mostly American dance music and is frequented by a young trendy crowd. It's open until the last customer leaves.

Shopping

For baskets of all shapes, beautiful wood handicrafts, and interesting ceramics made by Pantanal Indians, head to **Casa de Artesão** (⊠ Rua Calógeras 2050, at Av. Afonso Pena ☏ 067/383–2633). It's open weekdays 8–6 and Saturday 8–noon. The **Feria Indígena,** adjacent to the Mercado Central and just across Avenida Afonso Pena from the Casa de Artesão, is a good place to shop for locally made crafts. It's open Tuesday through Sunday 8–5. The massive **Shopping Campo Grande** (✉ Av. Afonso Pena 4909) has everything you'd expect in an American- or European-style mall—from a Carrefours department store to a food court with McDonald's. The many boutiques are what make this place shine.

BRASÍLIA & THE WEST A TO Z

To research prices, get advice from other travelers, and book travel arrangements, visit www.fodors.com.

AIR TRAVEL

CARRIERS Airlines that serve Brasília include American Airlines, British Airways, Air Canada, Gol, VASP, Varig, and TAM. The west is served by Gol, Varig, and TAM.

🛪 Airlines & Contacts **American Airlines** ☎ 61/321-3322 ⊕ www.aa.com. **British Airways** ☎ 61/327-2333 ⊕ www.ba.com. **Air Canada** ☎ 61/328-9203 ⊕ www.aircanada.com. **TAM** ☎ 61/365-1000 in Brasília, 62/207-4539 in Goiânia, 65/682-3650 in Cuiabá, 67/763-4100 in Campo Grande ⊕ www.tamairlines.com. **Varig** ☎ 61/327-3455 in Brasília, 62/207-1743 in Goiânia, 65/682-1140 in Cuiabá, 67/763-0000 in Campo Grande, 0800/99-7000 nationwide ⊕ www.varig.com. **VASP** ☎ 61/365-1425 in Brasília, 62/207-1350 in Goiânia, 65/682-3737 in Cuiabá, 67/763-2389 in Campo Grande, 0800/99-8277 nationwide ⊕ www.vasp.com.br.

AIRPORTS & TRANSFERS

The Aeroporto Internacional de Brasília (BSB), 12 km (7 mi) west of the Eixo Monumental, is considered South America's first "intelligent" airport, with computer-controlled communications and baggage-handling operations.

Major western airports are Aeroporto Santa Genoveva (GYN), in Goiânia; Aeroporto Marechal Rondon (CGB), in Cuiabá; and Aeroporto Internacional de Campo Grande (CGR).

🛪 Airport Information **Aeroporto Internacional de Brasília** ☎ 61/365-1224. **Aeroporto International de Campo Grande** ✉ 7 km (4 mi) west of downtown Campo Grande ☎ 67/368-6093. **Aeroporto Marechal Rondon** ✉ 7 km (4 mi) south of Cuiabá ☎ 65/614-2500. **Aeroporto Santa Genoveva** ✉ 6 km (4 mi) northeast of Goiânia ☎ 62/265-1500.

AIRPORT To get from the international airport in Brasília to the city center, taxis
TRANSFERS are your only real option (city buses, which cost about R$1, don't have room for your luggage). Trips to the hotel sectors along the Eixo Monumental take roughly 15 minutes and cost about R$23. Double-check costs at the dispatcher booth near the arrival gate, and reconfirm the fare with your driver.

The western airports are all close to their respective cities, so a taxi is your best bet. The fare into Goiânia and Campo Grande is about R$15; into Cuiabá it's R$20. Though buses (about R$2) serve the airports, they don't have space for luggage and often pull up well away from the terminals. To use them, you need to understand each city's layout fairly well.

BUS TRAVEL

The interstate bus station is the Estação Rodoferroviária. For trips to Goiânia (three hours), try Araguaina. Expresso São Luiz buses make the 12-hour journey to Cuiabá. To make the 14-hour trip to São Paulo, try Real. Itapemirim buses run to and from Rio de Janeiro (17 hours) and Belo Horizonte (11 hours).

Within the city itself, virtually all buses depart from Estação Rodoviária. Route names (usually coinciding with the final destination) and departing times appear on digital displays. Rides within the Plano Piloto cost about R$1. There are also a few air-conditioned express buses, which make fewer stops and cost about R$2.50. Of these, the Terminal Rodoferroviária and Palácio da Alvorada buses are good for sightseeing along the Eixo Monumental.

Bus Information Araguaina ☎ 61/233-7566 or 0800/62-1011. **Estação Rodoferroviária** ⊠ Westernmost tip of Eixo Monumental ☎ 61/233-7200. **Estação Rodoviária** ⊠ Eixo Monumental, at intersection of Asa Norte and Asa Sul ☎ 61/223-0557 and 61/223-3247. **Expresso São Luiz** ☎ 61/233-7961. **Itapemirim** ☎ 61/361-4505 or 0800/99-2627. **Real** ☎ 61/361-4555.

Although the distances in the west are great, buses remain the primary mode of transportation because of high airfares and limited air service. A dazzling array of companies have regular bus service connecting Brasília and Goiânia (three hours, R$23); Goiânia and Cuiabá (13 hours, R$110); Goiânia and Cidade de Goiás (2½ hours, R$16); Cuiabá and Campo Grande (10 hours, R$70); Cuiabá and Chapada dos Guimarães (two hours, R$15); and Campo Grande and Corumbá (seven hours, R$65). There's less frequent service between Brasília and Pirenópolis (2½ hours, $3) and between Pirenópolis and Goiânia (two hours, R$16).

Andorinha has frequent service between Campo Grande, Cuiabá, and Corumbá. Auto Viação Goinésia operates most of the buses between Pirenópolis and both Brasília and Goiânia.

The major western cities are fairly compact, so you won't need to worry about taking municipal buses, except perhaps to the airport or the interstate bus depot. The one exception is Campo Grande, where the shopping area is quite a distance east along Avenida Afonso Pena. Bus fares in the western cities are about R$1.80. Beware that during rush hours buses become overly crowded and claustrophobic.

Bus Information Andorinha ⊠ Corner of Dom Aquino and Joaquim Nabuco, upstairs inside Rodoviária, Campo Grande ☎ 67/383-5314. **Auto Viação Goinésia** ⊠ Terminal Rodoviário L Norte, Brasília ☎ 61/562-0720. **Rodoviária de Campo Grande** ⊠ Dom Aquino and Joaquim Nabuco, east of downtown ☎ 67/783-1678. **Rodoviária de Cuiabá** ⊠ Av. Marechal Deodoro, Alvorada, north of city center ☎ 65/621-2429. **Rodoviária de Goiânia** ⊠ Av. Goiás, Ferroviário Norte sector ☎ 62/224-8466.

CAR RENTAL

Expect to pay at least R$175 a day for a compact car with air-conditioning, including insurance and taxes. Because the roads are in such bad shape, a 15% surcharge is added to car rentals in Campo Grande and Cuiabá.

Brasílian rental agencies include Avis, Hertz, Localiza, and Unidas. Rental companies with offices in the western region include Avis, Hertz, Localiza, and Unidas.

🚘 Major Agencies **Avis** ☎ 61/365-2344 in Brasília, 67/325-0072 in Campo Grande, 65/682-7360 in Cuiabá, 0800/55-8066 nationwide. **Hertz** ☎ 61/365-2816 in Brasília, 65/682-6767 in Cuiabá, 0800/14-7300 nationwide.

🚘 Local Agencies **Localiza** ☎ 61/365-2782 in Brasília, 65/624-7979 in Cuiabá, 0800/99-2000 nationwide. **Unidas** ☎ 61/365-2266 in Brasília, 67/363-2145 in Campo Grande, 0800/12-1211 nationwide.

CAR TRAVEL

BRASÍLIA Brasília is connected with the rest of the country by several major highways. BR 050 is the shortest way south to São Paulo (1,015 km/632 mi). From the city of Cristalina (113 km/70 mi south of Brasília), it's another 612 km (380 mi) on BR 040 to Belo Horizonte. The westbound route, BR 060, runs to Goiânia and the Pantanal and intersects with BR 153, the north–south Transbrasiliana Highway, which stretches another 1,930 km (1,200 mi) north to Belém in the Amazon. BR 020 runs northeast from Brasília to Salvador (1,450 km/900 mi).

When they were first built, Brasília's wide north–south and east–west multilane highways—with their nifty cloverleafs, overpasses, and exits—allowed quick access to all major points. Nowadays you can expect traffic jams at rush hour. Parking is easy in the residential areas but can be tricky in the commercial sectors.

GOIÁS & THE WEST Driving isn't recommended to visit the western attractions, as in some stretches highways are in bad shape and there is heavy truck traffic. Also consider that Brazilian truck drivers are frightening in their disregard for basic rules of the road. Further, getting around on your own by car is difficult without a very good working knowledge of Portuguese. Outside the cities, few people speak English, making it hard to get directions if you get lost. In short, it's best to avoid traveling to and within the west by car.

EMERGENCIES

In Brasília, Drogaria Rosário is open 24 hours a day and has delivery service. There's a late-night pharmacy in Cuiabá near the corner of Avenida Getúlio Vargas and Rua Joaquim Murtinho. In Campo Grande try the late-night pharmacy at the corner of Avenida Afonso Pena and Rua 14 de Julho. Elsewhere in the region, use the 24-Hour Pharmacy Hotline.

🚑 Contacts in Brasília **Drogaria Rosário** ✉ SHCS 102, Bl. C, Lj. 05 ☎ 61/323-5901, 61/323-1818 for deliveries. **Hospital de Base do Distrito Federal** ✉ S. Hospitalar Sul ☎ 61/225-0070.

🚑 Contacts in the West **Hospital Ernestina Lopes Jayme** ✉ Rua dos Pirineus, Pirenópolis ☎ 62/331-1530. **Hospital Santo Antônio** ✉ Rua Quinco Caldas, Chapada dos Guimarães ☎ 65/791-1116. **Hospital Santa Casa** ✉ Rua Eduardo Santos Pereira 88, Campo Grande ☎ 67/321-5151. **Hospital Santa Casa** ✉ Praça Seminário 141, Cuiabá ☎ 65/624-4222. **Hospital Santa Helena** ✉ Rua 95 No. 99, S. Sul, Goiânia ☎ 62/219-9000.

🚑 General Numbers **Ambulance** ☎ 192. **Fire** ☎ 193. **Police** ☎ 190. **Tropical Disease Control Hotline** ☎ 61/225-8906. **24-Hour Pharmacy Hotline** ☎ 132.

ENGLISH-LANGUAGE MEDIA

In Brasília, Livraria Saraiva has the best selection of English-language books, magazines, and newspapers. Livraria Sodiler is also a good choice for magazines and paperbacks. Elsewhere in the west, English-language reading material is hard to come by, but try newsstands at the airports.

🗐 Bookstores **Livraria Saraiva** ⊠ SCS, Q. 1, Bl. H, Lj. 28 🖷 61/323-4115. **Livraria Sodiler** ⊠ Aeroporto Internacional, Upper Concourse, EC 14 🖷 61/365-1967.

HEALTH

In Brasília and throughout the west, stick to bottled water (and check that restaurants use it to make juice and ice). Malaria is quite rare in tourist areas. Yellow fever is of greater concern. It's best to get a yellow fever shot before arriving, but if you decide to travel at the last minute, it is possible to get shots at the airport; all airports have a Ministry of Health booth (open 8–5). Dengue fever, for which there is no vaccination or preventive medication, has also appeared around the Pantanal. The best way to prevent it is to avoid being bitten by mosquitoes. Pousadas and hotels in the Pantanal have insect-tight screened windows, doors, and verandas. Use insect repellent with DEET at all times.

MAIL, INTERNET & SHIPPING

Fax services are available at major *correio* (post office) branches and hotels. Most city hotels have full-fledged business centers. Smaller establishments and pousadas offer only the slowest Internet dial-up connections; Internet cafés are practically nonexistent.

🗐 Major Shipping Service **DHL** ⊠ SCS, Q. 06, Bl. A, Suite 1A, Brasília 🖷 61/225-9263.
🗐 Post Offices **Brasília post office** ⊠ SBN, Q. 1, Bl. A, Brasília. **Correio Campo Grande** ⊠ Av. Calógeras 2309, at corner of Rua Dom Aquino, Campo Grande ⊠ Rua Barão do Rio Branco, across from bus depot, Campo Grande. **Correio de Cuiabá** ⊠ Praça da República, center of town, just south of tourist office, Cuiabá ⊠ Aeroporto Marechal Rondon, 2nd floor. **Correio de Goiânia** ⊠ Praça Cívica 11, off Av. Tocantins, Goiânia.

MONEY MATTERS

Banking hours are weekdays 10–4 in major cities; 10–3 in the interior. Major banks are equipped with ATMs (dispensing reais), but only a few but only a few are available 24 hours—usually only those at airports and shopping malls. Outside state capitals, most ATMs operate from 8 AM–10 PM. Most ATMs run on the Plus network; if your card is only affiliated with Cirrus, plan accordingly. Banco do Brasil is the best establishments for cashing traveler's checks, with relatively low fees and decent exchange rates. Throughout the region, the better hotels will either exchange money for you (though rates aren't great) or tip you off to the area's best *casas de câmbio* (exchange houses).

In Goiânia, the BankBoston across from the Castro's Park Hotel has an ATM. Goiânia's main Banco do Brasil is open weekdays 10–6; there's also one at the airport. In Pirenópolis Banco do Brasil ATMs are available from 6 AM to 10 PM.

Banco do Brasil's main Cuiabá branch is in the middle of town and is open weekdays 10–4, with ATMs that operate from 6 AM to 10 PM; there are also ATMs at the airport. Several little câmbios line Rua Cândido Mariano, including Guimel He Tour, which is open weekdays 8:30–6 and offers good rates.

All the major banks have offices in the center of Campo Grande, along Avenida Afonso Pena. Try Banco do Brasil, which is open weekdays 10–5; there are also a branch and several ATMs at the airport.

🖪 **American Express** ⊠ Beltour, CLS 410, Bl. A, Lj. 29, Brasília ☎ 61/244–5577. **Banco do Brasil** ⊠ SBN, Q. 01, Bl. A, Brasília ☎ 61/310–2000 ⊠ Aeroporto Internacional, Brasília ☎ 61/365–1183 ⊠ Av. Afonso Pena at Rua 13 de Maio, Campo Grande ⊠ Av. Getúlio Vargas and Rua Barão de Melgaço, Cuiabá ⊠ Av. Goiás 980, Centro, Goiânia ⊠ Av. Sizenando Jayme 15, Centro, Pirenópolis. **BankBoston** ⊠ SCS, Q. 06, Bl. A, Lj. 200, Brasília ☎ 61/321–7714 or 0800/55–1784. **Citibank** ⊠ SCS, Q. 06, Bl. A, Lj. 186, Brasília ☎ 61/225–9250. **Guimel He Tour** ⊠ Rua Cândido Mariano 402, Cuiabá ☎ 65/624–1667. **Kammoun Câmbio** ⊠ SHS, Q. 3, Bl. J, Brasília ☎ 61/321–1983.

SAFETY

Although Brasília doesn't have as much crime as Rio and São Paulo, be cautious at night and at any time on buses or in bus terminals. For the most part, the western cities are safe, but—as in Brasília—you should always be cautious when going out at night, particularly near bus terminals. The southern and western parts of Goiânia are safest. In Cuiabá steer clear of the embankment at night.

TAXIS

BRASÍLIA Fares in Brasília are lower than in the rest of the country, and most cabs are organized into cooperatives with dispatchers. It's best to call for one of these "radio taxis," particularly in the evening; unlike those in other Brazilian cities, some offer discounted rates for cabs ordered by phone—inquire when calling.

🖪 Taxi Companies **Rádio Táxi** ☎ 61/325–3030. **Rádio Táxi Cidade** ☎ 61/321–8181.

THE WEST As most of the tourist areas in western cities are compact, you rarely need a cab except for trips to the airport, the bus depot, or to and from your hotel at night. But they're all metered, so you shouldn't have to haggle. They're safe and comfortable, and you can hail them on the street. Tips aren't expected.

🖪 Taxi Companies **CooperTáxi** ⊠ Campo Grande ☎ 61/3361–1111. **Rádio Táxi Cuiabana** ⊠ Cuiabá ☎ 65/322–6664

TELEPHONES

Area codes in the region are as follows: Brasília, 61; Goiânia and Pirenópolis, 62; Cuiabá, 65; and Campo Grande, 67. You can call long distance from all pay phones—they work with prepaid magnetic cards. Before making a long-distance call from a pay phone, you must choose a long-distance carrier and dial its designated access code prior to dialing the area code and number. Rates vary depending on time of day and promotions; check with the operator before dialing. You can choose from several companies: the most popular are Embratel (access code 021), Intelig (access code 023), and Telebrasília/Brasil Telecom (access code 014). Embratel and Intelig are the only ones that work throughout the country. The others are regional, and whether they work depends on if you're in the city or regional area to which they pertain. To sum up, to make a phone call, dial 0 + (21 or 23) + the city code + the phone number.

TOURS

BRASÍLIA Most hotels have an associated travel agency that arranges tours. Popular excursions include a basic day trip along the Eixo Monumental, a shorter night version with stops at clubs, and an uncanny "mystical tour" to the cult communities around town. ESAT Aero Táxi can arrange helicopter tours of the Plano Piloto and other Distrito Federal sights. The shortest flight (10 minutes) costs R$80 per person (minimum four people per flight). MS Turismo offers city tours as well as trips into the cerrado. VoeTur offers a variety of tours.

🖪 Brasília Tour Operators **ESAT Aero Táxi** ⊠ Monumental Axis at TV Tower ☏ 61/323-8777. **MS Turismo** ⊠ SHCS/EQS 102/103, Bl. A, Lj. 04/22 ☏ 61/224-7818. **VoeTur** ⊠ Brasília Shopping, SCN, Q. 05, Bl. A, Lj. 235-A ☏ 61/327-1717.

THE WEST In Pirenópolis Estação Aventura has bus, bike, or horseback tours of the ecological spots surrounding the town. Diniz of Ecotur is another good Pirenópolis guide who offers similar "ecological" trips. In Goiânia check with Pireneus Tour for in-state tours to Caldas Novas, Pirenópolis, and Goiás.

Arriving in one of the Pantanal's gateway cities without having a tour already booked isn't a problem. Just be careful when choosing a guide upon arrival—some budget travelers have had bad experiences. To avoid being overcharged, compare prices. Also be sure your guide has adequate equipment, sufficient knowledge about area wildlife, and good English-language skills.

In southern Pantanal you may choose to book tours out of Bonito, where more than a dozen establishments vie for your business—you will need to contact local agents because all local attractions require booking. PantTour is a reliable operator with good knowledge of the best spots in the region.

Pantanal Adventure in Cuiabá, Pérola do Pantanal in Corumbá, and Impacto Turismo in Campo Grande run large tours into the north and south of the Pantanal—including longer river trips in luxurious riverboats (locally known as "hotel-boats") that are equipped with many amenities and comfortable air-conditioned cabins. These boat tours usually stop in fazendas for treks into the wetlands by horseback, 4x4 vehicle, by zodiac, and by foot—whatever it takes to get the best animal sightings. The cost is about R$150 per person, per day, with everything included; most tours last 4–7 days.

🖪 Tour Operators **Ecotur** ⊠ Rua Emílio 21, Pirenópolis ☏ 62/331-1392. **Estação Aventura** ⊠ Rua da Prata 9, Pirenópolis ☏ 62/331-1069. **Impacto Turismo** ⊠ Rua Padre João Crippa 496, Campo Grande ☏ 67/325-1333 ᵬ 67/384-8179 ⊕ www.impactotour.com.br. **Pantanal Adventure** ⊠ Rua Commandante Costa 649, Cuiabá ☏ 65/333-6352 ⊕ www.pantanaladventure.com.br. **Pérola do Pantanal** ⊠ Rua Manoel Cavassa 255, Corumbá ☏ 067/231-1460 ⊕ www.peroladopantanal.com.br. **PantTour** ⊠ Rua Senador Felinto Müller

578, Bonito ☎ 67/255-1000 🖷 67/255-1707. **Pireneus Tour** ✉ Rua 87 No. 560, Suite 106, S. Sul, Goiânia ☎ 62/281-8111 🖷 62/281-8116 ⊕ www.pireneustour.com.br.

VISITOR INFORMATION

BRASÍLIA   Visit the main office of the Federal District Tourism Development Agency (ADETUR). There's a small information kiosk at Praça dos Três Poderes (across from the Panteão da Pátria).

🔝 Brasília Tourist Info **ADETUR** ✉ SDC, Centro de Convenções Ulisses Guimarães, 1st floor ☎ 61/325-5730.

THE WEST   Goiás's AGETUR has a lot of information, but it's far from comprehensive. In Pirenópolis you can collect information at PIRETUR. The staff members in Campo Grande's Morada dos Baís can give you information about everything under the sun in Campo Grande and environs. SEDTUR, in Cuiabá, doesn't have much information; your hotel is probably a better option.

🔝 The West Tourist Info **AGETUR** ✉ Rua 30 at Rua 4, Centro de Convenções, Goiás ☎ 62/217-1000. **Atendimento Turismo** ✉ Praça Central, Bonito ☎ 67/251-1799. **Morada dos Baís: Centro de Informação Turística e Cultura** ✉ Av. Noroeste at Av. Afonso Pena, Campo Grande ☎ 67/324-5830. **PIRETUR** ✉ Rua do Bom Fim s/n, Pirenópolis, ☎ 62/331-1299 Ext. 119. **SEDTUR** ✉ Praça da República 131, Cuiabá ☎ 65/624-9060.

SALVADOR & ENVIRONS

6

Updated by
Joan Gonzalez

IN "THE LAND OF HAPPINESS," as the state of Bahia is known, the sun shines almost every day. Its Atlantic Ocean shoreline runs for 900 km (560 mi), creating beautiful white-sand beaches lined with coconut palms—while inland is Parque Nacional da Chapada Diamantina (Chapada Diamantina National Park), with 152,000 hectares (375,000 acres) of mountains, waterfalls, caves, natural swimming pools, and hiking trails. And in Bahia's capital, Salvador da Bahia, the beat of bongo drums echoing through the narrow cobblestone streets of Pelourinho (the Old Town) is a rhythmic reminder of Brazil's African heritage.

Salvador was the most important port in the southern hemisphere until the 18th century. Although Portuguese navigator and explorer Pedro Alvares Cabral's first sighting of Brazil, on April 22, 1500, was 705 km (438 mi) south of Salvador, at what is now Porto Seguro, Salvador became the first capital of the new country. Portugal's monarch, Dom João III, had established a "captaincy" as the governing body in each district of their New World, with each head reporting directly to Portugal. By 1549 he realized a central authority was needed and appointed Tomé de Sousa as Brazil's first governor-general, with orders to establish a colonial capital in Bahia. Hence the city of Salvador was established on a bluff overlooking the vast Baía de Todos os Santos (All Saints' Bay). Salvador held the honor until 1763, when the capital was moved to Rio de Janeiro. In 1960 the capital was again moved, this time to a new city carved out of the hinterlands and named Brasilia.

Salvador is often called just "Bahia," as if it were the only city in this northeast state, but as attractions in other regions become better known, especially with the opening of new hotels, resorts, and *pousadas* (inns), Salvador may find that it needs to emphasize that although it is in the state of Bahia, its name is Salvador.

Salvador's downtown is built on two levels. The upper level (Cidade Alta) is on the bay side and its historical district is indeed the city's heart. Known locally as Pelourinho, or just Pelô, it is still undergoing a massive restoration started in 1968 by then-mayor António Carlos Magalháes. The project didn't gain momentum until 1991, when the former mayor, having been elected governor of the state for the third time ordered IPAC (Instituto do Patrimóio Artistico e Cultural da Bahia) to study the possibility of restoring the entire area. Today more than 500 of the 2,982 buildings have been restored, earning Salvador the reputation of having the finest examples of baroque architecture in South America. Many of these restored buildings are now occupied by businesses such as bars, restaurants, museums, and shops that sell everything from clothing, film, musical instruments, and handicrafts to precious stones.

The Cidade Baixa (Lower City) fronts the Atlantic Ocean and is known as the Comércio (commercial area). This is where you find most of the luxury hotels, parks, and modern malls. Its star attraction is the Mercado Modelo, the most touristy but also one of the most fascinating places in town, with its impromptu entertainment and dozens of stalls that sell everything from Bahian lace dresses and musical instruments to amulets believed to ward off evil or bring good luck.

Although Brazil's culture is a blend of those of European, African, and indigenous peoples—a blend that is uniquely Brazilian—the historical and cultural influence in Bahia is predominately African. It is estimated that more than 4 million slaves were brought to Brazil from Africa during the 1500s to work sugar plantations in Portugal's colonies. By contrast, only around 600,000 were shipped to the United States. It was the large slave population in Brazil that enabled Africans to retain their customs more easily there than in other countries. The indigenous tribes, forced to work with the Portuguese to harvest *pau-brasil* (brazilwood) trees either fled inland to escape slavery or were integrated into the European and African cultures.

On June 7, 1494, representatives of the crowned heads of Spain and Portugal met in Tordesillas, Spain, and signed the Treaty of Tordesillas. Spain was exploring the Pacific side of the South American continent and Portugal the Atlantic. An imaginary line was drawn from the Arctic to Antarctica, and "for the sake of peace and concord," the two countries agreed not to invade or lay claim to any present or future discoveries in the other's territory.

Unfortunately, although Spain and Portugal held to the agreement, it had not been signed by the French, English, or Dutch. Though the French and English posed no real threat to Brazil, the Dutch ignored the treaty and in 1602 set up the powerful Dutch East India Company, destroying Portugal's Asian spice-trade monopoly. They also started taking a keen interest in Brazil's profitable sugar enterprises and even sent botanists to catalog the nation's flora. In 1621, convinced that sugar was a hot commodity, they launched an all-out attack on northeastern Brazil and took over several captaincies. However, the Portuguese fought on and finally drove the Dutch out in 1654.

Today Bahia is waging a different battle. As Brazil's fourth-largest state, it is struggling to juggle a tremendous growth spurt while preserving as much of its natural assets as possible. The race is on to keep its rivers pure and to preserve the Atlantic rain forests, coral reefs, beaches, mangroves, swamplands, and Chapada Diamantina mountain range with its strange rock formations, caves, and waterfalls. Vast areas are being designated as parks and protected areas in a valiant effort to strike a balance between progress and preservation. But one thing will never change—Salvador, Bahia's capital, will always be exuberantly alive with the music, art, dance, religions, and cuisine of Africa.

About the Restaurants

Brazilians love to eat and they love to eat out. Breakfast may be just a cup of coffee (or rather, half coffee and half hot milk), but lunches are large and dinners are even bigger. Dinner starts late, usually after 9. Thimble-size cups of strong sweet coffee keep Brazilians going between meals, a habit easy to pick up if you're a coffee lover. Restaurants often serve hot pepper sauce on the side of all dishes, along with farofa or farinha, which do a delicious job of soaking up sauces. And most Bahian restaurants are happy to prepare simpler fish or shrimp dishes even if they're not on the menu.

6

If you have 5 days

If you are arriving in 🏨 **Salvador ❶ – ⓭** ⚐ on an overseas flight, spend your first day resting. Have dinner at one of the city's best, Trapiche Adelaide, or see a show at Solar do Unháo (reserve ahead). On your second day start early exploring Pelourinho to get the flavor of Salvador and have a light lunch at Uauá, in an old colonial house, or Escola Senac (reservations essential). After lunch continue your exploration of the historic district then take the **Elevador Lacerda** down to the **Mercado Modelo ❿** for an eclectic shopping experience. On the third day take a guided tour on a schooner or go on your own by ferry, catamaran, or *peguena lancha* (small boat) across the Bay of All Saints to the **Ilha de Itaparica (Itaparica Island)** and spend a pleasant day on its beaches. On the fourth day either take a guided tour or, for more freedom, rent a car and visit the fishing village of **Santo Antônio**—about a two-hour drive north of Salvador. Walk over the sand dunes to the beach for a swim, buy some handicrafts from the villagers sitting on their porches along the only street, and head back toward Salvador, stopping at the former fishing village (now a tourist village) of **Praia do Forte** for lunch at the Pousada Sobrado da Vila. Buy some more handicrafts and visit the **Projeto Tamar** at the end of the street along the beach before returning to your hotel in Salvador. On the fifth day finish your shopping or exploring, and then relax until your return flight.

If you have 7 days

Follow the itinerary above, but on Day 4 check in at the Pousada Porto da Lua in 🏨 **Praia do Forte** for three nights. The pousada is on Praia do Forte's 7-mi white-sand beach near the **Projeto Tamar.** Have lunch at your pousada and then relax and enjoy this laid-back former fishing village. If you're there during turtle-hatching season, you can help baby turtles find their way back to their home at sea. Activities include sailing, windsurfing, horseback riding, and visiting nearby parks, rivers, and forests.

If you have 10 days

Follow the seven-day itinerary, but on the fourth day check in for just two nights in 🏨 **Praia do Forte**. On the sixth day take a bus, rent a car, or fly on Nordeste Airlines to Lençóis, in the interior of Bahia. Go hiking, horseback riding, exploring caves, swimming in natural pools, or mountain climbing, or just absorb one of Bahia's most beautiful reserves, 🏞 **Parque Nacional da Chapada Diamantina.** In the small colonial town of Lençóis stay at the Pousada de Lençóis or the Canto das Aguas hotel. If you have a rental car, an alternative is to stay in the nearby town of Andaraí at the Pousada Sincorá. The owners speak English, and you're just a short hike away for some spectacular scenery. Spend two full days in Chapada Diamantina and return to 🏨 **Salvador ❶ – ⓭** for an overnight. If you are flying between Salvador and Lençóis, it may be possible to connect with your flight back home, which would give you an extra day in the reserve. Alternatively, if you only want to unpack once in 10 days, spend your entire vacation at the 🏨 **Costa Do Sauípe Resort** 76 km (47 mi) north of Salvador.

About the Hotels

Lodging options range from modern high-rises with an international clientele and world-class service to cozy, family-run *pousadas* (inns) on remote beaches or in fishing villages. Apartment hotels, where guest quarters have kitchens and living rooms as well as bedrooms, are also options.

WHAT IT COSTS In Reais				
	$$$$	**$$$**	**$$**	**$**	**¢**
RESTAURANTS	over $60	$45–$60	$30–$45	$15–$30	under $15
HOTELS	over $500	$375–$500	$250–$375	$125–$250	under $125

Restaurant prices are for a dinner entrée. Hotel prices are for two people in a standard double room in high season, excluding taxes.

Exploring Bahia

Bahia has many good secondary roads and excellent highways, making a rental car an option if you like to explore on your own. The best driving tour is from Salvador north along the coast, picking up the Linha Verde (Green Highway, an extension of BA 099) at Praia do Forte. Along the way are fishing villages, endless beaches, restaurants, and small hotels and pousadas. Public bus service is excellent.

To visit most attractions south of Salvador, since there is good local air service, the best choice is to fly between cities and then rent a car or contact a local tour operator, especially if you are visiting Porto Seguro (723 km/450 mi from Salvador) or Caravelas (865 km/537 mi from Salvador) for a boat trip to the Arquipelago de Abrolhos (Abrolhos Archipelago), Bahia's first underwater marine park. The main highway between Salvador and the border of the state of Espírito Santo—BR 101— runs 65 km (40 mi) or more inland and not along the coastal beaches.

Chapada Diamantina, Bahia's largest designated Environmental Protection Area, is 427 km (265 mi) inland and is one of Bahia's most spectacular attractions. Comfortable buses make the 7- to 8-hour trip between Salvador and Lençóis, the nearest town to Chapada Diamantina, twice a day. There is a good airport 25 km (16 mi) from Lençóis, but there are not, at this writing, any regularly scheduled flights from Salvador. Check with your international carrier or with domestic airlines in Brazil, as flight information is changing rapidly.

Bahia's most beautiful coastal area is the Costa do Coqueiros (Coconut Coast), with 190 km (118 mi) of beautiful beaches that run north from the outskirts of Salvador to the village of Mangue Seco, on the border of the state of Sergipe. The city of Salvador has 50 km (31 mi) of beaches fronting its many neighborhoods, including those around Baía de Todos os Santos (All Saint's Bay). The closest beach to the center of town and the one with the best swimming area is Porto da Barra, a bay with calm waters, where Tomé de Souza, the city's founder, first arrived. The coastal areas south of Salvador are the Dendê Coast, where the palms

6

Bahian Cuisine

When African slaves arrived in Bahia, they insinuated coconut milk, *dendê* (palm) oil, and hot spices into Portuguese and Indian dishes, transforming them into something quite new. Additional basic raw materials are lemon, coriander, tomato, onions, dried shrimp, salt, and hot chili peppers. Seafood is the thing in Bahia, and most regional seafood dishes are well seasoned, if not fiery hot. The ubiquitous *moqueca* is a regional seafood stew made with fish and/or shellfish, dendê oil, coconut milk, onions, and tomatoes, cooked quickly in a clay pot over a high flame. Other classics include *vatapá*, a thick puréelike stew made with fish, shrimp, cashews, peanuts, and a variety of seasonings; *caruru*, okra mashed with ginger, dried shrimp, and palm oil; *ximxim de galinha*, chicken marinated in lemon or lime juice, garlic, and salt and pepper and then cooked with dendê and peanut oil, coconut milk, tomatoes, and seasonings; and *efo*, a bitter chicorylike vegetable cooked with dried shrimp. A popular snack is *acarajé*, a pastry deep-fried in palm oil and filled with mashed *feijão fradinho* (black-eyed peas or beans), usually eaten with *camarão* (sun-dried shrimp) and *pimenta* (hot-pepper sauce). A variation is *abará*, peas or beans boiled in a banana leaf instead of fried. Note that palm oil is high in saturated fat and hard to digest; you can order these dishes without it.

Beaches

The Atlantic waters that wash in over the sands are warm year-round. From Bahia's capital of Salvador north to the state of Sergipe and south to the state of Espírito Santo are 900 km (560 mi) of beautiful beaches. Most beaches are wall-to-wall people on the weekends. If you don't mind a crowd, it's fun to soak up both sun and beach culture, which includes live music, sand sports, the briefest of swimwear, firewater drinks, and spicy seafood snacks. Few beaches have functioning bathrooms, though some have public showers that run on one-minute tokens that cost only a few centavos. Don't leave belongings unattended. The comfortable *ônibus executivo* (executive bus; marked ROTEIRO DAS PRAIAS) runs from Praça da Sé to Flamengo Beach, stopping at all the beaches along the way. As a rule, the farther away from the port the better is the beach.

Carnaval

As Bahia's distinctive *axé* music (a merging of African, Jamaican, and typical Bahian) rhythms have gained popularity, so has Salvador's Carnaval (Carnival), competing with Rio de Janeiro's more traditional and elaborate celebrations. In Salvador, Carnaval means dancing night after night through the streets following the earsplitting music of *trios elétricos* (bands on sound trucks); watching parades of groups such as the Filhos de Gandhi (Sons of Gandhi), a Carnaval association founded by striking stevedores in 1949, whose members dress in white tunics and turbans—the relics of Africa's Muslim conversions; and it means moving freely to ancient, mesmerizing rhythms produced by such famous percussion groups as Ilê Aiyê and Casa do Olodum. This movable feast formally lasts a week in February or March but begins in spirit January 1 with the Bom Jesus dos Navegantes (Festival of the Good Jesus of the Mariners). Hundreds of boats paddle, sail, or motor through All Saints' Bay carrying the image of the Bom Jesus dos Navegantes from Conceic(cx)ão da Praia church to the chapel at Boa Viagem, a procession of faith, and continues into Lent in small towns outside Salvador with street festivals called *micaretas*.

grow that produce palm oil used in Bahian cooking; the Cocoa Coast, where cocoa beans are produced; the Discovery Coast at Porto Seguro, where the Portuguese first landed; and the Whale Coast near Bahia's southern towns of Caravelas and Alcobaça. You can catch a boat from Caravelas to the Abrolhos Archipelago, where humpback whales go to mate and give birth from June to November.

Timing

Peak seasons are from November to April (South American summer) and the month of July, when schools have breaks. Make reservations far in advance for stays during these months, especially if you plan to visit during Carnaval (February or March). As the weather is sunny and warm year-round, consider a trip in the off-season, when prices are lower and the beaches less crowded.

SALVADOR

Though the city of Salvador, founded in 1549, lost its status as capital of Brazil in 1763 when that honor was given to Rio (and later to Brasília), it remains the capital of Bahia. At least 70% of its 2,250,000 population is classified as Afro-Brazilian. African rhythms roll forth everywhere—from buses and construction sites to the rehearsals of percussion groups. The scents of coriander, coconut, and palm oil waft around corners, where turbaned women in voluminous lace-trim white dresses cook and sell local delicacies.

Churches whose interiors are covered with gold leaf were financed by the riches of the Portuguese colonial era, when slaves masked their religious beliefs under a thin Catholic veneer. And partly thanks to modern-day acceptance of those beliefs, Salvador has become the fount of Candomblé, a religion based on personal dialogue with the *orixás*, a family of African deities closely linked to both nature and the Catholic saints. The influence of Salvador's African heritage on Brazilian music has also turned this city into one of the most stirring places to spend Carnaval, the bacchanalian fling that precedes Lent and only one of more than 20 festivals punctuating the local calendar.

Exploring Salvador

Salvador sprawls across a peninsula surrounded by the Baía de Todos os Santos on one side and the Atlantic Ocean on the other. The original city, referred to as the Cidade Histórica (Historic City), is divided into the *Cidade Alta* (Upper City) and *Cidade Baixa* (Lower City). The Cidade Baixa is a commercial area—known as Comércio—that runs along the port and is the site of Salvador's largest market, Mercado Modelo. You can move between the Upper and Lower cities on foot, by *comum* (taxi; literally, common), or via the landmark Elevador Lacerda, behind the market.

From the Cidade Histórica you can travel north along the bay to the Forte Monte Serrat and the hilltop Igreja de Nosso Senhor do Bonfim. You can also head south to the point, guarded by the Forte Santo Antônio da Barra, where the bay waters meet those of the Atlantic. Salvador's southern tip is home to the trendy neighborhoods of Vitória, Barra, Ondina, and Rio Vermelho, which are full of museums, theaters, shops, and restaurants. The beaches that run north from the tip and along the Atlantic coast are among the city's cleanest. Many are illuminated at night and have bars and restaurants that stay open late. Consider a guided tour as an introduction to Salvador.

Numbers in the text correspond to numbers in the margin and on the Salvador Cidade Histórica map.

Cidade Alta

The Cidade Alta neighborhood of Pelourinho, or Pelô, is on UNESCO's list of World Heritage sites and is a captivating blend of European and African cultures. It contains some of the most significant examples of colonial and baroque architecture in the Americas. Along its winding and sometimes steep streets, whose cobbles were laid by slaves, restored 17th- and 18th-century buildings, now house museums, galleries, shops, and cafés. The buildings, all freshly painted in bright pastel colors, add to the festive atmosphere of Cidade Alta, along with the sounds of street musicians and their *axé* music, a blend of local, African, and Jamaican rhythms.

A GOOD WALK Early morning is a good time for a walk in Cidade Alta, Salvador's historic Pelourinho neighborhood. Whether coming by taxi or bus (there's a bus terminal nearby on Rua Chile), start at the **Elevador Lacerda** ▶. If arriving at the lower level, take the elevator to the Upper City, exiting onto the Municipal Square (mainly a parking lot), where you have a spectacular view of the Todos os Santos Bay and, unfortunately, also of the "temporary" mayor's office (erected around 1987, it was supposed to have been replaced in two years), an oblong cement building on columns with large, round, yellow pipes around the sides. Also on the square is the **Palácio Rio Branco** ❶. Turn left onto Rua da Misericórdia, heading northeast past the Igreja da Misericórdia and through the Praça da Sé (named after a colonial church, the Igreja da Sé, which was demolished in 1933) to the large square, **Terreiro de Jesus** ❷. On your left, at the northwest end of the square, is the 17th-century **Catedral Basílica** ❸. Next to the cathedral is the **Museu Afro-Brasileiro** ❹. From here walk along the south side of the Terreiro de Jesus Square and through the Praça Anchieta, with its statue of the patron saint of Salvador, São Francisco de Xavier, on a cross—to the 18th-century baroque **Igreja de São Francisco** ❺ and the Igreja da Ordem Terceira de São Francisco. Walk back to the Terreiro de Jesus Square, turn right when you reach the square to the **Igreja São Domingos de Gusmão da Ordem Terceira** ❻. Continue to **Fundação Casa de Jorge Amada/Museu da Cidade** ❼, where you can see memorabilia of the author of such famous titles as *Dona Flor e Seus dos Maridos* (*Dona Flor and Her Two Husbands*), as well as exhibits on Candomblé. The Rua Alfredo de Brito leads into the famed plaza called **Largo do Pelourinho** ❽. To the north stands the baroque **Igreja de Nossa Senhora do Rosário dos Pretos** ❾. If you're hungry, a good place for a restful lunch is Casa de Gamboa, south of the Largo de Pelourinho.

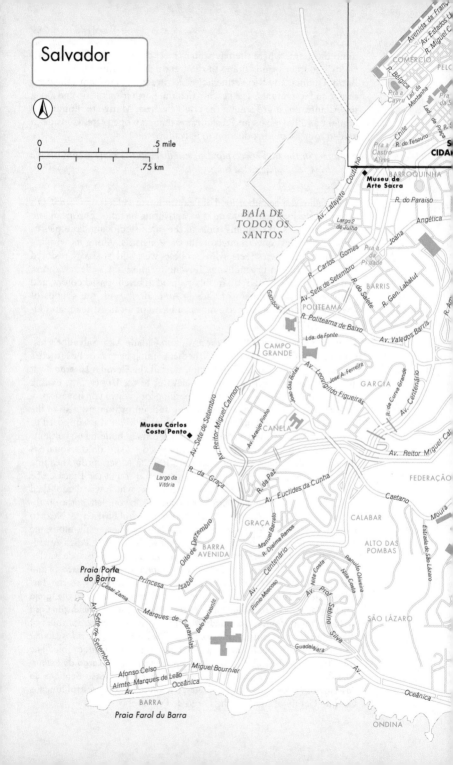

da Fran,
Estados Unidos
R. Miguel Calmon
O
PELOURINHO

1 - 12

SETE PORTAS
José Joaquim Seabra
SAÚDE
Lad. do Hospital
NAZARÉ
R. STO. AGOSTINHO
Bandeirantes
MATATU

Pra a
da S
Terreiro
de Jesus
R. S. Francisco
José
**SEE SALVADOR
CIDADE HISTÓRICO
MAP**

NHA

so

élica

Av. Castelo Branco

Iltana Angélica

R. da Telebahia

Lad. do Pepino

R. Frederico Costa

Bonocô

R. Cosme de Farias

Av. Leal

R. B. Vista de Brotas
R. Afonso de Carvalho Filho

Av. Dom João VI

DANIE
LISBO

R. Amparo do Tororó

Av. Presidente Costa E. Silva

DIQUE DO
TORORÓ

Av. General Graça Lessa

Urbino de Aguiar

N. Sra do
Guadalupe

ENGENHO VELHO
DE BROTAS

Lad. do

Av. Vasco da Gama

VILA
AMÉRICA

GARCIA

R. Ferreira Santos

ACUPE

Miguel Calmon

ALTO DO
SOBRADINHO

Moura

RAÇÃO

Av. Garibaldi

R. Sérgio de Carvalho

Ladeira do Bogum

ENGENGO VELHO
DA FEDERAÇÃO

R. Apolinário de Santana

R. das Palmeiras

R. Dep. Newton
Moura Costa

CAMPUS
UFBA

Av. Cardeal da Silva

Parque
Jo o XXIII

R. Adémar de Barros

R. Macapá

Parque
Zoobot nico

Av. Garibaldi

R. Almirante Barroso

R. João Gomes

ca

Av. Oceânica

TO PRAIA C
PRA
PRAIA STE

TIMING Simply walking this route will take about three hours. Pelourinho, with its music, cafés, restaurants, and shops, is a place that can be explored several times over a period of days and yet always seem new.

WHAT TO SEE **Catedral Basílica.** Hints of Asia permeate this 17th-century masterpiece, ❸ though it is a rather simple structure. Note the Asian facial features and clothing of the figures in the transept altars; the 16th-century tiles from Macao in the sacristy; and the intricate ivory-and-tortoiseshell inlay from Goa on the Japiassu family altar, third on the right as you enter. A Jesuit who lived in China painted the ceiling over the cathedral entrance. ✉ *Terreiro de Jesus, Pelourinho* ☎ *071/321–4573* 🎟 *Free* ⊘ *Tues.–Sat. 8–11 and 3–6, Sun. 5–6:30.*

❼ **Fundação Casa de Jorge Amado/Museu da Cidade.** The Jorge Amado House contains Bahia's most beloved writer's photos and book covers, as well as a lecture room. Amado lived in the Hotel Pelourinho when it was a student house, and he set the locale of many of his books in this part of the city. Next door is the Museu da Cidade, with exhibitions on Candomblé orixás. ✉ *Rua Alfredo Brito and Largo do Pelourinho, Pelourinho* ☎ *071/321–0122* 🎟 *R$3* ⊘ *Fundação weekdays 9:30 AM–10 PM. Museum Tues.–Fri. 10–5, weekends 1–5.*

❾ **Igreja de Nossa Senhora do Rosário dos Pretos.** Guides tend to skip over the Church of Our Lady of the Rosary of the Blacks, which was built in a baroque style by and for slaves between 1704 and 1796. It's worth a look at the side altars to see statues of the Catholic church's few black saints. Each has a fascinating story. ✉ *Ladeira do Pelourinho s/n, Pelourinho* ☎ *No phone* 🎟 *Free* ⊘ *Weekdays 8–5, weekends 8–2.*

❻ **Igreja São Domingos de Gusmão da Ordem Terceira.** The baroque Church of the Third Order of St. Dominic (1723) houses a collection of carved processional saints and other sacred objects. Such sculptures often had hollow interiors and were used to smuggle gold into Portugal to avoid taxes. Asian details in the church decoration are evidence of long-ago connections with Portugal's colonies of Goa and Macau. Upstairs are two impressive rooms with carved wooden furniture used for lay brothers' meetings and receptions. ✉ *Terreiro de Jesus, Pelourinho* ☎ *071/242–4185* 🎟 *Free* ⊘ *Mon.–Sat. 8–noon and 2–5.*

❺ **Igreja de São Francisco.** The famous 18th-century baroque Church of St. FodorsChoice Francis has an active monastery. Listen for the sound of African drums ★ in the square outside as you take in the ceiling, painted in 1774 by José Joaquim da Rocha, a mulatto who founded Brazil's first art school. The ornate cedar-and-rosewood interior writhes with images of mermaids, acanthus leaves, and caryatids—all bathed in gold leaf. Guides say that there's as much as a ton of gold here, but restoration experts maintain there's much less, as the leaf used is just a step up from a powder. A Sunday-morning alternative to crowded beaches is to attend a mass here (9–11 and 11–11:45). Stay until the end, when the lights go off, to catch the wondrous subtlety of gold leaf under natural light. The **Ordem Terceira de São Francisco** (☎ *071/321–6968*), part of the complex, has an 18th-century Spanish plateresque sandstone facade—the only of its kind in Brazil—that is carved to resemble Spanish silver altars that are made by beating

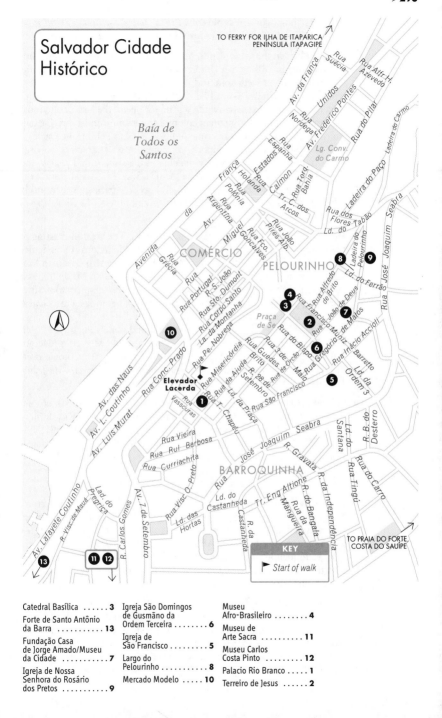

Salvador Cidade Histórico

Baía de Todos os Santos

TO FERRY FOR ILHA DE ITAPARICA
PENÍNSULA ITAPAGIPE

COMÉRCIO

PELOURINHO

Praça de Sé

Elevador Lacerda

BARROQUINHA

KEY

⚑ Start of walk

TO PRAIA DO FORTE,
COSTA DO SAUÍPE

the metal into wooden molds. ✉ *Praça Padre Anchieta, Pelourinho* ☎ *071/322–6430* 🎫 *Free* 🕙 *Mon.–Sat. 8–noon and 2–5, Sun. 8–noon.*

★ ❽ **Largo do Pelourinho** (Pelourinho Square). This small plaza commemorates the day in 1888 when Dom Pedro II freed the slaves. It was at this spot where slaves were sold and tied to a pillory and publicly beaten, which was legal in Brazil until 1835 (the word *pelourinho* means "whipping post"). The plaza is now the setting for one of the largest and most charming groupings of Brazilian colonial architecture and a thriving cultural renaissance. There are four public stages in Pelourinho, at least two of which have music nightly, all named after characters in Jorge Amado novels. There is usually dancing in the streets on Tuesday and Sunday evenings. The **Dia & Noite** (☎ 071/322–2525) association organizes Largo do Pelourinho's music shows. It publishes a monthly schedule that's available in tourist offices and hotels. ✉ *Rua Alfredo de Brito at Ladeira do Taboão.*

❹ **Museu Afro-Brasileiro** (Afro-Brazilian Museum). The most interesting of
FodorśChoice the three museums in the Antiga Facilidade de Medicinos (Old Faculty
★ of Medicine) building and former Jesuit school is the Afro-Brazilian Museum, next to the Catedral Basílica. The Afro-Brazilian Museum has a collection of more than 1,200 pieces of a religious or spiritual nature, including pottery, sculpture, tapestry, weavings, paintings, crafts, carvings, and photographs. There's an interesting display on the meanings of Candomblé orixás, with huge carved wood panels portraying each one. The other two museums are the Memorial de Medicina (Memorial to the Old Faculty of Medicine) and the Museu Arqueologia e Etnologia (Archaeology and Ethnology Museum). ✉ *Terreiro de Jesus, Pelourinho* ☎ *071/321–0983* 🎫 *R$3* 🕙 *Weekdays 9–5.*

❶ **Palácio Rio Branco.** Salvador's Chamber of Commerce and Bahíatursa, the state tourist office, now occupy the beautiful Palácio Rio Branco, erected on the Municipal Square in 1919 for the governor of Bahia. This was the site of the original headquarters of the colonial government of Brazil. The large square is near the entrance to the Elevador Lacerda, which connects upper and lower Salvador. ✉ *Rua Chile 2, Pelourinho* ☎ *071/241–4333* 🕙 *Tues.–Sat. 10–6.*

❷ **Terreiro de Jesus.** A large square with three churches and a small crafts fair, Terreiro de Jesus opens the way to historic Salvador. Where nobles once strolled under imperial palm trees, men today practice capoeira— a stylized dancelike fight with African origins—to the *thwang* of the *berimbau,* a rudimentary bow-shape musical instrument. If you stop to watch and take photographs of the capoeira fighters, you are expected to leave a financial contribution.

Cidade Baixa & Beyond

The Lower City is Bahia's commercial and financial center. In the port large cruise ships and small boats jockey for space. Ferryboats and catamarans leave from here for Ilha de Itaparica (Itaparica Island). It is busy during the day but is practically deserted at night, especially near the base of the Lacerda Elevator. Take a taxi between restaurants or hotels at night.

A GOOD WALK You can travel between the Cidade Alta and the Cidade Baixa aboard the popular **Elevador Lacerda** ☛. Exiting the elevator in the Lower City, cross the Praça Visconde de Cairú to the **Mercado Modelo** ⑩ for some shopping and people-watching. From here you have several options. If you head north along the bay and past the port, you come to the terminal where you can catch a ferry or hop a schooner for **Ilha de Itaparica.** Or you can head due south by cab to one of several museums: the **Museu de Arte Sacra** ⑪, with its religious paintings, or the **Museu Carlos Costa Pinto** ⑫, with art and artifacts gathered by private collectors. Another option is to visit the tip of the peninsula, which is marked by the **Forte de Santo Antônio da Barra** ⑬, with its lighthouse, a nautical museum, and a popular beach.

TIMING No need to arise at dawn, but the earlier you get started the better for a full yet relaxing day. If you're starting from the Upper City, take the elevator down to the Mercado Modelo. The market can easily be done in an hour unless you're really in a browsing mood and want to visit all 300-plus stalls. The trip to either the nearby Ilha de Itaparica or to one or more of the museums will fill up a leisurely afternoon, with time for lunch.

WHAT TO SEE **Elevador Lacerda.** For just a few centavos, ascend 236 feet in a minute ☛ in this elevator that runs between the Praça Municipal, in the Upper City, and Praça Visconde de Cairú and the Mercado Modelo. Built in 1872, the elevator ran on hydraulics until its 1930 restoration, when it was electrified. Bahians joke that the elevator is the only way to "go up" in life. A word of caution—when the elevator is crowded, watch out for pickpockets.

⑬ **Forte de Santo Antônio da Barra.** Fort St. Anthony has guarded Salvador since 1583. The lighthouse, Farol da Barra, wasn't built until 1696, after many a ship wrecked on the coral reefs and sandbanks. The fort now houses the **Museu Nautico** (☎ 071/264–3296), with exhibitions of old maps, navigational equipment, artillery, model vessels, and remnants of shipwrecks found by Brazil's first underwater archaeological research team. The museum is open Tuesday–Sunday 9–7. An eatery, Café do Farol, is open Tuesday through Sunday, from 9 AM to 11 PM. The Praia (beach) do Farol da Barra, which starts at the fort and runs east along Avenida Oceánica, is calm, with small waves, and is popular with locals, especially on weekends. ⌧ *Av. 7 de Setembro s/n, Barra* ☎ *No phone* 🖅 *R$2* ☼ *Thurs.–Tues. 9–7.*

★ **Ilha de Itaparica.** The largest of 56 islands in the Baía de Todos os Santos, Itaparica, was originally settled because its ample supply of fresh mineral water was believed to have rejuvenating qualities. Its beaches are calm and shallow, thanks to the surrounding reefs. The ferry ride takes 45 minutes. Another option is a slightly longer but very pleasant schooner cruise and tour that can include lunch and music. You can always take a schooner to the island, opt out of the tour group lunch, and take a taxi to the restaurant of your choice. Then you can enjoy an afternoon stroll before catching the ferry back to Salvador. Fares range from US$2 to US$10, depending on services. Catamarans, ferries, and *pequena lanchas* (small boats) leave for the island every hour. **Bahiatursa** (⊠ On right, just before exit to Mercado Modelo, Praça Visconde de Cayru 250 ☎ 071/241–0242) can provide information. The office is open Monday–Saturday 9–6 and Sunday 9–2. Volkswagen vans (*kombis*) provide transportation around the island. ⊠ *Ferries and catamarans leave from Terminal São Joaquim at other end of Porto de Salvador, Av. da França. Small boats leave from Terminal Turítico Maritimo in front of Mercado Modelo.*

⑩ Mercado Modelo. This enclosed market may not be the cheapest place to buy handicrafts—and you do have to bargain—but it must be experienced. Some of the many items you find here are *cachaça* (a strong Brazilian liquor made from sugarcane), cashew nuts, pepper sauces, cigars, manioc flour, dried shrimp (an integral part of Bahian cooking), leather goods, hammocks, lace, musical instruments, African sculptures, and gems. Outside, you can hear the nasal-voiced *repentistas,* folksingers who make up songs on the spot. Notice the blue *azulejos* on the building with Gothic-style windows. If you are entering the market from the back (having come down the Elevador Lacerda from the Upper City, just inside the door along the back wall are a post office and a tourist office where you can pick up maps and brochures. ⊠ *Praça Visconde de Cayru 250, Comércio* ☎ *Free* ☉ *Mon.–Sat. 9–6, Sun. 9–2.*

⑪ Museu de Arte Sacra. Housed in a former Carmelite monastery, the museum and the adjoining Igreja de Santa Teresa (St. Theresa Church) are two of Salvador's best-cared-for repositories of religious objects. An in-house restoration team has worked miracles that bring alive Bahia's 1549–1763 golden age as Brazil's capital and main port. See the silver altar in the church, moved here from the demolished Sé (Church), and the blue-and-yellow-tile sacristy replete with a bay view. ⊠ *Rua do Sodré 276, Centro* ☎ *071/243–6511* ☎ *R$5* ☉ *Weekdays 11:30–5:30.*

⑫ Museu Carlos Costa Pinto. A collection of more than 3,000 objects, including furniture, crystal, silver pieces, and paintings collected from around the world by a wealthy couple, is on display at this museum. Among the collection are examples of gold and silver *balangandãs* (or *pencas*), chains with large silver charms in the shapes of tropical fruits and fish, which were worn by slave women around the waist. A prized slave was given a chain by her master, who continued to reward loyalty and service with gifts of charms, sometimes freeing the slave after her chain was full. The balangandã usually included a *figa*—a closed fist with a thumb sticking out through the fingers—which, according to African legend, could increase warriors' fertility. In Brazil it's simply considered a good-luck charm. For it to work, though, it must always be a gift. ⊠ *Av. 7 de Setembro 2490, Vitória* ☎ *071/336–6081* ☎ *R$11* ☉ *Mon. and Wed.–Fri. 2:30–7, weekends 3–6.*

Urban beaches. In general, the farther east and northeast from the lighthouse point, the better are the city beaches. Some Salvadorans, especially singles, swear by the Cidade Baixa beaches **Praia Porto da Barra** and **Praia Farol da Barra,** which are frequented by a colorful mix of people who live nearby and tourists staying at neighboring hotels. To avoid large crowds, don't go on weekends. Regardless of when you go, keep an eye on your belongings; petty thievery has been reported. There are no bathrooms, but you can rent a beach chair for about R$2. The corner of Porto da Barra closest to the Grande Hotel da Barra is a gay hangout. Porto da Barra is north from the lighthouse, while the Farol da Barra starts at the lighthouse and goes around the corner east along Avenida Oceánica to the hotel districts of Ondina and Rio Vermelho, where the beaches intermittently suffer pollution problems. One of the nicest beaches along Avenida Oceánica is **Praia Corsário** (Third Bridge Beach), a wide stretch popular with surfers and the young crowd. There are beach huts where you can sit in the shade and enjoy seafood and an ice-cold beer or soft drink from the kiosks. The beach follows Avenida Oceánica and Avenida Otávio Mangabeira northeast past the convention center and is near the Parque Metropolitan de Pituaçu. Another nice beach is the **Praia Itapuã**, near the Sofitel hotel and the Farol de Itapuã. The next good beach is **Praia Stella Maris,** also popular with surfers and the young crowd. It is 18 km (11 mi) north of downtown.

Elsewhere on the Península Itapagipe

There's a tendency to think of the Itapagipe Peninsula as Salvador, but, actually, Salvador only occupies the small southern tip of the V-shape peninsula. To the west of the peninsula is the Baía de Todos os Santos, which flows into the Atlantic Ocean at the peninsula's tip. Some of Bahia's most beautiful beaches are along the southern coast of the peninsula.

WHAT TO SEE **Igreja de Nosso Senhor do Bonfim.** A procession of women dressed in petticoat-puffed Empire-waist white dresses and adorned with turbans and ritual necklaces comes here the Thursday before the third Sunday in January to wash the steps with holy water. Built in the 1750s, the simple church has many ex-votos—wax, wooden, and plaster replicas of body parts—objects of devoted prayer believed to be capable of miraculous cures. Many figures in Catholicism have a counterpart deity in Candomblé; Nosso Senhor do Bonfim's is Oxalá, the father of all the gods and goddesses. Thus are the seemingly bizarre mixture of figurines found in the shops opposite the church: St. George and the Dragon, devils, Indians, monks, sailors, and warriors, plus ex-votos that include house keys and Volkswagens for the devotees of consumerism. ⊠ *Praça do Senhor do Bonfim, Alto do Bonfim, 8 km (5 mi) north of Historical District, near Baía de Todos os Santos* ☎ *071/316–2196* 🎟 *Free* ☉ *Tues.–Sun. 8–noon and 2:30–6:30.*

Forte Monte Serrat. Built in 1500 and named for the Shrine of the Black Virgin at Montserrat, near Barcelona, the white fort is still used by the Brazilian military. There's a church by the same name nearby, rarely open, with a renowned carving of St. Peter. ⊠ *Follow Av. Oscar Pontes along Baía de Todos os Santos north from Lower City to the point just before Bonfim church* 🎟 *Free* ☉ *Tues.–Sun. 9:30–noon and 1:30–5:30.*

Where to Eat

You can easily find restaurants serving Bahian specialties in Barra, a neighborhood full of bars and sidewalk cafés. There are also many good spots

CloseUp

SPIRITUAL SALVADOR

BRAZIL IS OFFICIALLY A ROMAN CATHOLIC COUNTRY and evidence of that can be found everywhere. There are beautiful churches and cathedrals—from the colonial to the baroque to the modern—across the nation. Most Brazilians wear a religious medal or two, bus and taxi drivers place pictures of St. Christopher prominently in their vehicles, and two big winter celebrations (in June) honor St. John and St. Peter. For many Brazilians, however, the real church is that of the spirits.

When Africans were forced aboard slave ships, they may have left their families and possessions behind, but they brought along an impressive array of gods. Foremost among them were Olorum, the creator; Yemanja, the goddess of the rivers and water; Oxalá, the god of procreation and the harvest; and Exú, a trickster spirit who could cause mischief or bring about death. Of lesser rank but still very powerful were Ogun, Obaluayê, Oxôssi, and Yansan, to name but a few.

The Catholic Church, whose spiritual seeds were planted in Brazil alongside the rows of sugarcane and cotton, was naturally against such religious beliefs. As a compromise, the slaves took on the rituals of Rome but kept their old gods. Thus, new religions—Candomblé in Bahia, Macumba in Rio, Xangó in Pernambuco, Umbanda in São Paulo—were born.

Yemanja had her equivalent in the Virgin Mary and was queen of the heavens as well as queen of the seas; the powerful Oxalá became associated with Jesus Christ; and Exú, full of deception to begin with, became Satan. Other gods were likened to saints: Ogun to St. Anthony, Obaluayê to St. Francis, Oxôssi to St. George, Yansan to St. Barbara. On their altars, crosses and statues of the Virgin, Christ, and saints sit beside offerings of sacred white feathers, magical beads, and bowls of cooked rice and cornmeal.

Salvadorans are eager to share their rituals with visitors, though often for a fee (you can make arrangements through hotels or tour agencies). The Candomblé temple ceremony, in which believers sacrifice animals and become possessed by gods, is performed nightly except during Lent.

Temples, usually in poor neighborhoods at the city's edge, don't allow photographs or video or sound recordings. You shouldn't wear black (white is preferable) or revealing clothing. The ceremony is long and repetitive, and there are often no chairs and there's no air-conditioning; men and women are separated.

A pãe de santo or mãe de santo (Candomblé priest or priestess) can perform a reading of the búzios for you; the small brown shells are thrown like jacks into a circle of beads—the pattern they form tells about your life. Don't select your mãe or pãe de santo through an ad or sign, as many shell readers who advertise are best not at fortune-telling but at saying "100 dollars, please" in every language.

in bohemian Rio Vermelho and a slew of places along the beachfront drive beginning around Jardim de Alah and also in Pelourinho. It's wise to order meat only in *churrascarias* (barbecued-meat restaurants) and to avoid it in seafood places. You may discover that in Bahia one main course easily serves two; ask about portions when you order. Don't order the spicy dishes unless you are used to highly spiced food.

African

$-$$ ✕ **Casa do Benin.** Both a restaurant and a museum, Casa do Benin honors the West African country of Benin, home to many of the slaves brought to Bahia. The cuisine is strictly Bahian, a blend of the Old and New worlds. Fish and shrimp are the featured dishes. Reservations are essential September through February. ⊠ *Rua Padre Agostinho Gomes 17, Pelourinho* ☎ *071/326–3127* ▤ *AE, DC, MC* ⊙ *Closed Mon.*

Brazilian

★ **$$-$$$** ✕**Casa da Gamboa de Conceição Reis.** A longtime favorite of Bahian writer Jorge Amado, this is a Bahian cooking institution. *Casquinha de siri* (breaded crab in the shell) comes as a complimentary starter; then try the *peixe com risoto de ostras* (grilled fish with oyster risotto), followed by a traditional dessert. ⊠ *Rua João de Deus 32, Pelourinho* ☎ *071/ 321–3393* ▤ *AE, MC, V* ⊙ *No dinner Sun.*

$$-$$$ ✕ **Solar do Unhão.** You get a lot for your money at this restaurant on the bay. There's a show every evening presenting different African traditions still alive today. In the 18th century the colonial estate housed a sugar mill that in the next century became a "snuff" factory. The Museu de Arte Moderna occupies a corner of the estate but is only open for special exhibitions. The restaurant is in former slave quarters and is said to be haunted. Dinner is buffet style, with regional and international dishes. ⊠ *Av. do Contorno 08* ☎ *071/329–5551* ⌕ *Reservations essential* ▤ *AE, MC, V.*

$$-$$$ ✕ **Trapiche Adelaide.** Near the Mercado Modelo in downtown Salvador,
Fodor'sChoice this is one of the best restaurants in town. It's known for its blending
★ of Bahian and international dishes. Having drinks before dinner on the deck overlooking the Todos os Santos Bay is a pleasant way to wind down after a day of sightseeing. ⊠ *Praça dos Tupinambás, Av. Contorno 02, Contorno* ⌕ *Reservations essential* ☎ *071/326–2211* ▤ *MC, V.*

$$ ✕ **Maria Mata Mouro.** At this intimate restaurant you almost feel as if you're at a friend's house for dinner. Bahian food is cooked with a lighter touch than in most restaurants. Try the *badejo* (grouper) in ginger. ⊠ *Rua Inácio Acciole 8, Pelourinho* ☎ *071/321–3929* ▤ *AE, V* ⊙ *Closed Sun.*

$ ✕ **Escola Senac.** The quality of the meal may depend on the expertise of the chef-in-training, but meals at this restaurant, which opened in 1975 as a cooking school, often reflect the skill of the excellent teachers. More than 40 typical Brazilian dishes are served buffet style in this old colonial house. ⊠ *Praça José de Alencar 13–19, Pelourinho* ☎ *071/321– 5502* ⌕ *Reservations essential* ▤ *No credit cards.*

$ ✕ **Uauá.** The cuisine here is representative of many Brazilian regions. The clientele, which includes most of the city, is devoted. There are two locations, one in Pelourinho and one at Itapuã Beach. ⊠ *R. Gregório de Matos 36, Pelourinho* ☎ *071/321–3089* ⊠ *Av. Dorival Caymi 46, Itapuã* ☎ *071/249–9579* ▤ *AE, DC, MC, V* ⊙ *Closed Mon.*

Eclectic

$$ ✕ **Boi Preto.** After the Jesuits were run out of Brazil, their herds of cattle roamed the country, and beef became a main source of food here. It is no longer roasted in a hole in the ground, but beef is still cooked to perfection at one of the best barbecue places in Salvador: Boi Preto (Black Bull). Seafood, including lobster, crab, and sushi, and more exotic fare, like alligator, are also on the menu. A piano bar keeps the atmosphere light. It is near the Convention Center. ⊠ *Av. Otávio Mangabeira s/n, Jardim Armação* ☎ *071/362–8844* ☰ *AE, MC, V.*

French

$$$$ ✕ **Chez Bernard.** Discerning *soteropolitanos* (the pompous but nonetheless correct term for natives of the city) find this to be undoubtedly the best French restaurant in town, as well as one of the oldest. Everything is worth trying. ⊠ *Gamboa de Cima 11, Aflitos* ☎ *071/329–5403* ☰ *AE, V* ☉ *Closed Sun.*

Seafood

$–$$ ✕ **Bargaço.** Good, typical Bahian seafood dishes are served at this old favorite. *Pata de caranguejo* (vinegared crab claw) is hearty and may do more than take the edge off your appetite for the requisite *moqueca de camarão* (shrimp stew) or *moqueca de siri mole* (soft-shell crab stew); try the *cocada baiana* (sugar-caked coconut) for dessert, if you have room. Reservations are essential September through February. ⊠ *Rua das Laranjeiras 28, Pelourinho* ☎ *071/231–3900* ☰ *AE, DC, MC.*

★ **$$–$$$** ✕ **Yemanja.** A bubbly underwater atmosphere—replete with aquariums and sea goddess murals—sets the tone for meals of traditionally prepared seafood dishes. The service is somewhat slow, and there's no air-conditioning, but most patrons don't seem to mind, concentrating instead on plowing through enormous portions of moqueca, a seafood mixture heavy with spices and *dendê* (palm oil), or *ensopado,* seafood cooked in a similar but lighter sauce. Reservations are essential on weekends and in the high season. ⊠ *Av. Otávio Mangabeira 4655, Jardim Armação* ☎ *071/231–3036* ☰ *AE, DC, MC, V.*

Where to Stay

There are only a few hotels in the Cidade Histórico. Heading south into the Vitória neighborhood along Avenida 7 de Setembro, there are many inexpensive establishments convenient to beaches and sights. In the yuppie Barra neighborhood, many hotels are within walking distance of cafés, bars, restaurants, and clubs. The resorts in the beach areas of Ondina and Rio Vermelho are a 20-minute taxi ride from downtown. High seasons are from December 21 to March and the month of July. Low seasons are after Carnaval until June 30 and from August 1 to December 20, when you may be able to get better rates.

$$$ 🏨 **Bahia Othon Palace Hotel.** A short drive from most sights, nightspots, and restaurants, this busy, modern hotel sits on a cliff overlooking Ondina Beach. Top local entertainers often perform at the hotel's outdoor park, and in high season the friendly staff organizes poolside activities and trips to better beaches. ⊠ *Av. Presidente Vargas 2456, Ondina 40170-010* ☎ *071/247–1044* 🖶 *071/245–4877* ⊕ *www.hoteis-othon. com.br* ⟿ *300 rooms, 25 suites* ⚒ *Restaurant, coffee shop, in-room safes,* *minibars, cable TV, pool, health club, sauna, dance club, free parking* ⊟ *AE, DC, MC, V.*

★ **$$–$$$** ⊞ **Catussaba Hotel.** Amid a garden of flowers and palm trees, this hotel has large rooms with balconies and ocean views. All rooms open directly onto a beach that's good for swimming. The airport is nearby, and the hotel is 40 km (25 mi) from the city center. It is near the Stella Maris Beach, an ideal spot for surfing, jet skiing, and body boarding. Stands on the beach sell food, soda, and beer. If you tire of saltwater and sand, head for the large, attractive pool area. ⊠ *Alameda da Praia, Itapuã 41600-270* ☎ *071/374–8000* 🖷 *071/374–4749* ⊕ *www.catussaba. com.br* ↘ *186 rooms, 4 suites* ⌂ *Restaurant, room service, minibars, cable TV, tennis court, pool, health club, sauna, bar, Internet, meeting rooms, travel services, convention center, free parking* ⊟ *AE, MC, V.*

$$ ⊞ **Hotel Sofitel Salvador.** The only hotel in Salvador with its own golf course, albeit a 9-hole one, the Sofitel is in a tropical park 27 km (4 mi) from the international airport between Itapuã Beach and the Abaeté Lagoon. It is also near the Carlos Costa Pinto Museum and the Itapuã Lighthouse. The hotel provides transportation to Salvador's Pelourinho historic district. Sofitel plans to open a second, 70-room hotel in Pelourinho in mid-2005 as part of a 16th-century architectural complex that includes the Convento do Carmo and Museum and the Church of Ordem Terceiro. The convent, museum, and church are protected as a National Historical Heritage site and have been closed for several years. In opening a small hotel at the site, the hotel agreed to conserve and protect the convent, museum, and church. ⊠ *Rua da Passargada s/n, Itapuã 41620-430* ☎ *071/374–9611, 800/763–4835 in U.S.* 🖷 *071/374–6946* ⊕ *www.sofitel.com* ↘ *197 rooms, 9 suites* ⌂ *2 restaurants, room service, in-room safes, cable TV, 3 tennis courts, 9-hole golf course, 2 outdoor pools, hair salon, health club, massage, boating, billiards, 3 bars, shops, baby-sitting, concierge, dry cleaning, Internet, business services, free parking, airport shuttle* ⊟ *AE, DC, MC, V.*

$$ ⊞ **Ondina Apart-Hotel Residência.** In the resort hotel district, a short drive from the sights, nightlife, and restaurants of Salvador, this outstanding beachside complex has simple modern furniture. Businesspeople and families opt for this hotel when they're staying in Salvador for extended periods. ⊠ *Av. Presidente Vargas 2400, Ondina 40170-010* ☎ *071/203–8000* 🖷 *071/203–8112* ↘ *100 rooms* ⌂ *Restaurant, coffee shop, in-room safes, minibars, cable TV, tennis court, pool, gym, bar, baby-sitting, laundry service, parking (fee)* ⊟ *AE, DC, MC, V.*

$–$$ ⊞ **Tropical Hotel da Bahia.** Owned by Varig Airlines and often included in package deals, this centrally located hotel is a bit tattered, but it's practical for those whose priority is Salvador's history and culture. The hotel is away from the beaches, but there's a free beach shuttle. Some rooms overlook the square where Carnaval begins. The Concha Acústica do Teatro Castro Alves, site of many big musical shows, is within walking distance; performers in those shows often stay here. ⊠ *Av. 7 de Setembro 1537, Campo Grande 40080-121* ☎ *071/336–0102* 🖷 *071/336–9725* ⊕ *www.tropicalhotel.com.br* ↘ *282 rooms, 10 suites* ⌂ *Restaurant, coffee shop, room service, cable TV, 2 pools, massage, sauna, bar, dance club, concierge, parking (fee)* ⊟ *AE, DC, MC, V.*

$ ⊞ **Caesar Towers.** Though it doesn't have sea views, Caesar Towers is
FodorsChoice in the Ondina district, with easy access to the historic center and the
★ beaches. Rooms are comfortable and have wicker furniture and tile
floors. From here it's only 8 km (5 mi) to downtown, 15 km (10 mi)
to the best beaches, and a short distance to the many restaurants and
bars of the Barra district. The breakfast buffet and the Alfredo di Roma
Italian restaurant are both excellent. ⊠ *Av. Oceánica 1545, Ondina
41140-131* ☎ *071/331–8200* ☐ *071/237–4668* ⇗ *133 rooms*
♨ *Restaurant, coffee shop, room service, in-room safes, kitchenettes,
minibars, cable TV, outdoor pool, health club, sauna, meeting room,
business center, laundry service, parking (fee)* ⊟ *AE, DC, MC, V*
⊠❙ *BP.*

$ ⊞ **Fiesta Bahia Hotel.** In the city's financial district and attached to the
convention center, the Fiesta has wheelchair-accessible rooms and rooms
with direct phone lines, fax and PC terminals, and queen-size beds—
amenities that distinguish it from its competitors. ⊠ *Av. Antônio Carlos Magalhães 711, Itaigara 41125-000* ☎ *071/352–0000* ☐ *071/352–
0050* ⊕ *www.fiestahotel.com.br* ⇗ *239 rooms* ♨ *Restaurant, coffee
shop, room service, in-room data ports, in-room safes, minibars, cable
TV, 2 pools, hair salon, health club, bar, nightclub, shops, business services, meeting rooms, free parking* ⊟ *AE, DC, MC, V.*

★ ¢ ⊞ **Hotel Bahia do Sol.** It may be simple, but this hotel has a prime location close to museums and historic sights. Front rooms have a partial
ocean view, but those in the back are quieter. ⊠ *Av. 7 de Setembro 2009,
Vitória 40080-002* ☎ *071/336–7211* ☐ *071/336–7776* ⇗ *86 rooms,
4 suites* ♨ *Restaurant, cable TV, bar, meeting room, free parking* ⊟ *AE,
DC, MC, V.*

★ ¢ ⊞ **Hotel Catharina Paraguaçu.** The sleeping areas at this intimate hotel
in a 19th-century mansion are small but comfortable and include six
split-level suites. It's family run and in a neighborhood of good restaurants and bars. The kitchen serves snacks and meals, from fettuccine to
salmon. It is wheelchair accessible, unusual for a pousada. ⊠ *Rua João
Gomes 128, Rio Vermelho 40210-090* ☎☎ *071/334–0089* ✎ *hotel-
catharina@svn.com.br* ⇗ *23 rooms, 6 suites* ♨ *Dining room, minibars,
cable TV* ⊟ *MC, V* ⊠❙ *BP.*

★ ¢ ⊞ **Pousada Ambar.** From this pousada, just cross a couple of streets
to enjoy the beautiful Barra Beach. The inn is also near banks, shopping malls, restaurants, and nightlife; bus stops are nearby. If you're
braving Salvador at Carnaval time, the parade passes noisily just two
blocks away on Avenida Oceânica. There's a nice terrace and courtyard. The living room has a television. ⊠ *Rua Afonso Celso 485, Barra
40140-080* ☎ *071/264–6956* ☐ *071/264–3791* ⊕ *www.ambarpousada.
com.br* ⇗ *5 rooms* ♨ *Fans, Internet; no room TVs* ⊟ *AE, MC, V*
⊠❙ *BP.*

★ ¢ ⊞ **Pousada das Flores.** The Brazilian-French owners have made this inn,
northeast of Pelourinho and within walking distance of the historical
district, one of the city's best budget options. Rooms are large and have
high ceilings and hardwood floors. For peace and quiet as well as an
ocean view, opt for a room on an upper floor. If you feel like splurging,
request the penthouse, which has a fantastic view of the harbor. Break-

fast is served on the patio. ✉ *Rua Direita de Santo Antônio 442, Santo Antônio 40301-280* 🕿 *071/243–1836* 🛏 *6 rooms, 3 suites* ⚐ *Fans* ▭ *AE, DC, MC, V.*

Nightlife & the Arts

Pelourinho is filled with music every night and has more bars and clubs than you can count. Most bars serve food as well as drink. Activity also centers along the seashore, mainly at Rio Vermelho and between the Corsário and Piatã beaches, where many hotels have bars or discos.

Salvador is considered by many artists as a laboratory for the creation of new rhythms and dance steps. As such, this city has an electric performing arts scene. See the events calendar published by Bahiatursa (the tourist office), or see local newspapers for details on live music performances as well as the rehearsal schedules and locations of the Carnaval *blocos* (organized groups of dancers and musicians). In Pelourinho groups often give free concerts on Tuesday and Sunday nights.

Nightlife

After dark Praça Terreirro de Jesus is a hot spot, especially on Tuesday and Saturday nights, when stages are set up here and at other squares around the city for live performances. Praça Terreirro is especially popular with tourists because it has been painted, cleaned up, and gentrified. Although there may be impromptu musical performances any night, you can always count on it on Tuesday.

BARS Enjoy live music and typical Bahian food at **Casquinha de Siri** (✉ Coqueiros de Piatã s/n, Piata 🕿 071/367–1234). The two branches of the traditional bar **Habeas Copos** (✉ Rua Marques de Leão 172, Barra 🕿 071/247–7895 ✉ Praça Quincas Berro D'Agua, Pelourinho 🕿 071/321–0430 ✉ Rua Marques de Leão 172, Barra 🕿 071/247–7895) are famous for their chicken. **Sancho Pança** (✉ Av. Otávio Mangabeira 112, Pituba 🕿 071/248–3571) is a great place for sangria and typical Spanish fare. Sooner or later you must have a *caipirinha* (lime and sugar-cane brandy cocktail) at **Cantina da Lua** (✉ Praça Terreirro de Jesus 2, Pelourinho 🕿 No phone).

DANCE SHOWS Shows at the **Moenda** (✉ Rua P, Quadra 28, Lote 21, Jardim Armação 🕿 071/231–7915 or 071/230–6786) begin daily at 8 PM. There are Afro-Brazilian dinner shows at the **Solar do Unhão** (✉ Av. do Contorno 08, Comércio, near Mercado Modelo 🕿 071/321–5551), which is open Monday through Saturday from 8 PM on. The entertainment is better than the food. The unforgettable Afro-Bahian show at the **Teatro Miguel Santana** (✉ Rua Gregório de Mattos 47, Pelourinho 🕿 071/321–0222) has the town's best folkloric dance troupes. This is an entertaining way to learn about African-Brazilian culture.

NIGHTCLUBS Have dinner or drinks and listen to quality jazz, blues, soul, and pop at the **French Quartier** (✉ Aeroclube Plaza complex, Av. Otávio Mangabeira s/n, Lote 1, Pituba 🕿 071/240–1491 ⊕ www.frenchquartier.com.br). Happy hour is between 6 PM and 8 PM. Dress isn't formal, but wear something nice. The view of the bay is fantastic, but ocean breezes are cool, so bring a coat or sweater. French Quartier opens at 5 PM every day. The **Queops disco** (⊠ Hotel Sol Bahia Atlântico, Rua Manoel Antônio Galvão 100, Patamares ☎ 071/370–9000) has a large dance floor and weekly shows by local bands. **Rock in Rio Café** (⊠ Av. Otávio Mangabeira 6000, Jardim Armação ☎ 071/371–0979) is in the shopping-and-entertainment complex Aeroclube Plaza. The atmosphere here is more like Miami than Salvador.

The Arts

CAPOEIRA   You can see capoeira on Tuesday, Thursday, and Saturday evenings at 7 at the Forte de Santo Antônio. Two schools practice here. The more traditional is the Grupo de Capoeira Angola. Weekday nights are classes; the real show happens on Saturday.

There are several capoeira schools in Salvador for anyone who wants to learn the art that trains both the mind and body for combat. Mestre Bamba (Rubens Costa Silva) teaches at **Bimba's Academy** (⊠ Rua das Laranjeiras 01, Pelourinho ☎ 071/322–0639). A 10-day course costs around R$70.

CARNAVAL   Afro-Brazilian percussion groups begin Carnaval rehearsals—which are
REHEARSALS   really more like creative jam sessions—around midyear. **Ilê Aiyê**, which started out as a Carnaval bloco, has turned itself into much more in its 25-year history. It now has its own school and promotes the study and practice of African heritage, religion, and history. Practices are held every Saturday night at Forte de Santo Antônio and should not be missed. Olodum, Salvador's most commercial percussion group, gained fame when it made a recording with Paul Simon. The group has its own venue, the **Casa do Olodum** (⊠ Rua Gregório de Matos 22, Pelourinho ☎ 071/321–5010). Pre-Carnaval rehearsals take place at Largo do Pelourinho Tuesday evenings and Sunday afternoons.

MUSIC, THEATER   **Casa do Comércio** (⊠ Av. Tancredo Neves 1109, Ramal ☎ 071/341–8700)
& DANCE   hosts music performances and some theatrical productions. All kinds of musicians play at the **Concha Acústica do Teatro Castro Alves** (⊠ Ladeira da Fonte s/n, Campo Grande ☎ 071/247–6414 or 071/339–8000), a band shell with great acoustics. Catch a free jam session with Salvador's best jazz and blues musicians between 7 PM and 10 PM some Saturdays at **Solar do Unhão** (⊠ Av. do Contorno 08, Comércio, near Mercado Modelo ☎ 071/321–5551), on the waterfront. The **Teatro ACBEU** (⊠ Av. 7 de Setembro 1883, Vitória ☎ 071/247–4395 or 071/336–4411) has contemporary and classic music, dance, and theater performances by Brazilian and international talent. See theatrical, ballet, and musical performances at the **Teatro Yemanja** (⊠ Jardim Armacão s/n, Centro de Convenções da Bahia ☎ 071/370–8494).

Sports & the Outdoors

Bicycling & Running

The park **Dique do Tororó** (⊠ Entrances at Av. Presidente Costa e Silva and Av. Vasco da Gama, Tororó) has a jogging track and a lake with luminous fountains and statues of Candomblé orixás. You can bike here,

CAPOEIRA: THE FIGHT DANCE

DANCE AND MARTIAL ARTS IN ONE, capoeira is purely Brazilian. The early days of slavery often saw fights between Africans from rival tribes who were thrust together on one plantation. When an owner caught them, both sides were punished. To create a smoke screen, the slaves accompanied the fights with music: singing and chanting and playing the traditional berimbau string–drum instrument (a bow-shape piece of wood with a metal wire running from one end to the other, and a hollow gourd containing seeds at the bottom). Tapped alternately with a stick and a coin, the berimbau's taut wire produces a twanging sound. When the master appeared, the fighters punched only the air and kicked so as to miss their opponents.

The fights have been refined into a sport that was once practiced primarily in Bahia and Pernambuco but has now spread throughout Brazil. Today's practitioners,

called capoeristas, swing and kick— keeping their movements tightly controlled, with only hands and feet touching the ground—to the beat of the berimbau without touching their opponents. The goal is to cause one's opponent to lose concentration or balance. Capoeira is traditionally performed in a roda (wheel), which refers both to an event of continuous capoeira and to the circle formed by players and instrumentalists. Strength, control, flexibility, artistry, and grace are the tenets of capoeira. In any exhibition the jogadors, or players, as they are called—with their backs bending all the way to the floor and their agile foot movements (to avoid an imaginary knife)—as well as the compelling music, make this a fascinating sport to watch.

too. At **Jardim dos Namorados** (⊠ Av. Otávio Mangabeira, Pituba) you can rent bikes, play volleyball, or perhaps join a soccer game. The **Parque Metropolitano de Pituaçu** (⊠ Av. Otávio Mangabeira s/n, Pituaçu), surrounding a lagoon, is the nicest public park in town. The park is an ecological reserve with a lake, bike rentals, and a track, plus bars and restaurants, as well as sculptures by artist Mário Cravo. Entrance to the park is free; hours are 8–5 Wednesday–Sunday.

Golf & Tennis
Hotel Sofitel Salvador (⊠ Rua Passárgada s/n, Itapuã ☎ 071/374–9611) offers day passes to its golf course and its tennis courts.

Soccer
Bahia and Vitória are the two best local teams, and they play year-round Wednesday and Sunday at 5 in the **Estádio da Fonte Nova** (⊠ Av. Vale do Nazaré, Dique do Tororó, Tororó ☎ 071/243–3322 Ext. 237). Tickets are sold at the stadium a day in advance. Avoid sitting behind the goals, where the roughhousing is worst. The best seats are in the *arquibancada superior* (high bleachers).

Shopping

Areas & Malls

For paintings, especially art naïf, visit the many galleries in the Cidade Alta and around the **Largo do Pelourinho** (⊠ Rua Alfredo de Brito at Ladeira do Taboão). The **Mercado Modelo** is your best bet for local handicrafts, such as lace, hammocks, wood carvings, and musical instruments.

Shopping Barra (⊠ Av. Centenário 2992, Barra) is the best shopping mall in Salvador. It isn't far from the historic center and has cinemas, restaurants, and local boutiques, as well as branches of the major Rio, São Paulo, and Minas Gerais retailers. It is open from 10 to 10 weekdays and from 9 to 8 on Saturday. Many hotels provide transportation to the mall, but you can take the Rodoviário bus line.

Specialty Stores

ART   Top local artists (many of whom use only first names or nicknames) include Totonho, Calixto, Raimundo Santos, Joailton, Nadinho, Nonato, Maria Adair, Carybé, Mário Cravo, and Jota Cunha. **Atelier Portal da Cor** (⊠ Ladeira do Carmo 31, Pelourinho ☎ 071/242–9466) is a gallery run by an artists' cooperative.

HANDICRAFTS   The **Casa Santa Barbara** (⊠ Rua Alfredo de Brito s/n, Pelourinho ☎ 071/244–0458) sells Bahian clothing and lacework of top quality, and at high prices. It's closed Saturday afternoon and Sunday. Of Salvador's state-run handicrafts stores, the best is the **Instituto de Artesanato Visconde de Mauá** (⊠ Praça Azevedo Fernandes 2, Porto da Barra ☎ 071/264–5440 ⊠ R. Gregorio de Mattos 27, Pelourinho ☎ 071/321–5638). Look for exquisite lace, musical instruments of African origin, weavings, and wood carvings. **Kembo** (⊠ Rua João de Deus 21, Pelourinho ☎ 071/322–1379) carries native handicrafts. The owners travel to reservations all over the country and buy from the Pataxós, Kiriri, Tupí, Karajá, Xingú, Waiwai, Tikuna, Caipós, and Yanomami, among others.

JEWELRY &   Stones found in Brazil include agate, amethyst, aquamarine, emerald,
GEMSTONES   and tourmaline. Prices are usually cheaper here than in comparable stores outside South America, but it's a good idea to have an idea of what stones are worth before you go. The well-known, reputable **H. Stern** (⊠ Largo do Pelourinho s/n, Pelourinho ☎ 071/322–7353) has several branches in Salvador, most of them in malls and major hotels. **Simon** (⊠ Rua Ignácio Accioli s/n, Pelourinho ☎ 071/242–5218), the city's most famous jewelers, allows you to peer through a window into the room where goldsmiths work.

ESTRADA DO COCO

Once you hit the outskirts of Salvador and head north, leaving the *capoeiristas* (capoeira players), baroque churches, and colonial mansions behind, you quickly relax traveling on the Estrada do Coco (Coconut Road). The sun is shining, coconut palms whisper in the breeze, and the largest village you come to is the turtle haven of Praia do Forte. Then you hit a highway called Linha Verde (Green Line), and if you keep going

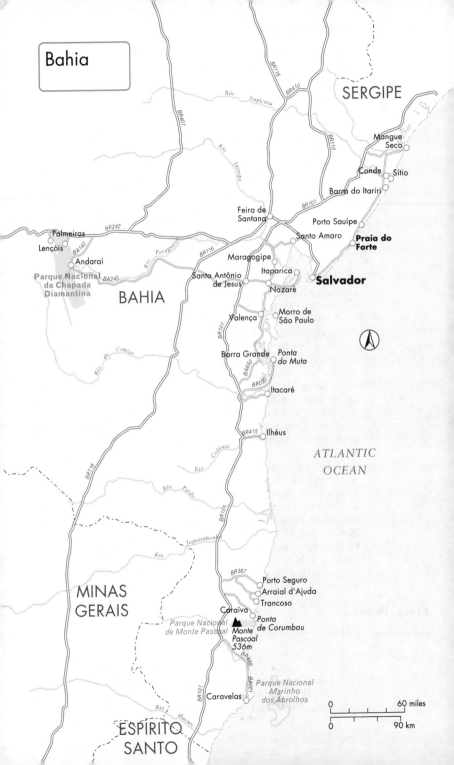

along this road, you reach Sergipe, the state to the north of Bahia. The little roads cutting east off Linha Verde are tempting because every road leads to a beautiful coastal beach.

Beaches

To reach some of Bahia's more pristine and less crowded beaches, head north of Salvador on the Estrada do Coco as far as the fishing village and turtle sanctuary of Praia do Forte, and then take Linha Verde (BA 099) up the coast. Bus transportation is readily available, but it's also a good area for a rental car. Beaches are all along the way, but if you have rented a jeep, turn off the main road and drive between the sand dunes to Santo Antônio (just before the entrance to Costa do Sauípe) and walk through the village with only 30 houses, up a sand dune, and then down onto a nearly deserted beach. Drinks are available in the little village store, handicrafts are sold by villagers, and sometimes a stand is open on the beach for drinks and snacks.

Barra do Jacuípe. A river runs down to the ocean at this long, wide, pristine beach lined with coconut palms. There are beachfront snack bars, and the Santa Maria/Catuense bus company operates six buses here daily. ⊠ *40 km (25 mi) north of Salvador.*

Guarajuba. With palm trees and calm waters banked by a reef, this is the nicest beach of them all, though it's lined with condos. The bus to Barra do Jacuípe continues on to Guarajuba, which has snack kiosks, fishing boats, surfing, dune buggies, and a playground. ⊠ *60 km (38 mi) north of Salvador.*

Itapuã. Frequented by artists who live nearby, Itapuã is polluted in some places but has a terrific atmosphere. Around K and J streets there are food kiosks, music bars, and amusement park rides. It was once a whale cemetery, and bones are still an occasional find. A mystical freshwater lagoon, the Lagoa de Abaeté, lies inland from Itapuã. Its black depths provide a startling contrast with the fine white sand of its shores. No one knows the source of these waters. City buses going to the lagoon leave from Campo Grande or Estação da Lapa. Tour operators include the lagoon on their beach tours, which cost about R$55. ⊠ *Take the Orla Marítima north to Itapuã, at Largo da Sereia (a square with a mermaid statue), follow signs for lagoon; 30-min drive from downtown.*

Piatã. Heading north and leaving the more built-up areas of the city behind, the first truly clean beach you'll come to is the wide Piatã. Its calm waters and golden sand attract families. ⊠ *20 km (13 mi) northeast of downtown Salvador.*

Praia do Forte

Fodor's Choice
★
72 km (45 mi) northeast of Salvador.

Praia do Forte was first settled in 1549 when Garcia D'Avila, a clerk for the Portuguese crown, arrived with Brazil's first governor-general, Tomé de Sousa. The clerk became a big landowner and introduced the young nation to cattle raising and coconut harvesting. To protect the coast, he built a medieval-style castle that served as a fort—hence the town's name, which means "Fortress Beach." The castle is just a shell, and there isn't too much to see, but it now has a helpful visitor center. Today the area's biggest attraction is the Projeto Tamar sea-turtle preservation project, which has greatly changed what used to be a sleepy fishing village. Now, instead of earning their living by killing turtles for meat, eggs, and shells, local fishermen are better paid to protect them. Jobs have also been provided by the bars, restaurants, pousadas, and shops that now line the three unpaved streets, which at this writing are being laid with brick. Almost everything in town is on the main street, Alameda do Sol.

On a relaxing day trip from Salvador, you can visit Praia do Forte's village, stop by the turtle project, and swim or snorkel. But there are several lodging options for longer stays, and although the nightlife is toned down a few decibels from that in Salvador, it's still lively. The town also has a beautiful coconut-lined beach. You can book a trip here through any Salvador tour operator or travel agent, and the Santa Maria/Catuense bus company has hourly service from the city. Renting a car is a nice option for exploring the surrounding area, especially if you're staying a couple days. There is a Localiza car-rental office at the village. Praia do Forte is an easy drive from Salvador over the excellent Linha Verde Highway.

Five of the seven turtle species in the world live in Brazil, and during the reproduction season more than 400,000 hatchlings are born along Brazil's 1,000 km (621 mi) of beach. On the beaches of Praia do Forte, **Projeto Tamar,** developed in 1980, has turned what was once a small, struggling fishing village into a tourist destination with a mission—to save Brazil's giant sea turtles and their hatchlings. During the nesting season (September through March), workers patrol the shore nightly to locate nests and move those found to be at risk to safer areas or to the open-air hatchery at the Tamar base, on the beach end of the village's main street. Here you can watch adult turtles in the swimming pools and see the baby turtles in the tanks that house them until they can be released to the sea. The base also has educational videos, lectures, and a gift shop where you can buy turtle-oriented gifts, like T-shirts with turtles parading across the front; proceeds help support the project. ⊠ *Base is on beach at end of Alameda do Sol* ☎ *071/876–1045* ⌲ *R$12.*

Swim or snorkel in the crystal-clear (and safe) waters of the **Papa Gente,** a 3-meter-deep (10-foot-deep) natural pool formed by reefs at the ocean's edge. Snacks are sold at little huts on the beach, but if you're really hungry, the restaurant in the Sobrado Da Vila Pousada is nearby.

If you have a couple of days to visit Praia do Forte, spend one of them on a jeep tour. These tours make their way through the **Reserva de Sapiranga,** with 600 hectares (1,482 acres) of secondary Atlantic forest that contains rare orchids and bromeliads. The reserve is a sanctuary for endangered animals. White-water rafting is possible on the Rio Pojuca, which flows through the park, and Lago Timeantube, where more than 187 species of native birds have been sighted. You can rent a car or preferably a jeep and drive yourself through the reserve or arrange for a tour

Fodor'sChoice
★

in town at the **Centro Turistico** (Tourist Center; ✉ Alameda do Sol s/n ☎ 071/676–1091 🖷 071/676–1392 ⊕ www.prdoforte.com.br). ✉ *Alameda do Sol* 🕾 *No phone* ✉ *R$3*.

Where to Stay & Eat

$$ ✕ **Sabor da Vila.** It isn't surprising that seafood fresh from the ocean is the specialty at this small modest restaurant on Praia do Forte's main street. The staff is friendly, and the kitchen will prepare your meal any way you want it. There are rooms for rent here; they're spartan but more than adequate. ✉ *Alameda do Sol* ☎ *071/676–1156* ▭ *No credit cards.*

¢ ✕ **Bar do Souza.** One of the best places to sample Bahia's version of fast food, *acarajés* (pastry deep-fried in palm oil and filled with mashed black-eyed peas), is at the Bar do Souza in Praia do Forte. Mashed black-eyed peas and the catch of the day are the main ingredients of most dishes. The restaurant serves up other excellent Bahian specialties, including fish stews, grilled lobster, and shellfish stew. It's a favorite with the locals, especially on Saturday night, when there's live music. The restaurant opens at 10 AM daily. ✉ *Alameda do Sol* 🕾 *No phone* ▭ *AE, MC, V.*

$ ✕🏠 **Pousada Praia do Forte.** You have your own thatch-roof bungalow with a hammock hanging on the open porch here. Bungalows are small, but you're only there to sleep—the beach and the pools that are left when the tide goes out are too inviting to miss. Redbrick paths curve through the landscaped grounds to 12 km (8 mi) of beaches lined with coconut trees and to the Tamar sea-turtle project. In the evening you can relax in the pousada's outdoor pool and take a walk on the beach, and then end the day with dinner in the restaurant, enjoying international and Bahian cuisine. ✉ *Av. do Farol s/n, Praia do Forte, Mata de São João, 48280-000* ☎ *071/676–1010* 🖷 *071/676–1033* 🖛 *19 bungalows* ♨ *Restaurant, fans, beach, pool* ▭ *DC, MC, V* ⦿ *MAP.*

¢ ✕🏠 **Sobrado Da Vila Pousada.** Leave your computer and pocket organizer at home and forget about time management, this is a laid-back pousada where you can kick back and relax. The rooms are plain but comfortable, and the restaurant is superb, with all Bahian specialties. If you've never tried a *queijo de coalho frito* (roasted cheese ball), try it here. You're right on the main drag, where nighttime action is very laid-back. ✉ *Alameda do Sol,* ☎ *071/676–1088* ⊕ *www.sobradodavila. com.br* 🖛 *22 rooms, 4 suites* ♨ *Restaurant, cable TV, refrigerators* ▭ *AE, MC, V.*

$$$$ 🏠 **Praia do Forte Eco Resort.** Relax on a hammock and contemplate the sea from your private veranda at this sprawling beachfront resort, which is around a curve in the beach from the sea-turtle project. Activities include kayaking, sailing, and bird-watching. All rooms face the ocean, and there are activities to keep you (and children) busy. You're within walking distance of the Praia do Forte village. The restaurant and other facilities are open only to resort guests. ✉ *Rua do Farol s/n, Praia do Forte, Mata de São João 48280-000* ☎ *071/676–1111* 🖷 *071/676–1112* ⊕ *www.praiadoforte.com* 🖛 *250 rooms, 2 suites* ♨ *2 restaurants, in-room safes, cable TV, 4 tennis courts, 5 pools, gym, beach, snorkeling, windsurfing, boating, 3 bars, dance club, children's programs* ▭ *AE, DC, MC, V* ⦿ *MAP.*

FodorsChoice ★

$ ⊞ **Pousada Porto da Lua.** Directly on the palm-lined beach, this two-story pousada has a nice dining room and a large veranda complete with hammocks. Ground-floor rooms are air-conditioned, while second-floor rooms have balconies with a hammock and are cooled with fans and the breeze that comes off the ocean. Off the lobby is a TV room that also has video equipment. Fax services are available. ⊠ *Praia do Forte, Mata de São João 48280-000* ☎ *071/676–1372* ▤ *071/676–1446* ⊕ *www.portodalua.com* ⟿ *22 rooms, 4 suites* ⟡ *Restaurant, some fans, in-room safes, minibars, beach, 2 bars, laundry services; no a/c in some rooms* ▤ *AE, MC, V* ⟦◎⟧ *BP.*

Costa do Sauípe Resort

114 km (71 mi) northeast of Salvador 42 km (26 mi) northeast of Praia Do Forte.

An hour's drive north from Salvador along the Atlantic coast brings you to the Costa do Sauípe resort complex. Its five hotels, convention center, re-created local village with six pousadas, and sports center are all part of a 500-acre development in an environmental protection area bordered by rain forest. To get around during your stay within the complex, you can either hop the resort van that makes continuous loops or take a horse and carriage.

If you prefer small lodgings to grand resorts, opt for a stay in one of the six themed pousadas (inns) in Vila Nova da Praia, a re-creation of a typical northeastern village, with cobblestone lanes, crafts shops, restaurants, bars, and street entertainment. Vila Nova da Praia is also a great place to find special gifts, especially ceramics, and to buy resort wear. Regardless of where you stay, you have access to all the resort's amenities, including those of the sports complex, with its 18-hole PGA golf course, 15 tennis courts, equestrian center, and water-sports facilities. All the hotels and pousadas within Costa do Sauípe share the same address. ⊠ *Km 76, Rodovia BA 099, Sauípe Linha Verde, Mata de São João, 48280-000.*

Where to Stay

Regardless of where you stay in Costa do Sauípe, you have access to all the resort's amenities, including an 18-hole golf course, 15 tennis courts, an equestrian center, water-sports facilities, 4 paddleball courts, 2 squash courts, and a soccer field.

$$$$ ⊞ **Breezes Costa do Sauípe.** At this all-inclusive family resort, kids are kept busy all day with circus workshops, which include trapeze and juggling lessons, and an extensive Kids' Club program. Meanwhile, resident tennis pros keep you busy on the courts. The spacious bilevel lobby and the main dining areas look out over a large free-form pool. Rooms, decorated with flowers, palm leaves, and lots of color, are a reminder that you're in a warm and sunny climate. Behind the pool is a beautiful, wide Atlantic beach. You can walk for miles; if you trek to the little village of San Antonio, you can buy souvenirs or a cold drink from the ladies sitting on their porches. In addition to the large buffet and grill at Breezes, there are four restaurants: Japanese, Italian, Bahian,

and Mediterranean. BBTUR has an office in the lobby where you can arrange tours or reconfirm airline tickets. The lobby gift shop has good maps and nice T-shirts. There is a strict no-tipping policy. Reservations are essential for all restaurants except for Jimmy's Buffet and the Tropical Restaurant by the pool. When Brazilian students are on holiday, Breezes can get pretty noisy; call ahead to check the schedule. ☎ 071/ 463–1000 🖷 071/463–1010 ⊕ www.superclubs.com ⟿ 308 rooms, 16 suites ♿ 5 restaurants, in-room data ports, in-room safes, cable TV, pool, wading pool, health club, windsurfing, boating, bicycles, billiards, Ping-Pong, recreation room, 3 bars, dance club, children's programs (ages 3–12), complimentary weddings, airport shuttle, travel services ☰ AE, DC, MC, V ⭘ AI.

$$$$ 🖭 **Sofitel Costa do Sauípe.** In the lobby, replicas of early sailing ships hang above a narrow pool, a hint that the hotel's theme involves not only sailing but also the discovery of Brazil. There are several cozy lobby sitting areas, each with its own TV. The Porão da Nau Pub & Club, off the lobby, is decorated in the style of a ship's hold, making it a unique place for drinks and dancing. If you'd rather enjoy a cocktail in the sun, head for the enormous poolside bar. The main restaurant, the Île de France, named for a luxurious French ship, serves fine French cuisine. Rooms look almost like the staterooms of an elegant ship with their dark-wood furniture and beige walls and drapes. Sliding-glass doors lead out to individual balconies with hammocks that overlook the gardens, with tall palm trees and the beautiful beach beyond. ☎ 071/467–2000 🖷 071/467–2001 ⊕ www.sofitel.com ⟿ 392 rooms, 12 suites ♿ 3 restaurants, coffee shop, room service, in-room data ports, in-room safes, minibars, cable TV, pool, gym, hair salon, hot tub, massage, sauna, beach, windsurfing, snorkeling, boating, bicycles, basketball, billiards, horseback riding, Ping-Pong, squash, bar, pub, dance club, shops, baby-sitting, children's programs (ages 3–12), dry cleaning, laundry service, business services, meeting rooms, airport shuttle, playground, concierge, car rental ☰ AE, DC, MC, V ⭘ MAP.

$$$$ 🖭 **Sofitel Suites & Resort.** This hotel is evocative of the days when large coconut groves filled the Bahian landscape. Public spaces and rooms are done in subdued shades of brown and gold, and wood and natural fibers are used throughout. From the lobby bar you can see the free-form pool, which surrounds small islands planted with coconut trees, and the Atlantic beyond. From the Tabuleiro bar-restaurant watch the chef prepare traditional Bahian dishes. The more sophisticated Casa Grande restaurant serves French and other international fare. Some suites are wheelchair accessible; all rooms have verandas and hammocks. ☎ 071/ 467–2000 🖷 071/467–2001 ⊕ www.sofitel.com ⟿ 198 suites ♿ 2 restaurants, room service, fans, in-room data ports, in-room safes, minibars, cable TV, pool, hair salon, 2 bars, shops, baby-sitting, children's programs (ages 3–12), playground, dry cleaning, airport shuttle, car rental ☰ AE, DC, MC, V ⭘ BP.

$$$ 🖭 **Marriott Costa do Sauípe Resort & Spa.** The view from your balcony is of the garden's swaying palm fronds and a clean sweep of beach. Inside your large room, the dark-wood furniture is offset by bright fabrics. Have drinks or a typical Brazilian meal at the poolside bar and

restaurant or retreat inside to the lobby bar or a restaurant with an ocean view that serves sushi, Korean barbecue, and other Asian cuisine. Dance the night away with the other guests in the ballroom. In addition to a list of facial and body treatments, the spa has shiatsu massage and hot-stone therapy. ☎ *071/465–3000* 🖷 *071/465–3001* ⊕ *www.marriott.com* 🛏 *239 rooms, 17 suites* ⚫ *3 restaurants, room service, in-room data ports, in-room safes, minibars, cable TV, pool, health club, spa, 2 bars, beach, baby-sitting, dry cleaning, laundry service, concierge, business services, airport shuttle* ▤ *AE, DC, MC, V* ⭐ *BP.*

$$$ ▦ **Renaissance Costa do Sauípe Resort.** The open-air lobby has a casual feel and a restaurant that looks out over sand dunes. If you opt to dine in the Mediterranean restaurant, your choices include specialties from Provence and southern Italy; some of the dishes are even cooked in a wood-burning oven. Fully equipped meeting rooms can accommodate gatherings of more than 300 people. Tile-floor rooms are breezy and pleasant and have high-speed Internet access. With breakfast and dinner included and a beautiful beach right out your door, it's a real bargain. ☎ *071/466–2000* 🖷 *071/466–2001* ⊕ *www.renaissancehotels.com/ ssabr* 🛏 *237 rooms, 17 suites* ⚫ *2 restaurants, snack bar, room service, in-room data ports, in-room safes, minibars, cable TV, pool, gym, sauna, beach, dry cleaning, laundry service, baby-sitting, meeting rooms, airport shuttle, concierge, business services, car rental* ▤ *AE, DC, MC, V* ⭐ *MAP.*

$ ▦ **Vila Nova da Praia.** The six Costa Sauípe pousadas in this planned village are nearly identical—all have the same amenities and are of equal quality—though each has a different theme and number of rooms. The village is very small, and the pousadas are close together. Resources available to anyone staying at the pousadas are banks, a convenience store, an ecotourism agency, a car-rental agency, a medical center, bars and restaurants, several kilometers of beaches, and shops selling clothing, jewelry, and handicrafts. Each pousada has its own pool.

Pousada Gabriela (20 rooms) resembles a mansion on a coconut plantation in the coastal town of Ilhéus, south of Salvador. It's named after a character from a Jorge Amado novel. With its bright colors, **Pousada Carnaval** (39 rooms) captures the spirit of Bahia's pre-Lenten festivities. Regional festivals are re-created on a small scale at **Pousada Maria Bonita do Agreste** (18 rooms) through music and food. There are two wheelchair-accessible rooms. Art and antiques fill **Pousada Torre** (28 rooms, 2 suites), giving you a real sense of Brazilian history. As its name implies, **Pousada do Pelourinho** (38 rooms) is a replica of a house in Salvador's historic district. **Pousada Aldeia** (20 rooms) makes you feel as if you're staying in a 16th-century coastal village. A sun deck has hammocks for lazy afternoons. ☎ *071/354–9696, 0800/56–9696 in Brazil* 🖷 *071/452–2420* ⊕ *www.costadosauipe.com.br* ⚫ *Dining room, in-room data ports, in-room safes, minibars, cable TV, pool, laundry service, airport shuttle* ▤ *AE, D, DC, MC, V* ⭐ *BP.*

SPORTS & THE **OUTDOORS** The **Costa do Sauípe Sports Complex** (☎ 071/353–4544) has an 18-hole golf course with a clubhouse, a tennis center with 15 courts, a water-sports center, an equestrian center that offers trail rides and ecological tours, a soccer field, and squash courts. There is also a small "farm" where you can learn how to milk a cow or watch a hog burrow in the mud. Your hotel staff members can help you make arrangements to participate in either the active or spectator sports of your choice.

Cachoeira

109 km (67 mi) northwest of Salvador.

This riverside colonial town dates from the 16th and 17th centuries, when sugarcane was the economy's mainstay. It has been designated a national monument and is the site of some of Brazil's most authentic Afro-Brazilian rituals. One of the most interesting is a festival held by the Irmandade da Boa Morte (Sisterhood of Good Death). Organized by descendants of 19th-century slaves who founded an association of black women devoted to abolition, it's held on a Friday, Saturday, and Sunday in the middle of August.

Devotion to Nossa Senhora da Boa Morte (Our Lady of Good Death) began in the slave quarters, where discussions on abolition and prayer meetings honoring those who had died for liberty took place. The slaves implored Our Lady of Good Death to end slavery and promised to hold an annual celebration in her honor should their prayers be answered.

The festival begins with a procession by the sisters who, heads held high, carry an 18th-century statue of their patron saint through the streets. The statue is adorned in a typical all-white Bahian dress that signifies mourning in the Candomblé religion practiced by many of the sisters. Sunday, the festival's main day, sees a solemn mass followed by a joyful procession that begins with the traditional samba *de roda,* which is danced in a circle. Other festival events include community suppers featuring local delicacies.

On an excursion to Cachoeira you can walk through the colorful country market and see architecture preserved from an age when Cachoeira shipped tons of tobacco and sugar downriver to Salvador. After Salvador it has the largest collection of baroque architecture in Bahia. To get to Cachoeira, take BR 324 north for about 55 km (34 mi), then head west on BR 420 through the town of Santo Amaro. The trip takes 1½ hours.

Restoration was completed in November 2002 of the **D'Ajuda Chapel,** built in the 16th century. The chapel was part of a R$8 million (US$2.3 million) program to restore 20 monuments and 50 private buildings and to revitalize streets and squares to attract more visitors. ⊠ *Largo D'Ajuda s/n* 🕾 *No phone* 🖃 *By donation* 🕙 *Inquire at Museu da Boa Morte to gain entrance to chapel.*

Next to Cachoeira's oldest church, the Nossa Senhora da Ajuda (circa 1595), and the D'Ajuda Chapel is the **Museu da Boa Morte,** with photos and ceremonial dresses worn by members of the Sisterhood of Our Lady of Good Death during their rituals and festivals. You may also meet some of the elderly but always energetic women whose ancestors protested slavery. The ladies at the museum will let you in to see the chapel and the church. ⊠ *Largo D'Ajuda s/n* 🕾 *075/725–1343* 🖃 *By donation* 🕙 *Weekdays 10–1 and 3–5.*

Where to Stay & Eat

¢ ✕▥ **Pousada do Convento.** You can stay overnight in one of the large rooms or have a good lunch at this one-time Carmelite monastery that dates from the 17th century. Reservations should be made early for overnight stays. ✉ *Praça da Aclamação s/n* ☎ *075/725–1716* ⤶ *26 rooms* ⌂ *Restaurant, minibars, pool, playground, meeting room* ▤ *AE, MC, V.*

WEST OF SALVADOR

Parque Nacional da Chapada Diamantina

427 km (265 mi) west of Salvador.

Fodor'sChoice **Chapada Diamantina National Park** has as many facets as the diamonds
★ that made it famous. But Chapada's jewel frenzy, which began in 1822 with the discovery of diamonds imbedded in its riverbeds, ended in 1889. Today it has been rediscovered as the perfect venue for adventure tourism that can be as rugged or as mild as you like but is always in a setting of incomparable beauty.

Chapada Diamantina has some of the most spectacular scenery in the world. A waterfall so clear it looks like glass, mysterious caves with ancient paintings, trails etched into the ground forever by *garimpeiros* (miners) who walked the same paths every day to the diamond mines, the tall peaks of the Sincorá Range, a cavern with a fossilized panther—these are just some of the sights in the 84,000-square-km (32,424-square-mi) park. Included in tours from Salvador is transportation to and from the region as well as the services of guides. You can also take a bus or plane from Salvador and arrange tours through agencies in Lençóis. Options for freelance guides range from local children who simply know the way in and out of the park to ecologists and other scientists. One interesting trek is a three-day bus-and-hiking journey to the **Cachoeira da Fumaça** (Glass Waterfall; ✉ Candombá Lodge, Capão Valley, Caeté-Açu, Chapada Diamantina, Bahia ☎ 075/ 344–1102 ⊕ www.gd.com.br/candomba), organized by Claude Samuel. The waterfall is 1,312 feet high, making it the tallest in Brazil and fifth highest in the world. The trip includes an overnight in a cave and is organized by Claude Samuel.

In the 19th century diamond miners, hauling supplies between the mining town of Lençóis and the Capão Valley, etched a trail so deep that it is still in use today by hikers visiting the Chapada Diamantina National Park. The Capão–Lençóis Trail is also used by farmers in the Capão Valley, who form donkey caravans to bring their produce to market in Lençóis. The trail crosses several ecosystems, including the *cerrado,* an area of dry and medium vegetation; the Mata Atlântica (Atlantic Forest); Campo Rupestre (stones); and Caatinga (very dry vegetation). The variation in ecosystems across a distance of 70 km (43 mi) between Lençóis and the valley is due to the changing altitudes and position of the sun. Hiking times depend on how many stops are

CloseUp

AFRO-BRAZILIAN HERITAGE

OF ALL OF BRAZIL'S STATES, *Bahia has the strongest links with its African heritage. There are few other countries with such a symphony of skin tones grouped under one nationality. This rich Brazilian identity began when the first Portuguese sailors were left to manage the new land. From the beginning Portuguese migration to Brazil was predominantly male, a fact that unfortunately led to unbridled sexual license with Indian and African women.*

The first Africans arrived in 1532, along with the Portuguese colonizers, who continued to buy slaves from English, Spanish, and Portuguese traders until 1855. All records pertaining to slave trading were destroyed in 1890, making it impossible to know exactly how many people were brought to Brazil. It's estimated that from 3 to 4.5 million Africans were captured and transported from the Sudan, Gambia, Guinea, Sierra Leone, Senegal, Liberia, Nigeria, Benin, Angola, and Mozambique. Many were literate Muslims who were better educated than their white overseers and owners.

It was common in the great houses of sugar plantations, which relied on slave labor, for the master to have a white wife and slave mistresses. However, cohabitation between white men and women of other races was openly accepted. It was also fairly common for the master to free the mother of his mixed-race offspring and allow a son of color to learn a trade or inherit a share of the plantation.

When the sugar boom came to an end, it became too expensive for slave owners to support their "free" labor force. Abolition occurred gradually, however. It began around 1871, with the passage of the Law of the Free Womb, which liberated all Brazilians born of slave mothers. In 1885 another law was passed, freeing slaves

over age 60. Finally, on May 13, 1888, Princess Isabel signed a law freeing all slaves.

The former slaves, often unskilled, became Brazil's unemployed and underprivileged. Although the country has long been praised for its lack of discrimination, this veneer of racial equality is deceptive. Afro-Brazilians still don't receive education on a par with that of whites, nor do they always receive equal pay for equal work. There are far fewer black or mulatto professionals, politicians, and ranking military officers than white ones.

Subtle activism to bring about racial equality and educate all races about the rich African legacy continues. For many people the most important holiday is November 20 (National Black Consciousness Day). It honors the anniversary of the death of Zumbi, the leader of the famous quilombo (community of escaped slaves) of Palmares, which lasted more than 100 years and was destroyed by bandeirantes (adventurers who tracked runaway slaves) in one final great battle for freedom.

made for refreshing swims or to admire the spectacular scenery of table-top mountains, waterfalls, and forests where orchids and bromeliads bloom and rare birds can be seen. Actual hiking time is 6–7 hours and is moderately strenuous. If you start from the valley rather than Lençóis, the hike is all downhill. The Capão Valley is 900 feet higher than Lençóis.

Claude Samuel, manager of the Pousada Candombá in the Capão Valley, assists in organizing the **Capão–Lençóis Trek** (✉ Candombá Lodge, Capão Valley, Caeté-Açu, Chapada Diamantina, Bahia ☏ 075/344–1102 ⊕ www.gd.com.br/candomba). The cost is around R$125 per person including the guide and food. Arrangements are made for transfers from the Lençóis Airport or from the town of Palmeiras, for guests coming by bus from Salvador. ✉ *From Salvador take BR 324 to Feira de Santana, then BR 116 and connect with BR 242* ☏ *No phone* 🎫 *Free* ⊙ *Daily 24 hrs.*

When gold and diamonds were discovered in the area in the early 17th century, fortunes were made, and the largest city, **Lençóis,** became so important that it even had a French consulate. When the boom ended, the city was forgotten. Since the park was established in 1985, Lençóis has enjoyed a renaissance. More than 250 mansions are in the process of being restored.

Where to Stay

$ 🏨 **Pousada Candombá.** Trails from the pousada lead to small villages, waterfalls (including the famous Fumaça Waterfall), rivers, caves, and green areas where birds, butterflies, plants, flowers, and fruit trees flourish, all surrounded by spectacular mountain scenery. It is 3 km (2 mi) from Caeté-Açu, a tiny village that has restaurants, a supermarket, a health center, and a few leftover hippies selling handmade jewelry and sandals made from discarded tires. The large rooms sleep 2–4 people. Both the rooms and chalets are basic. The altitude at the Pousada is 2,850 feet. The Capão–Lençóis Trek is arranged here, as are other guided tours. Hot water is provided by solar heaters and the sauna is warmed by heated rocks. A wine cellar has a good selection of wines, and the video and games room entertains when all else fails. ✉ *Capão Valley, Caeté-Açu, Vale do Capão, Palmeiras 46940–000* ☏ *075/344–1102* ⊕ *www.gd.com. br/candomba* 🛏 *4 rooms, 5 chalets* ⚐ *Restaurant, sauna.*

¢ 🏨 **Pousada de Lençóis.** On the edge of Lençóis and next to the Parque Nacional da Chapada Diamantina is this homey pousada. A stay in one of its extralarge rooms (some sleep up to five people) truly makes you feel as if you're a guest in someone's country house. The large pool is surrounded by flower gardens. The restaurant and bar are open to the public, and an in-house tour agency arranges park trips. ✉ *Av. Tancredo Neves 274, Bloco B, Sala 336, Lençóis 41820-020* ☏ *071/358–9395* 📠 *071/358–0114* 🛏 *36 rooms* ⚐ *Restaurant, in-room safes, minibars, cable TV, pool, gym, bar, travel services* ☱ *V* ⎮⎮*BP.*

★ ¢ 🏨 **Pousada Sincorá.** Named after the mountain range in the Parque Nacional da Chapada Diamantina, this pousada is in the foothill village of Andaraí, close to Lençóis and to several trails and remarkable scenery. It has an excellent library with English-language books and magazines.

The owners, Helder and Ana Maria Madeira, speak English; he's a guide and she's the cook. There are two double and three triple rooms. You can get help hiring local guides and arrange for transportation to and from the park. ✉ *Av. Paraguaçu s/n, Andaraí 46830-000, turn left on to BA 142 just before Lençóis,* ⌨ *5 rooms* ⌂ *Dining room, cable TV, laundry service* 🖃 *V* ⏣ *BP.*

SALVADOR & ENVIRONS A TO Z

To research prices, get advice from other travelers, and book travel arrangements, visit www.fodors.com.

AIR TRAVEL

CARRIERS Flights from major cities in Brazil are easy, but with the exception of TAP from Portugal (⇨ Air Travel *in* Smart Travel Tips A to Z), flights from other countries usually require a change of plane and airline in Rio de Janeiro or São Paulo. Non-Brazilian citizens must purchase tickets for Gol, a low-cost carrier, in person and with cash.

🖪 Airlines & Contacts **Gol** ☎ 0300/789-2121, 021/3398-5132, or 021/3398-5136 ⊕ www. voegol.com.br. **Nordeste Linhas Aéreas** ☎ 071/377-0130 ⊕ www.voenordeste.com.br. **TAM** ☎ 071/204-1167 ⊕ www.tamairlines.com. **VARIG** ☎ 071/204-1395 or 0800/99-7000 ⊕ www.varig.com.br. **VASP** ☎ 071/204-1304 or 0800-998-277 ⊕ www.vasp.com.br.

AIRPORTS & TRANSFERS

The Aeroporto Deputado Luís Eduardo Magalhães, 37 km (23 mi) northeast of Salvador, accommodates international and domestic flights.

🖪 Airport Information **Aeroporto Deputado Luís Eduardo Magalhães** ✉ Praça Gago Coutinho s/n, São Cristovão ☎ 071/204-1010.

AIRPORT In Salvador avoid taking *comum* (common) taxis from the airport; driv-
TRANSFERS ers often jack up the fare by refusing or "forgetting" to turn on the meter. Opt for one of the prepaid *cooperativa* (co-op) taxis, which are white with a broad blue stripe; the cost is R$79–R$113 for the 20- to 30-minute drive downtown. The *ônibus executivo,* an air-conditioned bus, runs daily from 6 to 9 at no set intervals; it costs about R$9 and takes an hour to reach downtown, stopping at hotels along the way. Drivers don't speak English, so write your hotel's address on a piece of paper to show to them. Several companies operate these buses, of which the largest is Transportes Ondina. The municipal Circular buses, operated by both Transportes Ondina and Transportes Rio Vermelho, cost mere centavos and run along the beaches to downtown, ending at São Joaquim, where ferries depart for Ilha de Itaparica.

🖪 Shuttles **Transportes Ondina** ✉ Av. Vasco da Gama 347 ☎ 071/245-6366. **Transportes Rio Vermelho** ✉ Av. Dorival Caymmi 18270 ☎ 071/377-2587.

BOAT & FERRY TRAVEL

Itaparica and the other harbor islands can be reached by taking a ferry or a launch from Salvador, by hiring a motorized schooner, or by joining a harbor schooner excursion—all departing from the docks behind the Mercado Modelo. Launches cost about R$2 and leave every 45 minutes from 7 to 6 from the Terminal Turístico Marítimo. The ferry takes passengers and cars and leaves every half hour between 6 AM and 10:30 PM from the Terminal Ferry-Boat. The fare is around R$2 for passengers and R$14–R$18 for cars, and it takes 45 minutes to cross the bay. You reach Cachoeira by a combination of boat and bus: boats depart weekdays at 2:30 from the Terminal Turístico Marítimo for the three-hour trip to Maragojipe; you then board a bus for the bumpy half-hour ride.

🚩 **Terminal Ferry-Boat** ⊠ Terminal Marítimo, Av. Oscar Ponte 1051, São Joaquim ☎ 071/321-7100 or 071/319-2890. **Terminal Turístico Marítimo** ⊠ Behind Mercado Modelo, Av. França s/n ☎ 071/243-0741.

BUS & METRÔ TRAVEL

Bus tickets are sold at the Terminal Rodoviário in Salvador, which is where all buses heading out of the city depart. Itapemirim has three buses a day to Recife (13 hours, R$90–R$125), Fortaleza (19 hours, R$150), and Rio (28 hours, R$200–R$375). Santa Maria/Catuense has hourly service to Praia do Forte starting at 7:30 AM, with the last bus returning to the city at 5:30 PM; tickets cost about R$11. Camurujipe has hourly service to Cachoeira between 5:30 AM and 7 PM. Comfortable Real Expresso buses make the seven-hour trip to Chapada Diamantina (Lençóis or Palmeiras) for about R$28, with departures at 11:30 PM daily and at 7 AM Tuesday, Thursday, and Saturday. Return is at 11:30 PM daily, with an additional departure at 7:30 AM Monday, Wednesday, and Friday.

Within Salvador, use the *executivo* (executive) buses. Although other buses serve most of the city and cost a pittance (R$1.40), they're often crowded and dirty and are favored by pickpockets. Fancier executivo buses (R$3.50) serve tourist areas more completely. The glass-sided green, yellow, and orange Jardineira bus (marked PRAÇA DA SÉ; R$6) runs every 40 minutes 7:30 to 7:30 daily from the Praça da Sé in Pelourinho to the Stella Maris Beach, traveling along the Orla Marítima series of avenues. Hop off when you see a beach you like. The Santa Maria/Catuense company operates six buses (marked PRAIA DO FORTE) daily that stop at Barra do Jacuípe Beach.

🚩 Bus Information **Camurujipe** ☎ 071/358-4704. **Comfortable Real Expresso** ☎ 071/450-2991 or 071/246-8355 ⊕ www.realexpresso.com.br. **Itapemirim** ☎ 071/358-0037. **Santa Maria/Catuense** ☎ 071/359-3474. **Terminal Rodoviário** ⊠ Av. Antônio Carlos Magalhães, Iguatemi ☎ 071/358-6633.

CAR RENTAL

Rental companies in Salvador include Avis, Hertz, and Localiza. The dearth of places to park in Salvador makes rental cars impractical for sightseeing in the Cidade Alta. Further, many soteropolitanos are reckless drivers, making driving a dangerous proposition, especially if you don't know your way around. That said, cars are handy for visits to outlying beaches and far-flung attractions.

🚩 Agencies **Avis** ⊠ Aeroporto Deputado Luís Eduardo Magalhães, Salvador ☎ 071/237-0155, 071/377-2276 at airport. **Hertz** ⊠ Aeroporto Deputado Luís Eduardo Magalhães, Salvador ☎ 071/377-3633. **Localiza** ⊠ Aeroporto Deputado Luís Eduardo Magalhães, Salvador ☎ 071/377-2272, 0800/99-2000 in Brazil ⊕ www.localiza.com.br ✉ Alameda do Sol s/n, Praia do Forte ☎ 071/676-0321, 0800/99-2000 in Brazil.

CAR TRAVEL

Two highways—BR 101 and BR 116—run between Rio de Janeiro and Salvador. If you take the BR 101, get off at the city of Santo Antônio/Nazaré and follow the signs to Itaparica, 61 km (38 mi) away. At Itaparica you can either take the 45-minute ferry ride to Salvador or continue on BR 101 to its connection with BR 324. If you opt for the BR 116, exit at the city of Feira de Santana, 107 km (67 mi) from Salvador and take the BR 324, which approaches the city from the north. Follow the signs marked IGUATEMI/CENTRO for downtown and nearby destinations. To reach Praia do Forte by car, take the Estrada do Coco north and follow the signs. To reach Cachoeira, take BR 324 north for about 55 km (34 mi), then head west on BR 420 through the town of Santo Amaro. The trip takes 1½ hours. To drive to Lençóis for Chapada Diamantina, take BR 324 to Feira de Santana and BR 116 to connect with BR 242. If you are going to Andarai to stay at the Posada Sincora, turn left onto BA 142 just before Lençóis.

EMERGENCIES

In an emergency, dial ☎ 192 for Pronto Socorro (first aid). In Salvador the office of the Delegacia de Proteção do Turista (Tourist Police) is down the steps at the back of the Belvedere at the Praça da Sé in Pelourinho. It deals as best it can (on a shoestring budget) with tourist-related crime after the fact. Officers, some of whom have rudimentary second-language skills, wear armbands that say POLÍCIA TURÍSTICA. There are also military-police foot patrols. For the nearest 24-hour pharmacy, dial 136 or ask at your hotel's front desk.

🏥 Emergency Services **Delegacia de Proteção do Turista** ☎ 071/320-4103.

🏥 Hospitals **Aliança Hospital** ✉ Av. Juracy Magalhães Jr. 2096 ☎ 071/350-5600. **Hospital Jorge Valente** ✉ Av. Garibaldi 2135 ☎ 071/203-4333. **Hospital Português** ✉ Av. Princesa Isabel 2, Santa Isabel ☎ 071/203-5555.

🏥 Hot Lines **Police** ☎ 190. **Pronto Socorro** (First Aid) ☎ 192.

🏥 24-Hour Pharmacies ☎ 136.

ENGLISH-LANGUAGE MEDIA

Graúna has many books in English. Livraria Brandão sells secondhand books in English and other foreign languages. Livraria Planeta (Aeroporto Deputado Luís Eduardo Magalhães) has English-language books, magazines, and newspapers.

🏥 Bookstores **Graúna** ✉ Av. 7 de Setembro 1448 ✉ Rua Barão de Itapoã, Porto da Barra. **Livraria Brandão** ✉ Rua Rui Barbosa 15B, Centro ☎ 071/3243-5383.

MAIL, INTERNET & SHIPPING

Salvador's main post office is in the Cidade Baixa's Praça Inglaterra. Other branches are in Pelourinho on Rua Alfredo de Brito, on the Avenida Princesa Isabel in Barra, the Rua Marques de Caravelas in Ondina, at the Barra and Iguatemi shopping centers, just inside the back door of the Mercado Modelo, and at the airport. The airport branch is open 24 hours; all others are open weekdays 8–5. All branches offer express-mail service. Make sure your letter or package has been stamped.

Most hotels and even many small pousadas have Internet services for a small fee. There are also Internet cafés scattered around the city. In Pelourinho, the historic district, try Internet Café.com, open Monday– Saturday 9–9.

🔒 Internet Cafés **Internet Café.com** ⊠ Rua Joãa de Deus 02 ☎ 071/331-2147.

🔒 Correio **Correio Pelourinho** ⊠ Rua Alfredo de Brito 43, Pelourinho ☎ 071/243-9383.

MONEY MATTERS

Never change money on the streets, especially in the Cidade Alta. Major banks have exchange facilities, but only in some of their branches. Try Citibank, which has good rates, Banco Económico, or Banco do Brasil, which also offers exchange services at its branches in the Shopping Center Iguatemi and at the airport. Credit cards and even dollars are welcome in most areas of tourist-friendly Brazil, but if you are traveling to villages or small towns, exchange at least what you think you will need for tips, taxis, restaurants, and purchases from street vendors or small shops while you are in Salvador.

🔒 Banks **Banco do Brasil** ⊠ Av. Estados Unidos 561, Comércio. **Banco Económico** ⊠ Rua Miguel Calmon 285. **Citibank** ⊠ Rua Miguel Calmon 555, Comércio.

SAFETY

The Centro Histórico area of Pelourinho has become one of the safest places in Salvador. There are friendly tourist police on almost every corner; however, that doesn't mean you shouldn't take normal precautions, especially at night. Stick to the main tourist areas and don't walk down streets that appear to be deserted. It's a good idea to stay away from any deserted area, even a beach. At night take a taxi (registered cabs only—they have identification stickers on the window) to wherever you want to go. The lower station of the Lacerda Elevator is renowned for crime, and pickpocketing is common on buses and in crowded places.

During Carnaval there are *huge* crowds in the streets. The recommendation is to join a bloco, which is surrounded by a rope with security guards. The tourist office, Bahiatursa (⇨ Visitor Information, *below*), can tell you how to join up with one, or contact a tour operator and join one of their groups, or watch it from one of the boxes installed along the route. If these options don't appeal to you, reread the safety instructions above.

TELEPHONES

Salvador's area code is 071. Public phones take cards that are sold in a variety of denominations at many shops.

TAXIS

Taxis in Salvador are metered, but you must convert the unit shown on the meter to reais using a chart posted on the window. Tipping isn't expected. You can hail a comum taxi (white with a red-and-blue stripe) on the street (they often line up in front of major hotels), or summon one by phone. If you bargain, you can hire a comum taxi for the day for as little as R$135. Try Ligue Taxi. The more expensive, though usually air-conditioned, *especial* (special) taxis also congregate outside major hotels, though you must generally call for them. Cometas is a reliable company.

🚹 Taxi Companies **Cometas** ☎ 071/244-4500. **Ligue Taxi** ☎ 071/357-7777.

TOURS
Salvador's large group tours are cursory, and their guides often speak minimal English; such tours are also targeted by hordes of street vendors. Private tours with an accredited Bahiatursa guide can be hired through your hotel or a travel agency or at a Bahiatursa office (⇨ Visitor Information). Prices vary depending on the size of the group but always includes a car that picks you up and drops you off at your hotel. Beware of guides who approach you at churches and other sights; they tell tall tales and overcharge you for the privilege.

Bahia Adventure Ecoturismo can help you arrange jeep tours and other adventure treks to the Reserva de Sapiranga, in the Praia do Forte area. BBTUR has excellent buses and vans; request an English-speaking guide ahead of time. The company has a full line of tours not only of Salvador but also of surrounding areas; there's also a branch in the lobby of the Breezes Costa do Sauípe resort. Odara Turismo, in the arcade at the Praia do Forte Eco Resort Hotel, arranges four-wheel-drive tours of the area plus horseback and hiking trips.

Though Tatur Tours specializes in African-heritage tours of Bahia, it also gives personalized special-interest city tours and arranges top-notch excursions from Salvador. Top Hilton Turismo offers the usual city tours and interesting boat cruises, including a trip around Baía de Todos os Santos in a trimaran and a schooner cruise to the islands. It also has a tour to the nudist beach at Massarandupió, along the northern coast. For trips to Chapada Diamante, Trekking Tours is your best bet.

Several travel agencies offer half-day minibus tours with hotel pickup and drop-off for about R$60–R$80. Agencies also offer daylong harbor tours on motorized schooners (R$80–R$90) and night tours (R$100–R$115) that include dinner and an Afro-Brazilian music-and-dance show. A beach tour that includes the Lagoa de Abaeté can be arranged as well, about R$80 a head including a car and a guide (minimum two people).

🚹 Tour Operators **Bahia Adventure Ecoturismo** ✉ Km 76, Rodovia BA 099, Costa do Sauípe, Mata de São João ☎ 71/464-2525 ⊕ www.bahiaadventure.com. **BBTUR** ✉ Vila Nova da Praia, Loja 22–23, Costa do Sauípe, Mata de São João ☎ 071/464-2121, 71/341-8800 in Salvador ✉ Av. Tancredo Neves 450, Edifício Suarez Trade Sala 1702, Pituba ☎ 071/341-8800. **Odara Turismo** ✉ Rua do Farol s/n, Praia do Forte, Mata de São João ☎ 071/876-1080. **Tatur Tours** ✉ Av. Antônio Carlos Magalhães 2573, Edifício Royal Trade, Pituba, Salvador ☎ 071/358-7216. **Top Hilton Turismo** ✉ Rua Fonte do Boi 05, Rio Vermelho, Salvador ☎ 071/334-5223. **Trekking Tours** ✉ Bahia Praia Hotel, Av. Oceániana 2483, Ondina, Salvador ☎ 071/332-5557.

VISITOR INFORMATION

Bahiatursa, the state tourist board, is the best source of information about areas outside of Salvador. Its main office is far from tourist attractions, but there are five other branches. Emtursa, Salvador's tourist board, is open weekdays 8–6. Through Emtursa, Salvador's city hall operates mobile tourist information units in the Central Histórico area (Pelourinho). Emtursa has bilingual receptionists and gives out leaflets with information on restaurants, tours, and prices.

🚩 Tourist Information **Bahiatursa** ✉ Edifício Sede do Centro de Convenções, Jardim Armação, Salvador ☎ 071/370-8400 ⊕ www.bahiatursa.ba.gov.br ✉ Aeroporto Internacional, 2 de Julho s/n, Salvador ☎ 071/204-1244 ✉ Av. Antônio Carlos Magalhães s/n, Terminal Rodoviário, Salvador ☎ 071/358-0871 ✉ Terreiro de Jesus s/n, Pelourinho, Salvador ☎ 071/321-0388 ✉ Mercado Modelo, Praça Visconde de Cairú s/n, Salvador ☎ 071/241-0240 ✉ Porto da Barra s/n, Barra, Salvador ☎ 071/247-3195 ✉ Av. do Farol s/n, Praia do Forte ☎ No phone ✉ Av. 22 de Abril 1067, Shopping Vitória Plaza Trade Center, Centro Porto Seguro ☎ 073/288-2578 ✉ Av. Senhor dos Passos s/n, Lençóis ☎ 075/334-1622. **Emtursa** ✉ Av. Vasco da Gama 206, Dique do Tororó 40240-090 ☎ 071/380-4200, 071/380-4281, or 071/380-4217 ⊕ www.emtursa. salvador.ba.gov.br.

RECIFE, NATAL
& FORTALEZA

7

Updated by
Brad Weiss

THE NORTHEASTERN CITIES ARE IMBUED WITH BRAZIL'S ESSENCE.
Churches, villas, and fortresses in Recife, Natal, and Fortaleza tell the
tale of Portuguese settlers who fought Dutch invaders and amassed fortunes from sugar. The beaches in and around these cities evoke Brazil's
playful side and its love affair with sun, sand, and sea. West of the cities,
the rugged, often drought-stricken *sertão* (bush) seems a metaphor for
Brazil's darker side—one where many people struggle for survival. This
warp and weave of history and topography is laced with threads of culture: indigenous, European, African, and a unique blend of all three that
is essentially Brazilian.

Throughout the region the influence of native peoples is a mere shadow
of long-ago days when they first worked with the Portuguese to harvest
pau-brasil (brazilwood) trees. Later the indigenous tribes either fled inland to escape slavery or were integrated into the European and African
cultures.

Although the Spanish and Portuguese had established rough territorial
boundaries in the New World with the 1494 Treaty of Tordesillas, the
French, English, and Dutch weren't inclined to respect the agreement,
which was made by papal decree. In the 16th century the Portuguese
crown established 15 "captaincies" (the forerunners of today's states)
as a way to protect Brazil from invaders. Each captaincy was assigned
a "captain," who governed the territory and collected taxes while also
defending it and ensuring its colonization. During this period many northeasterners made huge profits either from sugar grown on plantations
they had established or in the trade of African slaves, who were forced
to work the cane fields and *engenhos* (mills).

Under the leadership of Duarte Coelho, the northeastern captaincy of
Pernambuco thrived. Coelho adeptly established good relations with the
area's native people and was among the first to employ African labor.
At one point Pernambuco had more sugar engenhos than any other captaincy. Olinda, its capital, was filled with the elegance and luxury that
only true sugar barons could finance. Recife, the capital of what is now
Pernambuco State, also began to evolve as a major port.

By 1549 it became clear to Portugal's monarch, Dom João III, that his
New World captaincies were failing for the most part. He appointed Tomé
de Sousa as Brazil's first governor-general and ordered him to establish
a colonial capital in the central captaincy of Bahia. Hence, the city of
Salvador was established on a bluff overlooking the vast Baía de Todos
os Santos (All Saints' Bay).

In 1611 Martim Soares Moreno was dispatched from Portugal to a captaincy farther in the northeast, with orders to fend off the French, who
were threatening the area. Captain Moreno fell in love with the place—
parts of which became the state of Ceará and its capital, Fortaleza—as
well as its people. He was especially taken with a native woman, whom
he married. (The love affair was immortalized in the 19th-century classic Brazilian novel *Iracema,* named for the Indian woman, by José de
Alencar. Contemporary Fortaleza's Mucuripe Bay has a famous statue
of Iracema by Corbiano Lins, a sculptor from Pernambuco.)

Although the French had posed an early threat to Brazil, it was the Dutch who truly tested its mettle. In 1602 they set up the powerful Dutch East India Company, which demolished Portugal's Asian spice-trade monopoly. Soon the Dutch began to look toward Brazil and its profitable sugar enterprises (they even sent botanists to catalog the nation's flora). In 1621, after the Dutch West India Company was established, Dutch attacks in northeastern Brazil began. They invaded and took over several captaincies, but the Portuguese drove them from one after another, finally ousting them entirely in 1654.

The coveted northeast still has much to offer explorers, and though it's experiencing a renaissance, the changes strike a balance between preservation and progress. Recife remains a place of beautiful waters, and nearby Olinda is still a charming enclave of colonial architecture—though bohemians have long since replaced sugar barons. On Ceará State's 570-km-long (354-mi-long) coast, Fortaleza continues to thrive against a backdrop of fantastic beaches with both new amenities and timeless white dunes. Although smaller and with a less storied past, Natal and the surrounding region are experiencing dizzying growth in tourism and other major industries.

Exploring Recife, Natal & Fortaleza

Several good main and secondary roads, some of them right along the coast, run north–south through the region. Still, considering the distances, it's best to fly between the cities. From each you can rent a car, take a bus, or sign up for a guided tour and explore other coastal communities or inland areas.

About the Restaurants

The restaurants (all of which are indicated by a ✕) that we list are the cream of the crop in each price category. Properties indicated by a ✕🏠 are lodging establishments whose restaurant warrants a special trip.

About the Hotels

The lodgings (all indicated with a 🏠) that we list are the cream of the crop in each price category. We always list the facilities that are available—but we don't specify whether they cost extra: when pricing accommodations, always ask what's included. Most hotels charge as little as half the rack rate during high season and significantly less during low season. Properties indicated by a ✕🏠 are lodging establishments whose restaurant warrants a special trip.

WHAT IT COSTS In Reais				
$$$$	**$$$**	**$$**	**$**	**¢**
RESTAURANTS over $60	$45–$60	$30–$45	$15–$30	under $15
HOTELS over $500	$375–$500	$250–$375	$125–$250	under $125

Restaurant prices are for a dinner entrée. Hotel prices are for two people in a standard double room in high season, excluding taxes.

If you have 5 days	Fly into **Recife** ❶–⓬ and go straight to 🏛 **Olinda** ☞, where you should spend two nights. In a day you can easily explore the colonial area. The next day spend a few hours in nearby Recife, which has several museums and sites worth visiting. On the third day either take a short flight or the four-hour bus ride to 🏛 **Natal**. Stay in the **Ponta Negra** area and use it as a base to explore the nearby beaches. Reserve one day to visit **Genipabu** and take a dune buggy ride through its remarkable sand dunes. Also head to **Praia de Pipa**—be sure to take the boat trip to see the dolphins.
If you have 7 days	Do the same as above, but make sure to get in a quick trip to 🏛 **Fernando de Noronha,** which has some of the most beautiful beaches on the continent. While there, you should scuba dive or snorkel, as the marine wildlife in the protected archipelago is spectacular. It's best to spend three days at Fernando de Noronha. You should be able to save a day from the itinerary above by skipping the Recife tour and by avoiding the trip between Recife and Natal: Fly from **Recife** ❶–⓬ to Fernando de Noronha but take the return flight to 🏛 **Natal**.
If you have 10 days	Follow the seven-day itinerary and tack on a trip to **Cariri** at the end of your trip. This will give you a taste for the vastly different landscapes and culture of the interior. Highlights are mysterious rock formations and well-preserved rock paintings. It takes about four hours by car from Natal to get to Cariri. You should go with a tour operator, as transport there is rather difficult.

Timing

High season corresponds to school vacations and Carnaval. So avoid a trip during July or between late December and mid-March. You will be rewarded with far better prices and significantly less crowded beaches. If you've come to partake in festivities, Olinda has one of the best Carnaval celebrations in the country. Also, the region has two of the most popular out-of-season Carnaval celebrations: Carnatal in Natal, on the first weekend in December; and Fortal in Fortaleza, on the last weekend in July. In general, weather is not a factor, as the Northeast is warm and sunny year-round.

RECIFE

Just over 3.2 million people call the capital of Pernambuco State home. This vibrant metropolis 829 km (515 mi) north of Salvador has a spirit that's halfway between that of the modern cities of Brazil's south and of the traditional northeastern centers. It offers both insight on the past and a window to the future.

It was in Pernambuco State, formerly a captaincy, that the most violent battles between the Dutch and the Portuguese took place. Under the Portuguese, the capital city was the nearby community of Olinda. But beginning in 1637 and during the Dutch turn at the reins (under the powerful count Maurício de Nassau), both Olinda and Recife were greatly developed.

The Dutch had hoped that Brazilian sugar planters wouldn't resist their rule, but many took up arms. In 1654, after a series of battles around Recife, the Dutch finally surrendered. In the 17th century Pernambuco maintained much of the affluence of the earlier sugar age by cultivating cotton. With several rivers and offshore reefs, Recife proved to be an excellent port and began to outgrow Olinda.

Today Recife is a leader in health care and design, among other things. It's also Brazil's third-largest gastronomic center—it's almost impossible to get a bad meal here. Nearby Olinda has been recognized by UNESCO as part of Humanity's Natural and Cultural Heritage. It has attracted artists who display their canvases on easels behind the iron-barred windows of well-preserved colonial homes.

Recife is built around three rivers and connected by 49 bridges. Its name comes from the *arrecifes* (reefs) that line the coast. Because of this unique location, water and light often lend the city interesting textures. In the morning, when the tide recedes from Boa Viagem Beach, the rocks of the reefs slowly reappear. Pools of water are formed, fish flap around beachgoers, and the rock formations dry into odd colors. And if the light is just right on the Rio Capibaribe, the ancient buildings of Recife Antigo (Old Recife) are reflected off the river's surface in a watercolor display.

Exploring Recife

Recife is spread out and somewhat hard to negotiate. Centro consists of three areas: Recife Antigo, the old city; Recife proper, with the districts of Santo Antônio and São José; and the districts of Boa Vista and Santo Amaro. The first two areas are on islands formed by the Rivers Capibaribe, Beberibe, and Pina; the third is made into an island by the Canal Tacaruna.

Centro—with its mixture of high-rises, colonial churches, and markets—is always busy during the day. The crowds and the narrow streets can make finding your way around even more confusing. With the exception of Recife Antigo, Centro is dead at night and should be avoided as a safety precaution.

Six kilometers (4 mi) south of Centro is the upscale residential and beach district of Boa Viagem, reached by bridge across the Bacia do Pina. Praia da Boa Viagem (Boa Viagem Beach), the Copacabana of Recife, is chockablock with trendy clubs and restaurants as well as many moderately priced and expensive hotels.

Numbers in the text correspond to numbers in the margin and on the Recife map.

A Good Tour

A visit to Santo Antônio's **Praça da República** ❶ ▶—with its stately palms, fountains, and statues—is a pleasant way to start your day and get your bearings. In and around the square are several landmark build-

Beaches

Urban sands are often lined by wide walkways and filled with beach-goers as well as vendors hawking coconut drinks and renting chairs and colorful umbrellas. The Atlantic waters throughout the region are warm year-round, and many beaches, particularly those near Fortaleza, have dunes high enough to ski down. The BA 099 highway, called the Linha Verde (Green Line), links cities and beaches and is part of an effort to protect Brazil's green spaces.

Carnatal & Fortal

Natal's Carnatal began in 1991, it was the country's first *carnaval fora da epoca*, or out-of-season Carnaval. More than a dozen other cities have since instituted similar celebrations, but this remains one of the largest. Always on the first weekend in December, it unites party seekers from throughout the country and beyond. There are about 10 blocos, each with room for 3,000 revelers. They travel along a 2-km (1-mi) route that starts just outside the soccer stadium. Performances are given by some of the country's top acts. Tickets often sell out early, especially for the more popular blocos. You can reserve tickets online through www.carnatal.com.br.

Fortal, in Fortaleza, is one of the country's foremost Carnaval fora da epoca celebrations. It is held the last week in July on a 4-km (2½-mi) stretch along the seaside Avenida Beira-Mar. Its scale is impressive: There are six blocos, each with 2,500 revelers. An average of 500,000 participate in the festivities each of the four days, 200,000 of them tourists. Like Carnatal, Fortal attracts top acts. For more information visit www.fortal.com.br.

Carnaval

In Recife people attend Carnaval *bailes* (dances) and *bloco* (percussion group) practice sessions for two months prior to the main festivities. The beat of choice is *frevo* (a fast-pace, frenetic music that normally accompanies a lively dance performed with umbrellas). Galo da Madrugada, the largest of Recife's 500 blocos, opens Carnaval and has drawn up to 20,000 costumed revelers. The blocos are joined by *escolas de samba* (samba schools or groups), escolas de frevo, *caboclinhos* (who dress in traditional Indian garb and bright feathers), and *maracatus* (African processions accompanied by percussionists). The highly animated Carnaval in Olinda, which lasts 11 days, is considered to be among the three best in Brazil, along with those in Rio and Salvador. Highlights include the opening events—led by a bloco of more than 400 "virgins" (men in drag)—and a parade of huge dolls (likenesses of famous northeasterners) made of Styrofoam, fabric, and papier-mâché.

Eating Out

Lobster, shrimp, crabs, and squid are found along the coast and on most menus. Also common is *carne de sol,* or sun-dried beef. It is generally served with rice, beans, and manioc root. The popular side dish *paçoca* is made with ground-up carne de sol, sliced onions, and manioc flour. A typical dessert is fried tapioca pancakes, often filled with bananas, grated coconut, or cheese. Fruits harvested in the region include pineapple, mango, guava, and cashew fruit. Sugarcane, which grows alongside many roadways, is pressed and made into *caldo de cana* (sugarcane juice), but is more often drunk in its distilled form—cachaça.

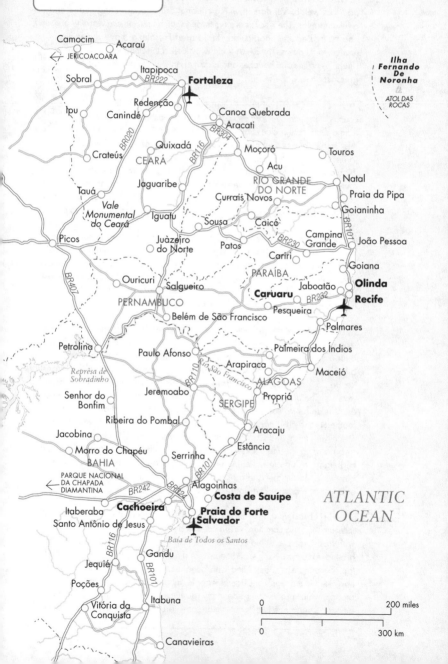

The Northeast Coast

Camocim
Acaraú
← JERICOACOARA
Sobral
Itapipoca
BR222
Fortaleza
Ipu
Redenção
Canindé
Canoa Quebrada
Aracati
Crateús
Quixadá
CEARÁ
Moçoró
BR116
BR304
Touros
Açu
RIO GRANDE
DO NORTE
Natal
Tauá
Jaguaribe
Currais Novos
Praia da Pipa
Goianinha
Vale
Monumental
do Ceará
Iguatu
Sousa
Caicó
Campina
Grande
João Pessoa
BR230
Picos
Juàzeiro
do Norte
Patos
Cariri
PARAÍBA
Goiana
BR101
Ouricuri
Salgueiro
Jaboatão
Caruaru
BR232
Olinda
Recife
BR407
PERNAMBUCO
Belém de São Francisco
Pesqueira
Petrolina
Paulo Afonso
Palmares
Palmeira dos Índios
Represa de
Sobradinho
Rio São Francisco
BR110
Arapiraca
ALAGOAS
Maceió
Senhor do
Bonfim
Jeremoabo
Propriá
SERGIPE
Ribeira do Pombal
Jacobina
Aracaju
Morro do Chapéu
Estância
BAHIA
Serrinha
BR101
PARQUE NACIONAL
DA CHAPADA
DIAMANTINA
←
BR242
BR324
Alagoinhas
Costa de Saúipe
Itaberaba
Cachoeira
Praia do Forte
Santo Antônio de Jesus
Salvador
BR116
Baía de Todos os Santos
ATLANTIC
OCEAN
Gandu
Jequié
BR101
Poções
Vitória da
Conquista
Itabuna
Canavieiras

Ilha
Fernando
De
Noronha

ATOL DAS
ROCAS

0   200 miles

0   300 km

ings, including the Palácio da Justiça. Behind it, on the Rua Imperador Dom Pedro II, is the **Igreja da Ordem Terceira de São Francisco** ❷. From this church follow Rua Imperador for about nine blocks to Travessa do Macêdo. On your right is the **Mercado de São José** ❸. Head west from the market, past the Praça Dom Vital, to Rua das Águas Verdes, where you find the Pátio de São Pedro and the **Catedral de São Pedro dos Clérigos** ❹. From the cathedral cross Avenida Dantas Barreto to the **Igreja e Convento do Carmo** ❺. Take Rua Mq. de Herval toward the Rio Capibaribe and cross Rua Floriano Peixoto to the **Casa da Cultura** ❻.

For a relaxing lunch, hop a cab to Rua do Bom Jesus in Recife Antigo and pick any restaurant. On that street is Latin America's oldest synagogue, **Sinagoga Kahal Zur Israel** ❼. After a quick visit, take another taxi to one of the city's forts or museums. In Recife Antigo, up Rua do Brum, is the **Fortaleza do Brum** ❽. Across the Ponte 23 de Setembro and along Avenida Sul and the waterfront is the **Forte das Cinco Pontas** ❾, in the São José district. Near the Rio Capibaribe as it curves northwest are the **Museo do Estado de Pernambuco** ❿ and the **Museo do Homem de Nordeste** ⓫. On the other side of the Capibaribe and 15 km (9 mi) out of town by way of Avenida Caxangá is the **Oficina Cerâmica Francisco Brennand** ⓬.

TIMING &
PRECAUTIONS

The walking portion of this tour takes 3–4 hours, longer if you linger at a café. Add another two or three hours if you visit one of the farther-flung forts or museums. Museum times change fairly frequently, so you may want to confirm before departing, especially for the more distant sites. Although petty thievery has been greatly reduced in Recife, take the normal precautions—be on guard against pickpockets, keep a tight hold on purses and cameras, and leave jewelry in the hotel safe.

What to See

❻ **Casa da Cultura.** In this 19th-century building, the old cells, with their heavy iron doors, have been transformed into shops that sell clay figurines, wood sculptures, carpets, leather goods, and articles made from woven straw. One of the cells has been kept in its original form to give you an idea of how the prisoners lived. There are areas for exhibitions and shows, such as the Monday, Wednesday, and Friday performances of local dances like *forró*, the *ciranda*, and the *bumba-meu-boi*. There are also clean public rest rooms. ⊠ *Rua Floriano Peixoto s/n, Santo Antônio* ☎ *081/3224–2850* ⊡ *Free* ☉ *Weekdays 9–7, Sat. 9–5, Sun. 9–2.*

❹ **Catedral de São Pedro dos Clérigos.** The facade of this cathedral, which was built in 1782, has fine wood sculptures; inside is a splendid trompe-l'oeil ceiling. The square surrounding the cathedral is a hangout for artists, who often read their poetry or perform folk music. It's lined with many restaurants, shops, and bars. A museum has exhibits on Carnaval and an art gallery. ⊠ *Pátio de São Pedro, São José* ☎ *081/3224–2954* ⊡ *Free* ☉ *Tues.–Fri. 8–11 and 2–4, Sat. 8–10:30.*

❽ **Fortaleza do Brum.** To safeguard their control, the Dutch wisely yet futilely built more than one fortress. In this one (c. 1629) you find reminders of those precarious days in the on-site **Museu Militar** (Military Museum), with its collection of old cannons, infantry weapons, and soldiers' utensils; there's even a skeleton of a soldier that dates from 1654. The fort also has a restaurant. ⊠ *Praça Luso-Brasileiro, Recife Antigo* ☎ *081/ 3224–4620* 🎫 *Free* ⊙ *Tues.–Fri. 9–4, weekends 2–4.*

❾ **Forte das Cinco Pontas.** The Dutch used mud to build the original five-sided fort in 1630. It was rebuilt in 1677 with stone and mortar; it now only has only four sides, but it has retained its original name. Inside is the **Museu da Cidade,** where maps and photos illustrate Recife's history. Before becoming a museum, it was used as a military headquarters and a prison. ⊠ *Largo das Cinco Pontas, São José* ☎ *081/3224–8492* 🎫 *Free* ⊙ *Weekdays 9–5, weekends 1–5.*

❺ **Igreja e Convento do Carmo.** The historic baroque-style church and convent are constructed of wood and white gold. The main altar has a life-size statue of Our Lady of Carmel. ⊠ *Praça do Carmo s/n, Santo Antônio* ☎ *081/3224–3341* 🎫 *Free* ⊙ *Weekdays 6:30 AM–8 PM, Sat. 7 AM–8 PM, Sun. 10–8:30. Mass weekdays at 6:30, 6, and 7; Sat. at 7; Sun. at 10 and 7.*

❷ **Igreja da Ordem Terceira de São Francisco.** Built in 1606, this church has beautiful Portuguese tile work. Don't miss the adjoining Capela Dourada (Golden Chapel), which was constructed in 1697 and is an outstanding example of Brazilian baroque architecture. The complex also contains a convent—the Convento Franciscano de Santo Antônio—and a museum displaying sacred art. ⊠ *Rua Imperador Dom Pedro II s/n, Santo Antônio* ☎ *081/3419–3287* 🎫 *Church free; museum R$2* ⊙ *Weekdays 8–11:30 and 2–5, Sat. 8–11:30.*

❸ **Mercado de São José.** In the city's most traditional market, vendors sell handicrafts, produce, and herbs. It's housed in a beautiful cast-iron structure that was imported from France in the 19th century. ⊠ *Trv. do Macêdo s/n, São José* ⊙ *Mon.–Sat. 6–6, Sun. 6–noon.*

❿ **Museu do Estado de Pernambuco.** The state historical museum is in a mansion once owned by a baron and seems more like a home filled with beautiful antiques than a museum. There's a grand piano, a dining-room table set with 18th-century china, an ornate 19th-century crib, and many beautiful paintings. ⊠ *Av. Rui Barbosa 960, Graça* ☎ *081/ 3427–9322* 🎫 *R$2* ⊙ *Tues.–Fri. 9–5:30, weekends 2–5:30.*

⓫ **Museu do Homem do Nordeste.** With three museums under one roof—one has displays about sugar, another anthropological exhibits, and the third regional handicrafts—the Museum of Northeastern Man offers great insight into Brazil's history. There are utensils made by indigenous peoples, European colonizers, and African slaves; religious articles used in Catholic and Candomblé rituals; and ceramic figurines by such artists as Mestre Vitalino and Mestre Zé. ⊠ *Av. 17 de Agosto 2187, Casa Forte* ☎ *081/ 3441–5500* 🎫 *Free* ⊙ *Tues. and Fri. 11–6, Thurs. 8–5, weekends 1–6.*

⓬ **Oficina Cerâmica Francisco Brennand.** In the old São José sugar refinery, this museum-workshop houses more than 2,000 pieces by the great (and prolific) Brazilian artist Francisco Brennand. Having studied in France, he was influenced by Pablo Picasso and Joan Miró, among others, and his works include paintings, drawings, and engravings as well as sculptures and ceramics. About 15 km (9 mi) from Recife Antigo, the museum's location

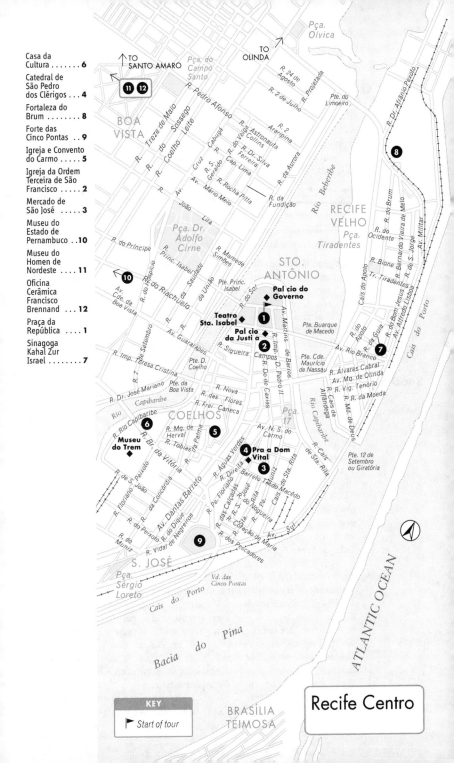

Pça.
Oivica

TO
OLINDA

TO
SANTO AMARO

Pça. do
Campo
Santo

R. 24 de
Agosto

R. Propatada

R. 2 de Julho

Pte. do
Limoeiro

R. Pedro Afonso

R. Treze de Maio

R. do Sossego

R. Coelho Leite

BOA
VISTA

R. Cabigá

R. da Veiga Collins

R. Astronauta

R. Araripina

R. 2

R. Dr. Silva Ferreira

R. da Aurora

R. S. Geraldo

R. Cap. Lima

R. Rocha Pitta

Cruz

Av. Mário Melo

R. da Fundição

Rio Beberibe

RECIFE
VELHO

R. do Ocidente

R. do Brum

R. Bernardo Vieira de Melo

R. de S. Jorge

Av. Militar

R. Dr. Afrânio Peixoto

Av. Alfredo Lisboa

8

João

Lira

Pça. Dr.
Adolfo
Cirne

R. do Príncipe

R. Princ. Isabel

Rio Capibaribe

R. da União

R. Saudade

R. Mamede Simões

Pça.
Tiradentes

STO.
ANTÔNIO

R. Bione

R. do Apolo

Tr. Tiradentes

Cais do Apolo

Av. da Cde. da Boa Vista

Av. Cde. da Boa Vista

R. do Riachuelo

Pte. Princ. Isabel

R. do Sol

Palácio do
Governo

1

Av. Martins de Barros

Pte. Buarque
de Macedo

R. do Bom Jesus

Av. Rio Branco

Cais do Porto

7

Teatro
Sta. Isabel

R. 7 de Setembro

Av. Guararapes

R. Imp. Teresa Cristina

Pte. D.
Coelho

Palácio
da Justiça

2

R. Siqueira

Campos

R. Imp. D. Pedro II

Pte. Cde.
Maurício
de Nassau

R. Álvares Cabral

Av. Mq. de Olinda

R. Vig. Tenório

R. da Moeda

R. da Guia

R. Dr. José Mariano

Rio Capibaribe

Pte. da
Boa Vista

R. Nova

R. das Flores

R. Frei Caneca

COELHOS

6

Museu
do Trem

R. Mq. de
Herval

R. Tobias

R. da Palma

5

Av. N. S. do
Carmo

Pça.
17

R. do Cais
de Sta. Rita

R. da Concórdia

R. Br. da Vitória

R. Mq. de
Herval

R. Águas Verdes

R. Direita

R. Pa. Floriano

4 Praça Dom
Vital

3

R. Barreto Teixeira

R. Tácio Macêdo

R. Muniz

Cais Alfândega

Cais de Sta. Rita

Pte. 12 de
Setembro
ou Giratória

R. de S. João

R. Floriano Peixoto

Av. Dantas Barreto

R. das Calçadas

R. José

R. Rita

R. do Nogueira

Cais do Sul

R. do Peixoto

R. do Dique

R. Vidal de Negreiros

R. do Coração de Maria

R. dos Pescadores

9

R. do
Muniz

S. JOSÉ

Pça.
Sérgio
Loreto

Vd. das
Cinco Pontas

Cais do Porto

ATLANTIC OCEAN

Bacia do Pina

KEY

▶ Start of tour

BRASÍLIA
TEIMOSA

Recife Centro

amid forest and fountains is almost as appealing as its displays. ⊠ *Km 16, Av. Caxangá, Várzea* ☎ *081/3271–2466* 🎫 *R$2* ⊙ *Weekdays 8–6.*

▶ ❶ **Praça da República.** Republic Square was originally known as the Field of Honor, a nod to those who were drawn and quartered here during the Republican movement of 1817. The structures around the square showcase the city's architecture from the 19th through the 20th centuries. Highlights include the Teatro Santa Isabel (St. Isabel Theater, 1850); the Palácio do Campo das Princesas, also known as the Palácio do Governo (Government House, 1841); and the Palácio da Justiça (Court House, 1930).

Recife Antigo. Most of Old Recife's colonial public buildings and houses have been restored. The area between Rua do Bom Jesus and Rua do Apolo is full of shops, cafés, and bars, making it the hub of downtown life both day and night; on some weekends there's dancing in the streets. A handicrafts fair is held every Sunday from 1 to 10 on Rua do Bom Jesus.

❼ **Sinagoga Kahal Zur Israel.** Opened in 2003 after a lengthy period of excavation and restoration, this synagogue was apparently Latin America's first. All that remain of the original synagogue are the walls and the ground, which can be viewed through glass floor panels. An excellent museum provides explanations of the Jewish experience in Brazil. Some monitors speak English. ⊠ *Rua do Bom Jesus 197, Recife Antigo* ☎ *081/3224–7376* ⊕ *www.arquivojudaicope.org.br* 🎫 *R$2* ⊙ *Weekdays 9–5, weekends 3–7.*

Beaches

★ **Boa Viagem.** Coconut palms line Recife's most popular beach, the 7-km-long (4-mi-long) Praia da Boa Viagem. A steady Atlantic breeze tames the hot sun, and reef formations create pools of warm water that are perfect for swimming. Sailors and fishermen beach their *jangadas* (handcrafted log rafts with beautiful sails), and vendors sell coconut drinks from kiosks. Avenida Boa Viagem separates a row of hotels and apartments from the beach, which is lined by a wide blue *calçadão* (sidewalk) that's perfect for runs, bike rides, or evening promenades. On weekend afternoons there's a handicrafts fair in Praça da Boa Viagem. Surfing and swimming beyond the reef are not recommended because of the presence of sharks. ⊠ *Just south of Recife.*

Cabo de Santo Agostinho. One of Pernambuco's finest beaches, Cabo de Santo Agostinho is good for swimming, though surfing has been banned due to the danger of shark attacks. In the town of Cabo de Santo Agostinho you can walk around the ruins of the Forte Castelo do Mar. ⊠ *35 km (22 mi) southeast of Recife.*

Gaibu. Quiet, beautiful Gaibu is surrounded by palm trees. Its blue waters are good for surfing, and it's also the site of volleyball competitions and fishing and sailing events. ⊠ *30 km (19 mi) south of Recife.*

Ilha de Itamaracá. This island is off the coast of the historic city of Igarassu. The best beach is Forte Orange, next to Coroa do Avião. ⊠ *39 km (24 mi) north of Recife, Igarassu.*

Maracaípe. Quiet Maracaípe Beach hosts surfing competitions; it hosted the World Surfing Games in 2000. Maracaípe is a tiny hamlet with three dune buggies, two beach bars, and a small hotel. The beach's appeal is seclusion and surfing. ⊠ *73 km (46 mi) southwest of Recife.*

Porto de Galinhas. You'll find cool, clean waves and several resorts at Porto de Galinhas. The beach, which follows the curve of a bay lined with coconut palms and cashew trees, gets crowded on weekends year-round. There are plenty of jangadas for rent; other boats can take you to the island of Santo Aleixo. ⊠ *70 km (43 mi) south of Recife.*

Tamandaré. Although it's in the middle of an important nature reserve, developers have their eye on Tamandaré. Come quick, before its beaches—such as Praia dos Carneiros and Praia de Guadalupe—become one big resort area. ⊠ *110 km (68 mi) south of Recife.*

Where to Eat

Brazilian

¢–$ ✕ **Parraxaxá.** Waiters wear the bent orange hats of Lampião, a Jesse James–like folk hero who made his way through the interior of the Northeast during the early 20th century. The buffet has a wide selection of the regional specialties Lampião might have encountered back in the day. Food is priced per kilo. ⊠ *Rua Baltazar Pereira 32, Boa Viagem* ☎ *081/3463-7874* ⊕ *www.parraxaxa.com.br* ▭ *MC, V.*

Eclectic

★ $–$$ ✕ **Leite.** Established in 1882, Leite is one of Brazil's oldest restaurants. Some tables are filled by the same people each day, and several waiters are following in the footsteps of generations of family members who have worked here. Roast lamb is a specialty. ⊠ *Praça Joaquim Nabuco 147, Santo Antônio* ☎ *081/3224-7977* ▭ *AE, DC, MC, V.*

Italian

$$ ✕ **Famiglia Giuliana.** This outstanding restaurant is in a replica of a medieval Italian castle, replete with a moat, candelabras, coats of armor, and a stained-glass ceiling. It's open from lunchtime until the last diner leaves. The seafood fettuccine is an excellent choice. ⊠ *Av. Eng. Domingos Ferreira 3980, Boa Viagem* ☎ *081/3465-9922* ▭ *AE, DC, MC, V.*

$–$$ ✕ **Barbarico Bongiovani.** A sophisticated setting and a high-quality Italian menu are the draws here. Try the scaloppine al Marsala. ⊠ *Av. Engenheiro Domingos Ferreira 2655, Boa Viagem* ☎ *081/3325-4268* ▭ *AE, DC, MC, V* ☾ *Closed Mon. No lunch Tues.–Sat.*

$–$$ ✕ **Buongustaio.** This Italian restaurant has a diverse menu for all palates. Although the dishes often change, you cannot go wrong if you order the lamb or cod. ⊠ *Rua Santo Elias 350, Espinheiro* ☎ *081/3241-1470* ▭ *DC* ☾ *Closed Sun.*

Portuguese

$$ ✕ **Tasca.** The menu is more Portuguese than Brazilian, so, not surprisingly, one of the best dishes is *bacalhau a calí* (codfish cooked with olive oil, onion, garlic, tomatoes, potatoes, and white wine). ⊠ *165 Rua Dom José Lopes, Boa Viagem* ☎ *081/3326-6309* ▭ *AE* ☾ *Closed Mon.*

Seafood

★ $–$$ ✕ **O Amphitrião.** At least one evening out in Recife Antigo is a must on your trip. Although there are many good restaurants along Rua Bom

Jesus, O Amphitrião stands out for its shrimp dish, *camarão Maurício de Nassau.* Space is limited inside, but most diners opt for the sidewalk tables. ⊠ *Rua do Bom Jesus 183, Recife Antigo* ☎ *081/3224–1436* ⊟ *AE, DC, MC, V* ⊘ *No dinner Sun.–Tues.*

$–$$ ✕ **Bargaço.** People come to this pleasant restaurant for the renowned dishes from the state of Bahia. If you don't mind a heavy dish, try the outstanding *moqueca baiana* (fish cooked with onion, tomatoes, peppers, parsley, and coconut milk). ⊠ *Av. Boa Viagem 670, Pina* ☎ *081/ 3465–1847* ⊟ *AE, DC, MC, V.*

Where to Stay

Most of Recife's top hotels are about 20 minutes from the airport, across from the Boa Viagem and Pina beaches or along Piedade Beach, in the municipality of Jaboatão dos Guararapes.

$$$–$$$$ 🏨 **Mar Hotel Recife.** Location is one of this hotel's main draws: it's a five-minute drive from the airport, a 20-minute drive from Recife Antigo, and very close to Boa Viagem. Rooms are only medium-size but are nicely decorated and well equipped with desks that have swivel chairs, two phone lines, and fax and modem lines. When you're ready to call it a day, you can relax by the pool, which has a soothing waterfall. ⊠ *Rua Barão de Souza Leão 451, Boa Viagem 51030-300* ☎ *081/3302–4444* 🖶 *081/3302–4445* ⊕ *www.marhotel.com.br* 🛏 *207 rooms, 30 suites* ⟁ *2 restaurants, minibars, cable TV, pool, health club, sauna, bar, meeting room* ⊟ *AE, DC, MC, V.*

$$$ 🏨 **Atlante Plaza Hotel.** Facing Recife's most popular beach, this high-rise's blue-glass windows make even the sky look pale. All rooms have sea views, but be sure to take a ride in the glass-enclosed elevator for a truly memorable ocean panorama. Ask for a room without carpets, as some have a faint mildew smell. A buffet breakfast is served in the Brasserie restaurant, where you can also have an á la carte or buffet lunch. The Mirage restaurant serves international or Brazilian dinners. ⊠ *Av. Boa Viagem 5426, 51030-000* ☎ *081/3302–3333* 🖶 *081/3302–3344* ⊕ *www. atlanteplaza.com.br* 🛏 *70 room, 27 suites* ⟁ *2 restaurants, minibars, cable TV, pool, health club, 2 bars, business services, meeting rooms, recreation room* ⊟ *AE, DC, V.*

$ 🏨 **Parthenon Golden Beach.** This beachfront apartment hotel is ideal for families or larger groups. Each spacious unit has one or two bedrooms, a living room, and a fully equipped kitchen. ⊠ *Av. Bernardo Vieira de Melo 1204, Piedade, Jaboatão dos Guararapes 54410-001* ☎ *081/ 3468–3002* 🖶 *081/3468–1941* ⊕ *www.accor.com.br* 🛏 *130 apartments* ⟁ *2 restaurants, minibars, cable TV, kitchenettes, pool, health club, sauna, 2 bars* ⊟ *AE, DC, MC, V.*

$ 🏨 **Recife Monte Hotel.** Just a block from Boa Viagem Beach, this hotel has all the amenities of a luxury hotel, including a lovely pool. A must during your stay here is the Sunday *feijoada* (Brazilian national dish consisting of black beans, smoked meats, oranges, and whatever else the chef may decide to throw in) in the Marruá restaurant. ⊠ *Rua dos Navegantes 363, Boa Viagem 51021-010* ☎ *081/3465–7422* 🖶 *081/ 3465–8406* ⊕ *www.recifemontehotel.com.br* 🛏 *152 rooms, 21 suites*

⚒ *Restaurant, minibars, cable TV, pool, hair salon, health club, sauna, bar* ☰ *AE, DC, V* ⦿| *BP.*

¢ 🏨 **Hotel do Sol.** This reasonably priced hotel faces Praia do Pina on Avenida Boa Viagem. Rooms are simple but comfortable. All have ocean views, some more direct than others. ⊠ *Av. Boa Viagem 978, Pina, 50030-010* ☎ *081/3091–0991* 🖶 *081/3465–5278* ⊕ *www.hsol.com.br* 📞 *69 rooms* ⚒ *Minibars, pool, bar* ☰ *DC, MC, V.*

¢ 🏨 **Recife Plaza.** Overlooking the Rio Capibaribe, this downtown hotel is simple and functional. Beds are a bit flimsy. Ask for a room with a river view. ⊠ *Rua da Aurora 225, Boa Vista 50060-000* ☎🖶 *081/ 3231–1200* ⊕ *www.recifeplazahotel.com.br* 📞 *80 rooms* ⚒ *Restaurant, minibars, pool, sauna* ☰ *AE, DC, MC, V.*

Nightlife & the Arts

Nightlife

Pólo Pina, the calçadão in the Pina district, is a popular area near the beach for nighttime activities. In the streets off Rua Herculano Bandeira you can find close to two-dozen bars and restaurants. Between Rua do Apolo and Rua do Bom Jesus (or Rua dos Judeus) in Recife Antigo, people gather in a seemingly endless variety of bars, cafés, and nightclubs. On Saturday the market in Praça de Boa Viagem comes alive with forró dancers.

BARS **O Biruta** (⊠ Rua Bem-te-vi 15, Brasília Teimosa ☎ 081/3326–5151) is a great spot to watch the moon rise over the beach. Chilled draft beer, tasty snacks, and excellent service make **Boteco** (⊠ Av. Boa Viagem 1660, Boa Viagem ☎ 081/3325–1428) one of the most popular bars in town. **Depois** (⊠ Av. Rio Branco 66, Recife Antigo ☎ 081/3424–7451) is in an old building in the heart of a bohemian neighborhood. Hits from the '60s and '70s are a hit with an over-30 crowd. **Galeria Joana D'Arc** (⊠ Rua Herculano Bandeira 500, Pina) is a cluster of small cafés and bars, among them Café Poire, Anjo Solto, Barnabé, and Oriente Médio. It's a premier gay and lesbian hangout.

DANCE CLUBS The **Calypso Bar** (⊠ Rua do Bom Jesus 147, Recife Antigo ☎ 081/ 3224–4855) is *the* place to dance to live music ranging from Caribbean rhythms to forró. You can fortify yourself with appetizers as well as drinks. **Downtown** (⊠ Rua Vigário Tenório 105, Recife Antigo ☎ 081/ 3424–6317), a club with a London pub look, is a good place to be on Wednesday night when local bands play. The club is popular with teenagers and twentysomethings. **Fashion Club** (⊠ Av. Fernando Simões Barbosa 266, Boa Viagem ☎ 081/3327–4040) is a hot spot Wednesday through Sunday, with a DJ, a laser show, a great dance floor, and three pubs. Sometimes there are live shows. The bar-restaurant **Sea Paradise** (⊠ Rua Almir B. Cunha s/n ☎ 081/3435–1740) has live music, a noteworthy fish stew, and day or night catamaran rides.

The Arts

Closed for 30 years, the **Teatro Santa Isabel** (⊠ Praça da República s/n, Santo Antônio ☎ 081/3224–1020), built in 1850, reopened in 2002 after a major restoration. The neoclassical theater is the setting for operas, plays, and classical concerts.

Sports & the Outdoors

Sailing

At Boa Viagem, fishermen with jangadas offer sailing or fishing trips. The waters are shallow and calm at Maria Farinha Beach, on the north coast at the mouth of the Rio Timbó. Here you can rent jet skis, take ultralight flights, and enjoy motorboat and catamaran rides.

Scuba Diving

For centuries the treacherous offshore reefs that gave Recife its name have struck fear into the hearts of sailors. Many a vessel has failed to navigate the natural harbor successfully. Seventeen wrecks have been identified as good and safe dives for underwater explorers of various experience levels. The *Vapor de Baixo* is one such ship. Bombed by the Germans during World War II, it's 20 meters (65 feet) down and is crawling with lobsters and turtles. Though diving is practiced year-round, visibility is best between October and May, when the wind and water are at their calmest. The **Seagate–Expedição Atlântico** (⊠ Av. Ministro Marcos Freire 257, Olinda ☎ 081/3426–1657 or 081/9972–9662 ⊕ www.seagaterecife.com.br), in Bairro Novo in Olinda, is a dive operation that offers courses, rents equipment, and runs trips for certified divers.

Shopping

Vendors at the **Mercado de São José** (⊠ Trv. do Macedo, São José) sell clothes and handicrafts as well as produce. It's open Monday–Saturday 6–6 and Sunday morning 6–noon. The **Feira Hippie** (Hippie Fair), held in the seafront Praça da Boa Viagem on afternoons starting at 4, has handicrafts.

Shopping Center Guararapes (⊠ Av. Barreto de Menezes 800, Piedade, Jaboatão dos Guararapes ☎ 081/3464–2211) has everything the Shopping Center Recife has but on a smaller scale. It's near Piedade Beach. The enormous **Shopping Center Recife** (⊠ Rua Padre Carapuceiro 777, Boa Viagem ☎ 081/3464–6000) is the perfect place for a day of shopping. In addition to a good variety of both Brazilian and international stores, you can find restaurants, banks, a post office, pharmacies, and a business center. It's not far from the Boa Viagem Beach.

SIDE TRIPS FROM RECIFE

Olinda

7 km (4 mi) north of Recife.

The name of Pernambuco State's original capital means "beautiful," and this must have been what came to mind when the first Europeans stood atop the forested hills and gazed at ocean and beach spread out before them. Today the town's natural beauty is complemented by colonial buildings painted in a rainbow of colors, making it a stunning slice of the old northeast.

Founded by the Portuguese in 1535, Olinda was developed further by the Dutch during their brief turn at running Pernambuco in the 1600s.

The narrow cobblestone streets of this UNESCO World Cultural Site curve up and down hills that, at every turn, offer spectacular views of both Recife and the Atlantic. The scenery is just as nice up close: many houses have latticed balconies, heavy doors, and stucco walls. The zoning laws are strict, resulting in a beautiful, compact city that artists, musicians, and intellectuals have made their own.

The city center is hilly but fairly easy to explore by foot. You may want to hire a guide to help provide some historical background on the city and its principal sites. Look for the official guides (they have ID cards) who congregate in the Praça do Carmo. They are former street children, and half the R$45 fee for a full city tour goes to a home for kids from the streets.

On Olinda's southern edge is the **Centro de Convenções Pernambuco,** one of the most modern convention centers in Latin America, which houses Empetur, the state tourism office. Cultural performances are often held in the center's theater and auditorium. ⊠ *Complexo de Salgadinho s/n* ☎ *081/3241–7966.*

The **Convento de São Francisco,** built in 1577, was the first Franciscan convent built in Brazil. The floors are Portuguese tile work, ceilings are frescoed, and walls are made of ground-up local coral. ⊠ *Rua Bispo Coutinho s/n* ☎ *081/3429–0517* ⌑ *R$1* ⊙ *Mon.–Sat. 7–noon and 2–5.*

The main chapel of the **Mosteiro de São Bento,** a Benedictine monastery, is considered one of Brazil's most beautiful. It once housed the nation's first law school. The 10 AM Sunday mass features Gregorian chants. ⊠ *Rua de São Bento s/n* ☎ *081/3429–3288* ⌑ *Free* ⊙ *Daily 7–11:30 and 2–6:30.*

The **Alto da Sé** is the most scenic spot for viewing Olinda, Recife, and the ocean. It's also a good place see some historic churches as well as to sample Bahia-style *acaraje* (black-eyed pea fritters) and Pernambuco's famous tapioca cakes. Have a seat at one of the outdoor tables here, or browse in the shops that sell handicrafts—including lace—and paintings. To get here, just walk up on Ladeira da Sé.

Built in 1540 and restored in 1654, the **Igreja da Misericórdia** (Mercy Church) has rich sculptures of wood, gold, and silver. It's atop the Alto da Sé. ⊠ *Rua Bispo Coutinho s/n* ☎ *081/3429–0627* ⌑ *Free* ⊙ *Daily noon–2:30.*

The last of many renovations to the 1537 **Igreja da Sé,** on the Alto da Sé, was in 1983. It has now been restored as much as possible to its original appearance. From its side terrace you can see the Old City and the ocean. ⊠ *Rua Bispo Coutinho s/n* ⌑ *Free* ⊙ *Daily 8–noon and 2–5.*

At the **Museu do Mamulengo-Espaço Tirida,** everyday life and northeastern folk tales are the stuff of shows, presented using some of the more than 300 puppets made of wood and cloth that are on display in this whimsical museum. ⊠ *Rua do Amparo 59* ☎ *081/3429–6214* ⌑ *R$2* ⊙ *Tues.–Fri. 9–5, weekends 10–5.*

The collection of sacred art and other objects in the **Museu de Arte Sacra de Pernambuco** tells the story of Olinda. ⊠ *Rua do Bispo Coutinho 726* ☎ *081/3429–0036* ⌑ *R$1* ⊙ *Weekdays 8–1.*

Where to Stay & Eat

\$–\$\$ ✕ **Oficina do Sabor.** Everything is tasty at this regional restaurant, but do try the *abóbora com camarão* (pumpkin stuffed with shrimp and served with a *pitanga* cherry sauce). ⊠ *Rua do Amparo 335* ☎ *081/3429–3331* 🖃 *AE, DC, MC, V* ☻ *Closed Mon.*

\$ ✕ **Goya.** The two artist-owners display their work on the walls of the colorful bilevel restaurant. Their creativity is also apparent in the preparation and presentation of French–Brazilian fusion dishes. The coconut shrimp is especially tasty. ⊠ *Rua do Amparo 335* ☎ *081/3429–3331* 🖃 *AE, DC, MC, V* ☻ *Closed Mon.*

\$ 🏨 **Hotel 7 Colinas.** This hotel sits in an off-street hollow amid the trees and flowers of a tangled garden. From here it's just a short hike up to Alto da Sé. Rooms are comfortably furnished, and all look out on the grounds. ⊠ *Ladeira de São Francisco 307, 53120-070* ☎ *081/3439–6055* ⊕ *www.hotel7colinasolinda.com.br* ⋈ *39 rooms* ⚲ *Restaurant, minibars, pool, bar, meeting room* 🖃 *AE, DC, V.*

\$ 🏨 **Pousada do Amparo.** A member of the exclusive Brazilian Roteiros de Charme group, this lovely pousada is made up of two colonial houses with 12-meter (39-foot) ceilings. Wood and brick details, original artwork, and an indoor garden lend considerable warmth to the cavernous spaces. ⊠ *Rua do Amparo 199, 53020-190* ☎ *081/3439–1749* 🖷 *081/3429–6889* ⊕ *www.pousadadoamparo.com.br* ⋈ *11 rooms* ⚲ *Restaurant, minibars, pool, sauna, bar* 🖃 *MC, DC, V.*

Fodor's Choice ★

¢–\$ 🏨 **Hotel Pousada Quatro Cantos.** In a converted mansion, this pousada has rooms that vary considerably in size and price. Carnaval decorations enliven the lobby. The Mercado da Ribeira is within walking distance. ⊠ *Rua Prudente de Morais 441* ☎ *081/3429–0220* ⊕ *www. pousada4cantos.com.br* ⋈ *16 rooms, 2 suites* ⚲ *Restaurant, minibars, bar* 🖃 *AE, DC, V.*

¢–\$ 🏨 **Pousada Peter.** You may wonder whether this grand mansion is a pousada or an art gallery. Peter Bauer, whose paintings have hung in many galleries, is both the owner and the resident artist. The large guest rooms lead out to a terrace where you can enjoy a view of the gardens, Olinda, and Recife. During Carnaval, for which the pousada has special packages, revelers dance along the street out front. ⊠ *Rua do Amparo 215, 53020-170* ☎🖷 *081/3439–2171* ⊕ *www.pousadapeter.com. br* ⋈ *8 rooms* ⚲ *Minibars, pool.*

Shopping

For crafts head to the **Casa do Artesão** (⊠ Rua de São Bento 170 ☎ 081/3429–2979). It's open weekdays 9–6 and Saturday 9–1. The **Mercado Eufrásio Barbosa** (⊠ Largo do Varadouro s/n ☎ 081/3439–1415) was once the site of the Royal Customs House, where goods from Europe were sold. It's now a tourist center—with handicrafts and snack bars. It's open Monday–Saturday 9–6. The **Mercado da Ribeira** (⊠ Rua Bernardo Vieira de Melo s/n, Ribeira ☎ 081/3439–9626) was once a slave market. Today you can find more than a dozen handicrafts shops that are open weekdays 9–8 and Saturday 9–noon.

Caruaru

134 km (83 mi) west of Recife.

Caruaru and its crafts center, Alto do Moura (6 km/4 mi south of Caruaru), became famous in the 1960s and '70s for clay figurines made by local artisan Mestre Vitalino. There are now more than 500 craftspeople working in Alto do Moura. All are inspired by Vitalino, whose former home is now a museum, open Monday–Saturday 8–noon and 2–6 and Sunday 8–noon. At the crafts center you can buy not only figurines, which depict northeasterners doing everyday things, but also watch the artisans work.

In Caruaru a great open-air market, **Feira de Artesanato**, is held every Saturday, when, as the songwriter Luis Gonzaga put it, "It is possible to find a little of everything that exists in the world." Look for pottery, leather goods, ceramics, hammocks, and baskets. ⊠ *Parque 18 de Maio.*

Where to Stay

¢ **Caruaru Park Hotel.** On the outskirts of town, the Caruaru Park's colorful rooms and chalets are sparsely decorated but neat and clean. Balconies have hammocks and decent views of town. ⊠ *Km 134, BR 232, 55030-400* ☎ *081/3722-9191* ⊟ *081/3722-7397* ↝ *68 rooms* ⌂ *Restaurant, minibars, cable TV, pool* ⊟ *AE, DC, MC, V.*

NATAL

Natal, with a population now exceeding 700,000, has been growing by leaps and bounds over the past decade. The capital of Rio Grande do Norte has become an important industrial center, yet no industry has had more effect on the economy than tourism. The past few administrations have invested heavily in the infrastructure and promotion, effectively placing it on the map as one of the prime tourism destinations in Brazil.

Although it has little in the way of historical or cultural attractions, the city's main asset is its location along one of the most beautiful stretches of coast in Brazil. In fact, Natal's foundation and much of its history have been all about location. In 1598 the Portuguese began construction of the Fortaleza dos Reis Magos in present-day Natal. Its location was strategic for two reasons. First, it was at the confluence of the Atlantic Ocean and the Rio Potengi. Second, it was near the easternmost point of the continent and therefore was closest to Europe and Africa. On December 25, 1599, the city was founded and named Natal, the Portuguese word for "Christmas."

Because of its valuable location, Natal was a target for the Dutch, who ultimately seized control of the city in 1633 and renamed it New Amsterdam. The Portuguese repossessed Natal after the Dutch abandoned the city in 1654. Yet it was never a major colonial center for the Portuguese. The city had to wait nearly three centuries to regain importance, again due to its location. In World War II the United States built several military bases in and around the city that they deemed "the springboard to victory"—its position at the far-eastern point of the continent made it ideal for launching aerial attacks into Europe.

Exploring Natal

Few tourists stay in the city itself, and many do not even visit. Nearly all head straight to Ponta Negra, a rapidly developing beach area 10 km (6 mi) south of the city center. Ponta Negra is still small enough that it can easily be explored on foot—most hotels and restaurants are on or just a few blocks from the beach. Natal's few museums and historic buildings are mostly clustered in Cidade Alta (Upper City), the oldest part of the city, and are within easy walking distance of each other. Just a kilometer to the northeast of Cidade Alta is Praia dos Artistas. It was formerly the center of tourist activity but has taken on a bit of a seedy quality. Its bars and clubs remain popular, but take taxis as night and avoid walking alone.

What to See

Forte dos Reis Magos. Natal owes its existence to this impressive five-sided fort. It was built by the Portuguese in 1598, one year before the founding of Natal, and controlled by the Dutch between 1633 and 1654. Visitors can see the old quarters, the chapel, and rusted cannons. ⊠ *Northern end of Av. Praia do Forte (continuation of Via Costeira that extends to Ponta Negra), Praia do Meio* ☎ *084/502–1099* ✆ *Free* ☉ *Daily 8–4:30.*

Museu Café Filho. Furniture, documents, and other objects belonging to the only Brazilian president from Rio Grande do Norte are displayed in this mansion. ⊠ *Rua da Conceição 601, Cidade Alta* ☎ *084/212–2496* ✆ *Free* ☉ *Tues.–Sun. 8–6.*

Museu Câmara Cascudo. This well-conceived museum has exhibits from a variety of disciplines: archaeology, paleontology, mineralogy, ethnography, and popular culture. A highlight is the collection of dinosaur fossils. ⊠ *Av. Hermes da Fonseca 1398, Tirol* ☎ *084/212–2795* ✆ *R$1* ☉ *Tues.–Fri. 8–11 and 2–5.*

Praça Sete de Setembro. The two most notable buildings around this center of old Natal are the Victorian-style governor's mansion, built in 1873, and the uninspiring cathedral, built in 1862. The square is rather lifeless except for in the month of December, when a play retelling the Christmas story is performed.

Beaches

Búzios. This beach has been endowed with great natural beauty yet does not usually have many visitors. The barrier reef creates an area of clear, calm waters ideal for bathing, snorkeling, and scuba diving. In the background are some impressive dunes, covered with palm trees and other vegetation. The modest infrastructure consists of just a few small pousadas and restaurants. ⊠ *RN 063 (Rota do Sol); 35 km (21 mi) south of Natal.*

Genipabu. Massive dunes have made this one of the best-known beaches in the country. The area is most commonly explored on thrilling, hourlong dune-buggy rides. You have two choices: *com emoção* (literally, "with emotion"), which rivals any roller-coaster, or *sem emoção* (without emotion), a little calmer but still fairly hair-raising. Buggy operators, who usually find you before you find them, charge around R$150 for five people. You can also explore the dunes on camels imported from southern Spain. Other activities include half-hour boat rides and sky boarding (also called sky surfing)—which is basically snowboarding down the dunes. The beach is attractive, although it gets very crowded during high season. Because Genipabu is close to Natal, it is primarily a day-trip destination. There are a few small pousadas and restaurants near the beach, but the town shuts down at night. Buses leave from the Rodoviário Velho every half hour or so. ⊠ *Take BR 101 north to Pitanguí access road; 10 km (6 mi) north of Natal.*

Maracajaú. The principal draw at Maracajaú is the large coral reef 7 km (4 mi) off the coast. Teeming with marine life, the sizable reef offers the best snorkeling in the Natal area. There are no hotels for overnight stays, but **Ma-noa Parque Aquático** (Ma-noa Aquatic Park; ⊠ Enseada Pontas dos Anéis ☎ 084/223–4333 ⊕ www.ma-noa.com.br) has all that day visitors require: a restaurant, water rides, a huge pool, boat trips to the reef with snorkeling equipment provided, and even transport to and from Natal hotels. Entrance to the park costs R$15, and the snorkel trip costs R$30. Go now, as the ecosystem will be not be able to handle the up to 1,000 daily visitors indefinitely. Ma-noa has a shuttle service from Natal. ⊠ *Take BR 101 north to Maracajaú access road; 70 km (42 mi) north of Natal.*

Pirangi do Norte. This long white-sand beach is an extremely popular summer vacation destination for residents of Natal. Boat rides to nearby coral reefs and beaches run frequently. Near the beach is the world's largest cashew tree, according to the *Guinness Book of World Records.* Its circumference measures 500 meters (1,650 feet), roughly 70 times greater than that of normal cashew trees. ⊠ *RN 063 (Rota do Sol); 28 km (17 mi) north of Natal.*

Ponta Negra. Nearly all tourism development has focused on or around this beach in the past few years. It has a multitude of pousadas, restaurants, and shops and even a few large resorts at the northern end. The beach itself, around 2½ km (1½ mi) long, can no longer be called pristine but is still reasonably clean and attractive. Large waves make it popular with surfers. Ponta Negra's distinguishing feature is the *Morro da Careca* (Bald Man's Hill), a 120-meter (390-foot) dune at the southern end. You can catch a taxi or a bus at various stops along the Via Costeira south of Natal. ⊠ *Via Costeira; 10 km (6 mi) south of Natal.*

Where to Eat

$$–$$$ ╳ **Raro Sabor.** Join Natal's high society for a few hours in this chic, pricey bistro near the Praia dos Artistas. The name means "rare flavor," but in reality the menu offers a mix of French and international classics. The *peixe saboroso ao molho de tangerina* (fish in tangerine sauce) is a winner. ⊠ *Rua Seridó 722, Petrópolis* ☎ *084/202–3411* ▭ *AE, DC, MC, V* ⊗ *Closed Mon.*

$–$$ ╳ **Peixada da Comadre.** If you were wondering where locals go for the town's best fish, this is it. The decor is rather simple, but tables in the back have excellent views of the Praia dos Artistas through large glass windows. Dishes are easily large enough for two. ⊠ *Rua Dr. José Augusto Bezerra de Medeiros 4, Praia do Meio* ☎ *084/202–3411* ⊟ *No credit cards* ⊘ *Closed Tues.*

$ ╳ **Piazzale Italia.** During the high season (July and December–mid-March), make a reservation, or you'll be among the many waiting outside, salivating from smells of fresh tomato sauce and garlic. The restaurant's popularity is a result of reasonable prices, proximity to the Ponta Negra Beach (a five-minute taxi ride), and skillful preparation of pasta and seafood dishes. Particularly recommended is the *tagliolini allo scoglio* (pasta with lobster, shrimp, and mussels). ⊠*Av. Dep. Antônio Florêncio de Queiroz 12, Ponta Negra* ☎ *084/236–2697* ⊟ *AE, DC, MC, V.*

★ $ ╳ **Tererê.** Consider fasting for several days before visiting what is considered by locals to be the town's best churrascaria. Unless you indicate otherwise, waiters bring choice cuts of beef, lamb, chicken, and pork until you have passed out on the table. If you're not as carnivorous as most Brazilians, you can sneak food off the salad table, which has a good selection of lighter fare. ⊠ *Estrada de Ponta Negra 2326, Ponta Negra* ☎ *084/219–4081* ⊟ *AE, DC, MC, V.*

¢–$ ╳ **Mangai.** Choose from more than 40 delicious regional specialties at this
FodorśChoice immensely popular per-kilo restaurant. Tourists and town residents eat
★ together at communal wood tables, which fit the typical rustic decor of the sertão. To top off your meal, consider ordering the *cartola,* a popular dessert made of caramelized banana, cheese, and cinnamon. ⊠*Av. Amintas Barros 3300, Lagoa Nova* ☎ *084/206–3344* ⊟ *V* ⊘ *Closed Mon.*

Where to Stay

$$$$ ▦ **Pestana Natal Beach Resort.** This attractive resort manages to avoid some of the traditional problems associated with megacomplexes: its beige color allows it to blend into its sandy surroundings, room furnishings all have original artwork and other strokes of personality, and personalized service makes guests feel like more than a number. ⊠ *Av. Senador Dinarte Mariz 5525, Via Costeira, 6 km north of Ponta Negra, 59090-001* ☎ *084/220–8900* 🖷 *084/220–8920* ⊕ *www.pestanahotels.com.br* ➷ *184 rooms, 5 suites* ♧ *2 restaurants, minibars, cable TV, pool, health club, sauna, bars, business center* ⊟ *AE, DC, MC, V.*

$$$ ▦ **Rifóles.** The eclectic architectural style of this hotel is both attractive and confusing; pirate and cave-painting motifs are cultivated through the use of materials such as old driftwood, plaster, marble, and *tijolo aparente*—locally produced beige bricks. The beach in front is uncrowded, as it is a mile or so from the busy part of Ponta Negra. You can also bathe in one of the two pools, but the nearby karaoke machine ruins any semblance of peace. Rooms are well equipped and adequately sized. ⊠ *Rua Cel. Inácio Vale 8847, Ponta Negra 59090-001* ☎ *084/646–5000* 🖷 *084/646–5005* ⊕ *www.rifoles.com.br* ➷ *110 rooms* ♧ *Restaurant, minibars, cable TV, 2 pools, sauna, bar, recreation room* ⊟ *AE, DC, MC, V.*

$$ ╳▦ **Manary Praia Hotel.** It is hardly surprising that this small all-star hotel
FodorśChoice was chosen as a member of the prestigious Roteiros de Charme group.
★ Both the service and decor reflect tremendous attention to detail. The

restaurant serves skillfully prepared dishes such as grilled seafood in the pretty pool area that overlooks the beach. The locations is ideal, as it is just beyond the crowded portion of Ponta Negra. The owner also runs Natal's only ecotourism operator, which offers top-flight trips to area beaches and fascinating inland destinations such as Cariri and Dinosaur Valley. ⊠ *Rua Francisco Gurgel 9067, Ponta Negra, 59090-050* 🕿🕿 *084/ 219–2900* ⊕ *www.manary.com.br* ⬐ *23 rooms, 1 suite* ⚭ *Restaurant, minibars, cable TV, pool, bar* ⊟ *AE, DC, MC, V.*

$ 🏨 **Divi-Divi.** Just one block from the beach, this small hotel offers great value to those willing to forgo a beachside location. Apart from the elevator, the three-story hotel seems more like a guesthouse. Rooms are thoughtfully decorated, well equipped, and comfortable. The small, stylish pool in front helps compensate for the lack of beach. ⊠ *Rua Elias Barros 248, Ponta Negra, 59090-140* 🕿 *084/219–2060* 🖷 *084/219– 4195* ⊕ *www.dividivi.com.br* ⬐ *32 rooms, 2 suites* ⚭ *Minibars, pool, bar, Internet* ⊟ *AE, DC, MC, V.*

$ 🏨 **O Tempo e o Vento.** The four-star quality rooms at this hotel are highly incongruous with the two-star quality lobby. Luckily, prices are more representative of the latter. The small hotel is just a block from the beach, with a pool in front. All rooms have balconies; request those with direct sea views, since they cost the same. ⊠ *Rua Elias Barros 66, Ponta Negra, 59090-140* 🕿🕿 *084/219–2526* ⊕ *www.otempoeovento. com.br* ⬐ *22 rooms* ⚭ *Minibars, pool, bar, Internet* ⊟ *DC, MC, V.*

¢ 🏨 **Residence Praia Hotel.** This modern hotel a block from Praia dos Artistas is a good option for those who want all major amenities but don't want to pay Ponta Negra prices. The hotel is easily recognizable by its blue-glass facade. Rooms are pleasant and colorful, with pastel-painted brick walls. The downside is that the area is no longer in vogue and can get a bit seedy at night. ⊠ *Av. 25 de Dezembro 868, Praia do Meio, 59010-030* 🕿 *084/202–4466* 🖷 *084/202–4411* ⊕ *www. residencepraia.com.br* ⬐ *118 rooms* ⚭ *Restaurant, minibars, cable TV, pool, meeting room* ⊟ *AE, DC, MC, V.*

Shopping

The best place to go for local crafts and artwork is the **Centro de Turismo** (⊠ Rua Aderbal de Figueiredo 980, Petrópolis 🕿 084/211–6149). Little shops are housed within the cells of the former prison. It's open daily 9–7. Natal also has several malls and shopping centers. The largest is **Natal Shopping** (⊠ Av. Senador Salgado Filho 2234, Candelária 🕿 084/ 235–8199). **Praia Shopping** (⊠ Av. Engenheiro Roberto Freire 8790, Ponta Negra 🕿 084/219–4313) is the most convenient shopping mall for those staying in Ponta Negra.

Nightlife & the Arts

Nightlife

Natal has a fairly active nightlife, supported by nearly year-round tourists. Some of the most frequented bars and clubs are in Praia dos Artistas. Other popular spots are scattered over the centro and Ponta Negra. Every Thursday the Centro de Turismo hosts a live forró band as part of the long-running "Forró com Turista" program, which is aimed at acquainting tourists with this important piece of local culture.

BARS You won't have to worry about getting stale beer at **Cervejaria Continental** (⊠ Av. Costeira 4197, Ponta Negra ☏ 084/202–1089), which is both a bar and brewery. For those staying in the resorts in the Via Costeira portion of Ponta Negra, it's the only watering hole within walking distance. A bar with character, **Taverna Pub** (⊠ Rua Dr. Manuel Augusto Bezerra de Araújo 500, Ponta Negra ☏ 084/236–3696) is in the basement of a stylized medieval castle. It's popular with locals in their twenties and tourists who stay in the hostel upstairs. A common nighttime destination for Ponta Negra tourists is **Praia Shopping** (⊠ Av. Engenheiro Roberto Freire 8790, Ponta Negra ☏ 084/219–4313), which has a cluster of small bars and restaurants. The gay and lesbian bar **Vice e Versa** (⊠ Rua Coronel Cascudo 127, Centro ☏ 084/222–2249), open Wednesday and Friday, is a favorite among locals.

DANCE CLUBS **Blackout** (⊠ Rua Chile 25, Ribeira ☏ 084/221–1282) heats up after midnight with live MPB (*música popular brasileira*), rock, and blues. **Downtown** (⊠ Rua Chile 11, Bairro da Ribeira ☏ 084/611–1950), modeled after typical London clubs, has live rock music Thursday through Saturday. **Chaplin** (⊠ Rua Presidente Café Filho 27, Praia do Meio ☏ 084/ 202–1199), near Praia dos Artistas, has three distinct environments, each with a different type of live music: *pagode* (a popular, mellow samba derivative), forró, and rock. A R$15 cover charge doesn't prevent up to 1,500 local youngsters and tourists from pouring in.

The Arts

Teatro Alberto Maranhão (⊠ Praça Augusto Severo, Ribeira ☏ 084/222– 3669), an impressive neoclassic structure built in 1898, hosts dance recitals, plays, and concerts. Local artists play regional music every Tuesday at 6:30 PM.

Sports & the Outdoors

Most outdoor activity options are found at the beaches outside Natal: Genipabu has dune-buggy rides, Maracajaú has prime snorkeling, and Búzios is great for scuba diving. Right alongside Ponta Negra is the **Parque das Dunas** (⊠ Av. Alexandrino de Alencar s/n ☏ 084/261– 6070), a 1,172-hectare (2,896-acre) protected area with 12 hiking trails. The terrain contains sand dunes and pieces of the rapidly disappearing Atlantic forest. You can call ahead to schedule a English-speaking guide.

SIDE TRIPS FROM NATAL

Praia da Pipa

85 km (51 mi) south of Natal.

This was a small fishing village until it was "discovered" by surfers in the '70s. Word of its beauty spread, and it is now one of the most famous and fashionable beach towns in the Northeast. It is also rapidly gaining a reputation for having an extremely active nightlife. Praia da Pipa receives a truly eclectic mix of people: hippies, surfers, foreign backpackers, Brazilian youth, and, most recently, high-end visitors attracted by the increasingly upscale restaurants and pousadas.

On either side of the town is a string of beaches with amazingly varied landscapes created by stunning combinations of pink cliffs, black volcanic rocks, palm trees, and natural pools. You can spend hours exploring the various beaches, most of which are deserted because they fall within environmentally protected areas. Another recommended activity is the boat ride to see dolphins, which often frequent the surrounding waters. The 90-minute boat ride leaves regularly from the north end of the principal beach and costs R$15.

For active travelers a good option is the **Santuário Ecológico de Pipa** (Pipa Ecological Sanctuary), a 120-hectare (300-acre) protected area. Sixteen short, well-maintained trails pass through Atlantic forest vegetation and allow for some great views of the ocean. ⊠ *Estrada para Tibau do Sul, 2 km (1 mi) northwest of town* ☎ *084/211–6070* ▢ *Free* ☉ *Daily 9–5.*

Where to Stay & Eat

$$–$$$ ✕ **La Provence.** This exquisite, unpretentious French restaurant is a true find. Among its specialties is the succulent *magret de canard avec pruneaux* (duck breast with prunes). ⊠ *Rua da Gameleira* ☎ *084/ 246–2280* ▤ *AE, DC, MC, V* ☉ *Closed May–June.*

$–$$ ✕ **Cruzeiro do Pescador.** This seafood restaurant has separate locations for lunch and dinner. Lunch is served in an open-air restaurant overlooking the ocean, while dinner is served in a more traditional locale in town. The owner's Portuguese background is apparent in delicious dishes like *arroz do mar* (squid, oysters, and shrimp over saffron rice). ⊠ *Lunch: Rua do Cruzeiro* ☎ *084/246–2338* ⊠ *Dinner: Rua da Gameleira* ☎ *084/246–2262* ▤ *DC, MC, V.*

$$ ▦ **Toca da Coruja.** This Roteiros de Charme member opened in 1991, when Pipa was still a fishing village. Although many pousadas have been built since, none can top Toca da Coruja. The chalets are more spacious and expensive than the apartments, but all are beautifully furnished. ⊠ *Av. Baía dos Golfinhos, 59173-000* ☎ *081/3439–6055* ⊕ *www.tocadacoruja.com. br* ⤳ *5 chalets, 6 apartments* ⚭ *Pool, sauna, bar* ▤ *AE, DC, MC, V.*

¢ ▦ **Pousada da Ladeira.** Made from local wood and tijolo aparente, this simple pousada has clean rooms—some with balconies overlooking the pool. Because it is right on the main road, it may not be the best choice for those looking for peace and quiet. ⊠ *Av. Baíáa dos Golfinhos, 59173-000* ☎ *084/246–2334* ▤ *081/3429–6889* ⊕ *www.pipa.com. br/fladeira.htm* ⤳ *34 rooms* ⚭ *Pool, bar* ▤ *AE, MC, DC, V.*

Cariri

333 km (200 mi) southwest of Natal.

This largely uninhabited region in the interior of Paraíba State is worth visiting for its spectacular **rock formations**. Its otherworldly appearance makes it ideal for those that tire of visiting only beaches. Only three other places in the world can compare in terms of the size, shape, and amount of rounded granite blocks (the others are in the Erongo Mountains of Namibia, the Hoggar region of Algeria, and the Australian outback). Despite this distinction, Cariri is seldom visited. Only one company, **Manary Ecotours** (☎ 084/219–2900 ⊕ www.manary.com.br) has tours to Cariri. Poor roads and a lack of public transport makes the trip difficult for independent travelers.

In Cariri tours visit several areas with enormous granite boulders; some lean against each other at precarious angles, and others have bottoms carved out so they look like helmets. On the way to Cariri, tours stop in **Ingá**, which has a huge monolith with mysterious prehistoric paintings. On the premises there is also a small, interesting museum with fossils and bones of prehistoric creatures that inhabited the area. At a site called **Saca de Lã**, huge rectangular rocks are mysteriously stacked upon each other. Visits include a trip into **Cabaçeiras**, a typical small town in the sertão.

Where to Stay

$ 🏨 **Hotel Fazenda Pai Mateus.** This typical sertão ranch has 11 housing units, each with two simple, comfortable apartments. Service is superb, and the locally grown food is excellent. The pool is a true blessing after hiking in the searing heat of the sertão. You can rent horses or bikes for R$10 per hour. ⊠ Off BR 412 ☎ 083/356–1250 ⊕ www.paimateus.com.br ⤵ 22 rooms ⚘ Restaurant, minibars, sauna, pool ▤ AE, DC, MC, V ⦿ FAP.

FORTALEZA

Called the "City of Light," Fortaleza claims that the sun shines on it 2,800 hours a year. And it's a good thing, too, as the coastline stretches far beyond city. To the east, along the Litoral Leste or the Costa Sol Nascente (Sunrise Coast), are many fishing villages. To the west, along the Litoral Oeste or the Costa Sol Poente (Sunset Coast), there are pristine stretches of sand. The shores here are cooled by constant breezes and lapped by waters with an average temperature of 24°C (72°F).

The city originally sprang up around the Forte de Schoonemborch, a Dutch fortress built in 1649. After the Portuguese defeated the Dutch, the small settlement was called Fortaleza Nossa Senhora da Assunção (Fortress of Our Lady of the Assumption). It didn't fully burgeon until 1808, when its ports were opened and the export of cotton to the United Kingdom commenced.

Today Fortaleza, a large, modern state capital with more than 2 million inhabitants, is Brazil's fifth-largest city. It's also on the move, with one of the country's newest airports, a modern convention center, a huge cultural center with a planetarium, large shopping malls, several museums and theaters, and an abundance of sophisticated restaurants. At Praia de Iracema there's a revitalized beachfront area of sidewalk cafés, bars, and dance clubs. But if you wander along the shore, you're still bound to encounter fishermen unloading their catch from traditional jangadas—just as they've done for hundreds of years.

Numbers in the text correspond to numbers in the margin and on the Fortaleza Centro Histórico map.

Exploring Fortaleza

Fortaleza is fairly easy to navigate on foot because its streets are laid out in a grid. Its business center lies above the Centro Histórico (Historic Center) and includes the main market, several shopping streets, and government buildings. East of the center, urban beaches are lined with high-rise hotels and restaurants. Beyond are the port and old lighthouse, from which Praia do Futuro runs 5 km (3 mi) along Avenida Dioguinho.

A Good Walk (or Two)

For a tour of the Centro Histórico, start at the **Teatro José de Alencar** ⑬ ↱, at Praça do José Alencar, alongside Rua General Sampaio. The theater is a good jumping-off point for a cab ride to the **Museu da Cachaça**. As an alternative, you can continue on the walk, heading toward the waterfront on Rua General Sampaio. Turn right at Rua São Paulo and then take another right onto Rua Floriano Peixoto. In a cluster between Rua Peixoto and Rua Sena Madureira (which becomes Rua Conde D'eu and then Avenida Alberto Nepomuceno as you walk toward the waterfront) are the **Palácio da Luz** ⑭, on your right; the **Igreja do Rosário** ⑮, on your left; the **Praça dos Leões** ⑯; and the **Museu do Ceará** ⑰, near Rua Dr. João Moreira. As you walk along Rua Conde D'eu and Avenida Nepomuceno, on your right is the **Catedral Metropolitana** ⑱. Across the street is the **Mercado Central** ⑲, where you can relax over lunch before exploring the 500-plus shops. If you feel like more walking, turn left on Rua Dr. João Moreira. On your right is the **Fortaleza de Nossa Senhora da Assunção** ⑳. Continue on to the **Passeio Público** ㉑ and walk across the park to the **Centro de Turismo e Museu de Arte e Cultura Populares** ㉒, on Rua Senador Pompeu near the waterfront.

On another day consider a stroll along the palm-lined seaside walkway east of the Passeio Público. From Praia Formosa you can walk to Praia de Iracema, which has some late-19th-century houses. Along the way you pass the Ponte Metálica (also called the Ponte dos Ingleses), a pier from which you might spot dolphins. Farther east are Praia do Meireles and Praia do Mucuripe, with the **Farol do Mucuripe** ㉓ and its Museu de Fortaleza. You can continue all the way to Praia do Futuro for a total seashore walk of 8 km (5 mi). Along the way you pass the statue of *Iracema* ㉔.

TIMING & PRECAUTIONS The tour of the Centro Histórico takes about three hours, much longer if you browse in the Mercado Central or explore the Centro de Turismo. Although a straight walk along the shore moving at a good clip would take roughly three hours, you might want to move at a more leisurely pace, stopping to enjoy the view and to rest. Be on guard against pickpockets—particularly in the historic district.

What to See

off the beaten path

BEACH PARK ACQUA CENTER – Just 30 minutes from downtown on the idyllic Porto das Dunas Beach is this enormous water park. A 14-story-high water slide dumps you into a pool at a speed of 105 kph (65 mph), or if you prefer slow-paced attractions, visit its museum, which has the country's largest collection of jangadas, the wooden sailing rafts used by fishermen. An open-air restaurant at the beach serves excellent seafood dishes. There is no bus from downtown, and a taxi costs around R$50. ⊠ *Rua Porto das Dunas 2734* 🕾 *085/361–3000* ⊕ *www.beachpark.com.br* 🖭 *R$59* ⊙ *July–mid-Dec., daily 10–5; mid-Dec.–June, Thurs.–Mon. 10–5.*

⑱ Catedral Metropolitana. Inspired by the cathedral in Cologne, Germany, the city cathedral was built between 1937 and 1963 and has a dominant Gothic look. Its two spires are 75 meters (250 feet) high, and it can accommodate 5,000 worshipers, who are no doubt inspired by its beautiful stained-glass windows. ⊠ *Praça da Sé s/n, Centro* 🕾 *085/231–4196* 🖭 *Free.*

Centro Dragão do Mar de Arte e Cultura. Not far from the Mercado Central, this majestic cultural complex is an eccentric mix of curves, straight lines, and angular and flat roofs. What's inside is as diverse as the exterior. There's a planetarium as well as art museums with permanent exhibitions of Ceará's two most famous artists, Raimundo Cela and Antônio Bandeira. Another museum presents Ceará's cultural history, with exhibits of embroidery, paintings, prints, pottery, puppets, and musical instruments. When you need a break, head for the center's romantic Café & Cultura, which serves a variety of cocktails made with coffee as well as little meat or vegetarian pies. The center's bookstore has English-language titles as well as souvenirs and cards. ⊠ *Rua Dragão do Mar 81, Praia de Iracema* 🕾 *085/488–8600* ⊕ *www.dragaodomar.org.br* 🖭 *Museums R$2, planetarium R$4* ⊙ *Tues.–Thurs. 9–9, Fri.–Sun. 10–10.*

㉒ Centro de Turismo. Originally a prison, this building was structurally changed in 1850 along simple, classical lines. It's now the home of the state tourism center, with handicraft stores as well as the Museu de Minerais (Mineral Museum) and the Museu de Arte e Cultura Populares (Popular Art and Culture Museum), whose displays of local crafts and sculptures are interesting. ⊠ *Rua Senador Pompeu 350, Centro* 🕾 *085/488–7410* 🖭 *R$2* ⊙ *Weekdays 7–6, Sat. 8–5, Sun. 8–noon.*

㉓ Farol do Mucuripe. Erected by slaves and dedicated to Princess Isabel, the monarch who eventually put an end to slavery, this lighthouse was inaugurated in 1846. Surrounded by a system of battlements, it operated for 111 years and was not deactivated until 1957. In 1982 it underwent a restoration and was designated a municipal historic monument. It now houses the Museu de Fortaleza, better known as the Museu do Farol, with exhibits on the city's history. ⊠ *Av. Vicente de Castro s/n, Mucuripe* 🕾 *085/263–1115* 🖭 *Free* ⊙ *Mon.–Sat. 8–5, Sun. 8–noon.*

㉐ Fortaleza de Nossa Senhora da Assunção. Built by the Dutch in 1649, this fort was originally baptized Forte Schoonemborch. In 1655 it was seized by the Portuguese and renamed after the city's patron saint, Nossa Senhora da Assunção. It was rebuilt in 1817 and is now a military headquarters. The city took its name from this fortress (*fortaleza*), which still has the cell where the mother of one of Ceará's most famous writers, José de Alencar, was jailed. ⊠ *Av. Alberto Nepomuceno s/n, Centro* 🕾 *085/231–9269* 🖭 *Free* ⊙ *Daily 8–4.*

Fortaleza Centro Histórico

ATLANTIC OCEAN

⓴ **Igreja Nossa Senhora do Rosário.** Built by slaves in the 18th century, it's one of the city's oldest churches and has a typical Brazilian colonial design. As the slaves who built it also worshiped in it, it is an important piece of African heritage in Ceará, a state considered a pioneer in the liberation of slaves. ✉ *Rua Rosário* ☎ *085/231–1998* 💲 *Donations accepted* ⊙ *Mon.–Sat. 7–6:30, Sun. 7:30 AM–10 PM.*

㉔ *Iracema.* Along the Praia do Mucuripe on Avenida Beira-Mar is the statue of *Iracema,* an Indian girl who waited at the port for her lover to return. Inspired by the work of Ceará writer José de Alencar, the statue shows Iracema with an arrow in her hand as she looks at Martinho, a Portuguese soldier seated in front of her, holding their son, Moacir.

⓳ **Mercado Central.** With four floors and more than 600 stores, this is *the* place to find handicrafts and just about anything else. It has elevators to take you from one floor to the next, but since it's built with an open style and has ramps that curve from one floor to the next, it's just as easy to walk up. ✉ *Av. Alberto Nepomuceno 199, Centro* ☎ *085/454–8724* ⊙ *Weekdays 7:30–6:30, Sat. 8–4, Sun. 8–noon.*

off the beaten path

MUSEU DA CACHAÇA – It's a toss-up whether coffee or cachaça is Brazil's national drink. This museum just west of Fortaleza offers tastings of the latter in a tavern. Of course, this happens after you tour the plant and learn the history of what has been a family business for four generations. In the tavern you see a 374,000-liter (98,736-gallon) wooden barrel, the largest in the world. ⊠ *Turn left off CE 65 just before small town of Maranguape; look for signs* ☎ 085/341–0407 ◻ *R$5* ⊙ *Tues.–Sat. 8–5.*

⑰ **Museu do Ceará.** Housed in the former Assembléia Provincial (Provincial Assembly Building), this museum's exhibits are devoted to the history and anthropology of Ceará State. ⊠ *Rua São Paulo s/n* ☎ 085/251–1502 ◻ *R$2* ⊙ *Tues.–Fri. 8:30–5, Sat. 8:30–noon, Sun. 2–5.*

⑭ **Palácio da Luz.** What was originally the home of the Portuguese crown's representative, Antônio de Castro Viana, was built by Indian laborers. In 1814 it became the property of the imperial government and served as the residence of the provincial president. The next important occupant was painter Raimundo Cefa. It now houses a display of his work and has been designated a historic landmark. ⊠ *Rua do Rosário* ☎ 085/231–5699 ◻ *R$5* ⊙ *Mon.–Sat. 8–noon and 2–5.*

㉑ **Passeio Público.** Also called the Praça dos Mártires, this landmark square dates from the 19th century. In 1824 many soldiers were executed here in the war for independence from the Portuguese crown. It has a central fountain and is full of century-old trees and statues of Greek deities. Look for the ancient baobab tree.

⑯ **Praça dos Leões (Praça General Tibúrcio).** Built in 1817, this square is officially named after a Ceará general who fought in Brazil's war against Paraguay. However, it's also commonly referred to as the Praça de Leões because of its bronze lions, which were brought over from Paris in the early 20th century.

▶ ⑬ **Teatro José de Alencar.** The José de Alencar Theater is a rather shocking example (especially if you come upon it suddenly) of the eclectic phase of Brazilian architecture. It's a mixture of neoclassical and art nouveau styles. The top of the theater, which looks as if it was designed by the makers of Tiffany lamps, really stands out against Ceará's perpetually blue sky. It was built in 1910 of steel and iron (many of its cast-iron sections were imported from Scotland) and was restored in 1989. It's still used for cultural events—including concerts, plays, and dance performances—and houses a library and an art gallery. Some of the tour guides speak English; call ahead for reservations. ⊠ *Praça do José Alencar, Centro* ☎ 085/252–2523 ⊕ *www.secult.ce.gov.br* ◻ *Free* ⊙ *Weekdays 8–6, Sat. 8–3.*

Beaches

Fortaleza's enchanting coast runs 22 km (14 mi) along the Atlantic between the Rio Ceará, to the west, and the Rio Pacoti, to the east. The feel of this great urban stretch of sand along with its scenery varies as often as its names: Barra do Ceará, Pirambu, Formosa, Iracema, Beira-Mar, Meireles, Mucuripe, Mansa, Titanzinho, Praia do Futuro, and Sabiazuaba.

In the city center and its immediate environs, feel free to soak up the sun and the ambience of the beaches, but stay out of the water—it is too polluted for swimming. However, you can find clean waters and amazing sands just a little way from Centro and beyond. Surfing is fine at several beaches, including those near the towns of Paracuru and Pecém, to the west of Fortaleza, and Porto das Dunas, to the east.

Fodor'sChoice
★

Canoa Quebrada. Hidden behind dunes, the stunning Canoa Quebrada Beach was "discovered" in the 1970s by French doctors working in the area. The spectacular scenery includes not only dunes with colored sands used to make pictures in bottles but also jangadas, red cliffs, and groves of palm trees. Carved into a cliff is the symbol of Canoa: a crescent moon with a star in the middle. Although it was initially settled by Italian hippies, the village itself has moved on with the times and now has good roads, several comfortable pousadas, and bars and restaurants. The best way to get here is on a trip offered by one of Fortaleza's many tour operators, but bus companies have daily departures from Fortaleza. ⊠ *Take BR 116 to BR 304; 164 km (101 mi) east of Fortaleza.*

Iguape. The white sand dunes at this beach are so high that people actually ski down them. The water is calm and clean. In the nearby village you find both fishermen and lace makers (lace is sold at the Centro de Rendeiras). There's also a lookout at Morro do Enxerga Tudo. Buses depart from Fortaleza for this beach several times daily. ⊠ *CE 040, 50 km (31 mi) east of Fortaleza.*

Flexeiras (or Fleixeiras). The ocean is always calm at this beach. Coconut trees, lagoons, and sand dunes surround it. During low tide the reefs surface, and you can see small fish and shells in the rocks. When the tide comes in and the natural pools form, you can grab your mask and go snorkeling. In a 5-km (3-mi) stretch between Flexeiras and Mundaú—another almost-deserted beach—there are several fishing villages and a working lighthouse. A river joins the ocean at Mundaú, forming a large S on the sand; on one side is a line of coconut trees and on the other, fishermen with their jangadas—the scene conveys the very essence of Ceará. Flexeiras is about a 90-minute drive from Fortaleza. You can take the Rendenção bus or arrange a trip here with a tour operator. As yet there are no luxury resorts here, but there are several simple, clean pousadas. ⊠ *CE 085, 177 km (110 mi) northwest of Fortaleza.*

Porto das Dunas. Its water-sports options, including surfing, and its sand dunes are enough to draw many people to this beach. But it has much more, including an all-suites hotel and a water park and entertainment complex that might make Disney jealous. You can get here on the *jardineira* bus from Centro or from along Avenida Beira-Mar. ⊠ *Take Av. Washington Soares, then follow signs to Estrada da Cofeco and Beach Park; 22 km (14 mi) southeast of Fortaleza.*

Where to Eat

Along Praia de Iracema and Praia do Mucuripe there are several good seafood restaurants. Be sure to try *lagosta ao natural* (lobster cooked in water and salt and served with homemade butter). Sun-dried meat with *paçoca* (manioc flour seasoned with herbs and red onions) and *caldeirada* (shrimp soup with vegetables and strong spices and herbs) are also popular regional dishes.

Brazilian

¢–$$ ✕ **Colher de Pau.** Ana Maria Vilmar and her mother opened this restaurant 10 years ago in a small rented house in the Varjota district. It became so popular that they had to open in a larger building down the street. The original place still serves meals to faithful patrons who are mostly locals; the newer branch is popular with visitors. At both branches the sun-dried meat is served not only with paçoca but also with banana and *baião-de-dois* (rice and beans). The shellfish dishes, many prepared using regional recipes, are also standouts. ⊠ *Rua Frederico Borges 204, Varjota* ☎ *085/267–3773* ⊠ *Rodovia dos Tabajaras 412, Praia de Iracema* ☎ *085/219–4097* ▤ *AE, DC, MC, V* ☺ *No lunch at Iracema branch.*

¢–$ ✕ **Caicó.** Locals come for arguably the city's most famous sun-dried meat and paçoca, though dishes of chicken and lamb are also recommended. Ambience is at a minimum in the simple, outdoor seating area on a busy road. ⊠ *Av. Engenheiro Santana Jr. 1002, Papicu* ☎ *085/234–1915* ▤ *AE, DC, V.*

Eclectic

$$–$$$ ✕ **Le Dinner.** The savvy mix of French and Asian cuisine blends well with this restaurant's sophisticated ambience and personalized service. The menu includes beef, poultry, and seafood selections. Reservations are essential on Friday and Saturday nights. ⊠ *Rua Afonso Celso 1020, Aldeota* ☎ *085/224–2627* ▤ *AE, DC, MC, V* ☺ *Closed Sun. and last 2 wks in Feb.*

$ ✕ **Santa Grelha.** The international fare with local accents smartly matches the attractive decor that employs traditional local materials. In a restored colonial house about a mile from the beach, Santa Grelha is off the tourist path. ⊠ *Rua Vicente Leite 1062, Papicu* ☎ *085/224–0249* ▤ *AE, V* ☺ *Closed Mon.*

French

$$–$$$ ✕ **La Marine.** Candles flicker on each table, and violin and cello music fills the air-conditioned dining room and sitting room. The flambéed dishes are the best: try the lobster in champagne. ⊠ *Av. Marechal Castelo Branco 400, Centro* ☎ *085/252–5253* ▤ *AE, DC, MC, V.*

$–$$ ✕ **La Bohème.** If you like original art, you must have dinner at La Bohème. Only one room inside this former colonial home is for dining; the others are part of an art gallery that you can wander through while waiting for your first course. Be sure to see the wall with photos from films of the 1930s. There's plenty of seating on the patio out front, where a small combo entertains, competing with a combo at a restaurant across the street. Although La Bohème specializes in French cuisine, it also has a small selection of regional seafood dishes. ⊠ *Rua dos Tabajaras 380, Praia de Iracema* ☎ *085/219–3311* ▤ *AE, DC, MC, V.*

FodorśChoice
★

Italian

¢–$$ ✕ **Pulcinella.** You can feast on this restaurant's classic Italian fare (sometimes given a regional twist) in either the air-conditioned dining room with a no-smoking section or in the alfresco seating area. Among the most popular dishes are spaghetti in garlic sauce with shrimp and pimiento and veal in a mushroom-and-herb sauce. ⊠ *Rua Osvaldo Cruz 640, Aldeota* ☎ *085/261–3411* ▭ *AE, DC, MC, V.*

Seafood

★ **$–$$$** ✕ **Cemoara.** A sophisticated decor with clean lines adds to the appeal of this traditional seafood restaurant. Although the *bacalão* (salt cod) selections are fabulous, you can't go wrong with the grilled lobster in a caper sauce or any of the flambéed dishes. The piano in the corner is there for a purpose: a musician accompanies your dinner with nice, soft music. Cemoara has air-conditioning and a no-smoking area. ⊠ *Av. Abolição 3340-A, Meireles* ☎ *085/263–5001* ▭ *AE, DC, MC, V.*

$–$$ ✕ **Al Mare.** Facing as it does out to the sea, it seems appropriate that the building housing this establishment is shaped like a ship. The grilled seafood *al mare*—a medley of fish, lobster, shrimp, octopus, and squid in an herb sauce—is the specialty. ⊠ *Av. Beira-Mar 3821, Mucuripe* ☎ *085/263–3888* ▭ *AE, DC, MC, V.*

¢ ✕ **Picanha Iracema Bar E Restaurante.** Although the decor is sparse, the location—amid Praia de Iracema's hopping nightlife—is terrific, and you can eat shrimp, fish, or steaks here for very little money. Top your meal off with an espresso that costs the equivalent of 5 U.S. cents. ⊠ *Av. Historiador Raimundo Girão 574* ☎ *085/219–0488* ▭ *DC, MC, V.*

Where to Stay

Most hotels are along Avenida Beira-Mar (previously known as Avenida Presidente John Kennedy). Those in the Praia de Iracema are generally less expensive than those along Praia do Mucuripe. Iracema, however, is also a more interesting area to explore, and it's full of trendy restaurants and bars.

$$$ 🏨 **Beach Park Suites Resort.** There's very little this pleasant all-suites resort doesn't offer. It faces the beautiful Porto das Dunas Beach, and the Beach Park Acqua Center—arguably the most fantastic facility of its kind in Latin America—is only a five-minute walk (hotel guests get a 20% discount on admission). All the spacious suites have balconies, and the dozens of pots of flowers in the lobby give the whole place a cheerful atmosphere. ⊠ *Rua Porto das Dunas 2734, Aquiraz 61700-000* ☎ *085/361–3000* 🖷 *085/361–3040* ⊕ *www.beachpark.com.br* ⌦ *198 suites* △ *Restaurant, minibars, cable TV, pool, 2 tennis courts, hair salon, health club, sauna, beach, bar, children's programs, Internet* ▭ *AE, DC, MC, V.*

★ **$$$** 🏨 **Caesar Park Hotel Fortaleza.** On Praia do Mucuripe, just a 15-minute drive from either the airport or Centro, this luxury hotel can certainly include "convenient location" in its list of features. Marble and black granite give the building a modern, sleek look. One of the on-site restaurants serves Brazilian fare, another French; the third, Mariko, is noteworthy for Japanese food and buffets of lobster, shrimp, sushi, sashimi, and oysters. The view from the pool area on the 20th floor is fantastic. The hotel has facilities for travelers with disabilities. ⊠ *Av. Beira-Mar 3980, Mucuripe 60165-050* ☎ *085/466–5000* 🖷 *085/263–1444* ⊕ *www.caesarparkfor.com.br* ⌦ *185 rooms, 45 suites* △ *3 restaurants, room service, in-room* *safes, minibars, cable TV, pool, health club, hot tub, massage, sauna, steam room, 2 bars, business services, convention center* ☰ *AE, DC, MC, V.*

$$ 🏨 **Parthenon Golden Flat.** The comfortable apartments here are perfect for families and visitors in the city for a long stay. Each unit has one or two bedrooms, a living room, and a fully equipped kitchen. If you get tired of preparing your own meals, you can head for the restaurant or the coffee shop. ☒ *Av. Beira-Mar 4260, Mucuripe 60165–121* 🖀🖀 *085/ 466–1323* ⊕ *www.accorhotels.com.br* ☞ *132 apartments* ⬩ *Restaurant, coffee shop, minibars, cable TV, pool, sauna, bar, playground* ☰ *AE, DC, MC, V.*

★ $ 🏨 **Holiday Inn.** Because of the way the Iracema Beach curves, all rooms here have either ocean or harbor views. There isn't anything opulent about the hotel, but rooms are well designed, large, and immaculate. Also, the location is great: a block off the beach and within walking distance of Centro Dragão do Mar, Ceará's largest cultural center. The pool is on the top deck, and there's a small French restaurant. ☒ *Av. Historiador Raimundo Girão 800, Praia de Iracema 60165-050* 🖀 *085/ 455–5000* 🖷 *085/455–5055* ⊕ *www.holiday-inn.com/fortaleza* ☞ *273 rooms* ⬩ *Restaurant, coffee shop, minibars, cable TV, pool, gym, sauna, bar, business services, convention center* ☰ *AE, DC, MC, V.*

$ 🏨 **Marina Park.** Designed to look like a huge ship, the resort overlooks a calm bay and is connected to a marina from which you can take boat trips. It is rather far from the center of everything, but it does have an uncrowded 5-km-long (3-mi-long) beach, as well as an enormous free-form pool. ☒ *Av. Presidente Castelo Branco 400, Praia de Iracema 60312–060* 🖀 *085/455–9595* 🖷 *085/253–1803* ⊕ *www.marinapark. com.br* ☞ *305 rooms, 10 suites* ⬩ *5 restaurants, coffee shop, in-room data ports, in-room safes, minibars, cable TV, 4 tennis courts, pool, hair salon, massage, sauna, dock, volleyball, bar, shops, children's programs, playground, business services, meeting room, helipad* ☰ *AE, DC, MC, V.*

$ 🏨 **Meliá Confort.** The Meliá hotel sits on a small hill right where the beach makes a big curve, affording guests a spectacular view of the beach and Mucuripe Bay. There's comfortable seating in the stylish lobby, where a spiral staircase leads up to meeting rooms. Tastefully decorated rooms are more like minisuites. ☒ *Av. Beira-Mar 3470, Mucuripe 60165-121* 🖀 *085/466–5500* 🖷 *085/466–5501* ⊕ *www.solmelia.com* ☞ *121 rooms, 13 suites* ⬩ *Restaurant, coffee shop, minibars, cable TV, gym, business services, meeting rooms* ☰ *AE, MC, V.*

★ $ 🏨 **Ponta Mar Hotel.** This refined and modern hotel is across the street from a popular beach. A handicrafts fair and a shopping plaza are nearby. Rooms are extralarge, and those with great sea views cost just R$15 more than those without. ☒ *Av. Beira-Mar 2200, Meireles 60165-121* 🖀 *085/248–9000* 🖷 *085/248–9001* ⊕ *www.pontamar.com.br* ☞ *265 rooms, 12 suites* ⬩ *Restaurant, minibars, cable TV, pool, bar, meeting rooms, business center, gym, Internet* ☰ *AE, DC, MC V.*

$ 🏨 **Praiano Palace.** This hotel is a surprisingly affordable option in the chic Praia do Meirles area. Its rooms are simple but comfortable, and nearly all have sea views. Windows alongside the lobby look out on a small garden and a waterfall. ☒ *Av. Beira-Mar 2800, Meireles 60165–121*

☎ 085/466–9500 🖷 085/242–3333 ⮡ 189 rooms ⌂ Restaurant, mini-bars, cable TV, pool, bar, business center, Internet ☰ AE, DC, MC, V.

$ ⊞ **Seara Praia.** There's plenty of action at the Meirles Beach across the street. The lobby is decorated with works by local artists. Rooms have tile floors, modern art, and furniture with clean, classic lines. For an ocean view, ask for a deluxe room or suite. Don't despair if such a room isn't available; simply head for the rooftop pool and deck and partake of the glorious sunsets. ⊠ Av. Beira-Mar 3080, Meireles 60165-121 ☎ 085/466–9600 🖷 085/242–5955 ⊕ www.hotelseara.com.br ⮡ 203 rooms, 14 suites ⌂ Restaurant, minibars, cable TV, pool, hair salon, bar, Internet ☰ AE, DC, MC, V.

$ ⊞ **Vila Galé Fortaleza.** This family-friendly resort is the newest, most up-scale hotel in the Praia do Futuro area. Extremely well run, it represents the Portuguese chain's foray into Brazil. Although the exterior lacks distinction, the grand lobby is impressive in its design and decor. Services and amenities are top-notch, which is fortunate since there's no nightlife to speak of in the area. ⊠ Av. Diaguinho 4189, Praia do Futuro 60182-001 ☎ 085/486–4400 🖷 085/486–4430 ⊕ vilagale.pt/homepage/hoteis/Fortaleza/HotelFortaleza.htm ⮡ 285 rooms, 15 suites ⌂ Restaurant, minibars, cable TV, pool, gym, sauna, bar, business services, meeting rooms, recreation room, children's programs ☰ AE, DC, MC, V.

¢ ⊞ **Malibu Praia Hotel.** Being six blocks from the beach means you do not pay a lot for a decent-size room with all major amenities. Its only major flaws are small beds and dim lighting. Tacky paintings and plastic flowers lend a comical touch to the lobby. ⊠ Av. Rui Barbosa, Iracema 60115-200 ☎ 085/261–5755 ⮡ 29 rooms ⌂ Restaurant, minibars ☰ AE, DC, MC, V.

Nightlife & the Arts

Nightlife

Fortaleza is renowned for its lively nightlife, particularly along Avenida Beira-Mar and Rua dos Tabajaras in the vicinity of Praia de Iracema. The action often includes live forró, the traditional and very popular music and dance of the northeast. As the story goes, U.S. soldiers based in Fortaleza during World War II always invited the townsfolk to their dances, saying they were "for all," which the Brazilians pronounced "forró."

BARS **Cais Bar** (⊠ Av. Beira-Mar 696, Praia de Iracema ☎ 085/219–1371) is a known hangout for artists and intellectuals. **Itapariká** (⊠ Av. Zezé Diogo 6801, Praia do Futuro ☎ 085/265–3213) is the place to feast on crabs while enjoying live daily MPB shows. Although it's open for lunch daily, Thursday is the only evening it remains open for dinner.

Kiss Disco Club (⊠ Travelessa Icó 12, Praia de Iracema ☎ 085/231–7615) is Fortaleza's premier gay nightclub. It is open Thursday through Saturday. The town's only microbrewery, **Lupus Bier** (⊠Rua Tabajaras 340, Praia de Iracema ☎085/224–4193) serves its own Belgian-style beers, plus pizza, pasta, and Japanese food. On Monday night—the most popular night for forró—check out the **Pirata Bar** (⊠ Rua dos Tabajaras 325, Praia de Iracema ☎ 085/219–8030), where as many as 2,000 people can move to the forró beat on the dance floor and in other areas inside or out.

Just outside Fortaleza are establishments that blend forró shows with *vaquejada,* a traditional rodeo in which farmhands try to wrangle bulls and wild horses. **Cajueiro Drinks** (⊠ Km 20, BR 116, Eusébio ☎ 085/275–1482) is a highly recommended venue for rodeo shows. On Sunday there are performances of local country music and a forró show.

For a lively mix of vaquejada with samba, reggae, forró, and other types of music, drop in at **Clube do Vaqueiro** (⊠ Quarto Anel Viário de Fortaleza, Km 14, BR 116, Eusébio ☎ 085/278–2000), especially on Wednesday, when there's usually a samba show. On Friday there's a forró show at **Parque do Vaqueiro** (⊠ Km 10, BR 020, after loop in intersection, Caucaia ☎ 085/296–1159).

A young crowd grooves to MPB and rock and roll at **Boite Domínio Público** (⊠ Rua Dragão do Mar 212, Praia de Iracema ☎ 085/219–3883). **Mucuripe Club** (⊠ Av. Beira-Mar 4430, Mucuripe ☎ 085/263–1006 ⊕ www.mucuripe.com.br) houses two separate clubs: Comodore is designed with a nautical theme and Submarino with an underwater theme. In Praia do Futuro Tuesday night is hottest at **Oásis** (⊠ Av. Santos Dumont 6061 ☎ 085/234–4970), when live music from years past draws a crowd to the large dance floor.

One of the latest and largest clubs, spread over 1,000 square meters (10,760 square feet), is **Abolição 3500** (⊠ Av. Abolição 3500 ☎ 085/466–7700). Flashback nights draw an older crowd, while European techno nights attract local youngsters.

The Arts

The large, white **Centro Dragão do Mar de Arte e Cultura** (⊠ Rua Dragão do Mar 81, Praia de Iracema ☎ 085/488–8600), near the Mercado Central, has several theaters and an open-air amphitheater that host live performances. There are also classrooms for courses in cinema, theater, design, and dance. The **Centro Cultural Banco do Nordeste** (⊠ Rua Floriano Peixoto 941, Centro ☎ 085/488–4100) often hosts plays, concerts, and art exhibitions.

The beautiful, early-19th-century **Teatro José de Alencar** (⊠ Praça José de Alencar, Centro ☎ 085/252–2523) is the site of many concerts, plays, and dance performances. Alongside the main theater is a smaller venue (it seats about 120 people) for more intimate events. There's also a small stage in the theater's garden.

Sports & the Outdoors

The sidewalk along Avenida Beira-Mar is a pleasant place for a walk, run, or bike, and there's usually a pickup volleyball or soccer game in progress on the beach—don't hesitate to ask the players whether you can join in. There are also running tracks and sports courts in the 25-km-long (16-mi-long) Parque do Cocó, on Avenida Pontes Vieira.

Futebol

Fortaleza's two futebol teams, Ceará and Fortaleza, haven't reached world-class status yet, but you can watch them play in the **Estádio Plácido Castelo** (⊠ Av. Alberto Craveiro s/n ☎ 085/295–2466), also known as Castelão.

Fortaleza's other futebol venue is the **Estádio Presidente Vargas** (✉ Av. Marechal Deodoro s/n ☎ 085/281–3225).

Scuba Diving

Off the coast of Ceará are some good dive sites with coral reefs, tropical fish, and wrecks. To rent equipment and arrange lessons and/or trips, contact **Projeto Netuno** (✉ Rua Osvaldo Cruz 2453, Dionísio Torres ☎ 085/264–4114 ⊕ www.pnetuno.com.br). If you're a novice, you can benefit from its courses, with presentations on equipment and dive techniques as well as marine biology.

Windsurfing

Open seas and constant trade winds make Ceará's beaches perfect for windsurfing. You can arrange lessons and rent equipment at the **Windclub** (✉ Av. Beira-Mar 2120, Praia dos Diários ☎ 085/248–8180).

Shopping

Fortaleza is one of the most important centers for crafts—especially bobbin lace—in the northeast. Shops sell a good variety of handicrafts, and others have clothing, shoes, and jewelry along Avenida Monsenhor Tabosa in Praia de Iracema. Shopping centers both large and small house branches of the best Brazilian stores. The biggest and most traditional mall is **Shopping Center Iguatemi** (✉ Av. Washington Soares 85, Água Fria ☎ 085/447–3577).

Markets and fairs are the best places to look for lacework, embroidery, leather goods, hammocks, and carvings. The large warehouse-style **Central de Artesanato do Ceará** (CEART; ✉ Av. Santos Dumont 1589, Aldeota ☎ 085/261–2401) sells all types of handicrafts, though at higher prices than elsewhere. The handicraft stores at **Centro de Turismo** (✉ Rua Senador Pompeu 350, Centro ☎ 085/488–7410 or 085/488–7411) are good options. More than 600 artisans sell their work at the nightly **feirinha de artesanato** (✉ Av. Beira-Mar, in front of Imperial Othon Palace), on Praia do Meireles.

For lace aficionados, a trip to the town of **Aquiraz** (✉ 30 km/19 mi east of Fortaleza), is a must. Ceará's first capital (1713–99) is today a hub for the artisans who create the famous *bilro* (bobbin) lace. On the beach called Prainha (6 km/4 mi east of Aquiraz) is the Centro de Rendeiras Luiza Távora. Here, seated on little stools, dedicated and patient women lace makers explain how they create such items as bedspreads and tablecloths using the bilro technique.

SIDE TRIPS FROM FORTALEZA

Vale Monumental do Ceará

158 km (98 mi) southwest of Fortaleza.

Ecological parks and huge monoliths fill the Vale Monumental do Ceará (Monumental Valley), an area of nearly 247,100 acres of sertão a two-hour drive over good roads from Fortaleza. Activities include mountain climbing, biking, hiking, horseback tours, paragliding, hang gliding, geology treks, and birding (400 species of birds have been identified).

Where to Stay

¢ ⊞ **Fazenda Hotel Parelhas.** It's called a hotel, but it's really a working farm that welcomes overnight guests. Horseback riding is free, and you can walk down a short path and fish in a small lake. There's also a very small pool. ⊠ *Km 133, Rodovia do Algodao, Quixeramobim 63800-000* ☎ *088/402–2847* 🖷 *088/441–1326* ⤢ *6 rooms* ⚲ *Pool* ▱ *No credit cards* ⑩ *FAP.*

Sports & the Outdoors

You can hire guides to take you on hikes along the Trilha das Andorinhas (Andorinhas Trail). The valley is filled with giant rocks sculptured by the elements into unusual formations. Trails have been mapped out for moderate hikes to grottos, caves (some of which have prehistoric etchings), lagoons, canyons, and tunnels. Contact **Sertão & Pedras** (⊠ Av. Plácido Castelo 1699, Quixadá ☎ 088/412–5995 ⊕ www.quixadanet. com.br/sertaopedras) to arrange a trek or rock-climbing/rappelling trips.

Thermal wind conditions are just right for paragliding off a mountaintop near the towns of Quixadá and Quixeramobim, about two hours southwest of Fortaleza (BR 116 to BR 122). One person's excursion of 6½ hours in the air made it into the *Guinness Book of World Records.* Once you're harnessed up, it's just a short downhill run before the wind grabs you and off you go. The most popular month for competitions is November because it's dry. Chico Santos at **Go Up Brazil** (⊠ Estrada das Canoas 722, Bloco 4, Apto. 207, São Conrado, Rio de Janeiro, RJ 22610–210 ☎ 021/3322–3165 ⊕ www.goup.com.br) can help you make arrangements for paragliding trips in the Vale Monumental. If you'd like to learn to paraglide, contact Claudio Henrique Landim, an instructor with **Escola de vôo Livre** (☎ 085/9984–1330). The course is R$680 for 30 hours.

Jericoacoara

Fodor'sChoice *300 km (186 mi) northwest of Fortaleza.*
★

It could be the sand dunes, some more than 30 meters (100 feet) tall; it could be the expanse of ocean that puts no limits on how far your eyes can see; or it could be that in the presence of this awesome display of nature, everyday problems seem insignificant. Jericoacoara, a rustic paradise on Ceará State's northwest coast, affects everyone differently but leaves no one unchanged—just like the sand dunes that change their shape and even their colors as they bend to the will of the winds.

In Jericoacoara, or Jerí, time seems endless, even though in the back of your mind you know you'll be leaving in a day or two (or a week or two, if you're lucky). It's the ultimate relaxing vacation, and not because there isn't anything to do. You can surf down sand dunes or ride up and down them in a dune buggy. Also, you can take an easy hike to the nearby Pedra Furada, or Arched Rock, a gorgeous formation sculpted by the waves.

Jerí is said to be one of the 10 most beautiful beaches in the world, yet it has managed to avoid mass tourism. Although a few more small businesses open every year, growth is tempered by its remoteness and its status as an Environmental Protection Area. The pousadas, restaurants, and bars that have sprung up are owned in large part by former tourists, especially from Europe, who were lured back to stay, as if by a siren's call.

The six-hour trip between Jericoacoara and Fortaleza can be arranged through **Marilha Tours** (⊠ Rua do Forró ☎ 085/433–9383).

Where to Stay & Eat

$–$$ ✕ **Carcará.** This highly regarded restaurant has a wide variety of seafood dishes, from local specialties to international favorites such as sashimi and seviche. You can choose between pleasant indoor and outdoor seating areas. ⊠ *Rua do Forró 530* ☎ *088/669–2013* ▤ *No credit cards* ⊘ *Closed Sun.*

★ **$** ▦ **Pousada Ibirapuera.** Wind chimes, candles, and mobiles help create a sense of peace and tranquility at this splendid pousada. Colorful duplex apartments have windows looking out into the garden and hammocks in front. The dining area is decorated with a mix of modern art and antiques. ⊠ *Rua S da Duna 06, 62598-000* ☎ *088/669–2012* ⊕ *www.jericoacoara.tur.br/ibirapuera* ⤳ *8 apartments* ⚄ *Minibars, bar; no room TVs* ▤ *AE, DC, MC, V.*

¢ ▦ **Casa do Turismo.** This pousada offers a choice of standard rooms or slightly more expensive duplex rooms. All have simple decoration but are well equipped. Inquire at the front desk about the pousada's full range of services, which include buggy trips, windsurfing rental, transport to Fortaleza, and GPS hikes. ⊠ *Rua das Dunas, 62598-000* ☎ *084/621–0211* ⊕ *www.jericoacoara.com* ⤳ *20 rooms* ⚄ *Minibars, refrigerators, cable TV, pool, bar* ▤ *AE, MC, DC, V.*

Sports & the Outdoors

A great option is a 9-km (5-mi) self-guided hike through the dunes using a handheld GPS (global positioning system) monitor. When you arrive at the oasislike Lagoa do Paraiso, you are picked up in a canoe and taken to a restaurant where Italian chef Fred treats you to a divine five-course meal. To arrange the trip, contact **Casa do Turismo** (☎ 084/621–0211 ⊕ www.jericoacoara.com).

FERNANDO DE NORONHA

322 km (200 mi) off the coast of Recife.

This group of 21 islands is part of the mid-Atlantic Ridge, an underwater volcanic mountain chain more than 15,000 km (9,315 mi) long. It was discovered in 1503 by the Italian explorer Amérigo Vespucci but was taken over by Fernando de Noronha of Portugal. Its attackers have included the French, Dutch, and English, but the Portuguese built several fortresses and, with cannons in place, fought them off. In later years the Brazilians took advantage of its isolated location and built a prison on one of the islands; it was later used as a military training ground. As word of its beauty and spectacular underwater life spread, however, it was turned over to Pernambuco State and designated a protected marine park. Today fierce regulations protect the archipelago's ecology.

The mountainous, volcanic main—and only inhabited—island of Fernando de Noronha is ringed by beaches with crystal-clear warm waters that are perfect for swimming, snorkeling, and diving. In summer surfers show up to tame the waves. There are shipwrecks to explore and huge turtles, stingrays, and sharks (14 species of them) with which to swim. Diving is good all year, but prime time is from December to March on the windward side (facing Africa) and from July to October on the leeward side (facing Brazil).

If you're an experienced diver, be sure to visit the *Ipiranga*, a small Brazilian destroyer that sank in 1987. It sits upright in 60 meters (200 feet) of water and is swarming with fish, and you can see the sailors' personal effects, including uniforms still hanging in closets. Another good site is the Sapata Cave, which has an antechamber so large that it has been used for marriage ceremonies (attended by giant rays, no doubt).

Well-maintained trails and well-trained guides make for enjoyable hikes. You can also enjoy the landscape on a horseback trek to the fortress ruins and isolated beaches where hundreds of seabirds alight. In addition, Projeto Tamar has an island base for its work involving sea turtles. One of the most fascinating exploring experiences, however, is an afternoon boat trip to the outer fringes of the Baía dos Golfinhos (Bay of the Dolphins), where dozens of spinner dolphins swim south each day to hunt in deep water.

There are two daily departures to Fernando de Noronha from both Recife and Natal; flight time from either is around an hour. Only 90 visitors are allowed here each day, and there's a daily tourist tax of R$28, including the day you arrive and the day you leave. Divers pay an additional R$20 a day. Bring enough reais to last the trip, as credit cards are not widely accepted and changing money is difficult.

Where to Stay & Eat

$–$$ ✕ **Ecologiku's.** This very small restaurant is known for its seafood, especially lobster. If you can't decide what to order, the *sinfonía ecologiku* is a sampling of every type of seafood on the menu. ⊠ *Near airport* ☎ *081/3619–1807.*

$–$$ ✕ **Tartarugão.** One of island's best restaurants also operates a little rent-a-buggy business on the side. The phenomenal steak is big enough for two people and comes with rice and a salad. ⊠ *Praia do Boldró; west side of island* ☎ *081/3619–1331.*

$$ ⌂ **Pousada Zé Maria Paraiso.** Although this friendly, popular pousada isn't on the beach, you can see the ocean, which is a 15-minute walk away. It sits atop a hill, surrounded by vegetation. ⊠ *Rua Nicie Cordeiro 1, Floresta Velha, 53990-000* ☎ *081/3619–1258* ⇨ *13 bungalows* ⌂ *Restaurant, cable TV, minibars, pool* ⊙ *FAP.*

$ ⌂ **Hotel Esmeralda do Atlântico.** As you might expect of a former military base, the rooms here are plain. They are, however, large, clean, and comfortable. ⊠ *Vila do Boldró, next to Praia do Boldró, 53990-000* ☎ *081/3619–1255* 🖷 *081/3619–1277* ⊕ *www.vistatur.com.br* ⇨ *48 rooms* ⌂ *Restaurant* ⊟ *AE, DC, MC, V* ⊙ *FAP.*

$ 🏨 **Pousada Dolphin.** The island's newest hotel is just a five-minute walk from the beach. Rooms are large and attractively decorated. ⊠ *Near Praia do Boldró, 53990-000* 🕿 *081/3465–7224* 📠 *18 rooms* ⚖ *Restaurant, minibars, pool, hot tub, sauna, bar, recreation room* 🖃 *AE, MC, V* ¶⊙¶ *MAP.*

Sports & the Outdoors

For dive trips, **Atlantis Divers** (⊠ Fernando de Noronha, Caixa Postal 20, 53990-000 🕿🕿 081/3619–1371 ⊕ www.atlantisnoronha.com.br) has excellent English-speaking staffers and good boats.

RECIFE, NATAL & FORTALEZA A TO Z

To research prices, get advice from other travelers, and book travel arrangements, visit www.fodors.com.

AIR TRAVEL

CARRIERS The main airlines operating in Recife, Natal, and Fortaleza are TAM, Varig, VASP, and Gol. Fernando de Noronha is a one-hour flight from Recife or Natal on Trip Airlines or Rio-Sul/Nordeste.

🖪 Airlines & Contacts **Gol** 🕿 0800/701-2131 in Fortaleza, 081/3464-4789 in Recife ⊕ www.voegol.com.br. **TAM** 🕿 085/261-5296 in Fortaleza, 084/201-2020 in Natal, 081/3341-8106 in Recife ⊕ www.tamairlines.com. **Trip Airlines** 🕿 084/234-1717 in Natal, 081/3619-1530 in Recife. **Varig** 🕿 085/477-5540 or 085/477-1720 in Fortaleza, 084/643-1100 in Natal, 081/3464-4440 Recife ⊕ www.varig.com. **VASP** 🕿 0300/789-1010 in Fortaleza, 084/211-4374 in Natal, 081/3216-2000 in Recife ⊕ www.vasp.com.br.

AIRPORTS & TRANSFERS

The Aeroporto Internacional Guararapes is 10 km (6 mi) south of Recife, just five minutes from Boa Viagem, and 15 minutes from the city center. In Natal, the Aeroporto Internacional Augusto Severo is 15 km (9 mi) south of the town center. The Aeroporto Internacional Pinto Martins, in Fortaleza, is 6 km (4 mi) south of downtown.

🖪 Airport Information **Aeroporto Internacional Augusto Severo** ⊠ BR 101, Parnamirim 🕿 084/643-1811. **Aeroporto Internacional Guararapes** ⊠ Praça Ministro Salgado Filho s/n, Imbiribeira, Recife 🕿 081/3464-4188. **Aeroporto Internacional Pinto Martins** ⊠ Av. Senador Carlos Jereissati, Serrinha, Fortaleza 🕿 085/477-1200.

AIRPORT In the lobby of Recife's airport, on the right just before the exit door, is a
TRANSFERS tourist information booth, and next to that is a taxi stand. You can pay at the counter; the cost is about R$23 to Boa Viagem and R$34 to downtown. The ride from the airport to Olinda costs R$34–R$45. There are also regular buses and microbuses (more expensive). The bus labeled AEROPORTO runs to Avenida Dantas Barreto in the center of the city, stopping in Boa Viagem on the way. To reach Olinda, take the AEROPORTO bus to Avenida Nossa Senhora do Carmo in Recife and then take the CASA CAIADA bus.

There are no buses connecting the Natal airport with Ponta Negra. Taxis cost around R$25. Fortaleza's fixed-price *especial* (special) taxis charge about R$23 for trips from the airport to downtown on weekdays, R$41 on weekends. City buses also run from here to the nearby bus station and Praça José de Alencar in Centro.

BUS & METRÔ TRAVEL

RECIFE The Terminal Integrado de Passageiros (TIP), a *metrô* terminal and bus station 14 km (9 mi) from the Recife city center, handles all interstate bus departures and some connections to local destinations. To reach it via metrô, a 30-minute ride, enter through the Museu do Trem, opposite the Casa da Cultura, and take the train marked RODOVIÁRIA. Several buses a day go to Salvador (12–14 hours, R$90), Fortaleza (12 hours, R$70), and Natal (four hours, R$30); there are also daily departures to Rio (40 hours, R$200) and frequent service to Caruaru (two hours, R$12).

In Boa Viagem you can take the PIEDADE/RIO DOCE bus to Olinda. Buses to Igarassu and Ilha de Itamaracá leave from the center of Recife, at Avenida Martins de Barros, in front of the Grande Hotel.

City buses cost R$1.10; they're clearly labeled and run frequently until about 10:30 PM. Many stops have signs indicating the routes. To reach Boa Viagem via the metrô, get off at the Joana Bezerra stop (a 20-minute ride) and take a bus or taxi (R$15) from here. Buses are free when using the metrô and vice-versa.

🚌 Bus & Metrô Information CBTU ☎ 081/3455-4533 ⊕ www.cbtu.gov.br. **Terminal Integrado de Passageiros** (TIP) ✉ Km 15, Rodovia BR 232, Curado, Jaboatão dos Guararapes ☎ 081/3452-2824.

NATAL Natal has two bus stations. For most destinations you use the Rodoviário de Natal, 5 km (3 mi) from Ponta Negra. It's often referred to as the *terminal nova* (new terminal). Several buses daily go to Praia da Pipa (1½ hours; R$7), Recife (four hours; R$30), Fortaleza (eight hours; R$75), and Rio de Janeiro (44 hours; R$205).

The other bus station, the Rodoviário Velho (old bus station), is downtown. Buses to Genipabu leave every half hour for the half-hour trip. The fare on city buses is R$1. Buses run fairly frequently between Ponta Negra and downtown. From Ponta Negra to downtown, look for buses marked CENTRO or CIDADE ALTA. On the return, look for buses marked PONTA NEGRA. Buses run between Ponta Negra and downtown.

🚌 Bus Information Terminal Rodoviário de Natal ✉ Av. Capitão Mor. Gouveia 1237, Cidade de Esperança ☎ 084/205-1000. **Rodoviário Velho** ✉ Praça de Augusto Severo ☎ No phone.

FORTALEZA The main bus station, Terminal Rodoviário João Tomé, is 6 km (4 mi) south of Centro. In low season you can buy tickets at the station right before leaving. São Benedito runs five buses daily to Beberibe and Morro Branco Beach (2½ hours; R$6.80), and three daily to Aracati and Canoa Quebrada (3½ hours; R$12). Expresso Guanabara and Itapemirim have five daily buses to Recife (12 hours; R$60–R$100), and one daily to Salvador (22 hours; R$133); in addition, Itapemirim has daily buses to Rio de Janeiro. Penha also runs buses to Rio (48 hours; R$305–R$375) and São Paulo (52 hours; R$268–R$375).

The fare on city buses is R$1.20. Those marked 13 DE MAIO or AGUA-NAMBI 1 or 2 run from Avenida General Sampaio and pass the Centro de Turismo; from here (Rua Dr. João Moreira), you can take the bus labeled CIRCULAR to Avenida Beira-Mar and Praia de Iracema and Praia do Meireles. From Avenida Castro e Silva (close to Centro de Turismo), PRAIA DO FUTURO and SERVILUZ buses run to Praia do Futuro. For beaches west of the city, take a CUMBUCO bus from Praça Capistrano Abreu on Avenida Tristão Gonçalves or from along Avenida Beira-Mar. For the eastern beach of Porto das Dunas and the water park, take a BEACH PARK bus from Praça Tristão Gonçalves or from along Avenida Beira-Mar.

🚌 Bus Information **Expresso Guanabara** ☎ 085/256-0214. **Itapemirim** ☎ 085/272-4511. **Penha** ☎ 085/272-4511. **São Benedito** ☎ 085/256-1999. **Terminal Rodoviário João Tomé** ✉ Av. Borges de Melo 1630, Fátima ☎ 085/256-2100.

CAR RENTAL

The principal rental companies in the region are Hertz, Avis, Interlocadora, Localiza, and Unidas.

🚗 Rental Agencies **Avis** ☎ 085/242-3115 for Fortaleza, 084/642-9065 for Natal. **Hertz** ☎ 085/242-5425 for Fortaleza, 084/463-1660 for Natal, 081/3381-2104 for Recife. **Localiza** ☎ 085/242-4255 for Fortaleza, 084/206-5296 for Natal, 081/3341-2082 or 081/3341-0477 for Recife. **Unidas** ☎ 081/3471-1562 for Recife.

CAR TRAVEL

RECIFE The main north–south highway through Recife is BR 101. To the north it travels through vast sugar plantations; it's mostly straight, with only slight slopes. To travel south, you also can take the scenic coastal road, PE 060, which passes through Porto de Galinhas Beach. To reach Caruaru, take BR 232 west; the trip takes 1½ hours. Because of horrible rush-hour traffic and careless drivers, it's best to rent a car only for side trips from Recife.

NATAL Natal lies at the northern end of BR 101, making it an easy trip from Recife, which is due south on BR 101. To reach Praia da Pipa, head south on BR 101 and then take RN 003 to the east. To Fortaleza, take BR 304 northwest and then head north on BR 116. Although traffic is increasing, it is still fairly easy and quick to drive around Natal.

FORTALEZA The main access roads to Fortaleza are the BR 304, which runs southeast to Natal and Recife and which is in good condition; the BR 222, which has a few poor sections and which travels west to the state of Piauí and on to Brasília; the BR 020 southwest, which goes to Picos, in Piauí State, and on to Brasília and is in decent shape; and the BR 116, which runs south to Salvador and has several stretches in poor condition. The CE 004, or Litoránea, links the coastal towns to the southeast as far as Aracati. Many of the secondary routes are paved, though there are also some dirt roads in fair condition.

Fortaleza is an easy city in which to drive. Major routes take you easily from one side of town to the other. Although rush hour sees traffic jams, they aren't nearly as bad as they are in other big cities.

EMERGENCIES

RECIFE 🆘 Emergency Services **Ambulance** ☎ 192.

🆘 Medical Clinics **Centro Hospitalar Albert Sabin** ✉ Rua Senador José Henrique 141, Ilha do Leite ☎ 081/3421-5411. **Real Hospital Português** ✉ Av. Portugal 163, Derby ☎ 081/3416-2211.

⚑ Pharmacies **Drogafácil** ✉ Av. Engenheiro Domingos Ferreira 3326, Boa Viagem ☎ 081/3326-6498. **Farmácia Casa Caiada** ✉ Rua Padre Carapuceiro 777, Boa Viagem ☎ 081/3465-1420.

NATAL ⚑ Emergency Services **Ambulance** ☎ 192.

⚑ Medical Clinics **Hospital Memorial** ✉ Av. Juvenal Lamartine 979, Tirol ☎ 084/211-3636. **Hospital Walfredo Gurgel** ✉ Av. Senador Salgado Filho s/n, Candelária ☎ 084/201-4233.

⚑ Pharmacies **Farmácia Búzios** ✉ Av. Praia dos Búzios 9036, Ponta Negra ☎ 084/219-3381. **Superfarma** ✉ Av. Praia de Ponta Negra 8936, Ponta Negra ☎ 084/219-3471.

FORTALEZA ⚑ Emergency Services **Ambulance** ☎ 192. **Surfing emergencies** ☎ 193.

⚑ Medical Clinics **Hospital Antônio Prudente** ✉ Av. Aguanambi 1827, Fátima ☎ 085/215-2007. **Hospital Batista** ✉ Rua Prof. Dias da Rocha 2530, Aldeota ☎ 085/261-2999.

⚑ Pharmacies **Farmácia Aldesul** ✉ Av. Abolicão 2625, Meireles ☎ 085/242-7071. **Farmácia Portugal** ✉ Av. Abolicão 2950, Meireles ☎ 085/242-4422.

ENGLISH-LANGUAGE MEDIA

RECIFE Livraria Brandão has used English-language books; the shop also sells books from stalls on Rua do Infante Dom Henrique. Livro 7 is a large emporium with a huge stock, including many foreign-language titles. You can find English-language books, magazines, and newspapers at Sodiler.

⚑ Bookstores **Livraria Brandão** ✉ Rua da Matriz 22, Boa Vista ☎ 081/3222-4171. **Livro 7** ✉ Rua Riachuelo 267, Boa Vista ☎ 081/3423-6419. **Sodiler** ✉ Guararapes Airport, Praça Ministro Salgado Filho s/n, Imbiribeira ☎ 081/3326-0883 ✉ Shopping Center Recife, Rua Padre Carapuceiro 777, Boa Viagem ☎ 081/3467-5091.

NATAL A.S. Book Shop has a decent selection of English-language books and periodicals.

⚑ Bookstores **A.S. Book Shop** ✉ Praia Shopping, Av. Engenheiro Roberto Freire 8790, Ponta Negra ☎ 084/219-5373.

FORTALEZA You can find English-language publications at Edésio.

⚑ Fortaleza Bookstores **Edésio** ✉ Rua Guilherme Rocha 185, Centro ☎ 085/231-3981.

MAIL, INTERNET & SHIPPING

Express-mail service is available at post offices in Recife, Natal, and Fortaleza. For Internet service in Fortaleza, try Company Office, which also has fax and secretarial services. Cyber-café Alô Brazil also provides Internet access. The Guararapes shopping center, just outside Recife, has Internet services at Cyber Café do Shopping Guararapes.

⚑ Internet Centers **Alô Brasil** ✉ Av. Monsenhor Tabosa 1001, Meireles, Fortaleza ☎ 085/263-3309. **Company Office** ✉ Caesar Park Hotel, Av. Beira-Mar 3980, Mucuripe, Fortaleza ☎ 085/263-1133. **Cyber Café do Shopping Guararapes** ✉ Av. Barreto de Menezes 800, near Piedade Beach, Jaboatão dos Guararapes, just south of Recife ☎ 081/3464-2488. **Interjato** ✉ Praia Shopping Av. Roberto Freire 3796, Ponta Negra, Natal ☎ 084/219-5510.

⚑ Overnight Services **Aeroexpress** ✉ Av. Campos Sales 463, Tirol, Natal ☎ 084/222-6304. **DHL** ✉ Av. Luciano Carneiro 2090, Fortaleza ☎ 085/227-5488 ✉ Av. Conselheiro Aguiar 1415, Recife ☎ 0800/701-0833 in Brazil. **FedEx** ✉ Km 10, BR 116, Fortaleza ☎ 085/274-1966.

⊞ Post Offices Recife Correio ⊠ Av. Gurarapes 250. **Natal Correio** ⊠ Av. Engenheiro Hilderando Góis 221. **Fortaleza Correio** ⊠ Rua Senador Alencar 38, Centro ⊠ Monsenhor Tabosa 111, Iracema.

MONEY MATTERS

RECIFE   Recommended *casas de câmbio* (exchange houses) in the city center include Mônaco Câmbio and Norte Câmbio Turismo. In Boa Viagem try Norte Câmbio Turismo or Colmeia Câmbio & Turismo. Banco do Brasil offers exchange services in several in-town locations as well as at its airport branch. Most banks are open weekdays 10–4.

⊞ **Recife Banks & Exchange Services Banco do Brasil** ⊠ Av. Dantas Barreto 541, Santo Antônio ⊠ Av. Conselheiro Aguiar 3600, Boa Viagem. **Colmeia Câmbio & Turismo** ⊠ Rua dos Navegantes 784, Loja 4, Boa Viagem. **Mônaco Câmbio** ⊠ Praça Joaquim Nabuco 159, Santo Antônio. **Norte Câmbio Turismo** ⊠ Rua Mathias de Albuquerque 223, Sala 508, Boa Viagem ⊠ Rua dos Navegantes 691, Loja 10, Boa Viagem.

NATAL   Money can be exchanged in the airport at VIP Câmbio or at Paria Câmbio in the Praia Shopping. Banco do Brasil has an office in Natal Shopping. Bank hours are generally weekdays 10–4.

⊞ **Natal Banks & Exchange Services Banco do Brasil** ⊠ Natal Shopping, Av. Senador Salgado Filho 2234, Candelária. **Praia Câmbio** ⊠ Praia Shopping, Av. Engenheiro Roberto Freire 8790, Ponta Negra. **VIP Câmbio** ⊠Aeroporto Internacional Augusto Severo, BR 101, Parnamirim.

FORTALEZA   The main Banco do Brasil branch is open weekdays 10–3; the Meireles branch on Avenida Abolição has the same hours. There are lots of casas de câmbio in Meireles as well.

⊞ **Fortaleza Bank Banco do Brasil** ⊠ Av. Duque de Caxias 560, Centro ☎ 085/255-3000 ⊠ Av. Desembarcador Moreira 1195, Aldeota ☎ 085/266-7800.

SAFETY

The three cities are not dangerous by São Paulo, Rio, or Salvador standards. Recife is considered the least safe of the three. A few problems occur in Boa Viagem—avoid the deserted Centro at night. In Natal Ponta Negra is still quite safe, but problems are more common at Praia dos Artistas. Don't wear expensive watches and jewelry—leave them and other valuables in hotel safes.

TELEPHONES

Recife's area code is 081, Natal's is 084, and Fortaleza's is 085. Public phones take cards, which are sold in a variety of denominations at many shops.

TAXIS

RECIFE   Taxis are cheap (fares double on Sunday), but drivers seldom speak English. All use meters. You can either hail a cab on the street or call for one. Recommended services are Coopertáxi, Radiotáxi Recife, and Teletáxi.

⊞ **Recife Taxi Companies Coopertáxi** ☎ 081/3424-8944. **Radiotáxi Recife** ☎ 081/3423-7777. **Teletáxi** ☎ 081/3429-4242.

NATAL   All taxis have meters and are easy to locate in Ponta Negra and downtown. Some of the best-known companies are Rádio Táxi, Rádio Táxi Relámpago, and Rádio Cooptáxi.

🔢 Natal Taxi Companies **Rádio Táxi** ☏ 084/221-5666. **Rádio Táxi Relámpago** ☏ 084/223-5444. **Rádio Cooptáxi** ☏ 084/205-4455.

FORTALEZA   You can call cabs or hail them on the street—all have meters. Fares are affordable, though they double on Sunday. Few drivers are English speakers. Reliable taxi services include Coopertáxi, Disquetáxi, Ligue Táxi, and Rádio Táxi.

🔢 Fortaleza Taxi Companies **Coopertáxi** ☏ 085/295-8258. **Disquetáxi** ☏ 085/287-7222. **Ligue Táxi** ☏ 085/231-7333. **Rádio Táxi** ☏ 085/287-5554.

TOURS

RECIFE   Agência Luck's vans pick up from all the hotels for city tours. Make arrangements for these and excursions outside Recife with Andratur. Catamarã Tours books day and night river trips by catamaran and other small boats from its office at the port in Recife Antigo on Praça Rio Branco (Marco Zero). You can make reservations for pousadas and land tours of Fernando de Noronha through Karitas Turismo Ltda.

Catamaran rides along the Rio Capibaribe pass Recife's grand houses, bridges, and mangrove swamps. There are two such excursions: The hour-long afternoon trip goes through the old rotating bridge and passes Recife Antigo and São José, the customs quay, the Santa Isabel Bridge, and the Rua da Aurora quays to the area near the Casa da Cultura. The two-hour-long night tour is aboard a slower—though more lively—vessel. The trip is like a party, with live music, drinks, and snacks. It passes the quays of São José Estelita (a set of restored warehouses) and then goes back by the Calanga Iate Clube, passing the ruins of the Casa de Banhos and running to the Rio Beberibe, from where there's a beautiful view of Olinda. Boats leave from near the Praça do Marco Zero in Recife Antigo.

In Olinda, the guides with official ID badges in the Praça do Carmo can show you around. Under any other circumstances, though, don't hire sightseeing guides who approach you on the street. Hire one through the museum or sight you're visiting, a tour operator, the tourist board, your hotel, or a reputable travel agency—and no one else.

🔢 Recife Tour Operators **Andratur** ✉ Av. Conselheiro Aguiar 3150, Loja 7, Boa Viagem ☏ 081/3465-8588. **Agência Luck** ✉ Rua Jornalista Paulo Bittencourt 163, Casa A, Derby ☏ 081/3421-3777. **Catamarã Tours** ☏ 081/3424-2845 or 081/3424-8930. **Catamaran reservations** ☏ 081/3436-2220. **Karitas Turismo Ltda.** ✉ Rua Agenor Lopes 292, Boa Viagem ☏ 081/3466-4300 ⊕ www.karitas.com.br.

NATAL   Manary Ecotours, the only ecotourism operator in Natal, runs professional trips to diverse destinations such as Cariri, Dinosaur Valley, and Praia da Pipa. Ma-noa has a hotel pickup service, allowing for easy day trips to their aquatic park in Maracajaú. A number of companies run dune buggy trips to Genipabu and other local beaches. These include Luck Natal Tour, Potiguar, and Protur.

🔢 Natal Tour Operators **Luck Natal Tour** ✉ Av. Praia de Ponta Negra 8820, Ponta Negra ☏ 084/219-2966. **Manary Ecotours** ✉ Rua Francisco Gurgel 9067, Ponta Negra ☏ 084/219-2900 ⊕ www.manary.com.br. **Ma-noa** ✉ Rua Doutor Horário 1889, Lagoa

Nova ☎ 084/223-4333 ⊕ www.ma-noa.com.br. **Potiguar** ✉ Rua Parde Lemos 78, Praia do Meio ☎ 084/202-4316. **Protur** ✉ Av. Engenheiro Roberto Freire 8337, Ponta Negra ☎ 084/642-2829.

FORTALEZA   Recommended operators include Ernanitur, Lisatur Viagens e Turismo Ltda., Nettour Viagem e Turismo, and Beach Sun Serviços e Turismo Ltda. For trips to Flexeiras, Jericoacoara, or other beach areas outside Fortaleza, OceanView Tours and Travel is a solid choice.

🎫 Fortaleza Tour Operators **Beach Sun Serviços e Turismo Ltda.** ✉ Rua Silva Jatahy 386, Meireles ☎☎ 085/248-2288. **Ernanitur** ✉ Av. Barão de Studart 1165, Aldeota ☎085/244-9363. **Lisatur Viagens e Turismo Ltda.** ✉Av. Dom Luiz 880, Sala 507, Aldeota ☎ 085/244-7812. **OceanView Tours and Travel** ✉ Av. Monsenhor Tabosa 1165, Meireles ☎ 085/219-1300.

VISITOR INFORMATION

RECIFE   The state tourist board in Recife is Empetur. It has several booths and a 24-hour information hot line, which is the number at the Guarapes airport booth. In Olinda contact the Secretaria de Turismo.

🎫 Recife Visitor Information **Empetur** ✉ Guararapes Airport, Praça Ministro Salgado Filho s/n, Imbiribeira ☎ 081/3462-4960 ✉ Praça Boa Viagem, Boa Viagem ☎ 081/3463-3621. **Secretaria de Turismo** ✉ Rua de São Bento 160, Olinda ☎ 081/3427-8183 ✉ Rua Bernardo Vieira de Melo, Mercado da Ribeira, Praça do Carmo, Olinda ☎ 081/3439-1660.

NATAL   SETUR is the state tourism board. Tourists can visit the main office or branches in Praia Shopping, Centro de Turismo, the bus station, or the airport. The main office is open 8–1 and 3–6 on weekdays; the other offices are open 8 AM–10 PM daily. SETUR also has a tourist hot line with English speakers available.

🎫 Natal Visitor Information **Disque Turismo** ☎ 0800/841-516. **SETUR** ✉ Rua Mossoró 359, Petrópolis ☎ 084/232-2500 ✉ Aeroporto Internacional Augusto Severo, BR 101, Parnamirim ☎ 084/643-1811 ✉ Centro de Turismo, Rua Abedal de Figueiredo 980, Petrópolis ☎ 084/211-6149 ✉ Praia Shopping, Av. Engenheiro Roberto Freire 8790, Ponta Negra ☎ 084/232-7248 ✉ Terminal Rodoviário de Natal, Av Capitão Mor. Gouveia 1237, Cidade da Esperança, ☎ 084/205-1000.

FORTALEZA   An English-language tourist information hot line, Disque Turismo, operates 24 hours a day. You can also get information through Ceará State's tourist board, SETUR, which has booths in several locations. The Cambeba booth is open weekdays 8–6; the Centro booth is open Monday–Saturday 8–6 and Sunday 8–noon; the booth in the João Tomé bus terminal is open daily 6 AM–9 PM. The municipal tourist board, Funcet, also has a booth open daily 8–noon and 2–6.

🎫 Fortaleza Visitor Information **Disque Turismo** ☎ 1516. **Funcet** ✉ Av. Pereria Filgueiras 4, Centro ☎ 085/252-1444. **SETUR** ✉ Centro Administrativo Virgílio Távora, Cambeba ☎ 085/488-3858 ✉ Aeroporto Internacional Pinto Martins, Av. Senador Carlos Jereissati, Serrinha ☎ 085/477-1667 ✉ Centro de Turismo, Rua Senador Pompeu 350, Centro ☎ 085/488-7412 or 083/488-7410 ✉ Terminal Rodoviário João Tomé, Av. Borges de Melo 1630, Fátima ☎ 085/256-4080.

THE AMAZON

8

MOST INTOXICATING DISH
Pato no tucupi with *jambu* leaf
(a mild stimulant) a Lá Em Casa ⇨*p.386*

BEST BOTTLED EMOTIONS
Love potions, sold at Ver-o-Peso ⇨*pp.383 and 390*

WORTH SINGING ABOUT
Teatro Amazonas opera house ⇨*p.406*

BIGGEST FISH TALE
Reeling in a 27-pound tucunaré ⇨*p.421*

WILDEST WAKE-UP CALL
Macaws and monkeys at
Ariaú Amazon Towers ⇨*p.410*

SEEING IS BELIEVING
Pink dolphins around Manaus ⇨*p.402*

SWEETEST WAY TO BEAT THE HEAT
Cairu's tropical fruit ice cream ⇨*p.382*

Updated by
Rhan Flatin

THE WORLD'S LARGEST TROPICAL FOREST SEEMS AN ENDLESS CARPET OF GREEN that's sliced only by the curving contours of rivers. Its statistics are as impressive: the region covers more than 10 million square km (4 million square mi) and extends into eight other countries (French Guiana, Suriname, Guyana, Venezuela, Ecuador, Peru, Bolivia, and Colombia). It takes up roughly 40% of Brazil in the states of Acre, Rondônia, Amazonas, Roraima, Pará, Amapá, and Tocantins. The Amazon forest is home to 500,000 cataloged species of plants and a river that annually transports 15% of the world's available freshwater to the sea, yet it's inhabited by only 16 million people. That's less than the population of metropolitan São Paulo.

Life centers on the rivers, the largest of which is the Amazon itself. From its source in southern Peru, it runs 6,300 km (3,900 mi) to its Atlantic outflow. Of its hundreds of tributaries, 17 are more than 1,600 km (1,000 mi) long. The Amazon is so large it could hold the Congo, Nile, Orinoco, Mississippi, and Yangtze rivers with room to spare. In places it is so wide you can't see the opposite shore, earning it the appellation Rio Mar (River Sea). Although there has been increasing urbanization in the Amazon region, between one-third and one-half of the Amazon's residents live in rural settlements, many of which are along the riverbanks, where transportation, water, fish, and good soil for planting are readily available.

Spaniard Vicente Pinzón is credited with being the first to sail the Amazon, in 1500. But the most famous voyage was undertaken by Spanish conquistador Francisco de Orellano, who set out from Ecuador on a short mission to search for food in 1541. Orellano was also familiar, no doubt, with the legend of El Dorado (the Golden One), a monarch whose kingdom was so rich in gold he covered his naked body in gold dust each day. Instead of gold or a lost kingdom, however, Orellano ran into natives, heat, and disease. When he emerged from the jungle a year later, his crew told a tale of women warriors they called the Amazons (a nod to classical mythology). This captivating story lent the region its name.

Much later, Portuguese explorer Francisco Raposo claimed to have found the ruins of a lost civilization in the jungle. He wrote: "We entered fearfully through the gateways to find the ruins of a city. . . . We came upon a great plaza, a column of black stone, and on top of it the figure of a youth was carved over what seemed to be a great doorway." Whatever Raposo saw was never again found. Unlike the highly organized Indian kingdoms and cities of Mexico and Peru, the Amazon natives were primarily nomadic hunter-gatherers.

Documented accounts indicate that early Portuguese contacts with the Indians were relatively peaceful. But it wasn't long before the peace ended, and the indigenous populations were devastated. Diseases brought by the Europeans and against which the Indians had no resistance took their toll; Portuguese attempts to enslave them did the rest. When the Portuguese arrived in Brazil, there were roughly 4.5 million Indians, many of them in the Amazon; today there are just over 300,000 in the nation and fewer than 200,000 in the Amazon.

In the late 19th century rubber—needed for bicycle and automobile tires—transformed Belém and Manaus from outposts to cities. Rubber barons constructed mansions and monuments and brought the most modern trappings of life into the jungle. The area attracted a colorful array of explorers, dreamers, and opportunists. In 1913 Brazilian adventurer Cândido Mariano da Silva Rondon (for whom the state of Rondônia is named) and former president Theodore Roosevelt came across a then-unknown river. Rondon named it Rio Roosevelt in honor of his traveling companion. In 1925 British adventurer Colonel Percy Fawcett, who had been seeking Raposo's lost city for years, disappeared into the jungle. In 1928 Henry Ford began to pour millions of dollars into vast rubber plantations. After much struggle and few results, the project was scrapped 20 years later.

Since the rubber era, huge reserves of gold and iron have been discovered. Land-settlement schemes and development projects, such as hydroelectric plants and major roadworks, have followed. Conservation has not always been a priority. Vast portions of tropical forest have been indiscriminately cut; tribal lands have again been encroached on; and industrial by-products, such as mercury used in gold mining, have poisoned wildlife and people. The 1988 murder (by a wealthy cattle rancher) of Brazilian activist Chico Mendes, who had made a name for himself lobbying for environmental issues abroad, brought still more global attention to the region. Although the Brazilian government has established reserves and made some efforts to preserve the territory, conservationists aren't satisfied.

And yet, 500 years after the first Europeans arrived, much of the Amazon has not been thoroughly explored by land. You can hear stories of lost cities and of unearthly creatures; stand on a riverboat deck and be astounded by the vastness of the mighty Rio Amazonas or charmed by wooden huts along a narrow waterway; and hike through dense vegetation and gawk at trees that tower 35 meters (150 feet). It's still a place where simple pleasures are savored and the mystical is celebrated.

Exploring the Amazon

Although there are regular flights and some bus routes through the Amazon, many visitors opt for the area's primary mode of transportation—boat. Though much slower, boats offer a closer look at Amazon culture, nature, and the river system, and they go just about everywhere you'd want to go. A trip along the Amazon itself, especially the 1,602-km (993-mi) four- to five-day journey between Belém and Manaus, is a singular experience. Averaging more than 3 km (2 mi) in width, but reaching a size of as much as 48 km (30 mi) across in the rainy season, there are many spots where it's impossible to see either bank. At night the moon and stars are often the only sources of light, reinforcing the sense of being in true wilderness.

Visiting outlying areas in the Amazon usually results in unforgettable adventures, but neotropical environments can be hostile, so prepare well and go with a companion if possible. It's a good idea to hire a guide or go with a tour company specializing in backcountry adventures. To join

Even 10 days is a short time to explore the region. Still, during a weeklong stay you can see some urban highlights and spend a little time on the river as well. The following independent itineraries start in Belém and end in Manaus, but it's fine to follow them in reverse order.

Numbers in the text correspond to numbers in the margin and on the Belém and Manaus maps.

8

**If you have
7 days**

Fly into ⊠ **Belém** ❶–⑯ ⊢ for two days of exploring the historic sites and natural reserves in and around the city. Then fly to ⊠ **Manaus** ㉔–㉟ for two days to see the meeting of the waters and to take a city tour that includes the **Teatro Amazonas** ❽. Then head out for a day or two to one of the famed jungle lodges, or sign up for an ecotour.

**If you have
10
days**

Spend two days in ⊠ **Belém** ❶–⑯ ⊢ exploring the city and its environs. On your third day travel by boat to ⊠ **Ilha do Marajó** for a two-day *fazenda* (ranch) stay. Return to Belém and fly to ⊠ **Manaus** ㉔–㉟ for two days to see the urban sights and the meeting of the waters. Spend your last few days at a jungle lodge outside Manaus, or go on an ecotour to see wildlife and villages.

**If you have
15
days**

After spending two days exploring ⊠ **Belém** ❶–⑯ ⊢ and two on a fazenda on ⊠ **Ilha do Marajó**, hop a riverboat for the two-day journey to ⊠ **Santarém**. Spend a day strolling the city before heading to **Alter do Chão**, an hour away. Then fly into ⊠ **Manaus** ㉔–㉟ to spend a day or two sightseeing before heading to a jungle lodge or out on an ecotour or fishing expedition.

---

a tour or to choose a destination, contact one of the tour companies we suggest, or consult with a state-run tour agency. Paratur in Belém and SEC in Manaus can also be helpful. Before departure make sure someone knows exactly where you are going and when you are returning. Tell them you will contact them as soon as you have phone access. Before you set out, make all your transportation arrangements, gather all the necessary supplies, and do some research so you are knowledgeable about the health and safety precautions you need to take. A small cut can turn into a bad infection, and a painful encounter with a stingray's barb can result in a ruined vacation. The more remote your destination, the more seriously you should heed the travel advice and health precautions in this book. (⇨ For information on health, *see* Health *in* The Amazon A to Z, *below,* and Health *in* Smart Travel Tips A to Z. For information on emergency evacuation insurance, *see* Insurance *in* Smart Travel Tips A to Z.) Your adventure can be wonderful, but you have to prepare well.

Boat Travel

Whatever the style, budget, or length of your Amazonian journey, there's a boat plying the river to suit your needs. Sleep in a hammock on the deck of a thatch-roof riverboat or in the air-conditioned suite of an upscale tour operator's private ship. Keep in mind that wildlife viewing is not good on boats far from shore. Near shore, however, the birding can be excellent. Binoculars and a bird guide can help, and shorebirds, raptors, and parrots can be abundant. Common in many parts of the river system are *boto* (pink dolphins) and *tucuxi* (gray dolphins). Look for them as they surface for air. To see the most wildlife, plan your travels to allow time in the forest and streams.

ADVENTURE CRUISES
Adventure cruises combine the luxury of cruising with exploration. Their goal is to get you close to wildlife and local inhabitants without sacrificing comforts and amenities. Near daily excursions include wildlife viewing in smaller boats with naturalists, village visits with naturalists, and city tours. Abercrombie and Kent, Aurora Expeditions, and INTRAV/ Clipper Cruises make these trips. They run from 9 to 16 days.

MACAMAZON BOATS
Longer boat routes on the lower Amazon are covered by MACAMA-ZON. Regular departures run between Belém, Santarém, Macapá, Manaus, and several other destinations. The boats are not luxurious but are a step above regional boats (⇨ *below*). You can get a suite for two from Belém to Manaus with air-conditioning and bath for about R$800. *Camarote* (cabin) class gets you a tiny room for two with air-conditioning and a shared bath. *Rede* (hammock) class is the cheapest and most intimate way to travel since you'll be hanging tight with the locals on the main decks. Hammocks are hung in two layers very close together, promoting neighborly chats. Arrive early for the best spots, away from the bar, engine, and bathrooms. Keep your valuables with you at all times and sleep with them. Conceal new sneakers in a plastic bag. In addition to a hammock (easy and cheap to buy in Belém or Manaus), bring two 4-foot lengths of ⅜-inch rope to tie it up. Also bring a sheet, since nights get chilly. MACAMAZON also runs a high-speed catamaran—with cushioned seats and air-conditioning—between Macapá and Belém (R$110). It takes 10 hours, about a third of the time that other boats take. It travels far from the riverbanks, so don't plan on seeing much.

OCEANGOING SHIPS
Some cruise ships call at Manaus, Belém, and Santarém as part of their itineraries. Most trips take place October through May. They range in length from 10 to 29 days, and costs vary. Two major lines making such journeys are Princess Cruises and Royal Olympic Cruises.

REGIONAL BOATS
To travel to towns and villages or to meander slowly between cities, go by *barco regional* (regional boat). A trip from Belém to Manaus takes about four days; Belém to Santarém is two days. The double- or triple-deck boats carry freight and passengers. They make frequent stops at small towns, allowing for interaction and observation. You might be able to get a cabin with two bunks (around R$400 for a two-day trip), but expect it to be claustrophobic. Most passengers sleep in hammocks with little or no space between them. Bring your own hammock, sheet, and two 4-foot sections of rope. Travel lightly and inconspicuously.

Booths sell tickets at the docks, and even if you don't speak Portuguese, there are often signs alongside the booths that list prices, destinations, and departure times. If you plan to sleep in a hammock, arrive at least one hour early to get a good spot away from the engine, toilets, and bar. Keep valuables with you in your hammock while you sleep, including

8

Archeology

The Santarém region has numerous areas with ancient pictographs and mounds of shellfish middens. Monte Alegre is great place to start. Another is Alenquer, just across the river from Santarém. Both villages are easily accessible by passenger boat, and both are typical river towns seldom visited by foreigners. Most sites require hiring a guide and a four-wheel-drive vehicle with a driver. Spend at least a half day at each site, starting at 6 AM. Be sure to take plenty of water and food for everyone involved, including the driver and guide.

Amazonian Cuisine

Who needs regular old beef or poultry when you can have water-buffalo steak, fried piranha, or duck in manioc sauce (*pato no tucupi*)? Or why not try the river fish with exotic Indian names such as *tucunaré*, *pirarucú*, *tambaquí*, *curimatã*, *jaraquí*, and *pacú*. The *pimenta-de-cheiro*, a local hot pepper, seriously spices things up. Side dishes often include *farinha* (coarsely ground manioc), *farofa* (finely ground manioc fried in margarine), red beans, and rice. Wherever you eat, beware of ordering endangered wildlife, such as caiman or armadillo, which remain (illegally) on some menus. For dessert try some of the fruits plentiful in this region, such as *cupuaçu* (creamy-white pulp with a unique flavor, reminiscent of soursop, used for desserts, jellies, and candies), *guaraná* (a small red fruit used in the popular Brazilian soft drink of the same name), and *açaí* (a small purple fruit used in soup and ice cream). Cerpa, one of the the region's most popular beers, is made near Belém.

Handicrafts

Handicrafts made by indigenous groups include woodcrafted and woven items, bows, arrows, blowguns, and jewelry and headdresses of seeds and feathers. (Note: U.S. Customs prohibits the import of endangered animal parts. Ask the storekeeper about such items before you buy.) In Belém you'll find *marajoara* pottery, which has the intricate designs used by the tribe of the same name. Vases and sculptures in Macapá often contain manganese—a shiny black mineral mined locally. All Amazon pottery is soft and breaks readily. Be sure it is packed exceptionally well.

River Villages

Anamá, Alenquer, Óbidos, Gurupá, and other Amazonian villages are wonderful places to visit. The docks and open markets are lively early in the day, and the community usually appreciates your interest. Many of these places rarely see foreigners. Inquire at tourist offices, ask at your hotel, or simply choose a place on the map. Someone at the boat docks can always tell you where your boat will be departing. All villages have food vendors. Your safest bet is a plate of rice and beans with beef, chicken, or fish. Smaller villages don't even have mineral water, and transportation is unreliable. Go well prepared and open-minded. In very small communities you may even be presented to the mayor or other town officials. Any attempt you make to communicate will be appreciated.

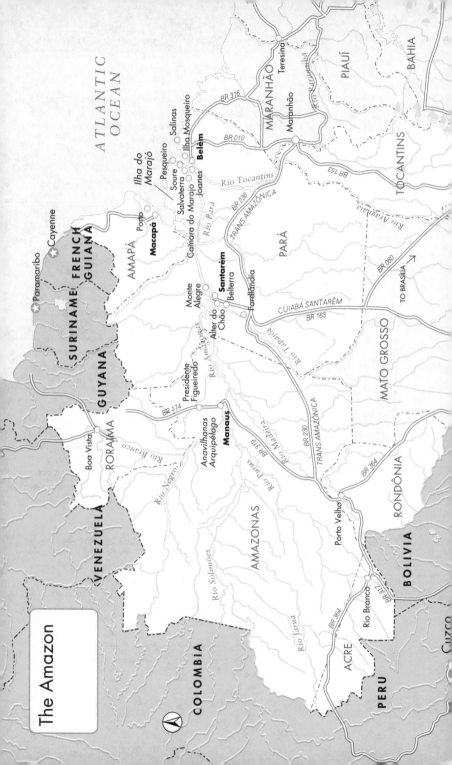

The Amazon

any new-looking clothing items (like sneakers), which you should conceal in a plastic bag. Sanitary conditions in bathrooms vary from boat to boat. Bring your own toilet paper, sunscreen, and insect repellent. Food is sometimes served, but the quality ranges from so-so to deplorable. Consider bringing your own water and a *marmita* (carry-out meal) if you'll be on the boat overnight. Many boats have a small store at the stern where you can buy drinks, snacks, and grilled *mixto quente* (ham-and-cheese) sandwiches. Fresh fruit and snacks are available at stops along the way. Be sure to peel or wash fruit thoroughly with bottled water before eating it.

TOURIST BOATS Private groups can hire tourist boats that are more comfortable than standard riverboats. They generally travel close to the riverbank and have open upper decks from which you can observe the river and forest. The better tour operators have a regional English-speaking expert on board— usually an ecologist or botanist. You can either sleep out on the deck in a hammock or in a cabin, which usually has air-conditioning or a fan. Meals are generally provided.

SPEEDBOATS You can take a speedboat to just about anywhere the rivers flow. Faster than most options, speedboats can be ideal for traveling between smaller towns, a morning of wildlife viewing, or visiting a place that doesn't have regular transportation, such as a secluded beach or waterfall. You design the itinerary, including departure and return times. Prices and availability vary with distance and locale. Contact tour agencies, talk with locals, or head down to the docks to find a boat willing to take you where you want to go. Work out the price, destination, and travel time before leaving. You may have to pay for the gas up front, but don't pay the rest until you arrive. For trips longer than an hour, bring water, snacks, and sunscreen.

Organized Trips

Most tour companies are based in Manaus, Belém, or Santarém. Tours vary considerably in price and quality and are from one day to three weeks in length. The majority are ecotours, fishing tours, cultural tours, and city tours, or a mixture of these. Some companies have longer educational tours, and trekking and camping trips. Your options include: joining an ecotour adventure, where you sleep in a hammock on a boat or in a luxury suite in a jungle hotel; sportfishing in out-of-the-way places on a fancy boat; or wildlife watching in backwater lakes in the early morning and walking through a *caboclo* (riverine people) village in the afternoon. For tour-operator information, *see* Tours *in* The Amazon A to Z *and* Tours & Packages *in* Smart Travel Tips A to Z.

ECOTOURS Boat- or land-based tours allow you to explore the flora, fauna, and people of the region. On boat-based tours a regional boat or yacht takes you to wildlife-viewing areas. You spend several days on your floating hotel, taking short departures to hike on a forest trail, visit with locals, do some fishing, or buzz along waterways in a motorboat searching for wildlife. The swimming is often excellent. Lodge-based trips are much the same, though obviously less mobile. Jungle lodges may or may not have accommodations superior to the boats, though you'll probably have more space and more opportunities to explore in the forest. The competence of guides and naturalists varies, so it's a good idea to meet them prior to departure. Educational ecotours (both boat- and land-based ones) provide highly trained naturalists or professors who provide plant, animal, and bird identification. Some companies offer assistance to researchers studying specific plants or animals.

FISHING TOURS   With 2,000 species of fish identified (and possibly up to 5,000), the Amazon has more species than the Atlantic. Many aquarium fish originate here, as does the legendary peacock bass. The *tucunaré*, as it's known in Brazil, is a hard-hitting fish that has been dubbed the "ultimate adversary." Reaching around 27 pounds (12 kilograms), it goes for flies and lures, and rarely disappoints. A number of companies have packages to remote fishing sites. Some are boat-based and some are lodge-based. Accommodations, prices, and tour quality vary, so shop around.

CULTURAL TOURS   Although Brazil limits visits to Indian reservations to researchers, if you have an interest in indigenous cultures you can learn about the Yanomami people on 11- or 15-day itineraries with Swallows and Amazons. Small boats take you along the Rio Negro to visit Yanomami communities that aren't part of a reservation and to spend several days with the people of one village. Amizade Limited takes its cultural trips a step farther. You can help the organization's volunteers and Brazilian students in various community-related projects.

CANOEING &   Paddling local wooden canoes by day and camping at night, you may
CAMPING   explore the rain forest that lines the banks of the Rio Negro (Black River) and perhaps continue along smaller tributaries. En route, you visit with local river people and see monkeys, iguanas, river dolphins, and caiman. Trips generally last 7 to 10 days.

Timing

The dry season (low water) between Belém and Manaus runs roughly from mid-June into December, and it's often brutally hot. Shortly before the new year, rains come more often and the climate cools a bit. The average annual temperature is 80°F (27°C) with high humidity. The early morning and the evening are always cooler and are the best times for walking around. The rainy season (high water) runs from December to June. "High water" means flooded forests and better boat access to lakes and wetlands for wildlife spotting. It also means flooded river beaches. Fishing is prime during low water, when fish move from the forest back into rivers and lakes, making them more accessible. Keep in mind that even the driest month has an average rainfall of 2 inches (compared with up to 13 inches during the wet season), so some kind of raingear is always recommended. Depending where you are in the Amazon, during the rainy season, it may rain every day, or three out of every four days, whereas during the dry season it may only rain one out of four days or less.

About the Restaurants

Reservations and dressy attire are rarely needed in the Amazon (indeed, reservations are rarely taken). Tipping isn't customary except in finer restaurants. Call ahead on Monday night, when many establishments are closed.

About the Hotels

Amazonia is still a wild place, and many lodges and towns are remote. Don't expect to be pampered. Room prices tend to be reasonable and include breakfast, but services and amenities may cost quite a bit extra. Laundry service, for example, can be outrageously expensive. When checking in, ask about discounts (*descontos*). During the slow season and often in midweek, you can get a discount of around 20%. Cry a little, as the Brazilians say, and you may get a larger discount. Paying with cash may lower the price. Hotel rooms have air-conditioning, TVs, phones, and bathrooms unless we indicate otherwise, but showers don't always have hot water. Jungle lodges and smaller hotels in outlying areas often lack basic amenities.

WHAT IT COSTS In Reais					
	$$$$	$$$	$$	$	¢
RESTAURANTS	over $60	$45–$60	$30–$45	$15–$30	under $15
HOTELS	over $500	$375–$500	$250–$375	$125–$250	under $125

Restaurant prices are for a dinner entrée. Hotel prices are for two people in a standard double room in high season, excluding taxes.

BELÉM

The capital of Pará State, Belém is a river port of around 1.3 million people on the south bank of the Rio Guamá, 120 km (74 mi) from the Atlantic, and 2,933 km (1,760 mi) north of Rio de Janeiro. The Portuguese settled here in 1616, using it as a gateway to the interior and an outpost to protect the area from invasion by sea. Because of its ocean access, Belém became a major trade center. Like the upriver city of Manaus, it rode the ups and downs of the Amazon booms and busts. The first taste of prosperity was during the rubber era. Architects from Europe were brought in to build churches, civic palaces, theaters, and mansions, often using fine, imported materials. When Malaysia's rubber supplanted that of Brazil in the 1920s, wood and, later, minerals provided the impetus for growth.

Belém has expanded rapidly since the 1980s, pushed by the Tucuruvi hydroelectric dam (Brazil's second largest), the development of the Carajás mining region, and the construction of the ALBRAS/Alunorte bauxite and aluminum production facilities. Wood exports have risen, making Pará the largest wood-producing state in Brazil. As the forests are cut, pastures and cattle replace them, resulting in an increase in beef production. In 2000 the state government began construction of a bridge network connecting Belém to outlying cities. The resulting increase in commerce has spurred economic growth in the region, though there is still considerable poverty and high unemployment. In the city highrise apartments are replacing colonial structures. Fortunately, local governments have launched massive campaigns to preserve the city's rich heritage while promoting tourist-friendly policies. This effort has earned state and federal government funds to restore historical sites in the

Belém area. Tourism is on the rise in the city and is becoming increasingly important for the city's economic well-being.

Exploring Belém

Belém is more than just a jumping-off point for the Amazon. It has several good museums and restaurants and lots of extraordinary architecture. Restored historical sites along the waterfront provide areas to walk, eat, and explore. Several distinctive buildings—some with Portuguese *azulejos* (tiles) and ornate iron gates—survive along the downtown streets and around the Praça Frei Caetano Brandão, in the Cidade Velha (Old City). East of here, in the Nazaré neighborhood, colorful colonial structures mingle with new ones housing trendy shops.

Cidade Velha

Cidade Velha (Old City) is the oldest residential part of Belém. Many of the houses are colonial with clay walls and tile roofs. Three stories is the tallest they get, though 15-floor apartment buildings are invading from the north. Much of Cidade Velha is middle-income with a variety of hardware, auto parts, and fishing supply stores. On its northwestern edge, the Forte Presépio lies along the banks of the Rio Guamá.

A GOOD WALK Begin at the **Igreja Nossa Senhora das Mercês** ❶ ⌐, a large pink church just northeast of the **Estação das Docas** ❷ and the **Ver-o-Peso** ❸ market. Walking southwest through the market, you pass the small dock where fishermen unload the day's catch. Turn left on Avenida Portugal (past the municipal clock), which borders Praça Dom Pedro II. Follow it to the large, baby-blue Palácio Antônio Lemos, which houses the **Museu de Arte de Belém (MABE)** ❹. Next door is the even larger white Palácio Lauro Sodré, with the **Museu do Estado do Pará** ❺ inside. Just behind this museum looms the golden church, **Igreja de São João Batista** ❻. From here head back toward Praça Dom Pedro II along Rua Tomásia Perdigão, and turn left onto Travessa Félix Roque. This takes you to the rear of the **Catedral da Sé** ❼ (the entrance faces Praça Frei Caetano Brandão). To your right as you exit is the **Museu de Arte Sacra** ❽, and just beyond is the **Casa das Onze Janelas** ❾ and the **Forte do Presépio** ❿. You can have a bite at the small restaurants in the Casa das Janelas and the Museu de Arte Sacra, or head back to Estação das Docas for a wider variety of food choices.

TIMING This tour takes close to three hours—longer if you linger in museums. Weekday mornings are best to catch the churches open.

WHAT TO SEE **Casa das Onze Janelas.** At the end of the 17th century, sugar baron Domin-❾ gos da Costa Barcelar built the neoclassical House of Eleven Windows as his private mansion. Today Barcelar's mansion is a gallery for contemporary plastic art and other visual art, including photography. The view from the balcony is impressive. Take a walk through the courtyard and imagine scenes of the past. This is where the aristocracy took tea and watched over the docks as slaves unloaded ships from Europe and filled them with sugar and rum. ⊠ *Praça Frei Caetano Brandão, Cidade Velha* ☎ *R$2, free Tues.* ⊙ *Tues.–Fri. 1–6, weekends 9–1.*

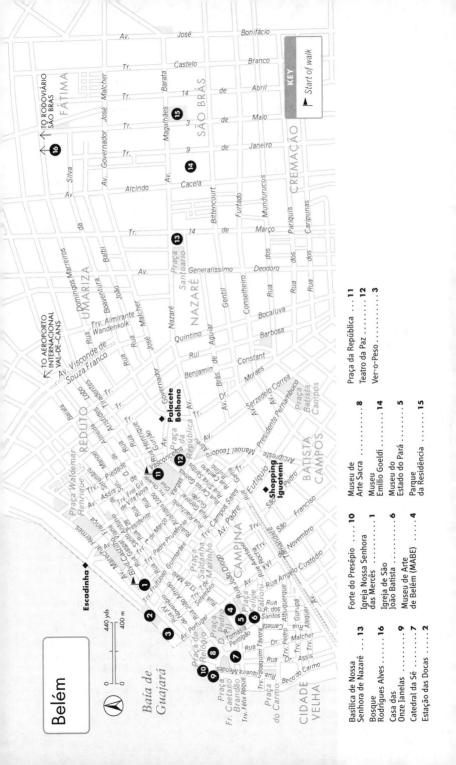

Belém

Baía de Guajará

TO AEROPORTO INTERNACIONAL VAL-DE-CANS ↗

↑ TO RODOVIÁRIO SÃO BRÁS

KEY

▲ Start of walk

❼ Catedral da Sé. In 1771 Bolognese architect Antônio José Landi, whose work can be seen throughout the city, completed the cathedral's construction on the foundations of an older church. Carrara marble adorns the rich interior, which is an interesting mix of baroque, colonial, and neoclassical styles. The high altar was a gift from Pope Pius IX. ⊠ *Praça Frei Caetano Brandão, Cidade Velha* ☎ *Free* ☉ *Tues.–Fri. 8–noon and 2–4, Sat. 5 PM–6:30 PM, Sun. 6 PM–7 PM.*

❷ Estação das Docas. Next to Ver-o-Peso market on the river, three former warehouses have been artfully converted into a commercial/tourist area. All have one wall of floor-to-ceiling glass that provides a full river view when dining or shopping. The first warehouse is a convention center, the second is full of shops and kiosks selling crafts and snacks, and the third has a microbrewery and 14 upscale restaurants. The buildings are air-conditioned and connected by glass-covered walkways and contain photos and artifacts from the port's heyday. A stroll outside along the docks provides a grand view of the bay. Tourist boats arrive and depart at the dock—a good place to relax both day and night. ⊠ *Boulevard Castilhos França s/n, Comercio* ☎ *091/212–5525* ☎ *Free* ☉ *Weekdays noon–1 AM, weekends 10 AM–1 AM.*

> **need a break?** The many regional flavors at ice cream shop **Cairu** include those unique to the Amazon, such as *taperebá, graviola,* and *cajá,* as well as the more familiar *coco* (coconut), mango, and chocolate. Juices, sandwiches, and soft drinks are also served. ⊠ *Estação das Docas, Boulevard Castilhos França s/n, Comercio* ⊠ *Conselheiro Furtado and Presidente Pernambuco* ⊠ *Travessa 14 de Março and João Balbi.*

❿ Forte do Presépio (Fort of the Crèche). Founded January 12, 1616, this fort is considered Belém's birthplace. From here the Portuguese launched conquests of the Amazon and watched over the bay. The fort's role in the region's defense is evidenced by massive English- and Portuguese-made cannons pointing out over the water. They are poised atop fort walls that are 3 yards thick in places. Renovations completed in 2002 unearthed more than two dozen cannons, extensive military middens from the moat, and native Tupi artifacts. A small museum of prefort indigenous cultures is at the entrance. Just outside the fort, cobblestone walkways hug the breezy waterfront. ⊠ *Praça Frei Caetano Brandão, Cidade Velha* ☎ *No phone* ☎ *R$4, free Tues.* ☉ *Tues.–Fri. 1–6, weekends 9–1.*

▶ **❶ Igreja Nossa Senhora das Mercês** (Our Lady of Mercy Church). Another of Belém's baroque creations attributed to Antônio Landi, this church is notable for its pink color and convex facade. It's part of a complex that includes the Convento dos Mercedários, which has served both as a convent and a prison, though not simultaneously. ⊠ *Gaspar Viana e Frutuosa Guimarães Comercio* ☎ *Free* ☉ *Mon.–Sat. 8–1.*

❻ Igreja de São João Batista (St. John the Baptist Church). Prodigious architect Antônio Landi finished this small octagonal church in 1777. It was completely restored in the late 1990s and is considered the city's purest example of baroque architecture. ☒ *Rua João Diogo and Rodriguês Dos Santos, Cidade Velha* ☜ *Free* ⊘ *Mon.–Sat. 6:30 AM–9 AM.*

❹ Museu de Arte de Belém (MABE). Temporary exhibits on the bottom level of the Metropolitan Art Museum are free to view. On the second level staff members hand you brown furry slippers that you must wear over your shoes to protect the wooden floors. The permanent collection of furniture and paintings dates from the 18th century through the rubber boom. The museum is housed in the Palácio Antônio Lemos (circa 1883), a municipal palace built in the imperial Brazilian style with French influences. ☒ *Praça Dom Pedro II s/n, Cidade Velha* ☎ *091/219–8228* ☜ *R$4, free Tues.* ⊘ *Tues.–Fri. 10–6, weekends 9–1.*

❽ Museu de Arte Sacra. A guided tour (call 48 hours in advance to reserve an English-speaking docent) begins in the early-18th-century baroque Igreja de Santo Alexandre (St. Alexander's Church), which is distinguished by intricate woodwork on its altar and pews. On the second half of the tour you see the museum's collection of religious sculptures and paintings. Temporary exhibitions, a gift shop, and a café are on the first floor. ☒ *Praça Frei Caetano Brandão, Cidade Velha* ☎ *091/219–1166* ☜ *R$4, free Tues.* ⊘ *Tues.–Fri. 1–6, weekends 9–1.*

❺ Museu do Estado do Pará. Pará State Museum is in the sumptuous Palácio Lauro Sodré (circa 1771), an Antônio Landi creation with Venetian and Portuguese elements. Consistently outstanding visiting exhibits are on the first floor; the second floor contains the permanent collection of furniture and paintings. ☒ *Praça Dom Pedro II, Cidade Velha* ☎ *091/219–1138* ☜ *R$4* ⊘ *Tues.–Fri. 1–6, weekends 9–1.*

★ ❸ Ver-o-Peso. Its name literally meaning "see the weight" (a throwback to the time when the Portuguese weighed everything entering or leaving the region), this market is a hypnotic confusion of colors and voices. Vendors hawk tropical fruits, regional wares, and an assortment of tourist kitsch. Most interesting are the *mandingueiras*, women who claim they can solve any problem with "miracle" jungle roots and charms for the body and soul. They sell jars filled with animal eyes, tails, and even heads, as well as herbs, each with its own legendary power. The sex organs of the pink river dolphin are a supposedly unrivaled cure for romantic problems. In the fish market you get an up-close look at pirarucu, the Amazon's most colorful fish and the world's second-largest freshwater species. Look for bizarre armored catfish species, such as the *tamuatá* and the huge *piraiba*. Across the street is a small arched entrance to the municipal meat market. Duck in and glance at the French-style pink-and-green-painted ironwork, imported from Britain. Be sure to visit Ver-o-Peso before noon, when most vendors leave. It opens around 6 AM. Leave your jewelry at home and beware of pickpockets. ☒ *Av. Castilhos França s/n, Comércio.*

Nazaré

Just east of the Cidade Velha, Nazaré's mango tree–lined streets create the sensation of walking through tunnels. Among the historic buildings there's a tremendous variety of pastel colors and European styles. Many of the newer buildings house elegant shops.

CloseUp

TALES FROM THE MIST

LEGENDS ARE AN INTEGRAL PART OF LOCAL CULTURE in the Amazon and are remarkably consistent throughout the region. Many are based on strange creatures that inhabit the rivers and jungle. One of the most widespread legends is that of the cobra grande (giant snake), which strikes fear into the hearts of many a river dweller. Popularized by the movie Anaconda (filmed near Manaus), the story involves sucuri (anaconda) snakes of epic proportions that terrorize. They're said to cause shipwrecks and to eat fleeing passengers whole.

Another extremely popular (and considerably less gruesome) legend is that of botos (dolphins) that take human form. Always dressed immaculately in white, they appear at parties and dance with the youngest, most beautiful girls. They lure the girls outside, where they seduce them, and then return to the water just before dawn. You can always tell a boto from its slightly fishy smell and the hole in the top of its head, which is covered by a hat.

Curupira appears as a nude and savage indigenous child, about six or seven years old, whose feet are turned backward. He is said to lure people into the jungle—causing them to become irreversibly lost. As the story goes, white men cut off his feet before killing him; a god sewed Curupira's feet on backward and returned him to the forest to exact revenge. Some people claim you can solicit Curupira's help for hunting and crop failures. As payment, you must bring him tobacco, matches, and a bottle of liquor—the latter of which he will down in one swig to seal the pact. If you ever tell anyone about the agreement, Curupira will hunt you down and stab you to death with his long, sharp fingernails.

Several tales explain the origins of important fruits and vegetables. Guaraná,

for example, was the name of a young child beloved by all. As the story goes, he was killed by the jealous god Jurupari, who disguised himself as a snake. Lightning struck as the village gathered around Guaraná's body and wept. At that moment the lightning god, Tupã, ordered the villagers to bury the child's eyes. The guaraná fruit (which actually resembles eyes) sprouted from the burial spot.

In the legend of Açaí, the chief of a starving tribe ordered all babies to be sacrificed to end the famine. The chief's daughter, Iaça, had a beautiful baby. Before its sacrifice, she found the child holding a palm tree, and then he suddenly vanished. The tree then became full of açaí (which is Iaça spelled backward) fruit, from which a wine was made that saved the tribe and ended the sacrifices.

The legend of the native water flower vitória régia begins with a beautiful girl who wished to become a star in the heavens. She trekked to the highest point in the land and tried in vain to touch the moon. Iaci—the god of the moon—was awed and enchanted by the girl's beauty. He knew that a mortal could never join the astral kingdom, so he decided to use his powers to immortalize the girl on earth instead. He transformed her into a stunning flower with an unmistakable, alluring scent. Realizing that he needed something fitting to help display this "star," he stretched a palm leaf and created a lily pad, and thus the vitória régia came to be.

A GOOD TOUR Begin near the south end of the **Praça da República** ⓫ ☞ just across Avenida President Vargas from the Hilton. There you'll find the large pink **Teatro da Paz** ⓬. After leaving the theater, veer left onto Avenida President Vargas and then left again onto Avenida Nazaré. Just beyond Avenida Generalíssimo Deodoro is the **Basílica de Nossa Senhora de Nazaré** ⓭. Avenida Nazaré becomes Avenida Magalhães Barata at this point. Continue east three more blocks to the **Museu Emilio Goeldi** ⓮. After touring the museum, consider going east another three blocks to the **Parque da Residência** ⓯ for a relaxing break and lunch, or take a short (R$17) taxi ride northeast to the **Bosque Rodrigues Alves** ⓰, a chunk of jungle in the middle of town.

TIMING It should take about 1½ hours to reach the Museu Emilio Goeldi. Plan to spend an hour or two here. If you need a break, the museum has a restaurant and a snack bar. Count on at least an hour at Bosque Rodrigues Alves.

WHAT TO SEE

FodorśChoice

★

⓭ **Basílica de Nossa Senhora de Nazaré.** It's hard to miss this opulent Roman-style basilica. Not only does it stand out visually, but there's an enormous *samauma* tree (kapok variety) filled with screeching white-winged parakeets in the plaza out front. Built in 1908 on the site where a *caboclo* (rural inhabitant) named Placido is said to have seen a vision of the Virgin in the early 1700s. The basilica's ornate interior is constructed entirely of European marble and contains elaborate mosaics, detailed stained-glass windows, and intricate bronze doors. In the small, basement-level Museu do Círio, displays explain the Círio de Nazaré festival, which is held each October to honor the city's patron saint. ⊠ *Av. Nazaré s/n at Av. Generalisimo Deodoro, Nazaré* ☎ *091/224–9614 museum* 🔊 *Free* ☉ *Basilica Mon. 6–11 and 3–5, Tues.–Sat. 6–11 and 3–7, Sun. 3–7; museum Tues.–Fri. 9–6.*

⓰ **Bosque Rodrigues Alves.** In 1883 this 40-acre plot of rain forest was designated an ecological reserve. Nowadays it has an aquarium and two amusement parks as well as natural caverns, a variety of animals (some in the wild), and mammoth trees. ⊠ *Av. Almirante Barroso, Marco* ☎ *091/ 226–2308* 🔊 *R$1* ☉ *Tues.–Sun. 8–5.*

★ ⓮ **Museu Emílio Goeldi.** Founded by a naturalist and a group of intellectuals in 1866, this complex contains one of the Amazon's most important research facilities. Its museum has an extensive collection of Indian artifacts, including the distinctive and beautiful pottery of the Marajó Indians, known as *marajoara*. A small forest has reflecting pools with giant *vitória régia* water lilies. But the true highlight is the collection of Amazon wildlife, including manatees, anacondas, macaws, sloths, and monkeys. ⊠ *Av. Magalhães Barata 376, Nazaré* ☎ *091/249–1230* 🔊 *Park R$2, park and museum R$4* ☉ *Tues.–Thurs. and weekends 9–noon and 2–5:30, Fri. 9–noon.*

⓯ **Parque da Residência.** For decades this was the official residence of the governor of Pará. Now it provides office space for the Secretaria de Cultura (SECULT; Executive Secretary of Culture), as well as public space. Within the park are a 400-seat theater, an orchid conservatory, an ice cream parlor, a restaurant, and shaded spots to relax and soak in the atmosphere. ⊠ *Av. Magalhães Barata 830, São Brás* ☎ *091/219–1200* 🖅 *Free* ☉ *Tues.–Sun. 9 AM–10 PM.*

▶ ⓫ **Praça da República.** At this square you'll find a large statue that commemorates the proclamation of the Republic of Brazil, an amphitheater, and several French-style iron kiosks. On Sunday vendors, food booths, and musical groups create a festival-like atmosphere that attracts crowds of locals. ⊠ *Bounded by Av. Presidente Vargas, Trv. Osvaldo Cruz, and Av. Assis de Vasconcelos.*

⓬ **Teatro da Paz.** A complete renovation of this 1878 neoclassical theater was finished in 2001. Concert pianos were acquired to facilitate production of operas. Greek-style pillars line the front and sides; inside, note the imported details such as Italian marble pillars and French chandeliers. Classical music performances are also held in the theater, which seats more than 800 people. English-speaking guides are available to give 20-minute tours. ⊠ *Av. da Paz s/n, Praça da República, Campina* ☎ *091/224–7355* 🖅 *Call for ticket prices* ☉ *Tues.–Fri. 9:30–11; tours Tues.–Fri. 12:30, 2:30, 4, and 5:30, Sat. 9:30, 11, and 12:30.*

Where to Eat

$–$$ ✕ **Dom Giuseppe.** From gnocchi to ravioli, flawless preparation of the basics distinguishes this Italian eatery from others. Everyone in town knows this, so reservations are a good idea—particularly on weekends. Don't leave without ordering a scrumptious *dolce* Paula (ice cream–and–brownie dessert). ⊠ *Av. Conselheiro Furtado 1420, Batista Campos* ☎ *091/241–1146* 🖃 *AE, DC, MC, V.*

¢–$$ ✕ **Casa Portuguesa.** Although it's in the heart of the commercial district, this restaurant does its best to replicate the charm of a Portuguese country home. Specialties include dishes with chicken and, of course, salted cod. ⊠ *Rua Senador Manoel Barata 897, Campina* ☎ *091/242–4871* 🖃 *AE, DC, MC, V.*

$ ✕ **Lá em Casa.** From inauspicious beginnings has emerged one of Belém's
Fodor'sChoice most popular restaurants. Regional cuisine, prepared to exacting spec-
★ ifications, has earned Lá em Casa its good reputation. Consider trying Belém's premier dish, *pato no tucupi* (duck in a yellow manioc–herb sauce served with the mildly intoxicating *jambu* leaf). Crabs on the half-shell covered with *farofa* (finely ground manioc fried in margarine) is another good choice, as is *açaí* sorbet for dessert. Sitting on the patio fringed by tropical vines and bromeliads, you feel like you're dining in the middle of the forest. ⊠ *Av. Governador José Malcher 247, Nazaré* ☎ *091/223–1212* 🖃 *AE, DC, MC, V.*

$ ✕ **Rodeio.** Grilled and roasted meats are the focus of this *churrascaria.* A reasonable fixed-price menu includes not only as many servings as you can eat but also salads and dessert. The wood interior, warm lighting, and excellent service make for a relaxing atmosphere. ⊠ *Padre Eutíquio 1308, Batista Campos* ☎ *091/212–2112* 🖃 *AE, DC, MC, V* ☉ *No dinner Sun., Mon.*

¢–$ ✕ **Miako.** Belém has a large Japanese community (second only to that of São Paulo), so there's no lack of Japanese restaurants. This one, however, is a tried-and-true favorite for excellent service, attractive wooden decor, and consistently good food. The sushi is terrific. ⊠ *Rua 1 de Março 76, Campina* ☎ *091/242–2355* ▤ *AE, DC, MC, V.*

¢ ✕ **Bom Paladar.** A convenient location across from Telemar and the Praça da República makes this pay-per-kilo restaurant a good choice for a quick lunch. The buffet table always has several main dishes, along with salads, beans, and rice. ⊠ *Riachuelo 357, Campina* ☎ *091/241–3723* ⊙ *Closed Sun. No dinner.*

¢ ✕ **Casa do Caldo.** Eight soups (out of 36) are featured every night for family dining in the "House of Soup." One price covers unlimited soup, toast, and dessert porridge. Try the crab soup with cilantro and the cow's-foot soup. It's air-conditioned and casual, with superb service. ⊠ *Rua Diogo Moia 266, Umarizal* ☎ *091/230–3110* ▤ *AE, V* ⊙ *Closed Mon.*

¢ ✕ **O Gato Comeu.** The best sandwiches in town are here. Try the Big Miau (fillet, vegetables, banana) or the Galinhão (chicken, vegetables, and banana). Sidewalk seating is best in the evening, so consider a stop here in conjunction with a stroll in adjacent Praça Batista Campos. ⊠ *Serzedelo Correa, Batisto Campos* ▤ *No credit cards* ⊙ *Closed Mon.*

¢ ✕ **Kanshari.** Lunches are strictly vegan at one of the few vegetarian restaurants in the city. Trained cooks work with soy products, vegetable protein, and whole grains to prepare an impressive buffet of Brazilian dishes. It's not far from the Hilton. ⊠ *Rua Gama Abreu 83, Campina* ☎ *091/252–2436* ▤ *No credit cards* ⊙ *Closed Sun. No dinner.*

Where to Stay

$$ ▥ **Hilton International Belém.** The Hilton's reliability and amenities are topped only by its location right on the Praça da República. Although rooms have few decorations, bland color schemes, and simple furniture, they are well equipped and comfortable. Executive rooms have the nicest views as well as access to a lounge with a VCR, a meeting area, and complimentary food and drink. ⊠ *Av. Presidente Vargas 882, Campina 66017-000* ☎ *091/217–7000, 800/445–8667 in U.S.* ▤ *091/225–2942* ⊕ *www.hilton.com* ☞ *361 rooms* ♢ *Restaurant, pool, hair salon, health club, sauna, 2 bars, convention center* ▤ *AE, DC, MC, V.*

$ ▥ **Equatorial Palace.** Widely considered to be one of the nicest hotels in town, the Equatorial Palace has a spacious dining hall and several shops (including a tour agency). The pool and bar are on the roof, with a nearly 360-degree view. The Nazaré location is within walking distance of the port, Centro, and Cidade Velha. ⊠ *Av. Braz de Aguiar 612, Nazaré 66035-000* ☎ *091/241–2000* ▤ *091/223–5222* ☞ *204 rooms, 7 suites* ♢ *2 restaurants, pool, bar, no-smoking rooms* ▤ *AE, DC, MC, V.*

$ ▥ **Hotel Regente.** This hotel has excellent service and a prime location for a reasonable price. Stained-glass windows and soft leather couches welcome you in an attractive lobby. Rooms on the 12th floor are nicer and more modern than those on other floors yet cost the same. ⊠ *Av. Governador José Malcher 485, Nazaré 66035-100* ☎ *091/3181–5000* ▤ *091/242–0343* ☞ *196 rooms, 6 suites* ♢ *Restaurant, pool, bar* ▤ *AE, DC, MC, V.*

¢–$ ▥ **Itaoca Hotel.** It comes as no surprise that this small, reasonably priced hotel has the highest occupancy rate in town. Its rooms are extremely comfortable, well equipped, and modern, and most have a fantastic view of the dock area and river. ✉ *Av. Presidente Vargas 132, Campina 66010-902* 🏨 *091/241–3434* 📋 *32 rooms, 4 suites* ⚐ *Restaurant, in-room safes, cable TV, meeting room* 🖃 *AE, DC, MC, V.*

¢ 🖩 **Manacá Hotel.** This small, bright-red hotel with a slanted brown-tile
Fodor'sChoice roof looks like a cross between a Monopoly™ hotel piece and a pagoda.
★ Cozy, artfully decorated common areas with soft lighting have more charm than those at larger places—for about a quarter of the price. It's a clean, simple alternative if you can live without a pool or a bar. Make sure to call ahead, since it's often booked during the week. ✉ *Trv. Quintino Bocaiuva 1645, Nazaré 66033-620* 🏨 *091/223–3335* 📋 *16 rooms* ⚐ *Cable TV; no room phones* 🖃 *AE, DC, MC, V.*

¢ 🖩 **Victoria Palace Hotel.** One of the quietest, friendliest, and safest hotels in town is a two-minute walk from the Basilica of Nazaré. It also provides some unique entertainment: Every morning at 5:45 in the enormous *samauma* tree in the square out front, hundreds of white-winged parakeets awaken, scream like crazy, and leave to feed for the day. At 5:30 PM they return to their roost and scream some more. If you're not sure where they are, exit the hotel and follow your ears. Don't be late. ✉ *Praça Justo Chermont Alam. Maria de Jesus 83, Nazaré* 🏨 *091/212–0734* 🏨 *091/225–1973* 📋 *21 rooms* ⚐ *Cable TV; no room phones* 🖃 *MC, V.*

Nightlife & the Arts

Nightlife

Doca Boulevard, about eight blocks east of Escadinha (the dock area used for boat trips), has many bars and dance clubs. The main nightlife strip is Avenida Visconde de Souza Franco, but there are several places a few blocks off it as well. For information about Brazilian music, *see* the Brazilian Music essay *in* Understanding Brazil.

BARS **Água Doce** (✉ Rua Diogo Móia 283, Umarizal 🏨 091/222–3383) specializes in *cachaça* (Brazilian sugarcane liquor). Listed on its menu are 182 kinds of cachaça and 605 different drinks, along with appetizers and entrées as well. Softly lighted with lots of tables, this place gets busy on weekends. It's open Tuesday–Sunday. If you prefer your music in a relaxed environment, head to **Cosanostra Caffé** (✉ Rua Benjamin Constant 1499, Nazaré 🏨 091/241–1068), which has live MPB (Música Popular Brasileira) and jazz. Catering to locals and expatriate foreigners alike, it serves food from an extensive menu until late in the night. **Roxy Bar** (✉ Av. Senador Lemos 231, Umarizal 🏨 091/224–4514) tops nearly everyone's list of hip spots at which to sip a drink and people-watch. **Strike 60** (✉ Rua Diogo Móia 123, Umarizal 🏨 091/212–1068) is a throwback to an American 1960s bowling-alley diner, Brazilian style. Sixties music is all that's played in this family-friendly place. Balls roll and pins crash on eight hardwood lanes. Beer and liquor are served.

DANCE CLUBS The hot spots for dancing are open on Friday and Saturday nights (only) and are all downtown. Mixed-age crowds frequent them no matter what the music. Prices vary depending on the show. Drinks are available but no food. All clubs except Signos have live music on occasion. Clubs open around 10 PM, though they don't get lively before 11 or midnight.

African Bar (⊠ Marechal Hermes 2, Reduto ☎ 091/241–1085) has one area with rock or pop playing, another with techno, and a third with regional dance music such as *brega*—a mix of country and rock with a lot of rude lyrics. **Bora Bora** (⊠ Rua Bernal do Couto 38, Umarizal ☎ 091/241–6364) attracts a dance crowd with country music on some nights and fast-paced *pagode* on others. **Signos** (⊠ Governador José Malcher 247, Nazaré ☎ 091/242–7702), underneath the Lá em Casa restaurant, has the fanciest decor of the clubs, with lots of mirrors and red booths. A DJ runs video clips of dance music on a huge screen. **Zeppelin Club** (⊠ Av. Senador Lemos 108, Umarizal ☎ 091/241–1330) has two dance floors with two kinds of music. Techno is mixed with American and Brazilian pop and rock.

EVENING
STROLLS
Nights in Belém are comfortable for walking. There are several popular locations that are relatively safe, but catch a cab to your hotel if you stay late.

Estação das Docas (⊠ Boulevard Castilhos França s/n, Comercio) has a long, broad sidewalk that passes between the bay and numerous restaurants. **Praça Batista Campos** (⊠ Av. Padre Eutíquio s/n, Batista Campos) has sidewalks, benches, and coconut vendors. Nearby residents come here to jog, walk, and date. **Ver-O-Rio** (⊠ Av. Marechal Hermes s/n, Umarizal) is on the edge of the bay. It has a small bridge and several small open-air restaurants.

The Arts

For information about cultural events, contact the state-run **Secretaria de Cultura** (SECULT; ⊠ Av. Governador Magalhães Barata 830, São Brás ☎ 091/219–1207), which prints a monthly listing of cultural events throughout the city.

Live music is played nightly at the **Estação das Docas** (⊠ Boulevard Castilhos França s/n, Comercio ☎ 091/219–1207). Weekdays shows usually consist of acoustic singers/guitarists. On weekends rock, jazz, and MPB bands play on a suspended stage that moves back and forth on tracks about 8 meters (25 feet) above patrons of the microbrewery and surrounding restaurants. Outstanding theatrical productions in Portuguese are presented at the **Teatro Experimental Waldemar Henrique** (⊠ Av. Presidente Vargas s/n, Praça da República, Campina ☎ 091/222–4762). **Teatro da Paz** (⊠ Av. da Paz s/n, Praça da República, Campina ☎ 091/224–7355) often hosts plays, philharmonic concerts, and dance recitals.

Sports & the Outdoors

Belém's two *futebol* (soccer) teams are Payssandú and Remo—neither of which is currently in the premier league. Still, attending a Brazilian match, regardless of the quality of the team, is a memorable experience. For Remo games head to **Estádio Evandro Almeida** (⊠ Av. Almirante Barroso s/n, Marco ☎ 091/223–2847). Payssandú plays at **Estádio Leônidas de Castro** (⊠ Av. Almirante Barroso s/n, Marco ☎ 091/241–1726).

Shopping

Indigenous-style arts and crafts are popular souvenir items in Belém. Some of them, however, can create problems with customs when returning home. Import regulations of Australia, Canada, New Zealand, the United Kingdom, and the United States strictly prohibit bringing endangered species (dead or alive) into those countries, and the fines can be hefty. Nonendangered wildlife and plant parts are also illegal to import, though there are some exceptions. Wooden and woven items, for example, are usually not a problem. Avoid headdresses and necklaces of macaw feathers and caiman teeth, and go for the marajoara pottery and the tropical fruit preserves (pack them carefully). For more information on customs *see* Customs and Duties *in* Smart Travel Tips A to Z.

Areas & Malls

Belém's main shopping street is **Avenida Presidente Vargas,** particularly along the Praça da República. **Icoaraci,** a riverside town 18 km (11 mi) northeast of Belém, is a good place to buy marajoara pottery. There are many boutiques and specialty shops in the neighborhood of **Nazaré.** To shop in air-conditioning, head for the upscale **Shopping Center Iguatemi** (⊠ Trv. Padre Eutíquio 1078, Batista Campos), a mall in the truest sense of the word. There are a few well-stocked music stores, a food plaza on the third floor, a bookstore on the first floor that has maps, and two department stores—Y. Yamada and Visão—with everything.

Markets

Ver-o-Peso (⊠ Av. Castilhos França s/n, Comércio) is one of the most popular markets in town. It sells fresh fruits, vegetables, fish, and meats. The city's largest concentration of vendors of medicinal plants and various concoctions) is clustered under a canvas roof in the outdoor section. There are lots of hammocks for sale. **Praça da República** (⊠ Bounded by Av. Presidente Vargas, Trv. Osvaldo Cruz, and Av. Assis de Vasconcelos) is busy only on weekends when *barracas* (small shops) pop up to sell electronic objects, paintings, snacks, artesan items, and regional foods. You can watch the action from a park bench while sipping a cold coconut or eating a slice of *cupuaçú* cake. It's a local favorite for Sunday-morning family strolls. A popular shopping district is **Comércio** (⊠ From Av. President Vargas take Senador Manoel Barata toward Cidade Velha). The streets are lined with shops selling hardware, fishing supplies, televisions, hammocks, and much more.

Specialty Shops

Artesanato Paruara (⊠ Rua Sezedelo Correo 15, Nazaré ☎ 091/248–4555) specializes in oils, stones, and other "mystical" items. **Casa das Ervas Medicinais** (⊠ Rua 28 de Setembro 130 ☎ 091/3087–3519) has dozens of kinds of medicinal plants, tinctures, syrups, oils, and soaps. A great souvenir shop, **Canto do Uirapurú** (⊠ Av. President Vargas 594, Campina) is well-stocked with medicinal plant concoctions, T-shirts, hats, pottery, and more. **Casa Amazonia Artesanatos** (⊠ Av. President Vargas 512, Campina ☎ 091/225–0150), though small, is packed with natural soaps, regional fruit preserves, pottery, and wood carvings. A short walk from Av. President Vargas, **Loja Jaguar** (✉ Sen. Manoel Barata 298, Comércio ☎ 224–9771) sells hammocks and *mosquiteiros* (mosquito nets). For photo needs visit **New Color** (✉ Av. President Vargas 356, Campina ☎ 091/212–2355), which is fast, friendly, and reliable. **Pólo Joalheiro** (✉ Rua 16 de Novembro s/n, Jurunas ☼ Tues.–Sat. 10–8) is a combination museum and high-priced jewelry and craft shops with Amazonian wares of gold, amethyst, and wood; pottery; and seeds and plant fibers. Museum admission is R$4; free on Tuesday.

SIDE TRIPS FROM BELÉM

Praia Outeiro

30 km (19 mi) north of Belém; about 45 min by bus.

The closest ocean beach to Belém is Salinas, a four-hour drive. River beaches like Outeiro and those at Ilha Mosqueiro are much closer. Depending on the season and time of day, river beaches are either expansive stretches or narrow strips of soft sand. Currents are rarely strong, and there's usually a large area of shallow water. Outeiro is generally crowded. The shoreline is eroded and dirty in places, but the swimming is good if you can handle muddy water. Restaurants line the beach with tables under trees. These are great places to have a cold drink, and snack on freshly boiled crabs, quail eggs, and salted shrimp. ✉ *Buses depart from Rodoviário São Brás, Av. Almirante Barroso s/n, São Brás* 🎫 *Bus ticket R$5.*

Ilha Mosqueiro

60 km (36 mi) from Belém; about 2 hrs by bus or car.

Most Belém residents head for one of 18 beaches on Ilha Mosqueiro, along the Rio Pará. Mosqueiro is about an hour from the city by bus. One of the most popular beaches, **Praia Farol,** is often crowded because it's close to **Vila,** the island's hub. At low tide you can walk to tiny, rocky Ilha do Amor (Love Island). In October and March the waves are high enough for river-surfing competitions. **Praia Morubira,** also close to Vila, has beautiful colonial houses and many restaurants and bars. The water is clear and the shore clean at **Praia Marahú,** but no bus from Belém travels here directly. You have to disembark in Vila and hop another bus. **Praia Paraíso** is lined with trees and has soft white sands and clear emerald waters. If you can't bear to leave at day's end, consider a stay at the Hotel Fazenda Paraíso. ✉ *Buses depart from Rodoviário São Brás, Av. Almirante Barroso s/n, São Brás* 🎫 *Bus ticket R$8.*

Where to Stay

¢ 🏨 **Hotel Fazenda Paraíso.** Wood-and-brick chalets with red-tile roofs accommodate as many as five people. Similarly designed apartments, which house up to three people, are more economical for singles and couples. The pool is configured in the shape of a clover. Be sure to make reservations—the hotel is very popular on weekends. ✉ *Beira-Mar, Praia do Paraíso, Ilha Mosqueiro 66915-000* ☎ *091/228–3950* 🛏 *12* *rooms, 10 chalets* ☒ *Restaurant, pool, beach, boating, horseback riding* ▭ *AE, DC, MC, V.*

Salinópolis

200 km (120 mi) east of Belém.

Commonly known as Salinas, this old salt port on the Atlantic coast is loaded with beaches. It lies south of the mouth of the Amazon River, just three to four hours from Belém on good roads, making it accessible to weekend beachgoers. Tourist center **Praia Atalaia** is Salinas's largest and most popular beach. The 14-km (9-mi) white-sand beach is expansive; the highest dunes have nice views. Behind them is the blackwater pond Lago Coca Cola, which sometimes dries up between September and January. Also visible are dunes encroaching on hotels and businesses, signs of poor coastal management. Atalaia has numerous restaurant–bars with simple, low-priced rooms for rent (R$25–R$45); expect no amenities, and bring your own towel and soap. The best places to eat and stay are in the middle of the beach, and some accept credit cards. Pampulha, David House, and Minha Deusa are good. They serve excellent seafood and other dishes at low prices (R$8–R$20). Beware of eating at other places. Shop around and choose a room with a secure window. A 10-minute walk from Atalaia is a quieter beach, **Praia Farol Velho,** which has few services. To get there, turn left at the entrance and walk around the point.

In the old section of downtown Salinas, known as **Centro,** life revolves around *Farol Velho* (the old light tower). Just across from the tower on Rua João Pessoa is Mercado Marissol with an excellent selection of fruits, vegetables, drinks, and convenience items. In the same vicinity are a pharmacy, an ice cream parlor, and a restaurant. The street changes dramatically at the beginning of the **Praia Maçarico.** The Maçarico strip, which sits back from the beach, is broad, clean, and dotted with benches and coco palms. On the strip are a couple of playgrounds, exercise stations, and some restaurants and hotels. The beach can get crowded. Maçarico is about a 10-minute walk downhill on João Pessoa toward the water. As you walk toward the beach, beware of the sidewalk on the left that occasionally drops off and has deep exposed gutters. **Praia Corvina,** near Maçarico, is a calmer spot. Upon entering Maçarico Beach, turn left and round the point to Corvina.

Buses run every couple of hours from the Belém *rodoviário* (bus terminal) and drop you off at the Salinas terminal. From there you can take a taxi about a mile to Centro and Maçarico Beach, or travel 20 minutes to Atalaia. Also, a rickety old bus travels between the beaches every hour, from around 6:30 AM to 10 PM. It takes some work to get to Salinas's more secluded beaches. Praia Maria Baixinha and Praia Marieta, for example, require a boat, as do island beaches. Ecotours can be arranged to mangrove forests to see scarlet ibis and other species. Talk to your hotel manager or *see* Tours *in* The Amazon A to Z.

Where to Stay & Eat

$–$$$ ✕ **Tucuruvi.** Due to its solid reputation, many followers from Belém frequent this churrascaria. Besides unlimited quantities of grilled meats, there are fish, chicken, and salads. ✉ *Maçarico strip, Rua João Pessoa s/n* ☎ *091/423–1119* ▭ *AE, DC, MC, V.*

¢ ✕ **Restaurante São Miguel.** A steady stream of local families filters in and out of this establishment. The menu is lengthy and varied, with regional dishes, burgers, fries, and more. It's one of the few places that serves breakfast. ✉ *Across from light tower, Rua João Pessoa 2465* ☎ *091/423–3301* ▭ *No credit cards.*

¢–$ ✕▦ **Hotel Clube Privé do Atalaia.** Just off the beach, this place has more amenities than any other in town. Breezy, spacious public areas, a wet bar, and water slides help you keep cool. The restaurant (¢–$$) specializes in shrimp and crab, but serves lots of fish and other dishes. ✉ *Estrada do Atalaia 10,* ☎ *091/3464–9000* 🖶 *091/3464–1210* ⊕ *www.privedocastanho.com.br/atalaia* ↘ *141 rooms* ⚭ *Restaurant, snack bar, 5 pools, sauna, video games room, pool tables, Ping-Pong, bar, shop* ▭ *AE, MC, V.*

★ ¢ ▦ **Hotel Salinópolis.** Right above Maçarico, this hotel has the best location in town. You can look down the length of the beach from the pool. It's only a 10-minute walk from the light tower. ✉ *Avenida Beira Mar 26, 68721-000* ☎ *091/423–1239* ↘ *35 rooms* ⚭ *Restaurant, pool, wading pool, lounge, shop* ▭ *AE, DC, MC, V.*

¢ ▦ **Pousada das Dunas.** Small, clean, and quiet, this place is excellent for those on a budget who don't want to rough it. The restaurant and bar open during the busy times. A four-bedroom house is available for rent next door. ✉ *Estrada do Atalaia 40* ☎ *091/464–1002* ↘ *13 rooms, 1 house* ▭ *No credit cards.*

¢ ▦ **Rango do Goiano.** Well situated on the Maçarico strip, this family-run place has compact but comfortable rooms. The restaurant (¢–$) offers full meals as well as soups and salads. Try the crab soup. ✉ *Rua João Pessoa 2165,* ☎ *091/423–3572* ↘ *5 rooms* ⚭ *Restaurant, bar* ▭ *MC, V.*

NIGHTLIFE During the week nightlife is almost nonexistent apart from a few folks gathered in a hotel bar or restaurant. On the weekends, though, and especially during holidays, things get lively. Altaia restaurant-bars serve drinks and crank the music. Beach bar **Marujo's** (✉ Praia Farol Velho) turns into a dance club at 10 PM on weekends.

SHOPPING The high-end boutique at **Hotel Clube Privé do Atalaia** (✉ Estrada do Atalaia 10 ☎ 091/3464–9000) has sunscreen, hats, crafts, T-shirts, and Salinas memorabilia. Otherwise, ask hotel staff for directions to Shopping Maçarico or Russi Russi.

BETWEEN BELÉM & MANAUS

The smaller communities between the Amazon's two major cities give the best picture of pure Amazonian culture. Life tends to be even more intertwined with the river, and the center of activity is the dock area in village after village. Even a brief stop in one of these towns provides an interesting window into the region's day-to-day life.

Ilha do Marajó

Soure is 82 km (49 mi) northwest of Belém.

With an area of roughly 49,600 square km (18,900 square mi), Ilha do Marajó is reputedly the world's largest river island. Its relatively unspoiled environment and abundant wildlife make it one of the few accessible places in the Amazon that feel isolated. The Aruã tribes that once inhabited the island resisted invasion by the British and Dutch but were eventually conquered by the Portuguese through trickery. Ilha do Marajó's western half is dominated by dense forest and its eastern half by expansive plains, wetlands, and savannas. The island is ideal for raising cattle and water buffalo and has a half-million water buffalo and more than a million head of cattle; the human head count is about 250,000. According to local lore, the arrival of the water buffalo was an accident, the result of the wreck of a ship traveling from India to the Guianas. A day trip to a local ranch or a stay at Fazenda Carmo gives you a close-up look at the unique lifestyle of the island's people as well as the chance to view some of its animals, both domesticated and wild. You may see caiman, toco toucans, monkeys, and capybara, the world's largest rodent. Hiking is better in the dry season and boating in the rainy season.

Camará, one of the island's most important ports, is where many boats from Belém dock. With almost 20,000 people, **Soure,** on the northeast coast, is Ilha do Marajó's largest town. Its many palm and mango trees, simple but brightly painted houses, and shore full of fishing boats make it seem more Caribbean than Amazonian. **Salvaterra,** a short boat ride south across the narrow Rio Paracauari, is smaller than Soure but equally charming. Enchanting **river beaches** are a short (and cheap) taxi ride from both Soure and Salvaterra.

Praia do Pesqueiro, 14 km (8 mi) north of Soure, is the island's most popular beach. When you stand on the white-sand expanse looking out at the watery horizon, the waves lapping at your feet, it's hard to believe you're not on the ocean. The beach has several thatch-roof restaurant–bars, making this an even more ideal place to spend an afternoon. You can travel here from Soure by taxi, by mototaxi (for one passenger), or by bike. Ask locals or hotel staff about bike rentals when you arrive in Soure.

The beach at **Caju Una,** a secluded fishing village, is breathtaking: a long strip of white sand with no vendors and few people. The village and its neighbor, Vila do Céu, are about a 45-minute drive (19 km/11 mi) north of Soure. Buses don't travel here, but you can hire a taxi (about R$40) or a mototaxi (about R$20) for an afternoon. A 20-minute, 4-km (2-mi) taxi ride northeast of Soure is **Praia do Araruna.** Rather than sandy stretches, it has a red-mangrove forest. In this eerie setting of twisted trees you almost expect Yoda to appear. More likely, it will be a flock of scarlet ibis. **Joanes,** 23 km (14 mi) southwest of Soure, was the island's first settlement. Poke around the ruins of a 16th-century Jesuit mission, bask on a beach, and have a meal in one of the seafood restaurants. A taxi from Soure costs about R$50.

Where to Stay & Eat

Local cuisine invariably involves the water buffalo, whether in the form of a succulent steak or in cheeses and desserts made with buffalo milk. There's also an array of local fish to try. Bring cash in small bills, as breaking large ones can be a challenge and credit cards are rarely accepted. In a pinch beer vendors can usually make change.

¢ ✕ **Angela's Bar.** Good fish at a low price on the beach is the reason to come here, though Angela has beef as well. A R$9 plate of fish, rice, farofa, and salad can serve two. ✉ *Praia Grande de Salvaterra s/n* ☎ *091/3765–1203.*

¢–$ ✕🖭 **Hotel Ilha do Marajó.** Clean rooms, solid creature comforts, and excellent facilities, including a lovely pool, are found here. During the rainy season mosquitoes infiltrate rooms. The outdoor restaurant (¢–$) has a view of the river and good food. Saturday evening sometimes brings performances of *carimbo*, local music with African and native rhythms. Package deals, arranged at Belém travel agencies, include transport to and from the dock in Camará and day trips to fazendas and beaches. English-speaking guides are available. ✉ *Trv. 2 No. 10, Soure 68870-000* ☎ *091/3741–1315 or 091/3765–1115 in Belém* 🛏 *32 rooms* ♨ *Restaurant, minibars, tennis court, pool, bar, recreation room* 🟰 *V.*

¢ ✕🖭 **Pousada dos Guarás.** This intimate pousada has private bungalows. Consider the package that includes transportation to and from the docks and trips to Soure shops, local fazendas, and beaches. Make arrangements with a travel agent in Belém. The restaurant (¢–$) has excellent food. Angela's Bar is a 15-minute walk along the beach. ✉ *Av. Beira-Mar (Praia Grande), Salvaterra 66860-000* ☎☎ *091/242–0904* 🛏 *20 rooms* ♨ *Restaurant, minibars, pool, beach, horseback riding, bar* 🟰 *AE, DC, MC, V.*

★ $$$ 🖭 **Fazenda Carmo.** As a guest in this small antiques-filled farmhouse, you're privy to simple comforts, wonderful hospitality, outstanding home-style meals prepared with farm-fresh ingredients, and fascinating activities. Take an early-morning canoe trip in search of howler monkeys, set off on horseback through wildlife-rich pastures, hop in a jeep for a muddy ride to an archaeological site, or take a dip in the small lake. The fazenda can accommodate 8–10 people, and stays are part of a package that includes meals, an English-speaking guide, and transportation to and from Camará (a 90-minute trip via van and boat). The minimum stay is three days. ✉ *Salvaterra* 🖭 *Amazon Star Tours, Rua Henrique Gurjão 236, Belém 66053-360* ☎ *091/212–6244* ♨ *No room phones, no room TVs* 🟰 *AE, MC, V* 🍴 *FAP.*

Nightlife

On Friday night there are usually live music and dancing at **Badalué** (✉ Trv. 14, Soure). The most popular music in the region is *brega,* which means "tacky." The name for this accordion-influenced music is appropriate, but don't be surprised if it grows on you. A **carimbo group** performs at the Hotel Ilha do Marajó on Saturday and sometimes in Soure on Wednesday or Friday. Ask at your hotel or ask a taxi driver for details.

Shopping

There are a few stores that sell sundries along Travessa 17 and Rua 3 in Soure. For marajoara pottery and ceramic figurines, try **Arte Caboclo** (⌧ Trv. 5 between Ruas 8 and 9, Soure). You can even see how the ceramics are made in the workshop at the back of the store, which is open daily 8–6. For sandals, belts, and other leather goods, head to **Curtume Marajó** (⌧ Rua 1, Bairro Novo), a five-minute walk from downtown Soure and next to the slaughterhouse. The workers here can give you a tour of the tannery. The shop's hours are 7–11 and 1–5 Monday–Saturday. **Núcleo Operário Social Marilda Nunes** (⌧ Rua 3 between Trv. 18 and Trv. 19, Soure) has stalls with everything from marajoara pottery and woven items to T-shirts and liquor. In theory, the hours are daily 7–noon and 2:30–6; the reality may be something else entirely.

Macapá

330 km (198 mi) northwest of Belém.

Macapá is on the north channel of the Amazon Delta and, like Belém, was built by the Portuguese as an outpost. Today it's the capital of and the largest city (150,000 people) in the Amapá State. It's also one of only five metropolises in the world that sit on the equator. Macapá's main lure is as a base for trips to see an extraordinary phenomenon—the *pororoca* (riptide). From March to May, when the Amazon floods, the tide produces waves as high as 4 meters (15 feet); the final stage of this event sounds like thunder as waters sweep into the forest along the riverbanks. The trip to the pororoca takes nearly two days by boat and costs about R$480 per person for a private cabin, meals, and an English-speaking guide.

Macapá's top man-made attraction is Brazil's largest fort, **Fortaleza de São José de Macapá.** Completed in 1782 after 18 grueling years, it is constructed of stones brought from Portugal as ship ballast. The well-preserved buildings house a visitor center, an art gallery, a meeting room, and a dance/music recital room. ⌧ *Av. Cândido Mendes s/n* ☎ *096/212–5118* ◻ *Free* ◷ *Tues.–Sun. 8–6.*

The **Marco Zero do Equador** is a modest monument to the equatorial line that passes through town. Although it consists of only a tall, concrete sundial and a stripe of red paint along the equator, there's a distinct thrill to straddling the line or hopping between hemispheres. The soccer stadium across the street uses the equator as its centerline. ⌧ *Av. Equatorial 0288* ☎ *096/241–1951* ◻ *Free* ◷ *Daily 9–noon and 2–8.*

Where to Stay & Eat

$ ✕ **Cantinho Baiano.** Because of the conservative tastes of the locals, the Salvador-born owner here began cooking specialties from Bahia State. These dishes, especially the seafood *moqueca* (fried fish in vegetable sauce), are a highlight. The excellent river view, soft music, and colorfully clad waiters add to the ambience. ⌧ *Av. Acelino de Leão 01* ☎ *096/223–4153* ▭ *MC, V* ◷ *No dinner Sun.*

¢–$ ✕ **Café Aymoré.** This is a local favorite for regional specialties such as maniçoba and *vatapá* (shrimp in flour and African palm oil). For those with more exotic tastes, it's the only restaurant in town with government consent to serve *tartaruga* (turtle), *jacaré* (caiman), and *capivara* (capybara). ⊠ *Av. Iracema Carvão Nunes 92* ☎ *096/223–2328* ⊟ *No credit cards.*

$ ⑆ **Hotel Atalanta.** Garishly pink and supported by towering Roman columns, this hotel seems out of place. Inside, you find stained-glass windows, small pink columns, and immaculate, comfortable guest rooms. The inconvenient location—10 blocks from the river in a residential neighborhood—is its only drawback. ⊠ *Av. Coaracy Nunes 1148, 68900-010* ☎☎ *096/223–1612* ⬐ *33 rooms, 3 suites* ⚐ *Minibars, gym, sauna, pool* ⊟ *AE, DC, MC, V.*

$ ⑆ **Novotel Macapá.** Partially obscured by palm trees, this three-story, white, colonial-style hotel is on well-manicured grounds. The interior is slightly worn, and the guest rooms aren't very impressive, despite modern amenities. Opt for one of the suites, which have balconies with exceptional river views. ⊠ *Av. Francisco Azarias Neto 17, 68900-080* ☎ *096/217–1350* ☎ *096/223–1115* ⬐ *74 rooms, 2 suites* ⚐ *Restaurant, in-room safes, minibars, tennis court, pool, bar* ⊟ *AE, DC, MC, V.*

¢ ⑆ **Frota Palace Hotel.** Clean and spacious, rooms here even have phones, which aren't easy to come by in this area. It's conveniently located in Centro, and the staff is friendly. ⊠ *Rua Tiradentes 1104, 68906-420* ☎ *096/223–3999* ⬐ *33 rooms* ⚐ *Restaurant, bar; no room phones* ⊟ *MC, V.*

Nightlife & the Arts

Macapá has a surprisingly active nightlife. If you like to bar-hop, head for the riverfront, where about 10 bars, some with music, are busy nearly every night. On weekends true night owls appreciate **Arena** (⊠ Rua Hamilton Silva s/n), which doesn't open until midnight. Most weekends and even sometimes during the week there's a play, a Philharmonic concert, or a dance recital in the **Teatro das Bacabeiras** (⊠ Rua Cândido Mendes 368 ☎ 096/212–5272). Admission is R$20.

Shopping

Although Macapá has a free-trade zone, neither the prices nor the selection is anything special. The largest concentration of shops is on Rua Cândido Mendes and Rua São José. The **Núcleo Artesanal** (⊠ Av. Engenheiro Azarias Neto 2201 ☎ 096/212–9156), an outstanding arts center, has two parts. The Casa do Artesáo sells works by local craftspeople and artists—from tacky souvenirs to exquisite paintings and pottery—and is open 8–6 Monday–Sunday. Visa is accepted. The Associação dos Povos Indígenas do Tumucumaque (APITU) has textiles, baskets, and other objects made by Amapá natives. It is open 8–noon and 2–6 weekdays and 3–8 Sunday.

Santarém

836 km (518 mi) west of Belém, 766 km (475 mi) east of Manaus.

Since its founding in 1661, Santarém has ridden the crest of many an economic wave. First wood, then rubber, and more recently minerals have lured thousands of would-be magnates hoping to carve their fortunes from the jungle. The most noteworthy of these may have been Henry Ford. Although he never actually came to Brazil, Ford left his mark on this country in the form of two rubber plantations southwest of Santarém—Fordlândia and Belterra. Today Santarém, a laid-back city of 242,000, has a new boom on the horizon—soybeans. As the highway BR 163 from Mato Grosso State improves (a federal government priority), it is becoming the fastest, cheapest route for hauling soybeans from Santarém to Atlantic seaports for international export. To meet the global demand for soybeans and to make enormous profits, Brazilian farmers are clearing vast tracts of forest south of town and all along the way to Mato Grosso. With this new boom, Santarém may change drastically in coming years. Perhaps the best place for walking is on the huge sidewalk along the river. You can watch boat traffic and check out some of the shops along the way.

Santarém-based trips can take you into a little-known part of the Amazon, with few foreign visitors, to places where the ecosystem is greatly different from those around Belém and Manaus. The area receives much less rain than either upstream or downstream, has rocky hills, enormous wetlands, and the Amazon's largest clear-water tributary, the Rio Tapajós.

The city is at the confluence of the aquamarine Rio Tapajós and the muddy brown Amazon. Seeing the meeting of these waters is second only to witnessing the pororoca outside Macapá. It's best viewed from the **Praça Mirante do Tapajós,** on the hill in the center of town and just a few blocks from the waterfront.

To learn more about Santarém's culture and history, head for the **Centro Cultural João Fona** (João Fona Cultural Center). This small museum has a hodgepodge of ancient ceramics, indigenous art, and colonial-period paintings and a library for more in-depth studies. ⊠ *Praça Barão de Santarém* ☎ *093/522–1383* ✉ *Free* ☉ *Weekdays 8–5.*

Where to Stay & Eat

¢–$$ ✕ **Mascote.** Since 1934 this has been one of the most popular and famous restaurants in town. The indoor dining area is enchanting, but the palm-lined patio is well-lighted and inviting and has a good view of the river and the plaza. An extremely varied menu includes pizzas, sandwiches, steaks, and seafood. ⊠ *Praça do Pescador s/n* ☎ *093/523–2844* ☰ *AE, DC, V.*

¢–$$ ✕ **Piracatu.** Just a five-minute taxi ride from downtown, this is the best fish house in town. You choose both the fish and how you want it prepared. The *surubim* (fish) soup is outstanding and easily serves two. ⊠ *Av. Mendoça Furtado 174, Prainha* ☎ *093/523–5098* ☰ *MC, V.*

¢–$ ✕ **Santo Antônio.** Fill up on *churrasco* (grilled meat) or with one of the regional specialties at this restaurant behind a gas station. The fish is always fresh, and a single portion serves two. The tucunaré, served on a searing-hot marble platter, is incredible. ⊠ *Av. Tapajós 2061* ☎ *093/523–5069* ☰ *MC, V.*

¢ ✕ **Delícias Caseiras.** A constant stream of locals filters in to fill up at the buffet table of this restaurant whose name means, roughly, "homemade

FORD'S IMPOSSIBLE DREAM

HENRY FORD SPENT MILLIONS of dollars to create two utopian company towns and plantations to supply his Model T cars with rubber tires. In 1927 he chose an area 15 hours southwest of Santarém. A year later all the materials necessary to build a small town and its infrastructure were transported by boat from Michigan to the Amazon. Small Midwestern-style houses were built row after row. Seringueiros (rubber harvesters) were recruited with promises of good wages, health care, and schools for their children. Fordlândia was born. Despite all the planning, the scheme failed. The region's climate, horticulture, and customs weren't taken into account. Malaria and parasites troubled the workers; erosion and disease plagued the trees.

Convinced that he had learned valuable lessons from his mistakes, Ford refused to give up. In 1934 he established another community in Belterra, just 48 km (30 mi) outside Santarém. Although some rubber was extracted from the plantation, production fell far short of original estimates. World War II caused further disruptions as German boats cruised the Brazilian coast and prevented food and supplies from arriving. Advances in synthetic rubber struck the final blow. Today some rusted trucks and electric generators, a few industrial structures, and many empty bungalows are all that remain of Ford's impossible dream.

delectables." Salads aren't noteworthy, but the chicken *milanesa* (breaded and fried) and beef Stroganoff are very good. ⊠ *Trv. 15 de Agosto 121, Centro* ☎ *093/523–5525* ▤ *No credit cards* ⊗ *No dinner.*

¢ ✕ **Mixtura Brasileira.** Excellent sandwiches and a self-service buffet keep the MB hopping. Try the beef fillet sandwich or the lasagna. ⊠ *Av. Tapajós 23, Centro* ☎ *093/522–4819* ▤ *MC, V* ⊗ *No dinner Mon.*

¢–$ ✕▦ **Belo Alter.** The white-sand beach is right outside the front door of this four-star establishment with an impressive range of room prices. Higher prices get you the amenities that come standard at city hotels— like air-conditioning—plus a view. Rooms without air-conditioning have fans. The restaurant (¢–$$) serves a variety of dishes, though it specializes in fish. ⊠ *Rua Pedro Texeira s/n,* ☎ *093/527–1230 or 093/527–1247* ➳ *24 rooms* ⌂ *Restaurant, fans; no a/c in some rooms, no room phones.*

¢ ▦ **Amazon Park Hotel.** The only "luxury" hotel in town has a decent location (a short taxi ride from Centro), and a gorgeous pool. Still, with little in the way of competition, it doesn't have much incentive to improve, as evidenced by the aging facilities and scantily furnished rooms. ⊠ *Av. Mendonça Furtado 4120, 68040-050* ☎ *093/523–2800* 🖷 *093/*

522–2631 ✆ *122 rooms* ♨ *Restaurant, minibars, pool, bar* ▭ *AE, DC, MC, V.*

¢ ▥ **Rio Dourado.** Reasonable rates get you simple but attractive accommodations, a convenient location, and friendly service in this peach-color hotel. The hotel has a nice view of an open market area and a bit of the waterfront from the dining area on the second floor (where you have breakfast). ⊠ *Rua Floriano Peixoto 799, 68005-080* ☎ *093/522–0320* ✆ *27 rooms* ♨ *Airport shuttle* ▭ *AE, DC, MC.*

¢ ▥ **Santarém Palace.** The front of the hotel is on a busy street with lots of bus traffic; request one of the rooms in the back—they are quieter and may have a view of the meeting of the waters. Facilities are clean and well maintained. ⊠ *Av. Rui Barbosa 726, 68005-080* ☎ *093/523–2820* ☏ *093/522–1779* ✆ *44 rooms* ♨ *Restaurant, minibars, meeting room* ▭ *DC, MC, V.*

Nightlife

Sunday afternoon can be sleepy in Santarém, but **Fun House!** (⊠ Av. Presidente Vargas 1721, Santa Clara ☎ 093/522–1787) is where everyone goes to dance off their extra energy. On Friday **La Boom** (⊠ Av. Cuiabá 694, Liberdade ☎ 093/522–1382) is *the* place to dance. One of the best places in town to get a drink is **Mascotinho** (⊠ Praça Manuel de Jesus Moraes s/n ☎ 093/523–2399). It has passable food and is usually breezy since it's on the river. Friday and Saturday nights are filled with MPB. **Sygnus** (⊠ Av. Borges Leal 2712, Santa Clara ☎ 093/522–4119), with a mix of Brazilian and international music, is popular on Saturday night.

Shopping

One of three artisan shops grouped together, **Loja Muiraquitã** (⊠ Rua Senador Lameira Bittencourt 131 ☎ 093/522–7164) sells an incredible variety of regional items including native musical instruments, locally mined minerals, and wood carvings. A reliable photo shop in town is **Foto Society** (⊠ Rui Barbosa 900, Centro ☎ 093/522–4828). If you're looking for a convenience store downtown that's loaded, head for **Center CR** (⊠ Rua Galdino Veloso with Dos Mártires, Centro).

Sports & the Outdoors

Santarém, at the hub of two very different river systems and forests, has a lot of outdoor options. Secluded beaches for swimming, forest trails for hiking, boats for exploring backwater areas and wildlife watching—they're all here. An American who knows the area particularly well is Steven Alexander, who has been living down here for nearly 30 years. He leads ecotours on occasion, especially to a forest preserve he has created outside town called **Bosque Santa Lúcia**. It has several trails with tree identification tags, troops of monkeys, and lots of birds and insects. Contact **Amazon Tours** (⊠ Trv. Turiano Meira 1084, Santarém ☎ 093/522–1928) for information on Steven Alexander's ecotours.

Monte Alegre

About 90 km (about 60 mi) northeast of Santarém.

Wedged on a hillside between fertile Amazon wetlands and *cerrado* (dry scrub forest), Monte Alegre area has long been a preferred site for human habitation. In the hills behind the town, carbon dating of middens below cave paintings indicates a human presence as long as 11,000 years ago, making them some of the earliest known in the Americas. Europeans also liked the site. A small band of Irish and English settled here in the 1570s, about 40 years before the Portuguese arrived in Belém. The site later became a missionary outpost—called Gurupatuba—for area natives. In 1758 it was incorporated as a village.

Today Monte Alegre is a city of around 80,000 souls. Its economy relies mostly on ranching, farming, and fishing. The town obviously has a rich history, but it is not well organized for tourism. There's no town map, for example, and the streets are confusing. Also, visiting hours for the few historic sites change often or don't exist. You can thoroughly enjoy Monte Alegre, however, if you walk around and talk to the locals. They're very helpful and may go out of their way to assist you. A short walking tour can give you a sense of the town. Begin at the Praça Fernando Guilhon in Cidade Alta (Upper City). The view over the Cidade Baixa (Lower City), and the Amazon River and wetlands is spectacular from here, especially at sunrise and sunset. Behind the praça is the Igreja de São Francisco (Church of St. Francis), which opens for mass at 6 AM and 7 PM. Descend the stairs at the overlook and walk down cobblestone Travessa do Matires toward the Cidade Baixa. In the commercial section you see Igreja Santa Lucia (Church of St. Lucia), with a small praça. Then head down to the river to watch the boat activity. Along the water you can get a *cafezinho* (small sweet coffee) and bakery item or fruit. Early or later is better since it's cooler.

Most foreign visitors are interested in cave paintings and wildlife. There are thousands of paintings in the hills behind town. You can hire a cab or a mototaxi to take you to the closest ones, about an hour away. The only guide who knows much about them is **Nelsí Sadeck** (☎ 093/533–1430 or 093/533–1215), a civil engineer who assisted archaeologists in exploring the paintings and in the dig sites; he works independently as a guide. Nelsí speaks no English (though you can e-mail him in English), but is patient and a good teacher. Contact him a few weeks in advance to hire him for a day of visiting the paintings (about R$120). He takes you out in a four-wheel-drive pickup that holds up to 10 people. It's hot, dusty, and bumpy, so take lots of water, a light lunch, snacks, and sunscreen. And wear sturdy shoes. Plan to leave around 6:30 AM to be back by 3 PM.

Though he is not a naturalist, Nelsí can also set up wildlife outings for you. Wildlife outings in Monte Alegre can be phenomenal, especially for bird-watching. What's exceptional is that there are two habitats to choose from. The cerrado hills merit some time, but the wetlands are where you'll find the most. Go early, and you may see hoatzins, horned screamers, and chestnut-fronted macaws.

Where to Stay & Eat

¢ ✕ **Marisco.** Fish dishes are the specialties at this friendly restaurant. Try the *tucunaré escabeche* (tucunaré fish in a coconut-milk sauce with tomato, onion, garlic, cilantro, and other spices). Beef and chicken are also served. ✉ *Rua 7 de Setembro* ☎ *093/9616–3990* ▬ *No credit cards.*

¢   ⨉🖩 **Hotel Restaurante Ceará.** Not far from the river in the Lower City, this hotel has rooms with a fan for R$20 and air-conditioned rooms for R$30. Rooms are sparse but clean. The TV is in the lounge. The restaurant (¢) serves plates of fish or meat with rice and beans. ☒ *Trv. Hermes da Fonseca 186* ☏ *093/533–1166* ↩ *8 rooms* ⚴ *Restaurant, some fans; no a/c in some rooms, no room TVs, no room phones* ▭ *No credit cards.*

¢   ⨉🖩 **Panorama I.** In the Cidade Alta and a little out of-the-way, these small chalets are quiet and private. A 100-yard walk takes you to an impressive overlook. The restaurant (¢) is rated by locals as the best in town. ☒ *Trv. Oriental 100* ☏ *093/533–1716* ↩ *4 chalets* ⚴ *Restaurant, cable TV; no room phones* ▭ *No credit cards.*

¢   🖩 **Hotel Panorama II.** Few hotels have a view as incredible as this one. Next to the praça on top of the hill, the veranda looks out over the Lower City and the Amazon. Rooms are clean and comfortable. Music at the bar next door can get noisy on the weekends. ☒ *Praça Fernando Guilhon 500* ☏ *093/533–1282* ↩ *6 rooms* ⚴ *Cable TV; no room phones* ▭ *No credit cards.*

Alter do Chão

About 30 km (about 20 mi) south of Santarém.

★   Of the cruises from Santarém on specially outfitted boats, the trip down the Rio Tapajós to the village of Alter do Chão, on the Lago Verde (Green Lake), is one of the best. The area has been called "the Caribbean of the Amazon," and when you see its clear green waters and its white-sand beaches you understand why. Buses also make the hour-long journey from Santarém to Alter do Chão regularly. From the village it's a short canoe ride across a narrow channel to the beach. Note that from April to July, when the water is high, the beach shrinks considerably.

Where to Stay

¢   🖩 **Pousada Tupaiulândia.** This pousada three blocks from the beach is one of the best places to stay in Alter do Chão. Large rooms are comfortable and air-conditioned. As this hotel is popular but small, reserve as far in advance as possible. ☒ *Rua Pedro Teixeira s/n, Alter do Chão 68109-000* ☏ *093/527–1157* ↩ *7 rooms* ⚴ *Restaurant, minibars* ▭ *V.*

MANAUS

Manaus, the capital of Amazonas State, is a hilly city of around 1.5 million people that lies 766 km (475 mi) southwest of Santarém and 1,602 km (993 mi) southwest of Belém. It was built on the banks of the Rio Negro 10 km (6 mi) upstream from its confluence with the Amazon. Founded in 1669, it took its name, which means "mother of the Gods," from the Manaó tribe. The city has long flirted with prosperity. Of all the Amazon cities and towns, Manaus is most identified with the rubber boom. In the late 19th and early 20th centuries it supplied 90% of the world's rubber. The industry was monopolized by rubber barons, whose number never exceeded 100 and who lived in the city, and spent enormous sums on ostentatious lifestyles. They dominated the region like feudal lords. *Seringueiros* (rubber tappers) were recruited. A few were from indigenous tribes, but most were transplants from Brazil's crowded and depressed northeast. Thousands flocked to the barons' plantations, where they lived virtually as slaves. Eventually conflicts erupted between the barons and the indigenous workers over encroachment on tribal lands. Stories of cruelty abound. One baron is said to have killed more than 40,000 native people during his 20-year "reign." Another boasted of having slaughtered 300 Indians in a day.

The 25-year rubber era was brought to a close thanks to Englishman Henry A. Wickham, who took 70,000 rubber-tree seeds out of Brazil in 1876. The seeds were planted in Kew Gardens in England. The few that germinated were transplanted to Malaysia, where they flourished. Within 30 years Malaysian rubber ended the Brazilian monopoly. Although several schemes were launched to revitalize the Amazon rubber industry, and many seringueiros continued to work independently in the jungles, the high times were over. Manaus entered a depression that lasted until 1967, when the downtown area was made a free-trade zone. The economy was revitalized, and its population jumped from 200,000 to 900,000 in less than 20 years. Then in the 1970s the industrial district was given exclusive free-trade-zone status to produce certain light-industry items. Companies moved in and began making motorcycles and electronic items. In the mid-1990s the commercial district lost its free-trade-zone status. Hundreds lost their jobs and businesses crumbled, but the light-industrial sector held strong and even grew. Today it employs 80,000, has the largest motorcycle factory in South America, and makes 90% of the TVs made in Brazil.

Manaus is the Amazon's most popular destination, largely because of the 19 jungle lodges in the surrounding area. The city's principal attractions are its lavish, brightly colored houses and civic buildings—vestiges of an opulent time when the wealthy sent their laundry to be done in Europe and sent for old-world artisans and engineers to build their New World monuments.

Exploring Manaus

Manaus is a sprawling city with few true high-rises. Although many hotels and sights are in the city center (Centro), it's neither large nor attractive, and it's congested. It is also exotic and hilly and is on the edge of a river one and a half times larger than the Mississippi.

Centro
Although Manaus is more spread out than Belém or Santarém, its downtown area has a lot going on. The floating docks are here, with tourist shops nearby. Open markets sell fish, meats, and all sorts of produce, while general stores ply machetes, hoes, hardtack, cassava flour, and boat motor parts to those pursuing a livelihood outside the city. Centro is also the most important historical section of the city. The Teatro Amazonas, the Customs House (Alfândega), and the Adolfo Lisboa Market are here, along with old churches, government buildings, and mansions. The result is a mix of neoclassic, Renaissance, colonial, and modern architecture.

A GOOD WALK Begin as early in the day as possible at the **Mercado Adolfo Lisboa** ⑰ ▶. Exit at its northeast end and take the first right onto Rua M. de Santa Cruz. Where it intersects with Avenida Eduardo Ribeiro, you see the **Alfândega** ⑱ on your left. Return to the intersection and cross Avenida Eduardo Ribeiro. On your left will be the **Hidroviária** ⑲ for regional boats, and just beyond it lies the raised walkway to the international section. Be sure to look down at the Porto Flutuante, a floating dock made by the British. It's where many large ships anchor. Return to Avenida Eduardo Ribeiro and begin walking up the left side; almost immediately you see the Relógio Municipal (Municipal Clock). Just behind it is the **Catedral da Nossa Senhora da Conceição** ⑳. From here turn right on Rua Quintino Bocaiuva, walk down to Avenida Lourenço da Silva Braga, and turn left to the **Usina Chaminé** ㉑. Exiting, turn left on Avenida Lourenço da Silva Braga, and take the second left onto Rua Lima Bacuri. Walk up to the first right on Rua Dr. Almínio, and go right again on Rua 7 de Setembro. Cross the bridge, and you see **Palácio Rio Negro** ㉒ on your right. Back on Rua 7 de Setembro, turn right and continue up to Avenida Duque de Caixas, where you see the **Museu do Índio** ㉓. From there head back toward Centro on Rua 7 de Setembro and turn right on Rua Barroso to go up to **Teatro Amazonas** ㉔. Cross Rua de Julho on Rua Tapajós to the **Igreja São Sebastião** ㉕.

TIMING Plan to spend 3–4 hours following the walk from start to finish. If it gets a bit long, you may want to take a taxi from the Museu do Índio to Teatro Amazonas or split it into two walks.

WHAT TO SEE **Alfândega.** The Customs House was built by the British in 1902 with ⑱ bricks imported as ship ballast. It stands alongside the floating dock that was built at the same time to accommodate the annual 12-meter (40-foot) rise and fall of the river. It's now home to the regional office of the Brazilian tax department, and the interior is of little interest. ⊠ *Rua Marquês de Santa Cruz s/n, Centro* ☎ *092/234–5481.*

⑳ **Catedral da Nossa Senhora da Conceição.** Built originally in 1695 by Carmelite missionaries, the Cathedral of Our Lady of the Immaculate Conception (also called Igreja Matriz) burned down in 1850 and was reconstructed in 1878. It's a simple, predominantly neoclassical structure with a bright, colorful interior. ⊠ *Praça da Matriz, Centro* ☎ *No phone* 🆓 *Free* ☉ *Usually Mon.–Sat. 9–5, but hours vary.*

⑲ **Hidroviária.** Everyone traveling by boat from the floating docks must go through the Water Transportation Terminal. There is one area for regional travelers and another for international travelers; both have food shops. The international area has high-end gift shops. ⊠ *Rua Marques de Santa Cruz 25, Centro* ☎ *092/621–4301.*

㉕ **Igreja São Sebastião.** This neoclassical church (circa 1888), with its charcoal-gray color and medieval characteristics, seems foreboding. Its interior, however, is luminous and uplifting, with white Italian marble, stained-glass windows, and beautiful ceiling paintings. The church has a tower on only one side. No one is sure why this is so, but if you ask, you may get one of several explanations: the second tower wasn't built because of lack of funds; it was omitted as a symbolic gesture to the poor;

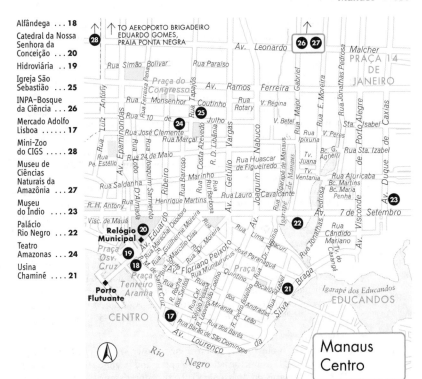

or the ship with materials for its construction sank. As you stroll through the church plaza and the one in front of the Teatro Amazonas, note the black-and-white Portuguese granite patterns at your feet. They are said to represent Manaus's meeting of the waters. ⊠ *Praça São Sebastião, Centro* 🕾 *No phone* 🖃 *Free* ☉ *Usually Mon.–Sat. 9–5, but hours vary; call ahead.*

▶ **⑰** **Mercado Adolfo Lisboa.** Vendors sell Amazon food products and handicrafts at this market. Built in 1882, it is a wrought-iron replica of the original Parisian Les Halles (now destroyed); the ironwork is said to have been designed by Gustave Eiffel himself. ⊠ *Rua dos Barés 6, Centro* 🕾 *092/234–8441* ☉ *Daily dawn–noon.*

㉓ **Museu do Índio.** The Indian Museum is maintained by Salesian Sisters, an order of nuns with eight missions in the upper Amazon. It displays handicrafts, weapons, ceramics, ritual masks, and clothing from the region's tribes. ⊠ *Rua Duque de Caxias 356, Centro* 🕾 *092/635–1922* 🖃 *R$5* ☉ *Weekdays 8:30–noon and 2–5, Sat. 8:30–noon.*

㉒ **Palácio Rio Negro.** The extravagant Rio Negro Palace was built at the end of the 19th century as the home of a German rubber baron. Later it was used as the official governor's residence. Today it houses some of the city's finest art exhibits and a cultural center. The Museu da Imagem e do Som, on the same property, has three daily screenings of art films and documentaries Tuesday through Friday and four screenings daily on weekends. ✉ *Av. 7 de Setembro 1546, Centro* ☎ *092/633–2850* ☞ *Free* ☉ *Tues.–Sun. 3–9.*

★ ㉔ **Teatro Amazonas.** The city's lavish opera house was completed in 1896 after 15 years. Its Italian Renaissance–style interior provides a clear idea of the wealth that marked the Amazon rubber boom. It has marble doorways, crystal chandeliers, handblown glass sconces from Italy, English wrought-iron banisters, and panels of French tiles. Italian frescoes depict Amazon legends. Operas and other events are presented regularly. Monday-evening performances are free and usually feature local artists of various musical genres. The Amazonas Philharmonic Orchestra plays Friday night and can be seen and heard practicing in the theater weekdays 9–2. A variety of foreign entertainers, from José Carreras to the Spice Girls, have performed here. Half-hour tours are conducted daily 9–4. ✉ *Praça São Sebastião s/n, Centro* ☎ *092/622–2420* ⊕ *www.teatroamazonas.com.br* ☞ *R$5* ☉ *Mon.–Sat. 9–4.*

㉑ **Usina Chaminé.** Transformed from a sewage treatment plant that never functioned, this art gallery displays exhibits and holds dance and theatre performances. Its neo-Renaissance style with hardwood floors and massive wood beams is another reason to visit. ✉ *Av. Lourenço da Silva Braga, Centro* ☎ *092/633–3026* ☞ *Free* ☉ *Tues.–Fri. 10–5, weekends 4–8.*

Elsewhere in Manaus

A GOOD TOUR   Take a cab to one of several far-flung in-town sights. The **INPA–Bosque da Ciência** ㉖ ☞ is northeast of the center, and beyond it is the **Museu de Ciências Naturais da Amazônia** ㉗. To the center's northwest is the **Mini-Zoo do CIGS** ㉘. If you have another day or two, consider an excursion to the Amazon Ecopark or the town of Presidente Figueiredo, both outside the city limits (⇨ Side Trips From Manaus, *below*).

TIMING   The tour should take from four and a half to six hours including travel time between the sights.

WHAT TO SEE   **INPA–Bosque da Ciência.** Used as a research station for the INPA (Instituto Nacional de Pesquisa da Amazônia), this slice of tropical forest is
㉖ home to a great diversity of flora and fauna. Some highlights include manatee tanks, caiman ponds, a museum, a botanical garden with an orchidarium, and nature trails. It's a great place for a walk in the shade. ✉ *Rua Otávio Cabral s/n, Aleixo* ☎ *092/643–3293* ☞ *R$2* ☉ *Tues.–Fri. 9–11 and 2–4, weekends 9–4.*

㉘ **Mini-Zoo do CIGS.** Here you can see dozens of animals native to the Amazon. The Brazilian army operates a jungle-survival training school here. Soldiers from around the globe come to participate in the two-year program. ✉ *Estrada do São Jorge 750, São Jorge* ☎ *092/671–6903* ☞ *R$2* ☉ *Tues.–Sun. 9–4:30.*

☞ ㉗ **Museu de Ciências Naturais da Amazônia.** The Natural History Museum of the Amazon has preserved specimens of insects, turtles, and fish on display. You can also view Amazon river fish in large tanks. ✉ *Estrada Belém s/n, Aleixo* ☎ *092/644–2799* ☞ *Free* ☉ *Mon.–Sat. 9–5.*

THE VANISHING INDIANS

THE INDIAN POPULATION WAS **4.5 MILLION** in 1500, when the Portuguese arrived in Brazil, with an estimated 1,400 tribes. From the beginning the Portuguese divided into two camps regarding the natives: the missionaries, who wanted to "tame" them and convert them to Catholicism, and the colonizers, who wished to enslave and exploit them. The missionaries lost, and when it became apparent that the Indians couldn't be enslaved, the infamous bandeirantes (assault forces) relentlessly persecuted the Indians to "liberate" tribal lands. Many Indians lost their lives defending their way of life, but the greatest killers were smallpox and influenza—European diseases against which they had no immunity. Slow but steady integration into Portuguese society caused the native population to dwindle.

Today, of Brazil's 328,000 remaining Indians, about 197,000 live in the Amazon. Each of the 220 societies has its own religious beliefs, social customs, and economic activities. The larger groups include the Manaó, Yanomami, Marajó, Juma, Caixana, Korubo, and Miranha. Each speaks one of the 170 distinct languages spoken by the indigenous peoples of Brazil; Tupi (with seven in-use derivations, including Tupi-Guarani) is the most widely spoken, followed by Macro Jê, Aruák, Karíb, and Arawá.

Throughout Brazil's history sporadic efforts were made to protect the Indians, but it was only in 1910 that the government established an official advocacy agency, the Service for the Protection of the Indians (SPI), founded by Cândido Mariana da Silva Rondon to support Indian autonomy, ensure respect for traditional practices, and help indigenous peoples to acquire Brazilian citizenship. In 1930 the SPI was abolished due to corruption and lack of funds. It was replaced in 1967 by the current governmental advocacy group, FUNAI (Fundação Nacional do Indio, or the National Indian Foundation). Although it has been highly criticized, FUNAI helped to get the first (and, thus far, only) Indian elected into office: Mario Juruna, an Indian chief, served as federal deputy from 1983 to 1987. The foundation has also defended the rights of Indians to protect their lands (it allows only legitimate researchers to visit reservations), which are increasingly targeted for logging, rubber extraction, mining, ranching, or the building of industrial pipelines and hydroelectric plants.

The Indians have always respected and understood their environment; their plight and that of the rain forest are closely linked. Conservation efforts to preserve the rain forest have called attention to some of FUNAI's issues, but for the Brazilian government the issue is complicated: rain-forest conservation is often overshadowed by economic development. Further, the Indians still lack many basic human rights, and violence (such as the 1998 murder of prominent activist Francisco de Assis Araujó) still sporadically occurs as the Indians continue to defend their way of life against outsiders.

Praia do Ponta Negra. Known as the Copacabana of the Amazon, this beach is next to the Hotel Tropical and has restaurants, bars, sports, and nightlife facilities (including an amphitheater).

Where to Eat

¢–$$$ ✕ **Suzuran.** For more than 20 years this festive restaurant has served the town's best Japanese food. If you can't decide between raw fish and fried favorites, don't. The *suzuran teishoku* platter has sushi, sashimi, shrimp and vegetable tempura, and grilled fish. ⊠ *Rua Teresina 155, Adrianópolis* ☎ 092/633–3570 ▤ *AE, DC, MC, V.*

$ ✕ **Canto da Peixada.** When Pope John Paul II came to Manaus in 1981, this restaurant was chosen to host him. The dining areas aren't elegant, but the fish dishes are outstanding, and there are 43 types of salad. One platter feeds two. ⊠ *Rua Emilio Moreira 1677, Praça 14* ☎ *092/234–1066* ▤ *V* ☻ *No dinner Sun.*

FodorśChoice
★

★ $ ✕ **Churrascaria Búfalo.** Twelve waiters, each offering a different cut of chicken, beef, or goat, scurry around this large, crowded restaurant. As if the delectable meats weren't enough, the table is also set with side dishes, including manioc root, pickled vegetables, and caramelized bananas. ⊠ *Rua Joaquim Nabuco 628-A, Centro* ☎ *092/633–3773* ⊕ *www. churrascariabufalo.com.br* ▤ *AE, DC, MC, V.*

$ ✕ **Moronguêtá.** Why not dine on deliciously prepared river fish while looking out over the meeting of the waters? The *costela de tambaqui no molho de camaráo* (tambaqui ribs in tomato-shrimp sauce) is amazing. It's only 15 minutes by taxi from downtown. ⊠ *Rua Jaith Chaves 30, Vila da Felicidede* ☎ *092/615–3362* ▤ *V.*

¢–$ ✕ **Fiorentina.** The green awning and red-and-white-check tablecloths are hints that this restaurant serves authentic Italian cuisine. Pasta dishes are delicious, especially the lasagna *fiorentina* (with a marinara and ground-beef sauce). ⊠ *Praça da Polícia 44, Centro* ☎ *092/215–2233* ▤ *AE, DC, MC, V.*

¢ ✕ **Filosóphicus.** Vegetarian buffet-style food here uses ingredients like whole grains, textured vegetable protein, and soy. It's on the second floor and tricky to find. ⊠ *Av. 7 de Setembro 752, 2nd floor, Centro* ☎ *092/234–2224* ▤ *No credit cards* ☻ *No lunch.*

Where to Stay

Although there are several decent in-town hotels, the jungle lodges outside town offer far more opportunity for adventure. Whether you choose a treetop lodge, a floating barge, or a cabana on a scenic lake, they usually have guides and exciting activities. Most offer swimming, nature walks, caiman "hunts" (the animals are blinded with flashlights, photographed, and released), piranha fishing, and canoe trips. Many lodges are near the Rio Negro, where mosquitoes are less of a problem because they can't breed in acidic black water. Unless otherwise noted, prices are for two-day, one-night packages, which generally include transport to and from the lodge, meals (not drinks), and a variety of activities that depend on the length of your stay.

Hotels

$$$ 🏨 **Hotel Tropical.** Nothing in the Amazon can match the majesty of this resort hotel. It's 20 km (12 mi) northwest of downtown and overlooks the Rio Negro, with a short path to the beach. In addition to the zoo, sports facilities, and two gorgeous pools, the Tropical has its own dock. The location is remote, far from Centro. The Tarumã restaurant is a reliable choice for dinners of regional and international fare. ✉ *Av. Coronel Teixeira 1320, Ponta Negra 69029-120* ☎ *092/659–5000* 🖷 *092/658–5026* ☞ *588 rooms, 8 suites* ♨ *2 restaurants, coffee shop, in-room safes, 4 tennis courts, 2 pools, gym, sauna, beach, dock, boating, basketball, bar, dance club, recreation room, shops, helipad, travel services* ▭ *AE, DC, MC, V.*

$ 🏨 **St. Paul.** If you're planning an extended stay, this apartment hotel in Centro is your best bet. Accommodations are immaculate and have living rooms and fully equipped modern kitchens. For stays of more than a week you may get a discount. ✉ *Av. Ramos Ferreira 1115, Centro 69010-120* ☎ *092/622–2131* 🖷 *092/622–2137* ☞ *45 apartments* ♨ *Kitchenettes, pool, gym, sauna* ▭ *AE, DC, MC, V.*

$ 🏨 **Taj Mahal.** Much of the charming East Indian artwork of the original hotel disappeared in the last renovation, although you can still see some in the lobby. Although the Taj Mahal is now more standardized, it's still a pleasant option, with a rooftop pool, a revolving restaurant, and a convenient location. Request a room with a river view. ✉*Av. Getúlio Vargas 741, Centro 69020-020* ☎☎ *092/627–3737* ☞ *144 rooms, 26 suites* ♨ *Restaurant, pool, hair salon, massage, sauna, bar, meeting room* ▭ *AE, DC, MC, V.*

¢–$ 🏨 **Lider Hotel.** Although far from luxurious, this hotel is clean, comfortable, and conveniently located in Centro. It's a good base from which to branch out on city tours. ✉ *Av. 7 de Setembro 827, Centro 69005-140* ☎ *092/621–9700* ☞ *60 rooms* ♨ *Restaurant, bar* ▭ *AE, DC, MC, V.*

¢ 🏨 **Central.** In the free-trade zone, this hotel is a good option if you're on a tight budget. Rooms are simple and clean, with standard amenities. ✉ *Rua Dr. Moreira 202, Centro 69005-250* ☎ *092/622–2600* 🖷 *092/622–2609* ☞ *50 rooms* ♨ *Minibars* ▭ *AE, DC, MC, V.*

¢ 🏨 **Manaós.** Across from Teatro Amazonas and just up the street from the busy part of downtown, this hotel is in a great spot. Rooms are small but are clean and have nice woodwork. The hotel staff is warm and friendly. ✉ *Av. Eduardo Ribeiro 881, Centro* ☎ *092/633–5744* 🖷 *092/232–4443* ✉ *manaos@argo.com.br* ☞ *39 rooms* ♨ *Restaurant, bar, Internet* ▭ *AE, DC, MC, V.*

Jungle Lodges

$$$$ 🏨 **Acajatuba Jungle Lodge.** You forget that the city is a mere four hours away at this thatch-hut lodge on Acajatuba Lake. Twenty individual screened cabins are elevated 1 meter (3 feet) aboveground and connected to the rest of the lodge by walkways. Lighting is provided by 12-volt batteries and kerosene lamps (generators would keep wildlife away), and there is no hot water, but what it lacks in luxury, it more than makes up for by putting you in the middle of the tropical forest. The boat leaves from the CEASA port near the Meeting of the Waters. ✉ *60 km (35 mi) west of Manaus, via boat along Rio Negro* 🕾 *Contact: Anaconda*

Turismo, Rua Lima Bacuri 345, Manaus 69005-220 ☎ *092/233–7642*
➥ *40 rooms* ♨ *Bar; no a/c, no room TVs, no room phones* ➡ *MC*
¶⊙¶ *FAP.*

$$$$ ⊞ **Amazon Lodge.** Nearly four hours by boat from Manaus, this lodge consists of rustic floating cabins with air-conditioning and baths. Because of its remote location, there is an excellent chance of spotting monkeys and birds. The English-speaking guides are knowledgeable and friendly. The minimum stay is two nights. Boats leave from the CEASA port near the Meeting of the Waters. ✉ *Lago Juma, 74 km (50 mi) south of Manaus* ⟟ *Heliconia Amazônia Turismo Ltda., Rua José Clemente 500, Room 214, Manaus 69010-070* ☎ *092/234–5915* 🖷 *092/633–7094* ➥ *14 rooms* ♨ *Restaurant, fishing, hiking* ➡ *No credit cards* ¶⊙¶ *FAP.*

★ **$$$$** ⊞ **Ariaú Amazon Towers.** Undoubtedly the most famous of the Amazon jungle lodges, Ariaú is composed of four-story wooden towers on stilts and linked by catwalks. The effect is more dramatic in the rainy season, when the river floods the ground below. Although the idea is to make you feel integrated with nature, the size of this complex generally prevents much of a sense of this, or much contact with wildlife for that matter. The exceptions are brightly colored macaws and adorable semi-wild monkeys that visit and make mischief. The lodge serves excellent food, though of limited variety, and has small comfortable rooms. Its most popular accommodation, sought by honeymooners and celebrities, is the Tarzan House, 30 meters (100 feet) up in the treetops. It can be had for R$2,300 above the price of any package. The lodge is two hours from Manaus. Boats depart near the Hotel Tropical. ✉ *Rio Ariaú, 60 km (40 mi) northwest of Manaus,* ⟟ *Rua Silva Ramos 41, Manaus 69010-180* ☎ *092/622–5000* 🖷 *092/233–5615* ➥ *291 rooms, 19 suites* ♨ *2 restaurants, 5 pools, dock, fishing, hiking, 4 bars, shops, helipad, auditorium, Internet; no room TVs* ➡ *AE, DC, MC, V* ¶⊙¶ *FAP.*

$$ ⊞ **Jungle Palace.** It's quite a sight to cruise down the Rio Negro and see the neoclassical columns of this "flotel" looming on the horizon. Built on a steel barge, this lodge combines remote location and luxury. Explore the region by day, and at night return to your air-conditioned cabin for a hot shower or to take a stroll on the observation deck. Catch your boat at the Hotel Tropical. ✉ *35 km (20 mi) west of Manaus via boat along Rio Negro* ⟟ *Rua Saldanha Marinho 700, Manaus* ☎ *092/633–6200* ➥ *42 rooms* ♨ *Restaurant, cable TV, pool, health club, bar, meeting room* ➡ *AE, MC, V* ¶⊙¶ *FAP.*

$$ ⊞ **Lago Salvador.** Although it's only a 45-minute boat ride from Manaus and a 15-minute ride from the Hotel Tropical, this lodge feels secluded. Four cabanas with three apartments each are on the shore of the lake from which the lodge takes its name. During the high-water season the lake flows over its shores to join the Rio Negro. Rooms are simple and comfortable, with running water. All of the small cabins have trails leading to them, but your guide will probably use the most direct route—paddling a canoe across the lake—to get you there. Boats leave from the Hotel Tropical. ✉ *15 km (10 mi) northwest of Manaus* ⟟ *Amazônia Expeditions, Hotel Tropical, Av. Coronel Teixeira 1320, Manaus 69029-120* ☎ *092/659–5119* 🖷 *092/658–4221* ➥ *12 cabins* ♨ *Restaurant, room service, fans, boating, hiking* ➡ *V* ¶⊙¶ *FAP.*

*Fodor's*Choice
★

Nightlife & the Arts

Pick up a copy of *Manaus Em Tempo* at any newsstand for event listings in Portuguese.

Nightlife

Boi bumbá (ox legend) music and dance—native to the central Amazon region—tells stories with tightly choreographed steps and strong rhythms. The amphitheater at Praia da Ponta Negra holds regular boi-bumbá performances. **Alegro** (⊠ Av. Djalma B 483 ☎ 092/216–5099), open every night, is a nightclub and restaurant with a varied Italian-heavy menu. The club plays MPB, rock, and *sertanejo* (country music from Ceará). For a traditional boi-bumbá experience in a nightclub environment, head to **Boiart's** (⊠ Rua José Clemente 500, Centro ☎ 092/637–6807), which is just across from the Teatro Amazonas. **Coração Blue** (⊠ Km 6, Estrada da Ponta Negra 3701 ☎ 092/658–4057) is an outdoor bar that has techno, *axé* (a Bahian rhythm), boi-bumbá, and dance music. Weeknights it's often the busiest place in town. A popular but somewhat highbrow dance club is the Hotel Tropical's **Studio Tropical** (⊠ Av. Coronel Teixeira 1320, Ponta Negra ☎ 092/659–5000), which plays high-energy dance music for a well-dressed clientele. It's open Thursday–Saturday.

The Arts

Teatro Amazonas (⊠ Praça São Sebastião s/n, Centro ☎ 092/622–2420) draws some of the biggest names in theater, opera, and classical music. Monday-evening performances are free. The Amazonas Philharmonic Orchestra plays every Friday night.

Sports & the Outdoors

Jet Skiing

Clube do Jet (⊠ Rua Praiana 13, access through Av. do Turismo, Ponta Negra ☎ 092/657–5435) rents equipment for about R$100 an hour on the Rio Negro.

Jungle & River Excursions

Though Belém, Santarém, and other communities are great places for jungle and river excursions, they don't have nearly the selection or number of visitors that Manaus has.

The most common excursion is a half- or full-day tourist-boat trip that travels 15 km (9 mi) east of Manaus to the point where the coffee-color water of the Rio Negro flows beside and gradually joins the coffee-with-cream-color water of the Rio Solimões. According to Brazilians, this is where the Amazon River begins. The waters flow alongside one another for 6 km (4 mi) before merging. Many of these meeting-of-the-waters treks include motorboat side trips along narrow streams or through bayous. Some also stop at the Parque Ecológico do Janauary, where you can see birds and a lake filled with the world's largest water lily, the *vitória régia*.

Nighttime boat trips into the forest explore flooded woodlands and narrow waterways. Some stop for trail hikes. Some companies take you by canoe on a caiman "hunt," where caimans are caught and released. Trips to the Rio Negro's upper reaches, where wildlife is a little wilder, are also offered. Such trips usually stop at river settlements to visit with local families. They may include jungle treks, fishing (they supply the gear and boat), and a trip to Anavilhanas, the world's largest freshwater archipelago. It contains some 400 islands with amazing Amazon flora, birds, and monkeys. To arrange any of these excursions, contact an area tour operator.

Soccer

Manaus's professional soccer teams, Rio Negro and Nacional, play at **Estádio Vivaldo Lima** (⊠ Av. Constantino Nery, Flores ☎ 092/236–3219). A taxi ride to the stadium and a ticket should each cost about R$20.

Shopping

Here, as in other parts of the Amazon, you can find lovely indigenous artisanal items made from animal parts. Macaws, for example, are killed in the wild for feathers to make souvenir items for tourists. As a result, there are no longer many macaws in the forests close to Manaus. Traveling home with items made from animal parts, certain types of wood, or plant fibers can result in big fines and even jail time, so beware.

Areas & Malls

The largest, most upscale mall is **Amazonas Shopping** (⊠ Av. Djarma Batista 482, Parque 10 ☎ 092/642–3555), with 300 stores with 38 restaurants. **Studio 5 Festival Mall** (⊠ Av. Rodrigo Octavio 2555, Vila da Felicidade ☎ 092/3048–7048) is a large mall.

Specialty Stores

Ecoshop (⊠ Centro ☎ 092/232–0409), in the Hidroviária International Terminal, sells regional art and a variety of indigenous crafts. One of the best places to buy all kinds of things, from fresh fish to hammocks and souvenirs, is **Mercado Adolfo Lisboa** (⊠ Rua Dos Barés 46, Centro), down along the water. **Museu do Índio** (⊠ Rua Duque de Caxias 296, Centro ☎ 092/635–7922) has a gift shop that sells traditional crafts such as necklaces made from seeds and feathers and baskets.

SIDE TRIPS FROM MANAUS

Amazon Ecopark

③⑥ *23 km (15 mi) northwest of Manaus.*

It's a half-hour boat ride from the Hotel Tropical, on the Tarumã River, to the Amazon Ecopark. The park has a monkey jungle, waterfalls, and birds and must be visited on a half- or full-day guided tour (R$126 or R$168 per person). You can also get a package (R$728 per person) and stay for one or more nights. ☎ 092/622–2612.

Beaches

Praia da Lua is 23 km (14 mi) southwest of Manaus. Praia do Tupé is 34 km (20 mi) northwest of Manaus.

Crescent-shape **Praia da Lua** can only be reached by boat on the Rio Negro, so it's clean and less crowded than other beaches. **Praia do Tupé**, a Rio Negro beach accessible only by boat, is popular with locals and tends to fill up on Sunday and holidays, when a special ship makes the trip from the city.

Presidente Figueiredo

107 km (64 mi) north of Manaus.

One of the Amazon's best-kept secrets is a two-hour drive north of Manaus. The town of Presidente Figueiredo (founded 1981) has dozens of waterfalls—up to 32 meters (140 feet) in height—and caves with prehistoric paintings and pottery fragments. The area was stumbled on during the construction of the BR 174 highway, the only highway that takes you out of the state (to Roraima and on to Venezuela), and was ultimately discovered by explorers looking for minerals, who had based themselves in Presidente Figueiredo. The area is excellent for swimming in black-water streams and hiking through upland forest. The town has several hotels and restaurants, and there's a hydropower plant and reservoir and an archaeology museum in the area. The Centro de Proteção de Quelonias e Mamiferos Aquaticos (Center for the Protection of Turtles and Aquatic Mammals) is in Balbina, 82 km (51 mi) north of town. The **Secretaria de Turismo** (⌧ Rua Das Araras 1 ☎ 092/324–0011) tourism office is next to the bus station and is open weekdays 8–noon and 2–6.

THE AMAZON A TO Z

To research prices, get advice from other travelers, and book travel arrangements, visit www.fodors.com.

AIR TRAVEL

BELÉM   All flights are served by Aeroporto Internacional Val-de-Cans, which is 11 km (7 mi) northwest of the city. Varig sometimes offers direct flights to Miami. Carriers that fly regularly to Rio, São Paulo, Brasília, and Manaus include TAM, Gol, VASP, Tavaj, and Varig. These carriers also have regular flights to Santarém, Macapá, and Marabá. Regional flights to smaller airports are offered by Penta and Meta.

The easiest route from the airport is south on Avenida Julio Cesár and then west on Avenida Almirante Barroso. The 20-minute taxi ride costs around R$25. There are also buses. Look for those labeled MAREX/PRES. VARGAS, for the Hilton and other hotels; MAREX/PRAÇA KENNEDY, for Paratur and the docks; or MAREX/VER-O-PESO, for Cidade Velha.

BETWEEN BELÉM   The only airport on Marajó is in Soure. It's very small and receives air
& MANAUS   taxis only. Norte Jet can take you there on a 30-minute (very expen-

sive) flight from Belém. Amazon Star Tours arranges these flights. Aeroporto de Macapá is 4 km (2 mi) northwest of town. Although buses make the journey regularly, hopping a taxi for the short, inexpensive ride is your best bet. Aeroporto Maria José is 14 km (23 mi) west of Santarém. Buses and taxis are plentiful.

MANAUS The international Aeroporto Brigadeiro Eduardo Gomes is 17 km (10 mi) south of downtown. Varig has a weekly direct flight to Miami. Most flights connect in São Paulo, where you can fly direct to Miami, New York, L.A., and Houston. VASP, Varig, TAM, and Tavaj have regular flights to and from Santarém, Belém, Brasília, Rio, and São Paulo. Tavaj and Rico also fly to smaller towns like Tabatinga, Parintins, and Tefé. The trip to Centro from the airport takes 20 minutes and costs R$30–R$45 by taxi. A trip on one of the city buses, which depart regularly during the day and early evening, costs R$1.50.

🛫 Airlines & Contacts **Meta** ☎ 091/522-1697 in Belém. **Penta** ☎ 091/222-7777 in Belém, 093/523-2220 in Santarém. **Norte Jet** ✉ Aeroporto Internacional Val-de-Cans ☎ 091/257-3780 🖒 Amazon Star Tours, Rua Henrique Gurjão 236, Campina ☎ 091/212-6244. **Rico** ☎ 092/652-1391 in Manaus. **TAM** ☎ 091/210-6400 in Belém, 092/652-1382 in Manaus ⊕ www.tamairlines.com. **Tavaj** ☎ 091/210-6257 in Belém, 092/652-1486 in Manaus. **Varig** ☎ 091/3083-4521 in Belém, 096/223-4612 in Macapá, 093/522-2488 in Santarém, 092/622-3161 in Manaus ⊕ www.varig.com.br. **VASP** ☎ 091/224-5588 in Belém, 096/223-2411 in Macapá, 092/622-3470 in Manaus ⊕ www.vasp.com.br.

🛬 Airport Information **Aeroporto Brigadeiro Eduardo Gomes** ✉ Av. Santos Dumont s/n, Manaus ☎ 092/652-1210. **Aeroporto de Macapá** ✉ Rua Hildemar Maia s/n, Santa Rita, Macapá ☎ 096/223-2323. **Aeroporto Internacional Val-de-Cans** ✉ Av. Julio Cesár s/n, Belém ☎ 091/210-6400. **Aeroporto Maria José** ✉ Rodovia Fernando Guilhon, Praça Eduardo Gomes s/n, Santarém ☎ 093/523-1990.

BIKE & MOTORCYCLE TRAVEL

On Ilha do Marajó one of the best ways to reach the beaches or to explore towns is to use a bike. Rates are less than R$2 an hour. You can find motorcycles to rent as well, though you'll have to ask around, since they're not advertised. The locals usually know who has equipment for rent.

🚲 Bike Rental **Bimba** ✉ Rua 4 between Trv. 18 and Trv. 19, Soure ☎ No phone.

BOAT & FERRY TRAVEL

BELÉM Most ships arrive and depart in the general dock area on the edge of downtown called the Escadinha. MACAMAZON ships and standard riverboats head to Santarém and Manaus from nearby Cais do Porto. The tourist-boat terminal, 20 minutes south of town on Avenida Alcindo Cacela (Praça Princesa Isabel), is where many excursions start.

BETWEEN BELÉM Arapari operates boats between Belém and Camará (Marajó) twice
& MANAUS daily Monday through Saturday. Although more expensive than other lines, it cuts the travel time from four hours to three. A ferry takes cars to Ilha do Marajó. Vans run from Camará to Soure and cost about R$10.

Although Macapá is very close to Ilha do Marajó's western side, most boats traveling to Macapá originate in Belém. Regional boats regularly make the 24-hour trip. If time is an issue, try the high-speed boats, which cut the journey down to 10 hours and cost R$110. Bom Jesus runs a "party boat," with restaurants, bars, and multiple decks, that makes the trip five times a week. You can rent hammock space for around R$75 (hammocks aren't provided). Boats dock in the nearby port town of Santana, where taxis await. The fare to Macapá is R$15–R$40, depending on how many other passengers the driver can gather. Buses run hourly.

Only regional boats make the two-day trip from Macapá to Santarém and onward to Manaus. They also go from Belém to Santarém, which takes about two and a half days. Taxis are always at the docks in Santarém. The cost to any of the nearby hotels in town is less than R$10.

MANAUS If you're looking for a boat to another town, a lodge, or a beach, visit the Hidroviária Regional Terminal. At the ticket or tourist information booths you can get information about prices and departure times and days to all the locations. You can also walk down to Porto Flutuante via the bridge behind the terminal to take a look at the regional boats. Their destinations and departure times are listed on plaques. To reach most Manaus-area beaches, catch a boat from Porto Flutuante. Sunday is the only day with regularly scheduled trips; boats transport great crowds for about R$8 per person. You can hire small craft to the beaches and other attractions, such as the meeting of the waters. Look for people wearing the green vests of the Associação dos Canoeiros Motorizados de Manaus near the Porto Flutuante or in the Escadinha area closer to the market in Belém. They can set you up with local boat trips at reasonable prices. You can also make arrangements through tour operators.

🚢 Boat & Ferry Information **Arapari** ☎ 091/9601-5312. **Bom Jesus** ✉ Av. Mendonça Junior 12, Macapá ☎ 096/223-2342. **Macamazon** ☎ 091/222-5604. **Ilha do Marajó Vans** ☎ 091/741-1441.

BUS TRAVEL

BELÉM The bus station in Belém, Rodoviário São Brás, is east of Nazaré. Reservations for buses are rarely needed. Boa Esperança makes the 209-km (125-mi) journey to Salinas Beach every couple of hours daily. Beira-Dão leaves every half hour on the 60-km (36-mi), two-hour, R$8 journey to Ilha Mosqueiro. Clearly marked buses to Outeiro Beach and the town of Icoaraci pass the bus station regularly and cost about R$1. Belém's local bus service is safe and comprehensive, but a little confusing. Ask a resident for guidance. You board buses at the rear, pay an attendant, and pass through a turnstile. Keep an eye on your belongings.

BETWEEN BELÉM In Soure buses to Camará pass by the riverside regularly. In Macapá there's
& MANAUS an outdoor terminal on Rua Antônio Coelho de Carvalho, a block from the fort. Catch the bus labeled B. NOVO/UNIVERSIDADE to the Marco Zero, a 20-minute ride. Buses from Santarém to Alter do Chão depart from Praça Tiradentes in the city center or from Avenida Cuiabá (near the Amazon Park Hotel). They make the journey back and forth five or six times a day and hourly on Sunday.

MANAUS The bus station in Manaus, Terminal Rodoviário Huascar Angelim, is 7 km (4 mi) north of the city center. The city bus system is extensive and easy to use. The fare is about R$1.50. Most of the useful buses run along Avenida Floriano Peixoto, including Bus 120, which goes to Ponta

Negra and stops near the Hotel Tropical. The Fontur bus, which costs about R$12, travels between Centro and the Tropical several times a day. To get to Presidente Figueiredo, take the bus labeled ARUANÃ, which runs regularly from the terminal and costs around R$15.

🚌 Bus Information **Beira-Dão** ☎ 091/226-1162. **Boa Esperança** ☎ 091/266-0033. **Rodoviário São Brás** ✉ Av. Almirante Barroso s/n, São Brás, Belém. **Terminal Rodoviário Huascar Angelim** ✉ Rua Recife 2784, Flores, Manaus ☎ 092/642-5805.

CAR RENTAL

In Belém rental cars cost between R$91 and R$162 a day. Several companies have offices at the airport and in town. There aren't any car-rental companies on Ilha do Marajó, but you can rent a car in Belém and transport it to the island on the ferry that leaves from Icoaraci. In Macapá you can rent from Locvel and in Santarém from Bill Car, though there are other companies. You can rent a car at the Manaus airport through Unidas Rent a Car.

🚗 Local Agencies **Bill Car** ✉ Av. Mendoço Furtado Santarém ☎ 093/522-1705. **Locvel** ✉ Av. Fab 2093, Macapá ☎ 096/223-7999. **Norauto** ✉ Av. Gentil Bittencourt 2086, Nazaré, Belém ☎ 091/249-4900. **Unidas Rent a Car** ✉ Aeroporto Brigadeiro Eduardo Gomes, Av. Santos Dumont s/n, Manaus ☎ 092/621-1575.

CAR TRAVEL

The BR 316 begins on the outskirts of Belém and runs eastward toward the coast and then south, connecting the city with Brazil's major northeastern hubs. To reach the beaches at Ilha Mosqueiro outside Belém, take BR 316 and then head north on PA 391. To reach Salinas Beach, take BR 316 to PA 324 and head north on PA 124. From Manaus BR 174 runs north to Boa Vista, and BR 319 travels south to Porto Velho, which is south of Manaus in Rondônia State. To get to BR 319, you have to take a ferry across the Amazon. You can go about 100 km (63 mi) on paved road. Then it turns to dirt or mud. Even if you're after adventure, don't think about driving to Porto Velho. A four-wheel-drive vehicle takes you farther than 100 km (62 mi) but won't get you across the rivers and lakes that take over the road farther south.

Although Belém has the most traffic of any Amazon city and what seems like more than its fair share of one-way streets, in-town driving is relatively easy. Parking is only tricky in a few areas, such as Avenida Presidente Vargas and the Escadinha. Traffic and parking problems don't exist in the region between Belém and Manaus. Manaus has its share but is calmer than Belém.

EMERGENCIES

Big Ben is a 24-hour pharmacy in Belém with many branches. Farmácia Teixeira in Soure may be open 24 hours (the pharmacies there rotate 24-hour duty). In Macapá Farmácia Globo is open 24 hours a day, and Santarém's only 24-hour pharmacy is Drogaria Droga Mil.

🚑 Emergency Contacts **Ambulance** ☎ 192 in Belém, 1520 in Macapá, 192 in Manaus. **Fire** ☎ 193 in Belém, 193 in Macapá, 093/522-2530 in Santarém, 092/611-5040 in Manaus. **Police** ☎ 190 in Belém, 190 in Macapá, 093/523-2633 in Santarém, 190 in Manaus.

Hospitals **Hospital e Maternidade Dom Luiz I** ☒ Av. Generalíssimo Deodoro 868, Umarizal, Belém ☎ 091/241-4144. **Hospital e Maternidade Sagrada Familia** ☒ Av. Presidente Vargas 1606, Santarém ☎ 093/522-1988. **Hospital e Pronto Socorro Municipal 28 de Agosto** ☒ Rua Recife s/n, Adrianópolis, Manaus ☎ 092/236-0326. **Pronto Socorro** ☒ Rua Milton Silva s/n, Macapá ☎ 096/421-1499 or 192. **Santa Severa** ☒ Rua 8 and Trv. 17, Soure, Ilha do Marajó ☎ 091/741-1459.

24-Hour Pharmacies **Big Ben** ☒ Av. Gentil Bittencourt 1548, Nazaré, Belém ☎ 091/241-3000. **Drogaria 24h** ☒ Boulevard Álvaro Maio 744, Centro, Manaus ☎ 092/633-6040. **Drogaria Droga Mil** ☒ Av. Magalhães Barata 674, Santarém ☎ 093/523-1000. **Farmácia Globo** ☒ Rua Leopoldo Machado 1902, Macapá ☎ 096/223-1378. **Farmácia Teixeira** ☒ Rua 2 s/n, Soure, Ilha do Marajó ☎ 091/741-1487.

HEALTH

Several months before you go to the Amazon, visit a tropical medicine specialist to find out what vaccinations you need. Describe your planned adventure, and get tips on how to prepare. Read about tropical diseases in the Amazon so you know the symptoms and how to treat them should you fall ill.

In a remote area the likeliest health issues are infection and dehydration. Infections are common from insect bites and cuts. Treat them quickly, so they don't worsen. Dehydration can result from gastrointestinal problems or inadequate water. Be sure to keep yourself hydrated with clean water, and learn what to do about gastrointestinal issues. Schistosomiasis, a water-borne parasite, is rarely a problem in the Amazon. However, rabies, Chagas' disease, malaria, and dengue fever are problematic. For information on tropical ailments, *see* Health *in* Smart Travel Tips A to Z.

Safety issues can quickly become health issues. Tropical forests are home to lots of ants, bees, spiders, scorpions, centipedes, and caterpillars, many of which bite or sting. Their unpleasant attacks largely can be avoided by wearing protective clothing and by not playing with them. If you are allergic to bites and stings, you should carry an adrenaline kit. Remember to check your shoes in the morning for small guests. Many plants have spines and thorns that may also result in wounds, so beware of where you place your hands and feet. Mosquitoes and gnats are abundant in some places. Only stronger versions of repellents with DEET (N,N-diethyl-m-toluamide) keep them away. A *mosquiteiro* (netting for hammock or bed) helps tremendously at night. Most lodges and hotels in mosquito-heavy areas provide these for guests. Ticks live in forests, too. If you find one on you, remove it and treat the site with disinfectant. Chiggers inhabit grassy areas and are nearly invisible. Repellent sprayed on shoes, socks, and pants helps, as does powdered sulfur. Anti-itch cream helps you sleep at night.

Other safety issues include water and larger creatures. Though you can swim in many places, get local information beforehand. Is the water too shallow to jump or dive? Are there rocks or dead trees just under the surface? Piranhas are rarely a problem, except as supporting actors in B movies, but ask your neighbors first. Freshwater stingrays are another potential peril. They hide in shallow water, and they're difficult to see, but if you step on one, you'll feel it. A sting from its barbed tail can be excruciating and long in healing. This bad memory can usually be avoided by dragging your feet as you move slowly through shallow areas or by heading directly to deeper water, where the rays can avoid you. Another unlikely though possible encounter is with venomous snakes. Bushmasters, fer-de-lance relatives, and several others are present though rarely seen. Shoes or boots and long pants are excellent preventive measures. Also, watch closely where you step, especially if you venture off a trail.

Throughout the region, avoid drinking tap water and using ice made from it. In the cities most restaurants buy ice made from purified water. Bottled water is generally easy to find. Beware of where you eat. Many of the street-side stands are not very clean. Over-the-counter remedies can ease some discomfort. For loose bowels, Floratil can be purchased without a doctor's prescription. Estomazil and Sorrisal are two remedies for upset stomach. They may contain aspirin. For more information on health *see* Health *in* Smart Travel Tips A to Z.

MAIL, SHIPPING & INTERNET
In Belém, NetG@mes Cyber Café provides Internet service for R$3 an hour and is open Monday–Saturday 8 AM–11 PM. Telemar, the phone company, offers Internet access for R$6 per hour. The central branch of the Belém post office is open weekdays 8–noon and 2–5. You can send faxes, and, as in all Brazilian post offices, SEDEX international courier service is available.

On Ilha do Marajó, the Soure post office is on Rua 2 between Travessa 13 and Travessa 14. The Macapá central post office is open weekdays 9–noon and 2–5. You can mail a letter at the Santarém post office weekdays 8–4. In Santarém, Henrique Art's Digitais is open Monday through Saturday 9–6, at R$5 per hour for Internet access.

In Manaus, Internext has 14 computers and charges R$3 per hour for Internet access. The most central Manaus post office is open weekdays 9–5 and on Saturday 9–1. Cybercity charges R$6 per hour for Internet access.
🌐 Internet Cafés **Cybercity** ⊠ Av. Getúlio Vargas 188, Centro, Manaus ☎ 092/234-8930. **Internext** ⊠ Av. Eduardo Ribeiro, Rio Negro Center 220, 2nd floor, Centro, Manaus ☎ 092/633-4409. **Henrique Art's Digitais** ⊠ Trv. 15 de Agosto 47, Centro, Santarém ☎ 093/523-4888. **NetG@mes Cyber Café** ⊠ Av. Nazaré 947, Loja 7, Nazaré, Belém ☎ 091/224-3344.
🌐 Post Offices **Belém post office** ⊠ Av. Presidente Vargas 498, Campina ☎ 091/212-1155. **Macapá central post office** ⊠ Av. Coroliano Jucá 125 ☎ 096/223-0196. **Manaus post office** ⊠ Rua Marechal Deodoro 117, Centro ☎ 092/622-2181. **Santarém post office** ⊠ Praça da Bandeira 81 ☎ 093/523-1178. **Soure post office** ⊠ Rua 2 s/n ☎ 091/741-1207.

MONEY MATTERS
In Belém the airport branch of the Banco do Brasil charges a hefty commission to cash traveler's checks. In town Banco Amazônia has the best rates; it's open weekdays 10–4. Casa Francesa Câmbio e Turismo is one of several exchange houses that offer comparable rates. ATMs are avail-

able at most bank branches in major cities. In smaller towns neither ATMs nor change are easy to come by: bring cash and lots of small bills. There are no exchange facilities on Ilha do Marajó. In Macapá you can exchange money at Banco do Brasil, which is open weekdays 11–2:30. You'll probably get a better rate at Casa Francesa Câmbio e Turismo. In Santarém you can exchange money at Banco do Brasil, which is open weekdays 10–1. At the airport in Manaus you can exchange money at Banco do Brasil and Banco Real. In town Cortez Câmbio has the best rates.

🏦 Banks & Exchange Services **Banco Amazônia** ⊠ Av. Presidente Vargas 800, Comércio, Belém ☎ 091/216-3252. **Banco do Brasil** ⊠ Aeroporto Internacional Val-de-Cans, Av. Júlio César s/n ☎ 091/257-1983 ⊠ Rua Independência 250, Macapá ☎ 096/223-2155 ⊠ Av. Rui Barbosa 794, Santarém ☎ 091/523-2600. **Casa Francesa Câmbio e Turismo** ⊠ Trv. Padre Prudêncio 40, Batista Campos, Belém ☎ 091/241-2716 ⊠ Rua Independência 232, Macapá ☎ 096/224-1418. **Cortez Câmbio** ⊠ Av. 7 de Setembro 1199, Centro, Manaus ☎ 092/622-4222.

PACKING

For remote travel in the Amazon, a small backpack is the most efficient way to carry your items. Plan for drenching downpours by bringing sufficient plastic bags, especially for important items. Other items to consider packing are: water bottle, filter, and purification tablets, sunscreen, insect repellent, hat, a good medical kit, knife, lightweight gold-miner's hammock (*rede de garimpeiro*), mosquito netting, sheet, 3 yards of ¼-inch rope, tent (if you're planning to camp), rain poncho, light shorts, pants, jacket, flashlight, batteries, matches, food, earplugs, sunglasses, camera, film, passport copy, credit card, cash, phone numbers, paper, and pen. For more information on packing *see* Packing *in* Smart Travel Tips A to Z.

SAFETY

In Belém watch out for pickpockets everywhere, but especially at Vero-Peso, on Avenida President Vargas, and in Comércio. Avoid walking alone at night or on poorly lighted streets, and don't wear jewelry, especially gold. Manaus has similar crime problems; beware in Centro near the docks. Santarém has some petty theft but is considerably safer. Still, be cautious at night. The smaller towns tend to be safer, though not all are. Ask locals or tour office personnel for more information. On sleepy Ilha do Marajó, your greatest personal safety concern may be getting hit on the head by a falling mango.

TELEPHONES

Throughout the region there are card-operated public phones. Cards are sold in newsstands and often in restaurants. The area code for Belém is 091. In Santarém it's 093, in Macapá it's 096, and in Manaus it's 092. You can make long-distance calls at Telemar. Hours vary depending on the city, but mostly they're open daily from 8 AM to 9 PM.

📞 **Telamazon** ⊠ Av. Getúlio Vargas 950, Centro, Manaus ☎ 092/621-6339. **Telepará** ⊠ Av. Presidente Vargas 610, Campina, Belém ⊠ Av. Rua Siqueira Campos 511, Santarém ☎ 091/523-2974.

TAXIS

There are plenty of taxis in Amazon cities, and they're easy to flag down. All have meters (except Marajó), and tips aren't necessary. Where meters don't exist, you have to bargain for the price. At odd hours call the taxi company. You can find them listed in the yellow pages, or call one of the companies below. Smaller towns also have mototaxis. They are much cheaper but only carry one passenger.

🚖 Taxi Companies **Coopertaxi** ☎ 091/257-1041 or 091/257-1720 in Belém. **Rádio Taxi** ☎ 096/223-5656 in Macapa. **Rádio Táxi Piauí** ☎ 091/523-2725 in Santarém. **Soure Taxis** ☎ 091/741-1336 in Soure. **Taxi Nazaré** ☎ 091/242-7867 in Belém. **Tucuxi** ☎ 092/800-5050 or 092/622-4040 in Manaus.

TOURS

For excursions in Belém as well as help with plane and hotel reservations, contact Angel Turismo in the Hilton Hotel. Valeverde Turismo has a tour boat and office at the Estação das Docas. Amazon Star can do just about everything.

Tour operators that arrange trips to Ilha do Marajó are based in Belém. Amapá Tours offers city and river tours and is the only company that arranges trips to see the pororoca. Santarém Tur can arrange boat trips on the Amazon and Arapiuns rivers, day trips to Alter do Chão, and city tours. Amazon Tours, run by knowledgeable, friendly American Steven Alexander, conducts half-day trips to a patch of forest he owns that's a half hour's drive southeast of Santarém.

In Manaus, Amazônia Expeditions can book stays at jungle lodges, tours to the meeting of the waters, and piranha fishing. They also have a floatplane, with half-hour flights starting at R$250. Fontur arranges boat and city tours. Another operator, Tarumã, can help with hotel arrangements and transportation in the city or on the river.

For information about fishing trips in Pará State, contact the Secretaria de Estado de Ciência, Tecnologia e Meio Ambiente (SECTAM).

🚖 Tour Information **SECTAM** ✉ Trv. Lomas Valentinas 2717, Marco ☎ 091/266-5000.
🚖 Tour-Operator Recommendations **Amapá Tours** ✉ Hotel Macapá, Av. Azarias Neto 17, Macapá ☎ 096/223-2553. **Amazon Explorers** ✉ Rua Nhamundá 21, Centro, Manaus ☎ 092/633-1978. **Amazon Star Tours** ✉ Rua Henrique Gurjão 236, Campina, Belém ☎ 091/212-6244. **Amazon Tours** ✉ Trv. Turiano Meira 1084, Santarém ☎ 093/522-1928. **Amazônia Expeditions** ✉ Hotel Tropical, Av. Coronel Teixeira 1320, Ponta Negra, Manaus ☎ 092/658-4221. **Angel Turismo** ✉ Hilton International Belém, Av. Presidente Vargas 882, Praça da República, Campina, Belém ☎ 091/224-2111. **Fontenele** ✉ Av. Assis de Vasconcelos 199, Reduto, Belém ☎ 091/241-3218. **Fontur** ✉ Hotel Tropical, Av. Coronel Teixeira 1320, Ponta Negra, Manaus ☎ 092/658-3052. **Lusotur** ✉ Av. Brás de Aguiar 471, Nazaré, Belém ☎ 091/241-1011. **Santarém Tur** ✉ Rua Adriano Pimentel 44, Santarém ☎ 093/522-4847. **Tarumã** ✉ Av. Eduardo Ribeiro 620, Centro, Manaus ☎ 092/648-8347. **Valeverde Turismo** ✉ Boulevard Castilhos França s/n, Campina, Belém ☎ 091/212-3388.

ECOTOURS Heliconia Amazônia Turismo Ltda., across the street from the Teatro Amazonas, can help any size group set up a tour of the Amazon region. Swallows and Amazons has an excellent reputation.

📳 Ecotour Operator Recommendations **Heliconia Amazônia Turismo Ltda.** ✉ Rua José Clemente 500, Room 214, Centro, Manaus ☎ 092/234-5915 🖷 092/633-7094 ⊕ www.heliconia-amazon.com. **Swallows and Amazons** ✉ Rua Quintino Bocaiuva 189, Manaus ☎🖷 092/622-1246 ⊕ www.swallowsandamazonstours.com.

FISHING TOURS Santana in Manaus has well-run peacock bass (*tucunaré*) sportfishing tours that are popular with North Americans. Augusto Albuquerque runs a small operation setting up fishing tours for small groups to out-of-the-way places.

📳 Fishing Tour Operator Recommendations **Augusto Albuquerque** ✉ Rua Cândidi Mariano 61, Centro, Manaus ☎ 092/232-1346. **Santana** ✉ Rua dos Andrades 106, Centro, Manaus ☎ 092/234-9814 🖷 092/233-7127 ⊕ www.santanaecologica.com.br.

VISITOR INFORMATION

Belemtur, the city tourist board, is open weekdays 8–noon and 2–6. Pará State's tourist board, Paratur, is open weekdays 8–6. Both agencies are well organized and extremely helpful. On Ilha do Marajó contact the Secretaria Municipal de Turismo. For information in Macapá, contact the state tourism authority, DETUR. In Santarém contact SANTUR. Amazonas State's tourism authority, the Secretaria de Estado da Cultura e Turismo, is open weekdays 8–6. The Manaus tourism authority, Manaustur, is open weekdays 8–2.

📳 Tourist Information **Belemtur** ✉ Av. Governador José Malcher 592, Nazaré, Belém ☎ 091/242-0900 or 091/242-0033. **DETUR** ✉ Rua Raimundo Álvares da Costa 18, Macapá ☎ 096/223-0627. **Manaustur** ✉ Av. 7 de Setembro 157, Centro, Manaus ☎ 092/622-4986 or 092/622-4886. **Paratur** ✉ Praça Maestro Waldemar Henrique s/n, Reduto, Belém ☎ 091/223-6198 or 091/212-0669 ⊕ www.paratur.pa.gov.br. **SANTUR** ✉ Rua Floriano Peixoto 777, Santarém ☎🖷 093/523-2434. **Secretaria de Estado da Cultura e Turismo** ✉ Av. 7 de Setembro 1546, Centro, Manaus ☎ 092/232-5550 ⊕ www.visitamazonas.com.br. **Secretaria Municipal de Turismo** ✉ Rua 2 between Trv. 14 and Trv. 15, Soure ☎ 091/3741-1327.

UNDERSTANDING
BRAZIL

A LAND OF CONTRAST
& DIVERSITY

NATIONAL PRIDE WAS STRONG IN 2003: the country had just declared war on hunger, launching the ambitious *Fome Zero* program; the Brazilian film *Cidade de Deus* (City of God) was nominated for best foreign film (though it didn't win); Brazil had won the *futebol* (soccer) World Cup for the fifth time in 2002; Gustavo "Guga" Kuerten was doing well and would probably rejoin the list of the world's 10-best tennis players in a year or so; and other globetrotting sports heroes such as Ronaldo were back in form.

In Brazil sports heroes are like royalty. Only state affairs are able, on occasion, to steal the limelight from them. Sports personalities can rivet the country's attention, forming an emotional chain across this vast land that links more than 175 million people. With the help of mass communication, even lesser princes, such as beach volleyball world champions, are often met by cheering crowds.

Brazilians rarely unite passionately behind weightier issues, but when they do, the effects are awesome. No one who was in the country in 1984 can forget the months of nationwide marches that nudged the military regime toward democratic elections for president after 20 years of dictatorship. Little more than a decade later, the movement to impeach the corrupt president, Fernando Collor de Mello, brought out similar crowds, not only politically organized groups but also citizens going about their everyday affairs. Housewives donned black as a sign of protest when they did their weekly shopping, and students made up their faces using war paint when they attended classes. Involving very little direct confrontation—and even less violence—these events seemed more like Carnaval (Carnival) than political revolution. But this is a style that makes sense in Brazil.

In this gigantic territory, larger than the continental United States and 250 times the size of Holland, contrasts are overwhelming. Brazil is a fabulously rich land, but it's full of inequalities. You're as apt to see five-star hotels and resorts as you are shantytowns. Shopping malls, McDonald's restaurants, and international banks stand side by side with street vendors peddling homemade foods and herbal medicines. Brazil's GNP is nearly US$795 billion (more than half that of Latin America as a whole), yet it also has a relatively high infant mortality rate (out of 1,000 babies born, 34 don't make it to their first birthday) and one of the world's worst distributions of wealth. The nation has more than 100 million acres of arable land; unequaled reserves of iron, bauxite, manganese, and other minerals; and mammoth hydroelectric power plants. Yet reckless mining and agricultural procedures—particularly in the Amazon—have poisoned rivers, created deserts, and dislodged entire Indian tribes. Further, the racial democracy for which Brazil is often praised is more evident in the bustling downtown markets than in the plush salons of suburban socialites.

It has been said that in this radiant land live a sad people, and certainly the feeling of *saudade* (nostalgia) is latent in much Brazilian poetry and music. Yet this plaintive tone vanishes as soon as the Carnaval season begins. In the heat of the South American summer (February or March, depending on the date of Easter), the country explodes in gaiety. From such cities as Rio de Janeiro, Salvador, and Recife—where hundreds of thousands dance in street parades—to the small towns of Pará or Goiás, Brazil comes alive. Carnaval season involves not only the days right before Lent (Friday through Ash Wednesday), but also months of rehearsal beforehand. And the sparks of passion flow over into other events throughout the year: religious festivals, ball games, weekend dances.

If you examine Brazil's demographics, you'll find other stark contrasts. You can drive through vast regions in the central *cerrados* (savannas), the southern pampas, or the northeastern *sertão* (arid interior) without seeing a soul and then, paradoxically, spend hours stuck in traffic in a major city. The bloated urban areas harbor nearly 80% of the population. They're like cauldrons that contain a stew of many races seasoned by regional customs and accents. Although Brazil is considered a Latin country—and the Portuguese language does, indeed, help to unify it—any type of person fits the Brazilian "mold." The country's racial composition reflects the historical contact among native peoples, Portuguese colonizers, African slaves, and immigrants from Germany, Italy, Japan, and even the United States.

In diversity, religion runs a close second to ethnicity. Although the almanac will tell you that Brazil is 70% Catholic, the people's spiritual lives are much more eclectic. Some estimates put the number of spiritualists—many of whom are followers of the 19th-century Belgian medium Alan Kardec—at 40 million. Candomblé, Macumba, Umbanda, and other cults inspired by African religions and deities abound. And, recently, Pentecostal sects have opened one church after another, performing exorcisms and miraculous "cures" in front of packed auditoriums. Most of these churches and cults welcome visitors of any creed or culture. Brazilians, it seems, are anything but sectarian.

Brazil is truly a land of contrasts, and any visit here is likely to be a sensuous adventure. A variety of cultures, beliefs, and topographies makes this warm nation a showcase of diversity. An array of nature's bounty—from passion fruit and papaya to giant river fish and coastal crabs—has inspired chefs from all over the world to come and try their hands at Brazilian restaurants (adding lightness and zest to the country's already exquisite cuisine). All over the land, spas with bubbling mineral water and soothing hot springs offer the best of both nature and technology. Whether you travel to the Amazon rain forest, the mountain towns of Minas Gerais, the urban jungle of São Paulo, or the immense central plateau surrounding Brasília, you'll plunge into an exotic mix of colors, rhythms, and pastimes.

Historical Notes

Colonial Days. Brazil was officially "discovered" in 1500, when a fleet commanded by Portuguese diplomat Pedro Álvares Cabral, on its way to India, landed in Porto Seguro, between Salvador and Rio de Janeiro. (There is, however, strong evidence that other Portuguese adventurers preceded him. Duarte Pacheco Pereira, in his book *De Situ Orbis,* tells of being in Brazil in 1498, sent by King Manuel of Portugal.)

Brazil's first colonizers were met by the Tupinamba, one group in the vast array of the continent's native population. Lisbon's early goals were simple: monopolize the lucrative trade of *pau-brasil,* the red wood (valued for making dye) that gave the colony its name, and establish permanent settlements. There's evidence that the Indians and Portuguese initially worked together to harvest trees. Later, the need to head farther inland to find forested areas made the pau-brasil trade less desirable. The interest in establishing plantations on cleared lands increased and so did the need for laborers. The Portuguese tried to enslave the indigenous peoples, but unaccustomed to toiling long hours in fields and overcome by European diseases, many natives either fled far inland or died. (When Cabral arrived, the indigenous population was believed to have been more than 3 million; today the number is scarcely more than 200,000.) The Portuguese then turned to the African slave trade for their workforce.

Although most settlers preferred the coastal areas (a preference that continues to this day), a few ventured into the hinterlands. Among them were Jesuit missionaries, determined men who marched inland in search of Indian souls to "save," and the infamous *bandeirantes* (flag bearers), tough men who marched inland in search of Indians to enslave. (Later they hunted escaped Indian and African slaves.)

For two centuries after Cabral's discovery, the Portuguese had to periodically deal with foreign powers with designs on Brazil's resources. Although Portugal and Spain had the 1494 Treaty of Tordesillas—which set boundaries for each country in their newly discovered lands—the guidelines were vague, causing the occasional territory dispute. Further, England, France, and Holland didn't fully recognize the treaty, which was made by papal decree, and were aggressively seeking new lands in pirate-ridden seas. Such competition made the Lusitanian foothold in the New World tenuous at times.

The new territory faced internal as well as external challenges. Initially, the Portuguese crown couldn't establish a strong central government in the subcontinent. For much of the colonial period it relied on "captains," low-ranking nobles and merchants who were granted authority over captaincies, slices of land often as big as their motherland. By 1549 it was evident that most captaincies were failing. Portugal's monarch dispatched a governor-general (who arrived with soldiers, priests, and craftspeople) to oversee them and to establish a capital (today's Salvador) in the central captaincy of Bahia.

At the end of the 17th century the news that fabulous veins of emeralds, diamonds, and gold had been found in Minas Gerais exploded in Lisbon. The region began to export 30,000 pounds of gold a year to Portugal. Bandeirantes and other fortune hunters rushed in from all over, and boatloads of carpenters, stonemasons, sculptors, and painters came from Europe to build cities in the Brazilian wilderness.

In 1763 the capital was moved to Rio de Janeiro for a variety of political and administrative reasons. The country had successfully staved off invasions by other European nations, and it had roughly taken its current shape. It added cotton and tobacco to sugar, gold, and diamonds on its list of exports. As the interior opened, so did the opportunities for cattle ranching. Still, Portugal's policies tended toward stripping Brazil of its resources rather than developing a truly local economy. The arrival of the royal family, which was chased out of Portugal by Napoléon's armies in 1808, initiated major changes.

The Empire & the Republic. As soon as Dom João VI and his entourage arrived in Rio, he began transforming the city and its environs. Building projects were set in motion, universities as well as a bank and a mint were founded, and investments were made in the arts. The ports were opened to trade with other nations, especially England, and morale improved throughout the territory. With the fall of Napoléon, Dom João VI returned to Portugal, leaving his young son, Pedro I, behind to govern. But Pedro had ideas of his own: he proclaimed Brazil's independence on September 7, 1822, and established the Brazilian empire. Nine years later, following a period of internal unrest and costly foreign wars, the emperor stepped aside in favor of his five-year-old son, Pedro II. A series of regents ruled until 1840, when the second Pedro was 14 and Parliament decreed him "of age."

Pedro II's daughter, Princess Isabel, officially ended slavery in 1888. Soon after, disgruntled landowners united with the military to finish with monarchy altogether, forcing the royal family back to Portugal and founding Brazil's first republican government on November 15, 1889. A long series of easily forgettable presidents, backed by strong coffee and rubber economies, brought about some industrial and urban development during what's known as the Old Republic. In 1930, after his running mate was assassinated, presidential candidate Getúlio Vargas seized power via military coup rather than elections. In 1945 his dictatorship ended in another coup. He returned to the political scene with a populist platform and was elected president in 1951. However, halfway through his term, he was linked to the attempted assassination of a political rival; with the military calling for his resignation, he shot himself.

The next elected president, Juscelino Kubitschek, a visionary from Minas Gerais, decided to replace the capital of Rio de Janeiro with a grand, new, modern one (symbolic of grand, new, modern ideas) that would be built in the middle of nowhere. True to the motto of his national development plan, "Fifty years in five," he opened the economy to foreign capital and offered credit to the business community. When Brasília was inaugurated in 1960, there wasn't a penny left in the coffers, but key sectors of the economy (such as the auto industry) were functioning at full steam. Still, turbulent times were ahead. Kubitschek's successor Jânio Quadros, an eccentric, spirited carouser who had risen from high-school teaching to politics, resigned after seven months in office. Vice-president João "Jango" Goulart, a Vargas man with leftist leanings, took office only to be overthrown by the military on March 31, 1964, after frustrated attempts to impose socialist reforms. Exiled in Uruguay, he died 13 years later.

Military Rule & Beyond. Humberto Castello Branco was the first of five generals (he was followed by Artur Costa e Silva, Emílio Médici, Ernesto Geisel, and João Figueiredo) to lead Brazil in 20 years of military rule that still haunt the nation. Surrounded by tanks and technocrats, the military brought about the "economic miracle" of the 1970s. However, it did not last. Their pharaonic projects—from

hydroelectric and nuclear power plants to the conquest of the Amazon—never completely succeeded, and inflation soared. Power was to go peacefully back to civil hands in 1985.

All hopes were on the shoulders of Tancredo Neves, a 75-year-old democrat chosen to be president by an electoral college. But just before his investiture Neves was hospitalized for routine surgery; he died of a general infection days later. An astounded nation followed the drama on TV. Vice-president José Sarney, a former ally of the military regime, took office. By the end of his five-year term, inflation was completely out of hand. Sarney did, however, oversee the writing of a new constitution, promulgated in 1988, and Brazil's first free presidential elections in 30 years.

Fernando Collor de Mello, a debonair 40-year-old from the state of Alagoas, took office in March 1990. Dubbed "the maharajah hunter" (an allusion to his promises to rid the government of idle, highly paid civil servants), Mello immediately set about trying to control inflation (his first step was to block all savings accounts in Brazil). His extravagant economic plans only became clear two years later with the discovery of widespread corruption involving his friend and campaign manager Paulo César "P. C." Farias. After an impeachment process, Collor was ousted in December 1992, and Brazil's leadership fell to Vice-President Itamar Franco. With his Plano Real, Franco brought inflation under control.

In 1994 Franco was replaced by Fernando Henrique Cardoso, the former secretary of the treasury. Following the dictates of the International Monetary Fund, Cardoso brought about relative economic stability, but at the price of recession, cuts in health and educational programs, and a soaring national debt. His policy of selling state-owned industries—from banks to mines to phone companies—was riddled with irregular practices.

In October 1998, taking advantage of a constitutional amendment that he personally engineered allowing for reelection, Cardoso won a second term, running against Workers Party candidate Luis Inácio Lula da Silva. He based his campaign on propaganda that promised a return to economic growth and an end to unemployment. Cardoso managed to avoid draconian economic measures and a 35% currency devaluation until the day after the election. Then, new taxes and budget cuts were announced, recession settled in, and unemployment soared. In 1999 Cardoso's popularity was at a record low, causing nationwide calls for his resignation. He held on—ruling with more gusto than his military predecessors—by churning out endless "temporary" executive decrees, which bypassed normal legislative procedures. Before the first quarter of 2001 was over, Cardoso had signed 48,000 such decrees in a seven-year period. The crowning reaction by Brazilians to what they saw as eight years of economic and political mismanagement came on October 27, 2002, with the landslide election of Lula da Silva over Cardoso's protégé, José Serra.

In Brasília, on January 1, 2003, the many acres between the Esplanada dos Ministérios and the Praça dos Três Poderes were jammed with a euphoric crowd—people carrying children and flags, street vendors peddling umbrellas and raincoats. On television, in Brazil and worldwide, millions of curious eyes watched as Lula da Silva, a 57-year-old former steelworker, born in dire poverty, took office with pomp and circumstance as the nation's new president. Elected with 52.7 million votes, his campaign had consistently emphasized themes of hope, love, and peace. People believed in him, hoping he would be up to the huge task that lay ahead. For the time being, whether he will succeed is anyone's guess.

As the local saying goes, patience and chicken soup harm no one. Brazilians know how to be patient and resilient under stress. Many of them see the careful but earnest first steps of the new government as a good omen. Economic recovery may be slow and political healing difficult, but it's almost impossible to lose faith in such a rich land. The dream is not over. Certainly, there are other victories in store for the coming years: a sports crown, beating inflation, or even (why not?) an Academy Award.

— by José Fonseca

Born and raised in Minas Gerais, journalist José Fonseca left Brazil at the start of the military dictatorship, earned a master's degree from the University of Kansas, and then spent more than 10 years in Europe and west Africa before returning to Brazil. Working as a environmental journalist, translator, and writer, he is now based in Porto Alegre, where he lives with his anthropologist wife and his cats and dogs.

CHRONOLOGY

1494 The Treaty of Tordesillas divides lands to be discovered in the New World between Spain and Portugal.

1500 On April 22 a Portuguese fleet commanded by 30-year-old Pedro Álvares Cabral lands on Brazil's easternmost point, near present-day Porto Seguro in the state of Bahia.

1502 On January 1 a Portuguese fleet commanded by Amerigo Vespucci first sights Guanabara Bay. Thinking it the mouth of a mighty river, he names it Rio de Janeiro (River of January).

1503 The name *Brasil* is used for the first time, taken from the Indian name of *pau-brasil* (brazilwood), valued for its red dye.

1532 The first Portuguese colony, called São Vicente, is established in the southern part of the land.

1549 A government seat is established in Salvador in the northeast to administer the colony as a whole and the unsuccessful system of 15 captaincies into which it had been divided in 1533. In the same year the first Africans are imported as slaves.

1554 A Jesuit mission is established at São Vicente, giving birth to the city of São Paulo.

1555–65 French forces hold Guanabara Bay.

1567 The Portuguese governor general establishes the city of Rio de Janeiro on Guanabara Bay.

1621 Dutch attacks on northeastern Brazil begin. These continue—with the Dutch gaining, holding, and then losing territory—for the next 30-odd years.

1633 Work begins on Rio's Benedictine monastery of São Bento, famed for its elaborate gold-leaf interior.

1654 The Dutch are completely ousted from the northeastern regions.

1694 Colonial forces find and destroy Palmares, the largest of the *quilombos* (communities formed in the forest by runaway slaves). Palmares and its leader, Zumbi, still appear in modern stories, films, and songs.

1695 Gold is discovered in Minas Gerais. Great inland colonial cities and churches are built with the sudden new wealth, and for the next century Brazilian gold enriches and supports the government of Portugal.

1720 Rio's landmark Glória church is built. Named Nossa Senhora da Glória do Outeiro (Our Lady of Glory on the Hill), the small baroque beauty stands on a low rise and looks out across Guanabara Bay.

1750 The Treaty of Madrid recognizes Portuguese rule of what is roughly today's Brazil.

1759 Jesuit priests are expelled from Brazil after 200 years of conflict with both colonial factors and the Portuguese government.

1763 With a shift away from wealth and power in the northeast, which had been based on sugar, to a newer center of influence in the southeast, based on gold, the capital is moved from Salvador to Rio de Janeiro.

1792 The Inconfidência Mineira, an independence movement based in Minas Gerais and spurred by repressive taxation policies, comes to an end when its leader, Tiradentes (Tooth Puller), is hanged in Rio de Janeiro.

1807 Portugal is conquered by Napoléon, and King João VI goes into exile in Brazil. With his court in Rio de Janeiro and with a new understanding of the colony from which he now directs all Portuguese affairs, he introduces reforms and permits Brazil to trade with other countries.

1814 Aleijadinho dies, leaving behind a timeless treasure of religious art in the churches of his native state of Minas Gerais.

1821 King João returns to Portugal. His son, Dom Pedro, is named Prince Regent of Brazil.

1822 On September 7 Pedro I proclaims the Brazilian Empire and independence from Portugal, partly to establish his own position and partly to continue the reforms begun by his father. The United States recognizes the new nation in 1824; Portugal does so in 1825.

1824 Austrian-born Empress Dona Leopoldina, wife of Pedro I, begins a campaign to populate the southern Brazilian countryside with European farmers. For the next 30 years colonists from Germany, Italy, and elsewhere settle in this region.

1831 Hoping to regain the throne of Portugal for himself, Pedro I abdicates in favor of his son, Pedro II, who is only five. Until 1840 the country suffers through a period of unrest and rebellion under a regency of political leaders.

1840–89 The reign of Pedro II brings further reforms and economic stability and earns the king the respect of Abraham Lincoln. But territorial skirmishes with neighboring countries bring the military to prominence.

1850 The importation of African slaves comes to an end.

1855 The first Carnaval celebration is held in Rio de Janeiro.

1871 All children of slaves are declared free.

1881 The Teatro Amazonas, modeled on the Paris Opera, opens in Manaus, capital of the Amazon.

1884 The first railway line takes passengers to the top of Corcovado, overlooking Rio de Janeiro.

1885 All slaves over the age of 60 are freed.

1888   On May 13 all remaining slaves (nearly a million people) are freed. Brazil begins to even more aggressively recruit agricultural laborers from Germany, Italy, Portugal, and Spain.

1889   A bloodless military coup overthrows Pedro II and sends him into exile in France. On November 15 the Republic of Brazil is founded.

1890–1910   Manaus and the Amazon region produce tremendous wealth in the rubber trade. At the same time, the wealth of coffee growers shifts power from Rio de Janeiro to São Paulo.

1894   Prudente de Morais is elected as Brazil's first nonmilitary president.

1906   Alberto Santos-Dumont brings glory to Brazil with the first self-propelled, heavier-than-air plane flight.

1908   The first Japanese immigrants arrive in Brazil to work on coffee plantations. Today most of their descendants are settled in São Paulo, which has the largest Japanese population of any city outside Tokyo.

1910   The government's first official Indian advocacy agency, the Service for the Protection of the Indians (SPI), is founded by adventurer Cândido Mariana da Silva Rondon, for whom the state of Rondônia was later named.

1912   The first cable car carries passengers to the top of Sugarloaf, at the mouth of Rio's Guanabara Bay.

1913   Rondon and former U.S. president Theodore Roosevelt mount the Rondon-Roosevelt Expedition into the Amazon.

1917   Ernesto dos Santos, known as Donga, records "Pelo Telefone" ("On the Telephone"), the first song designated a samba. It's the hit of the year and forever changes the music of Carnaval.

1922   A "Week of Modern Art" is held in São Paulo, celebrating the latest ideas in painting and poetry. It crystallizes and legitimizes the newest styles and trends and encourages artists to find a truly Brazilian way to adopt them.

1923   The Copacabana Palace opens on Rio's famed beachfront and continues for decades as a mecca for gamblers (until 1946, when gambling is outlawed in Brazil), international high society, and countless celebrities and heads of state.

1927   Henry Ford makes the first of two unsuccessful attempts to establish his own rubber plantation in Brazil.

1930   With the support of the military, Getúlio Vargas becomes president and assumes dictatorial powers, but he introduces many social reforms and is initially extremely popular.

1931   The monumental statue of Cristo Redentor (Christ the Redeemer) is unveiled atop Corcovado, rising 30 meters (100 feet) above the 701-meter (2,300-foot) granite peak.

1938   Brazil is the first country in Latin America to send a national soccer team to the World Cup finals.

1942 Brazil declares war on Germany and sends 25,000 troops to fight in Italy.

1945 Getúlio Vargas is forced out of office by the military.

1950 Vargas becomes president again, this time elected by the people.

1951 In Rio during the early 1950s, Ipanema's dirt roads and beach cottages are replaced with fashionable, expensive apartments and shops.

1954 Again threatened by a military coup, Vargas commits suicide in the presidential palace.

1956 The new president, Juscelino Kubitschek, announces plans to attract foreign investments and develop Brazilian industry. He also promises to make real an old Brazilian dream of a new capital city.

1958 With Pelé on the team, Brazil wins the World Cup.

1959 João Gilberto's first album, *Chega de Saudade* (*No More Sadness*), which includes his famous "Desafinado" ("Out of Tune"), firmly establishes bossa nova as Brazil's most popular new music. In the same year the film *Orfeu Negro* (*Black Orpheus*) brings to the world the colors of Rio's Carnaval and the brilliance of Brazilian music.

1960 On April 19, after four years of furious work, President Kubitschek inaugurates the new capital city of Brasília, designed by Oscar Niemeyer and Lúcio Costa.

1964 *Getz/Gilberto,* the album that includes Astrud Gilberto's famous vocals on "The Girl from Ipanema," is released and becomes an instant classic around the world. In the same year a military coup ousts President João Goulart, and the generals begin a 20-year period of repression, runaway inflation, and enormous national debt.

1967 The current governmental Indian advocacy group, FUNAI (Fundação Nacional do Indio, or the National Indian Foundation), is established.

1970 Copacabana's beach is widened and the now-famous mosaic sidewalks designed by Roberto Burle Marx are installed on Avenida Atlântica.

1973 Singer-songwriter Chico Buarque releases "Cálice," a song whose title means "chalice" but sounds the same as "shut up" in Portuguese, turning it into a song of protest against governmental repression. From 1969 until 1972, just prior to its release, Buarque and fellow musician Caetano Veloso had been in exile.

1981–83 Following a brief economic boom in the late 1970s, a period of deep recession leads to the downfall of the military government.

1984 Rio's Sambadrome, designed by Oscar Niemeyer, opens for Carnaval.

1985 José Sarney becomes president. His Cruzado Plan fails to control inflation.

1988 A new constitution returns freedoms, ends censorship, and guarantees rights for Indians. In the same year Chico Mendes, a spokesman for the rain forest and its rubber tappers, is murdered.

1989 In this year's election, Luiz Ignácio da Silva, known as Lula, a trade union leader, comes to national prominence, but he loses to Fernando Collor de Mello. Chief Raoni of the Megkroniti tribe embarks on a worldwide tour with the rock musician Sting to garner support for Brazil's Indians and to raise overall environmental consciousness.

1990 The day after he takes office, Collor de Mello orders harsh fiscal constraints that only briefly stem the growth of inflation.

1991 Brazil takes the lead in forming MERCOSUL, a trade alliance that includes Argentina, Paraguay, and Uruguay.

1992 The United Nations holds the Earth Summit in Rio de Janeiro. In December Collor de Mello, brought down by corruption scandals, resigns the presidency on the brink of impeachment.

1994 Fernando Henrique Cardoso is elected president. His Plano Real finally stabilizes the economy and curbs inflation. Brazil takes the lead in building more trade alliances and expands its role in international affairs.

1999 After a constitutional amendment, Cardoso is permitted to run for a second term and wins. Despite bumps in the road, the Brazilian economy appears stable and progress continues.

2001 An economic crisis in Argentina, a major trading partner, causes the real to fall in relation to the dollar, but the Brazilian economy remains strong and on track.

2002 After running for office three times, Lula (Luiz Ignácio da Silva) is voted president in a much-anticipated election. He vows to combat hunger and poverty in Brazil. Singer Gilberto Gil is appointed minister of culture.

2003 In his first year in office, Lula aimed at preventing inflation from rising again. The economy slowed down as unemployment rates rose. Still, popular support for Lula's administration remained strong.

BRAZIL AT A GLANCE

Understanding Brazil

Name in Portuguese: Brasil
Capital: Brasília
National anthem: Hino Nacional Brasileiro
Type of government: Federative republic
Administrative divisions: 26 states, 1 federal district (Brasília)
Independence: September 7, 1822, from Portugal
Constitution: October 5, 1988
Legal system: Each state has its own judicial system; disputes between states and matters outside the jurisdiction of state courts are settled by federal courts
Suffrage: Voluntary between 16 and 18 years of age and over 70; compulsory over 18 and under 70 years of age
Legislature: Bicameral Congresso Nacional (National Congress), comprising the Federal Senate and the Chamber of Deputies. Senate has 81 members, representing each state and the federal district of Brasilia. The Chamber of Deputies has 513 members, directly elected
Population: 182,032,604
Fertility rate: 2.05 children per woman
Life expectancy: Female 68, male 60
Literacy: Total population 83.3%; male 83.3%, female 83.2%
Language: Portuguese
Ethnic groups: White (includes Portuguese, German, Italian, Spanish, Polish) 55%, mixed white and African 38%, African 6%, other (includes Japanese, Arab, Amerindian) 1%
Religion: Catholic 73.8%, Protestant 15.4%, no religion 7.3%

Geography and Environment

Land area: 8,511,965 square km (3,286,470 square mi); slightly larger than the continental United States; occupies nearly 50% of South America
Coastline: 7,367 km (4,578 mi); bordered by the Altantic Ocean to the east
Border countries: Argentina 1,224 km, Bolivia 3,400 km, Colombia 1,643 km, French Guiana 673 km, Guyana 1,119 km, Paraguay 1,290 km, Peru 1,560 km, Suriname 597 km, Uruguay 985 km, Venezuela 2,200 km
Terrain: Highlands and some mountains in the south; Amazon Basin and flat and rolling lowlands in the north; cerrado in central Brazil, with savannah, woodland, and dry forest
Land use: Forests 58%, pasture 22%, crops 6%, other 14%
Natural resources: Bauxite, gold, iron ore, manganese, nickel, phosphates, platinum, tin, uranium, petroleum, hydropower, timber
Natural hazards: Droughts in northeast, floods and some frost in the south
Flora: 45,000 species (22% of world total)
Fauna: 524 mammal species (131 endemic), 517 amphibian species (294 endemic), 1,677 bird species (191 endemic), 468 reptile species (172 endemic), 3,000 freshwater fish species, and 1.5 million insect species; Brazil ranks first in the world for numbers of species of primates, amphibians and plants; third for bird species; and fourth for species of butterflies and reptiles
Endangered species: 395
Environmental issues: Deforestation in Amazon Basin and subsequent endangerment of plant and animal species; illegal wildlife trade; air and water pollution in Rio de Janeiro, São Paulo, and some other large cities; land degradation and water pollution due to mining activities; wetland degradation; oil spills

Economy

Currency: reais (singular: real)
GDP: $1.34 trillion
Per capita income: $7,250
Inflation: 7.7%
Unemployment: 6.4%
Work force: 79 million (services 53%, agriculture 23%, industry 24%)
Debt: $232 billion
Major industries: Textiles, shoes, chemicals, cement, lumber, iron ore, tin, steel, aircraft, motor vehicles and parts, other machinery and equipment.
Agricultural products: Coffee, soybeans, wheat, rice, corn, sugarcane, cocoa, citrus, beef

Exports: $57.8 billion
Major export products: Manufactures, iron ore, soybeans, footwear, coffee, autos
Major export partners: U.S. 20.5%, Argentina 9.5%, Netherlands 7.1%, Japan 5.9%, Germany 4.7%, other European Union 27.1%
Imports: $57.7 billion
Major import products: Machinery and equipment, chemical products, oil, electricity, autos and auto parts
Import partners: U.S. 23.6%, Argentina 11.0%, Germany 10.4%, Japan 5.4%, other European Union 25.4%

Did You Know?

• Brazil is the fifth largest country in the world after Russia, Canada, the United States, and China.

• Brazil is the second largest producer of gold.

• 60% of the world's precious stones is found in Brazil.

• Diamonds mined in Brazil are more resistant to scratching than those mined in Africa.

• Nearly half of the world's supply of cocoa is from Brazil.

• Brazil has never won a gold medal for soccer at the Olympics.

• Aviator Alberto Santos-Dumont, from Minas Gerais, flew Europe's first airplane in 1906.

• Soccer superstar Pelé scored 1,279 goals, more than any player in history.

• The Pantanal has the world's largest tract of swamp, about 42,000 square miles.

• In the 1988 mayoral election in Rio, a chimp heading the "Brazilian Banana Party" came in third place, with 400,00 votes.

• Brazil has nearly 40 political parties.

• The country has the sixth largest population in the world, but there are only 15 people per square mile.

BRAZILIAN MUSIC: THE HEARTBEAT OF THE COUNTRY

Nothing in the world sounds like the music of Brazil. Whether you're listening to a rousing samba on a restaurant radio, a soothing bossa nova in a beachside café, or an uplifting Afro-Brazilian spiritist song on the street, you know instantly that you're hearing the country's beating heart. And even a short list of musical styles—which are as often linked to rhythms and dances as they are to tunes and lyrics—rolls off the tongue like an ancient chant: *axé, bossa nova, forró, frevo, maracatu, samba, tropicalismo.* Many of these are divided into subcategories, with varying types of lyrics, singing styles, arrangements, and instrumentation. Some also fall into the supercategory of *música popular brasileira* (MPB, or Brazilian popular music). All fill the ear with a seamless and enchanting blend of European, African, native Indian, and regional Brazilian sound.

History explains the eclecticism. The Portuguese colonists brought the Western tonal system and the music of the church with them to Brazil. When they arrived, they encountered the music of the native Indians, which was almost exclusively percussive. The African slaves added fresh, varied rhythms and a love for choral singing to the mix. In a country this large, it isn't surprising that different regions would develop their own styles as well. From the northeast alone come forró, which uses the accordion to its best and most rhythmic advantage; axé, a Bahian blend of samba and reggae; maracatu, a percussive beat derived from Afro-Brazilian religious traditions, and frevo, a fast-pace dance music, the last two most associated with Recife's Carnaval.

Although varied, Brazilian music is always characterized by complex rhythms and layers of textured sounds. Performers often embrace the use of violins, accordions, and flutes in their compositions. Some, such as Hermeto Pascoal and Naná

Vasconcelos, have innovative keyboard or percussion styles; others, such as Milton Nascimento, incorporate moving choral arrangements. Very often, musical groups have a percussionist armed with chimes, rattles, and shells, all used so subtly as to belie the word *noisemaker.* Most distinctive of all is the squeaking sound of the *cuíca,* and a solo on this samba instrument, made from a metal can, will always bring an audience to its feet.

Samba: The Spirit of Carnaval

The music for which Brazil is perhaps most famous is believed to have its roots in *lundu,* a Bantu rhythm reminiscent of a fandango yet characterized by a hip-swiveling style of dance, and *maxixe,* a mixture of polka as well as Latin and African rhythms. The earliest references to samba appear in the late 19th century, and one theory suggests the term comes from the Bantu word *semba,* meaning "gyrating movement." "Pelo Telefone" ("On the Telephone"), the first song actually designated a samba, was recorded in 1917. By the 1930s samba was being played in Rio de Janeiro's Carnaval parades, and by the 1960s it was the indisputable music of Carnaval. Today its many forms include the pure samba *de raiz* (literally, "roots samba"), the popular *pagode,* based on a small guitarlike instrument called a *cavaquinho,* and the samba *canção* (the more familiar "samba song").

Samba evokes the spirit of Carnaval, regardless of when it's played. In cities such as Rio, Salvador, and São Paulo, entire neighborhoods are divided into *escolas de samba* (samba schools), which work all year on costumes, floats, dances, and music to prepare for the pre-Lenten festivities. Composers who might have remained unknown, such as Carlos Cachaça and the legendary Cartola, have become revered *sambistas* thanks to Carnaval and its escolas. Some schools also recruit well-known samba singers such as Martinho da Vila to perform what they hope will be the winning composition in the Carnaval competitions. Although today's Carnaval is big business, it manages to remain honest to this great country's soul. Costumed dancers still swirl, drums still thunder, and sweating faces still smile through it all. The opening line of one samba from Rio's Portela School says it all: "Samba may suffer, but it never dies."

Bossa Nova & Beyond

Although Brazilian music has a long, rich history, it wasn't until the 1959 film *Black Orpheus* that it reached the outside world in a big way. The movie retells the Greek legend of Orpheus and Eurydice, only this time the tragic love story is set amid Rio de Janeiro's Carnaval. It's a great film, but what most people treasure is the beauty of its music, by Antônio Carlos Jobim (known affectionately as "Tom") and Luís Bonfá.

In the early 1960s things happened that caused the world to listen ever more closely to Brazilian music. Artists and intellectuals began gathering in the cafés and apartments of Rio's chic Zona Sul neighborhoods of Copacabana, Ipanema, and Leblon. From the mix of personalities and the air of creative freedom arose a sound never heard before. It came first from the voice and the guitar of a young songwriter named João Gilberto. He sang in an understated, breathy way, and when he recorded the song "Desafinado," he virtually stated a new philosophy of music. The title means "out of tune," and, indeed, a few listeners thought he was. Melodic lines went in unexpected directions and ended in surprising places, and under those melodies was a cool, intricate rhythm.

During this period Tom Jobim and his frequent collaborator, Vinicius de Moraes (former diplomat, lifelong poet and lyricist, and later singer), met daily at a corner café in Ipanema. And every day, while seated at their preferred table, they saw the same beautiful teenage girl pass along the street between the beach and her home. They felt compelled to pay tribute both to her beauty and to the way she made them feel; so they composed a song. Tom wrote the music, Vinicius the lyrics, and "The Girl from Ipanema" was born. Today that café is known as Garota de Ipanema, the song's title in Portuguese, and the street that it's on has been renamed in honor of Vinicius.

Already influenced by Miles Davis and the cool California jazz made popular by Chet Baker, Gerry Mulligan, and others, American jazz musicians began heading to Rio. The great saxophonist Stan Getz was among the first to arrive. He teamed up with Tom Jobim and João Gilberto to record an album. At the last minute it was decided that João's wife, who wasn't actually a singer, would perform both the Portuguese and English versions of "The Girl from Ipanema." Soon, Astrud Gilberto was a star, and the song became the quintessential bossa nova hit.

Loosely translated, the term *bossa nova* means "new thing," and its greatest songs are recorded time and again, presenting ever-new challenges to each generation of performers. The latest include Bebel Gilberto, daughter of João Gilberto, who in 2000 released *Tanto Tempo (So Much Time)*—an album mixing electronic music and bossa that topped the charts in both Europe and the United States.

The politically turbulent late 1960s and 1970s saw the development of the tropicalismo movement. Musicians and intellectuals like Caetano Veloso, Chico Buarque, Tom Zé, and Gilberto Gil began using such contemporary instruments as the electric guitar and keyboard in their works. They also combined rock-and-roll and avant-garde experimentation with samba and other traditional rhythms. Often the tunes were upbeat, though the lyrics, which were frequently written in double and triple entendres, were critical of social and political injustices.

Tropicalismo sparked such heated debate that an angry Veloso once harangued a São Paulo audience for being unwilling to accept anything new. Despite this controversy, the music gained a strong enough following that it brought about the attention and disapproval of the military regimes. Some of its performers were arrested; others had to live abroad for several years.

The tendency to mix traditional rhythms with electric instruments spawned *samba rock* and its major star Jorge Ben, a.k.a. Jorge Benjor, whose hit "Taj Mahal" was copycatted on Rod Stewart's "Do Ya Think I'm Sexy?" Jorge Ben and other groups, including the now-revered Mutantes, would later be considered the first Brazilian rock acts.

From the 1970s on, Jamaican reggae became part of the Brazilian mix. Gilberto Gil's recordings of classic Bob Marley songs, including "No Woman, No Cry," honor their source and yet have a richness all their own. The dreadlocked singer Carlinhos Brown and his group, Timbalada, as well as several other groups from the state of Bahia, blend reggae sounds with the traditional rhythms of northeastern Brazil. São Luís do Maranhão, nicknamed "reggae capital of the country," is in the state of Maranhão, in the northeast.

The two following decades witnessed the birth and consolidation of Brazilian rock and pop music. The process culminated in the early '90s with the rise of the MPopB generation, whose idol was the now-defunct Chico Science and his *mangue beat* band Nação Zumbi. MPopB mixes hip-hop, funk, rock, traditional rhythms, and electronic beats.

During the latter half of the 20th century, Brazilian musicians collaborated with or influenced several U.S. performers. Tom Jobim recorded two classic albums with Frank Sinatra and appeared again on Sinatra's *Duets* album. Wayne Shorter introduced Milton Nascimento to North America as a vocalist on his 1975 album, *Native Dancer*. Paul Simon found inspiration in the music of Bahia for his *Rhythm of the Saints* album. David Byrne has championed many Brazilian singers with his compilations of Brazilian music. And James Taylor has recorded and often performed with Nascimento. The song "Only a Dream in Rio" appears on albums by each man, and they made a memorable appearance together at the 2001 Rock in Rio music festival.

Brazilian Voices

One of the greatest strengths of Brazilian music is its number of extraordinary female vocalists. Although Carmen Miranda may always have a special place in many hearts, by general agreement the country's greatest woman singer was Elis Regina, who died in 1982 at the age of 37. Her pure voice, perfect diction, emotional performance, and wonderful melodic sense made her unique. Among her many great albums, those recorded with Tom Jobim and Milton Nascimento are considered the best. For samba, the recordings made by Clara Nunes, who also died at an early age, are *the* classics for most Brazilians.

Today singers such as Gal Costa, Maria Bethânia (Caetano Veloso's sister), Beth Carvalho, Elba Ramalho, Alcione, Marisa Monte, Daniela Mercury, Ivete Sangalo, and Adriana Calcanhoto fill concert halls at home and abroad. Far from the top charts, Virginia Rodrigues applies a voice of operatic quality to both beautiful ballads and impassioned songs in praise of the *orixás* (African spiritual deities), whereas Teresa Cristina's renditions of traditional sambas de raiz judiciously add her name to the ever-growing list of excellent Brazilian female voices.

Another characteristic of the country's singers is making their voices heard in forms of expression other than popular music. Several have written film scores. Milton Nascimento has composed a mass. Chico Buarque and Vinicius de Moraes are highly regarded poets; Buarque is also a novelist and playwright. Caetano Veloso has written a lengthy memoir and meditation on music called *Verdade Tropical* (*Tropical Truth*). Gilberto Gil has held a seat on Salvador's city council and in early 2003 became minister of culture. Brazil's greatest artists are often more than mere pop stars, and the country acknowledges their efforts. Vinicius de Moraes isn't the only one with a street named in his honor. And though many Brazilians still refer to Rio's international airport as Galeão, after the death of Antônio Carlos Jobim, it was renamed for him.

A Few Notes of Your Own

The following anthologies provide good samplings of Brazilian singers, composers, and styles. If you like these, you can seek out CDs by individual artists.

Brasil: a Century of Song (Blue Jackel). This box set with a 48-page booklet and four CDs comprises the best of folk and traditional songs (Carmen Miranda, Pena Branca e Xavantinho), carnival music (Paulinho da Viola, Mangueira), bossa nova (João Gilberto, Toquinho e Vinícius), and MPB (Marisa Monte, Ivan Lins).

Brazil Classics 1: Beleza Tropical (Sire). The 18 tracks, compiled by David Byrne, include songs by Milton Nascimento, Caetano Veloso, Jorge Ben, Maria Bethânia, Gal Costa, and Chico Buarque.

Brazil Classics 2: O Samba (Sire). David Byrne compiled these 15 tracks that include sambas by Alcione, Clara Nunes, Beth Carvalho, Martinho da Vila, and others.

For updated info and complete discographies, you can refer to the **All Brazilian Music Guide** (⊕ www.allbrazilianmusic. com).

— by Alan Ryan

Novelist and journalist Alan Ryan has written extensively about Brazilian music, literature, and culture for many newspapers and magazines. He lives in Rio de Janeiro.

BOOKS & MOVIES

Books

On the nonfiction front, Joseph A. Page provides a fascinating, highly readable overview of Brazilian history and culture in his book *The Brazilians*. Along the same lines is Marshall C. Eakin's *Brazil: The Once and Future Country*. A short but good new history by Brazilian scholar Boris Fausto is *A Concise History of Brazil*. Social anthropologist Claude Lévi-Strauss discusses his research of Amazonian peoples in *Tristes Tropiques,* a book that's part travelogue, part scientific notebook—with many interesting observations and anecdotes.

Chris McGowan's *The Brazilian Sound: Samba, Bossa Nova, and the Popular Music of Brazil* provides an overview of the country's 20th-century music. Also recommended is *Bossa Nova: The Story of the Brazilian Music That Seduced the World,* by Ruy Castro. Christopher Idone's *Brazil: A Cook's Tour* has more than 100 color photos and 100 recipes. *Eat Smart in Brazil,* by Joan and David Peterson, is a good introduction to Brazilian food, with history, color photos, recipes, and a detailed glossary.

Fiction lovers should try John Grisham's captivating *The Testament,* in which a lawyer voyages to the Pantanal Wetlands to search for a missionary who has inherited a fortune. Several Jorge Amado titles, which are usually set in his native Bahia, are available in English, including *Dona Flor and Her Two Husbands*; *Gabriela, Clove and Cinnamon*; and *The War of the Saints.*

Movies

City of God (2002), the story of adolescents living in the violent favelas of Rio, was nominated for an Academy Award for Best Foreign Film in 2003. A chilling fictional account of street kids in São Paulo is *Pixote* (1981). In 1969, following the military takeover of the Brazilian government, Marxist revolutionaries kidnapped an American diplomat in protest. *Four Days in September* (1998) is an entertaining and well-executed film that tells the story of these young revolutionaries. *Central Station* (1998) is a heartwarming tale of the unlikely friendship between an orphaned street child and a middle-aged woman who is soured on life. *Bus 174* (2002) is a highly acclaimed documentary about a bus hijacking that took place Rio in 2000. *Black Orpheus* (1956) is one of the best known Brazilian films. It won an Academy Award in 1960 and is based on the Greek tragedy of Orpheus, set in a Rio favela around Carnaval. The 1999 update, *Orfeu,* brings the tale into modern times.

The lighter side of Brazilian culture is explored in movies such as *Bossa Nova* (2000), a romantic comedy set in Rio, and *Tieta de Agreste* (1996), the story of a successful businesswoman who returns to her home in a small village in the Northeast. The latter has some lovely shots of the northeastern landscape. For more views of the Brazilian countryside, see *Bye, Bye Brazil* (1979), which follows a group of traveling entertainers from the Northeast to the Amazon jungle; *Me, You, Them* (2000), a story of woman in the Northeast who forms a series of unusual romantic relationships; and *Behind the Sun* (2001), a depressing film that portrays two feuding families in the Northeast of 1910. The acclaimed *Dona Flor and Her Two Husbands* (1978) follows a Bahian woman through joys and hardships. *The Boys from Brazil* (1990), not to be confused with the similarly named drama about hunting Nazis in Brazil, is a BBC documentary about Brazilian soccer.

MENU GUIDE

Portuguese	English

General Dining

Acompanhamento	Side dish
Almoço	Lunch
Café da manhã	Breakfast
Entradas	Appetizers
Jantar	Dinner
Prato principal	Main course
Prato do dia	Daily special

Dining Establishments

Café	Coffee shop; also serves small meals or snacks
Churrascaria	Brazilian barbecue restaurant
Confeitaria/doceria	Pastry shop
Lanchonete	Snack bar
Pastelaria	Shop that sells fried Brazilian-style pastry with fillings
Quilo	Buffet restaurant where food is charged by its weight
Restaurante	Restaurant
Sorveteria	Ice-cream parlor

Café da Manhã

Cereais	Cereal
Geléia	Jam
Iogurte	Yogurt
Manteiga	Butter
Mel	Honey
Omelete	Omelet
Ovos	Eggs
−Cozidos	Hard-boiled
−Quentes	Soft-boiled
−Fritos/estrelados	Fried
−Mexidos	Scrambled
Pão	Bread
Queijo	Cheese
Torrada	Toast
Requeijão	Brazilian-style cream cheese

Peixes e Frutos do Mar (Fish and Seafood)

Atum	Tuna
Badejo	Similar to sea bass
Camarão	Shrimp

Caranguejo	Crab
Lagosta	Lobster
Lula	Squid
Mexilhão	Mussels
Molusco/marisco	Clams
Ostra	Oyster
Pescado	Another word for "fish"
Pirarucu	Amazon river fish
Pitu	Giant prawn
Robalo	Snook
Salmão	Salmon
Sardinha	Sardine

Carne e Aves (Meat and Poultry)

Ao ponto	Medium (cooking instructions)
Bife/filé	Steak
Carne de vaca/boi	Beef
Carneiro	Lamb
Carne de porco	Pork
Chouriço/ lingüiça/ salsicha	Sausage
Frango/galinha	Chicken
Mal passado/bem passado	Rare/well done
Pato	Duck
Peito	Breast
Peru	Turkey
Presunto	Ham
Toucinho	Bacon

Legumes/Verduras (Vegetables)

Alcachofra	Artichoke
Alface	Lettuce
Batata	Potato
Cebola	Onion
Cenoura	Carrot
Chuchu	Type of squash
Cogumelo	Mushroom
Couve	Collard greens
Couve-flor	Cauliflower
Repolho	Cabbage
Espinafre	Spinach
Feijão	Beans
Mandioca	Manioc, cassava
Milho	Corn
Palmito	Palm heart
Pepino	Cucumber

Pimentão	Sweet pepper
Quiabo	Okra

Frutas/Castanhas (Fruits/Nuts)

Abacaxi	Pineapple
Abacate	Avocado
Açaí	Dark-purple Amazon fruit
Banana	Banana
Caqui	Persimmon
Carambola	Starfruit
Castanha de caju	Cashew nuts
Castanha-do-pará	Brazil nuts
Cereja	Cherry
Coco	Coconut
Cupuaçu	Amazon fruit used in desserts and juice
Framboesa	Raspberry
Goiaba	Guava
Graviola	Cherimoya (tropical fruit)
Laranja	Orange
Limão	Lime
Lima	Lemon
Maçã	Apple
Mamão papaia	Papaya
Manga	Mango
Maracujá	Passion fruit
Melancia	Watermelon
Melão	Melon
Morango	Strawberry
Pêra	Pear
Pêssego	Peach
Tomate	Tomato
Toranja	Grapefruit
Uva	Grape

Lanches (Snacks) and Fast Food

Batata frita	French fries/potato chips
Cachorro quente	Hot dog
Coxinha	Chicken rolled in dough and fried
Empada, empadinha	Pastry shell filled with cheese, shrimp or chicken
Mandioca frita	Fried manioc
Misto quente	Toasted ham-and-cheese sandwich
Pão de queijo	Cheese rolls

Pipoca	Popcorn
Salgado	Savory snacks like empadas, pão
de queijo, or coxinhas	
Sanduíche	Sandwich
X-burger	Cheeseburger (pronounced *sheesh-*
burger)	

Sobremesas (Desserts)

Arroz doce	Rice pudding
Baba-de-moça	Dessert of egg yolk, coconut milk,
and syrup	
Biscoito/bolacha	Cookie
Bolo	Cake
Canjica	Dessert of sweet corn and coconut
milk	
Cocada	Similar to a coconut macaroon
Pudim	Custard
Sorvete	Ice cream

Bebidas (Beverages)

Água de coco	Coconut water
Água mineral (com gás/sem gás)	(Carbonated/still) mineral water
Batida	Cachaça blended with fruit and ice
Cachaça, pinga	Sugar cane liquor
Café	Coffee
–Preto	Black (without milk)
–Com leite	With milk
Cafezinho	Small cup of strong and sweet cof-
fee	
Caipirinha	Cachaça mixed with sugar, ice, and
crushed lime	
Cerveja	Beer
Chá (com leite/limáo:	Tea (with milk/lemon)
Chá/café gelado	Iced tea/coffee
Chocolate quente	Hot chocolate
Chopp	Draught beer
Com água/soda	With water/soda
Com gelo	On the rocks
Guaraná	Tropical fruit soft drink
Leite (frio/quente)	(Cold/hot) milk
Limonada	Lemonade
Refrigerante	Soft drink
Suco (de laranja)	(Orange) juice
Vinho (tinto/branco)	(Red/white) wine
Vitamina	Fruit blended with milk

Other Useful Words

Açúcar	Sugar
Alho	Garlic
Arroz	Rice
Azeite	Olive oil
Cardápio	Menu
Colher	Spoon
Conta/nota	Bill
Dendê	Palm oil
Faca	Knife
Farinha	Flour
Farofa	Manioc flour sautéed in butter
Garfo	Fork
Manteiga	Butter
Molho	Sauce
Pimenta	Pepper
Sal	Salt
Salada	Salad
Sopa/caldo	Soup

BRAZILIAN RECIPES

The sumptuous stews, luscious desserts, and tasty side dishes of Brazil reflect the country's spirit, especially when the dishes are homemade. We've gathered a selection of typical dishes from local sources—from the omnipresent *feijoada* (black beans and pork stew) to the rich dessert *quindim* (egg and coconut custard).

Coxinha de galinha

Brazilians eat *coxinhas* (mock chicken legs) as a snack, but you can also try them as an appetizer.

Ingredients:
3-pound chicken, cut into pieces
3 tablespoons olive oil
3 cloves garlic, minced
1 medium onion, chopped
1 bay leaf
Salt and pepper to taste
1 cup rice flour
2 cups milk
1 cup reserved chicken broth
3 egg yolks, beaten
1 tablespoon butter
1 malagueta pepper (or any red chili pepper), finely chopped
4 cups fine bread crumbs
2 eggs, beaten
Vegetable oil for frying

Directions:
Sauté the chicken in olive oil. Add garlic, onion, bay leaf, salt, and pepper to taste. Cover with water and simmer until done. Remove chicken and reserve 1 cup broth. Take the meat off the bones. Reserve 15 thin strips of chicken and finely chop the remainder. Whisk together the flour, milk, and reserved broth until smooth and cook over medium heat until thickened, stirring constantly. Remove from heat and stir in egg yolks, butter, chicken and malagueta pepper. Adjust the seasonings to taste. Return to heat and stir until quite thick. Completely cool mixture in refrigerator. Take an amount the size of a large egg and shape it around a reserved strip of chicken, forming an oval dough ball. Roll in bread crumbs, dip into beaten eggs, and cover with another layer of bread crumbs. Fry in hot oil until golden brown.

Feijoada

Since it was first created from pork odds and ends by Bahia's African slaves, this black-bean stew with roasted and boiled meats has become Brazil's national dish. *Feijoada* is eaten with rice, collard greens (see next recipe), cracklings, and pepper sauce. Try it with the unbeatable *caipirinha* (lime and sugarcane brandy cocktail), as Brazilians from all over the country often do.

Ingredients:
2 cups (1 pound) black beans, rinsed and picked over
¾ pound pork butt or shoulder, trimmed of fat
6 ounces slab bacon
½ pound smoked pork sausages
½ pound hot Portuguese sausage such as *linguiça*
1 or 2 pounds ham hock or shank, cut into 1-inch rounds
1 large yellow onion, chopped
Seasoning:
3 garlic cloves, minced and sautéed in 1 tablespoon vegetable oil
6 green onions, including tops, chopped
1 yellow onion, chopped
Large handful of chopped fresh parsley (about ½ cup)
2 bay leaves, crumbled
1½ tablespoons dried oregano, crushed
Salt and ground black pepper to taste
Chopped fresh cilantro or parsley

Directions:
Soak the beans overnight in enough water to cover by several inches. Drain.

Place the drained beans in a saucepan and add enough water to cover by 3 inches. Bring to a boil, reduce the heat to low, cover, and simmer until the beans are tender, 2–2½ hours. Add additional water as needed to keep the beans covered.

While the beans are cooking, prepare the meats. Preheat an oven to 375 degrees. Dice the pork butt or shoulder and the bacon into ½-inch cubes. Place the pork, whole sausages, and bacon in a large baking pan. Roast until well done. The sausages will be ready after 35–40 minutes and the other meats after 45–60 minutes.

Cook the ham hock at the same time as the meats are roasting. In a saucepan combine the ham hock rounds and onion with water to cover. Bring to a boil, reduce the heat to a simmer, and cook until tender, about 1 hour. Remove the ham hock rounds from the water and remove the meat from the bones, if desired; set aside. Or leave the rounds intact for serving alongside the beans. Strain the cooking liquid into a bowl. Add the strained onions from the liquid to the beans. Add the cooking liquid to the beans if needed to keep them immersed.

Once the beans are almost cooked, check to make sure there is plenty of cooking liquid in the pot. It should be rather soupy at this point. Cut the sausages into rounds and add them and all the other cooked meats to the pot. Then add all the seasonings to the pot, including the salt and pepper. Simmer for another 30 minutes, or until the beans are very tender.

Taste and adjust the seasonings. Sprinkle with chopped cilantro or parsley just before serving.

Couve na manteiga (Collard greens in butter)

This is one of the traditional side dishes that go with *feijoada*, but collards are also part of the regular Brazilian fare.

Ingredients:
4–5 bunches of collard greens (or kale)
Butter (use ½ tablespoon for every cup of shredded collards)

Directions:
Wash the collard greens. Remove the stems and roll the leaves tightly together. Slice into very thin strips with a sharp knife.

Shortly before serving, melt the butter and add collard greens. Cook over high heat stirring constantly until collard greens just start to wilt. Sprinkle with salt and serve.

Arroz de carreteiro (Truck driver's rice)

Rice is eaten daily by the majority of Brazilians. It is usually a side dish, but it can also be made into main courses such as this one: a rice with dried beef dish typical of the South.

Ingredients:
2 pounds dried, salted beef
5 small cloves garlic, minced
3 small onions, chopped
2–3 tablespoons vegetable oil
2 cups rice
4 cups water (to cook rice)
Salt and pepper to taste
½ cup parsley, chopped
½ cup scallions, chopped
Cayenne pepper (optional) to taste

Directions:
Cut meat into small cubes, about ½-inch on each side. Cover with water and soak overnight or boil for 15 minutes to rehydrate the meat and remove the salt. Drain. Fry the onions and garlic in oil until limp. Add meat and fry until browned. Add salt, black pepper, and cayenne pepper. Mix in rice and cook 5 minutes. Add boiling water and boil for 2 minutes. Cover and simmer until the rice is of the desired consistency. Top with parsley and scallions.

Camarão na moranga (Winter squash with shrimp)

Winter squash with shrimp is a rich, luscious entrée from the Northeast. Serve it with pure white rice.

Ingredients:
1 winter squash, medium
3 tablespoons oil
2 pounds medium-size shrimp, deveined
8 jumbo shrimp for decoration, deveined
Salt and white pepper to taste
Juice of 1 lemon
2 tablespoons butter

2 onions, chopped
1 teaspoon sweet paprika
1 teaspoon mustard powder
2 teaspoons flour
2 cups cream
1¾ cups cream cheese, softened

Directions:
Coordinate preparation of the squash and shrimp. Cut off and discard the top of the squash, remove all seeds and stringy fibers and rub the outside surface with 2 table-spoons of oil. Bake 1 hour at 250 degrees. The squash will not darken appreciably during this time.

While the squash is baking, season the shrimp with salt and white pepper and sprinkle with lemon juice. Heat the butter and the remaining oil in a pan and fry the onions until limp but not dark. Add the shrimp, including the jumbo shrimp, and sauté until pink, approximately 2 minutes on each side. Remove the jumbo shrimp and set aside. Season the remaining shrimp with paprika and mustard. Mix the flour with the cream and add it to the shrimp mixture. Stir over low heat until thickened. Add the cream cheese and continue to stir over low heat until the cheese is melted. Adjust the seasonings.

Remove the squash from the oven to a serving plate. Pour the shrimp mixture into the squash. Decorate the rim of the squash with the reserved jumbo shrimp.

Quindim

Quindim is a yolk-sugar-coconut pudding. Don't think about your cholesterol!

Ingredients:
1 cup grated coconut
1 tablespoon butter
¾ cup sugar
5 egg yolks
1 egg white, beaten into stiff peaks

Directions:
Preheat oven to 350 degrees. In a large bowl mix the coconut, butter, and sugar. Add the egg yolks one by one, mixing well. Finally, blend in the egg white. Grease a regular muffin pan, then fill the wells evenly with the mixture. Add boiling water to a large baking dish, placing the muffin pan in it so as not to float. Bake until the top of the puddings are golden brown (30–40 minutes). Allow them to cool before turning upside down to unmold. Serve after refrigerating for at least 2 hours.

How & Where

To buy some of the usual ingredients used in Brazilian dishes, try the Mexican section of your local supermarket. Specialty items such as coconut milk and *mandioca* (cassava) flour are sold in a few super-markets, but your best bet is a Latin grocery or deli. You can buy some more unusual ingredients or Brazilian products online at **Via Brasil** (⊕ www.viabrasil.com).

BRAZILIAN PORTUGUESE VOCABULARY

Words and Phrases

	English	Portuguese	Pronunciation
Basics			
	Yes/no	Sim/Não	**see**ing/nown
	Please	Por favor	pohr fah-**vohr**
	May I?	Posso?	**poh**-sso
	Thank you (very much)	(Muito) obrigado	(**moo**yn-too) o-bree **gah**-doh
	You're welcome	De nada	day **nah**-dah
	Excuse me	Com licença	con lee-**ssehn**-ssah
	Pardon me/what did you say?	Desculpe/O que disse?	des-**kool**-peh/o.k. **dih**-say?
	Could you tell me?	Poderia me dizer?	po-day-**ree**-ah mee dee-**zehrr**?
	I'm sorry	Sinto muito	**seen**-too **moo**yn-too
	Good morning!	Bom dia!	bohn **dee**-ah
	Good afternoon!	Boa tarde!	**boh**-ah **tahr**-dee
	Good evening!	Boa noite!	**boh**-ah **noh**ee-tee
	Goodbye!	Adeus!/Até logo!	ah-**deh**oos/ah-**teh loh**-go
	Mr./Mrs.	Senhor/Senhora	sen-**yor**/sen-**yohr**-ah
	Miss	Senhorita	sen-yo-**ri**-tah
	Pleased to meet you	Muito prazer	**moo**yn-too prah-**zehr**
	How are you?	Como vai?	**koh**-mo **vah**-ee
	Very well, thank you	Muito bem, obrigado	**moo**yn-too **beh**-in o-bree-**gah**-doh
	And you?	E o(a) Senhor(a)?	eh oh sen-**yor** (**yohr**-ah)
	Hello (on the telephone)	Alô	ah-**low**

Numbers

	English	Portuguese	Pronunciation
	1	um/uma	oom/**oom**-ah
	2	dois	**doh**ees
	3	três	**treh**ys
	4	quatro	**kwa**-troh

5	cinco	**seen**-koh
6	seis	**seh**ys
7	sete	**seh**-tee
8	oito	**oh**ee-too
9	nove	**noh**-vee
10	dez	**deh**-ees
11	onze	**ohn**-zee
12	doze	**doh**-zee
13	treze	**treh**-zee
14	quatorze	kwa-**tohr**-zee
15	quinze	**keen**-zee
16	dezesseis	deh-zeh-**seh**ys
17	dezessete	deh-zeh-**seh**-tee
18	dezoito	deh-**zoh**ee-toh
19	dezenove	deh-zeh-**noh**-vee
20	vinte	**veen**-tee
21	vinte e um	**veen**-tee eh **oom**
30	trinta	**treen**-tah
32	trinta e dois	**treen**-ta eh **doh**ees
40	quarenta	kwa-**rehn**-ta
43	quarenta e três	kwa-**rehn**-ta e **treh**ys
50	cinquenta	seen-**kwehn**-tah
54	cinquenta e quatro	seen-**kwehn**-tah e **kwa**-troh
60	sessenta	seh-**sehn**-tah
65	sessenta e cinco	seh-**sehn**-tah e **seen**-ko
70	setenta	seh-**tehn**-tah
76	setenta e seis	seh-**tehn**-ta e **seh**ys
80	oitenta	ohee-**tehn**-ta
87	oitenta e sete	ohee-**tehn**-ta e **seh**-tee
90	noventa	noh-**vehn**-ta
98	noventa e oito	noh-**vehn**-ta e **oh**ee-too
100	cem	**seh**-ing
101	cento e um	**sehn**-too e **oom**
200	duzentos	doo-**zehn**-tohss
500	quinhentos	key-**nyehn**-tohss

700	setecentos	seh-teh-**sehn**-tohss
900	novecentos	noh-veh-**sehn**-tohss
1,000	mil	meel
2,000	dois mil	**doh**ees meel
1,000,000	um milhão	oom mee-lee-**ahon**

Colors

black	preto	**preh**-toh
blue	azul	a-**zool**
brown	marrom	mah-**hohm**
green	verde	**vehr**-deh
pink	rosa	**roh**-zah
purple	roxo	**roh**-choh
orange	laranja	lah-**rahn**-jah
red	vermelho	vehr-**meh**-lyoh
white	branco	**brahn**-coh
yellow	amarelo	ah-mah-**reh**-loh

Days of the Week

Sunday	Domingo	doh-**meehn**-goh
Monday	Segunda-feira	seh-**goon**-dah **fey**-rah
Tuesday	Terça-feira	**tehr**-sah **fey**-rah
Wednesday	Quarta-feira	**kwahr**-tah **fey**-rah
Thursday	Quinta-feira	**keen**-tah **fey**-rah
Friday	Sexta-feira	**sehss**-tah **fey**-rah
Saturday	Sábado	**sah**-bah-doh

Months

January	Janeiro	jah-**ney**-roh
February	Fevereiro	feh-veh-**rey**-roh
March	Março	**mahr**-soh
April	Abril	ah-**breel**
May	Maio	**my**-oh
June	Junho	gy**oo**-nyoh
July	Julho	gy**oo**-lyoh
August	Agosto	ah-**ghost**-toh
September	Setembro	seh-**tehm**-broh
October	Outubro	owe-**too**-broh
November	Novembro	noh-**vehm**-broh
December	Dezembro	deh-**zehm**-broh

Useful Phrases

Do you speak English?	O Senhor fala inglês?	oh sen-**yor fah**-lah een-**glehs?**
I don't speak Portuguese.	Não falo português.	nown **fah**-loh pohr-too-**ghehs**
I don't understand (you)	Não lhe entendo	nown ly**eh** ehn-**tehn**-doh
I understand	Eu entendo	**eh**-oo ehn-**tehn**-doh
I don't know	Não sei	nown say
I am American/ British	Sou americano (americana)/ inglês/inglêsa	sow a-meh-ree-**cah**-noh (a-meh-ree-**cah**-nah)/ een-**glehs** (een-**glah**-sa)
What's your name?	Como se chama?	**koh**-moh seh **shah**-mah
My name is . . .	Meu nome é . . .	mehw **noh**-meh eh
What time is it?	Que horas são?	keh **oh**-rahss **sa**-ohn
It is one, two, three . . . o'clock	É uma/São duas, três . . . hora/horas	eh **oom**-ah/**sa**-ohn **oo**mah, **doo**-ahss, **treh**ys **oh**-rah/**oh**-rahs
Yes, please/No, thank you	Sim por favor/ Não obrigado	seing pohr fah-**vohr**/ nown o-bree-**gah**-doh
How?	Como?	**koh**-moh
When?	Quando?	**kwahn**-doh
This/Next week	Esta/Próxima semana	**ehss**-tah/**proh**-see-mah seh-**mah**-nah
This/Next month	Este/Próximo mêz	**ehss**-teh/**proh**-see-moh mehz
This/Next year	Este/Próximo ano	**ehss**-teh/**proh**-see-moh **ah**-noh
Yesterday/today tomorrow	Ontem/hoje amanhã	**ohn**-tehn/**oh**-jeh/ ah-mah-**nyan**
This morning/ afternoon	Esta manhã/ tarde	**ehss**-tah mah-**nyan** / **tahr**-deh
Tonight	Hoje a noite	**oh**-jeh ah **noh**ee-tee
What?	O que?	oh **keh**
What is it?	O que é isso?	oh **keh** eh **ee**-soh
Why?	Por quê?	pohr-**keh**
Who?	Quem?	**keh**-in
Where is . . . ?	Onde é . . . ?	**ohn**-deh **eh**
the train station?	a estação de trem?	ah es-tah-**sah**-on deh train
the subway station?	a estação de metrô?	ah es-tah-**sah**-on deh meh-**tro**

the bus stop?	a parada do ônibus?	ah pah-**rah**-dah doh **oh**-nee-boos
the post office?	o correio?	oh coh-**hay**-yoh
the bank?	o banco?	oh **bahn**-koh
the hotel?	o hotel . . . ?	oh oh-**tell**
the cashier?	o caixa?	oh **kah**y-shah
the museum?	o museo . . . ?	oh moo-**zeh**-oh
the hospital?	o hospital?	oh ohss-pee-**tal**
the elevator?	o elevador?	oh eh-leh-vah-**dohr**
the bathroom?	o banheiro?	oh bahn-**yey**-roh
the beach?	a praia de . . . ?	ah **prah**y-yah deh
Here/there	Aqui/ali	ah-**kee**/ah-**lee**
Open/closed	Aberto/fechado	ah-**behr**-toh/feh-**shah**-doh
Left/right	Esquerda/direita	ehs-**kehr**-dah/dee-**ray**-tah
Straight ahead	Em frente	ehyn **frehn**-teh
Is it near/far?	É perto/longe?	eh **pehr**-toh/**lohn**-jeh
I'd like to buy . . .	Gostaria de comprar . . .	gohs-tah-**ree**-ah deh cohm-**prahr** . . .
a bathing suit	um maiô	oom mahy-**owe**
a dictionary	um dicionário	oom dee-seeoh-**nah**-reeoh
a hat	um chapéu	oom shah-**peh**oo
a magazine	uma revista	**oo**mah heh-**vees**-tah
a map	um mapa	oom **mah**-pah
a postcard	cartão postal	kahr-**town** pohs-**tahl**
sunglasses	óculos escuros	**ah**-koo-loss ehs-**koo**-rohs
suntan lotion	um óleo de bronzear	oom **oh**-lyoh deh brohn-zeh-**ahr**
a ticket	um bilhete	oom bee-ly**eh**-teh
cigarettes	cigarros	see-**gah**-hose
envelopes	envelopes	eyn-veh-**loh**-pehs
matches	fósforos	**fohs**-foh-rohss
paper	papel	pah-**pehl**
sandals	sandália	sahn-**dah**-leeah
soap	sabonete	sah-bow-**neh**-teh
How much is it?	Quanto custa?	**kwahn**-too **koos**-tah
It's expensive/cheap	Está caro/barato	ehss-**tah kah**-roh / bah-**rah**-toh
A little/a lot	Um pouco/muito	oom **pohw**-koh/**moo**yn-too
More/less	Mais/menos	**mah**-ees /**meh**-nohss

Enough/too much/too little	Suficiente/ demais/ muito pouco	soo-fee-see-**ehn**-teh/ deh-**mah**-ees/ **moo**yn-toh **pohw**-koh
Telephone	Telefone	teh-leh-**foh**-neh
Telegram	Telegrama	teh-leh-**grah**-mah
I am ill.	Estou doente.	ehss-**tow** doh-**ehn**-teh
Please call a doctor.	Por favor chame um médico.	pohr fah-**vohr shah**-meh oom **meh**-dee-koh
Help!	Socorro!	soh-**koh**-ho
Help me!	Me ajude!	mee ah-**jyew**-deh
Fire!	Incêndio!	een-**sehn**-deeoh
Caution!/Look out!/ Be careful!	Cuidado!	kooy-**dah**-doh

On the Road

Avenue	Avenida	ah-veh-**nee**-dah
Highway	Estrada	ehss-**trah**-dah
Port	Porto	**pohr**-toh
Service station	Posto de gasolina	**pohs**-toh deh gah-zoh-**lee**-nah
Street	Rua	**who**-ah
Toll	Pedagio	peh-**dah**-jyoh
Waterfront promenade	Beiramar/ orla	behy-rah-**mahrr**/ **ohr**-lah
Wharf	Cais	**kah**-ees

In Town

Block	Quarteirão	kwahr-tehy-**rah**-on
Cathedral	Catedral	kah-teh-**drahl**
Church/temple	Igreja	ee-**greh**-jyah
City hall	Prefeitura	preh-fehy-**too**-rah
Door/gate	Porta/portão	**pohr**-tah/porh-**tah**-on
Entrance/exit	Entrada/ saída	ehn-**trah**-dah/ sah-**ee**-dah
Market	Mercado/feira	mehr-**kah**-doh/ **fey**-rah
Neighborhood	Bairro	**buy**-ho
Rustic bar	Lanchonete	lahn-shoh-**neh**-teh
Shop	Loja	**loh**-jyah
Square	Praça	**prah**-ssah

Dining Out

A bottle of . . .	Uma garrafa de . . .	**oo**mah gah-**hah**-fah deh
A cup of . . .	Uma xícara de . . .	**oo**mah **shee**-kah-rah deh
A glass of . . .	Um copo de . . .	oom **koh**-poh deh
Ashtray	Um cinzeiro	oom seen-**zehy**-roh
Bill/check	A conta	ah **kohn**-tah
Bread	Pão	**pah**-on
Breakfast	Café da manhã	kah-**feh** dah mah-**nyan**
Butter	A manteiga	ah mahn-**tehy**-gah
Cheers!	Saúde!	sah-**oo**-deh
Cocktail	Um aperitivo	oom ah-peh-ree-**tee**-voh
Dinner	O jantar	oh **jyahn**-tahr
Dish	Um prato	oom **prah**-toh
Enjoy!	Bom apetite!	bohm ah-peh-**tee**-teh
Fork	Um garfo	**gahr**-foh
Fruit	Fruta	**froo**-tah
Is the tip included?	A gorjeta esta incluída?	ah gohr-**jyeh**-tah ehss-**tah** een-clue-**ee**-dah
Juice	Um suco	oom **soo**-koh
Knife	Uma faca	**oo**mah **fah**-kah
Lunch	O almoço	oh ahl-**moh**-ssoh
Menu	Menu/ cardápio	me-**noo** / kahr-**dah**-peeoh
Mineral water	Água mineral	**ah**-gooah mee-neh-**rahl**
Napkin	Guardanapo	gooahr-dah-**nah**-poh
No smoking	Não fumante	nown foo-**mahn**-teh
Pepper	Pimenta	pee-**mehn**-tah
Please give me	Por favor me dê	pohr fah-**vohr** mee **deh**
Salt	Sal	sahl
Smoking	Fumante	foo-**mahn**-teh
Spoon	Uma colher	**oo**mah koh-ly**ehr**
Sugar	Açúcar	ah-**soo**-kahr
Waiter!	Garçon!	gahr-**sohn**
Water	Água	**ah**-gooah
Wine	Vinho	**vee**-nyoh

INDEX

456 < Index

FODOR'S KEY TO THE GUIDES

America's guidebook leader publishes guides for every kind of traveler. Check out our many series and find your perfect match.

FODOR'S GOLD GUIDES

America's favorite travel-guide series offers the most detailed insider reviews of hotels, restaurants, and attractions in all price ranges, plus great background information, smart tips, and useful maps.

COMPASS AMERICAN GUIDES

Stunning guides from top local writers and photographers, with gorgeous photos, literary excerpts, and colorful anecdotes. A must-have for culture mavens, history buffs, and new residents.

FODOR'S CITYPACKS

Concise city coverage in a guide plus a foldout map. The right choice for urban travelers who want everything under one cover.

FODOR'S EXPLORING GUIDES

Hundreds of color photos bring your destination to life. Lively stories lend insight into the culture, history, and people.

FODOR'S TRAVEL HISTORIC AMERICA

For travelers who want to experience history firsthand, this series gives in-depth coverage of historic sights, plus nearby restaurants and hotels. Themes include the Thirteen Colonies, the Old West, and the Lewis and Clark Trail.

FODOR'S POCKET GUIDES

For travelers who need only the essentials. The best of Fodor's in pocket-size packages for just $9.95.

FODOR'S FLASHMAPS

Every resident's map guide, with dozens of easy-to-follow maps of public transit, restaurants, shopping, museums, and more.

FODOR'S CITYGUIDES

Sourcebooks for living in the city: thousands of in-the-know listings for restaurants, shops, sports, nightlife, and other city resources.

FODOR'S AROUND THE CITY WITH KIDS

Up to 68 great ideas for family days, recommended by resident parents. Perfect for exploring in your own backyard or on the road.

FODOR'S HOW TO GUIDES

Get tips from the pros on planning the perfect trip. Learn how to pack, fly hassle-free, plan a honeymoon or cruise, stay healthy on the road, and travel with your baby.

FODOR'S LANGUAGES FOR TRAVELERS

Practice the local language before you hit the road. Available in phrase books, cassette sets, and CD sets.

KAREN BROWN'S GUIDES

Engaging guides—many with easy-to-follow inn-to-inn itineraries—to the most charming inns and B&Bs in the U.S.A. and Europe.

BAEDEKER'S GUIDES

Comprehensive guides, trusted since 1829, packed with A–Z reviews and star ratings.

OTHER GREAT TITLES FROM FODOR'S

Baseball Vacations, The Complete Guide to the National Parks, Family Vacations, Golf Digest's Places to Play, Great American Drives of the East, Great American Drives of the West, Great American Vacations, Healthy Escapes, National Parks of the West, Skiing USA.
